THE HANDBOOK OF MORTGAGE-BACKED SECURITIES

THE HANDBOOK OF MORTGAGE-BACKED SECURITIES

Fifth Edition

FRANK J. FABOZZI

Editor

McGraw-Hill

New York   Chicago   San Francisco
Lisbon   London   Madrid   Mexico City
Milan   New Delhi   San Juan   Seoul
Singapore   Sydney   Toronto

Library of Congress Cataloging-in-Publication Data

The handbook of mortgage-backed securities / [edited] by Frank J. Fabozzi—5th ed.
    p. cm.
    Includes bibliographical references.
    ISBN 0-07-135946-X
    1. Mortgage-backed securities—United States.   2. Portfolio management—United States.
I. Fabozzi, Frank J.
HG4655 .H36   2001
332.63'23—dc21   00-053702

McGraw-Hill

A Division of The McGraw·Hill Companies

3 4 5 6 7 8 9 0 DOC/DOC 0 9 8 7 6 5 4 3

ISBN 0-07-135946-X

This book was set in Times Roman by Carlisle Communications, Ltd.

Printed and bound by R. R. Donnelley & Sons Company.

This publication is designed to provide accurate and authoritative information in regard to the subject matter covered. It is sold with the understanding that neither the author nor the publisher is engaged in rendering legal, accounting, futures/securities trading, or other professional service. If legal advice or other expert assistance is required, the services of a competent professional person should be sought.

—From a Declaration of Principles jointly adopted by a Committee
of the American Bar Association and a Committee of Publishers

CONTENTS

SECTION VII

NON-U.S. MORTGAGE-BACKED PRODUCTS

PREFACE

⑥

The fifth edition of *The Handbook of Mortgage-Backed Securities* is designed to provide not only the fundamentals of these securities and the investment characteristics that make them attractive to a broad range of investors, but also extensive coverage on the state-of-the-art strategies for capitalizing on the opportunities in this market. The book is intended for both the individual investor and the professional manager.

To be effective, a book of this nature should offer a broad perspective. The experience of a wide range of experts is more informative than that of a single expert, particularly because of the diversity of opinion on some issues. I have chosen some of the best known practitioners to contribute to this book. Most have been actively involved in the evolution of the mortgage-backed securities market.

DIFFERENCES BETWEEN THE FOURTH AND FIFTH EDITIONS

Money managers must justify their management and transaction costs to clients. Consequently, all money managers eventually must demonstrate to their clients how much *value* they've added to portfolio performance above and beyond what could have been achieved by employing a lower-cost, buy-and-hold strategy. As the editor of *The Handbook of Mortgage-Backed Securities,* I am effectively the portfolio manager of the assets of this book—the chapters. The fifth edition must justify to my current clients (those who purchased the fourth edition of the *Handbook*) why they should not follow a buy-and-hold strategy of simply continuing to use the fourth edition and reduce advisory fees and transaction costs (i.e., the cost of this book). In short: What value has been added to the fourth edition?

The differences between the fourth and fifth editions are summarized in the following section. The number of chapters has been increased from 39 chapters to 42 chapters. Twenty-nine of the chapters are either new or have been substantially revised. Consequently, this book can be characterized as a new book, reflective of the dynamic changes that have occurred in this market in terms of new product development (particularly nonagency mortgage-backed securities) and advances in technologies since the publication of the fourth edition in 1995.

SUMMARY OF DIFFERENCES BETWEEN FOURTH AND FIFTH EDITIONS

The fourth edition has 39 chapters and an appendix, divided into the following eight sections:

    I. Mortgages and Pass-Through Securities

   II. Prepayment Behavior and Forecasting

  III. Stripped Mortgage-Backed Securities

  IV. Collateralized Mortgage Obligations

   V. Commercial Mortgage-Backed Securities

  VI. Valuation Techniques and Risk Measurement

 VII. Hedging Strategies

VIII. Accounting and Tax Considerations

The fifth edition has 42 chapters and an appendix, divided into the following seven sections:

    I. Mortgages and Pass-Through Securities

   II. Stripped Mortgage-Backed Securities and Collateralized Mortgage Obligations

  III. Credit-Sensitive Mortgage-Backed Securities

  IV. Prepayment Modeling

   V. Valuation Techniques, Relative Value Analysis, and Portfolio Strategies

  VI. Commercial Mortgage-Backed Securities

 VII. Non-U.S. Mortgage-Backed Products

The following chapters are new or substantially revised:

  1. Overview of the Mortgage Market

  3. Securities Backed by Adjustable-Rate Mortgages

  4. Prepayment Penalty Mortgage-Backed Securities

  6. Building an MBS Index: Conventions and Calculations

13. Inverse Floating-Rate CMOs

14. Nonagency CMOs

15. Securities Backed by Closed-End Home Equity Loans

16. Securities Backed by Manufactured Housing Loans

17. Mortgage Credit Analysis

18. Credit Performance of High LTV Loans

19. Overview of Recent Prepayment Behavior and Advances in Its Modeling

Frank J. Fabozzi

CONTRIBUTORS

James S. Anderson
Managing Director
First Union Securities, Inc.

Nichol Bakalar
Vice President
Deutsche Banc Alex. Brown Inc.

Alexander Batchvarov
Managing Director
Merrill Lynch & Co.

Anand K. Bhattacharya, Ph.D.
Executive Vice President
Countrywide Capital Markets, Inc.

Jeffrey D. Biby
Senior Vice President
Lehman Brothers Inc.

Joel W. Brown, CFA
Mortgage Credit Analyst
Stein, Roe & Farnham, Inc.

Michael Bykhovsky
President and CEO
Applied Financial Technology, Inc.

S. Esther Chang
Research Analyst
Countrywide Capital Markets, Inc.

Kristina L. Clark
Assistant Vice President
First Union Securities, Inc.

Patrick Corcoran, Ph.D.
Vice President
J.P. Morgan Securities Inc.

Ed Daingerfield
Managing Director
Nomura Securities International, Inc.

Xavier De Pauw
Assistant Vice President
Merrill Lynch & Co.

Lev Dynkin, Ph.D.
Managing Director
Lehman Brothers Inc.

Frank J. Fabozzi, Ph.D., CFA
Adjunct Professor of Finance
School of Management
Yale University

Sean Gallop

Lang Gibson
Vice President
Fixed Income Research
First Union Securities, Inc.

Bennett W. Golub, Ph.D.
Managing Director
BlackRock, Inc.

Laurie Goodman, Ph.D.
Managing Director and Head
Mortgage Strategy Group
UBS Warburg

Richard Gordon
Director
First Union Securities, Inc.

Brian Hargrave
Associate
Lehman Brothers Inc.

Lakhbir S. Hayre, DPhil.
Managing Director
Salomon Smith Barney

Jeffrey Ho
Director
Mortgage Strategy Group
UBS Warburg

David S. Horowitz, CFA
Portfolio Manager
Miller, Anderson & Sherrerd

R. Russell Hurst
Director
First Union Securities, Inc.

Jay Hyman, Ph.D.
Senior Vice President
Lehman Brothers Inc.

David P. Jacob
Managing Director and Head of Research and
Structuring
Nomura Securities International, Inc.

Vadim Konstantinovsky, CFA
Vice President
Lehman Brothers Inc.

Michael Levine
Senior Managing Director
Mortgage Trading
Bear, Stearns & Co. Inc.

Vito Lodato
Managing Director
Prudential Securities Inc.

Linda Lowell
Senior Vice President
Asset Backed Research
Greenwich Capital Markets, Inc.

Bruce Mahood

Satish M. Mansukhani
Managing Director
Bear, Stearns & Co. Inc.

Srinivas Modukuri
Vice President
Lehman Brothers Inc.

Cyrus Mohebbi, Ph.D.
Managing Director
Prudential Securities Inc.
and
Adjunct Professor
New York University

Mortgage Research Group
Lehman Brothers Inc.

Errol Mustafa, Ph.D.

Kumar Neelakantan
Vice President
ABS Research
Credit Suisse First Boston

Philip O. Obazee
Vice President
Quantitative Research
First Union Securities, Inc.

Alessandro Pagani
Director, Research Analyst
Banc One Capital Markets

Joshua R. Phillips
Vice President
Nomura Securities International, Inc.

Vincent Pica
President of Capital Finance
Prudential Securities Inc.

Ganesh Rajendra
Vice President
Merrill Lynch & Co.

Chuck Ramsey
CEO
Mortgage Risk Assessment Corp.

Scott F. Richard, DBA
Portfolio Manager
Miller, Anderson & Sherrerd

Nancy Roth
Vice President
Lehman Brothers Inc.

Anthony B. Sanders, Ph.D.
Professor of Finance and Galbreath
Distinguished Scholar
The Ohio State University

Glenn Schultz, CFA
Director, Senior Research Analyst
Banc One Capital Markets

V.S. Srinivasan
Associate Director
Bear, Stearns & Co. Inc.

William M. Wadden IV
Senior Vice President and Principal
Stein, Roe & Farnham, Inc.

Karen Weaver, CFA
Managing Director
Global Head of Securitization Research
Deutsche Banc Alex. Brown Inc.

Trudy Weibel
Assistant Vice President
Deutsche Banc Alex. Brown Inc.

Dale Westhoff
Senior Managing Director
Bear, Stearns & Co. Inc.

Michael L. Winchell

Eugene Xu
Director
Deutsche Banc Alex. Brown Inc.

David Yuen, CFA
Portfolio Strategist/Risk Manager
Franklin Templeton Investments

Wembo Zhu
Vice President
Merrill Lynch & Co.

Thomas Zimmerman
Director
Mortgage Strategy Group
UBS Warburg

THE HANDBOOK OF MORTGAGE-BACKED SECURITIES

MORTGAGES AND PASS-THROUGH SECURITIES

CHAPTER 1

OVERVIEW OF THE MORTGAGE MARKET

Anand K. Bhattacharya, Ph.D.
Executive Vice President
Countrywide Capital Markets, Inc.

Frank J. Fabozzi, Ph.D., CFA
Adjunct Professor of Finance
School of Management
Yale University

S. Esther Chang
Research Analyst
Countrywide Capital Markets, Inc.

A *mortgage* is a loan secured by the collateral of some specified real estate property and is a contractual agreement between the lender and the borrower that pledges the property to a lender as a security for the repayment of the loan through a series of payments. The mortgage also entitles the lender (the *mortgagee*) the right of foreclosure on the loan if the borrower (the *mortgagor*) fails to make the contracted payments.

The types of real estate properties that can be mortgaged are divided into two broad categories: residential properties and nonresidential properties. Residential properties include single-family structures, such as houses that accommodate one to four families, and multifamily structures, like condominiums, cooperatives, and apartments in which more than four families reside. Nonresidential properties include commercial structures such as office buildings, retail malls, hotels, assisted care facilities, and farm properties.

Mortgages can also be divided into two types of loans, the conventional loan and the nonconventional loan. A nonconventional loan is one that is backed by the full faith and guarantee of the U.S. government. Such loans are provided by federal agencies such as the Federal Housing Administration (FHA), the Veterans Administration (VA), and the Rural Development Administration (RDA). Conventional loans are those that do not carry any form of government guarantee.

The market where these funds are borrowed is called the *mortgage market,* which comprises the primary and secondary market. The primary market provides the actual loan to a borrower, whereas the secondary market channels liquidity into the primary market by way of purchasing packages of loans from lenders. Hence, the mortgage sector of the debt market is by far the largest in the world. At over $5 trillion in size it is larger than all consumer debt, bank commercial loans, and corporate debt combined.[1] The national homeownership rate is now at 67%,[2] and the mortgage market has undergone significant structural changes over the decades to accommodate the rapid growth. Innovations have occurred, and continue to occur, in terms of the design of new mortgage instruments in the primary market and the development of products that use pools of mortgages as collateral for the issuance of securities in the secondary market. Such securities are called *mortgage-backed securities* (MBS). These securities may be sold to investors, either as pass-throughs or in structured form, known as *collateralized mortgage obligations* (CMOs), to meet specific prepayment, maturity, and volatility tranching requirements of investors.

The focus of this chapter is the structure of the residential mortgage market and the wide range of products available within the residential mortgage sector.

PARTICIPANTS IN THE MORTGAGE MARKET

There are many participants in the mortgage market including a variety of players within the financial sector, such as commercial banks, thrift institutions, money managers, pension funds, insurance companies, securities dealers, trust departments, corporate treasury departments, corporations, and private investors. The industry can be categorized into four groups: mortgage originators, mortgage servicers, mortgage insurers, and mortgage investors.

Mortgage Originators

The original lender is called the *mortgage originator.* Mortgage originators include commercial banks, thrifts, mortgage bankers, life insurance companies, and pension funds. The three largest originators for all types of residential mortgages are commercial banks, thrifts, and mortgage bankers, originating more than 95% of annual mortgage originations. Over the years, with the consolidation in the thrift industry, the majority of mortgages are currently originated by banks and mortgage bankers.

Originators may generate income for themselves in one or more ways. First, they typically charge an origination fee. This fee is expressed in terms of *points,* where each point represents 1% of the borrowed funds. For example, an origination fee of 2 points on a $100,000 mortgage is equal to $2,000. Originators also charge application fees and certain processing fees.

The second source of revenue is the profit that might be generated from selling a mortgage at a price higher than par. This profit is called *secondary marketing profit.* Should mortgage rates rise, an originator will realize a loss when the mortgages are sold in the secondary market. Typically, in such instances, part or

---

1. *Fannie Mae and the Mortgage Industry in the E-Commerce Age,* May 8, 2000. See www.fanniemae.com/markets/stock/ecommerce.
2. U.S. Department of Housing and Urban Development, April 21, 1999.

all the losses may be "recovered" from gains in hedge instruments. Finally, the mortgage originator may hold the mortgage in its investment portfolio.

A potential homeowner who wants to borrow funds to purchase a home will apply for a loan from a mortgage originator. Upon completion of the application form and payment of an application fee, the mortgage originator will perform a credit evaluation of the applicant. The three primary factors in determining whether the funds will be lent are *capacity, credit,* and *collateral.* The assessment of these attributes is typically conducted by measures such as *payment-to-income* (PTI) and *debt-to-income* (DTI) *ratio* for capacity, the *loan-to-value* (LTV) *ratio* for collateral, and the credit worthiness of the borrower.

The PTI includes the principal, interest, taxes, and insurance (PITI), and the DTI includes the components of the PITI as well as other debt that may be recorded on the borrower's credit report, such as other installment debts that may include auto loan, credit cards, and student loans. The PTI/DTI is the ratio of monthly payments (mortgage and real estate tax, and other debt such as credit cards) to monthly income, and measures the ability of the borrower to make monthly payments. Also referred to as the *front-end/back-end ratio,* if the PTI/DTI is reported as 28/36, for instance, 28% of the applicant's income will be applied to the mortgage and real estate tax payments, and 36% of the income will be applied to all outstanding debt including mortgage and real estate tax payments. Therefore, the lower the PTI/DTI ratio is, the greater the likelihood is that the borrower will be able to make the required payments.

The difference between the purchase price of the property and the amount borrowed is the borrower's down payment. The LTV is the loan-to-value ratio of the amount of the loan to the market (or appraised) value of the property. The lower this ratio is, the lower the amount that is borrowed, and the more protection the lender has if the applicant defaults and the property has to be repossessed and sold.

The credit worthiness of the mortgagor is evaluated by relying heavily on credit reports obtained from credit reporting bureaus such as Experian, Trans Union, and Equifax, and credit scores such as FICOs, which represent a numerical assessment of the applicant's credit worthiness.

After a mortgage loan is closed, a mortgage originator can either (1) hold the mortgage in its portfolio, (2) sell the mortgage to an investor who will either hold the mortgage or who will aggregate the mortgage in a pool of mortgages to be used as collateral for the issuance of a mortgage-backed security (MBS), or (3) use the mortgage as collateral for the issuance of a MBS. When a mortgage is used as collateral for the issuance of a security, the mortgage is said to be *securitized.*

Conduits

When originators intend to sell mortgages, they will obtain a commitment from the potential investor who will buy them. Potential buyers include three government-sponsored enterprises (GSEs) and several private companies. As these agencies and private companies pool the mortgages and sell them to other investors, they are called *conduits* and operate exclusively in the secondary mortgage market to support mortgage lending in the primary market. When these conduits buy mortgages, they provide more loanable funds to lenders who in turn are able to make more loans to homebuyers.

The three GSEs, the Federal Home Loan Mortgage Corporation (Freddie Mac), the Federal National Mortgage Association (Fannie Mae), and the Government National Mortgage Association (Ginnie Mae) only purchase conforming mortgages (discussed later). Congress created Fannie Mae in 1938 as a part of several economic recovery measures during the Great Depression to support the housing industry. Since then they have revised their charter and operate to increase the availability and affordability of homeownership for low-, moderate-, and middle-income homebuyers, along with Freddie Mac, which was also chartered by Congress in 1970. Together these two GSEs hold 17% of the mortgages in the market. Ginnie Mae was created in 1968 as a part of the Department of Housing and Urban Development (HUD) to serve low- to moderate-income families. Unlike Fannie Mae and Freddie Mac, which are privately owned companies, Ginnie Mae is still a wholly owned government entity.

The GSEs were created to facilitate the primary mortgage market so that homebuyers would have better access to financing. By taking an active role in the secondary mortgage market, the GSEs have served to ameliorate imbalances of mortgage credit distribution that may occur in certain regional, capital deficient areas. The GSEs also have managed to keep mortgage rates lower by purchasing large volumes of mortgage assets, creating MBS, and channeling funds from investors to the primary markets by standardizing loans and intermediating the credit associated with loans. Today the GSEs are the largest providers of funds for home mortgages.

A *conforming mortgage* is one that meets the underwriting standards established by these GSEs for being in a pool of mortgages underlying a security that they guarantee. Three underwriting standards established by these agencies in order to qualify as a conforming mortgage are (1) a maximum PTI, (2) a maximum LTV, and (3) a maximum loan amount, which typically increase each year to keep pace with inflation. If an applicant does not satisfy the underwriting standards, the mortgage is called a *nonconforming mortgage*. Loans that exceed the maximum loan amount are called *jumbo mortgages*.

Mortgages acquired by the GSEs are held as investments in their portfolio or securitized, whereas private conduits such as the Residential Funding Corporation (a subsidiary of General Motors Acceptance Corporation) and Chase Manhattan Mortgage Corporation that buy both conforming and nonconforming mortgages, will typically securitize the mortgages that they purchase rather than hold them as an investment. Such securitizations are called *private-label executions*.

Mortgage Channels

As product offerings by mortgage originators have evolved, so too have the channels by which they are made available to borrowers and distributed to investors. Prior to the revolution of Internet-related technology, the mortgage business comprised three channels: retail, wholesale, and correspondent. The *retail channel* deals directly with consumers, the so-called "brick-and-mortar" shops where the loans are originated. The *wholesale channel* provides a medium where loans are purchased from brokers who originate the loans, and the *correspondent channel* enables the purchase of loans from a network of smaller, independent entities. The difference between the wholesale channel and the correspondent channel is that the members of the latter group are actual subsidiaries of lending institutions and are able to originate, underwrite, and fund mortgages among other functions, whereas the members of the former group act as an intermediary between a borrower and many potential lenders. Usually the distinguishing factor between wholesale and correspondent is the ability to fund the loan. Typically the funding of the loan in the wholesale channel is conducted by the ultimate buyer of the loan.

With the advent of the Internet and e-commerce the roles of the three channels have undergone many changes as well. Foremost of these changes, though, has taken place on the consumer end as the proliferation of mortgage-related web sites has expanded the knowledge base of the borrower. Consumers are now able to gather all the pertinent information regarding the loan process and the myriad types of mortgage products available and as a result have more options available to them. However, although the Internet has served to increase the mortgage knowledge of consumers, the process of obtaining a mortgage still requires human intermediation, and it may be a while before the mortgage lending process becomes completely automated.

Among the new developments within the retail channel has been the creation of online lending. The new "clicks-and-bricks" concept has enabled lenders to offer applications on their web sites, to provide preapprovals on loans, and to offer ancillary products such as insurance and other financial products and services. For consumers "clicks-and-bricks" allow them to make electronic loan payments, see their statements online, and even make purchases of products and services in one central location.

Mortgage Servicers

Every mortgage loan, both securitized and nonsecuritized, must be serviced. *Servicing* a loan entails the collection of monthly payments and forwarding the proceeds to owners of the loan, sending payment notices to mortgagors, reminding mortgagors when payments are overdue, maintaining records of principal balances, administering an escrow balance for real estate taxes and insurance purposes, initiating foreclosure proceedings if necessary, and furnishing tax information to mortgagors when applicable. Those who service mortgage loans include bank and commercially related entities and mortgage bankers.

Servicers obtain their revenue from several sources. The primary source is the servicing fee, which is a fixed percentage of the outstanding mortgage balance, and declines over time as the mortgage balance amortizes. The second source of servicing income derives from the interest that can be earned from the escrow balance that the borrower often maintains with the servicer. The third source of revenue is the float earned on the monthly mortgage payment because of the delay permitted between the time the servicer receives the payment and the time that the payment must be sent to the investor. Fourth, there are several sources of ancillary income such as charging late fees if the payment is not made on time, receiving commissions for cross-selling borrowers for life and other insurance products, and generating fees from selling mailing lists. Finally, for servicers who are also lenders their portfolio of borrowers are in addition a potential source for other loans such as second mortgages, automobile loans, and credit cards.

Mortgage Insurers

Mortgage insurance protects the lender against loss in the event of default by the borrower. Hence, insurance at the loan level minimizes the credit risk of the loan, whereas GSEs minimize risks at the secondary level when securities are created with the loans. The amount of mortgage insurance required varies as it is dependent on the type and term of the loan but is usually required on loans with LTV ratios greater than 80%. The amount insured will be some percentage of the loan and may decline as the LTV ratio declines. By law, when the LTV ratio becomes less than 80%, the mortgage insurance must be lifted. Although the insurance is required by the lender, its cost is borne by the borrower, usually through a higher contract rate. However, recent years have witnessed the advent of a new type of mortgage insurance program where the premiums are paid by the lender and result in a higher note rate for the mortgagor.

At the loan level there are three main types of mortgage insurance: insurance provided by a government agency which only applies to nonconventional loans, regular private mortgage insurance, and lender-paid mortgage insurance.

The federal agencies that provide mortgage insurance are the FHA, VA, and the RDA. Private mortgage insurance can be obtained from a mortgage insurance company such as the Mortgage Guaranty Insurance Company and the PMI Mortgage Insurance Company. Lender-paid mortgage insurance enables the borrower to incorporate the insurance cost into the interest rate or by adding origination points to the loan amount. It is important to note that little similarities exist between the mortgage insurance provided by the government agencies and that provided by lenders and insurance companies. The insurance provided by the federal agencies such as Ginnie Mae derives from the full faith and guarantee of the government, whereas Fannie Mae and Freddie Mac have an implicit guarantee of the government.[3]

Insurance provided by lenders and insurance companies, however, is purchased. For private mortgage insurance premiums are paid by the borrower on a predetermined schedule, and for lender-paid mortgage insurance the premiums are either financed into the loan amount or paid up-front. Another form of insurance, *hazard insurance,* may be required for mortgages on properties located in

---

3. In recent years the privileged status of Fannie Mae and Freddie Mae in the capital markets concerning their abilities to borrow at preferential rates has been an issue of heavy debate, with the privatization of these agencies offered as one alternative to solve the dual status of the agencies (private shareholder organization with ties to the U.S. Treasury).

geographical areas where the occurrence of natural disasters such as floods and earthquakes is more frequent.

When mortgages are pooled by a private conduit and securities are issued, additional insurance for the pool is typically obtained to enhance the credit of the security. This occurs because the major rating agencies require external credit enhancement to obtain investment grade ratings. Factors considered by the rating agencies to assess the credit quality of a pool of mortgages, in addition to the credit quality of the individual mortgages, are the credit ratings of the mortgage insurer, the underwriting standards and procedures of the originator, and the quality of the operations of the servicer. This insurance may take the form of a corporate guarantee or a "wrap" from a rated insurer. Alternatively, the issuer may decide to self-insure by subordinating a certain portion of the cash flows in a "senior-subordinated" ("senior-sub") structure. These various forms of credit enhancement are discussed in later chapters. Historically, the usage of "senior-sub" structure increases as an execution vehicle as the asset class becomes mature and liquid.

PREPAYMENT RISK

The homeowner has the option to prepay the mortgage in whole or in part at any time. Typically a penalty is not imposed on the homeowner for prepaying the mortgage unless it is stated contractually. That is, the loan is repaid at par value at any time. Because of the prepayment option granted to the homeowner, an investor in a mortgage cannot be certain of the cash flow. A 30-year mortgage could turn out to have a maturity of a year or one of 30 years. The uncertainty about the cash flow due to the prepayment option granted the homeowner is called *prepayment risk.*

An investor is exposed to prepayment risk for an individual mortgage and for a pool of mortgages. Consequently any security backed by a pool of mortgages exposes an investor to prepayment risk.

Prepayments occur for one of several reasons. First, homeowners prepay the entire mortgage when they sell their home. The sale of a home can result from (1) a change of employment that necessitates moving, (2) the purchase of a more expensive home ("trading up"), or (3) a divorce in which the settlement requires sale of the marital residence, among other reasons. Second, in the case of homeowners who cannot meet their mortgage obligations, the property is repossessed and sold. The proceeds from the sale are used to pay off the mortgage in the case of a conventional mortgage, and for those that are insured the balance is paid by the insurer. Third, if property is destroyed by fire, or if another insured catastrophe occurs, the insurance proceeds are used to pay off the mortgage balance. Finally, the borrower may refinance the loan if the current mortgage rate falls by a sufficient amount below the contract rate.

Prepayment risk also has implications for the performance of a mortgage. The performance is similar to that of a callable bond, a fact that should not be surprising given that a mortgage can be conceptualized as the long portion in a fixed-rate instrument and a short call option on interest rates.

The key in analyzing an individual mortgage or a pool of mortgages is the projection of prepayments, which incorporates macroeconomic variables as well as loan level attributes. All primary dealers and several vendors have developed prepayment models. A discussion of these models is provided in other chapters in this book. At this point it is sufficient to say that there is not one prepayment model for all the mortgage designs that we review in the next section.

EVOLUTION OF MORTGAGE INSTRUMENTS

The design of mortgages has undergone significant changes since the Great Depression in response to changing consumer needs and the ability of originating institutions to devise alternative funding methods. At that time most borrowers had mortgages that resembled balloon loans in which the principal was not amortized, or only partially amortized at the maturity date. Sometimes the bank could even ask for repayment of the outstanding balance on demand or upon relatively short notice, even if the mortgagor was fulfilling his or her obligation. Such a system of mortgage financing proved to be inefficient and contributed to the further contraction of the financial markets.

As the government sought to resuscitate the housing market, one of its solutions was to encourage the use of a new type of mortgage instrument that would alleviate the type of problems that had been associated with balloon loans. The new type of mortgage was structured as a fixed-rate, level-payment, fully amortized loan ("level-payment mortgage" for short) and met the requirements to be insured by the then newly created FHA.

While the level-payment mortgage is still a prevalent form, lenders have come to offer myriad single-family mortgage loan structures to borrowers over the years. These include such traditional structures as tiered-payment mortgages, balloon mortgages, and "two-step" mortgages, as well as recent innovative structures such as revolving lines of credit, rate reduction mortgages, and reverse mortgages to meet the unique needs of mortgagors.

As many of these new products find their way into the secondary market, investors are presented with both opportunities and challenges. The opportunities include the chance to invest in new securities that may provide a better portfolio fit than other mortgage products have to date. Some of these loan types are likely to become permanent features of both the primary and secondary mortgage market; others are likely to disappear, such as one of the mortgage designs discussed subsequently, the graduated payment mortgage.

Level-Payment Mortgage

With the level-payment mortgage the borrower pays interest and repays principal in equal installments over the term of the loan. Thus, at the end of the term the mortgage has been fully amortized. Each monthly mortgage payment for a level-payment mortgage is due on the first of each month and consists of

1. Interest of 1/12 of the fixed annual interest rate times the amount of the outstanding mortgage balance at the beginning of the previous month

2. A repayment of a portion of the outstanding mortgage balance (principal)

The difference between the monthly mortgage payment and the portion of the payment that represents interest equals the amount that is applied to reduce the outstanding mortgage balance. The monthly mortgage payment is designed so that after the last scheduled monthly payment of the loan is made, the outstanding mortgage balance is zero (i.e., the mortgage is fully repaid).

To illustrate a level-payment mortgage, consider a 30-year (360-month), $100,000 mortgage with a 9.5% mortgage rate. The monthly mortgage payment would be $840.85.[4] Exhibit 1–1 shows how each monthly mortgage payment is divided between interest and repayment of principal. At the beginning of month 1 the mortgage balance is $100,000, the amount of the original loan. The mortgage payment for month 1 includes interest on the $100,000 borrowed for the month. The interest rate is 9.5%, so the monthly interest rate is 0.0079167 (0.095 divided by 12). Interest for month 1 is therefore $791.67 ($100,000 × 0.0079167). The $49.18 difference between the monthly mortgage payment of $840.85 and the interest of $791.67 is the portion of the monthly mortgage payment that represents repayment of principal. This $49.18 in month 1 reduces the mortgage balance.

The mortgage balance at the end of month 1 (beginning of month 2) is then $99,950.81 ($100,000 − $49.19). The interest for the second monthly mortgage payment is $791.28, the monthly interest rate (0.0079167) times the mortgage balance at the beginning of month 2 ($99,950.81). The difference between the $840.85 monthly mortgage payment and the $791.28 interest is $49.57, representing the amount of the mortgage balance paid off with that monthly mortgage

---

4. The monthly mortgage payment can be calculated using the following formula:

$$MP = MB_0 \frac{[i(1 + i)^n]}{[(1 + i)^n - 1]}$$

where

MP = monthly mortgage payment ($);
n = number of months;
MB_0 = original mortgage balance ($);
i = simple monthly interest rate (annual interest rate/12).

For our hypothetical mortgage

$$n = 360, \quad MB_0 = \$100,000, \quad i = 0.0079167 \, (= 0.095/12)$$

$$MP = \$100,000 \left[\frac{0.0079167(1.0079167)^{360}}{(1.0079167)^{360} - 1} \right] = \$840.85$$

EXHIBIT 1-1

Amortization Schedule for a Level-Payment, Fixed-Rate Mortgage*

Month	Beginning Mortgage Balance	Monthly Mortgage Payment	Interest for Month	Principal Repayment	Ending Mortgage Balance
1	$100,000.00	$840.85	$791.67	$ 49.19	$99,950.81
2	99,950.81	840.85	791.28	49.58	99,901.24
3	99,901.24	840.85	790.88	49.97	99,851.27
4	99,851.27	840.85	790.49	50.37	99,800.90
5	99,800.90	840.85	790.09	50.76	99,750.14
6	99,750.14	840.85	789.69	51.17	99,698.97
7	99,698.97	840.85	789.28	51.57	99,647.40
8	99,647.40	840.85	788.88	51.98	99,595.42
9	99,595.42	840.85	788.46	52.39	99,543.03
10	99,543.03	840.85	788.05	52.81	99,490.23
...	...	...	...	...	...
...	...	...	...	...	...
...	...	...	...	...	...
98	92,862.54	840.85	735.16	105.69	92,756.85
99	92,756.85	840.85	734.33	106.53	92,650.32
100	92,650.32	840.85	733.48	107.37	92,542.95
101	92,542.95	840.85	732.63	108.22	92,434.72
102	92,434.72	840.85	731.77	109.08	92,325.64
103	92,325.64	840.85	730.91	109.94	92,215.70
104	92,215.70	840.85	730.04	110.81	92,104.89
105	92,104.89	840.85	729.16	111.69	91,993.20
106	91,993.20	840.85	728.28	112.57	91,880.62
...	...	...	...	...	...
...	...	...	...	...	...
...	...	...	...	...	...
209	74,177.40	840.85	587.24	253.62	73,923.78
210	73,923.78	840.85	585.23	255.62	73,668.16
211	73,668.16	840.85	583.21	257.65	73,410.51
212	73,410.51	840.85	581.17	259.69	73,150.82
...	...	...	...	...	...
...	...	...	...	...	...
...	...	...	...	...	...
354	5,703.93	840.85	45.16	795.70	4,908.23
355	4,908.23	840.85	38.86	802.00	4,106.24
356	4,106.24	840.85	32.51	808.35	3,297.89
357	3,297.89	840.85	26.11	814.75	2,483.14
358	2,483.14	840.85	19.66	821.20	1,661.95
359	1,661.95	840.85	13.16	827.70	834.25
360	834.25	840.85	6.60	834.25	0.00

*Mortgage loan, $100,000; mortgage rate, 9.5%; monthly payment, $840.85; term of loan, 30 years [360 months].
Source: From Frank J. Fabozzi (ed.), *The Handbook of Fixed Income Securities*, p. 18, Chapter 2, 4th ed.

payment. Notice in Exhibit 1–1 that the last monthly mortgage payment is sufficient to pay off the remaining mortgage balance. When a loan repayment schedule is structured in this way so that the payments made by the borrower will completely pay off the interest and principal, the loan is said to be fully amortizing. Exhibit 1–1 is then referred to as an *amortization schedule.*

As Exhibit 1–1 shows, the portion of the monthly mortgage payment applied to interest declines each month, whereas the part applied to reducing the mortgage balance increases. Since the monthly mortgage payment is fixed while the mortgage balance declines, a larger part of the monthly payment is applied to reduce the principal in each subsequent month and the interest decreases.

What was ignored in the amortization is the portion of the cash flow that must be paid to the servicer of the mortgage. The servicing fee is a specified portion of the mortgage rate. The monthly cash flow from a mortgage loan, regardless of mortgage design, can therefore be decomposed into three parts:

1. The servicing fee

2. The interest payment net of the servicing fee

3. The scheduled principal repayment

For example, consider once again the $100,000, 30-year level-payment mortgage with a rate of 9.5%. Suppose the servicing fee is 0.5% per year. Exhibit 1–2 shows the cash flow for the mortgage with this servicing fee. The monthly mortgage payment is unchanged, although the amount of the servicing fee, like the interest, declines each month as the mortgage balance declines.

Graduated Payment Mortgage

Although the level-payment mortgage may appeal to most mortgagors, the fixed nature of the payment may place a financial burden on individuals in the early years of the mortgage, especially if such individuals expected their incomes to increase. In order to address such a predicament, the *graduated payment mortgage* (GPM) was introduced by the FHA in 1979. With this mortgage design both the interest rate and the term of the mortgage are fixed, as they are with a level-payment mortgage. However, the monthly mortgage payment for a GPM is smaller in the initial years than for a level-payment mortgage with the same contract rate but larger in the remaining years of the mortgage term.

The terms of a GPM plan include (1) the mortgage rate, (2) the term of the mortgage, (3) the number of years over which the monthly mortgage payment will increase (and when the level payments will begin), and (4) the annual percentage increase in the mortgage payments.

Since the monthly mortgage payments in the earlier years of a GPM are generally not sufficient to pay the entire interest due on the outstanding mortgage balance, the difference between the monthly mortgage payment and the accumulated interest is added to the outstanding mortgage balance so that there is negative amortization. However, the higher-level mortgage payments in the later years of the GPM are designed to amortize fully the outstanding mortgage balance, which is, by then, greater than the original amount borrowed.

EXHIBIT 1–2

Cash Flow for a Mortgage with Servicing Fee*

Month	Beginning Mortgage Balance	Monthly Mortgage Payment	Net Interest for Month	Servicing Fee	Principal Repayment	Ending Mortgage Balance
1	$100,000.00	$840.85	$750.00	$41.67	$ 49.19	$99,950.81
2	99,950.81	840.85	749.63	41.65	49.58	99,901.24
3	99,901.24	840.85	749.26	41.63	49.97	99,851.27
4	99,851.27	840.85	748.88	41.60	50.37	99,800.90
5	99,800.90	840.85	748.51	41.58	50.76	99,750.14
6	99,750.14	840.85	748.13	41.56	51.17	99,698.97
7	99,698.97	840.85	747.74	41.54	51.57	99,647.40
8	99,647.40	840.85	747.36	41.52	51.98	99,595.42
9	99,595.42	840.85	746.97	41.50	52.39	99,543.03
10	99,543.03	840.85	746.57	41.48	52.81	99,490.23
...	...	...	...	...	...	...
...	...	...	...	...	...	...
...	...	...	...	...	...	...
98	99,862.54	840.85	696.47	38.69	105.69	92,756.85
99	92,756.85	840.85	695.68	38.65	106.53	93,650.32
100	92,650.32	840.85	694.88	38.60	107.37	92,542.95
101	92,542.95	840.85	694.07	38.56	108.22	92,434.72
102	92,434.72	840.85	693.26	38.51	109.08	92,325.64
103	92,325.64	840.85	692.44	38.47	109.94	92,215.70
104	92,215.70	840.85	691.62	38.42	110.81	92,104.89
105	92,104.89	840.85	690.79	38.38	111.69	91,993.20
106	91,993.20	840.85	689.95	38.33	112.57	91,880.62
...	...	...	...	...	...	...
...	...	...	...	...	...	...
...	...	...	...	...	...	...
209	74,177.40	840.85	556.33	30.91	253.62	73,923.78
210	73,923.78	840.85	554.43	30.80	255.62	73,668.16
211	73,668.16	840.85	552.51	30.70	257.65	73,410.51
212	73,410.51	840.85	550.58	30.59	259.69	73,150.82
...	...	...	...	...	...	...
...	...	...	...	...	...	...
...	...	...	...	...	...	...
354	5,703.93	840.85	42.78	2.38	795.70	4,908.23
355	4,908.23	840.85	36.81	2.05	802.00	4,106.24
356	4,106.24	840.85	30.80	1.71	808.35	3,297.89
357	3,297.89	840.85	24.73	1.37	814.75	2,483.14
358	2,483.14	840.85	18.62	1.03	821.20	1,661.95
359	1,661.95	840.85	12.46	0.69	827.70	834.25
360	834.25	840.85	6.25	0.35	834.25	0

*Mortgage loan, $100,000; mortgage rate, 9.5%; servicing fee, 0.5%; monthly payment, $840.85; term of loan, 30 years [360 months].

Growing Equity Mortgage

A variation of the GPM that does not have negative amortization is the *growing equity mortgage* (GEM), which has a fixed-rate mortgage whose monthly mortgage payments increase over time. Rather, the higher monthly mortgage payments serve to pay down the principal faster and to shorten the term of the mortgage. For example, a 30-year, $100,000 GEM loan with a contract rate of 9.5% might call for an initial monthly payment of $840.85. However, the GEM payment would gradually increase, and the GEM might be fully paid in only 15 years.

Fixed-Rate Tiered-Payment Mortgage

Fixed-rate tiered-payment mortgages (TPMs) were also designed to provide originators with the ability to offer borrowers a low initial payment in the era of high interest rates of the early 1980s, when buy-down and graduated payment mortgage lending programs flourished.

Buy-down origination programs carried market accrual rates and subsidized the payments in the early years with payments from a separate account typically established by the builder or owner of the property. Graduated payment mortgages also carried near-market accrual rates and allowed the mortgage to experience negative amortization in the early years of its life. On the other hand, most adjustable-rate mortgages relied on low initial rates, employed payment caps, and allowed the mortgage to amortize negatively in order to maintain a low payment schedule for some time into the future.

Tiered-payment mortgages provide the payment advantage in a unique way. The mortgage carries a market accrual rate and a 15-year or, less commonly, 30-year final maturity, but the payment is calculated based on an interest rate as much as 300 to 500 basis points (bps) lower than the actual interest rate on the loan (even lower for some 30-year loans). The structure does not allow negative amortization. Therefore, it stipulates that if the payment is less than the amount required to pay the interest due on the loan based on the actual interest rate, then the difference between the borrower's payment and the amount required to pay the entire interest accrued must be made up from a subsidy account established by the borrower, seller, builder, or other party. The payments are adjusted annually and allowed to increase by a maximum of 7.5% per year until the payment fully amortizes the loan over its remaining term.

The primary way TPMs differ from GPMs is that TPMs do not experience negative amortization and typically carry a 15-year maturity. TPMs differ from buy-downs because any initial subsidy to the borrower's payment (from the interest shortfall account) is typically much smaller than that required by a buy-down loan and is also frequently funded by the borrower.

Unlike ARMs (discussed later in the chapter), TPMs have a certain payment schedule with relatively moderate annual payment increases. The interest-only (IO) nature of the earliest total cash flows on the mortgage (including any necessary subsidies) also allows the payment to be based on an extremely low accrual rate, much lower than can be profitably offered on most ARMs.

Prepayment Penalty Mortgage

To minimize the prepayment risk, lenders developed mortgage products that incorporated penalties for prepaying the loans. These prepayment penalty loans offer a lower mortgage rate to borrowers who agree not to refinance their mortgage for a set period of time, the common terms being 3 or 5 years. As an incentive for the borrower, the prepayment penalty loans offer rates that are usually 25 to 50 bps lower than nonprepayment penalty loans, and the borrower may refinance after the lockout period.

The two popular prepayment penalty loan structures are

1. Five-year lockout period—the borrower would have to pay 6 months of interest on any prepaid principal that exceeds 20% of the original loan balance, or 20% of 80% of the original loan balance depending on the program.

2. Three-year lockout period—the borrower would have to pay 2% of any prepaid amount that exceeds 20% of the original balance. If the mortgage rate is less than 4%, then the penalty structure is the same as 1 above.

Adjustable-Rate Mortgage

In high interest rate environments many financial institutions holding fixed-rate mortgages that are funded with short-dated liabilities faced a mismatch between the duration of its mortgages and its liabilities. To deal with this problem, shorter duration mortgages were developed.

An *adjustable-rate mortgage* (ARM) is a loan that usually has a lower start rate and a contract rate that is reset periodically in accordance with some specified index rate, such as the rate on U.S. Treasury securities, the London Interbank Offered Rate (LIBOR), the Eleventh (11th) District Cost of Funds (COFI or ECOFI), or the prevailing prime rate.

Outstanding ARMs call for resetting the contract rate either every month, 6 months, 1 year, 2 years, 3 years, or 5 years. In recent years ARMs typically have had reset periods of 6 months, 1 year, or 5 years. The contract rate at the reset date is equal to a reference rate plus a spread. The spread is typically between 200 and 300 bps, reflecting market conditions, the features of the ARM, and the increased cost of servicing an ARM compared to a fixed-rate mortgage.

Index Rate

Three categories of index rates have been used in ARMs: (1) market-determined rates, (2) calculated rates based on the cost of funds for the thrifts, and (3) LIBOR (the rate at which banks lend money to one another). The most popular market-determined rates are Treasury-based rates and LIBOR. The index rate will have an important impact on the performance of an ARM and how it is priced.

Indexes for the cost of funds for thrifts are calculated based on the monthly weighted average interest cost for liabilities of thrifts. The two most popular indexes are COFI and the National Cost of Funds Index (NCOFI), the former being the most popular. Whereas the NCOFI is rarely used, the COFI is still widely utilized by thrifts in the 11th District states to match asset returns and liability costs. However, one of the limitations of this index is that it is heavily influenced by the high costs of a few dominant thrift institutions that exist due to consolidation in the industry.

The 11th District includes the states of California, Arizona, and Nevada, and the index value is derived from the averages of their cost of funds, which is reported with a one-month lag. For example, June's 11th District COFI is reported in July. The contract rate for a mortgage based on the 11th District COFI is usually reset based on the previous month's reported index rate. For example, if the reset date is August, the index rate reported in July will be used to set the contract rate. Consequently there is a 2-month lag by the time the average cost of funds is reflected in the contract rate. This obviously is an advantage to the borrower and a disadvantage to the investor when interest rates are rising. The opposite is true when interest rates are falling.

The NCOFI which is reported with approximately a 1.5-month delay, is calculated based on all federally insured savings and loan institutions. Rather than using an average, a median cost of funds for the S&Ls is calculated, and the contract rate is typically reset based on the most recently reported index value.

Features of Adjustable-Rate Mortgages

To encourage borrowers to accept ARMs rather than fixed-rate mortgages, mortgage originators generally offer an initial contract rate that is less than the prevailing market mortgage rate. This below-market initial contract rate, set by the mortgage originator based on competitive market conditions, is commonly referred to as a *teaser rate*. One-year ARMs typically offer a 100 bps spread over the index rate. Suppose also that the index rate is 6.5% so that the initial contract rate should be 7.5%. The mortgage originator might set an initial contract rate of 6.75%, a rate 75 bps below the current value of the reference rate plus the spread.

A pure ARM is one that resets periodically and has no other terms that affect the monthly mortgage payment. However, the monthly mortgage payment, and hence the investor's cash flow, are affected by other terms. These are due to (1) periodic caps and (2) lifetime rate caps and floors. Rate caps limit the amount that the contract rate may increase or decrease at the reset date. A lifetime cap sets the maximum contract rate over the term of the loan.

Fixed/Adjustable-Rate Mortgage Hybrids

Another type of mortgage loan structure that has experienced growing popularity is the *fixed/adjustable-rate mortgage hybrid*. A hybrid ARM combines features of a fixed-rate loan with that of an ARM. The loan is fixed for a specified period (usually 3, 5, 7, or 10 years) and then resets annually afterward. Like regular ARMs, hybrids offer an initial mortgage rate that is lower than a 30-year fixed-rate loan but do not have a reset after one year. For instance, one popular hybrid structure carries a fixed rate for 5 years, and thereafter has a floating rate which resets every 6 months at a margin over the 6-month CD index. Like many other

ARMs, the coupon is subject to both periodic and lifetime limitations on the rate change. Other fixed/ARM hybrids turn into one-year Treasury ARMs, or monthly 11th District COFI ARMs after their fixed period. In many cases the first coupon reset is not subject to any periodic caps that may apply to later coupon resets; instead, it is subject only to the lifetime cap. Some hybrid ARMs also provide a convertibility option, which allows the borrower to convert the loan into a fixed-rate mortgage during a specified period called the conversion window. Although other types of conversion windows exist, the typical window is 60 months long and starts at month 1 or month 12. The rate for the new loan is then usually set between 3/8% and 5/8% above the fixed 30-year mortgage rate.

At first glance the hybrid mortgage structure may appear to be straightforward in terms of its valuation since it combines two types of products with which the market is familiar. However, such a combination in itself presents some unique valuation challenges. One issue is determining the appropriate prepayment model for the valuation as borrowers may prepay the loan as they would a fixed-rate loan or that of an ARM loan. Historically these two borrower groups have responded differently to similar refinancing incentives. Another issue relates to the pricing of such mortgages as they become fully floating. Current markets conventionally price these mortgages at par at the end of the fixed period.

Balloon Mortgages

Most single-family balloon mortgages originated today carry a fixed rate and a 30-year amortization schedule. They typically require a balloon repayment of the principal outstanding on the loan at the end of 5 or, more commonly, 7 years, although other balloon dates are possible. Balloon mortgages are attractive to borrowers because they offer mortgage rates that are significantly lower than generic 30-year mortgages in a steep yield-curve environment. In turn the short final maturity of balloon mortgage pools offers investors substantial performance stability.

Nowadays many balloon mortgage contracts are actually hybrids that contain certain provisions allowing the borrower to take out a new mortgage from the current lender to finance the balloon repayment with minimal requalification requirements. In order for the new loan to qualify for a Fannie Mae pool, for instance, the borrower receiving the new loan to finance a balloon payment must not have been delinquent on payments at any time during the 12 preceding months, must still be using the property as a primary residence, and must have incurred no new liens on the property. In addition, the interest rate on the new loan must be no more than 500 bps greater than the rate on the balloon loan. If these conditions are met, Fannie Mae requires no additional requalification of the borrower taking out a new mortgage to meet a balloon payment and will accept the resulting mortgage in a generic Fannie Mae pool.

Whether or not investors need to concern themselves with the refinancing option offered to the borrower in conjunction with issuance of the balloon loan depends primarily on what form the balloon investment takes. For instance, investors who own agency balloon mortgages can ignore the refinancing options offered to borrowers because the agency guarantees the ultimate balloon repayment to the investor in the case of borrower default. Investors in balloon mortgages with credit support provided in another manner, on the other hand, should carefully assess the sufficiency of that support to meet borrower shortfalls at the balloon date, as the rating agencies do when assigning credit ratings to MBS backed by pools of such loans.

It is possible, of course, that the nature of the refinancing option may influence borrower prepayment behavior before the balloon date, affecting both agency and nonagency balloon mortgage holdings. On this particular issue there are at least two schools of thought on the likely prepayment behavior of balloon borrowers. One theory suggests that conforming balloon borrowers have selected this type of mortgage because they believe that they are likely to move before the balloon date, and thus pools backed by these mortgages will prepay faster than otherwise similar pools backed by generic fixed-rate loans. A second theory suggests that the lower rate offered to balloon borrowers will tend to attract a wide range of borrowers, including marginal borrowers, so that the balloon pools would prepay similarly to or perhaps more slowly than generic 30-year pools. However, prepayment rates on balloon securities have in general been faster than those of other mortgage products with similar refinancing incentives, suggesting that balloon borrowers tend to be a self-selected group with a shorter than average borrowing horizon.

"Two-Step" Mortgage Loans

Similar to the concept of the balloon loan is another mortgage design, the two-step loan structure, in which a loan carries a fixed rate for some period, usually 5 or 7 years, and then resets once. However, unlike a refinancing option the rate reset occurs without any action on the part of the borrower. The rate reset, which can be based on any rate, does not consist of a repayment of the initial loan and the origination of a new one. Fannie Mae's two-step mortgage program calculates the reset rate by adding 250 bps to the weekly average 10-year constant maturity Treasury (CMT) yield, and has a life cap of 600 bps. Essentially the two-step mortgage is an adjustable-rate mortgage with a single reset, and hence, a pool backed by two-step loans has a 30-year final maturity rather than the shorter final maturity of a balloon pool. The borrower is compensated for assuming the rate reset risk by an initial mortgage rate that is lower than the generic 30-year fixed rate, the difference depending on the steepness of the yield curve.

For the lender or investor who holds the two-step mortgage, an additional option has been extended to the borrower since the program allows for an extension of the loan when the available market rate at the reset date is more than 250 bps above the 10-year Treasury rate. If the available mortgage rate from other lenders is less than 250 bps above that of the 10-year Treasury, the borrower can prepay the two-step loan and achieve financing at a lower rate. In a rational world without transaction costs this two-step loan would have to trade at wider levels than a balloon loan with a maturity equal to the reset date of the two-step loan because the two-step is short one additional option that has some positive value.

However, not all borrowers will have the ability to prepay, and since there are transaction costs associated with refinancing a loan, the reset may actually have some positive value to investors. For instance, it is likely that at the reset date there will be some borrowers in the pool who are unable to prepay their two-step loans, even if the new rate is higher than currently available fixed rates because they are unable to qualify for the new loan. They may be unemployed, for instance, or the value of the property may have declined, requiring an additional down payment. Also, the difference between the new rate on the two-step and the current mortgage rate may not be large enough to compensate borrowers for the costs of arranging a new loan.

For example, a two-step mortgage that resets at 250 bps over the 10-year Treasury when generic mortgage rates are 200 bps over the 10 years may not experience significant prepayments, but it would offer enhanced value to investors. However, since points are usually charged for the origination of a mortgage, the borrowers also may consider how long they expect to remain in their home. A borrower with a relatively short horizon over which to amortize the points on a new loan is more likely to accept the reset even if it means paying a relatively high mortgage rate versus the prevailing market rate.

The additional value offered by these types of borrower behavior also might be a function of the form of the investors' two-step mortgage holdings. Take, for instance, a nonagency pool where only the weakest borrower credits remained after a rate reset that was significantly above the prevailing market rates. Such a pool could suffer an impairment in value as a result.

Rate Reduction Mortgages

Another trend within mortgage originations has been the development of *rate reduction programs.* Lenders such as Countrywide introduced the "eEasy Rate Reduction Loan" program that effectively enables borrowers to reduce their rate by paying a fee up-front and bypass the refinance process in a declining interest rate environment. Under this program a borrower takes out a traditional fixed-rate loan which includes a convertible option to lower the rate to the new, lower prevailing rate at a later time by paying a fee that equates to 2.5 points of the unpaid principal balance to modify the loan. Instead of taking the lengthy steps of refinancing, the terms of the loan, such as the interest rate, can be converted with a mere phone call or visit to the web site. The borrower may opt to reduce his or her rate once a month but must pay the 2.5% fee each time, which can be paid up-front with homeowner's own funds by adding to the remaining loan balance, or taking a slightly higher interest rate. The borrower also can, under certain circumstances, extend the term of the loan beyond the remaining term.

Reverse Mortgages

Reverse mortgages are designed for senior homeowners who want to convert their home equity into cash. Fannie Mae, for instance, offers two types of reverse mortgages for senior borrowers. "The Home Keeper Mortgage" is an adjustable-rate conventional reverse mortgage for borrowers who are at least 62 years of age, and who either own the home outright or have a very low unpaid principal balance. The maximum amount that can be borrowed is based on the homeowner's age, the property's value, and the interest rate. The borrower will not have to repay the loan until he or she no longer occupies the home as the principal residence and cannot be forced to sell or vacate the home to pay off the loan as long as the property is maintained. The other type of reverse mortgage, "Home Keeper for Home Purchase," enables senior borrowers to buy a new home with a combination of personal funds and calculated amount of reverse mortgage that is based on the borrower's age, the number of borrowers, the adjusted property value, and the equity share option chosen.

Growth of "Alternative" Mortgage Loans

While the product design of mortgages has continued to evolve, in recent years lenders also have started to make loans to borrowers with blemished credit, reduced documentation with nonstandard specifications, and even loans that require less down payment than previously, or do not need any down payment at all. Addressing the distinctive needs of various mortgagors in the changing mortgage market, lenders have come to offer such specialized programs as high-LTV, Alt-A, and subprime loans.

High-LTV

Traditionally for a conventional, conforming loan borrowers typically were required to make a down payment of 20% when qualifying for a mortgage. However, a mortgagor with good credit today has the option of making a lesser down payment or no down payment, resulting in loans with higher LTVs. For those interested in conventional, nonconforming loans there are programs available with 103% LTV that require no down payment because 100% of the home's price as well as an additional 3% for closing costs can be financed into the mortgage.

Alt-A

Alt-A loans are made to borrowers whose qualifying mortgage characteristics do not meet the underwriting criteria established by the GSEs. For instance, the borrower may be self-employed and not be able to provide all the necessary documentation for income verification. In such respects Alt-A loans allow reduced or alternate forms of documentation to qualify for the loan. An Alt-A loan borrower, however, should not be confused with borrowers who have blemished credits (discussed subsequently). The typical Alt-A borrower will have a credit score high enough to obtain an A standing, which is especially important to the originator since the score must compensate for the lack of other necessary documentation. With respect to LTV, Alt-A loans tend to fall within a range of 60% to 90%, which is usually just below 80%. What is appealing to borrowers about the Alt-A program is the flexibility that the program offers in terms of documentation, and they will pay a premium for the privilege. Typically rates on Alt-A loans range between 75 to 125 bps above the prime rate.

Subprime Mortgage

Borrowers who apply for subprime loans vary from those who have or had credit problems due to difficulties in repayment of debt brought on by an adverse event, such as job loss or medical emergencies, to those that continue to mismanage their debt and finances. The distinguishing feature of a subprime mortgage is that the potential universe of subprime mortgagors can be divided into various risk grades, ranging from A− through D. The risk gradation is a function of past credit history and the magnitude of credit blemishes existing in the history. Additionally, some of the higher grades in this loan category also have been labeled as "fallen angels" to indicate the fact that the credit worthiness of such borrowers was hampered by a life event, such as job loss or illness. Since such borrowers tend to have lower credit scores and pose greater credit risk, subprime mortgages command premium pricing over standard mortgages. Higher interest rates and loan fees commanded by lenders for subprime loans have therefore created a lucrative niche in the mortgage industry, and as a result have spawned innovations in product offerings.

In the past subprime lending was an arena dominated by specialized, nonbank lenders. However, as financial turmoil erupted within the bond and equity markets in the late 1990s, some of the specialized lenders were forced to close down due to high levels of loan losses, whereas well-capitalized financial institutions found an opportunity to enter. Along with the entrance of mainstream lenders the potential profitability of the subprime sector also appealed to the interests of GSEs such as Fannie Mae and Freddie Mac, a development that has generated some healthy debate in the industry.

Fannie Mae, for instance, introduced a product, the "Timely Payment Rewards Mortgage," in 1999, which was designed to target A− borrowers. This program prices the loans at 100 bps over the rate for Fannie Mae's prime quality loans, which is 200 bps below the subprime rate for similar credit quality, with the additional incentive of reducing the rate by another 100 bps after the borrower has made 24 monthly payments without delinquency. Freddie Mac also introduced a similar program, the "Affordable Merit Rate Mortgage," which gives borrowers up to 4 years to earn a 100 bps reduction in their rate. The program extends to 4 years so that if the borrowers are delinquent on a payment within the first 24 months, they can be reevaluated for a rate reduction on the 36th or the 48th month. These programs are designed for those with mild credit impairment and provide the borrowers with an incentive to make timely payments.

In sharp contrast to the market for prime mortgages the secondary market for subprime mortgages is not quite as developed. Additionally, since the late 1990s, where the industry was dominated by specialty finance companies who relied mainly on securitization to liquefy the loans, the industry has undergone severe consolidation, where the current market is dominated by a few well-capitalized lenders. However, it is not clear whether the consolidation is completely over as banks faced with the possibility of higher capital requirements and onerous capital reserves for residuals may find this business profitable on an ongoing basis.

CONCLUSION

As indicated in this chapter, the basic design of the mortgage has undergone several changes in response to changing market conditions and varying consumer demands. At the same time the market for securities created by using these mortgages also has continued to expand. In addition, as budget surpluses continue to grow and government debt is retired, the potential for additional investors to enter the mortgage fold also appears to be healthy. With changing demographic and socioeconomic conditions indicating that economic security is at parity with the quality of life, it is our contention that there will be an emergence of the "non-W-2" culture with a greater degree of variation in employment status and income. This suggests the continued proliferation of innovative mortgage instruments that focus on attributes such as portability, expandability, auto-refinancing, and fusion of first and second liens.

CHAPTER 2

MORTGAGE PASS-THROUGH SECURITIES

Linda Lowell
Senior Vice President
Asset Backed Research
Greenwich Capital Markets, Inc.

The pass-through market received its major impetus in the 1980s, growing from $11 billion at the end of 1980 to $914 billion at the end of 1989. As of June 2000, the pass-through market amounted to almost $2 trillion. Only U.S. Treasury issuance, with about $3.5 trillion outstanding, is larger. (The tradable Treasury market is actually smaller—the Treasury component of fixed income indices is closer to $1.7 trillion.) The bulk of that production has been fostered by the U.S. government through government or government-sponsored housing agencies whose missions include promoting a secondary market for home mortgage debt.

Burgeoning investor interest drove this tremendous growth. Underlying this interest is the fact that agency mortgage-backed securities represent the highest credit quality while offering excess expected yield compared to comparable Treasury and corporate securities. A variety of forces have accelerated this demand, including the growth of the collateralized mortgage obligation (CMO) market, permitting investors to buy mortgage cash flows across a spectrum of maturity sectors and to partition the prepayment risks. In addition, risk-based capital requirements established for banks and thrifts in 1989 assigned low risk weightings to agency pass-throughs and CMOs. In the mid-1990s several developments encouraged a dramatic shift in focus from CMOs back to pass-throughs on the part of many fixed income investors. Perhaps the most sweeping and enduring of these was the growing practice of evaluating portfolio managers' performance against a bond market index. Mortgage-backed securities (MBS) are represented in the common indices by the outstanding agency pass-through market. As a consequence an expanding number of portfolio managers find it difficult not to hold some portion of their portfolios in the pass-through market. Finally, the ongoing refinement and acceptance of prepayment and option-modeling techniques has encouraged demand and enabled the growth of a significant class of leveraged and hedged investors.

This chapter is intended to provide an overview of the variety of pass-through types and an introduction to the general structure and analysis of fixed-rate level payment pass-throughs, the largest and most frequently traded type of MBSs. The discussion then focuses on the cash flows and other features of pass-throughs that distinguish them from noncallable corporate or Treasury debt instruments and that give them their market properties. The chapter concludes with a discussion of the economic or total rate of return performance of pass-throughs in various interest rate scenarios and the relative value analysis of these securities. Methodologies for analyzing pass-through securities are discussed in greater detail in later chapters.

WHAT IS A MORTGAGE PASS-THROUGH SECURITY?

Pass-through securities are created when mortgages are pooled together and undivided interests or participations in the pool are sold. Typically the mortgages backing a pass-through security have the same loan type (fully amortizing level payment, adjustable-rate, etc.) and are similar enough with respect to maturity and loan interest rate to permit cash flows to be projected as if the pool were a single mortgage. The originator (or another institution which purchases this right) continues to service the mortgages, collecting payments and "passing through" the principal and interest, less the servicing, guarantee, and other fees, to the security holders. The security holders receive pro-rata shares of the resultant cash flows. A portion of the outstanding principal is paid each month according to the amortization schedule established for the individual mortgages. In addition, and this is a critical feature of mortgage pass-through securities, the principal on individual mortgages in the pool can be prepaid without penalty in whole or in part at any time before the stated maturity of the security. This characteristic has important implications for the cash flow and market performance of the security, as will be explored in detail later.

Mortgage originators (savings and loans, commercial banks, and mortgage bankers) actively pool mortgages and issue pass-throughs. In the case of mortgages meeting agency size and underwriting requirements the originator obtains the guarantee of one of three federally sponsored agencies: the Government National Mortgage Association (GNMA), or "Ginnie Mae"; the Federal National Mortgage Association (FNMA), or "Fannie Mae"; and the Federal Home Loan Mortgage Corporation (FHLMC), or "Freddie Mac." (These are referred to as "conforming mortgages.") A significant volume of mortgages is directly purchased, pooled, and securitized by FNMA (Federal National Mortgage Association) and FHLMC (Federal Home Loan Mortgage Corporation) as well. A significant volume of nonconforming mortgages are securitized by private issuers too.

The pass-through structure has proved to be an excellent vehicle for securitizing many different types of mortgage instruments available to home buyers. As a result, large amounts of balloon and adjustable-rate mortgages have been securitized. As new mortgage vehicles become popular with borrowers and mortgage originators, the agencies have proven willing to introduce new security types (e.g., relocation mortgages or mortgages with prepayment lockouts).

AGENCY PASS-THROUGH SECURITIES

The vast majority of regularly traded pass-throughs are issued and/or guaranteed by federally sponsored agencies. Differences among the agencies—the nature of their ties to the U.S. government, their stated role in national housing policy, and so forth—as well as among the types of loans eligible for securities carrying their guarantees, can affect the characteristics and relative value and performance of their pass-throughs. In addition, differences can exist among the programs which influence the investment characteristics of the securities.

Generally the market classifies agency pass-throughs into two groups: those guaranteed by GNMA and backed by government-sponsored or guaranteed loans and those guaranteed by FHLMC and FNMA and backed by "conventional" mortgages that "conform" to their loan amount and underwriting standards. Because GNMA is an agency in the Department of Housing and Urban Development (HUD), its guarantee carried the full faith and credit of the U.S. government. By contrast, FHLMC and FNMA are not government agencies; they are government-sponsored entities (GSEs) which exist pursuant to government housing policy. FHLMC and FNMA are for-profit corporations (their stock is exchange-traded) that are regulated by the federal government. As such, their guarantee does not carry the full faith and credit of the U.S. government. Instead, it is backed by emergency drawing rights on the U.S. Treasury. However, the rating agencies consider FNMA and FHLMC securities eligible collateral for triple-A securities "due to their close ties with the U.S. government." The market generally trades FNMAs and FHLMCs as if they were triple-A or government agency issues.

The market perceives a difference in credit quality between GNMA and FHLMC/FNMA, and consequently demands a risk premium for the conventional agency pass-throughs. All other factors being equal, this would translate into a higher yield for the GSE-guaranteed issues. However, all else is not equal. Fundamental and technical issues influence the price behavior of the securities and over time have tended to swamp differences in credit quality.

Differences between the prepayment characteristics of government mortgage loans and those of conventional loans give rise to differences in securities' cash flows and price performance over different interest scenarios. GNMAs are backed by FHA and VA loans, which may be assumed by subsequent buyers. By contrast, conventional loans are due on sale. As a result prepayments of government loans resulting from home sales are less likely in higher interest rate environments than prepayments of conventional loans. Prepayment rates are also influenced by borrower characteristics and underlying home values. The FHA insurance and VA guarantee provide implicit housing subsidies to people with moderate incomes and to veterans. Borrowers tend to be first time borrowers and purchasers of moderately priced homes. (Currently the amounts of loans pooled in GNMAs are limited to $203,000 and to $252,700 in both FHLMCs and FNMAs.) Less expensive homes have proven to have more stable values and turnover rates over the course of entire housing cycles than more expensive homes. As we discuss in more detail later in this article, investors' expectations of prepayment behavior are a chief determinant of pass-through values.

The pressure of supply and demand also plays an important role in obscuring any credit risk spread differential between GNMA and conventional agency pass-throughs. Only a subset of the market prefers the explicit government guarantee, while at present the vast majority of MBS investors prefer the greater liquidity of conventional agency securities. (At the end of 1990 GNMAs accounted for close to 38% of outstanding MBS, conventional agency pass-throughs for another 57%, and private issues for about 5%; by the end of the decade GNMA's share had dropped to under 27%, the conventional agencies' share was little changed, and private MBS became more than 11%.) Another significant technical force arises from the CMO market, where the prepayment profile of conventional mortgages and the ancillary costs of underwriting an agency CMO have to date been more conducive to the creation of FNMA/FHLMC CMOs. (A CMO or *collateralized mortgage obligation* is a structured security backed by pools of agency pass-throughs or nonconforming conventional loans.) This "CMO bid" is an important component of total demand for agency pass-throughs.

GOVERNMENT NATIONAL MORTGAGE ASSOCIATION PASS-THROUGH SECURITIES

The oldest and best-known group of pass-through securities is guaranteed by GNMA. As discussed, the mortgage pools underlying GNMA (Government National Mortgage Association) pass-through securities are made up of FHA-insured or VA-guaranteed mortgage loans and GNMA's guarantee carries the full faith and credit of the U.S. government.

Furthermore, the GNMA pass-through security is what is known as a *fully modified* pass-through security, which means that regardless of whether the mortgage payment is made, the holder of the security will receive full and timely payment of principal as well as of interest.

GNMA administers two primary pass-through programs, the original GNMA program (GNMA I), in existence since 1970, and GNMA II, established in 1983. The GNMA I and II programs are further divided into pool types depending on the type and term of the mortgages and other characteristics of the pool. The largest of these is the "SF" (single-family) pool type, backed by a 30-year fixed-rate mortgages. The GNMA SF pool type is created in both the GNMA I and GNMA II programs. Single-family mortgages with original maturities of 15 years are part of the same SF pool type; these pools are sometimes called "midgets." Other GNMA pool types include adjustable-rate (ARM) loans as well as once more commonly originated graduated payment (GPM), growing equity (GEM), and buy-down (BD) loans. Smaller amounts of GNMA II SF, 15-year SF, GPM, GEM, and BD pools are also created. Mobile home loans (MH) and project loans (PL) are also securitized. Project loan securities are normally backed by a single FHA-insured loan for multifamily housing, hospitals, and similar public benefit housing-related projects. Construction loans (CL) for projects are also securitized as CL pool types.

Among the various agency and private pass-through programs, GNMA I pools are the most homogeneous. All mortgages in a pool must be the same type and be less than 12 months old. Ninety percent of the pooled mortgages backing 30-year pass-throughs must have original maturities of 20 or more years. The mortgage interest rates of GNMA I pools must all be the same and the mortgages must be issued by the same lender. GNMA I payments have a stated 14-day delay (payment made on the 15th day). Minimum pool size for GNMA I pools is $1 million.

The changes introduced with GNMA II include the ability to assemble multiple issuer pools, thereby allowing for larger and more geographically dispersed pools, as well as securitization of smaller portfolios. Also, a wider range of coupons is permitted in a GNMA II pool (the excess coupon income over the lowest rate is retained by the issuer or servicer as servicing income and is not passed through). Issuers are permitted to take greater servicing fees, ranging from 50 to 150 basis points (bps). GNMA Is and IIs also differ in permitted payment delay; GNMA I payments are received with a 15-day delay, whereas GNMA IIs have an additional 5-day delay passing through principal and interest payments because issuer payments are consolidated by a central paying agent. The minimum pool size for GNMA IIs is $250,000 for multilender pools and $1,000,000 for single-lender pools.

In the early 1990s, GNMA enhanced the GNMA I and II programs with a platinum pool type, allowing investors to recombine smaller pools into a new, single pool in amounts of $10 million and up. Below a certain remaining principal amount pools become harder to trade.[1] For a fee investors can recombine smaller GNMA I pools only into a single platinum pool.

FEDERAL NATIONAL MORTGAGE ASSOCIATION MORTGAGE-BACKED SECURITIES

The Federal National Mortgage Association is the oldest of the three agencies, but was the last agency player to enter the pass-through market. FNMA was created in 1938 to provide liquidity to housing lenders. In 1968 the agency was split into GNMA and the private corporation FNMA, which was charged with the mission of promoting a secondary market for conventional mortgages on midpriced housing and seasoned FHA/VA single- and multifamily mortgages. The first FNMA MBS were issued in 1981. FNMA is, in effect, a quasi-private corporation. While a number of federal constraints on its activities exist, it does not receive a government subsidy or appropriation, its stock is traded on the New York Stock Exchange, and it is taxed at the full corporate rate. In addition to holding loans purchased from originators in its portfolio, FNMA also may securitize and sell the mortgages. FNMA pools mortgages from its purchase programs and issues MBS to originators in exchange for pooled mortgages. Like GNMA, FNMA guarantees the timely payment of principal and interest for all securities it issues. Similarly, its securities are not rated by the rating agencies.

Analogous to the 30-year GNMA SF, FNMA's 30-year conventional security, pool type CL (conventional loan) is backed by level-payment mortgages fully

---

1. "Good delivery" requirements on a TBA trade for over $1 million are three pools per million for coupons below 11% and five pools per million for coupons of 11% or higher. See footnote 5 on TBA and generic pass-through trades.

amortizing in 16 to 30 years. FNMA also issues securities under pool-type CI backed by conventional mortgages amortizing in 8 to 15 years, FNMA CIs. These are analogous to 15-year GNMA SFs and are sometimes called "dwarfs." Seven-year balloon mortgages are securitized under the pool type CX. The agency also has played a significant role in issuing adjustable- and variable-rate mortgage pass-throughs. In addition, it administers programs to securitize FHA and VA 30-year loans and FHA-insured project loans under pool type GL. Other loan types securitized include GEM, GPM, relocation, co-op, and 20-year mortgages and an extensive range of adjustable-rate mortgages. In recent years product lines have been added for high LTV (97%), pledged asset, and biweekly mortgages. In addition, the agency guarantees pools of multifamily mortgages.

Pool size starts at $1 million and more than one originator may join together to form pools. FNMA pools may contain aged mortgages, and underlying mortgage rates may range from 0 to 200 bps above the pass-through coupon rate. For a fee FNMA also permits investors to exchange small, older pools with the same coupon for a single MEGA certificate in amounts of $10 million and up.

The agency's web site provides current product information: http://www.fanniemae.com.

FEDERAL HOME LOAN MORTGAGE CORPORATION PARTICIPATION CERTIFICATES

FHLMC was created in 1970 to promote an active national secondary market for conventional residential mortgages, and has been issuing mortgage-backed securities (MBS) since 1971. At its creation FHLMC was governed as an entity within the Federal Home Loan Bank System, with stock held by member thrift institutions. The 1989 Financial Institutions Reform, Recovery, and Enforcement Act (FIRREA) restructured FHLMC to give it a market-oriented corporate structure similar to that of FNMA under the regulatory control of the Department of Housing and Urban Development (HUD).

The agency pools a wide variety of fixed- and adjustable-rate mortgages under its Gold Participation Certificate (PC) program. Standard fixed-rate PC programs include 30-, 20-, and 15-year mortgages. The nonstandard conventional loan PCs include 5- and 7-year balloon mortgages, biweekly mortgages (paid every 2 weeks), mortgages on cooperative shares, extended buy-down mortgages, newly originated assumable mortgages, relocation loans (made to relocating employees under special lending arrangements established between large employers and mortgage bankers) and second mortgage loans. In addition, FHLMC will pool FHA/VA loans under its Gold program. Pooling criteria for Gold PCs have evolved over the years: Currently the interest rates on the underlying mortgage may range as much as 250 bps above the pool coupon rate. Loans may be any age. Twenty-year loans may be pooled separately or included in standard or nonstandard PC pools containing 30-year mortgages. Up to 10% of the conventional mortgages in a standard PC pool (by original principal balance) may be a nonstandard mortgage other than second, biweekly, or balloon mortgages so long as the combination of these types does not exceed 15% of the original principal balance. The minimum pool size for fixed-rate Gold PCs is $1,000,000 (fixed-rate mini-PCs, containing standard and some nonstandard mortgage types, are pooled with a minimum pool size of $250,000). FHLMC also allows investors to repackage small, older pools in a single GIANT pool.

Prior to October 10, 1994 FHLMC distinguished between Gold securities issued in swap transactions with mortgage originators (guarantor pools) and those backed by mortgages purchased in cash transactions with mortgage originators (cash pools). The cash program allowed the underlying mortgage rates to vary from 25 and 75 bps above the pool coupon (after October 1, 1993; before that time the range between the highest and lowest bps could not exceed 100 bps, with the highest no more than 200 bps above the pool coupon). Minimum pool size for cash pools was $50 million. The guarantor program was originally established in the 1980s to provide liquidity to the thrift industry by allowing originators to swap pooled mortgages for PCs backed by those same pools (hence they were called swap PCs). This program quickly became popular with mortgage bankers and grew to account for the bulk of FHLMC pass-through production.

The Gold guarantee provides for timely payment of interest and scheduled principal and ultimate payment of all principal without offset or deduction. Gold PCs have a stated payment delay of 14 days. Prior to June 1990 most FHLMC pass-throughs were issued with "modified" guarantees and they all had 44-day payment delays. A modified guarantee provides timely payment of interest and eventual payment of principal. These securities are now referred to as the 75-day-delay PCs since the payment was made on the 45th day and mortgage payments are made 30 days in arrears (due on the first day of the next month); the total delay on those securities was 75 days. The 75-day-delay securities may be exchanged for Gold PCs.

The agency's web site, http://www.freddiemae.com, is an excellent source of additional information on its pass-through programs.

Private Pass-Through Securities

In the 1980s mortgage pass-throughs were commonly issued by private entities, such as banks, thrifts, homebuilders, and private conduits. These issues were referred to as conventional, private label or double-A pass-throughs. They were not guaranteed or insured by a government agency or GSE. Instead, their credit was enhanced by pool insurance, letters of credit, guarantees or subordinated interests, and they were rated by one or more credit rating agencies. With the advent of the REMIC tax rules, multiclass CMO-type structures with credit enhancement in the form of several levels of subordinated interests became far more popular. The refinancing boom of the early 1990s fed the growth of this "whole loan" CMO market, dominated by mortgage banking firms and Wall Street conduits. Pass-through "execution" became rare for 30-year loans, although 15-year mortgages are commonly packaged as a single senior tranche (pass-through). Today all forms of private MBS account for 11% of the MBS market (agency CMOs are not included to avoid double counting).

The loans backing private pass-throughs and CMOs typically are those conventional loans that do not qualify for FHLMC and FNMA programs. (Normally it is more profitable for originators of conforming loans—i.e., loans that do qualify—to use the agency programs). When the borrower enjoys a "prime" or "A" credit standing, the most typical reason conventional loans do not qualify for agency securities is that the principal balance exceeds the agency maximum ($252,700 for 2000). These nonconforming conventional loans are commonly referred to as "jumbos." Other characteristics of nonconforming loans include limited or no documentation of income (for reasons of speed or convenience to the borrower), loans on second or vacation homes or investor properties, and so forth. In the mid-1990s it became common practice to segregate these loans, dubbed "alternative criteria" or "Alt-A" loans from jumbo loans in separate securities, to capitalize on observed differences in their prepayment behavior.

MORTGAGE AND PASS-THROUGH CASH FLOWS

The investment characteristics and performance of pass-throughs cannot be evaluated without a thorough understanding of what cash flows are received by the investor. Analysis of the cash flow pattern begins with the simplest case, the payment stream of a single mortgage, assuming a fixed mortgage rate, level payments, and no prepayment of principal. Following that the effects of servicing fees (the amount retained by a servicer reduces the cash flow to pass-through holders) and, most important, prepayments are incorporated into the analysis.

Standard residential fixed-rate mortgages are repaid in equal monthly installments of principal and interest (hence, the term *level payment*). The payment amount is determined such that, for a given interest rate, principal payments retire the loan as of the final payment date. In the early years most of the monthly installment consists of interest. Over time the interest portion of each payment declines as the principal balance declines until, near maturity, almost all of each payment is principal.

Under the assumption that all the mortgages have the same interest rates and maturities, a "scheduled" cash flow pattern can be projected for the pool. In other words, the pool is treated as if it were an individual mortgage. Exhibit 2–1 shows the scheduled cash flow pattern for a $1 million pool of 10%, 30-year mortgages, assuming no prepayments or servicing fees. Note that the proportion of the payment that is interest declines as the proportion of principal increases over time. It is important to understand that, even without considering prepayments, the projected cash flows calculated by this procedure are *estimates*. The alternative to assuming all loans have the same interest rate and maturity would be to calculate the payments for each loan individually and then aggregate them. This is far too inefficient an approach and the loan level data are not provided by agencies or servicers. Instead, the scheduled cash flows from a pool are estimated using the weighted average of loan interest rates, or coupons (WAC) as the pool's mortgage rate and the weighted average of loan maturities (WAM) as the pool's maturity.[2] It is possible

---

2. The WAC and WAM are computed using as weights the principal amount outstanding. Sometimes the WAC is referred to as the pool's "gross WAC" and the pool coupon rate referred to as the "net WAC."

E X H I B I T   2–1

Scheduled Mortgage Pool Cash Flows*

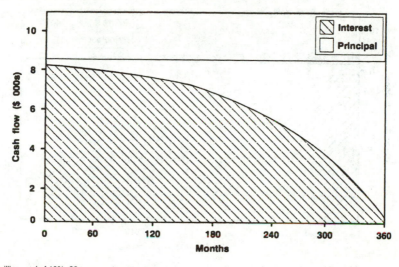

*$1 million pool of 10%, 30-year mortgages.
Note: Assumes no prepayments.

to project the payments with reasonable accuracy when pools are fairly homogeneous, as GNMA pools are. (The discrepancy arises from the fact that amortization is not a "linear" function. Individual loans will be paying principal and interest at different rates depending on the age and term of the loan.[3]) The accuracy of projected amortization schedules using WAC and WAM statistics is reduced somewhat when a wide range of coupons, maturities, and seasonings is permitted in a pool.

The cash flow from a pass-through certificate is similar but not identical to the cash flow from the underlying pool of mortgages. The differences arise from the deduction of servicing fees (and a servicing delay in the receipt of payments,

3. Actually, assuming an original principal amount of $1, three parameters are needed to calculate scheduled interest and principal: term, coupon, and age. The term and the coupon are used to calculate a full series of monthly P&I payments (180, 240, or 360 payments) and the age is used to roll off payments already estimated to have been made. The term "WAM" is normally used to indicate the remaining maturity of pools so that WAM equals the pool term minus the age. This usage is accurate if all loans in a pool have the same terms. For example, the average age of underlying loans in a 30-year pool (term 360 months) with a WAM of 359 months (WAM + AGE = TERM) is 1 month. This assumption works less well when, as in conventional pools, loans of different ages and different original terms (20-year with 30-year) can be pooled together. For instance, a 30-year pool can have an original (at issue) WAM of 352. If all the loans are 30-year loans, then the average loan age is 8 months. If an uncertain number of loans have 20-year terms, then 8 months is only an estimate of the pool's age, impounding additional uncertainty in the projected cash flows. The agencies provide different statistics to help the market resolve some of this uncertainty. The agencies now update their WAM statistics for pools monthly to capture the changing contents of the pool. In addition, FHLMC and GNMA provide an actual weighted average loan age, updated monthly (WALA).

E X H I B I T   2–2

Scheduled Mortgage-Backed Security Cash Flows*

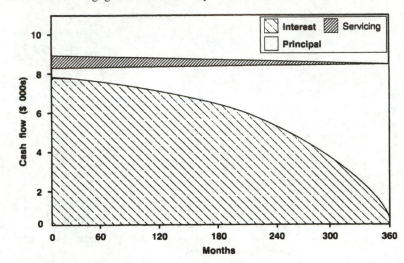

*$1 million pool of 10%, 30-year mortgages and a 9.5% pass-through certificate.
Note: Assumes no prepayments.

discussed subsequently) so that the scheduled total monthly cash flow from the mortgage pool is level, whereas the cash flow from the corresponding pass-through is not. The servicing fee is defined as a percentage of the outstanding principal and is subtracted from the interest paid on the underlying mortgages. The remaining interest income is passed through to the security holder as coupon income. (In other words, servicing is equal to the WAC less the coupon.) Thus, the dollar amount of servicing fee decreases as principal declines. As a consequence the total cash flows to pass-through owners increase slightly over the term. The cash flows from a pass-through certificate with a 9.5% coupon (the difference between the 10% WAC and a 0.5% servicing fee) are depicted in Exhibit 2–2. The graph shows that the decline in servicing fees leads to slightly increasing cash flow over time.

The possibility that individual loans will prepay is the critical issue for investors evaluating mortgage securities. Individual loans can be paid off prior to pool maturity because the borrower sells the property or refinances. *The possibility of prepayments means that cash flows cannot be predicted with certainty.* Assumptions concerning the likely prepayment pattern must be made in order to estimate the cash flows.

Exhibit 2–3 depicts the cash flow patterns for the 9.5%, 30-year pass-through in the previous example when a prepayment assumption is introduced. The cash flow pattern shown in the diagram is based on the assumption that a constant fraction of the remaining principal is prepaid each month (in this case, at a constant prepayment rate of 0.5% per month). The cash flow is no longer level in each month over the period. Instead, it declines each month as both prepayments and scheduled

E X H I B I T   2–3

Scheduled and Unscheduled Mortgage-Backed Security Cash Flows*

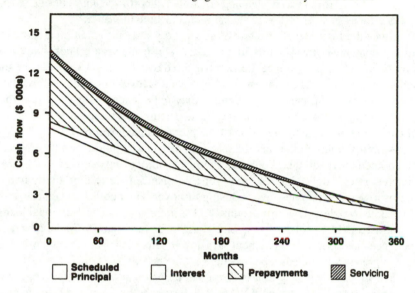

*$1 million pool of 10%, 30-year mortgages, and a 9.5% pass-through certificate.

principal payments reduce the remaining principal balance of the pool. The reader should note that prepayments lower the total amount of interest paid over the life of the pass-through in addition to accelerating the return of the principal.

DETERMINANTS OF PREPAYMENT RATES

The chief determinant of a pass-through's investment performance is the effect of prepayments on cash flows actually received. For this reason MBS investors devote considerable attention to the underlying causes of prepayments and to projecting prepayments over the investment horizon. The causes of prepayments generally fall under two categories—refinancing and mobility. Homeowners tend to refinance when the current market mortgage rate is far enough below the rate on their existing mortgage to lower their monthly payment significantly.[4] The difference in payments must be at least great enough to permit the homeowner to recover the loan fees and other costs of refinancing over some reasonable period of time. In the 1980s a common rule of thumb put this lower mortgage rate at 200 bps below the existing mortgage's rate.

---

4. Actually prepayments can arise from a third source, cash-out refinancings. In this case homeowners refinance in order to realize paid-in equity or increases in appraised home value. Homeowners may be more likely to refinance for this purpose when they can pay the same or a lower rate of interest, but in many situations the need to do so (home improvement or expansion, illness or education expenses, etc.) is not interest-rate sensitive.

Aggressive marketing by mortgage banking firms, the leading originators of loans securitized in GNMA and conventional agency securities, have resulted in no-point and even no-fee loan terms. In such a lending environment borrowers may consider an interest rate cut as small as 50 bps sufficient inducement to refinance.

Since the future level of interest rates is very difficult to anticipate, the resulting prepayments are also difficult to predict. Refinancings are a negative event for pass-through investors since they are triggered by a fall in market rates and the principal returned must be reinvested at lower yields. Investors who purchase their high coupon pass-throughs at a premium may experience additional losses because the principal is repaid at par and must remain outstanding to earn interest sufficient to recover the future value of the premium paid over par.

Mobility refers to the fact that at any time, in any mortgage rate environment, homeowners sell their homes and move. Mobility is also linked to the level of interest rates. Higher interest rates act as a disincentive to buy a new home, whereas lower interest rates favor housing turnover. The due-on-sale clause, now enforceable by federal law, ensures this kind of prepayment of conventional loans. By contrast, GNMA pools, made up of assumable government-insured mortgages, experience this form of prepayment at a lower rate. An assumable loan is less likely to prepay when it has a below-market interest rate.

The chief indicator of a pass-through's prepayment risk is the average underlying mortgage rate—the pool WAC. The farther below current mortgage rates a pool's WAC is, the slower the pool is expected to prepay. Likewise, prepayments are faster for pools with above-market-rate WACs. It follows that securities with higher pass-through coupons are expected to pay faster than those with lower coupons, but investors must not lose sight of the fact that the pass-through coupon is less than the underlying mortgage rates by the amount of servicing and guarantee fees. In the case of GNMA I securities the coupon precisely indicates the underlying mortgage rate since every mortgage in the pool must have the same rate and 50 bps are stripped off. However, with conventional agency (and private issue) pools, there is considerable room for variation in underlying mortgage rates above the coupon. For example, we know GNMA SF 8s have a WAC of 8.50%. By contrast, as of November 1, 1994, in aggregate, FNMA CL 8s (18,304 pools with a current principal balance of $45.9 billion) had a WAC of 8.554%, whereas FHLMC gold 8s (10,230 pools, $56.6 billion) had a WAC of 8.594%.

Nonetheless, because the WAC is indicated by the coupon of a GNMA I security and can be assumed on average for a conventional pass-through, the market uses the coupon as a short-hand indication of prepayment risk and trades pass-throughs accordingly. The most fundamental relative value distinctions among pass-throughs are made on the basis of prepayment risk between GNMAs and conventionals and among discount, current, and premium coupon securities. To satisfy investor preference, the vast majority of pass-through pools are issued with a whole or half coupon (8, 8.5, 9, etc.) and securities with quarter, eighth, or other coupon groups are illiquid. The current coupon is usually defined as the pass-through with a whole or half coupon priced the closest to but below par. Under normal market conditions this is also the coupon class where most new supply is entering the market.

The age or *seasoning* of a pool is another key determinant of prepayment behavior and, accordingly, of relative value within and across coupon classes. Normally some months or years elapse after a mortgage is closed before the borrower is willing or able to go to the effort and expense of moving or refinancing. As a result, prepayment rates increase from a very low level during the early years of a pass-through's life to level off sometime after 12 to 60 months (depending on the program and coupon). As a result, newly issued pass-throughs will demonstrate low prepayment rates but show significant rates of increase from month to month. Likewise, the prepayment rates of fully seasoned securities will be relatively stable. "Seasoned" means that the pass-through has been outstanding long enough for this process to have occurred and prepayments to have reached a steady state appropriate for the interest rate environment. When the loans are unrefinanceable, the steady state is characterized by a pronounced seasonal prepayment pattern, reflecting the fact that housing turnover is highly seasonal. When a security is refinanceable, the steady state is indicated by a slowing of the rate at which prepayments accelerate from month to month. In general lower coupons season more slowly than higher coupons. Historically GNMAs have seasoned more slowly than conventionals because the loans are assumable.

Depending on the characteristics of current tradable supply and the prevailing interest rate environment, some degree of price tiering can exist in coupons or coupons groups. For example, investors will pay a premium for seasoned discounts over new pools on the assumption that principal will be returned more quickly. Similarly, very seasoned premium coupons are valued in sustained rally environments because they tend to be less responsive to refinancing opportunities. One of the explanations for this effect is that, as years pass, the interest portion of the monthly payment declines, lowering the total savings a cut in rate would produce. Another is that when pools are exposed to repeated refinancing opportunities over time, the borrowers remaining in the pool are somewhat less likely to respond to the next opportunity. This effect is often termed "burnout."

Considerable attention has been given to identifying the factors underlying prepayment activity in mortgage pass-throughs and specifying them in econometric models which can be used to project prepayments. These factors include the economic incentive, the weighted average age of the pool, burnout, and seasonality. More recent models have attempted to capture other influences on borrower behavior such as price appreciation (depreciation) and macroeconomic factors. Prepayment modeling is discussed in greater detail in Section IV.

The unique securitization and cash flow characteristics of mortgage pass-throughs give rise to important differences from Treasury and corporate securities. These are summarized in Exhibit 2–4.

Measuring Prepayments

In order to facilitate the evaluation and trading of MBS, the market has evolved a variety of conventions for quantifying prepayments. The oldest and simplest of these was the prepaid life assumption employed by secondary market traders of

E X H I B I T   2–4

Features of Pass-Through, Government, and Corporate Securities Compared

	Pass-Throughs	Treasuries
Credit risk	Generally high grade; range from government guaranteed to A (private pass-throughs)	Government guaranteed
Liquidity	Good for agency issued/guaranteed pass-through	Excellent
Range of coupons (discount to premium)	Full range	Full range
Range of maturities	Medium- and long-term (fast-paying and seasoned pools can provide shorter maturities than stated)	Full range
Call protection	Complex prepayment pattern; investor can limit through selection variables such as coupon, seasoning, and program	Noncallable (except certain 30-year bonds)
Frequency of payment	Monthly payments of principal and interest	Semiannual interest payment
Average life	Lower than for bullets of comparable maturity; can only be estimated due to prepayment risk	Estimate only for small number of callable issues; otherwise, known with certainty
Duration/interest rate risk	Function of prepayment risk; can only be estimated; can be negative when prepayment risk is high	Unless callable, a simple function of yield, coupon, and maturity; is known with certainty
Basis for yield quotes	Cash flow yield based on monthly payments and a constant CPR, assumption	Based on semiannual coupon payments and 365-day year

whole loan mortgages. At that time the 12-year prepaid life assumption was the industry standard for quoting mortgage yields. Under this convention a 30-year pass-through is treated like a single mortgage prepaying in the twelfth year of its life (or, no loans prepay until the twelfth year, when they all prepay). Other prepaid life assumptions were used, such as 7-year prepaid life, but the 12-year as-

EXHIBIT 2–4

Continued

	Corporates	Stripped Treasuries
Settlement	Once a month	Any business day
Credit risk	High grade to speculative	Backed by government guarantees
Liquidity	Generally limited	Fair
Range of coupons (discount to premium)	Wide range for few issuers	Zero coupon (discount securities)
Range of maturities	Full range	Full range
Call protection	Generally callable after initial limited period of five to ten years	Noncallable
Frequency of payment	Semiannual interest (except Eurobonds, which pay interest annually)	No payments until maturity
Average life	Minimum average life known, otherwise a function of call risk	Known with certainty
Duration/interest rate risk	Function of call risk; can be negative when call risk is high	Known with certainty; no interest-rate risk if held to maturity
Basis for yield quotes	Based on semiannual coupon payments and 360-day year of twelve 30-day months	Bond equivalent yield based on either 360- or 365-day year, depending on sponsor
Settlement	Any business day	Any business day

sumption was the standard. During the 1970s and mid-1980s, however, interest rates and, in turn, prepayments became far more volatile. Prepaid life assumptions could not be adjusted for actual prepayment experience or the differences in coupon, maturity, seasoning, and other security characteristics which began to appear as the pass-through market evolved.

Recognizing the problems with the prepaid life assumptions, traders and investors began using the termination experience collected on FHA-insured mortgages issued since 1970 to model expected prepayments. These data are published periodically by HUD in the form of a table of 30 numbers indicating the probability of survival of a mortgage at any given year up to maturity. Prepayment rates (the percentage or fraction of principal prepaying in a year) are implicit in these survivorship rates. An example of an FHA series converted to prepayment rates is graphed in Exhibit 2–5. Its advantage was that it linked prepayments to age; pre-

E X H I B I T   2–5

PSA Versus FHA CPR Series

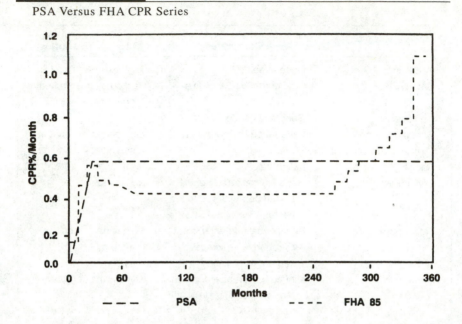

payments rise rapidly in the first 30 months and then level off (the staircase pattern in the last years was an interpolation provided by FHA actuaries). Given a pool's age, prepayments over the remaining months to maturity could be projected based on the FHA series of annual rates. Faster or slower prepayment speeds were expressed as a multiple of the base table. For instance, "0% of FHA" means no prepayments, "100% of FHA" refers to the average rate, and "200% of FHA" means twice the FHA rate.

The FHA experience was welcomed in the early years of the mortgage market before huge databases of actual prepayment experience were accumulated which allowed the market to link prepayment behavior to other factors besides age. As the market's empirical understanding of prepayment behavior grew, the shortcomings of the FHA series became more problematic. For one, the underlying data are from assumable FHA mortgages and can be misleading when applied to conventional pass-throughs. Moreover, FHA experience did not provide a consistent standard because a new series is published each year or so, often based on different statistical manipulations of the underlying data. For instance, prior to FHA 83, all mortgages back to 1957 were included; subsequently all mortgages prior to 1970 were excluded. Extrapolation was used to a greater degree to derive experience for years not covered by actual data. Similarly, through 1981 each year's data were equally weighted; starting in 1982 mortgages issued in the 1980s were given additional weight. For instance, in 1986 investors could conceivably be pricing MBS based on 1981, 1983, 1984, or 1985 FHA statistics.

Conditional Prepayment Rates

As the market expanded during the mid-1980s, large Wall Street firms making markets in pass-throughs developed the capability to report historical prepayments on individual pools as well as on specific coupons within programs and, within coupons, groups of pools with various degrees of seasoning. These reports allowed investors and traders to form empirical views on prepayment behavior and to base projections of future prepayments on the aggregate response of generic pass-throughs to actual interest rate environments. The fundamental measure employed in these reports was the conditional prepayment rate (CPR) or single monthly mortality (SMM). This measure has become the principal means traders and investors employ to quantify prepayment activity in pass-throughs. The CPR measures prepayments as a fraction or percentage of the remaining principal balance at the beginning of the measurement period (hence, "conditional" on the principal balance). Thus, it can be employed to express an average or compound rate over many periods, or a single-period rate. The resulting rate sometimes is expressed as an annualized percentage. (In recent years CPR has increasingly come to refer to an annualized prepayment rate, SMM to the monthly rate.) This simple quantification is intuitive and easy to incorporate into pricing and yield formulas. In calculating yields, investors may employ a single or "constant" CPR assumption across the term of the investment to project the cash flows. The use of a constant CPR is the most common (hence, it is sometimes thought that CPR stands for "constant prepayment assumption"). Some analytic tools allow investors to project pass-through cash flows using a series (sometimes called a "vector") of varying CPR assumptions reflecting historical experience or projections from formal prepayment forecast models.

The PSA Prepayment Standard

The Public Securities Association (PSA) introduced a standard prepayment model for the purpose of valuing CMOs. The intention was to replace with a single standard the proliferation of FHA experience tables that were being used to project cash flows on the underlying collateral when CMO issues were structured and priced. It is not really a model; more correctly, it is a measurement standard or yardstick, expressed as a series of 360 monthly prepayment rates expressed as annual CPRs. It begins at 0.2% in the first month and increases by 0.2% in each successive month until month 30, when the series levels out at 6% per year until maturity. Prepayments are measured as simple linear multiples of this schedule. For instance, 200% PSA is 0.4% per year in the first month, 0.8% per year in the second month, and 12% per year after month 30. Market participants often speak of the first 30 months of the series as the "ramp" and speak of securities seasoned 30 months as "off the ramp." Exhibit 2–5 compares the PSA standard to the 1985 FHA series.

One advantage of the PSA CPR series is that it does reflect the normal increase in CPRs that occurs as the pool ages. (Since a CMO issue effectively "carves up" the cash flow from pass-through collateral among a series of bond classes with short, intermediate, and long average lives, it is important to be as realistic as possible when projecting the amount of cash available in the early years to pay off the bonds with the shortest expected average lives.) This effect is also captured by the FHA series, but the PSA series of CPRs do not display the fluctuation in prepayment rates found in the FHA series. After month 30, using the PSA is equivalent to applying a constant CPR over the remaining life of the pool. The PSA standard was intended to simplify the comparison and analysis of CMOs but has increasingly been used to express prepayment speeds in the fixed-rate pass-through market (ARM speeds are expressed in CPR terms). This practice can be confusing and even misleading. For instance, for very new securities, a relatively small CPR can be reported as a very large PSA because the divisors are so small on the "foot of the ramp." A similar sort of illusion is created when the monthly prepayment rates on new securities go up but not as fast as suggested by the PSA ramp. In this case it will appear as if reported speeds, in PSA terms, are going down, when in fact the CPRs are going up. Thirty months is much too long a seasoning period for conventional securities and is too long for GNMAs if they become refinanceable. Furthermore, differences in prepayments between fast-paying and slow-paying pools are not proportional over the lives of the pools. Relying on a PSA prepayment assumption, without considering the CPRs, and hence the actual magnitudes of the cash flows which it expresses, can result in mistaken security valuations and investment decisions. Finally, the PSA standard should not be used with securities backed by loans making balloon payments at maturity.

EVALUATING PASS-THROUGH SECURITIES YIELD, AVERAGE LIFE, AND DURATION

The price of a pass-through is the present value of the projected cash flows discounted at the current yield required by the market, given the specific interest rate and prepayment risks of the security in question. Generic[5] agency pass-throughs trade on price, subject to supply and demand forces. That means the required yield and the prepayment assumption may both have to be imputed from the price. Increasingly the market has gravitated toward using econometric models (or a median of Street firms' prepayment models) to fix the prepayment assumption given the current level of interest rates. It is then an easy matter to find the yield. Investors use the yield-to-maturity on the projected cash flows (given the prepayment assumption) at a given market price as the basis for determining if the anticipated investment return is a good value relative to other investment alternatives.

Yield is useful for determining relative value but it is a poor predictor of future performance. Yield-to-maturity is a poor predictor of any bond's performance because it assumes that (1) all cash flows are reinvested at an interest rate equal to the yield and (2) the security is held to maturity. Further, there is the implication that the market values cash flows received at different times at the same average yield.

---

5. The most generic pass-through is a coupon class of a specific agency program with a whole or half coupon. This security trades "TBA" or "to be announced," meaning that the seller may deliver at settlement a pool or pools of any age that meet the description (subject to good delivery guidelines established by the PSA). A year class within a coupon class may be stipulated (based on WAM). In most circumstances it would trade at a premium to the TBA price.

EXHIBIT 2–6

Effect of Reinvestment Rate on Realized Yield from Monthly Payments on a 9.5% Pass-Through Priced at 99 8/32 to Yield 9.54%

Reinvestment Rate (%)	Realized Cash Flow Yield (%)	Change from Expected Yield (%)
4	5.93	−37.84
6	7.16	−24.95
8	8.48	−11.11
10	9.87	3.46
12	11.33	18.76
14	12.84	34.59
16	14.41	51.05

Note: Assumes 0.50% service fee and no prepayments.

Deviations from the first assumption are particularly significant for pass-throughs owing to their monthly coupon and principal payments since interest on these payments compounds monthly in the yield calculation instead of semiannually on coupon payments only, as with Treasury and corporate bonds. Exhibit 2–6 demonstrates how much the realized return or internal rate of return on the cash flows can vary when reinvestment rates that are different from the yield-to-maturity are used to project the total cash flows to be received from a pass-through. The second assumption is as unrealistic for MBS as it is for Treasury and corporate bonds. If an investment is not held to maturity, the realized yield will be affected by any capital gain or loss on the remaining cash flows, as market yields and prices are likely to have changed since the initial investment was made.

More importantly, the yield anticipated on a pass-through can vary significantly depending on the prepayment rate used to project the cash flows. If the pass-through is priced at par, changes in prepayment speeds do not affect the yield calculation. (Actually the yield does not change if the security was purchased at its *parity price* [slightly less than 100], which adjusts par for the payment delay. The delay lowers yield at a given price by moving the cash flows further out into the future.) No matter when the principal is returned, the security will continue to yield its coupon rate on the remaining principal. At faster speeds the earlier receipt of principal offsets the loss of coupon income, and at slower speeds additional coupon income offsets the additional delay in return of principal. However, if the security is purchased at a premium, faster than expected prepayments will reduce the yield: Prepayments shorten the amount of time the principal remains outstanding to earn above-market coupon payments, thereby lowering the total cash flows. In a similar fashion, the yield of a discount security increases with faster prepayments as the time required to earn the discount is shortened. Principal purchased at, say, 90% of its value, is returned at 100%. The effect of prepayments on yield for securities purchased close to, above, or below par is shown in Exhibit 2–7.

E X H I B I T 2–7

Effect of Different Prepayment Rates on the Cash Flow Yield of Discount, Current, and Premium Coupon Pass-Throughs*

CPR (%/yr)	Price 89 20/32	Price 99 28/32	Price 105 4/32
2	8.78	9.57	10.67
4	8.97	8.58	10.57
6	9.18	9.58	10.46
8	9.39	9.59	10.35
10	9.62	9.60	10.23
12	9.85	9.62	10.11
18	10.58	9.65	9.74
24	11.37	9.68	9.33

*Assumes 9.5% coupon is priced closest to par.

Two additional issues requiring brief discussion arise from the differences between the cash flow characteristics of mortgage securities and those of Treasury or corporate bonds. First, the difference in payment timing between pass-throughs and bonds with semiannual coupons and bullet principal payments means their yields are not directly comparable. The greater frequency of payments increases the value of a pass-through of a given coupon compared to traditional corporate or government debt. Interest compounds monthly. This monthly compounding gives pass-through securities a yield advantage over other securities of the same coupon. Quoted cash flow yields, however, do not reflect the advantage. For instance, a 10.00% cash flow yield is equivalent to a 10.21% bond yield. In order to compare pass-through yields to yields on other securities, it is necessary to adjust the mortgage yield upward to its bond equivalent yield (BEY). Basically the monthly coupons are treated as if they are collected and reinvested at the cash flow yield rate until the end of each semiannual or other period. The accumulated (compounded) amount is larger than the sum of the face amount of six monthly coupons.

The second, the payment delay, does not alter the level of payments, but it does affect their timing. In effect it pushes the stream of payments further out in time and effectively lowers the current value of the payment stream. There are two sources of payment delay in pass-throughs. Mortgage payments are made in arrears; that is, interest accrues during the month (on a 30-day basis) and is payable, along with a scheduled principal amount, on the first day of the second month. Second, there is a further delay as the servicer collects payments due (a 15-day grace period is typical) before the holder of the corresponding pass-through receives the payment. An investor in a GNMA single-family pass-through, for example, does not receive payment until the 15th day of the second month (a 14-day actual delay plus 30 days for the accrual period plus 1 amounts to a 45-day stated

EXHIBIT   2–8

The Effect of Payment Delay on Pass-Through Yield and Price

Stated Delay	Yield	Change	Price	Change (%)
30	9.59		99 8/32	
45	9.54	−0.05	98 27/32+	−0.39
50	9.53	−0.06	98 23/32+	−0.52
55	9.51	−0.08	98 19/32	−0.66
75	9.45	−0.14	98 2/32	−1.20

Note: Assumes 9.5% coupon, 99 8/32 price, 9.59% yield, and no prepayments.

delay). FNMA securities have a stated delay of 55 days, which means the first payment takes place on the 25th day of the second month. Older FHLMC securities have a 75-day delay, whereas newer Gold PCs have 45-day delays.

Delay decreases the current value of the stream of payments: The greater the delays, the lower the price is for a given cash flow yield. Similarly, for a given yield and payment stream yield declines as delay increases. Yield and cash flows held equal, GNMA securities with lower delays will trade at higher prices than FNMAs or FHLMCs, and FNMAs will trade higher than FHLMCs. The effect of varying the delay on the yield, price held constant, and the price, yield held constant, for a 9.5% coupon pass-through is indicated in Exhibit 2–8. For instance, assuming the security has a price of 99:08 points, adding 15 days to a stated delay of 30 days lowers the yield to 9.54% from 9.59%. In price terms the table indicates that the difference in delay between otherwise comparable Gold and FNMA 9.5s is worth about 8+/32 point.

The interest rate and age of a mortgage (or WAC and WAM of the underlying loans in a mortgage pool), as we have noted, determine the rate at which scheduled principal is expected to be paid to the investor. In general, for the same principal amount and term, the higher the mortgage rate is, the greater the interest payments will be, and accordingly, the lower the principal payments are in the early years of the mortgage. A look at any of the cash flow figures should make apparent the effect of age on cash flows. All other things being equal, age affects the cash flow by establishing the amount of principal included in a given monthly payment and the number of payments remaining. As the security ages a greater proportion of the payments will be principal. For pass-throughs purchased at a given discount price older pass-throughs will have higher yields—more principal is returned sooner at par. Age has the opposite impact on premium securities; at the same price and coupon older pass-throughs have lower yields since less principal is outstanding for shorter periods of time to earn high coupon income while principal is coming back to the investor at par. In either case the further the price of the security is from par, the greater the impact of seasoning on the yield. The yields for securities that are near par are not significantly affected.

The natural variability of expected cash flows from a pass-through investment makes it difficult as well to determine the degree of risk undertaken. A fundamental measure of the risk in any investment is its term, or longevity. Because the principal is returned throughout the pass-through's life, maturity is not a good measure of the longevity of this form of debt. The likelihood of prepayments amplifies this deficiency. For these reasons a preferred measure for MBS, including pass-throughs, is the average elapsed time until the principal is returned. *Average life* is calculated as the weighted average time to principal repayment, with the amount of the principal paydowns (both scheduled and prepaid) as the weights. Average life expresses the average number of years that each principal dollar will be outstanding. Clearly the higher the prepayment rate is, the sooner the principal is returned, and hence the shorter the average life is. It also should be apparent from the definition that average life declines as a security ages.

Determining a pass-through's interest rate risk, or duration, with certainty also is impossible. Modified, or cash flow, duration[6] is as sensitive to the prepayment assumption used to project a pass-through's cash flows as are its yield and average life. As a result a duration can significantly misestimate the actual price change of pass-throughs when interest rates decline and the market changes its estimates of prepayment risk. More importantly, a pass-through's duration changes as the expected prepayment rates used to calculate its change in response to changes in the general level of interest rates. Pass-through duration lengthens in a bear market and shortens in a bull market. As a result a pass-through's price can decline more quickly than a Treasury with the same duration at the outset when interest rates rise. Similarly, pass-through prices increase more slowly for successive declines in the general level of interest rates. This characteristic of a pass-through's price behavior is generally referred to as "negative convexity." It is also observed in the phenomenon called "coupon compression." This term refers to the fact that price spreads between coupons shrink as the coupon—and the prepayment expectation—increases. In other words, at a given point in time the market might price GNMA 7s 3:06 points above GNMA 6.5s and GNMA 8.5s only 2:24 points above GNMA 8s.

Modified duration, then, is not a good prospective measure of a pass-through's price risk because it reflects a static prepayment assumption. Approaches taken by the market to adjust for this shortcoming include effective duration, empirical duration, and option-adjusted duration. Effective durations are measured by calculating the relative change in price that would result, assuming a large enough shift in rates (e.g., 25, 50, or 100 bps up and down) to generate a change in the prepayment assumption. The new prepayment rates are used to cal-

---

6. Macaulay duration is defined as the weighted average time to receipt of the present value of both principal and interest cash flows. With a routine adjustment this expression is equivalent to the first derivative of price with respect to yield. That is, *modified duration* expresses the percentage change in price that would occur for a small change in yield, assuming cash flows are fixed. Since prepayments are also interest rate sensitive, this assumption is violated. Duration shrinks or grows with interest rate shifts and it drifts with time.

culate a new price given the shifted yields; solving for the percentage price change per 1 bp of yield shift produces the effective duration. Empirical durations are determined by a statistical analysis of actual price changes for observed changes in market yields so that an empirical duration captures the duration implied by actual trading behavior. Option-adjusted duration is computed similarly to an effective duration using option pricing models. Which measure of price risk an investor uses depends on the horizon, the strategy, and the mortgage instrument. For instance, a short-term hedge may work best when constructed using an empirical measure of price behavior, whereas an effective or OA duration may be a better indicator of interest rate risk over a longer investment horizon.

The cash flows from pass-throughs, particularly as they reflect monthly amortization, delays, and the likelihood of prepayments, give rise to the major differences between pass-throughs on the one hand and Treasury and corporate bonds on the other. The differences among these instruments are summarized in Exhibit 2–4.

Relative Value Analysis

The chief objective of any investment evaluation technique is to identify the securities which provide the highest return for a given level of risk. Yield-to-maturity or the internal rate of return on a bond's cash flows is traditionally used to order investment opportunities in fixed income instruments. For securities of comparable risk the highest yielding security would be the cheapest and most attractive. With mortgage pass-throughs the difficulty is determining the degree of risk. Credit risk is normally assumed away, but the interest rate risk and the yield of a mortgage pass-through are uncertain at the time the investment decision is made. Nonetheless, the mortgage market has adapted traditional techniques of bond analysis in order to make relative value comparisons to other fixed income sectors and across sectors of the pass-through and CMO markets.

The first comparison made between pass-throughs and other instruments is to Treasury instruments, typically the on-the-run Treasury with the maturity closest to the pass-through's average life. Average life is not the best basis on which to compare a monthly pay mortgage security to a bullet Treasury, but it approximates maturity. (The better comparison would be between securities of comparable price sensitivity, or duration). Given the widespread acceptance of prepayment models, most participants now use a median of dealer prepayment projections (such as those published on Bloomberg Capital Markets screens or by the Bond Market Association on Telerate) as the consensus of market prepayment expectations. For instance, as of October 26, 1994 the market price for GNMA 8s was 98:08, and the median of dealer prepayment projections, assuming interest rates are unchanged, was 135% PSA to yield 8.92 (assuming a WAM of 349, representative of the coupon class). At that speed the pass-through had an average life of 9.6 years and provides a yield spread to the 10-year Treasury of 106 bps. That is, the pass-through would provide 106 bps additional yield to a comparable Treasury benchmark if interest rates are unchanged and the prepayment assumption is on target.

This spread to a Treasury benchmark[7] can be used to make rudimentary relative value distinctions between pass-throughs. (Is an FNMA or FHLMC pool of FHA/VA loans cheap to a GNMA with the same coupon? Or, is an FHLMC 6.5 rich compared to a GNMA 8?) It fails to account for the much greater uncertainty in the pass-through than in the Treasury cash flows. That is, the pass-through is cheap to the Treasury only in the very unlikely case that interest rates are unchanged and the median of street firms' prepayment projections is correct. In other scenarios the 106 bps of the base case yield may not compensate an investor for holding the pass-through instead of the Treasury. For instance, if interest rates fall sharply, the pass-through investor must reinvest monthly principal and interest in lower yielding securities while the Treasury investor has locked in a higher coupon on the entire principal until the maturity date. Worse, falling interest rates accelerate prepayments. As an example of how badly the pass-through yield can be reduced by reinvesting rapid prepayments at a lower rate, assume yields drop 200 bps instantaneously. If interest cash flows, now returned at 350% PSA, are reinvested at a yield of 200 bps less than the original pass-through yield, or in the case of the Treasury alternative at the Treasury yield less than 200 bps, the GNMA 8.5 would yield 7.18%, the Treasury 7.32% (the expected yield was 7.86%). That is, instead of yielding 106 bps more than the 10-year Treasury, as anticipated at the time of purchase, the GNMA 8.5 yields 14 bps less than the Treasury. Altogether the GNMA 8.5 provides 120 bps less yield than anticipated at the time of purchase.

The prepayment uncertainty in mortgage cash flows, then, makes it difficult to make a relative value determination between a pass-through and a Treasury. Many market participants adjust by looking at the pass-through's yield across a range of prepayment/interest rate scenarios (using a model or a street consensus projection). The yield in each scenario can be compared to the yield of the Treasury security with a maturity closest to the pass-through's average life (or to capture the slope of the yield curve, an interpolated Treasury). The most attractive MBS would be the one that provides the widest spread to Treasuries across the scenarios deemed the most likely.

Traditional yield-to-maturity techniques can be adjusted for the greater complexity of pass-through cash flows, but they are ultimately arbitrary and even misleading. To overcome many of the shortcomings of static cash flow analysis, many market participants have adopted option-adjusted spread (OAS) simulation models. In brief, their objective is to evaluate explicitly the option to prepay given the current yield environment, a process for modeling likely changes in interest rates for realistic levels of interest rate volatility, and a prepayment model that links prepayment activity to interest rate levels. Different analytic techniques may be used to arrive at such models, but the basic outputs will include measures of yield and yield spread over Treasuries that are adjusted for the average exercise of the prepayment option

---

7. For premium pass-throughs with rapid prepayment expectations and consequently short average lives, the yield-to-the-average life, or to the curve, is preferable because it picks up the value of the curve when the curve is upwardly sloped. It is found by interpolating between the on-the-run Treasury yields at the expected average life of the pass-through.

over a wide range of interest rate paths. Other outputs include option-adjusted measures of price sensitivity or duration. Rich-cheap analysis is conducted using these measures in the same way as with older techniques: Investments with similar risk characteristics are compared to identify superior value. The difference is that the investor has the advantage of being able to compare a theoretical value to the actual market spread to make a better informed investment decision.

Total Return Analysis

Yield is not commonly used to describe the historical investment performance of a pass-through. Instead, the total rate of return is used. The actual or economic return received by an investor is the sum of interest and principal payments as well as any reinvestment income received over a holding or measurement period, plus any capital gain or loss if the bond is sold at the end of the period. If the bond is not sold, the total return calculation takes into account any appreciation or depreciation in market price as of the end of the period.

Total returns also can be projected to support trading and investment decisions. Such analysis, if performed with adequate care, overcomes many of the shortcomings of yield. For one thing assumptions about interest rate and prepayment scenarios can be used to project principal and interest payments and to reinvestment income over the period, as well as market prices at the end of the measurement horizon. The results, however, are highly dependent on the terminal prices. Some investors perform total rate of return analysis in a static cash flow calculator by using a prepayment model and assuming that the current spread curve for pass-throughs holds at the end of the horizon. That is, the remaining cash flows are projected for the specific interest rate scenario and, given their resultant average life, priced at the required spread currently observed for a pass-through of the same average life. This approach is rough but it can help to build intuition regarding the performance of pass-throughs in different scenarios. A better approach is OAS-based. It prices the remaining cash flows at the same option-adjusted spread (OAS) to Treasuries as demonstrated by the security at the beginning of the period. This approach has the advantage of incorporating a mathematical expectation rather than a point estimate of the required spread.

Projected returns for new discount and current coupon FNMA pass-throughs and for a seasoned premium coupon FNMA securities are depicted in Exhibit 2–9. At the time that these total rates of return were calculated, the 8.5% coupon was the current coupon. That is, it was priced closest to but below par. Current new production was centered on this coupon. These were calculated holding OAS constant to determine the terminal pricing. Readers should note the differences in projected total return performance between pass-throughs from different coupon sectors of the market. The current coupon 8.5 outperforms in the base case, owing to its higher base case yield. As interest rates rise, the discount extends somewhat, underperforming the current and premium rates. At the same time prepayments slow on the current coupon 8.5, extending its duration and hurting its performance in rising rate scenarios. By contrast, the seasoned premium has a shorter duration and yield at the

EXHIBIT 2–9

Total Rates of Return on Selected Conventional Pass-Throughs over a
One-Year Horizon*

Interest Rate Shift (Basis Points)	Discount	Current	Seasoned Premium
−250	22.00	18.15	15.37
−200	20.55	17.20	13.81
−150	17.88	15.88	12.42
−100	15.09	14.13	11.16
−50	12.30	12.07	9.99
0	9.57	9.78	8.87
50	6.95	7.32	7.76
100	4.44	4.80	6.60
150	2.03	2.31	5.38
200	−0.29	−0.12	4.13
250	−2.51	−2.46	2.86

*Assumes 8.5% coupon priced closest to but below par.

outset of the horizon—and consequently, underperforms in the base case. However, its short duration is more stable owing to the seasoned prepayment pattern, limiting price declines somewhat as rates rise. The 10% premium coupon helps to buffer price declines as well. In the rally scenarios the long duration of the discount gives it the superior performance, although rising prepayment risk begins to limit price gains mostly. The current coupon 8.5 performs less well as its duration shortens more rapidly. The shorter duration of the seasoned premium results in smaller price appreciation; this effect is accentuated in the increasingly bullish scenarios as its prepayments accelerate and its duration shortens sharply.

Total return projections are typically used in making relative value assessments. In this context the investor would prefer the securities offering the greatest return advantage over comparable Treasuries in the anticipated interest rate scenarios.

SUMMARY

In this chapter the investment characteristics of mortgage pass-through securities and the various types of securities are explained. In the next chapter agency adjustable-rate mortgage securities are discussed. While the basic factors that influence prepayments are reviewed, a more detailed discussion of prepayment modeling is provided in Section IV. Cash flow yield and duration are parameters often used to describe the investment characteristics of these securities. Later chapters discuss the limitations of these measures in greater detail and suggest better methodologies for valuing pass-throughs, as well as estimating and hedging their price volatility.

CHAPTER 3

SECURITIES BACKED BY ADJUSTABLE-RATE MORTGAGES

Satish M. Mansukhani
Managing Director
Bear, Stearns & Co. Inc.

An adjustable-rate mortgage (ARM) has a coupon rate that tracks interest rate movements. In general an ARM floats off a benchmark index plus a margin, bound on each reset date by periodic and lifetime caps. Homeowners choosing fixed-rate financing lock in their borrowing costs, whereas they face the uncertainty of fluctuating interest rates when choosing adjustable-rate financing. This basic characteristic attracts a specific type of homeowner, leading to inherently different risks of investing in ARMs rather than fixed-rate mortgages (FRMs).

Since the introduction of ARMs in the 1980s banks and thrifts have been the largest investors. The short duration of ARMs make these a good asset/liability management tool to match the floating liabilities of depository institutions. Moreover, during the last few years ARMs have appealed to a variety of new investors, ranging from money managers to international financial institutions. As investor understanding and analytical techniques have improved, so too has demand. Even traditional mortgage investors, who had previously invested only in FRM passthroughs and collateralized mortgage obligations (CMOs), have turned to ARMs as a short duration alternative.

In this chapter we explain the structural characteristics of ARMs and how these characteristics affect the value and risk profile of ARMs. Further, we discuss a variety of methods to discern relative value.

THE ARM MARKET

ARM securities constitute about 13.6% of the total amount of mortgage securities currently outstanding. The greater affordability permitted by adjustable-rate financing (due either to lower rates on ARMs versus FRMs or to the added appeal

This chapter is reprinted from the author's chapter, "Valuation and Analysis of ARMs," Chapter 10, in Frank J. Fabozzi, (ed.), *Advances in Fixed Income Valuation Modeling and Risk Management* (New Hope, PA: Frank J. Fabozzi Associates, 1997).

of below-market teaser rates) make ARMs an attractive choice, particularly among first-time home buyers. The interest rate environment has a large bearing on a homeowner's choice. In periods of low-fixed-rate mortgages homeowners typically opt for a fixed-rate mortgage, seizing an opportunity for low-cost financing that may not recur in the foreseeable future. When interest rates are high (and especially if the yield curve is positively sloped), homeowners are inclined toward ARMs since they are priced off the front end of the curve.

Prior to 1991 when rates on FRMs were relatively high, ARM originations tracked the spread between fixed- versus adjustable-rate financing. However, when fixed mortgage rates have been unusually low, this relationship has not held despite ARMs offering a rate incentive over FRMs. Notably during 1993 homeowners could not turn down the opportunity of a 7% fixed-rate mortgage. Thus, both the absolute level of interest rates and the shape of the yield curve interactively impact ARM market share. Further, alternative mortgage products, such as 5- and 7-year balloons, have wooed homeowners away from adjustable-rate financing. When the yield curve was flat in 1995, an interesting innovation was "hybrid" ARMs. These offer the safety of a fixed-rate mortgage for an initial period of 3, 5, 7, or 10 years, floating annually thereafter.

The three mortgage agencies—Government National Mortgage Association (GNMA), Federal National Mortgage Association (FNMA), and Federal Home Loan Mortgage Corporation (FHLMC)—dominate ARM issuance. Twenty-four percent of the overall ARM market consists of nonagency securities. The three agencies issue ARMs under different guidelines. All GNMA ARMs are issued under the GNMA II program. GNMA ARMs pools are comprised of mortgages insured by the Federal Housing Administration (FHA). [Prior to September 1995 GNMA ARMs also included loans guaranteed by the Department of Veterans Affairs (VA).] Additionally, GNMA ARMs are multiple issuer pools, in that separate issuers can contribute loans to one single pool. FHLMC ARMs are originated under either the cash or guarantor programs. Under the cash program FHLMC buys mortgages outright for cash. The guidelines of this program make it better suited for the pooling of new production loans. In the guarantor program lenders swap mortgages in return for the participation certificate (PC security) created from these very mortgages. A guarantor ARM can be either a margin or a WAC ARM. Mortgages underlying the margin program are homogeneous in terms of reset and convertibility dates. On the other hand, a WAC ARM contains mortgages that may have different characteristics (reset, conversion dates, life caps, etc.) but float off a common index. The characteristics of the resulting PC security are weighted averages of the underlying loans. Also, FHLMC has a GIANT program, which pools together existing FHLMC PCs into larger, more diversified and liquid securities. Correspondingly FNMA offers the flex and mega programs.

From a trading perspective the ARM market can be segregated into TBA (to-be-announced) and specified pool sectors. Since new production GNMA ARMs are the most homogeneous, they trade on a TBA basis enabling investors to finance them in the dollar roll market. Older GNMA ARMs, however, trade on a pool-specific basis. Similarly, most FNMA and FHLMC ARMs trade on a pool-specific basis due to the heterogeneity of conventional securities. The one exception is COFI-indexed ARMs, which trade as TBAs. Generally TBA instruments consist of recently originated (2 to 3 years old) loans. However, the Public Securities Association (PSA) does not place any origination date restrictions on the underlying loans for TBA-eligible COFI ARMs. As a result thrifts sporadically securitize large portions of their COFI loan portfolio causing large monthly swings in TBA COFI origination.

Among fixed-rate mortgages relative value opinions are primarily based on differences in homeowner profile, seasoning, coupon, and so on. ARMs have the added intricacy of different indices, net margins, caps and floors, reset frequencies, lookbacks, payment caps, negative amortization, and convertibility features. These are discussed in detail in a later section.

DURATION OF FLOATING-RATE SECURITIES

Before immersing ourselves into the intricacies of ARM valuation, we would like briefly to reintroduce the concept of duration. *Duration* measures the interest rate sensitivity of a bond and is calculated as the percentage price change for a parallel 100 basis point (bp) rate shift.

We can illustrate the duration of a capped floating-rate instrument, such as an ARM, by starting with a pure floater. The coupon rate of a pure floater perfectly tracks changes in interest rates. Thus, as shown in Exhibit 3–1, a pure floater has a duration of zero, that is, no interest rate risk. The price of a pure floater remains constant since it will always pay the prevailing market rate. An investor in a pure floater, however, faces credit risk of its issuer. With incremental constraints, like caps and floors, the duration of a security extends (see Exhibit 3–1). The following section introduces various contractual features highlighting their impact on ARM security valuation.

ARM STRUCTURAL CHARACTERISTICS

Index

The ARM coupon resets off a given benchmark index. Banks and thrifts favor ARM securities pegged off an index which most closely matches their funding costs. Some common indices are reviewed here.

Weekly Average Yield of Constant Maturity 1-Year Treasuries
U.S. government securities' dealers report daily closing prices of the most actively traded bills, notes, and bonds to the Federal Reserve Bank of New York. Yields are then computed by the Treasury Department. The Federal Reserve publishes this index, which is the weekly average yield of the actively traded securities with a constant maturity of one year, in its weekly statistical H.15 release. This report is available at the start of the week for the previous Monday to Friday period (accessible on Telerate page 7052). The index is not the yield of the 52-week Treasury bill; however, the two will be closely related.

EXHIBIT 3-1

Interest Rate Sensitivity Analysis of Pure, Capped, and Capped/Floored Floaters

		Reference Rate								
		−300	−225	−150	−75	Flat	75	150	225	300
Pure	Price	100:00	100:00	100:00	100:00	100:00	100:00	100:00	100:00	100:00
Floater	ROR	0.80	1.562	2.216	3.070	3.839	4.610	5.385	6.162	6.941
	Duration	NA	0.00	0.00	0.00	0.00	0.00	0.00	0:00	NA
9%	Price	99:29	99:21+	99:6+	98:14+	97:12	95:31+	94:7+	92:5	89:26
Capped	ROR	3.426	3.986	4.304	4.357	4.117	3.503	2.474	1.092	−0.600
Floater	Duration	NA	0.48	0.82	1.23	1.69	2.19	2.71	3.18	NA
9% cap/	Price	103:17	101:19+	99:31+	98:18+	97:12	95:31+	94:7+	92:5	89:26
3% floor	ROR	6.952	5.867	5.041	4.446	4.117	3.503	2.474	1.092	−0.600
Floater	Duration	NA	2.33	2.02	1.76	1.78	2.19	2.71	3.18	NA
Effective	Price	123:20+	117:5+	111:1+	105:10+	99:29+	94:28	90:3	85:19+	81:12
Fixed rate	ROR	23.411	18.309	13.341	8.532	3.898	−0.560	−4.892	−9.078	−13.13
	Duration	NA	7.17	7.12	7.05	6.97	6.90	6.89	6.78	NA
Reference Treasury Curve					1-year	2-year	3-year	5-year	7-year	10-year	30-year
					3.44	4.11	4.60	5.52	6.06	6.56	7.38

11th District Cost of Funds Index (COFI)

The Federal Home Loan Bank of San Francisco calculates the monthly index, which reflects the actual interest expenses of all savings institutions headquartered in Arizona, California, and Nevada. These three states make up the 11th District of the Federal Home Loan Bank System. The COFI index is *not* a market interest rate. Savings institutions rely on medium- and long-term maturity fixed-rate deposits as primary funding. Since these deposit rates are not affected by changing market interest rates until the deposit matures, the total interest expense paid by savings institutions in a particular month largely reflects interest rates that were prevalent in previous months or years. This creates a natural 6- to 9-month lag in the index because longer deposits must mature before they are rolled into new deposits. This causes the index to register smaller and delayed moves relative to other short-term rates. The updated COFI index for the prior monthly period is obtained by calling (415) 616-2600, after 6 p.m. Eastern time on the last business day of every month. Historical and updated values of the index are available on Telerate page 7058.

National Monthly Median Cost of Funds Index

SAIF-insured depository institutions report monthly cost of funds data to their regulator, the Office of Thrift Supervision (OTS). After ranking all the institutions by cost of funds, the OTS reports the statistical median, which is the value of the index. Although similar to the 11th District COFI, the primary difference between the two is that the Monthly Median calculation uses the *current* month's liabilities as the base, whereas the 11th District COFI calculation uses the *average* liabilities of the current and prior month. Further, the 11th District COFI is a weighted average measure, whereas the National Median COFI is a median. The updated value of this index can be obtained by calling the Office of Thrift Supervision at (202) 906-6988, or by referring to Telerate page 7058.

6-Month LIBOR

The London Interbank offer rate (LIBOR) is the rate at which major international banks offer to place deposits with one another for maturities ranging from overnight up to 5 years. Six-month LIBOR, which is commonly used for ARMs, is the rate offered for 6-month U.S. dollar denominated deposits. Updated values are available daily in *The Wall Street Journal* and on Telerate page 7050.

6-Month CD

This rate is calculated by the Federal Reserve Bank of New York. It reflects the average of the dealer offering rates on nationally traded certificates of deposit with a maturity of 6 months. The Federal Reserve publishes this index in its weekly statistical H.15 release (accessible on Telerate page 7052).

    Exhibit 3–2 illustrates historical levels of the most commonly used indices. Movements in the 1-year CMT, 6-month LIBOR, and 6-month CD are closely correlated, whereas the 11th District COFI and National Median COFI lag interest rates. Exhibit 3–3 provides a breakdown of the ARM market by index.

EXHIBIT 3–2

Historical Levels of Commonly Used Arm Indices

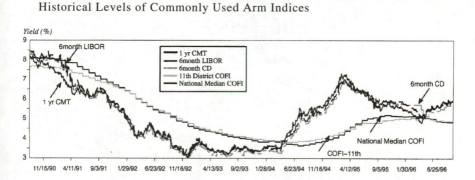

EXHIBIT 3–3

ARM Agency and Nonagency Issuance Market Share by Index

Index	Market Share (%)
1-year CMT	58.39
COFI	24.04
6-month LIBOR	8.46
1-month LIBOR	2.09
3-year Treasury	1.62
6-month CD	1.06
Other	4.34

The index of an ARM will affect its duration. The more an index lags market interest rates, the more a security will behave like a fixed-rate security rather than a pure floater. Thus the duration of COFI-indexed ARMs is largely derived from the lagging nature of the index.

Net Margin

The *net margin* is the spread above the index that an ARM coupon adjusts to. Almost all GNMA ARMs have a 150 bp net margin. However, conventional ARMs carry a wider range of net margins depending on loan underwriting guidelines. Let us consider a sample 6.5% ARM with a net margin of 150 bps (security A1). At an index level of 7% the coupon rate resets to a fully indexed rate of 8.5% (see Exhibit 3–4).

E X H I B I T   3–4

Net and Gross Margins

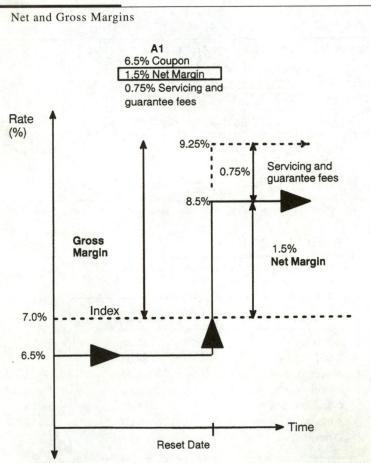

Gross Margin

The *gross margin* is the net margin plus servicing and guarantee fees. Therefore, the coupon of the ARM security plus the gross margin equals the actual loan rate charged to the homeowner. If the servicing and guarantee fees on the sample ARM just introduced are 75 bps, then the gross mortgage rate will be 9.25% (see Exhibit 3–4).

Loans underlying GNMA ARMs tend to have more homogeneous features than FNMA and FHLMC ARMs. However, the gross borrowing rate may vary from loan to loan within a given GNMA ARM security. With inadequate loan level data on GNMA ARMs, market convention has assumed a gross margin of 225 bps on GNMA ARMs issued prior to 1995 and 275 bps on post-1995 originations. In actuality a particular loan may have a different gross margin since mortgage bankers may incorporate different excess servicing when underwriting these loans. For example, in environments when business volume is low mortgage bankers have been known to generate revenues by originating loans with higher gross margins.

Periodic Cap and Floor

Periodic caps/floors limit how much the ARM rate can reset *relative to the current coupon rate*. An important feature of periodic caps and floors is that they are path dependent. They do not represent absolute constraints, but rather, are relative constraints. Since the periodic cap/floor is relative to the current coupon rate, the strike level of the periodic caps and floors change from reset to reset. The periodic cap protects homeowners from facing "payment shock" (a large jump in their monthly payment).

Exhibit 3–5 examines the reset mechanism with periodic caps. Note the two-example ARMs, A1 and A2, with a 1 and 2% periodic cap/floor, respectively. Like A1, A2 also has a 6.5% coupon rate but a 225 bp net margin. The 1% cap on A1 limits its adjustment to a 7.5% coupon, bringing the cap 100 bps "in-the-money," whereas an uncapped security would reset to a fully indexed rate of 8.5%. Likewise, the 2% periodic cap on A2 is 75 bps "in-the-money." The net margin determines the extent to which a cap is "in- or out-of-the-money." In general for a given periodic cap the higher the net margin is, the *greater* the likelihood that the cap is in-the-money.

Exhibit 3–6 illustrates rate adjustments on the sample ARMs when the index drops to 3%. The fully indexed rate on these securities will be 4.5% and 5.25%, respectively. However, the 1% floor on A1 limits its downward adjustment to 5.5%, bringing the floor 100 bps in-the-money. Correspondingly the 2% floor on A2 is "at-the-money" as its coupon adjusts to the fully indexed rate. In contrast to the interaction between net margin and periodic caps, the larger the net margin is, the *lesser* the likelihood that a floor is in-the-money.

Investors commonly ignore periodic floors while focusing solely on the caps. All else being equal, periodic caps hinder the performance of ARMs when rates rise, and periodic floors enhance their performance when rates fall. Periodic

E X H I B I T 3–5

Periodic Caps

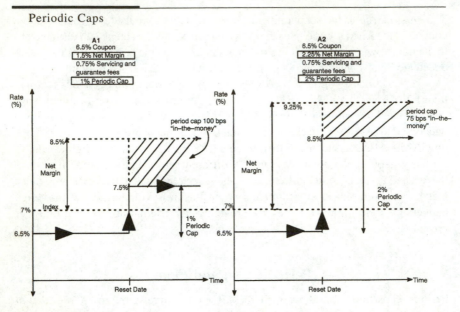

caps and floors raise the duration of an ARM by preventing the coupon rate from keeping pace with market rate movements, making the security behave more like a fixed-rate bond. Generally the lower the caps and the higher the floors are, the greater the duration extension will be. GNMA ARMs have an annual cap/floor of 1% movements relative to their prior coupon rate. On the other hand, conventional ARMs have either 1% *semiannual* caps and floors or 2% *annual* caps and floors. Thus, 1% capped GNMA ARMs have longer durations than 2% capped conventional ARMs.

Lifetime Cap

The lifetime cap sets the maximum coupon rate over the life of a loan. Unlike the periodic cap, which is path dependent and relative, the lifetime cap is an absolute level and therefore supersedes the periodic caps. Once market rates surpass a given level, the ARM becomes "capped" out and behaves like a fixed-rate security unless rates subsequently decline. Securities with similar lifetime caps but with different net margins will "cap" out at different levels of the index. Let us consider securities A1 and A2 again, both with a life cap of 10%. Since A1 has a net margin of 150 bps, the coupon will cap when the index hits 8.5% (10% − 1.5%), whereas the coupon on A2 will cap at an index level of 7.75% (see Exhibit 3–7).

EXHIBIT 3–6

Periodic Floors

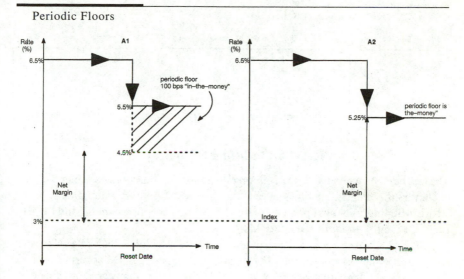

EXHIBIT 3–7

Effect of Lifetime Caps

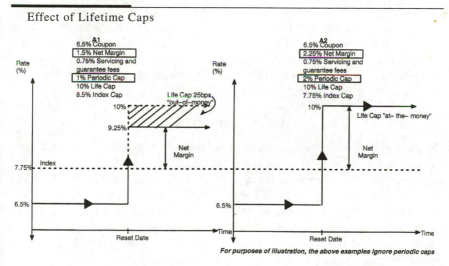

For purposes of illustration, the above examples ignore periodic caps

The lifetime cap increases the duration of an ARM. The lower the index cap is, the longer the duration of the ARM will be. All GNMA ARM securities have lifetime caps 5% points above the original coupon rate. Correspondingly most conventional ARMs have lifetime caps pegged about 5 to 6% above the original coupon.

EXHIBIT 3–8

GNMA ARM Production Schedule

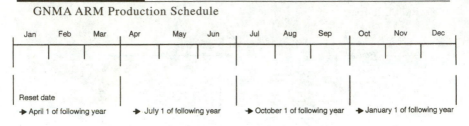

Reset Date and Frequency

The *reset date* is when the ARM coupon rate adjusts to market rates. The reset frequency is the number of times a year that the ARM coupon rate adjusts. Most ARMs offer a semiannual or an annual reset. Some exceptions are monthly resetting COFI and 1-month LIBOR ARMs.

GNMA ARMs are issued on a quarterly rolling schedule which determines the specific reset date of the security. For example, all GNMA ARM securities issued during the first quarter of a year reset on April 1 of the following year, those issued in the second quarter reset on July 1 of the following year, and so on (see Exhibit 3–8—GNMA ARM production schedule). Since the security has a single reset date, it is called a *bullet reset*. Conventional ARMs, on the other hand, generally offer stratified resets because the underlying loan reset dates are distributed throughout the year.

The further out the reset dates are, the longer the duration is; the closer the reset dates are, the shorter the duration is. The more delayed the reset dates are, the longer is the lag before an ARM fully adjusts to market rates, making the ARM behave more like a fixed-rate instrument.

Index Lookback

The *lookback period* is the time between the index determination date and the reset date. ARMs issued by different issuers vary considerably in terms of their lookback features. We present the coupon reset adjustment process for GNMA, FNMA, and FHLMC ARMs in Exhibits 3–9 and 3–10).

Exhibit 3–9 illustrates a sample GNMA ARM pool with an April 1, 1996 reset date. The lookback period of 30 calendar days refers to the index rate as of Saturday, March 2, 1996. The index value is obtained from the most recently available H.15 release as of that date or the prior business day.

Exhibit 3–10 compares the lookback and reset procedures for FNMA and FHLMC WAC PC ARM securities. The primary difference between the two are

- In the case of FNMA ARMs both the underlying loans and security reset simultaneously. In the case of FHLMC WAC ARM PCs the security coupon adjusts 30 days after the loan coupon adjustment (compare loans versus PC/pool reset for FHLMC/FNMA ARM in Exhibit 3–10).

- The payment delay after the security adjusts is 55 days for FNMA and 75 days for the PC issues.

E X H I B I T   3–9

GNMA ARM Rate Adjustment

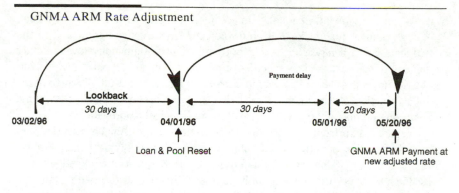

E X H I B I T   3–10

FHLMC WAC PC ARM Rate Adjustment

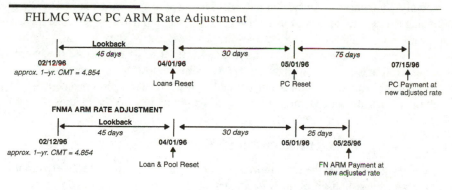

The lookback features are crucial in a highly volatile rate environment. For example, between February and May 1996, the 1-year CMT rate rose by 65 bps. Ignoring the lookback period could result in a 65-bp error in estimating the coupon reset, leading to misstating the yield by 10 to 15 bps. Further, investors typically disregard the reset lag between coupon adjustments on the underlying loans versus the overlying security.

Because of the lookback and payment delays FNMA ARM securities take 100 days (over 3 months) and FHLMC WAC PC ARM securities take over 150 days (6 months) for interest payments to reflect market rates. Thus, shorter lookbacks translate into shorter durations. Conversely, longer lookbacks translate into longer durations.

Payment Adjustment Cap/Floor and Reset Frequency

The payment cap/floor limits the percentage change of the borrower's monthly payment. This is a common feature in COFI-indexed ARMs. TBA-eligible COFI ARMs have an *annual* payment cap/floor of 7.5%. This implies that, on an annual basis, the monthly payment can neither increase nor decrease by more than 7.5%. Payment caps/floors are similar to periodic caps/floors since both shield the borrower from payment shock.

Negative Amortization

Negative amortization is the capitalization of interest payments, accrued to principal. This is a common feature in COFI-indexed ARMs. Mortgages originated in the United States are typically level-paying mortgages. Upon origination a level monthly paying amortization schedule is specified, a portion of which is applied toward principal write down and the remainder applied toward interest due. Initially most of the payment is applied toward interest due, and as the principal balance keeps declining, an increasing portion of the payment goes toward principal amortization.

Negative amortization arises due to two reasons: a mismatch between payment and rate adjustment frequencies and the imposition of payment caps. For example, in a rapidly rising interest rate environment, frequent rate adjustments increase the interest portion of the monthly payment without a corresponding increase in the monthly payment amount. If the interest due surpasses the amount of the monthly payment, the unpaid interest will be added to the principal outstanding, leading to negative amortization. As a general rule of thumb a 200-bp instantaneous upward move in the COFI index causes immediate negative amortization.

However, there are contractual limits on negative amortization. In general the maximum negative amortization on COFI-indexed ARMs is limited to 110 to 125% of the original outstanding principal balance. Once this limit is reached, any payment caps are waived and the borrower's monthly payment is increased.

Payment Recast and Recast Frequency

Payment recast forces the full amortization of a mortgage. In a negatively amortizing mortgage a cutoff point is necessary to force the eventual paydown of the balance to zero. The payment recast overrides any payment caps and establishes a new amortization schedule. The payment recast frequency is generally 5 years.

Convertibility

ARM borrowers may choose between convertible or nonconvertible ARM loans. Convertibility allows the homeowner to change from adjustable-rate into fixed-rate financing. This option is typically exercisable during the first 5 years after origination. However, the option does have a cost in the form of higher up-front fees. Upon exercising the conversion option, the loan will carry a coupon equal to the then prevailing fixed rate plus a premium (0.25 to 0.75%). Typically the conversion rate is based on the FNMA or FHLMC 30- or 60-day mandatory delivery rate. Despite the premium it is generally assumed to be cheaper to convert an adjustable-rate loan rather than refinancing it. The exercise of the conversion option represents a prepayment for the security holder. As one would expect, a convertible ARM would tend to have a more rate-sensitive prepayment profile than a nonconvertible ARM.

Exhibit 3–11 summarizes generic ARM characteristics and presents PSA guidelines on TBA-eligible GNMA and FNMA COFI ARMs.

Summary of Generic ARM Characteristics

	Conventional			GNMA	Impact on Duration (holding all else equal)
Index	1-year CMT	6-month LIBOR	11th District COFI	One-year CMT	
Periodic cap	2% annual	1% semiannual	NA on monthly 1% on semiannual 2% on annual	1% annual	Decreases with larger caps/floors
Lifetime cap	6% over original coupon	5–6% over original coupon	Greater than 12%	5% over original coupon	Decreases with higher index caps
Reset frequency	12 months	6 months	Monthly Semiannual Annual	12 months	Decreases with shorter resets
Lookback	45 days	45 days	45 days	30 days	Decreases with shorter lookbacks
Payment cap and frequency	NA	NA	7.5% Annually	NA	Decreases with larger caps
Negative amortization	NA	NA	110–125%	NA	
Payment recast frequency	NA	NA	5 years	NA	
Net margin	150–250 bps	150–250 bps	Generally 125 bps	150 bp	
Gross margin	215–315 bps	215–315 bps	Generally 200 bps	Assumed to be 225 bps	
Convertible	Allowed	Allowed	Allowed	Not allowed	

Specifications of TBA-eligible FNMA 11th District COFI ARMs

1. 12% and higher original life cap
2. 125 bps margin or higher
3. Fully indexed
4. 25- to 40-year maturities
5. 2-, 3-, 4-month lag is allowable within each million-dollar lot
6. Adjustable monthly, +/– 7.5% payment cap

Specifications of TBA-eligible GNMA ARMs

1. All pools must be multiple issuer pools
2. 150 bps margin or higher
3. Reset off the one-year CMT index annually
4. Coupons should be the same on all pools
5. 1% annual cap
6. All pools should have a lifetime cap equal to 500 bps above the original coupon
7. The settlement date implies the reset date that must apply to all pools

RELATIVE VALUE TOOLS FOR ADJUSTABLE-RATE MORTGAGES

ARMs can be viewed as hybrids, sometimes performing like an uncapped floater, and sometimes like a fixed-rate security. The tighter the caps and floors are, the more the ARM will mimic a fixed-rate security. In fact, one can think of a fixed-rate security as a limiting case of an ARM, with caps and floors that equal the MBS coupon rate. A fixed-rate mortgage security is generally viewed as

Fixed-rate MBS = Long noncallable bond + short prepayment option

Likewise, an ARM is generally viewed as

Adjustable-rate MBS = Long pure floater + long floors + short caps + short prepayment option

The *best* relative value measure is one that correctly values each component of the security—caps, floors, and prepayment options.

Net Effective Margin

The *net effective margin* (NEM) measures the difference between the yield of the ARM security (at an assumed constant prepayment speed and current index) and the current value of the index over which the ARM security resets. It helps to indicate the income spread if the investor were funding liabilities resetting over the same index. Hence, NEM is a popular gauge among banks and thrifts.

The NEM is similar to the *discount margin* (DM) measure used to value floating-rate securities like CMO floaters. However, there is one key difference between the two measures. Whereas NEM assumes semiannual compounding, DM uses monthly compounding.

NEM has limited usage being a static measure. If interest rates and prepayments indeed turn out to be static, the NEM would be an appropriate relative value measure. However, the world is rarely static. Let us consider the sample securities, A1 and A2, to illustrate. The two bonds are similar except that one has a 1% periodic cap, a net margin of 150 bps, and the other has a 2% periodic cap, a net margin of 225 bps. The coupon rate adjustment for the two securities is shown in Exhibit 3–12. The two securities are assumed to prepay at the same constant prepayment rate. NEM is calculated using these projected cash flows.

The drawback of the NEM calculation is that it ignores the *full* impact of the caps and floors and the prepayment option. Even the value of the periodic caps that are currently in-the-money is measured only with respect to the current value of the index. Further, NEM is only useful as a relative value measure within a specific universe of ARM securities using the same index. It falls short when comparing ARMs with different indices and against other mortgage/fixed income instruments.

Despite its problems the simplicity of the calculation, easy replication, and long-standing prevalence continues to support its use as an initial valuation screen.

EXHIBIT 3–12

Calculating Yield/NEM on ARMs

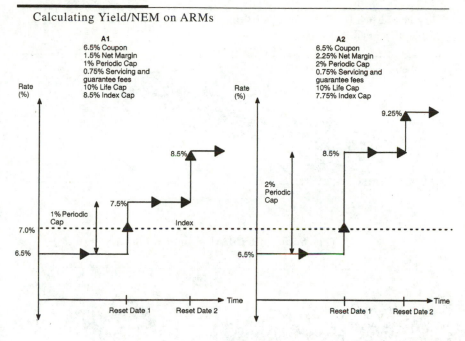

Curve-Adjusted Yield/NEM

Although NEM and yield are static measures they can still be useful. As investor understanding and analytical techniques constantly improve, the markets do price in the various embedded options, reflected in the widening/tightening of these static spreads.

Let us consider an investor trying to ascertain relative value between FRM and ARM pass-throughs. Curve shape should exert a larger impact on the valuation of ARMs than on FRMs. Given a steeper curve and higher implied forward rates, periodic and lifetime caps are more likely to go in-the-money. Hence, the spread represented by the NEM/yield is less likely translated into realized total return. In an attempt to net out the impact of curve shape on the spread valuation of ARMs, we analyze daily yield spreads between par-priced 30-year FNMA FRMs and par-priced GNMA ARMs, plotting them against the 1/10-year spread. We restrict the analysis to par-priced securities in order to screen out the prepayment characteristics generally associated with discount and premium securities. Since the duration of par-priced FRMs is higher than that of par-priced GNMA ARMs, swapping from the former and into the latter entails a yield give up. According to the scatter plot (see Exhibit 3–13), a steeper curve implies a greater yield give up, whereas a flatter curve reduces the yield give up. Notably, observations outside the 95% confidence intervals indicate relative cheapness/richness. The plot identifies

E X H I B I T   3–13

Par-Priced FNMA FRM Yield/Par-Priced GNMA ARM Yield Versus 1- to
10-Year Spread

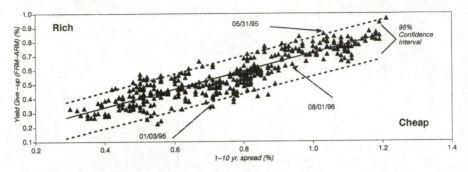

Time Series of FRM/ARM Spread Model

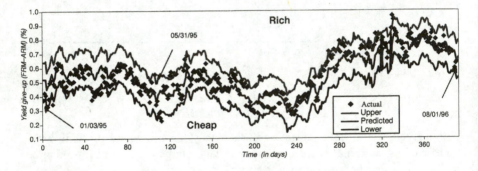

two historical points when GNMA ARMs proved to be cheap (1/03/95) and rich
(5/31/95) versus FRMs. The time series graphs plot the daily actual spreads versus the predicted and the 95% confidence bands.

This analysis serves only as an initial screen on relative value since the
yields are calculated under static prepayment assumptions. Our scatter plot assumes a lifetime prepayment assumption of 8% CPR on the GNMA ARMs. Yields
on FRMs are generated using the Bear Stearns' prepayment models. Additionally,
the analysis uses history as a benchmark. Relative cheapness/richness is determined by comparing current versus prior spreads for similar curve shape.

Similar analysis is replicated by examining the NEM of GNMA ARMs and
netting out the influence of curve shape. In this case we use the 1/2-year and 1/10-
year spread as the independent variables. The dependent variables are the difference between the NEM and the 1/2-year and 1/10-year spread, respectively (see

EXHIBIT 3–14

Par-Priced GNMA ARM NEM Versus 1- to 2-Year Spread

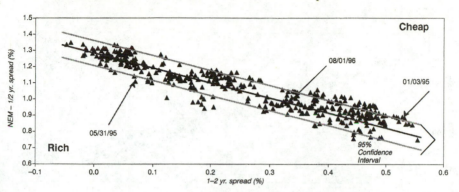

Time Series of 1- to 2-Year Spread Model

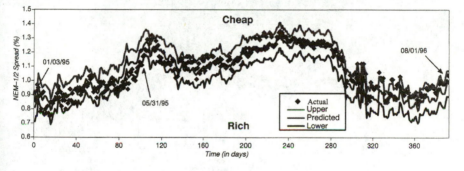

Exhibits 3–14 and 3–15). This helps to measure the income that will most likely be earned. The analysis helps to identify risk/reward with any outliers, indicating relative cheapness/richness.

Market Implied Returns

This is a simple tool used to examine intercoupon relationships (see Exhibit 3–16). The analysis assumes that when interest rates shift in parallel by 50, 100, 150 bps, then the terminal price of a security will be that of the adjacent coupon 50, 100, 150 bps higher/lower, as the case may be, than the security being examined. Thus, in studying GNMA 6% ARMs, the base case horizon period returns are obtained by assuming unchanged prices and historical speeds (3- or 6-month averages depending

EXHIBIT 3–15

Par-Priced GNMA ARM NEM—1- to 10-Year Spread Versus 1- to 10-Year
Spread

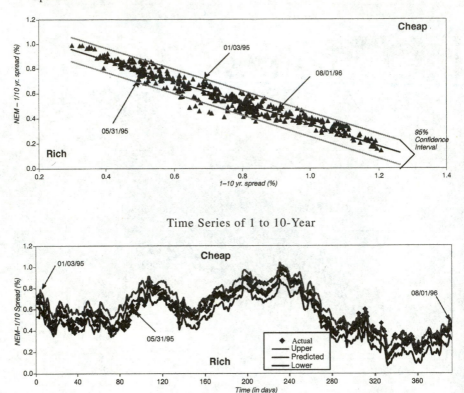

Time Series of 1 to 10-Year

on the rate environment) over the horizon period. In a down 50 scenario the projected returns are obtained by assuming a horizon price and historical speeds of the
adjacent coupon 50 bps higher, that is, GNMA 6.5% ARMs. The analysis is simplistic in that it assumes that a security will behave exactly like the adjacent coupon
when rates move. Reinvestment rates are adjusted in up/down scenarios from a
base case reinvestment rate equal to the fed funds rate.

The drawback of the analysis is that it can only be used to value homogeneous securities. Given the diversity of ARM securities, the analysis is limited to
examining intercoupon relationships between TBA GNMA ARMs. TBA GNMA
ARMs are issued with coupons, lifetime caps, periodic caps, and so on, that
change in increments of 50 bps, making the technique easily applicable. Further,
they are issued with the same reset date, eliminating any complications arising
from varying reset dates on valuations.

The advantage of the analysis is that it incorporates factual information
available in the market. However, actual price changes, even if the curve experi-

E X H I B I T   3–16

Adjacent Coupon Analysis of GNMA ARMs

Using 3-Month Speeds, 3:00 p.m. Closing Prices as of July 25, 1996				
Rate Movement		**−50**	**0**	**+50**
Reinvestment Rate		**4.75**	**5.25**	**5.75**
GNMA	Coupon	5.5	5.0	4.5
5.0	Three-month speed (CPR)	3.7	1.9	0.1
	Terminal price	97:12+	95:25	94:17
	Projected 12-month ROR	6.99	5.39	4.08
GNMA	Coupon	6	5.5	5.0
5.5	Three-month speed (CPR)	6.1	3.7	1.9
	Terminal price	98:28+	97:12+	95:25
	Projected 12-month ROR	7.19	5.79	4.21
GNMA	Coupon	6.5	6.0	5.5
6.0	Three-month speed (CPR)	11.9	6.1	3.7
	Terminal price	100:01	98:28+	97:12+
	Projected 12-month ROR	7.08	6.13	4.74
GNMA	Coupon	7.0	6.5	6.0
	Three-month speed (CPR)	14.8	11.9	6.1
	Terminal price	101:4	100:01	98:28+
	Projected 12-month ROR	7.21	6.40	5.46
12-Month ROR Pickups (in basis points)				
	5.5 over 5	20.5	39.7	13.2
	6 over 5.5	(11.4)	33.8	52.8
	6.5 over 6	13.4	27.3	72.0

enced parallel 50, 100, or 150 bp moves, may not be exactly the same as those implied by the adjacent coupons. For example, technical supply/demand forces may
have an unforeseeable impact on actual pricing (particularly in the case of the
GNMA ARM sector where monthly supply influences market pricing).

Despite the disadvantages the model has had good predictive value in examining the intercoupon relationships in the past. Exhibit 3–16 illustrates the results as of July 25, 1996. The analysis reflects the relative cheapness of GNMA
5.5 and 6.5% ARMs, as highlighted by their projected returns across all scenarios,
and the relative richness of GNMA 6% ARMs.

Option-Adjusted Spread (OAS)

The OAS methodology values a security under thousands of possible interest rate
scenarios. Compared to static yield and NEM measures, OAS assigns probabilities

to scenarios other than the base case. The application of OAS to ARM valuation involves four basic steps:

1. A large sample of potential risk-free rate paths are generated, using a probabilistic model that is consistent with the current term structure and assumed level of volatility.

2. For each path of risk-free rates a corresponding path for the ARM index is generated.

3. For each rate scenario cash flows are generated that reflect prepayment variability, and all contractual features affecting cash flows, such as the periodic and lifetime caps and floors, reset frequency, teaser rates, and so on.

4. A value of the security is found for each scenario by discounting the cash flows at the projected risk-free rates plus a spread; this generates a distribution of values for the security; for a given price the OAS is the spread such that the average of the distribution of values equals that price.

Valuing ARMs using OAS is superior to making relative value comparisons based on static measures. OAS captures the effect of yield-curve shape on the valuation of the embedded options—caps, floors, and prepayments. Further, OAS is a dynamic measure which investors can use as a yardstick to compare ARMs against other fixed income securities.

There are some drawbacks of relying solely on OAS as a relative value tool. The output generated by an OAS model is contingent upon the inputs; namely, the quality of the prepayment model and the ability to value accurately the caps and floors. OAS calculations depend significantly on the robustness and predictive power of the underlying prepayment model. Further, volatility assumptions have an impact on the valuation of the embedded caps and floors. Most OAS models use a single volatility assumption as opposed to utilizing volatility curves, as is the practice in the derivatives market. The sensitivity of OAS values to the interactive effects of any errors in prepayment projections and cap valuations make it crucial to question these inputs prior to making relative value judgments based on OAS.

Finally, market participants generally assume that higher yielding OAS securities are more valuable. In practice, however, different securities trade within their respective OAS trading range. Thus, GNMA ARMs, for example, trade within a different range from GNMA FRMs. Further, under technical supply/demand conditions, a security's high OAS valuation could reflect the outcome of further widening as opposed to a prudent investment opportunity. Although an advancement over static measures, OAS should not be employed blindly.

Swap Spreads to a Benchmark Index

All the analytical measures discussed earlier help to gauge relative value of ARMs. However, apart from OAS all the tools either do not fully value the various embedded options or require homogeneity among the securities to identify relative value. The heterogeneity among ARM securities make it difficult to answer

E X H I B I T   3–17

ARM Asset Swaps: Example Trade

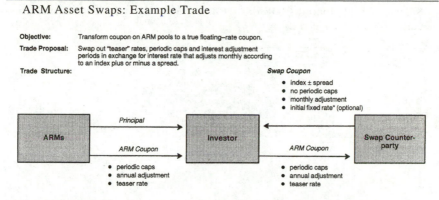

Objective: Transform coupon on ARM pools to a true floating-rate coupon.

Trade Proposal: Swap out "teaser" rates, periodic caps and interest adjustment periods in exchange for interest rate that adjusts monthly according to an index plus or minus a spread.

*Initial rate can be fixed until first ARM adjustment, for a higher spread over the index.

realistic questions such as: Should an investor buy TBA GNMA ARMs or specified GNMA ARMs? GNMA ARMs or conventional ARMs? While OAS aims to answer these questions, it falls short due to the various reasons already discussed. Further, it fails to isolate where the arbitrage opportunity lies, that is, is the high OAS due to undervaluing the prepayment option and/or the caps and floors?

Generally investors in floating-rate securities aim to take limited risk and capture a spread to their cost of funding. Hence, the cheapest security would be the one that, net of all the underlying options, prepayment and caps, translates to the highest spread over a benchmark index. The practice to swap ARM interest cash flows into an uncapped interest cash flow has been in place since 1994. For GNMA ARMs swap dealers offer to swap the underlying ARM interest cash flows with coupon adjustment constraints into uncapped cash flows indexed to 1-month LIBOR. Investors have the choice to remove both periodic and lifetime caps or simply remove the periodic caps and lift the lifetime caps. Exhibit 3–17 illustrates the working of a swap using GNMA ARMs. Swaps on GNMA ARMs are generally structured with a stated maturity of 10 years.

Swap spreads on TBA GNMA ARMs help to ascertain relative value between ARMs and other floating-rate sectors. For instance, Exhibit 3–18 presents spreads over 1-month LIBOR on par-priced TBA GNMA ARMs. This is commonly used to compare ARMs against other floating-rate securities such as asset-backed floaters. Since the swap is generally structured such that at the end of 10 years the investor retains the remainder of the ARM with the caps and floors, investors need to consider the impact of this "tail" risk. It is becoming increasingly common for swap dealers to sell the "tail" to a third party, thus increasing the attractiveness of the swap to traditional buyers of floating-rate instruments.

Swap spreads also assist in studying intercoupon relationships. Typically lower dollar priced securities swap to higher spreads because of the call risk associated with higher dollar priced securities, which the swap dealer assumes.

E X H I B I T   3–18

Spreads over 1-Month LIBOR on GNMA ARM Collateral Priced Closest to Par (10-Year Uncapped Swap)

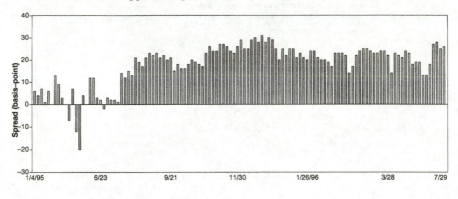

E X H I B I T   3–19

Intercoupon Swap Spreads: GNMA 6–GNMA 6.5

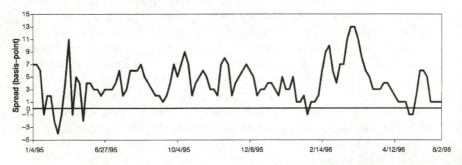

Exhibit 3–19 plots the historical difference between swap spreads on GNMA 6s over GNMA 6.5s. A negative spread, that is, when GNMA 6.5s swap to *higher* spreads than GNMA 6s, generally indicates a buying opportunity for the higher dollar priced securities.

Technology from the derivatives market can be used to value caps and floors and indicate swap levels on most conventional ARMs. This makes the universe of ARM securities—teasers versus fully indexed, low versus high caps, GNMAs versus conventionals, TBA versus specified, and so on—easily comparable against each other and helps to identify investment opportunities.

In summary, comparing swap spreads on ARM securities provides an objective measure, netting out the interactive effect of various ARM characteristics on investment performance.

CONCLUSION

This chapter serves as an introduction to the market and issues that investors should consider when trying to ascertain relative value of ARM securities. Continued technological advancements in valuing ARM securities will lead to the increasing appeal of this sector to a variety of institutional investors. The development of state-of-the-art tools that help to encapsulate differences between the structural characteristics of the variety of ARM securities will help to identify relative value opportunities in a transparent yet comprehensive manner.

CHAPTER **4**

PREPAYMENT PENALTY MORTGAGE-BACKED SECURITIES

Anand K. Bhattacharya, Ph.D.
Executive Vice President
Countrywide Capital Markets, Inc.

As part of ongoing innovation in mortgage lending, originators have increasingly developed products, which meet the dual needs of borrowers and investors. One such innovation that has been developed by the mortgage banking community to reduce borrowing rates to mortgagors as well as to mitigate prepayment risk to investors are *prepayment penalty mortgages* (PPMs). Although the usage of prepayment penalties is fairly standard in subprime mortgage lending, the main purpose of this feature in the prime mortgage arena is to reduce the note rate paid by the borrower in return for the imposition of a penalty in the event of a refinance. In the early days of mortgage lending, due to the dominance of portfolio lending over secondary market disposition, most mortgages were originated with prepayment clauses that were applicable over the life of the mortgage. However, in the 1980s, due to the prevalence of higher interest rates, such mortgages became virtually nonexistent. With the advent of the refinancing wave of the 1990s, such mortgages came into vogue again in a reincarnated form that was originated in a more structured legal and secondary market environment and with less onerous penalties.

Given the relatively recent nature of the PPM market and the availability of a reasonable data time series, the objective of this chapter is to evaluate the efficacy of these provisions in the determination of prepayments. As part of this evaluation we also offer our thoughts on associated relative value issues. Additionally, we outline the complex web of regulations, at both the federal and state levels that affect the imposition and efficacy of prepayment penalties.

Research and computational assistance by Bill Berliner, Esther Chang, and Nick Trosper is gratefully acknowledged.

LEGAL FRAMEWORK FOR IMPOSITION
OF PREPAYMENT PENALTIES

A host of federal and state regulations govern the imposition of prepayment penalties. As a general rule the relevant laws for the regulation of prepayment penalties are those enacted at the state level. However, in certain instances, especially with respect to adjustable-rate mortgages and balloon loans, federal laws typically override state regulations subject to certain exceptions. As a starting point lenders are prohibited from imposing prepayment penalties upon the sale of a property. The Garn–St. Germain Depository Institutions Act of 1982 provides lenders a federal preemption of any state law restrictions on due-on-sale clauses for residential mortgages. Whereas lenders are permitted to accelerate the principal balance upon the transfer of the property, lenders are prohibited from imposing any prepayment fees occurring due to the early payment of principal as a result of the due-on-sale clause.

As noted earlier, the ability of independent mortgage bankers to impose prepayment penalties is governed by state regulations. Additionally, the imposition of prepayment penalties is also affected by the interest rate of the loan since certain states require a different license in order to originate loans over specified interest rates. Although the specifics of prepayment penalties may vary in each state, regulations at the state level typically restrict prepayment penalties on residential mortgages along the following dimensions:

• Complete prohibition of prepayment penalties
• Caps on the amount of prepayment fees that can be charged
• Restrictions on the amount of penalties that can be charged for higher note rates or for balances below a certain threshold limit.

In addition to independent mortgage originators, state-chartered thrifts and non-federally chartered commercial banks are also governed by state regulations in the imposition of prepayment penalties.[1] Federally chartered thrifts and banks are governed by federal regulations, which can preempt the applicability of state laws. However, with respect to "alternative mortgage" instruments such as adjustable-rate mortgages (ARMs) and balloon loans, the ability of state-regulated institutions to charge prepayment penalties is governed by the Alternative Mortgage Transactions Parity Act (Parity Act) of 1982. The objective of this regulation was to eliminate the discriminatory impact that federal regulations had upon nonfederally chartered housing creditors in an environment of high fixed-rate mortgages. Under this law state-chartered institutions and other housing creditor entities were allowed to make "alternative mortgages," such as ARMs and balloon loans, irrespective of state law restrictions as long as such loans were made in accordance with federal regulations. The practical effect of this act was to permit penalties in states where such restrictions were prohibited or to enable lenders to charge penalties higher than those mandated by state law. In order for the federal preemption to apply, state-chartered banks are required to comply with any applicable reg-

---

1. A summary of the prepayment penalties in different states by product type is provided in Appendix B. Although every attempt has been made to ensure that this information is accurate, state laws are subject to change and this information should not be relied upon in lieu of definitive legal counsel.

ulations of the Office of the Comptroller of the Currency (OCC), whereas state-chartered thrifts and independent mortgage companies must comply with applicable laws of the Office of Thrift Supervision (OTS). Under the current regulations of the National Credit Union Administration (NCUA), credit unions are not permitted to make loans with prepayment penalties. Exceptions to the federal preemption of state statutes are allowed if the state legislature had enacted legislation within 3 years of the passage of the Parity Act overriding the federal preemption. As part of the passage of the Parity Act, each state was expressly allowed the opportunity to opt out of preemption provisions between October 15, 1982, and October 15, 1985, by enacting legislation indicating the state's decision not to be governed by the provisions of the Parity Act.

In practice, as part of the regulatory process, the OTS has issued rulings that ratify the applicability of the preemption in the case of closed- and open-ended first and second lien ARMs and balloon loans on owner occupied properties. However, the OCC recognizes the federal preemption only for ARMs, which are used to purchase or refinance one- to four-family properties. Despite the apparent clarity of the federal preemption, the validity of the law has been challenged. A recent example of this occurred in Virginia, where some lenders were found to be charging as much as 5% of the loan balance in prepayment penalties despite the fact that state regulations limited such penalties to 2% of the loan balance. However, federal courts upheld the federal preemption of state laws on grounds that Virginia had not opted out of the provisions of the Parity Act within the specified time period.[2]

PREPAYMENT PENALTY LOAN STRUCTURES

The basic structure of a prepayment penalty loan allows a lower mortgage rate to borrowers who agree not to refinance their mortgage for a specified period of time (3 or 5 years, depending on the structure). After the penalty period is over, the borrower may refinance without incurring prepayment penalties. Typically such loans offer rates that are usually about one-fourth of a point lower than loans that do not have such provisions. The existing size of the market for prepayment penalty mortgage-backed securities (MBS) is described in Exhibit 4–1.

In the prime mortgage arena, loans with prepayment penalties can be typically classified along the following dimensions[3]:

- For both 3- and 5-year prepayment penalty loans, partial prepayments up to 20% of the original loan amount in any consecutive 12-month period are permissible.

- Three- or five-year lockout periods during which partial prepayments up to 20% of the original loan balance are allowed. In the 3-year lockout loan the typical prepayment penalty is the lesser of 2% of any amount prepaid within 3 years that exceeds 20% of the original balance, or 6 months of interest on the amount by which the prepayment exceeds 20% of the original loan balance. In the 5-year

---

2. See U.S. District Court, Eastern District of Virginia, Richmond Division, in *National Home Equity Mortgage Association vs. Joseph Face,* Commissioner of Financial Institutions, Virginia State Corporation et al., September 10, 1999.
3. The major originators of PPMs are Countrywide Home Loans, Bank of America, and First Nationwide.

EXHIBIT 4–1

Prepayment Protected Pools by Origination Year, FNMA Versus FHLMC

FNMA Prepayment Protected Pools by Origination Year			FHLMC Prepayment Protected Pools by Origination Year		
Coupon	Original Issued*	Current Outstanding	Coupon	Original Issued*	Current Outstanding*
1999			**1999**		
6.0	496.5	484.7	6.0	275.6	269.7
6.5	968.4	948.8	6.5	255.4	248.8
7.0	633.8	625.9	7.0	69.1	68.7
7.5	104.1	103.1	7.5	19	18.7
8.0	29.8	29.4	8.0	6.7	6.4
Total	2232.6	2191.9	Total	625.8	612.3
1998			**1998**		
6.0	2111.7	2010.5	6.0	420.5	403
6.5	2538.8	2345.8	6.5	364.9	336.9
7.0	273.8	241.7	7.0	52.1	45.2
7.5			7.5	3.1	2.6
8.0			8.0	3.2	2.5
Total	4924.3	4598	Total	843.8	790.2
1997			**1997**		
6.0	87.1	80.7	6.0		
6.5	618.7	551	6.5	32.6	29.6
7.0	865.4	731.3	7.0	252.6	209.7
7.5	594.2	423.6	7.5	47.2	37.6
8.0	80.1	46.9	8.0	3.5	3.1
Total	2245.5	1833.5	Total	335.9	280
1996			**Other Pools**		
6.0			**1999**		
6.5	41.1	33.9	5.5	3.8	3.7
7.0	370.6	283.5	8.5	3	3
7.5	409.4	282.1	9.0	2.7	2.6
8.0	68.9	44	**1998**		
Total	890	643.5	8.5	2.3	1.4
Other			Total	11.8	10.7
1995					
6.0	42.6	41.6	**Total—All**	**1,817.3**	**1,693.2**
1992					
8.0	28	27	**FNMA and FHLMC Totals**		
Total	70.6	68.6		12,180.3	11,028.7
Total—All	**10,363.0**	**9,335.5**			

*In $ millions.
Source: Muller Data Corp. and Countrywide Securities Corp. as of January 11, 2000.

lockout loan the typical premium is 6 months interest on any amount prepaid in the first 5 years of the loan that exceeds 20% of the original principal balance.

- The servicer is required to enforce the premium and typically retains the premium paid by the mortgagor.

In response to the development of this market segment both FNMA and FHLMC have been issuing securities collateralized by prepayment penalty mortgages since 1996. With respect to the FNMA program the initial classification distinguished these securities only with respect to the amortization term—15- and 30-year. However, FNMA recently revamped the prepayment penalty program to create the following classifications of prepayment penalty MBS:

- K0: loans with a 3-year penalty and an initial term of 180 to 360 months
- K1: loans with a 3-year penalty and an initial term of less than 180 months
- K2: loans with a 5-year penalty and an initial term of 180 to 360 months
- K3: loans with a 5-year penalty and an initial term of less than 180 months
- KL: 30-year mortgages that carry a penalty other than 3- or 5-year terms
- Kl: 15-year mortgages that carry a penalty other than 3- or 5-year terms

The FHLMC program, which began funding PPMs in March 1997, also includes A-minus prepayment protection 15- and 30-year single-family mortgages (since April 1999) in the existing prepayment premium categories, which are classified as follows:

- P0: 30-year mortgage with a 3-year period penalty and 2% prepayment premium
- P1: 15-year mortgage with a 3-year period penalty and 2% prepayment premium
- P2: 30-year mortgage with a 5-year period penalty and 6 months' interest prepayment premium
- P3: 15-year mortgage with a 5-year period penalty and 6 months' interest prepayment premium

For both the FNMA and FHLMC programs the prepayment penalty MBS are not considered good delivery for TBA securities, even after the penalty period has expired.

THE DYNAMICS OF THE PREPAYMENT PENALTY

With respect to the structural characteristics of prepayment penalty loans the effect of the prohibition is to raise the threshold at which the mortgagor prepays the loan. Alternatively, due to the penalty associated with refinancing the loan, the rate on newer loans has to be significantly lower such that the interest savings from the new loan combined with the costs of refinancing are greater than the penalty associated with the loans. In order to establish a generalized framework for establishing the efficacy of the prepayment penalty, consider the example of a 5-year prepayment penalty loan with a principal balance of $100,000 and a note rate of 8%. As noted earlier, the penalty associated with this loan is 6 months of interest for prepayments that exceed 20% of the principal balance. In the event of refinance the penalty equivalent to 6 months of interest would be determined as $100,000 × 0.80 × (0.008/12) × 6 = $3,200.[4] Assuming the market pricing for 100 basis points (bps) worth of additional coupon, as determined by the difference between current coupon (priced at par) and 1% higher coupon (priced at 104) is 4 points, the additional refinancing threshold for equivalent coupon prepayment penalty mortgages would be 80 bps ($3,200/4,000). Therefore, in addition to any drop in rates that would make refinancing feasible, interest rates would have to drop by another 80 bps for loans with prepayment penalties to refinance.

Because of this muted response to interest rate changes during the penalty period, securities collateralized by such loans have desirable convexity attributes. At the same time there are several reasons for lenders to originate such mortgages. As a result of dampened prepayment behavior the value of the retained servicing asset is likely to be higher than that associated with nonprotected mortgages. In the event of refinance-related prepayments, lenders collect and retain the relevant prepayment penalties, which serve to subsidize the impairment associated with the servicing asset. Along this vein one of the issues that has been raised with respect to prepayment penalty loans is that servicers may not enforce the penalty in situations where the originator could refinance the loan and continue to service the loan cash flows. However, since the value of the penalty, which the servicer retains, is typically greater than the value of the servicing, the economics of retaining the servicing at the expense of not enforcing the penalty would be prohibitive, causing such concerns to be unfounded.

Nonetheless, it is an interesting question to investigate the motivation of those borrowers that opt for prepayment penalty mortgages. Given that the typical interest rate advantage of prepayment protected mortgages is one-quarter point lower than that of similar nonprotected mortgages, the monthly interest rate savings on a typical conventional loan are not that significant in comparison to the penalty. For instance, assuming a conventional loan limit of $252,700 with a 20% down payment resulting in a mortgage loan of $202,160 at a 30-year nonprotected note rate of 8%, the monthly payment is $1,483.38. Assuming the imposition of a 5-year prepayment penalty clause on the mortgage, which reduces the rate to 7.75%, the monthly payment is $1,448.30, leading to a difference of about $35.08 per month. Therefore, in return for monthly savings of $35.08 per month, which translates into a savings of $2,104.80 over the entire 5-year lockout period, the mortgagor may have to incur a penalty of 6 months' interest, equivalent to (0.8 × 202,160) × (0.0775 × 0.5) = $6,267 any time over the next 5 years, assuming curtailments are negligible.[5] Therefore, from a behavioral perspective it is our contention that since the amount of the prepayment penalty overwhelms the interest savings from prepayment penalty mortgages, there is a certain degree of self-selection in the mortgagor populace that is attracted to such mortgages. Unless such mortgagors have fairly strong opinions on the

---

4. *Freddie Mac Securities Bulletin,* vol. 6, no. 5, May 1999.
5. For the sake of simplicity, we assume that there are no curtailments during the prepayment penalty period resulting in the amount of the prepayment penalty being virtually identical during the lockout period.

future direction of interest rates, given the associated "media" effect associated with rallying markets and the relative ease of refinancing due to technological innovations, the refinancing option is a fairly expensive option to give up at a relatively lower cost.

In view of this observation the basic thrust of our contention is that such mortgagors give up the refinancing option because they are comfortable with their choice of housing and associated mortgage payments and use the penalty mortgage to obtain a lower rate. This decision of obtaining a prepayment penalty mortgage is apt to take on an added degree of importance in a rising rate environment. An implication of this observation is that prepayment penalty mortgages are also likely to lead to a lower degree of turnover than generic mortgages. At the same time we also recognize that some mortgagors with short holding periods are likely to take out prepayment penalty mortgages to take advantage of lower rates, especially in a high interest rate environment. For such mortgagors this "rate arbitrage" behavior may be a sound economic decision, as the mortgagor does not have to pay the penalty in the event of the sale of the property.

PREPAYMENT DYNAMICS OF PPMs

In view of the structural characteristics of PPMs it is reasonable to expect that prepayments during the lockout period would be determined mainly by borrower mobility. However, given our self-selection hypothesis, which suggests that the primary users of PPMs are borrowers with a lower mobility propensity, it is not unreasonable to expect the turnover of such mortgages to be generally lower than that of generics. Still, the prepayment behavior of such mortgages at the expiration of the penalty period can be subject to certain vagaries. At first blush it appears that at the expiration of the lockout period the prepayment behavior of these mortgages should approximate that of generics, especially for current coupons and discounts. For premium PPMs one could argue that since such mortgages have not experienced the same degree of burnout as generic premiums, the prepayment behavior of such securities could be temporarily faster. However, in view of vibrant growth in the real estate market over the last several years it is plausible to surmise that at the expiration of the prepayment penalty there is a certain degree of pent-up demand for either missed refinancing opportunities (rate or term) or appreciation-driven "cash-out" refinancings. The implication of this observation is that prepayments on PPMs could be faster across the board for a period of time after expiration of the lockout period. Once this pent-up demand is exhausted, the prepayment behavior of PPMs should revert to that of generics in the course of time.

The empirical testing of these propositions poses several challenges. First, with the exception of one originator, First Nationwide, PPMs issued by other originators are still in the lockout period. Countrywide Home Loans, Inc.'s (CHL) production, consisting mainly of 5-year PPMs, comprises the majority of this outstanding amount.[6] Second, comparisons of summary statistics, such as

---

6. Since the rejuvenation of PPMs in 1996 the predominant part of earlier First Nationwide production was mortgages with 3-year lockouts, whereas Countrywide's production has mainly been loans with 5-year penalties.

EXHIBIT 4-2

Refinancing Curves for First Nationwide Prepayment Penalty Pool Versus Generic at 1-Month CPR (%)

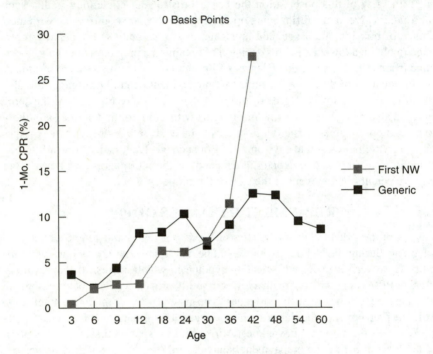

Source: Muller Data Corp. and Countrywide Securities Corp. as of November 30, 1999.

periodic CPRs between PPMs and generics, are likely to lead to biased results, as the aggregate prepayment patterns of PPMs are apt to be muted. In order to address these issues, our analysis is focused on developing refinancing incentive curves for 3-year PPMs since the prepayment behavior of these loans is no longer constrained by the penalty. These incentive curves were compared with similar curves for equivalent coupon generics to ascertain differences in prepayment and to provide empirical support for our propositions. By subtracting the FHLMC reference rate from the coupon rate of the MBS and grouping the prepayment patterns, refinancing curves for various incentives were developed. For instance, the zero refinance incentive curve for the respective categories was developed by stratifying loans in which the difference between the note rate of the underlying loans and the current mortgage rate, as indicated by the FHLMC reference rate, was zero.

An analysis of the comparisons of the refinancing incentive curves in 50 bps, zero, and negative 50 bps leads to some fairly interesting conclusions. These results are presented in Exhibits 4–2 through 4–5. With respect to 3-year PPMs an

EXHIBIT 4-3

Refinancing Curves for First Nationwide Prepayment Penalty Pool Versus Generic at 1-Month CPR (%)

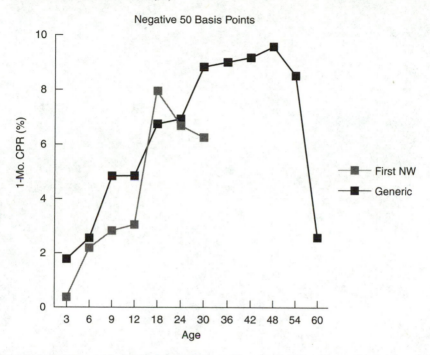

Source: Muller Data Corp. and Countrywide Securities Corp. as of November 30, 1999.

evaluation of these results in Exhibits 4–2 through 4–4 yield the following generalized conclusions:

- During the lockout period 3-year PPMs indicate a lower degree of turnover than generic securities with equivalent refinancing incentives. This observation is apparent under the zero refinancing incentive where the turnover component of generics is faster. This finding also supports the argument that mortgagors with a lower mobility propensity are attracted to PPMs. In a negative refinancing regime the turnover component of PPMs and generics is fairly close primarily owing to the "lock-in" effect on the part of generic mortgagors.

- The desirable convexity features of PPMs during the lockout period are visible in the positive refinancing regime where there is a convergence between the prepayment behavior of generics and PPMs. Due to the dual effects of turnover and refinancing-generated savings, the observed behavior of generics is significantly faster than PPMs during the lockout period.

EXHIBIT 4-4

Refinancing Curves for First Nationwide Prepayment Penalty Pool Versus
Generic at 1-Month CPR (%)

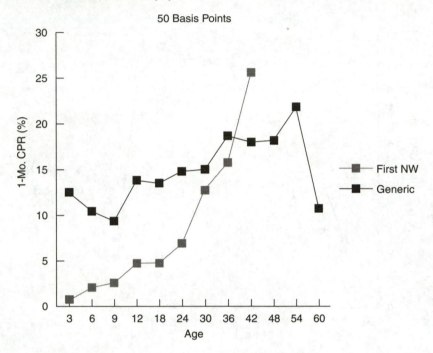

Source: Muller Data Corp. and Countrywide Securities Corp. as of November 30, 1999.

- With respect to 3-year PPMs, which are the only prepayment penalty mortgages where the penalty period has expired, there is a spike in the prepayment behavior of PPMs after the expiration of the lockout period. This suggests that a certain degree of pent-up demand leads to a high degree of refinancing behavior on the part of mortgagors with prepayment penalty mortgages. Given our earlier observations about the lower mobility propensity of such mortgagors, it seems reasonable to conclude that this behavior is primarily driven by "cash-out" refinancings, especially given the recent documented appreciation of real estate.

- Our analysis of 5-year PPM yields similar qualitative results as those of 3-year PPMs. However, because such loans are still within the penalty period, our analysis is incomplete with respect to any cash-out refinancing issues.

RELATIVE VALUE CONSIDERATIONS

The pricing of prepayment penalty mortgages is at discount (premium) to to-be-announced (TBA) pricing for discount (premium) MBS. Since PPMs are not considered good delivery for TBA programs, some of this pricing presumably

E X H I B I T   4–5

Comparative Analysis of PPMs Versus Generics

Coupon (%)	Discount to TBA	OA Spread	OA Duration	OA Convexity	Yield	Prepay Model
6.0 PPyPen	- 25/32	147.1	5.41	0.17	7.74	100% for 36 mos, 150% for 6 mos, 100% thereafter
TBA		129.8	5.45	0.11	7.57	
6.5 PPyPen	- 16/32	137.2	5.11	-0.15	7.70	100% for 36 mos, 150% for 6 mos, 100% thereafter
TBA		126.2	5.15	-0.20	7.60	
7.0 PPyPen	- 10/32	130.2	4.79	-0.61	7.75	100% for 36 mos, 150% for 6 mos, 100% thereafter
TBA		123.9	4.82	-0.67	7.69	
7.5 PPyPen	- 5/32	127.2	4.01	-1.08	7.87	100% for 36 mos, 150% for 6 mos, 100% thereafter
TBA		124.4	4.05	-1.11	7.85	

Source: Countrywide Securities Corp. as of March 22, 2000.

reflects the opportunity costs of giving up favorable roll opportunities as well as exit costs for nongeneric securities. Although the benefits of premium PPMs are fairly readily apparent owing to the dampened prepayment behavior that occurs as a result of the penalty, it is our contention that the seasoned discount PPM sector has the maximum degree of embedded value. Additionally, as noted in Exhibit 4–5, this discount to TBA pricing increases as the PPM coupon decreases. Intuitively, while the discount to TBA pricing appears logical for below-par PPMs, the pricing does not change as the PPM approaches the end of the penalty period. In our opinion PPMs have the maximum degree of embedded value prior to the end of the lockout period. Given the observed prepayment behavior for PPMs after the lockout period, which suggests that there is a spike in prepayments, we also contend that the maximum degree of this embedded value lies within the deepest discounts, as such PPMs are priced with the maximum concession to TBAs.

The results of our analysis as part of testing these propositions, which were conducted with 3-year PPMs, are presented in Exhibit 4–5. In this analysis the critical assumption concerns the increases in speeds, modeled at 150% of generic model speeds for 6 months after the lockout period. Assuming that our thesis regarding self-selection based on motivational considerations for mortgagors who chose PPMs and the associated but not related observation about the prepayment spike at the lockout period is correct, the results should be qualitatively similar for 5-year PPMs. In fact, given that the pent-up demand period with 5-year PPMs is longer, it is also possible that the ensuing spike in prepayments could be of a greater magnitude than that for 3-year PPMs. An evaluation of our analysis reveals the following noteworthy observations:

- Due to the discount pricing of the PPMs, the spike in prepayments leads to desirable performance characteristics, such as shorter effective durations and higher effective convexity metrics.

- The entire discount PPM sector exhibits a higher degree of embedded value, as measured by the difference in the higher OASs of PPMs versus OASs for generic MBS.

- The degree of embedded value and the enhanced performance characteristics are higher for lower coupons. Since this performance is partially determined by the pricing concession to TBAs, these results also indicate the maximum degree of underpricing in the deep discount PPMs sectors.

SUMMARY

Although the incorporation of prepayment penalties in the mortgage contract is fairly standard in the subprime and commercial arena, this feature is mainly used in the prime mortgage world to provide a lower rate to the mortgagor. In return for a lower mortgage rate, typically one-quarter point, the obligor agrees not to refinance the mortgage without paying a fee, which is usually 6 months of interest. In the computation of this penalty 20% of the original balance is not excluded from the penalty calculation nor is the penalty enforceable upon the sale of the property. Over the years the current form of the penalty in prime mortgages has been governed by a maze of state and, in certain cases, preemptive federal regulations.

The dynamics of the prepayment behavior of PPMs during the lockout period are rather easily comprehensible and indicate that PPMs are likely to experience, on an aggregate basis, a slower prepayment rate than generics. At the same time the turnover component of prepayments for PPMs should be equal to or less than that of generics. With respect to prepayment behavior of such mortgages after the lockout period, our research, based on data from 3-year PPMs, indicates that there is a significant spike in the paydown pattern. This is consistent with our thesis that a process of self-selection governs the choice of PPMs on part of the obligor. Such individuals are comfortable with their choice of housing and exhibit a lower mobility propensity as the value of the foregone option, namely, that the additional cost of refinancing emanating due to the penalty is significantly greater than the reduction in note rates. However, given the recent appreciation in real estate such mortgagors have a certain degree of pent-up demand, which leads to the observed spike in prepayment behavior.

The market pricing of PPMs does not take into account the possibility of this prepayment behavior. As a result premiums are priced as a payup to generics, whereas discounts are priced at a concession to market benchmarks. Additionally, the higher the premium coupon, the greater the payup. Conversely, the lower the discount coupon, the greater the absolute value of the concession. In our opinion herein lies the opportunity, assuming the validity of our hypothesis. Although our analysis does not negate the value of premiums during the lockout period, our results suggest that the hidden opportunity lies in investing in deep discount seasoned PPMs. The ability to reap additional value-added attributes such as spread and convexity due to the accretion of the discount is best when the investment horizon spans the period immediately prior to the end of the penalty provision and ends at the time when there is convergence of PPM speeds.

APPENDIX A

States Allowing Prepayment Penalties— Fixed-Rate Mortgages

There are 36 states and the District of Columbia that permit prepayment penalties on fixed-rate first mortgages and 9 states that allow penalties with specific restrictions. Alaska, Iowa, New Jersey, New Mexico, and Vermont do not allow prepayment penalties on fixed-rate first mortgages.

States allowing prepayment penalties with restrictions on fixed-rate first mortgages are as follows:

- Illinois: State restriction requires that rate must be less than or equal to 8% in order to impose a penalty.
- Louisiana: Loan amount must be greater than or equal to $25,000.
- Maine: Rate must be less than 12%.
- Maryland: Rate must be less than or equal to 8%.
- North Carolina: Loan amount must be greater than or equal to $100,000.
- Oklahoma: Rate must be less than or equal to 13%.
- Pennsylvania: Loan amount must be greater than $50,000.
- South Carolina: Loan amount must be greater than $100,000.
- Wyoming: APR must be less than or equal to 18%.

APPENDIX B

States Allowing Prepayment Penalties— Adjustable-Rate Mortgages (ARMs)

There are 33 states and the District of Columbia that allow prepayment penalties on adjustable-rate first mortgages and 9 states that allow penalties with specific restrictions. In these nine states many of the restrictions associated with fixed-rate mortgages are applicable with the following exceptions:

• Prepayment penalty is allowed in Maine on first lien ARMs.

• ARMs in New York must have a 5-year fixed rate.

In addition to Alaska, Iowa, New Jersey, New Mexico, and Vermont, which also prohibit penalties on fixed-rate mortgages, California, Maine, and Wisconsin prohibit penalties on first lien ARMs. However, with respect to alternative mortgages, such as ARMs, federal preemption under the Alternative Mortgage Transaction Parity Act allows for the imposition of prepayment penalties except in the states that overrode the Parity Act.

States that overrode the Parity Act are as follows:

• Arizona: Has no restrictions on prepayment penalties

• Maine: Does not allow prepayment penalties on ARMs

• Massachusetts: Permits penalty with a specific prepayment structure (see State Laws in following table)

• New York: Permits penalty with a specific prepayment structure (see State Laws in following table)

• South Carolina: Does not allow prepayment penalties on ARMs.

State Laws and Restrictions on Prepayment Penalties

Fixed-Rate, Adjustable, and Subprime Mortgages

State	Ability to Enforce Penalty on:							Preemption on O/O ARMs[b]		Restrictions
	Fixed-Rate		ARMs			B/C[a]				
	First Mortgage	Junior Liens	First Mortgage	Junior Liens	Fixed	O/O ARMs[c]	N/O/O ARMs	First Mortgage	Junior Liens	
Alabama	Yes	Yes	Yes	Yes	Yes	Yes	Yes	Yes	Yes (OTS) No (OCC)*	No penalty is allowed on loan amounts less than $2,000.
Alaska	No	No	No	No	No	Yes	No	Yes	Yes (OTS) No (OCC)*	Penalty is only permitted on federally insured loans.
Arizona	Yes	Yes	Yes	Yes	Yes	Yes	Yes	No	No	No restriction on loan amounts greater than $5,000 is allowed.
Arkansas	Yes	Yes	Yes	Yes	Yes	Yes	Yes	Yes	Yes (OTS) No (OCC)*	Penalty is not allowed on "agricultural" property. On subprime O/O ARMs, penalty is allowed on agricultural property.
California	Yes	Yes	No[d]	No	Yes	Yes	No	Yes	Yes (OTS) No (OCC)*	1. For fixed-rate loan originated by CA real estate broker penalty may be charged in first 7 years and is limited to 6 months' interest on amount by which aggregate prepayments in a 12-month period exceeds 20% of unpaid principal balance at the time of prepayment.

State							Notes
							2. For all other fixed-rate loans penalty may be charged only in first 5 years and is limited to 6 months' interest on amount by which prepayments in any 12-month period exceeds 20% of the original principal balance. 3. For subprime loans prepay penalty is limited to first 5 years of the loan with penalty of 6 months' interest on prepayments in excess of 20% of original balance. Not allowed on ARMs under certain conditions.[e]
Colorado	Yes	Yes	Yes	Yes	Yes	Yes	Penalty is not allowed on loans that are subject to Colorado Consumer Credit Code ("CCCC"). Penalty is not allowed on junior lien loans if APR is greater than 12%. A first lien on a property previously owned free and clear with an APR greater than 12% is subject to the CCCC. A prepay penalty may not be charged on such loans.
Connecticut	Yes	Yes	Yes	Yes	Yes	Yes (OTS) No (OCC)*	Penalty is limited to 5% of the balance prepaid and may only be imposed in first 3 years if loan is made by a lender licensed under Connecticut's Secondary Mortgage Act.

(Continued)

91

State Laws and Restrictions on Prepayment Penalties (*Continued*)

Fixed-Rate, Adjustable, and Subprime Mortgages

State	Ability to Enforce Penalty on:							Preemption on O/O ARMs[b]		Restrictions
	Fixed-Rate		ARMs		Fixed	B/C[a]				
	First Mortgage	Junior Liens	First Mortgage	Junior Liens		O/O ARMs[c]	N/O/O ARMs	First Mortgage	Junior Liens	
Delaware	Yes	Yes	Yes	Yes	Yes	Yes	Yes	Yes	Yes (OTS) No (OCC)*	
Washington DC	Yes	Yes	Yes	Yes	Yes	Yes	Yes	Yes	Yes (OTS) No (OCC)*	Penalty is limited to first 3 years of loan (from date of execution of loan). Maximum amount is 2 months' advance interest on the aggregate prepayments made in a 12-month period that exceed one-third of the original principal amount. For subprime O/O ARMs it is the business' decision to use state law.
Florida	Yes	Yes	Yes	Yes	Yes	Yes	Yes	Yes	Yes (OTS) No (OCC)*	
Georgia	Yes	Yes	Yes	Yes	Yes	Yes	Yes	Yes	Yes (OTS) No (OCC)*	

State									Comments
Hawaii	Yes	Yes	Yes	Yes	Yes	Yes	Yes	Yes (OTS) No (OCC)*	Penalty is limited to prepayments in first 5 years and is limited to 6 months' interest at maximum interest rate allowed by law for the loan applied to prepayments in excess of 20% of the original principal in any 12-month period for loans originated under Financial Services Loan Co. Act[f] for junior lien loans for APR greater than 12%. Penalty is allowed for junior lien loans if APR is less than or equal to 12% and not originated by Financial Services Loan Co.
Idaho	Yes	Yes	Yes	Yes	Yes	Yes	Yes	Yes (OTS) No (OCC)*	For junior lien loans penalty is limited to prepayments in first 3 years. Penalty may not exceed 6 months' interest on the average monthly balance for the prior 6 months.
Illinois	Yes (if rate is less than or equal to 8%)	Yes (if rate is less than or equal to 8%)	No	Yes	No	Yes	No	Yes (OTS) No (OCC)*	Penalty is not allowed if loan rate is greater than 8% unless the loan is FHA or VA.
Indiana	Yes	Yes	Yes	Yes	Yes	Yes	Yes	Yes (OTS) No (OCC)*	For junior lien loans penalty is limited under Consumer Credit Code to 2% of unpaid balance at the time of prepayment and may only be imposed in first 3 years.

(Continued)

State Laws and Restrictions on Prepayment Penalties (*Continued*)

Fixed-Rate, Adjustable, and Subprime Mortgages

| State | Ability to Enforce Penalty on: | | | | | | | Preemption on O/O ARMs[b] | | Restrictions |
| | Fixed-Rate | | ARMs | | | B/C[a] | | | | |
	First Mortgage	Junior Liens	First Mortgage	Junior Liens	Fixed	O/O ARMs[c]	N/O/O ARMs	First Mortgage	Junior Liens	
Iowa	No	Yes (if original loan amount is greater than $25,000)	No	Yes (if original loan amount is greater than $25,000)	No	Yes	No	Yes	Yes (OTS) No (OCC)*	
Kansas	Yes	No	Yes	No	No	Yes		Yes	Yes (OTS) No (OCC)*	On ARMs penalty is only allowed if loan is prepaid in first 6 months. On fixed-rate loans with interest less than or equal to FHLMC plus 1.5% penalty is allowed if prepaid in first 6 months. If loan rate exceeds FHLMC plus 1.5%, loan must be made under State's Consumer Credit Code ("CCC") and penalty is not permitted. For subprime loans penalties are only allowed if loan is prepaid in first 6 months. (Also, see new law for additional restrictions.)

State									Comments
Kentucky	yes	Yes (if loan is greater than $15,000)	Yes	Yes (if loan is greater than $15,000)	Yes	Yes	Yes	Yes (OTS) No (OCC)*	
Louisiana	Yes (if rate is greater than or equal to $25,000)	No	Yes (if rate is greater than or equal to $25,000)	Yes	Yes	Yes	Yes	Yes (OTS) No (OCC)*	Penalty is limited to 5% of unpaid principal balance if prepaid in first year; 4% of unpaid principal balance if prepaid in second year; 3% of unpaid principal balance if prepaid in the third year; 2% of unpaid principal balance if prepaid in the fourth year; 1% of unpaid principal balance if prepaid in the fifth year. No limitation on FHA or VA loans.
Maine	Yes (if rate is less than 12%)	No	No	Yes (if rate is less than 12%)	No	No	No	No	
Maryland	Yes (if rate is less than or equal to 8%)	No	Yes (if rate is less than or equal to 8%)	No	Yes	No	Yes	Yes	If loan rate is less than or equal to 8%, penalty is allowed in amount up to 2 months' interest on amount of prepayments in any 12-month period in excess of one-third of original loan amount.
Massachusetts	Yes	Yes	Yes	Yes	Yes	Yes	No	No	Penalty not allowed on property assessed at a value less than $40,000. For O/O loans penalty is allowed for prepayments in first year and is limited to lesser of 3 months' interest or balance of first year's interest. Additional 3 months' interest penalty is allowed if prepayments is to refinance loan with another lender for nonsubprime loans.

(Continued)

State Laws and Restrictions on Prepayment Penalties (*Continued*)

Fixed-Rate, Adjustable, and Subprime Mortgages

| | Ability to Enforce Penalty on: | | | | | | | | Preemption on O/O ARMs[b] | | | |
| | Fixed-Rate | | ARMs | | | B/C[a] | | | | | | |
State	First Mortgage	Junior Liens	First Mortgage	Junior Liens	Fixed	O/O ARMs[c]	N/O/O ARMs	First Mortgage	Junior Liens	Restrictions
Michigan	Yes	No	Yes	No	Yes	Yes	Yes	Yes	Yes (OTS) No (OCC)*	Penalty is only allowed for prepayments made during first 3 years and may not exceed 1% of the unpaid principal balance at the time of payoff. For subprime loans it is business' decision to use state law.
Minnesota	Yes	Yes	Yes	Yes	No	Yes	No	Yes	Yes (OTS) No (OCC)*	Penalty is allowed for prepayments made in full during first 42 months (unless property is sold). Penalty may not exceed 2% of unpaid principal balance or 60 days, interest. Borrower must sign statutory form waiving right to prepay without penalty. For subprime O/O ARMs a waiver form for the prepayment penalty is needed.
Mississippi	Yes	Yes	Yes	Yes	Yes	Yes	Yes	Yes	Yes (OTS) No (OCC)*	Penalty allowed for full prepayment made in first 5 years as follows: 5% of unpaid principal balance if prepaid in first year; 4% of unpaid principal balance if

State							Comments
Missouri	Yes	Yes	Yes	Yes	Yes	Yes	Yes (OTS) No (OCC)*	prepaid in second year; 3% of unpaid principal balance if prepaid in the third year; 2% of unpaid principal balance if prepaid in the fourth year; 1% of unpaid principal balance if prepaid in the fifth year. No limitation on FHA or VA loans.
Montana	Yes	Yes	Yes	Yes	Yes	Yes	Yes (OTS) No (OCC)*	Penalty allowed for prepayment made in full in first 5 years. Penalty may not exceed 2% of unpaid principal balance at time of prepayment.
Nebraska	Yes	Yes	Yes	Yes	Yes	Yes	Yes (OTS) No (OCC)*	If lender is an installment loan licensee, penalty is only allowed for prepayments made in the first 2 years. Penalty is not allowed on same lender refinance and may not exceed 6 months' interest on 30% of the original principal balance. For subprime loans penalty is permitted unless lender is an installment loan licensee.
Nevada	Yes	Yes	Yes	Yes	Yes	Yes	Yes (OTS) No (OCC)*	
New Hampshire	Yes	Yes	Yes	Yes	Yes	Yes	Yes (OTS) No (OCC)*	Penalty must be in boldface type.
New Jersey	No	No	No	No	Yes	No	Yes (OTS) No (OCC)*	

(Continued)

State Laws and Restrictions on Prepayment Penalties (*Continued*)

Fixed-Rate, Adjustable, and Subprime Mortgages

| | Ability to Enforce Penalty on: | | | | | | | Preemption on O/O ARMs[b] | | Restrictions |
| | Fixed-Rate | | ARMs | | B/C[a] | | | | | |
State	First Mortgage	Junior Liens	First Mortgage	Junior Liens	Fixed	O/O ARMs[c]	N/O/O ARMs	First Mortgage	Junior Liens	
New Mexico	No	No	No	No	No	Yes	No	Yes	Yes (OTS) No (OCC)*	
New York	Yes	Yes	No (Unless a 5-year fixed-rate period on loan)	No	Yes	No		No	No	Penalty is allowed on B/C fixed-rate loans if prepayment is made in full in the first year. No penalty is allowed on subprime O/O ARMs.
North Carolina	Yes (if loan amount is greater than or equal to $100,000) See Restrictions	Yes (if loan amount is greater than $25,000) See Restrictions	Yes (if loan amount is greater than or equal to $100,000) See Restrictions	Yes (if loan amount is greater than $25,000) See Restrictions	Yes (if loan amount is greater than or equal to $100,000)			Yes		For fixed- and adjustable-rate junior liens in amount greater than $25,000 but less than $100,000, penalty is allowed in amount up to 2% of unpaid principal balance if prepaid in the first 3 years. For subprime fixed-rate loan, amount must be greater than or equal to $100,000.
North Dakota	Yes	Yes	Yes	Yes	Yes	Yes	Yes	Yes	Yes (OTS) No (OCC)*	

								OTS/OCC	Notes
Ohio	Yes	Yes	Yes	Yes	Yes	Yes	Yes	Yes	Yes (OTS) No (OCC)*	Penalty is allowed only for prepayments made in full in the first year. Penalty may not exceed 1% of original principal balance. Penalty is not allowed on same lender refinance.
Oklahoma	Yes (if rate is less than or equal to 13%)	Yes (if rate is less than or equal to 13%)					Yes		Yes (OTS) No (OCC)*	
Oregon	Yes	Yes	Yes	Yes	Yes	Yes	Yes	Yes	Yes (OTS) No (OCC)*	Statutory "Notice to Borrower" language must be in note. For junior liens penalty is allowed if prepayments are made in full in the first year. Penalty may not exceed 2% of unpaid principal balance.
Pennsylvania	Yes (if loan amount is greater than $50,000)	Yes (if loan amount is greater than $50,000)	Yes (if loan amount is greater than $50,000)	Yes	Yes	Yes	Yes	Yes	Yes (OTS) No (OCC)*	For subprime O/O ARMs penalty is also allowed on loans less than or equal to $50,000. For other subprime loans amount must be greater than $50,000.
Rhode Island	Yes	Yes	Yes	Yes	Yes	Yes	Yes	Yes	Yes (OTS) No (OCC)*	Penalty allowed for full prepayment made in first year. Penalty may not exceed 2% of unpaid principal balance.
South Carolina	Yes (if loan amount is greater than $100,000)	No	Yes (if loan amount is greater than $100,000)	No	Yes (if loan amount is greater than $100,000)		No		No	

(Continued)

State Laws and Restrictions on Prepayment Penalties (*Continued*)

Fixed-Rate, Adjustable, and Subprime Mortgages

| State | Ability to Enforce Penalty on: | | | | | | | Preemption on O/O ARMs[b] | | Restrictions |
| | Fixed-Rate | | ARMs | | | B/C[a] | | | | |
	First Mortgage	Junior Liens	First Mortgage	Junior Liens	Fixed	O/O ARMs[c]	N/O/O ARMs	First Mortgage	Junior Liens	
South Dakota	Yes	Yes	Yes	Yes	Yes	Yes	Yes	Yes	Yes (OTS) No (OCC)*	Penalty is restricted to 1.5% if loans are made by South Dakota savings and loans.
Tennessee	Yes	Yes	Yes	Yes	Yes	Yes	Yes	Yes	Yes (OTS) No (OCC)*	No penalty is allowed on loans made by industrial loan and thrift companies.
Texas	Yes	No	Yes	No	No	Yes	Yes	Yes	Yes	No penalty is allowed if rate is greater than 18%. No penalty is allowed if loans secured by homesteads (i.e., O/O properties) if rate is greater than 12% or the loan is an (a)(6) "home equity" loan under the Texas constitution. For subprime loans penalty is allowed on homesteads if the rate is less than 12%. For subprime O/O ARMs penalty is permitted regardless of rate. For homesteads Texas constitution overrides federal preemption.
Utah	Yes	No	Yes	No	Yes	Yes	Yes	Yes	Yes (OTS) No (OCC)*	

Vermont	No	No	No	No	No	No	Yes	Yes (OTS) No (OCC)*	
Virginia	Yes	Yes	Yes	Yes	Yes	Yes	Yes	Yes (OTS) No (OCC)*	If original loan amount is less than $75,000 penalty is limited to 1% of unpaid principal balance. If original loan amount is greater than or equal to $75,000 on O/O properties, penalty is limited to 2% of unpaid principal balance. No penalty is allowed if prepayment is made due to sale of property. For junior liens penalty is only allowed if loans are made by bank, savings institutions, industrial loan associations, or credit unions. Penalty is not allowed if loans are made by other institutions.
Washington	Yes (if APR is less than or equal to 12%)	Yes	Yes (if APR is less than or equal to 12%)	Yes	Yes	Yes	Yes	Yes (OTS) No (OCC)*	For subprime loans penalty is not permitted if licensed under Consumer Loan Act only and is not otherwise exempt from licensing.
West Virginia	Yes	Yes	Yes	No	Yes	Yes	Yes	Yes (OTS) No (OCC)*	Penalty allowed in first 3 years in amount not to exceed 1% of the original principal balance. No penalty is allowed on loans made by industrial loan companies or Second Mortgage Act licensee.

(Continued)

State Laws and Restrictions on Prepayment Penalties (*Continued*)

Fixed-Rate, Adjustable, and Subprime Mortgages

| | Ability to Enforce Penalty on: | | | | | | | Preemption on O/O ARMs[b] | | |
| | Fixed-Rate | | ARMs | | | B/C[a] | | | | |
State	First Mortgage	Junior Liens	First Mortgage	Junior Liens	Fixed	O/O ARMs[c]	N/O/O ARMs	First Mortgage	Junior Liens	Restrictions
Wisconsin	Yes	Yes (if original loan amount is greater than $25,000 or APR is less than or equal to 10%)	No	Yes (if original loan amount is greater than $25,000 or APR is less than or equal to 10%)	Yes	Yes		Yes	Yes (OTS) No (OCC)*	Penalty is allowed on fixed-rate loans for prepayments made during first 5 years. Penalty may not exceed 6-months' interest on amount of prepayments in any 12-month period which exceeds 20% of original principal balance.
Wyoming	Yes (if APR is less than or equal to 18%.)	No	Yes (if APR is less than or equal to 18%.)	No	Yes (if APR is less than or equal to 18%.)	Yes		Yes	Yes (OTS) No (OCC)*	

[a]This chart only lists applicable restrictions and structures for B/C first liens on owner-occupied ("O/O") and nonowner-occupied ("N/O/O") ARMs and owner-occupied fixed-rate loans.

[b]Federal preemption: Alternative Mortgage Transactions Parity Act of 1982 (the "Parity Act") 12 U.S.C. section 3801. Under this federal law state-chartered depository institutions and other "housing creditors" are permitted to make "alternative mortgages," which include adjustable-rate and balloon loans, regardless of any state law restrictions, provided the loans meet all applicable federal regulations. The only exception is if the state legislature enacted legislation within 3 years overriding the federal preemption. Five states overrode the Parity Act and, as indicated on the chart, include Arizona, Maine, Massachusetts, New York, and South Carolina. The purpose of the Parity Act was to permit parity, or a level playing field, between federally chartered depository institutions which were authorized to charge prepayment penalties regardless of the state law and state-chartered institutions and other mortgage lenders. The effect of the Parity Act in states which did not override it is either (1) to allow a penalty in a state which did not allow a penalty on ARM or balloon loans or (2) to allow an increased penalty over what would otherwise be permitted.

To take advantage of the federal preemption, state-chartered banks must comply with any applicable regulations of the Office of the Comptroller of Currency (OCC), whereas credit unions would be subjected to the regulations of the National Credit Union Administration. However, under current law credit unions are not permitted to make loans with prepayment penalties. Therefore, no loan closed by a credit union can have a prepayment penalty. Savings institutions and other "housing creditors," such as independent mortgage banking companies like Countrywide, are subject to the regulations of the Office of Thrift Supervision (OTS) and must be licensed as required under state law.

The OTS has issued letters stating that state law restrictions on prepayment penalties are preempted by the Parity Act with respect to ARM and balloon loans on owner-occupied properties, whether the loans are in first or a junior position, or open-end or closed-end. The most significant OTS requirement that needs to be adhered with respect to ARM loans is that the late charge cannot be imposed except for payments that are 15 days late (i.e., the late charge cannot be imposed for payments that are only 10 days late.) The OCC's position is that the federal preemption is available only for ARM loans, the process of which are used to purchase or refinance a one- to four-family housing.

It should be understood that a state regulator or a borrower's attorney might take the position that the federal preemption is ineffective despite the apparent clarity of the law.

[c]Where state law allows prepayment penalties without restriction, company uses CA penalty structure.

[d]CA laws regarding certain "variable-rate" loans also restrict prepayment penalties. These restrictions are not listed here due to the availability of federal preemption to allow prepayment penalties on ARMs.

[e]Laws affecting ARM loans in CA do not permit prepayment penalty if borrower prepays within 90 days after rate adjustment.

[f]A license is required under the Financial Services Loan Co. Act to permit junior lien loans to exceed 12% APR.

[*]Federal preemption under the Alternative Mortgage Parity Act is not available under the rules of the Office of the Comptroller of Currency unless it is to purchase property.

Source: The information contained in this table was provided courtesy of the law firm of Kirkpatrick and Lockhart, Washington, DC office. For further information please contact Phillip L. Schulman, (202) 778-9027, of that office. Please be advised that state laws and regulations are subject to change from time to time and that the information may need to be updated following publication. The information contained in this table is not a legal opinion and should not be relied on in lieu of advice from the reader's counsel.

CHAPTER 5

TRADING, SETTLEMENT, AND CLEARING PROCEDURES FOR AGENCY MBS

Jeffrey D. Biby
Senior Vice President
Lehman Brothers Inc.

Srinivas Modukuri
Vice President
Lehman Brothers Inc.

Brian Hargrave
Associate
Lehman Brothers Inc.

Investors new to agency mortgage-backed securities (MBS) quickly learn that they offer return and risk characteristics that are unlike other fixed income investments. These differences arise because MBS are collateralized by residential mortgages and because the homeowner has the option to prepay at any time.

The features of agency MBS have led to specialized trading practices and back office procedures unlike those of the government and corporate bond markets. These procedures have evolved to ensure smooth-running and liquid markets, although they may seem somewhat arbitrary to investors new to the MBS market. This chapter focuses on the basics of how agency *pass-through* securities trade, settle, and clear—and why.

TBA TRADING: TURNING POOL-SPECIFIC SECURITIES INTO GENERIC SECURITIES

Every agency pass-through *pool* is unique, distinguished by features such as size, prepayment characteristics, and geographic concentration or dispersion. However, most agency pass-through securities trade on a generic or to-be-announced (TBA) basis. In a TBA trade the seller and buyer agree to the type of security (i.e., agency, program), coupon, face value, price, and settlement date at the time of the trade, but they do not specify the actual pools to be traded. Two days before settlement, the seller identifies or announces the specific pools to be delivered to satisfy the commitment. (Appendix A shows how a typical MBS transaction unfolds from the trade date to receipt of the first monthly payment.)

TBA trading improves the liquidity of similar pass-through mortgage pools by making them *fungible*. In effect, agency MBS trade as though their primary characteristics—*weighted average coupon* (WAC), *weighted average maturity* (WAM), and *prepayment* history—are equal to the average of all similar pools outstanding, even though each pool is unique. Generally speaking, this is a reasonable assumption. Since most TBA trades are composed (at a minimum) of securities from several pools, their distinct characteristics tend to blend together into a close approximation of generic securities.

Investors can specify particular pool characteristics at the time of the trade. These requests may be fairly general (e.g., current coupon Fannie Maes composed of newly issued pools) or quite specific (e.g., Fannie Mae 8s with WAC between 8.60% and 8.65%). The major mortgage securities dealers use sophisticated computer systems to process allocations, allowing dealers to fulfill particular investor specifications at minimal cost.

Other market participants that benefit from TBA trading are the mortgage bankers, commercial banks, and thrifts that originate residential mortgages and sell them into the secondary mortgage market in securitized form. Most mortgage application processes allow a borrower to lock in a mortgage rate at some point prior to closing. After this rate lock, the mortgage originator is exposed to *interest rate risk:* the risk that the value of the mortgage may change as market rates change before the mortgage is sold. Actual MBS pools can be formed only after mortgages close; while they are in the pipeline, pool characteristics may shift if applicants withdraw their applications or postpone closing, fail to meet underwriting standards, or change loan amounts. Originators frequently hedge their pipelines of rate-locked mortgages by *selling* them into the *forward* market as mortgage securities for TBA delivery months (or more) in the future. TBA trading allows originators to sell prospective mortgage securities before they know the specific collateral characteristics of the pools. Without the TBA mechanism, mortgage pools could not be sold until they had been formed, and originators would have to hedge their pipelines using Treasury futures or Treasury or MBS options. Using TBA forward sales to hedge pipelines is more efficient and has probably resulted in lower mortgage rates for borrowers.

SETTLEMENT PROCEDURES
FOR AGENCY PASS-THROUGHS

TBA trades of agency pass-throughs settle monthly according to a schedule established by the Bond Market Association (BMA), the trade association for primary dealers in U.S. government and municipal securities. The BMA releases a schedule for the upcoming 6 months on a quarterly basis. It divides all agency pass-through programs into four groups, each group settling on a different day

EXHIBIT 5–1

BMA Call-Out Settlement Schedule, August 2000

Class Call-out	Products
A	30 Yr. FNMA
	30 Yr. FHLMC Gold
	30 Yr. FHLMC 75 day delay
B	15 Yr. FNMA
	15 Yr. GNMA I and II
	15 Yr. FHLMC Gold
	15 Yr. FHLMC 75 day delay
C	30 Yr. GNMA I and II
D	Balloons
	ARMS/VRMs
	Multifamily/GPMs

AUGUST

		1	2	3	4
7	8	9	10	11
14	15	A 16	17	18
B 21	22	C 23	D 24	25
28	29	30	31	

of the month. Two business days before settlement (the pool notification or call-out date), sellers must provide buyers with pool information by 3 p.m. Eastern Standard Time (EST). Exhibit 5–1 shows the BMA schedule for August 2000. Exhibit 5–2 shows typical pool information provided on the call-out date. BMA scheduling is designed to distribute settlement activity as evenly as possible over a series of days. As market trends affect the distribution of activity, BMA modifies its schedules.

The monthly schedule was established for two main reasons. Dealers must await pool *factors* released near the beginning of the month before security trades can be settled. The factor is used to determine the current face value of securities. In addition, dealers can more easily create tradable blocks if all pools for a month of trading are specified on the same day; the larger the inventory of pools, the easier it is to meet the requirements of each buyer. Thus, the monthly settlement schedule helps ensure liquidity in the agency MBS market.

BMA GOOD DELIVERY GUIDELINES

BMA good delivery guidelines are summarized in the following discussion.

Notification

To qualify for delivery on the settlement date, the seller must provide the buyer with pool information by 3 p.m. EST 2 days prior to settlement (this is known as the 48-hour rule). The seller must also indicate the face value of securities to be

EXHIBIT 5-2

Sample Pool Information for $1 Million Trade

Customer Name	Original Contract	Coupon	Price
ABC Management	$1,000,000.00	8.5%	101 10/32 (101.3125)

Trade Date	Settlement Date	Security	Trade Specifications
7/19/00	8/16/00	FNMA 30 year	None

Pool No. Issue Date	Coupon Rate Maturity Date	Original Face Factor	Current Face Delivery Date	Principal Accrued Interest Total Due
1	8.5%	$525,149.00	$525,149.00	$ 532,041.58
8/1/00	8/1/30	1.00000000	8/16/00	$ 1,859.90
				$ 533,901.48
2	8.5%	$475,150.29	$474,838.90	$ 481,071.16
7/1/00	7/1/00	0.99934464	8/16/00	$ 1,681.72
				$ 482,752.88
	Total original face	$1,000,299.29	Total principal	$1,013,112.74
	Total current face	$ 999,987.90	Total accrued interest	$ 3,541.62
			Total due	$1,016,654.36

delivered. This information is transmitted electronically via the Electronic Pool Notification (EPN) system. International investors are subject to these requirements and should pay close attention to time differences.

Variance

The face value to be settled must be within 0.01% of the value agreed upon at the time of the trade. For example, in a $1 million trade a seller can deliver any face amount greater than or equal to $999,900 and less than or equal to $1,000,100. A previous variance allowance of 2% was reduced to the current 0.01% to significantly limit the option value created by the wider allowance, as well as facilitate the more timely flow of pool information.

Pools

(Good Combo Rule): Each million dollars traded can consist of up to three pools (or five pools if the coupon is 11% or higher). An investor buying a $10 million security could receive as few as 1 pool and as many as 30 pools, or 3 pools per million.

Changes

In the event of early notification, the seller can modify any of the pool information, such as substituting pools or providing a different face amount, as long as the pools have not been delivered. However, the seller must notify the buyer of any changes by 12:15 p.m. EST (instead of 3 p.m.) in order to deliver the pools two business days later.

Failure to Deliver

Occasionally, sellers cannot provide pool information by the notification date or cannot deliver pools on the settlement date. Sometimes an originator must delay a delivery date with a dealer, or a dealer may not be able to cover a short position in TBAs. In these cases, a *fail* occurs.

All sellers have a strong economic incentive to deliver pools as soon as possible because buyers pay only the amount agreed to plus accrued interest through the original settlement date, and they do not pay until the securities are delivered. In the meantime the buyer can invest the funds at short-term rates. A seller that delivers pools after the *record date* must also advance monthly payments to buyers. Buyers who are particularly averse to fails sometimes request settlement after the official settlement date. By giving the dealer more time to assemble appropriate pools, the buyer further minimizes the possibility of a fail.

These good delivery guidelines were established because of certain unique characteristics of the mortgage market. In part, they help mortgage originators manage their *mortgage pipelines* more efficiently by defining widely accepted criteria under which mortgage securities can be sold and traded generically. As noted above, mortgage originators can hedge pipeline risk by selling mortgage securities that do not yet exist into the forward market, based on expectations that loans in the pipeline will close and be securitized by the settlement date.

These guidelines also help facilitate trading activity in other ways. Amortization and prepayment of mortgage pools mean that securities will rarely have current face values in convenient multiples of $1,000, making the good combo and variance rule essential both for combining awkward pools or securities and for ensuring that buyers are not forced to accept delivery of a large number of splintered pools. The notification rule gives the parties to a trade time to prepare for settlement and ensure that the trade goes smoothly.

Although most TBA trades conform to the BMA guidelines, trades can be negotiated to settle in whatever fashion is satisfactory to both the buyer and seller. For example, two parties may agree to trade a TBA security on any day of the month. They could also agree to change the amount of variance or allow no variance at all.

TRADING AND SETTLEMENT PROCEDURES FOR OTHER MBS PRODUCTS

Nonagency MBS and REMICs (backed by both agency and nonagency collateral) are composed of specified pools and do not trade on a TBA basis. New issues settle on the date provided in the prospectus. In the secondary market, these securities trade on an issue-specific basis and generally settle on a corporate basis (5 business days after the trade). Unlike TBA securities, they have nothing to gain from a monthly settlement schedule whereby pools are pieced together to create more generic totals.

CLEARING PROCEDURES FOR MBS

There are currently two methods for clearing (that is, settling) MBS trades: *physical delivery* and *electronic book-entry transfer.* Physical delivery is still used for only a small portion of nonagency securities. As shown in Exhibit 5–3, all agency and most nonagency MBS trades are cleared through the electronic book-entry transfer systems of Fedwire and the Depository Trust Company (DTC). Fedwire, a system maintained by the Federal Reserve System, handles Freddie Mac and Fannie Mae securities. PTC and DTC, established and owned by a consortia of securities dealers and institutional investors, clear Ginnie Mae and nonagency securities, respectively. Plans call for Ginnie Mae securities to move to the Fedwire system in the near future.

E X H I B I T   5–3

MBS Classified by Clearinghouse

Clearinghouse	Securities Cleared
Fedwire	FHLMC/FNMA
Depository Trust Company	GNMA
	Most nonagency REMICs and pass-throughs
Physical delivery	Some nonagency REMICs and pass-throughs

Electronic book-entry systems are also used to transfer principal (amortization and prepayments) and interest payments to investors. On the record date (the last day of the month for MBS and various dates for derivative securities), each system identifies the current holders of each MBS. These holders receive the next monthly payment.[1] Each investor also receives a monthly report from the clearinghouse indicating the securities owned and interest and principal received.

To invest in MBS cleared through book-entry transfer, buyers have several choices. Securities can be removed from the book-entry systems and physically delivered, but the cost of removal is substantial. Alternatively, investors can hold an account with a bank that is a member of the appropriate clearing systems. Or investors can have a dealer hold the securities on their behalf and send monthly payments at no expense. This option is attractive to many investors because it considerably reduces their paperwork.

SUMMARY

Investors new to agency mortgage-backed securities (MBS) quickly discover that the trading, settlement, and clearing procedures for these securities differ from those for government and corporate securities. These differences arise due to the intrinsic features of agency MBS and the needs of mortgage originators who sell new securities into the secondary market.

- *Although each agency pass-through pool is unique, most trade on a generic or to-be-announced (TBA) basis.* In a TBA trade investors receive specific pool information 2 days before settlement. TBA trading is essential to market liquidity because it makes agency pools fungible (interchangeable). However, TBA trading is not obligatory; investors can request specific pools or characteristics.

- *Trading in agency pass-throughs may take place on any business day, but TBA securities usually settle on one specific date each month.* The Bond Market Association (BMA) releases a monthly schedule that divides all agency pass-throughs into four groups, each settling on a different day. BMA has also established good delivery guidelines to ensure that settlement procedures are fair and efficient. Although most TBA trades conform to the BMA schedule and guidelines, trades can be negotiated to settle in whatever fashion is satisfactory to the buyer and seller.

- *Like most government and corporate securities, agency pass-throughs generally clear through electronic book-entry systems.* Although physical delivery is possible, the cost of removing mortgage securities from book-entry systems is substantial. The Depository Trust Company (DTC) controls GNMA products, and Fedwire handles FNMA and FHLMC securities. These systems also transfer monthly payments to investors.

---

1. Each agency has established a *payment delay* that gives it time to process monthly payments received from mortgage originators and distribute them to the appropriate investors. The actual payment delays are 14, 19, 24, 44, and 14 days for Ginnie Mae I, Ginnie Mae II, Fannie Mae, Freddie Mac, Freddie Mac Guarantor, and Freddie Mac Gold PC, respectively.

APPENDIX A

What Happens When an Investor Buys a Mortgage-Backed Security?

We now follow a sample trade through the settlement and clearing procedures for agency pass-throughs. Exhibit 5–4 provides a timeline from the date of the trade to receipt of the first monthly payment. Exhibit 5–5 shows the calculation of principal and interest components of the purchase price and the first monthly payment. Procedural details vary, depending on the dealer, customer, and security purchased.

On July 9, 2000, Joe Investor of ABC Management calls a dealer to buy a mortgage-backed security. After some discussion about the advantages and relative value of various securities, Joe decides to buy a 30-year Fannie Mae pass-through with $1 million face value and a coupon of 8 1/2%. He agrees to pay a price of 161 10/32, and he does not specify any pool characteristics. The dealer tells Joe that ABC will receive pool information on Monday, August 14 (the call-out date) and will receive the security two business days later on Wednesday, August 16. On July 24, ABC receives confirmation of the terms of the trade.

Sometime before 3 p.m. EST on August 14, ABC receives electronic notification that in 2 days it will receive two pools (though the guidelines allow from 1 to 3) with the characteristics shown in Exhibit 5–2. One of the pools is new; it was issued on August 1 and has a 1.00 factor. The other has just begun to pay principal; it was issued on July 1 and has a factor slightly less than 1.00. ABC will receive slightly less than the face value requested, as allowed by the variance rule. On the settlement date, ABC must pay the agreed-upon price plus accrued interest from August 1 to August 16, a total of $1,016,654.36.

EXHIBIT 5–4

Trade, Settlement, and Clearance Timeline for a Sample 30-year Fannie Mae Security

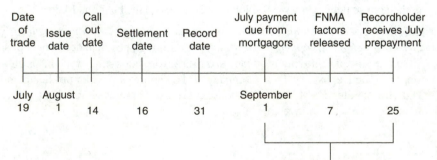

E X H I B I T 5-5

Purchase Price and First Monthly Payment for ABC's Purchase of 30-Year Fannie Mae Securities

Trade Date: **July 19 (Thursday)**			
Face value	$1,000,000.00		
Coupon	8.5%		
Price	101 10/32 (101.3125)		
Call Out Date: **August 14 (Monday)**	**Pool No. 1**	**Pool No. 2**	**Total**
Original face value	$525,149.00	$475,150.29	$1,000,299.29
Factor	1.00000000	0.99934464	
Current face value	$525,149.00	$474,838.90	$ 999,987.90
Original Settlement Date: **August 16 (Wednesday)**	**Pool No.1**	**Pool No. 2**	**Total**
Principal	$532,041.58 ($525,149 × 101.3125)	$481,071.16 ($474,838.90 × 1.1.3125)	$1,013,112.74
Accrued interest	$1,859.90 (8.5% × 15/360 × $525,149)	$1,681.72 (8.5% × 15/360 × $474,838.90)	$3,541.62
Total due for purchase			$1,016,654.36
FNMA Releases August Pool Factors: **September 7 (Thursday)**	**Pool No. 1**	**Pool No. 2**	
Factor	0.9994214	0.99872234	
Monthly Payment Date: **September 25 (Monday)**	**Pool No. 1**	**Pool No. 2**	**Total**
Principal[a]	$303.85 ($525,149 × (1.0 − 0.9994214))	$295.69 ($475,150.29 × (0.99934464 − 0.99872234))	$ 599.54
Interest[b]	$3,719.81 (8.5% × 30/360 × $525,149)	3,363.44 (8.5% × 30/360 × $474,838.90)	$ 7,083.25
Total payment received			$ 7,682.78

[a] Principal payment is based on difference between the previous factor and current factor. It includes scheduled amortization and prepayments.
[b] Interest payment is based on the previous month's face value.

On the August 16 settlement date, ABC receives notification that Fedwire has credited its securities account and debited its reserve (cash) account according to the terms of the transaction.

On the last day of August (the record date), Fedwire takes a snapshot of the location of all MBS in its system and registers ABC as the new holder of record for the security purchased. On the fifth business day of the month (September 7), Fannie Mae pool factors for July are released; this information is used to determine the payment of principal and interest due to ABC. Fannie Mae pass-through payments are made 24 days after the beginning of the month to the holder at the last record date. Therefore, on September 25, ABC receives notification that Fannie Mae has transferred a payment including principal (amortization and prepayments) and interest to its account via Fedwire based on August factor information. ABC will continue receiving monthly payments until it sells the pools.

What if the Dealer Fails to Deliver?

A fail can occur on either the call-out or settlement date. PSA guidelines prohibit delivery of securities until 2 business days after pool information has been provided; if the dealer does not give ABC the pool information until August 15, settlement cannot occur until August 17. If the dealer fails to deliver the pools on time, it will make every effort to deliver them as soon as possible. If it cannot deliver the pools identified on the call-out date, it can substitute other pools, but it cannot deliver them until two business days after notifying ABC of the change. Meanwhile, ABC can use the money set aside for purchase of the security to generate short-term interest; the dealer must bear the *cost of fail* for each day it fails to deliver the security.[2]

If the dealer delivers the security after the record date, the dealer will receive the payment for August. If the security is delivered after the record date and before the payment date, the dealer must advance the monthly payment to ABC. If delivery occurs after both the record and payment dates, then the dealer must send the payment along with the security. Thus in any fail scenario, ABC can earn short-term interest on the cash for purchase of the security at the expense of the dealer, and ABC earns monthly payments. In the rare instances of a fail, the buyer always comes out ahead.

---

2. Cost of fail: The opportunity cost of fund between the original and actual settlement dates, for which the buyer does not compensate the dealer.

CHAPTER 6

BUILDING AN MBS INDEX: CONVENTIONS AND CALCULATIONS

Lev Dynkin, Ph.D.
Managing Director
Lehman Brothers Inc.

Jay Hyman, Ph.D.
Senior Vice President
Lehman Brothers Inc.

Vadim Konstantinovsky, CFA
Vice President
Lehman Brothers Inc.

Nancy Roth
Vice President
Lehman Brothers Inc.

Lehman Brothers produces and publishes a family of rules-based indices that cover a broad universe of fixed income securities. Producing an index involves four basic steps. First, the set of securities that will comprise the index at any given time is identified according to a fixed set of rules. All securities in the index are then priced by an appropriate combination of trader quotes and matrix-pricing techniques. Returns of all securities in the index are computed based on the beginning-of-period and end-of-period prices as well as on the interim cash flows. Finally, the index return is calculated as a market-weighted average of individual security returns.

While the same basic methodology is used in the production of each index, the specific trading practices and conventions prevalent in each market need to be reflected in the calculation of index returns. In the case of mortgage-backed securities (MBS) a number of issues pose challenges at each of these steps.

The decentralized origination of mortgage debt leads to an unmanageable number of investable securities, or "pools." For the purposes of building an index groups of similar pools are combined to form a more manageable set of generic aggregates. Such an aggregation, while solving the problems caused by a large

The authors thank Andy Sparks and Prafulla Nabar for helpful discussions.

number of securities, raises the related issue of how to price this universe given that obtaining quotes even for every single generic (let alone every single pool) on a daily basis is not realistic. Computing returns for mortgage-backed securities is also nontrivial because of such unique characteristics of the mortgage market as once-a-month settlement, payment delays, and delayed reporting of the pool factors. The task of aggregating individual securities into an index is further complicated by the fact that settlement dates and factor reporting dates are staggered through the month for different classes of MBS.

To deal effectively with all these issues, Lehman Brothers has developed a set of conventions which lead to a well-behaved index with meaningful index returns and statistics and facilitate combining MBS securities with government and corporate bonds into mixed indices. The conventions and assumptions used in computing MBS index prices and returns are explained in detail in the subsequent sections. A special section is dedicated to the precise calculations of index returns.

To compute returns on mortgage portfolios, investors must face all the preceding intricacies and more. Various portfolio accounting systems have their own ways of dealing with the special characteristics of MBS securities. These differences in convention can make comparing portfolio and index returns difficult. A separate section of this chapter focuses on several issues specific to portfolio returns and should help investors to understand better their portfolios' performance against the MBS index.

AGGREGATING POOLS INTO MBS GENERICS

There are currently more than half a million existing mortgage pools. This universe is so big that creating a pool-based index is infeasible. Fortunately, the investment characteristics of fixed-rate mortgage pools are relatively homogeneous along such dimensions as issuer, program, coupon, and loan origination year. MBS market participants view most mortgage pools belonging to categories defined along these dimensions as fungible. As a result, an index based on such aggregates would adequately represent the mortgage market. Using aggregates in the index reflects the fact that most mortgage pass-throughs trade on a generic basis. Investors typically place orders to buy and sell "Ginnie Mae 30-year 7s of 1996" or "Fannie Mae 15-year 6s of 1997" without specifying actual pools.

To create generic aggregates, pools are grouped along the three most important dimensions: agency/program (sector), coupon, and origination year. As a result, a universe of approximately 3,200 generics, or annual aggregates, is created.[1] These generics are then treated as individual securities for the purposes of pricing and computing returns and statistics. The amount outstanding for each generic is set to the sum of those of the included pools; statistics such as weighted average maturity (WAM) and weighted average coupon (WAC) are market-weighted averages of the individual pool data. The MBS index is then built from the mortgage generics. The process of selection among these generics is basically

---

1. Over the period from 1991 through 1999 this number has fluctuated between 2,343 and 3,836.

EXHIBIT 6–1

Index Participation of MBS Sectors

Sector Code	Cusip Code	Sector Description	In the Index
GNa	GNA	GNMA I single family 30 years	Yes
GNb	GNB	GNMA II single family 30 years	Yes
GNc	GNC	GNMA buydown 30 years	No
GNd	GND	GNMA I graduated payment 30 years	No
GNe	GNE	GNMA II graduated payment 30 years	No
GNf	GNF	GNMA I single family "midget" 15 years	Yes
GNg	GNG	GNMA II single family "midget" 15 years	No*
GNh	GNH	GNMA manufactured home class B 15 years	No
FHa	FHA	FHLM cash single family 30 years	Yes
FHb	FHB or FGB (gold)	FHLM guarantor and gold single family 30 years	Yes
FHc	FHC or FGC (gold)	FHLM guarantor and gold FHA/VA 30 years	No*
FHd	FHD or FGD (gold)	FHLM guarantor and gold single family 15 years	Yes
FHe	FHE	FHLM cash single family 15 years	No*
FHf	FGF	FHLM 5-years balloon	Yes
FHg	FGG	FHLM 7-years balloon	Yes
FHh	FGH	FHLM gold single family 20 years	Yes
FNa	FNA	FNMA conventional long term 30 years	Yes
FNb	FNB	FNMA government long term 30 years	Yes
FNc	FNC	FNMA conventional intermediate 15 years	Yes
FNd	FND	FNMA 7-years balloon	Yes
FNe	FNE	FNMA conventional long term 20 years	Yes

*These sectors are not explicitly excluded from the index. However, currently they comprise no generics with outstanding balances above the $150 million index threshold.

the same as that used to produce all other Lehman Brothers indices.[2] Each generic must have a total outstanding balance of at least $150 million and a remaining term of at least 12 months to be included in the MBS index. Certain less liquid sectors, like GNMA Manufactured Housing, Buydown, and Graduated Payment mortgages, are excluded from the MBS index altogether. Exhibit 6–1 presents a list of all MBS sectors indicating which of them are currently in the MBS index.

Within each sector pools are first grouped by pool coupon in increments of 0.250%.[3] Thus the maximum pool coupon variation within each generic is limited to ±0.125% around the generic's coupon. Each coupon group is then broken down by origination year. Importantly, a pool is mapped to a particular origination year based on the weighted average origination year of the underlying loans, not the

---

2. *A Guide to the Lehman Global Family of Fixed Income Indices,* Lehman Brothers, March 2000.
3. "Quarter-coupon" generics are currently excluded from the index.

year when these loans were securitized to create the pool. This approach creates generics that are more homogeneous with respect to their prepayment characteristics which depend on the underlying mortgages. It is especially important for relatively new pools composed of seasoned loans.

The resulting aggregates are then assigned eight-character identifiers, or "generic cusips." This convention reflects the three dimensions along which pools are aggregated. The first three letters represent sector (see the "Cusip code" column in Exhibit 6–1). The three digits following the sector code represent a coupon. The first two digits show the whole part of the coupon. The third shows the number of eighths and may be 0, 2, 4, or 6. Finally, the last two digits of the eight-character cusip show the origination year. Thus FNC07497 denotes a 15-year Fannie Mae with a coupon of 7.5% issued in 1997.

Exhibit 6–2 shows the current composition of a single most liquid generic in each sector of the MBS index. This exhibit highlights the drastic differences in liquidity between the various sectors of the mortgage market. A single generic may be composed of several thousand pools in the most liquid sectors or just a handful in the least liquid ones. Also, the various pools that comprise a given generic may still exhibit significant diversity due to various demographic, geographic, and other effects. For instance, while the average pool "factor" (fraction of the original pool balance still outstanding) for FNMA 6.5 of 1998 (FNA06498) is 0.874, the standard deviation is 0.092, indicating that the factor for a given pool from this group could easily be below 0.80 or above 0.95.

For the purposes of computing returns and any other analytics each pool is "mapped" onto a generic security to which it contributed its outstanding balance. The mapping of a particular pool to a generic may occasionally change over time. This is because every individual pool is backed by a large number of individual mortgage loans. Although these loans will typically be fairly homogeneous, their origination dates are not necessarily all in the same calendar year. As the underlying loans prepay, each at its own rate, the average origination date for a given pool may migrate from one year to the next. Pool mappings are recalculated each month based on the weighted average loan age (WALA) reported for each pool by the agencies.[4] For example, a FHLM pool of 15-year single-family loans issued in March 1999 with a WALA of 5 months will be put into a generic with a 1998 origination year. By December 2000, though, uneven prepayments might bring the WALA of this pool to 22, in which case the pool would be mapped into 1999 origination. While the weighted average coupon (WAC) of a pool might similarly drift over time, this will never cause a change in pool mapping since

---

4. By subtracting WALA from the current date, we arrive at the weighted average origination date for the pool. FNMA does not report pool WALA. Because of loan curtailments (extra principal payments made by home owners) remaining WAM cannot be used to compute WALA. Instead, for FNMA pools original (as of the pool issue date) WALA is calculated as the original maturity minus WAM at the pool issue date. The pool weighted average origination date is then determined by subtracting the original WALA from the pool issue date.

EXHIBIT 6–2

Most Liquid Generics in Each Sector of the MBS Index, June 2000

Code	Cusip	Sector Description	Outstanding ($ million)	Pools	Factors Avg.	St. Dev.
FNA	FNA06498	FNMA conventional long term 30 years	106,829	9929	0.874	0.092
FGB	FGB06498	FHLM gold single family 30 years	85,017	6498	0.863	0.089
GNA	GNA06498	GNMA I single family 30 years	35,289	5194	0.907	0.069
FNC	FNC06098	FNMA conventional intermediate 15 years	27,545	3628	0.843	0.067
FGD	FGD06098	FHLM gold single family 15 years	22,463	2160	0.830	0.063
GNB	GNB06498	GNMA II single family 30 years	16,251	157	0.917	0.069
FNE	FNE06498	FNMA conventional long term 20 years	4,777	543	0.855	0.083
FGH	FGH06498	FHLM gold single family 20 years	3,632	13	0.849	0.043
GNF	GNF06493	GNMA I single family 15 years	1,872	1789	0.346	0.074
FNB	FNB07099	FNMA government long term 30 years	1,413	17	0.977	0.014
FND	FND07096	FNMA 7-years balloon	1,233	729	0.304	0.131
FGG	FGG05499	FHLM 7-years balloon	1,147	196	0.920	0.071
FHB	FHB08487	FHLM guarantor single family 30 years	502	3855	0.071	0.048
FGF	FGF06497	FHLM 5-years balloon	238	160	0.421	0.154
FHA	FHA09489	FHLM cash single family 30 years	176	16	0.032	0.007

pools are mapped based on the pass-through (pool) coupon, which is set when the pool is created and never changes.

All three agencies have programs for the secondary aggregation of existing pools. They are known as "platinum pools" (Ginnie Mae), "giant pools" (Freddie Mac), or "mega pools" (Fannie Mae). These programs allow holders of multiple pools with small remaining balances to consolidate their holdings. Swapping many small and illiquid pools for one large pool improves liquidity, simplifies back-office operations, and reduces custodial costs. These securities do not participate in the creation of generic aggregates. Because all the underlying pools are already part of some generics, these "pools of pools" do not participate in the creation of aggregates to prevent double counting.

PRICING MBS GENERICS

Collecting Quotes and Matrix Pricing

The Lehman Brothers mortgage trading desk selectively quotes to-be-announced (TBA) prices and price spreads over TBA for seasoned issues.[5] The quotes are provided for the most liquid sectors and origination years within them on a per coupon basis. For the nonquoted issues mapping procedures have been established and are periodically reviewed to reflect the current trading patterns of particular mortgage sectors, coupons or seasoning categories.

As shown in Exhibit 6–3, there are four levels of detail in quoting MBS prices. For the most liquid sectors (GNMA I 30-year, FNMA 30- and 15-year) the trading desk provides both TBA prices and explicit over-TBA price spread quotes for certain origination years within those sectors. At the next level (GNMA II 30-year, FHMLC Gold 30- and 15-year) only TBA prices are quoted directly, while the price spreads of the preceding three most liquid sectors are used for seasoned issues. Pass-throughs with long payment delays (FHMLC cash and guarantor 30- and 15-year) are priced at a fixed spread (currently, 16/32) below the prices of similar issues in conventional sectors. Finally, all other sectors use a single set of TBA price quotes for all origination years.

The set of origination years for which over-TBA price spreads are provided is chosen separately for each sector and coupon level to best represent the way the market trades. Typically the years for which spreads are quoted for a particular coupon will correspond to those years in which a particular coupon saw significant issuance. Those origination years that are not directly quoted in one way or another are normally mapped to the nearest quoted *later* year. Exhibit 6–4 illustrates how this mapping approach is used to price all 8% FNMA 30-year conventional single-family pass-throughs from a set of quotes for selected origination years (shown in boldface).

---

5. For a detailed description of TBA trading, see Chapter 5.

EXHIBIT 6–3

Types of MBS Price Quotations

Code	Sector	TBA	Seasoned
Quoted TBA prices and selectively quoted over-TBA spreads for seasoned issues			
GNA	GNMA I single family 30 years	Quoted	Quoted/mapped spreads
FNA	FNMA conventional long term 30 years	Quoted	Quoted/mapped spreads
FNC	FNMA conventional intermediate 15 years	Quoted	Quoted/mapped spreads
Quoted TBA prices and comparable sectors' over-TBA spreads for seasoned issues			
GNB	GNMA II single family 30 years	Quoted	GNA over-TBA spreads
FGB	FHLM gold single family 30 years	Quoted	FNA over-TBA spreads
FGD	FHLM gold single family 15 years	Quoted	FNC over-TBA spreads
Freddie Mac non-gold			
FHA	FHLM cash single family 30 years	N/A	FNA price minus 16/32
FHB	FHLM guarantor single family 30 years	N/A	FNA price minus 16/32
FHD	FHLM guarantor single family 15 years	N/A	FNC price minus 16/32
FHE	FHLM cash single family 15 years	N/A	FNC price minus 16/32
A single quote for TBA and seasoned issues			
GNF	GNMA I single family 15 years	Quoted	
FND	FNMA 7-years balloon	Quoted	
FGF	FHLM 5-years balloon	Quoted	
FGG	FHLM 7-years balloon	Quoted	
FNB	FNMA government long term 30 years	Quoted	
FNE	FNMA conventional long term 20 years	Quoted	
FGH	FHLM gold single family 20 years	Quoted	

EXHIBIT 6–4

Thirty-Year Single-Family FNMA 8% (as of June 30, 2000)

Origination Year	PSA Settlement Price	Spread over TBA (32nds)	Outstanding Market Value ($ million)
2000	100.406	0	10,036
1999	100.406	0	5,233
1998	100.406	0	402
1997	100.406	0	2,958
1996	100.563	5	5,043
1995	100.563	5	3,006
1994	100.656	8	3,072
1993	100.906	16	1,396
1992	100.906	16	6,857
1991	100.906	16	1,910
1990	100.906	16	282
1989	100.906	16	107
1988	100.906	16	95
1987	101.219	26	418
1986	101.219	26	212
1985	101.219	26	33
1984	101.219	26	26
1983	101.219	26	19
1982	101.219	26	17
1981	101.219	26	11
1980	101.219	26	20
1979	101.469	34	21
1978	101.469	34	72
1977	101.469	34	99
1976	101.469	34	137
1975	101.469	34	85
1974	101.469	34	82
1973	101.469	34	42

Adjusting Quotes to Obtain Index Prices

Once a price quote is obtained for a generic MBS, it must be adjusted for the difference between index and market settlement conventions. A single standard settlement day each month is designated by the Bond Market Association (formerly Public Securities Association, or PSA) for each sector of the MBS market. Quoted prices for MBS generics are always for this standard PSA settlement. The MBS index, however, uses a same day settlement convention to reflect the current market

EXHIBIT 6–5

Fifteen-Year MBS (PSA Class B), June 2000

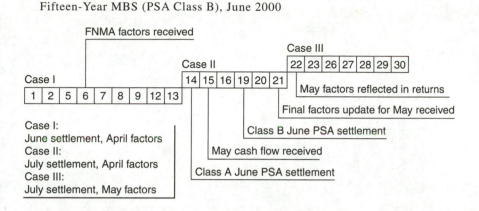

value of securities held by the index.[6] The discrepancy between the settlement convention used for quotes and for pricing the index necessitates price adjustments of two types. First, a pure adjustment of forward prices to spot prices reflects the cost of carry. More importantly, when the index and PSA settlement dates are in different months, the index price includes one more payment of principal and interest.

Let us consider the calculation of the index price for FHLMC 15-year 7 of 1999 (FGD07099) on June 2, 2000. As shown in Exhibit 6–5, the June PSA settlement date for this sector was on the 19th of the month. The quoted price for PSA settlement as of the 2nd was 97.72 (Exhibit 6–6). With accrued interest of 0.35 as of the 19th, the settlement payment based on this quote would be 98.07. The present value of this payment as of the 2nd (discounting by a GNMA repo rate standard for all pass-throughs in the index) is 97.76. The index price for immediate settlement on the 2nd is backed out by subtracting the accrued interest of 0.02 from this present value and equals 97.74. The exact formula is given in Case I later in the chapter.

In this first example the calculation of the index price simply adjusts the PSA settlement quote for the cost of carry until settlement. This is sufficient because a purchase which settles on June 2nd will entitle the buyer to the identical set of cash flows as a purchase which settles on June 19th since each monthly cash flow belongs to the owner of record at the end of the month. The situation at or near the end of the month is different. The quote on June 26th is for July PSA settlement. Such a purchase will entitle the buyer to receive cash flows from this security starting in August. However, a purchase for immediate settlement (or an existing position) would entitle the owner to an additional payment of principal and interest in July. In this case the index settlement price is backed out to match the sum of the present values of the following two quantities. The first principal and

---

6. This settlement convention for the MBS index has been in place since October 1994 (see *Revised Methodology for Calculating MBS Index Returns*, Lehman Brothers, October 1994). Most other Lehman Brothers indices follow the next calendar day settlement convention.

EXHIBIT 6-6

15-Year Single-Family FHLMC Gold 7 of 1999, June 2000

MBS Index Settlement			PSA Settlement				MTD Returns (%)			
Date	Price	Accrued	Date	Price	PSA	SMM	Price	Coupon	Paydown	Total
05/31/00	96.88	0.58	06/19/00	96.84	344	0.493	−0.79	0.589	0.0198	−0.189
06/01/00	97.34	0.00	06/19/00	97.31	344	0.493	0.470	−0.001	0.0247	0.493
06/02/00	97.74	0.02	06/19/00	97.72	344	0.493	0.880	0.019	0.0249	0.924
06/05/00	98.02	0.08	06/19/00	98.00	344	0.493	1.162	0.078	0.0254	1.265
06/06/00	98.02	0.10	06/19/00	98.00	344	0.493	1.162	0.098	0.0255	1.285
06/07/00	97.92	0.12	06/19/00	97.91	344	0.193	1.065	0.118	0.0257	1.209
06/08/00	97.80	0.14	06/19/00	97.78	344	0.493	0.937	0.138	0.0258	1.100
06/09/00	97.80	0.16	06/19/00	97.78	344	0.493	0.935	0.158	0.0260	1.119
06/12/00	97.95	0.21	06/19/00	97.94	344	0.493	1.089	0.217	0.0265	1.333
06/13/00	98.07	0.23	06/19/00	98.06	344	0.493	1.215	0.237	0.0266	1.479
06/14/00	98.24	0.25	07/20/00	98.19	344	0.493	1.392	0.257	0.0268	1.676
06/15/00	98.24	0.27	07/20/00	98.19	344	0.493	1.390	0.277	0.0268	1.694
06/16/00	98.55	0.29	07/20/00	98.50	344	0.493	1.703	0.297	0.0268	2.026
06/19/00	98.39	0.35	07/20/00	98.34	344	0.493	1.542	0.356	0.0268	1.925
06/20/00	98.24	0.37	07/20/00	98.19	344	0.493	1.384	0.376	0.0268	1.787
06/21/00	97.99	0.39	07/20/00	97.94	344	0.493	1.132	0.396	0.0268	1.554
06/22/00	97.87	0.41	07/20/00	97.81	363	0.586	1.006	0.415	0.0298	1.451
06/23/00	97.74	0.43	07/20/00	97.69	363	0.586	0.879	0.435	0.0298	1.344
06/26/00	97.92	0.49	07/20/00	97.88	363	0.586	1.063	0.494	0.0298	1.587
06/27/00	97.95	0.51	07/20/00	97.91	363	0.586	1.093	0.514	0.0298	1.636
06/28/00	97.89	0.53	07/20/00	97.84	363	0.586	1.028	0.534	0.0298	1.592
06/29/00	98.07	0.54	07/20/00	98.03	363	0.586	1.214	0.553	0.0298	1.798
06/30/00	98.18	0.58	07/20/00	98.16	363	0.586	1.321	0.593	0.0298	1.944

interest cash flow (which would be received in July) is discounted from the payment date back to the present. The position remaining after this paydown is valued by discounting the quoted price and the appropriate accrued interest from the PSA settlement date back to the present. This calculation is complicated by the fact that the July cash flow, which is the subject of this adjustment, is not yet known. Rather than projecting it using a proprietary (and subjective) prepayment model, the next month's single monthly mortality (SMM), or percentage of outstanding prepaid, is assumed to equal the most recently observed one. The exact formulas are given in Cases II and III in the calculations section of this chapter. The only difference between the two is that in Case II the June SMM is projected based on that of April, whereas in Case III the May SMM is used.

Although all events that affect the MBS index are essentially monthly in nature, they occur scattered throughout the month. The PSA subdivides the market into five classes, A through E, of MBS securities, with a distinct settlement date for each. Similarly, the agencies issue monthly pool factor reports on different days for different types of pass-throughs. There also may be one or more updates following the initial factor release. To simplify index calculations, our convention is to address each of these monthly events *simultaneously for all securities* in the index. Thus all securities in the index switch to their respective next month PSA settlement dates as soon as the earliest class (Class A) switches. As a result, the *month* of PSA settlement is always the same for all securities in the index. Similarly, pool factor updates are not applied to the index database in a piecemeal fashion as they come in. Instead, factors are updated all at once after the last factor update is received. Currently, the last factor update for the previous month is received on the 15th business day of each month. Starting on the next business day, the SMM computed from the previous month's factors begin to serve as the estimate for the current month's prepayment.

This convention ensures that all securities progress through the same sequence of calculations in the course of a month despite their individual characteristics. Exhibit 6–5 provides an example that helps to clarify this process. For the PSA Class B generic shown, the Case I calculation (based on a quote for June settlement) could have been applied until the Class B settlement date of June 19th. However, starting on the 14th of the month (the Class A settlement date), the entire index is quoted for July settlement. Similarly, the switch from Case II (based on April factors) to Case III (May factors) is delayed from the 6th, when factors were received for this particular security, until the 22nd, when all index pool factors are updated.

COMPUTING RETURNS

Returns on Individual Generics

Because mortgage pass-throughs are amortizing securities, the realized return on them always consists of two parts—the return on the portion of the initial investment that is still in securitized form and the return on the portion paid out as cash. Thus all return calculations will be affected by the remaining balance and the paid down amount numbers, which in their turn depend on the current month prepayment estimate.

Which month prepayment is used as an estimate in computing month-to-date returns depends on how far into the month we have advanced. Exhibit 6–6 traces month-to-date returns for a particular Freddie Mac pass-through. At the beginning of June the May factors are not yet available for some securities in the index, so the April prepayment (PSA of 344 for this particular pass-through) is used as an estimate for all securities in the index. When on the 16th business day (in June of 2000 that was the 22nd), the factors get updated for the index, May prepayment (PSA of 363 for this security) begins to serve as an estimate in calculating month-to-date returns.

These switches in prepayment estimates may lead to discontinuities in the daily sequence of month-to-date returns. If prepayments do not change much from one month to the next, the effect is negligibly small. When there is a significant change in prepayments, this discontinuity can become noticeable (particularly in the paydown return). Those investors who closely monitor month-to-date returns need to be aware of this potential discontinuity. As can be seen in Exhibit 6–6, on the 22nd of June there was a small jump in paydown return.

The coupon return calculation for the MBS index reflects the fact that the 30/360 day count convention used for MBS makes monthly coupon flows independent of the actual number of days in a particular month. In the end-of-month return calculation accrued interest is brought up to the full monthly coupon (30 days accrual) regardless of the actual number of days in the month. For the end-of-month calculations, the MBS index is assumed to settle always on the last day of the month, whether or not it is a business day. So if the last business day happens to be the 27th of the month, the accrued interest on that day will jump from 26 days worth up to the full monthly coupon. For an 8% pass-through, for example, the accrued interest will go from $8 \times 26/360$ (0.578%) directly to $8 \times 30/360$ (0.667%) instead of to $8 \times 27/360$ (0.600%).

One thing common to all Lehman Brothers indices is the no-reinvestment assumption. In the calculations of month-to-date coupon and paydown returns of the MBS index an asymmetry is introduced. When the index settlement date is before the cash flow payment date (1 + agency delay), the value of the future cash flow is discounted. But after the payment date, the cash flow already received is not reinvested forward and used "as is." This effect can be clearly seen in Exhibit 6–6. Up to the cash flow payment date (through June 14th) the paydown return is increasing as the coming payment is discounted over fewer days. From that day on it stays constant (except for the one jump due to the prepayment estimate switch on the 22nd).

Finally, let us comment on the definition of the paydown return. For the purposes of the Lehman Brothers MBS index both interest and principal components of the received cash flow contribute to the paydown return, whereas the coupon return is based only on the surviving portion. Importantly, because the beginning or "base" value for all return calculations is the last day of the previous month, on the very first day of the current month the mortgage security "sheds" one cash flow. Thus the full paydown return for the month is realized on the first day of the month.

Exhibit 6–7 traces the daily sequence of the MBS index returns for June 2000. Beside the month-to-date returns we show "daily returns,"[7] which better highlight the conventions described previously. As this exhibit shows, the same return patterns demonstrated and explained earlier for an individual generic are seen at the index level as well.

Calculations

For the purposes of the index return calculations there are three important days within each month (see Exhibit 6–5):

- t_{cf}—the day on which the cash payment of interest and principal is received by the bondholders of record (1 + agency delay).

- t_{psa}—the current month PSA settlement date for Class A, on which all mortgage securities in the index switch to the next month settlement.

- t_f—the next business day after the day of the last factor update (from that day on the previous month SMMs are used as the current month prepayment estimates). Currently it is the 16th business day of the month (so the switch to the next month PSA settlement always happens earlier, i.e., t_{psa} is always before t_f).

We present the end-of-month return calculations as well as three cases of the daily month-to-date returns calculations depending on where the index settlement date is relative to the preceding three dates. In each case we show how the PSA price is converted into the index price and how all returns are computed.

To make notation more intuitive and clear, we mark calculation components with the names of calendar months for a particular example, rather than with abstract subscripts like i and $i + 1$. In all formulas we assume that calculations take place as we progress through the month of April.

For all cases let us define the following:

$t_{psa}^{Apr}, t_{psa}^{May}$	PSA settlement dates for a particular MBS in April and May
$t_{end}^{Mar}, t_{end}^{Apr}$	the last calendar days of March and April
C	monthly coupon (annual coupon in percent/12)
r	daily repo rate (annualized 1-month GNMA repo/360)
$P(t, s)$	price at time t for settlement on s
$A(s)$	accrued interest at settlement on s
$BV = P(t_{end}^{Mar}, t_{end}^{Mar}) + C$	base value for all returns calculations during April

---

7. A *daily* return is defined as the difference between two consecutive month-to-date returns.

EXHIBIT 6-7

Daily MBS Index Returns for June 2000

Date	MTD Returns (%)				Daily Returns (%)			
	Price	Coupon	Paydown	Total	Price	Coupon	Paydown	Total
05/31/00	**-0.575**	**0.588**	**0.033**	**0.045**				
06/01/00	0.548	-0.002	0.035	0.581	0.548	-0.002	0.035	0.581
06/02/00	1.009	0.018	0.035	1.062	0.461	0.020	0.000	0.481
06/05/00	1.416	0.077	0.036	1.529	0.407	0.059	0.001	0.467
06/06/00	1.430	0.097	0.036	1.563	0.014	0.020	0.000	0.034
06/07/00	1.275	0.117	0.036	1.428	-0.155	0.020	0.000	-0.135
06/08/00	1.097	0.137	0.036	1.270	-0.178	0.020	0.000	-0.158
06/09/00	1.072	0.157	0.036	1.266	-0.024	0.020	0.000	-0.004
06/12/00	1.227	0.216	0.037	1.480	0.155	0.059	0.000	0.215
06/13/00	1.392	0.236	0.037	1.665	0.165	0.020	0.000	0.185
06/14/00	1.602	0.256	0.037	1.895	0.209	0.020	0.000	0.229
06/15/00	1.612	0.276	0.037	1.925	0.010	0.020	0.000	0.030
06/16/00	1.986	0.295	0.037	2.319	0.374	0.020	0.000	0.394
06/19/00	1.818	0.355	0.038	2.211	-0.167	0.059	0.000	-0.108
06/20/00	1.650	0.374	0.038	2.062	-0.168	0.020	0.000	-0.148
06/21/00	1.261	0.394	0.038	1.693	-0.390	0.020	0.000	-0.370
06/22/00	1.080	0.414	0.042	1.536	-0.181	0.019	0.005	-0.157
06/23/00	0.917	0.433	0.042	1.392	-0.163	0.020	0.000	-0.143
06/26/00	1.149	0.493	0.042	1.684	0.233	0.059	0.000	0.292
06/27/00	1.183	0.512	0.042	1.738	0.034	0.020	0.000	0.053
06/28/00	1.103	0.532	0.042	1.678	-0.080	0.020	0.000	-0.060
06/29/00	1.383	0.552	0.042	1.978	0.280	0.020	0.000	0.300
06/30/00	**1.505**	**0.591**	**0.042**	**2.138**	0.121	0.039	0.000	0.161

$F^{\text{Jan}}, F^{\text{Feb}}, F^{\text{Mar}}$ factors at the end of January, February, and March, respectively

$S^{\text{Feb}} = \dfrac{F^{\text{Feb}}}{F^{\text{Jan}}}$ monthly survival rate for February

$S^{\text{Mar}} = \dfrac{F^{\text{Mar}}}{F^{\text{Feb}}}$ monthly survival rate for March

Case I. Month-to-Date[8] Returns Calculation Before t_{psa}

April settlement, February factors

This is the simplest case in terms of the index price calculation because only the discounting from the PSA settlement date back to the index settlement date needs to be done.

$$\text{Index price } (P(t, t)) = \frac{P(t, t^{\text{Apr}}_{\text{psa}}) + A(t^{\text{Apr}}_{\text{psa}})}{(1 + r)^{(t^{\text{Apr}}_{\text{psa}} - t)}} - A(t) \qquad (6\text{-}1)$$

$$\text{Price return} = \frac{1}{BV} \times [S^{\text{Feb}} \times (P(t, t) - P(t^{\text{Mar}}_{\text{end}}, t^{\text{Mar}}_{\text{end}}))] \qquad (6\text{-}2)$$

$$\text{Coupon return}[9] = \frac{1}{BV} \times \left[S^{\text{Feb}} \times \left(\frac{C}{(1 + r)^{(t_{\text{cf}} - t)}} + A(t) - C \right) \right] \qquad (6\text{-}3)$$

Paydown return =

$$\frac{1}{BV} \times \left[(1 - S^{\text{Feb}}) \times \left(\frac{100}{(1 + r)^{(t_{\text{cf}} - t)}} - P(t^{\text{Mar}}_{\text{end}}, t^{\text{Mar}}_{\text{end}}) + \frac{C}{(1 + r)^{(t_{\text{cf}} - t)}} - C \right) \right] \qquad (6\text{-}4)$$

Or, after the current month cash flow has been received

$$\text{Coupon return} = \frac{S^{\text{Feb}} \times A(t)}{BV} \qquad (6\text{-}5)$$

$$\text{Paydown return} = \frac{1}{BV} \times [(1 - S^{\text{Feb}}) \times (100 - P(t^{\text{Mar}}_{\text{end}}, t^{\text{Mar}}_{\text{end}}))] \qquad (6\text{-}6)$$

---

8. Calculations on any particular day use the previous business day close, so the reported returns are for the period from the beginning of the month through the previous business day.
9. On the first day of the month, when accrued interest is zero, coupon return may actually be a small negative number as the present value of C is less than C itself (see Exhibit 6–6).

Case II. Month-to-Date Returns Calculation Between t_{psa} and t_f

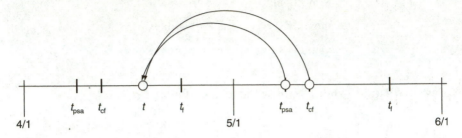

May settlement, February factors

This and the following cases differ from Case I in that the index price must be adjusted for the unknown future cash flow, which needs to be "reinstated."

Index price $(P(t, t)) =$

$$\frac{S^{\text{Feb}} \times (P(t, t_{\text{psa}}^{\text{May}}) + A(t_{\text{psa}}^{\text{May}}))}{(1 + r)^{(t_{\text{psa}}^{\text{May}} - t)}} + \frac{(1 - S^{\text{Feb}}) \times 100 + C}{(1 + r)^{(t_{\text{cf}} - t)}} - A(t) \qquad (6\text{--}7)$$

All the formulas for the returns calculations are the same as in Case I.

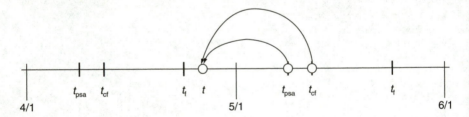

May settlement, March factors

Case III. Month-to-Date Returns Calculation After t_f
This case differs from Case II in that the March prepayment is used to compute both the index price and returns.

Index price $(P(t, t)) =$

$$\frac{S^{\text{Mar}} \times (P(t, t_{\text{psa}}^{\text{May}}) + A(t_{\text{psa}}^{\text{May}}))}{(1 + r)^{(t_{\text{psa}}^{\text{May}} - t)}} + \frac{(1 - S^{\text{Mar}}) \times 100 + C}{(1 + r)^{(t_{\text{cf}} - t)}} - A(t) \qquad (6\text{--}8)$$

$$\text{Price return} = \frac{1}{BV} \times [s^{\text{Mar}} \times (P(t,t) - P(t_{\text{end}}^{\text{Mar}}, t_{\text{end}}^{\text{Mar}}))] \qquad (6\text{--}9)$$

$$\text{Coupon return} = \frac{1}{BV} \times \left[s^{\text{Mar}} \times \left(\frac{C}{(1 + r)^{(t_{\text{cf}} - t)}} + A(t) - C \right) \right] \qquad (6\text{--}10)$$

Paydown return

$$= \frac{1}{BV} \times \left[(1 - S^{\text{Mar}}) \times \left(\frac{100}{(1 + r)^{(t_{cf} - t)}} - P(t_{\text{end}}^{\text{Mar}}, t_{\text{end}}^{\text{Mar}}) + \frac{C}{(1 + r)^{(t_{cf} - t)}} - C \right) \right] \tag{6-11}$$

Or, after the current month cash flow has been received

$$\text{Coupon return} \quad = \quad \frac{S^{\text{Mar}} \times A(t)}{BV} \tag{6-12}$$

$$\text{Paydown return} \quad = \quad \frac{1}{BV} \times [(1 - S^{\text{Mar}}) \times (100 - P(t_{\text{end}}^{\text{Mar}}, t_{\text{end}}^{\text{Mar}}))] \tag{6-13}$$

Case IV. End-of-Month Returns Calculation

The only difference from Case III is that the accrued interest equals the full monthly coupon.

Index price $(P(t_{\text{end}}^{\text{Apr}}, t_{\text{end}}^{\text{Apr}})) =$

$$\frac{S^{\text{Mar}} \times (P(t_{\text{end}}^{\text{Apr}}, t_{\text{psa}}^{\text{May}}) + A(t_{\text{psa}}^{\text{May}}))}{(1 + r)^{(t_{\text{psa}}^{\text{May}} - t_{\text{end}}^{\text{Apr}})}} + \frac{(1 - S^{\text{Mar}}) \times 100 + C}{(1 + r)^{(t_{cf} - t_{\text{end}}^{\text{Apr}})}} - C \tag{6-14}$$

$$\text{Price return} \quad = \quad \frac{1}{BV} \times [S^{\text{Mar}} \times (P(t_{\text{end}}^{\text{Apr}}, t_{\text{end}}^{\text{Apr}}) - P(t_{\text{end}}^{\text{Mar}}, t_{\text{end}}^{\text{Mar}}))] \tag{6-15}$$

$$\text{Coupon return} \quad = \quad \frac{S^{\text{Mar}} \times C}{BV} \tag{6-16}$$

$$\text{Paydown return} \quad = \quad \frac{1}{BV} \times [(1 - S^{\text{Mar}}) \times (100 - P(t_{\text{end}}^{\text{Mar}}, t_{\text{end}}^{\text{Mar}}))] \tag{6-17}$$

The total return is always the sum of the price return, coupon return, and paydown return.

Aggregating Generics' Returns into the Index Return

Returns on the MBS index are computed as market value weighted averages of the individual generics' returns. As a result, the index returns are determined not only by the price changes but by the index composition as well. While that is true for all Lehman Brothers indices, this effect is more pronounced for the MBS index due to mortgage prepayments and new issuance. As Exhibit 6–8 shows, the relative weight of a particular generic may change significantly in the course of a single year. As higher coupons prepay quickly, and most of the new issuance is at market

EXHIBIT 6–8

Changes in Relative Weights of Selected Generics in the MBS Index

Date	MBS Index MV ($ billions)	FNMA Conventional 30-Year 7 of 1994		FNMA Conventional 30-Year 7 of 1999	
		MV ($ billions)	% Index MV	MV ($ billions)	% Index MV
1/31/99	1,712.0	10.4	0.61	N/A	N/A
2/28/99	1,741.6	10.1	0.58	0.1	0.01
3/31/99	1,765.5	9.9	0.56	0.4	0.02
4/30/99	1,791.0	9.7	0.54	1.0	0.06
5/31/99	1,797.6	9.5	0.53	1.8	0.10
6/30/99	1,790.6	9.2	0.51	3.3	0.18
7/31/99	1,790.1	9.0	0.50	6.3	0.35
8/31/99	1,797.4	8.8	0.49	11.2	0.62
9/30/99	1,836.2	8.8	0.48	18.2	0.99
10/31/99	1,855.5	8.7	0.47	24.3	1.31
11/30/99	1,860.8	8.6	0.46	28.4	1.53
12/31/99	1,855.9	8.4	0.45	32.0	1.72
1/31/00	1,838.5	8.2	0.45	35.2	1.92
2/29/00	1,862.7	8.2	0.44	38.0	2.04
3/31/00	1,878.3	8.2	0.44	38.8	2.07
4/30/00	1,872.3	8.1	0.43	38.7	2.07
5/31/00	1,867.3	8.0	0.43	38.4	2.06
6/30/00	1,938.9	8.0	0.41	39.0	2.01

EXHIBIT 6–9

Price Deviation from Par for the MBS, Treasury, and Corporate Indices, 1989–1999

	MBS	Treasury	Corporate
Average of absolute deviations of index price from par	2.60	6.68	3.81
Average of absolute values of differences between coupon and yield	0.63	1.26	0.77

level, the MBS index composition tends to gravitate toward the current coupon. This effect is illustrated by Exhibit 6–9. As shown here, the MBS index price tends to stay closer to par than that of the Lehman Brothers Treasury or Corporate indices as its weighted average coupon follows the market yield more closely.

MANAGING PORTFOLIOS AGAINST THE MBS INDEX

When comparing the performance of an MBS portfolio against the Lehman Brothers MBS index, it is important to understand how and why return calculations differ.

An index measures value and changes in value of a particular market. There is no notion of ownership of the component securities in an index (i.e., no buying and selling), yet this is a critical factor in the context of portfolio performance measurement, especially in the MBS sector. Portfolios that are benchmarked against an index are generally actively traded and are typically marked-to-market on a daily basis. Changes in these daily valuations are the basis of performance measurement.

In this section we describe a few of the more significant ways in which performance measurement for an actively traded MBS portfolio differs from the Lehman Brothers MBS index return methodology. The list is not exhaustive in that it does not include some of the more advanced, yet common, trading practices such as dollar rolls, short positions, and hedging. However, issues that are of concern to most portfolio managers are discussed in the following topics:

• Pools versus aggregates

• Delivery variance

• Income accrual

• Reinvestment

• Transactions

• Profit and loss versus total return

Pools Versus Aggregates

As previously described, the Lehman Brothers MBS index consists of a set of generic securities, derived from the universe of agency-backed pools. Those generics have to satisfy the rules for index inclusion. Using aggregates rather than pools makes the task of producing an index feasible, but using aggregates as proxies for pools in a portfolio will only provide approximation of actual performance.

From month to month the set of pools that map to a particular aggregate can change. This may be due to the slight changes in the average origination year of the loans underlying a pool, causing some pools to drift to an aggregate with an adjacent origination year. It also may be due to the fact that new issuance during the course of the year means new pools are added to a particular aggregate. In this case an aggregate actually may grow in size from one month to the next. Therefore, it is possible that over time the particular aggregate to which a pool is mapped may no longer closely approximate the pool's characteristics.

It is also important to understand that cash flows for any pool and its associated aggregate will be different. Cash flows for pools are defined by the behavior of the underlying loans. Coupons and scheduled principal are based on the standard mortgage formulas, and all prepayments are passed through to the investor. Since the composition of an aggregate changes, however, and in particular, since it can actually grow in size, using the cash flows of the constituent pools could result in patterns that do not make sense, such as negative amortization. Therefore, cash flows for aggregates for a given performance period are calculated based on the average WAM and conditional prepayment rate (CPR) of the constituent pools that month (and *not* aggregated from the underlying pools).

Furthermore, cash flows may differ simply because any pool or group of pools in a portfolio that map to a particular aggregate is likely to be a very small subset of all the pools that make up the aggregate. By definition this subset will have a similar indicative profile (i.e., similar WAC, WAM, and WALA), but it may have a different demographic profile. For example, the subset of pools in a portfolio may be concentrated in a small geographic area, whereas the pools that comprise the aggregate are more geographically diverse. Demographics can play a large part in how mortgages prepay.

Delivery Variance

When pass-throughs are traded on a TBA or generic basis, the exact pools and exact amounts that will be delivered are not known until 2 days before settlement. According to the current PSA requirements, good delivery can be within 0.01% of the original face value of the TBA trade. This aspect of the pass-through market is well understood by most participants, and traders use their delivery option to take advantage of price movements. Similarly, a good back office takes advantage of the option to deliver the worst performing pools (such as fast-paying premium coupon securities) as long as they constitute good delivery.

When mortgage pools are purchased for a portfolio in this fashion, the exact amount that gets marked-to-market is unknown until the allocation date 2 days before settlement. An estimate must then be used to calculate performance until the delivery amount is known; after delivery calculations are done on the actual amount. This kind of estimation is not required in the MBS index because all amounts are known and fixed for the period of performance measurement.

Income Accrual

In the MBS market trades settle once a month according to the PSA schedule for the various classes of agency/coupons, typically around the middle of the month. Buying a mortgage pass-through results in immediate exposure of the portfolio to price risk, but there is no interest accrual until the trade settles. Between the trade date and the settlement date, the position is considered pending. After the settlement date the position becomes an outright holding. Once an outright holding is sold, there is no more price risk associated with the position, but income continues to accrue until the settle date of the sale is reached. In summary, a portfolio is exposed to price risk from trade date to trade date and accrues interest from settlement date to settlement date.[10]

In the MBS index there are no pending positions. Once a security is included in the index, it contributes to performance similarly to an outright holding in a portfolio. This is because in the MBS index, settlement dates, by convention, are the same as the "trade" or pricing dates. Therefore, price changes and daily accrual are included in the return calculation for the entirety of a holding period. When comparing performance of a portfolio against the MBS index, it is important to understand these timing differences. For the period of time when a pending position is not earning interest, a portfolio may be at a disadvantage relative to the index.

Imposing the MBS index date conventions on a portfolio is difficult. Active portfolio managers often execute transactions (buys or sells) and then unwind the position while it is still pending for the same settlement date.[11] As a result, there is a realized price gain or loss for the portfolio, but there is no interest income at all. This type of trading must be taken into account by any system that calculates MBS portfolio performance but has no relevance in the context of the MBS index.

Reinvestment

If an MBS portfolio is at a disadvantage relative to the MBS index for those times or situations when interest is not accruing, it has an advantage over the index when it comes to reinvestment. Mortgage pass-throughs have monthly cash flows that consist of interest and principal (both scheduled and unscheduled). Therefore, reinvestment of cash flows plays a much larger role in managing a mortgage portfolio than it does for most other fixed income investments whose cash flows are less frequent.

The return calculations for the MBS index effectively assume a 0% reinvestment rate for cash flows from the payment date through the end of the performance period. At the end of the month all the accumulated cash is assumed to be invested in the next month's index. This is equivalent to a delayed reinvestment into the market. Until the end of the month, though, the cash does not participate in valuations. The magnitude of the reinvestment return that the index would have achieved depends on the rate of prepayment and on prevailing short-term interest rates. At times of high prepayment reinvestment return is typically moderated by low interest rates. In any event the reinvestment return foregone by the index is modest. In 1993, a year of high prepayment, the MBS index reinvestment return (assuming reinvestment at the Fed Funds rate) would have been on average 0.6 bp/month (basis point per month). Slower prepayments in 1996 would have brought this down to 0.3 bp/month.

In actual portfolios as cash flows are received, they are normally reinvested back into the market immediately. But even when funds are temporarily kept as cash (or more likely, as low-risk, low-yielding cash equivalents such as U.S. Treasury bills), they remain part of the portfolio and continue to have an impact on performance.

---

10. Some systems include all remaining accrual after a pending sale on the trade date rather than continuing to include it in daily marked-to-market reports.
11. There is still delivery risk in this type of trading, especially if the trades are executed with different dealers.

Transactions

For the purposes of return calculations membership in the MBS index is fixed once a month (on the last business day of the previous month). Returns are calculated on this fixed set of securities (either daily or for the whole month) and are linked across month boundaries via compounding to provide performance results for longer historical time frames. For actively traded portfolios, however, membership can change daily. Furthermore, positions, either pending or outright, may be traded in their entirety or in multiple lots at (potentially) different prices. These issues need to be considered when calculating portfolio returns.

If the set of securities is fixed (i.e., no transactions) for a given period of time, then performance is calculated from the starting and ending market values of the security plus any intervening cash flow. If the mix of securities changes, then the performance period must first be broken down into subperiods defined by those days on which there are transactions.[12] Then, depending on how much detail must be captured, some algorithm is used to look at all the opening values (i.e., existing positions plus any new purchases) and closing values (i.e., remaining positions plus any sales) of the security and arrive at a set of returns.

For example, the simplest algorithm would be to calculate an average starting value or cost from all the opening positions and an average ending value from all the closing positions. If it is necessary to keep track of realized versus unrealized returns, then some algorithm for pairing off positions and trades must be employed.

Profit and Loss Versus Total Return

When reviewing portfolio performance, investors typically measure how much each market sector within their holdings contributes to the total. When breaking down performance in this fashion it is sometimes useful to look at results in terms of dollars (profit and loss) rather than percentages (total return). This is true any time the basis, or the beginning market value upon which return is calculated, is either not well defined or when it changes. With static portfolios the basis is well defined and fixed, and portfolio total return can be defined as the market-weighted average of the returns of the component securities. This is equivalent to taking the sum of the profit or loss in dollars of each security in the portfolio and dividing that sum by the portfolio basis. When the contents of the portfolio change over the holding period, however, this relationship breaks down.

Profit and loss, therefore, is a reasonable framework for analyzing performance of an actively traded portfolio, either in addition to or instead of per-

---

12. In the 1997 AIMR (Association for Investment Management and Research) *Performance Presentation Standards Handbook,* daily performance periods are recommended. AIMR also requires, as part of compliance, that time-weighted rates of return be used.

centage return.[13] The main disadvantage of using profit and loss is that it is difficult to rank portfolios of different sizes based on excess profit; for this, percentage return is a more appropriate measure.

CONCLUSION

The Lehman Brothers MBS index serves as a basis for performance evaluation and risk measurement for a large number of MBS portfolios and mortgage components of diversified portfolios. Its published returns are based on a number of common conventions that allow aggregating results for different MBS securities and across a variety of other asset classes. Disparate settlements, the timing of pool factor updates, cash flow delays, evolution of outstanding balances, all make the MBS return computations particularly dependent on index conventions. The "buy and hold" nature of the MBS index makes return comparisons and especially attribution of performance challenging for actively traded portfolios. Sensibility and consistency of index construction techniques, conventions, and calculations determine the ultimate success of an MBS index as a widely accepted benchmark.

Investors managing MBS portfolios against a stable duration target or a fixed liability stream may attempt to hedge away the negative convexity and to maintain a desired duration by applying dynamic hedging techniques. Dynamically hedged portfolios have risk/return characteristics that are different from those of unhedged MBS and, consequently, require special performance benchmarks. Standard industry benchmarks measure performance on an unhedged basis and do not reflect the hedging costs inherent in dynamic portfolio strategies. Recently we have developed a framework for building "duration-stabilized" performance benchmarks for dynamically hedged MBS portfolios.[14] The MBS index described in this chapter represents the core holdings, while a leveraged position in a liquid hedge instrument is used to maintain the overall duration at the desired level. Using this framework, investors who bear the cost of dynamic duration hedging can design a custom benchmark by choosing the target duration and hedging instruments that are most closely aligned with their needs.

---

13. Because the market value of an index is usually orders of magnitude larger than a portfolio, it is necessary to normalize the size of the index to the size of the portfolio before meaningful comparisons can be made.
14. L. Dynkin, J. Hyman, V. Konstantinovsky, and R. Mattu, "Constant-Duration Mortgage Index," *Journal of Fixed Income,* vol. 10, no. 1 (2000), 79–96.

CHAPTER 7

COLLATERALIZED BORROWING VIA DOLLAR ROLLS

Jeffrey D. Biby
Senior Vice President
Lehman Brothers Inc.

Srinivas Modukuri
Vice President
Lehman Brothers Inc.

Brian Hargrave
Associate
Lehman Brothers Inc.

The mortgage securities market offers investors a specialized form of reverse repurchase agreement known as a *dollar roll*. A dollar roll is a collateralized short-term financing, where the collateral is mortgage securities. These transactions provide security dealers with a liquid and flexible tool for managing temporary supply/demand imbalances in the market. *An investor initiates a dollar roll by delivering securities to a dealer and agreeing to repurchase similar securities on a future date at a predetermined price.* The investor assumes some delivery risk at the end of the roll period, for unlike a normal reverse repurchase agreement, the dealer is not obligated to return the identical securities to the investor. In return for this privilege, the dealer extends a favorable borrowing rate to the investor that may be anywhere from a few basis points to several points below current repo market rates.

This chapter first introduces collateralized borrowing via the dollar roll transaction. Second, it describes a methodology for calculating the cost of funds using an example of a typical transaction. Third, it describes the risks to the calculated cost of funds due to prepayments, the delivery option, and adverse selection. Fourth, it takes a snapshot view of the dollar roll market for 30-year agency securities using breakeven analysis. Finally, it displays dollar roll prices (drops) and their associated borrowing costs for GNMA securities for the 12-month period from July 1999 to June 2000, offering some insights into TBA (to be announced) GNMA trading.

DOLLAR ROLL DEFINED

A dollar roll can be thought of as a collateralized borrowing, where an institution pledges mortgage pass-throughs to a dealer to obtain cash. The dealer is said to "roll in" the securities. In contrast to standard reverse repurchase agreements, the dealer is not obliged to return securities that are identical to the originally pledged collateral. Instead, the dealer is required to return collateral that is "substantially the same."[1] According to the American Institute of Certified Public Accountants, substantially the same standard is met by mortgage pass-throughs that meet the following conditions:

1. Be collateralized by similar mortgages, for example, one- to four-family residential mortgages

2. Be issued by the same agency and be a part of the same program

3. Have the same original stated maturity

4. Have identical coupon rates

5. Be priced to have similar market yields

6. Satisfy "good delivery" requirements

The flexibility in returning collateral has value for a dealer because it provides a convenient avenue for covering a short position. That is, a trader may require a particular security for delivery this month and, by entering into a dollar roll agreement, can effectively extend a delivery obligation to next month. If a dealer were required to return the identical security sold, as in the case of a standard repurchase agreement, the dealer would be unable to cover a short position. Dollar rolls offer dealers a convenient way to obtain promised mortgage securities, avoiding much of the cost of failing to make timely delivery. In theory, the dealer (the short coverer) will be willing to pay up to the cost of failure to deliver for the short-term opportunity to borrow or purchase securities required to meet a delivery commitment. For this reason most dollar rolls are transacted close to the monthly settlement date for mortgage-backed securities. Dollar rolls also allow dealers to even out the supply and demand for mortgage securities in the current settlement month and "back" months. Primary market mortgage originators frequently sell anticipated new mortgage security production in the forward market, for delivery 1 to 3 months (or more) in the future. This expected supply provides liquidity to the dollar roll market, by ensuring that dealers will have the securities required to close out dollar roll transactions.

In return for this service, dealers often offer dollar roll financing at extremely cheap rates and on flexible terms. Unlike most collateralized borrowings, there is no haircut, or requirement for overcollateralization. The investor gets 100% of the full market price, not a four- to six-point haircut as in a 1- to 3-month reverse repo. Dollar roll transactions are generally opened or closed as of the settlement date of each month, with the terms set some time prior to settlement. They typically cover the 1-month period between consecutive settlement dates, but they

---

1. A detailed discussion of "substantially the same" can be found in The American Institute of Certified Public Accountants, Statement of Position 90-3, February 13, 1990. This definition has also been incorporated into *Financial Accounting Standards Board*, SFAS No. 125, *Accounting for Transfers and Servicing of Financial Assets and Extinguishment of Liabilities*, June 6, 1996. Investors should discuss these issues with an accountant to ensure that the transaction receives the desired accounting treatment.

may also extend over multiple months, for up to 11 months. The dollar roll market also allows investors to negotiate more flexible borrowing windows. Terms can be arranged for 34, 44, or 89 days (reverse repos tend to centralize around 30-, 60-, or 90-day intervals) thus enabling the investor to exploit short-term investment opportunities, such as certificates of deposit or banker's acceptances.

DOLLAR ROLL: COST OF FUNDS EVALUATION

In calculating the actual cost of funds obtained through a dollar roll, there are several key considerations:

1. *Price of securities sold versus price of securities repurchased.* In a positive carry (or a positively sloped yield curve) environment, the repurchase price will be lower than the original purchase price. The drop (dollar roll price) is the difference between the initial and ending prices plus the difference between the dealer's bid/ask prices.

2. *Size of coupon payments.*

3. *Size of principal payments,* both prepayments and scheduled amortization.

4. *Collateral attributes of securities rolled in and securities rolled out.*

5. *Timing.* The position of settlement dates within the months of the transaction impacts the accrued interest (paid to the seller at each end of the transaction). The days between settlements is the length of the borrowing period.

Each of these factors can influence the effective cost of funds implied by the dollar roll. For illustrative purposes the calculations for a typical roll are described in the following section.

Breakeven Drop Calculation

As a form of collateralized borrowing, a dollar roll has an implied cost of funds that can be evaluated in comparison with other financing alternatives. Conceptually, the effective cost of funds arises from the fact that the pass-through security (along with the corresponding principal and interest payments) is pledged to the lender in exchange for cash, and subsequently repurchased at a lower price, as specified by the drop. Therefore, for any cost-of-funds assumption, we can calculate the breakeven drop at which the dollar roll delivers that same cost of funds. In other words, we can calculate the drop at which the investor would be indifferent between borrowing via the roll or using alternative financing means. This calculation is demonstrated in the following example.

On July 18, 2000, an investor is evaluating a long position in GNMA pass-through securities. The investor holds $1 million of GNMA 8.5s trading on a TBA basis. These securities are currently trading for an August 23rd settlement at a price of 101 27/32nds, with a weighted average maturity (WAM) of 357 months. The investor can either finance the securities for an additional month in a dollar roll agreement or via an alternative source of funding. For simplicity we assume

E X H I B I T   7–1

Breakeven Drop Calculation

Beginning market value		
Current price at 101-27	$1,018,438	($1,000,000 × 101 27/32/100)
22 days accrued interest	5,194	(8.5% × 22/360 × $1,000,000)
Total	1,023,632	
Future value		
Payment received:		
Coupon interest	$7,083	(8.5% × 30/360 × $1,000,000)
Scheduled principal	559	Standard amortization schedule
Prepaid principal	6,383	Based on 7.4% CPR
Total payments received	14,025	
Future value of carry	14,041	((1 + (6.63% × 6/360)) × $14,025)
Remaining principal:		
$993,058 at 101-27	1,011,368	($993,058 × 101 27/32)
20 days accrued interest	4,689	(8.5% × 20/360 × $993,058)
Future value of principal and carry	1,030,098	
Less financing costs	(5,467)	($1,023,632 × 6.63% × 29/360)
Total future value	1,024,631	
Less beginning market value	(1,023,632)	
Implied dollar value of the drop	999	
Implied value of the drop (32nds)	3.22	($999/$993,058 × 100 × 32)

that the investor's alternative cost of funding is the current 1-month LIBOR rate of 6.63%. In Exhibit 7–1 we analyze the breakeven drop at which the investor would be indifferent between the roll and the alternative source of funding.

The initial market value of $1,023,632 including accrued interest, is the amount the investor is faced with financing. Holding the securities for an additional month, the investor will receive positive carry in the form of both a coupon and principal payment. For a GNMA I pass-through this payment will be received on September 15th. The coupon payment is $7,083. The principal payment consists of prepaid principal and scheduled principal amortization. Though the security has minimal prepayment history, the investor estimates an annual conditional prepayment rate (CPR) of 7.4%, based on prior month actual rates (it is worth noting that the prepayment assumption represents a significant risk that will be discussed later). Given this prepayment assumption, a weighted average coupon (WAC) of 9.00% and weighted average maturity of 357 months, the total principal received will be $6,942—$6,383 of prepaid principal and $559 of scheduled amortization. Thus the total payment received on September 15th is $14,025, which can be reinvested for an additional 6 days to the September 21st settlement date. Assuming a reinvestment rate equal to current 1-month LIBOR (6.63%), this will yield a future value from principal and interest of $14,041. The future value of the remaining principal plus accrued interest is then added to the carry to arrive at a future value before financ-

EXHIBIT 7–2

Implied Cost of Funds Calculation

Beginning market value		
Current price at 101-27	$1,018,438	($1,000,000 × 101 27/32/100)
22 days accrued interest	5,194	(8.5% × 22/360 × $1,000,000)
Total	1,023,632	
Future value		
Payment received:		
Coupon interest	$7,083	(8.5% × 30/360 × $1,000,000)
Scheduled principal	559	Standard amortization schedule
Prepaid principal	6,383	Based on 7.4% CPR
Total payments received	14,025	
Future value of carry	14,041	((1 + (6.63% × 6/360)) × $14,025)
Remaining principal:		
$993,058 at **101-22**	1,009,816	($993,058 × 101 22/32)
20 days accrued interest	4,689	(8.5% × 20/360 × $993,058)
Future value of principal and carry	1,028,546	
Less beginning market value	(1,023,632)	
Implied dollar cost of financing	4,914	
Implied percent cost of financing	5.96%	($4,914/$1,023,632 × 360/29)

ing of $1,030,098. We then subtract the cost of financing the initial market value for 29 days to get a total future value of $1,024,631. By comparing this figure with the initial market value, we see that the investor has gained $999 of positive net carry this month. It is important to note that this is net carry, which means it is in excess of the cost of financing. In the context of the dollar roll, the lender, who holds the securities for the month, would capture this net carry. Thus the borrower would reduce the repurchase price to be paid by an amount that corresponds to this positive carry. To convert the positive carry amount to a price basis, we simply divide the $999 by the expected end of period principal ($993,058) and then divide by 3,200 to convert to 32nds. The end result is a breakeven drop of 3.22/32nds.

Implied Cost of Funds

Now that the intuition of the drop has been established, we will evaluate an actual dollar roll trade by comparing the implied cost of funds with alternative funding sources in Exhibit 7–2. We will utilize the same security as in the previous example, with the exception that we now have an actual market quoted drop of 5/32nds.

We calculate the implied cost of funding using a methodology very similar to that of Exhibit 7–1, the only difference being that the drop is reflected in the future price and we instead solve for a cost of financing. As demonstrated in the previous example, the net positive carry the lender gains from holding the collateral is offset by a lower repurchase price. In Exhibit 7–2, we reflect this lower price in our calculation of the future value of the principal. In this case the drop of 5/32nds is greater than the previously calculated 3.22/32nds. Intuitively, we would then expect the implied cost of funding to be lower than in our previous example, offsetting the lower repurchase price. As can be seen in Exhibit 7–2, by subtracting the beginning market value of $1,023,632 from our newly calculated future value of $1,028,546, we get an implied dollar cost of funding of $4,914. Consistent with our analysis, this is lower than the dollar cost of funding of $5,467 in Exhibit 7–1. Converting to an annual rate, the implied cost of funds in the dollar roll is 5.96% versus 6.63% previously.

How is this implied cost of funding utilized? Quite simply, if we still assume that the investor's alternative cost of funds is the 1-month LIBOR rate of 6.63%, the dollar roll represents a more economically attractive means of financing the securities position. Specifically over the 1-month period, the investor is able to save an annualized 67 basis points in financing costs.

RISKS

The cost calculation presented above is subject to risk arising from two sources. The first is prepayment uncertainty. If the security is trading close to par, then this risk is minimal; however, dollar rolls for securities that trade away from par involve increased prepayment risk. The second source of risk is the problem of adverse selection; investors are likely to be returned pools that exhibit less desirable characteristics. The impact of each of these risks is described below.

Prepayment Risk

In our example we used an estimated prepayment rate of 7.4% CPR. An increase in prepayment speed reduces the future value of the "hold" alternative because the investor receives principal payments at par, while the security is priced at a premium. If the security actually pays down at 16% CPR, the effective cost of borrowing is reduced to 5.76%, a reduction of 20 basis points over the expected borrowing cost of 5.96%.

Exhibit 7–3 extends the example by presenting a sensitivity analysis of the effective cost of funds under various prepayment assumptions. Different prepayment rates can significantly change the effective cost of funds for GNMA 8.5s. This makes the dollar roll a useful tool for institutions that have faster prepayment expectations over a given period as compared with the general market. The reverse is true for discounts, as prepayments are made at par, the "hold" alternative becomes more attractive relative to the dollar roll. In other words, an increase in prepayment speed will increase the effective cost of funds for a discount security. For dollar roll transactions with securities priced at or near par, prepayments become less important.

Adverse Selection Risk

Because the dealer is not obliged to return the identical collateral, the dealer and the investor both have a clear incentive not to deliver collateral with attractive attributes. For example, were the investor to roll a more seasoned security (which

EXHIBIT 7-3

Dollar Roll CPR Sensitivity of the GNMA 8.5 Priced at 101-27
with a Drop of 5/32nds

	Annual CPR (%)					
	0.0%	4.0%	8.0%	12.0%	16.0%	20.0%
Effective cost of funds	6.12%	6.03%	5.95%	5.86%	5.76%	5.66%

generally trades at a higher price), the security returned would likely be a lower-priced TBA, thus the investor would lose out by the amount of the payup on the seasoned issue. As a consequence both parties usually transact the dollar roll with pools that are either average or less attractive than the universe of deliverable securities. As long as both parties recognize this, there is little chance that one party or the other will be affected negatively.

Investors who wish to use high-quality specified securities for dollar rolls can stipulate that the securities returned must be of similar quality and/or that the drop be increased in recognition of the securities' more attractive attributes. As long as the lender and the borrower recognize that dollar rolls, like all TBA transactions, trade to the lowest common denominator, both parties will benefit from the transaction.

BREAKEVEN AND SENSITIVITY ANALYSIS

As we have previously demonstrated, the dollar roll can be evaluated using the effective cost of funds. A more robust breakeven analysis recognizes the dollar roll breakeven as a function of the size of the drop, the prepayment rate, as well as the cost of funds. In Exhibit 7–1, we calculated a breakeven drop based on a firm's reinvestment rate and estimate of prepayments. If the offered drop exceeds the breakeven level, the dollar roll makes economic sense. In Exhibit 7–2, we calculated the effective cost of funds for a given prepayment rate and drop. If the alternative cost of funds exceeds this effective rate, then again the dollar roll makes sense. Alternatively, a breakeven prepayment rate can be calculated, with estimated prepayments above the breakeven level making the dollar roll attractive in a premium security (and unattractive in a discount). In addition to the breakeven prepayment analysis, an investor would be well-advised to evaluate prepayment sensitivity on premium and discount securities, similar to the one constructed in Exhibit 7–3. A complete example of a breakeven-sensitivity analysis for a group of traded pass-throughs appears in Exhibit 7–4.

To illustrate the use of the breakeven-sensitivity analysis, we offer the following example. Suppose an investor is evaluating a dollar roll on a GNMA 9. The quoted dollar drop is 3/32nds for a 1-month roll. Using the previous month's CPR, the effective cost of funds is calculated at 6.82%, 20 basis points above the current

EXHIBIT 7-4

Dollar Roll Breakeven and Sensitivity Market Analysis for Selected 30-Year Coupons, July 24, 2000*

Type	Coupon (%)	Price	Drop (32nds)	1-Month CPR (%)	WAM	Effective Cost of Funds (%)	Breakeven Values (Target Fin. Rate: 6.62%)		Effective Cost of Funds Sensitivity (bp)	
							CPR (%)	Drop (32nds)	Additional 1/32 Drop	Additional 1% CPR
GNMA	9.0	103-05	3	11.7	355	6.82	16.7	3.5	(37)	(4)
GNMA	8.5	102-04	5	7.4	357	5.92	NA	3.0	(38)	(3)
GNMA	8.0	100-27	4	2.0	357	6.07	NA	2.5	(38)	(1)
GNMA	7.5	99-05	3	1.4	357	6.12	NA	1.5	(38)	1
GNMA	7.0	97-06	2	5.6	346	6.32	15.5	1.0	(40)	3
GNMA	6.5	94-29	2	5.9	342	6.16	13.6	1.0	(40)	6
FNMA	9.0	102-23	3	33.6	357	5.99	18.3	1.5	(36)	(5)
FNMA	8.5	101-21	4	20.9	358	6.01	NA	2.5	(37)	(2)
FNMA	8.0	100-09	4	5.0	358	6.08	NA	2.5	(38)	(1)
FNMA	7.5	98-17	3	2.5	358	6.17	35.0	2.0	(39)	1
FNMA	7.0	96-18	3	5.6	346	5.98	22.4	1.5	(40)	4
FNMA	6.5	94-14	3	6.8	342	5.85	18.7	1.0	(41)	6
FHLMC	9.0	102-28	3	18.7	357	6.63	18.7	3.0	(37)	(4)
FHLMC	8.5	102-01	6	13.6	358	5.41	NA	3.0	(38)	(3)
FHLMC	8.0	100-15	5	5.2	358	5.70	NA	2.5	(38)	(1)
FHLMC	7.5	98-23	4	2.5	358	5.78	53.5	2.0	(39)	2
FHLMC	7.0	96-23	4	5.9	349	5.60	31.0	1.5	(40)	4
FHLMC	6.5	94-18	4	7.3	343	5.48	24.1	1.0	(40)	6

*Target financing rate is 1-month LIBOR.

1-month LIBOR rate. Upon review of the breakeven levels, the investor sees that prepayments would have to rise to 16.7% before the effective cost of funds drops to 6.62% and that the breakeven drop is 3.5/32nds. From this analysis the investor concludes that the dollar roll trade is not attractively priced. However, the cost-of-funds sensitivity to a 1% change in CPR is −4 basis points, and the breakeven CPR is relatively close to the previous month's actual. Given this sensitivity, if the investor forecasts a pickup in prepayment speed, the trade may become attractive.

As mentioned, dollar roll deliveries are made on a TBA basis. As a general rule a borrower will not use a security for a dollar roll that investors are willing to pay a premium for in the "specified pool" market. This is true because the borrower is likely to end the dollar roll with a security that trades in the TBA market (with a lower price). Against this background, the breakeven/sensitivity analysis should be based only on those securities likely to be traded in the TBA market.

To offer a longer term perspective, Exhibit 7–5 shows the 1-month dollar roll prices (drops), along with the computed effective annual cost of funds (using actual prepayments for TBA loans) for GNMA 8s, compared to the 1-month LIBOR rate. This analysis of the bids on GNMA dollar rolls shows some interesting aspects of TBA trading activity and highlights some attractive financing opportunities that were available over the period. Dollar rolls with coupons near current production levels tend to offer the most attractive financing opportunities. This is primarily due to large forward sales of these coupons by mortgage originators wishing to hedge their pipelines. Heavy activity of this type tends to depress forward prices, thus increasing the drop. This translates into attractive opportunities for holders of these coupons.

Dollar roll drops can vary significantly over the course of a year. For example, rolls generally collapse and LIBOR spikes in December as year-end balance sheet constraints temporarily dislocate the market. In 1999 this effect was compounded by Y2K concerns heading into the new year.

SUMMARY

Dollar rolls often offer an attractive means of borrowing at low cost primarily because they allow dealers to cover their short positions. We have focused our discussion of dollar rolls on GNMA fixed-rate pass-throughs, but it should be noted that there are also very active markets for dollar rolls in conventional fixed-rate and ARM pass-throughs and that similar cost-of-funds savings can be found in these transactions. This chapter has demonstrated a methodology for calculating the effective cost of funds obtained through dollar rolls, and outlined the primary risks associated with the cost-of-funds calculation.

E X H I B I T 7–5

GNMA 8s Historical Dollar Rolls, July 1999 through June 2000

Coupon	July 1999	Aug. 1999	Sept. 1999	Oct. 1999	Nov. 1999	Dec. 1999	Jan. 2000	Feb. 2000	Mar. 2000	Apr. 2000	May 2000	June 2000
Thirty-year mortgage rate	7.61%	7.92%	7.92%	7.85%	7.86%	7.96%	8.31%	8.43%	8.33%	8.25%	8.63%	8.37%
Roll bids (drops) in 32nds	5	7	6	6	5	4	5	8	6	6	4	5
Effective cost of funds	4.86%	5.25%	5.42%	4.87%	4.95%	2.96%	3.95%	6.13%	4.27%	5.03%	3.68%	3.76%
One-month LIBOR rate	5.18%	5.21%	5.38%	5.42%	5.41%	6.48%	5.79%	5.92%	5.94%	6.13%	6.48%	6.66%

STRIPPED MORTGAGE-BACKED SECURITIES AND COLLATERALIZED MORTGAGE OBLIGATIONS

CHAPTER **8**

STRIPPED MORTGAGE-BACKED SECURITIES

Lakhbir S. Hayre, DPhil.
Managing Director
Salomon Smith Barney

Vincent Pica
President of Capital Finance
Prudential Securities Inc.

Vito Lodato
Managing Director
Prudential Securities Inc.

Cyrus Mohebbi, Ph.D.
Managing Director
Prudential Securities Inc.
and
Adjunct Professor
New York University

In 1983 FHLMC launched the collateralized mortgage obligation (CMO) structure that enabled issuers to tailor-make mortgage securities according to investor coupon, maturity, and prepayment risk specifications. In July 1986, FNMA introduced a new addition to the mortgage security product line—stripped mortgage-backed securities (SMBS). By redistributing portions of the interest and/or principal cash flows from a pool of mortgage loans to two or more SMBS, FNMA developed a new class of mortgage securities that enabled investors to take strong market positions on expected movements in prepayment and interest rates. As the mortgage pass-through market has matured, the number of derivative products available has increased to give investors a broad range of choices to help them achieve their investment goals. In addition to straight interest-only (IO) securities, and principal-only (PO) securities, investors may now choose from a wide array of synthetic coupons from each strip issue. Investors are able to fine-tune their derivatives to match their desired sensitivity to interest rate, prepayment, and market risk.

SMBS are highly sensitive to change in prevailing interest and prepayment rates and tend to display asymmetric returns. SMBS certificates that are allocated large proportions or all the underlying principal cash flows tend to display very attractive *bullish* return profiles. As market rates drop and prepayments on the underlying collateral increase, the return of these SMBS will be greatly enhanced since principal cash flows will be returned earlier than expected. Conversely, SMBS that

---

Dr. Hayre was Director of Mortgage Research in the Financial Strategies Group at Prudential Securities Inc. when this chapter was written.

are entitled to a large percentage or all the interest cash flows have very appealing *bearish* return characteristics since greater amounts of interest cash flows are generated when prepayments of principal decrease (typically when market rates increase).

OVERVIEW OF THE SMBS MARKET

The SMBS market has grown substantially since the introduction of the first SMBS in July 1986 (see Exhibit 8–1). In total, an estimated $207.6 billion agency SMBS in 434 issues have come to market as of June 2000. FNMA has been the predominant issuer of SMBS with 319 issues totaling $135.3 billion.

Types of SMBS

Strip securities exist in various forms. The first and earliest type of mortgage strip securities are called *synthetic-coupon pass-through securities*. Synthetic-coupon pass-throughs receive fixed proportions of the principal and interest cash flow from a pool of underlying mortgage loans. Synthetic-coupon pass-throughs were introduced by FNMA in mid-1986 through its "alphabet" strip program. IOs and POs, the second and most common type of strip security, were introduced by FNMA in January 1987. IOs and POs received, respectively, only the interest or only the principal cash flow from the underlying mortgage collateral. A third type of strip security, the *CMO strip* is also popular among issuers and investors. As

E X H I B I T   8–1

Growth of SMBS Market

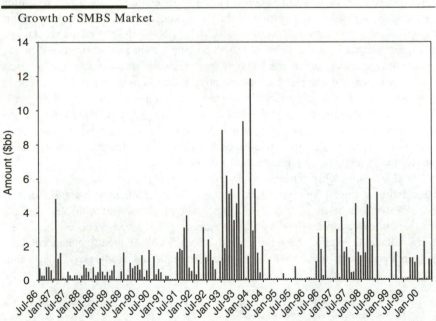

implied by their name, *CMO strips* are tranches within a CMO issue that receive only principal cash flows or have synthetically high coupon rates.

Development of the SMBS Market

The First Mortgage Strip—FNMA SMBS "Alphabet" Strip Securities

FNMA pioneered the first stripped mortgage security in July 1986 through its newly created SMBS Program. For each issue of SMBS Series A through L, FNMA pooled existing FHA/VA and GPM mortgage loans that had been held in its portfolio and issued two SMBS pass-through certificates representing owner-ship interest in proportions of the interest and principal cash flows from the un-derlying mortgage loan pool. Alphabet strips were subsequently called synthetic discount- and premium-coupon securities since the coupon rate of the alphabet strip was quoted as the percentage of the total principal balance of the issue.[1] In total, 12 alphabet strip deals were issued by FNMA in 1986 totaling $2.9 billion.

The FNMA SMBS Trust Program and IOs and POs

The successive and current FNMA strip program, the SMBS Trust Program begun in 1987, provides a vehicle through which deal managers (e.g., investment banks) can swap FNMA pass-throughs for FNMA SMBS Trust certificates. In the swap-ping process, eligible FNMA pass-through securities submitted by the deal man-agers are consolidated by FNMA into one FNMA Megapool Trust. In return, FNMA distributes to the deal manager two similarly denominated SMBS certifi-cates evidencing ownership in the requested proportions of that FNMA Megapool Trust's principal and interest cash flows.[2]

To date, the majority of FNMA SMBS Trusts have contained IO and PO se-curities. IOs and POs represent the most leveraged means of capturing the asym-metric performance characteristics of the two cash flow components of mortgage securities. Although IOs and POs can be combined in different ratios to create synthetic-coupon securities, some investors have shown a preference for one-certificate synthetic securities due to their bookkeeping ease. In late 1993, FNMA added another feature to their SMBS structure. In addition to IO and PO classes, FNMA SMBS Trusts contained a provision for exchanging IOs and POs for another class with a synthetic coupon. The synthetic-coupon classes that are available are determined in the prospectus supplement for each Trust and generally range from 0.5% to double the coupon on the underlying collateral in 50 basis point increments.

---

1. For example, a strip that receives 75% interest and 50% principal of the cash flow from a FNMA 10% would be a synthetic 15% coupon security since the 7.50% coupon is expressed as a 100% principal (i.e., 7.50% coupon / 50% principal = 15.00% coupon / 100% principal). By the same logic, a strip security from a FNMA 10% that receives 50% interest and 1% principal would be a 5,000% coupon security.
2. FNMA tightly restricts the type of collateral that can be placed in Trust. For example, all mortgage securities must have the same prefix (be of the same loan type) and be within certain WAC and WAM range to correspond with preliminary pricing. Moreover, the minimum initial principal balance of each SMBS Trust must be $200 million.

Exchanges are executed for a small fee and may be reversed back into IO and PO components as well as into any other available combination, provided the proportions of IO and PO are correct. To promote liquidity in the SMBS market, all FNMA SMBS certificates (except FNMA SMBS Series L) have a unique conversion feature that enables like denominations of both classes of a FNMA SMBS issue or Trust to be exchanged on the book-entry system of the Federal Reserve Banks for like denominations of FNMA MBS certificates or Megapool certificates. Because of the potential for profitable arbitrages, the aggregate price of the two classes of any same FNMA issue or Trust tend to be slightly higher than the price of comparable-coupon and remaining-term FNMA pass-through certificates.

All FNMA SMBS pass-throughs (alphabet and Trusts) have the same payment structure, payment delays, and FNMA guarantee as regular FNMA pass-throughs. As of June 2000, 307 FNMA SMBS Trust deals have come to market, totaling approximately $132.4 billion.

Private Issuance
Investment firms began to issue private-label SMBS in late 1986. Many of these private-labels SMBS were issued through REMIC structures. Since one class of REMIC issue must be designated the residual interest, the super-premium coupon class of many of these private-label SMBS is often the residual interest of the REMIC deal. Unlike investing in FNMA SMBS, investors who purchase these residual securities are responsible for the tax consequences of the entire REMIC issue.

Developments in the SMBS Market

A number of developments have occurred in the SMBS market that have further enhanced its depth and efficiency.

PO-Collaterized CMOs
Profitable arbitrage opportunities led to the introduction of CMO securities collaterized by POs. PO-collateralized CMOs allocate the cash flow from underlying PO securities between several CMO tranches with different maturities and prepayment patterns. The potential for profitable arbitrages with PO securities has enhanced the efficiency of the SMBS market by effectively placing a floor on the price potential of POs and a price ceiling on corresponding IOs in a given market environment.

CMO Strip Securities
Strip securities are included in CMO issues as regular-interest (nonresidual) CMO tranches. CMO strip securities that pay only principal, large proportions of interest cash flows (relative to principal cash flows), or only interest over the underlying mortgage collateral's life are termed PO securities, "higher-interest" securities, and IO securities respectively; they tend to have performance characteristics similar to FNMA SMBS. Other types of CMO strip securities receive initial and

ongoing collateral principal or interest in cash flows after other classes in the CMO issue are retired or have been paid. These types of strip CMO securities are structured as PO or IO PACs, TACs, or Super-POs and perform differently from FNMA SMBS.

FHLMC Stripped Giant Program

FHLMC is also a participant in the SMBS market. In October 1989, FHLMC announced the Stripped Giant Mortgage Participation Certificate Program. As of June 2000, FHLMC had issued 108 FHLMC Giant PO and IO PCs, totaling approximately $66.6 billion.

FHLMC's Stripped Giant Program is similar to FNMA's swap SMBS Trust Program. Deal managers submit FHLMC PCs to FHLMC; FHLMC, in turn, aggregates these PCs into Giant pools and issues Strip Giant PCs representing desired proportions of principal and interest to the deal manager. All FHLMC Strip PCs have the same payment structure, payment delays, and payment guarantee as regular FHLMC PCs. Like FNMA SMBS, FHLMC Giant Strip IOs and POs have a conversion feature that allows them to be exchanged for similarly denominated FHLMC PCs. Under the FHLMC Gold MACS (Modifiable and Combinable Securities) program, IO and PO securities may be exchanged for synthetic-coupon classes that have been predetermined in the prospectus supplement for a fee.

GNMA Collateral for SMBS

In 1990 FNMA began to issue SMBS collaterized by GNMA pass-through certificates. Since the beginning of 1990, FNMA has issued 76 trusts that have had underlying GNMA collateral. FHLMC began to issue GNMA-backed SMBS in 1993 and has issued 7 GNMA strips to date. The increased availability of GNMA SMBS has further broadened the investor base of SMBS, enhanced the liquidity of the SMBS market and increased the number of hedging alternatives available to GNMA investors.

Buyers of SMBS

The asymmetric returns of SMBS appeal to a broad variety of investors. SMBS can be used effectively to hedge interest rate and prepayment exposure of other types of mortgage securities, such as CMO residual and premium-coupon mortgage pass-through securities. SMBS can also be combined with other fixed income securities such as U.S. Treasuries and mortgage securities to enhance the total return of the portfolio in varying interest rate scenarios. Insurance companies and pension funds with conservative duration-matching needs frequently use SMBS as a method of tailoring their investment portfolio to meet the duration of liabilities and thus minimize interest rate risk.

SMBS are used by various types of investors to accomplish their investment objectives. Insurance companies, pension funds, money managers and other total rate of return accounts use SMBS to improve the return of their fixed income portfolios.

PO securities, which tend to have long durations, enable pension funds to more effectively manage the duration of their portfolios. Thrift institutions and mortgage bankers often use PO securities to hedge their servicing portfolios or use IO securities as a substitute for servicing income.[3]

Investment Characteristics

SMBS enable investors to capture the performance characteristics of the principal or interest components of the cash flows of mortgage pass-through securities. These individual components display contrasting responses to change in market rates and prepayment rates. Principal-only (PO) SMBS are bullish instruments, outperforming mortgage pass-through in declining interest rate environments. Interest-only (IO) SMBS are bearish investments that can be used as a hedge against rising interest rates.

Variation of Interest and Principal Components with Prepayments

The cash flows that an MBS investor receives each month consist of principal and interest payments from a large group of homeowners. The proportion of principal and interest in the total payment varies depending on the prepayment level of the mortgage pool. Exhibit 8–2 illustrates these cash flows for $1 million 30-year FNMA current-coupon pass-through securities at various PSA prepayment speeds.

Exhibit 8–2a shows the principal component of the monthly cash flows. Since the interest is proportional to the outstanding balance, Exhibit 8–2a can also be viewed as showing the decline in the mortgage balance at the various prepayment speeds.

At a zero prepayment level, the interest and principal cash flows in Exhibit 8–2 compose a normal amortization schedule. In the earlier months of the security's life, the cash flows primarily contain interest payments. This occurs because interest payments are calculated based on the outstanding principal balance remaining on the mortgage loans at the beginning of each month. As the mortgage loans amortize, the cash flows increasingly reflect the payment of principal. Toward the end of the security's life, principal payments make up the bulk of the cash flows.

Prepayments of principal significantly alter the principal and interest cash flows received by the mortgage pass-through investor. Homeowners who prepay all or part of their mortgage loans return more principal to the investor in the earlier years of the mortgage security. All else being equal, an increase in prepayments has two effects:

1. The time remaining until return of principal is reduced as shown in Exhibit 8–2a. At 100% PSA, the average life of the principal cash flows is 11.8 years, whereas at faster speeds of 200 and 300% PSA, principal is returned in average time periods of 7.8 years and 5.7 years, respectively.

---

3. According to the applicable risk-based capital guidelines, strip securities that are backed by agency (FNMA, FHLMC, and GNMA) pass-through securities (agency-issue or private-label issue) are in the 100% risk-based category for thrift institution and commercial banks.

Principal Component of Monthly Cash Flows

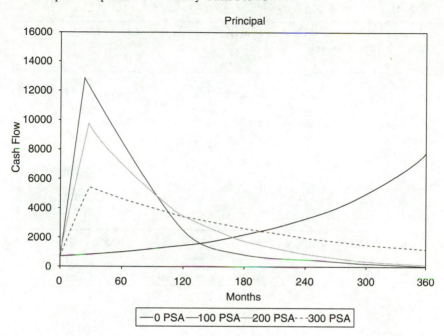

Total Amount of Interest Cash Flows

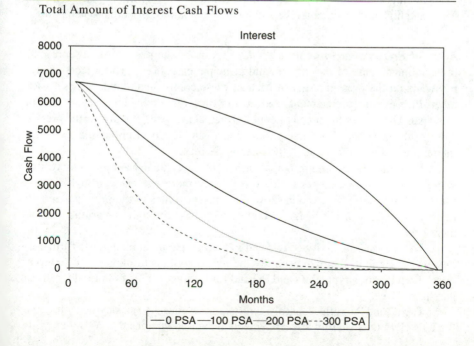

EXHIBIT 8–3

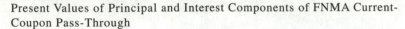

Present Values of Principal and Interest Components of FNMA Current-Coupon Pass-Through

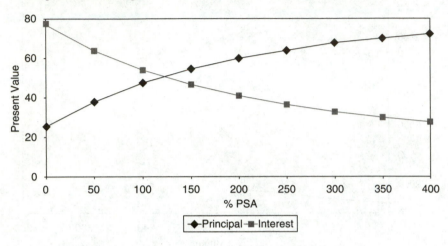

2. The total amount of interest cash flows is reduced, which is shown in Exhibit 8–2*b*. This occurs because interest payments are calculated based on the higher amount of principal outstanding at the beginning of each month and higher prepayment levels reduce the amount of principal outstanding.

Effect of Prepayment Changes on Value   A mortgage pass-through represents the combined value of the interest and principal cash flows. The effects of prepayments on the present value of each of these components tend to offset each other. Increases in prepayments reduce the time remaining until repayment of principal. The sooner the prepayment of principal is repaid, the higher the present value of the principal. Conversely, since increasing levels of prepayments reduce interest cash flows, the value of the interest decreases.

   Thus, the interest and principal cash flows individually are much more sensitive to prepayment changes than the combined mortgage pass-through. This is illustrated in Exhibit 8–3, which shows the present values of the principal and interest components of a FNMA current-coupon pass-through at various prepayment levels.

   The greater sensitivity of IOs and POs to prepayment changes is further illustrated in Exhibit 8–4, which shows the realized yields to maturity (or internal rates of return) for a typical IO and PO and for the underlining collateral for given purchase prices.

   The IO and PO reflect sharply contrasting responses to prepayment changes; the IO's yield falls sharply as prepayments increase, whereas the PO's yield falls

EXHIBIT 8-4

Realized Yields to Maturity for Typical IO and PO

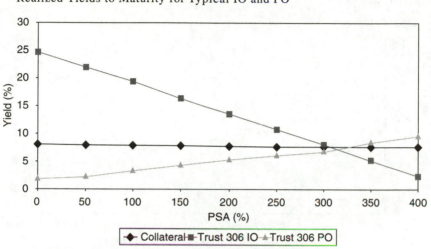

sharply as prepayments decrease. The yield of the underlining collateral is, on the other hand, relatively stable since it is assumed to be priced close to par.

Price Performance of SMBS   The discussion above indicates that prepayment speeds are by far the most important determinant of the value of an SMBS. Since the price response of an SMBS to interest rate changes is determined, to a large extent, by how the collateral's prepayment speed is affected by interest rate changes, we begin with a discussion of mortgage prepayment behavior.

The Prepayment S Curve   The prepayment speed of an MBS is a function of the security's characteristics (such as coupon and age), interest rates, and other economic and demographic variables.[4] Although detailed prepayment projections generally require an econometric model, the investor can obtain some insight into the likely behavior of an SMBS by examining the spread between the collateral's gross coupon and current mortgage rates.

This spread is generally the most important variable in determining prepayment speeds. With respect to this spread, prepayment speeds have an S shape; speeds are fairly flat for discount coupons (when the spread is negative and prepayments are caused mainly by housing turnover), they start increasing when the spread becomes positive, they surge rapidly until the spread is several hundred basis points, and then they level off when the security is a high premium. At this

---

4. Prepayment modeling is discussed in Section IV of this book.

EXHIBIT 8–5

Prepayment S Curve

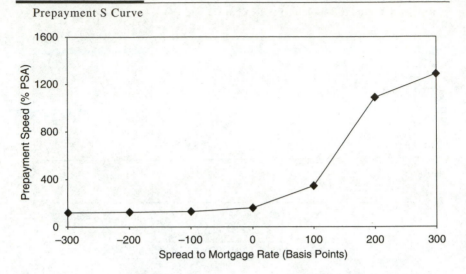

point, there is already substantial economic incentive for mortgage holders to refinance, and further increases in the spread lead to only marginal increases in refinancing activity. This S curve is illustrated in Exhibit 8–5, which shows projected long-term prepayments for current coupon collateral for specified changes in mortgage rates.

In the remainder of this section, we make repeated reference to Exhibit 8–5, since the performance of an SMBS can be explained to a large extent by the position of its collateral on the prepayment S curve.[5]

---

5. However, the investor should note that not all aspects of prepayment behavior are explained by the spread between the coupon and the mortgage rate. The projected prepayments shown in Exhibit 8–5 are long-term averages. Month-to-month prepayment rates vary (for example, due to seasonality) even if mortgage rates do change. If a substantial and sustained decline in mortgage rates occurs, then mortgage holders exposed to mortgage refinancing incentives for the first time initially exhibit a sharp increase in prepayments. This gradually decreases as the homeowners most anxious and able to refinance do so. This non-interest rate–related decline in the prepayment speeds of premium coupons usually is referred to as "burnout." The projected speeds shown in the declining-rate scenarios are the average of the high early speeds and lower later speeds.

For seasoned coupons that have experienced a heavy refinancing period, burnout implies that prepayments may be less responsive to decline in interest rates. This applies to the majority of premium coupons currently outstanding. The age effect on prepayments is well known. Prepayment speeds are low for new mortgages and increase gradually until the mortgages are 2 to 3 years old, after which the age is less important. This means that, other things being equal, an IO is worth more if it is collaterized by new FNMA 8s, for example, than by seasoned FNMA 8s.

EXHIBIT 8–6

Projected Price Paths for a Current Coupon IO and PO for Parallel Interest Rate Shifts

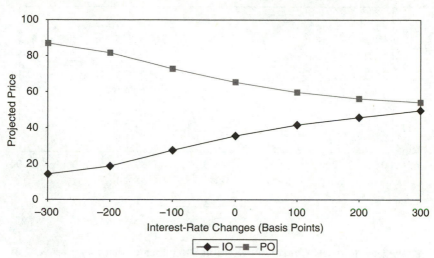

Projected Price Behavior   Exhibit 8–6 gives projected price paths for a current coupon IO and PO for parallel interest rate shifts.[6]

The projected price behavior of the SMBS as interest rates change can be explained largely by the prepayment S curve in Exhibit 8–5.

• As rates drop from current levels, the collateral begins to experience sharp increases in prepayment. Compounded by lower discounted rates, this causes substantial price appreciation for the PO. For the IO, however, the higher prepayments outweigh the lower discount rates and the net result is a price decline.

• If the rates drop by several hundred basis points, the collateral becomes a high-premium coupon and prepayments plateau. The rates of price appreciation of the PO and price deprecation of the IO both decrease. Eventually the IO's price starts to increase, as the effect of lower discount rates start to outweigh the effect of marginal increases in prepayments.

• If rates rise, the slower prepayments and higher discount rates combine to cause a steep drop in the price of the PO. The IO is aided initially by the slower prepayments, giving the IO negative duration, but eventually prepayments plateau on the slower side of the prepayment S curve and the IO's price begins to decrease.

---

6. The prices are calculated to give an option-adjusted spread (OAS) of 120 basis points in all cases. A discussion of OAS analysis is given in the next section. Note that if it is also priced at an OAS of 120 basis points, the collateral price is just the sum of the IO and PO prices.

EXHIBIT 8–7

IO and PO Effective Durations for Current or Low Coupon Collateral

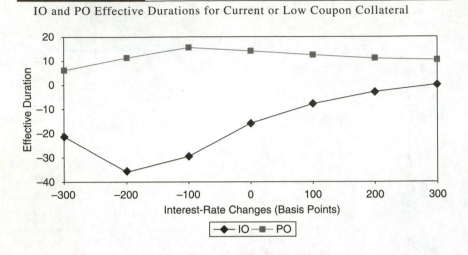

Effective Duration and Convexity   Exhibit 8–6 indicates that for current or low-premium collateral, POs tend to have large, positive effective durations whereas IOs have large, negative effective durations.[7]

The effective durations in Exhibit 8–7 reflect the price paths in Exhibit 8–6:

- For the PO, as rates decline the effective duration initially increases, reflecting its rapid price appreciation as prepayments surge. Note that this is in complete contrast to traditional measures such as Macaulay or modified duration, which, reflecting the shortening of the PO, would actually decrease. As rates continue to drop, the PO's effective duration levels off and then decreases, reflecting both

---

7. Effective duration is a measure of the proportional price change if interest rates change by a small amount. Let Price (0) be the current price of a security. Let Price (Δ) be the price if interest rates increase by a small amount Δ *y* and Price (−Δ) be the price if interest rate decrease by a small amount Δ. Then

$$\text{Effective duration} = \frac{\text{Price}(-\Delta) - \text{Price}(\Delta)}{\text{Price}(0) \times 2\Delta y} \times 100$$

This formula is straightforward: We take the total price change (the difference in the new prices) and divide by the initial price (the 100 is a scaling factor).

To obtain the projected price and durations, we have, for simplicity, assumed parallel shifts in interest rates. In practice, of course, rates do not move in parallel (typically, short-term rates tend to be more volatile than long rates). However using nonparallel yield-curve shifts raises questions which, although interesting, are best left for another book. For example, suppose the yield curve shifts such that short rates move twice as much as long rates, and we compute the corresponding price change. The effective duration will be twice as large if we compare the price change against the change in short rates (i.e., Δ *y* = change in short rates) as opposed to comparing the price change against the change in long rates (i.e., Δ *y* = change in long rates).

EXHIBIT 8–8

IO and PO Convexities

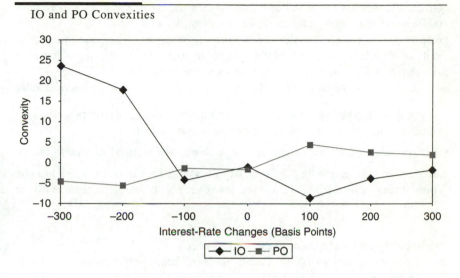

a leveling off of prepayments and the fact that, to calculate the effective duration, we are dividing by an increasing price. If rates increase, the PO's duration
decreases but remains positive.

- For the IO, the effective duration is initially negative and decreases rapidly as
rates drop, before eventually increasing and becoming positive after prepayments
plateau. If rates increase, the duration increases and eventually becomes positive.

Convexity measures the rate of change of duration and is useful in indicating whether the trend in price change is likely to accelerate or decelerate. It is calculated by comparing the price change if interest rates decrease with the price
change if rates increase.[8] Exhibit 8–8 shows the convexities obtained using the
projected prices in Exhibit 8–6.

Comparing Exhibits 8–6 and 8–7 shows that the convexity indicates how the
duration is changing. When the duration is increasing (as in the case of the PO
when rates begin to decline from the initial value), the convexity is positive, and

---

8. Convexity is calculated by comparing the price change if rate move up or down by small amounts. Let

$$\Delta P^+ = \text{Price (0)} - \text{Price (}\Delta\text{)}$$
$$\Delta P^- = \text{Price (}-\Delta\text{)} - \text{Price (0)}$$

where ΔP^+ and ΔP^- are the price changes if rate increases or decreases by Δy, respectively.
Then

$$\text{Convexity} = \frac{\Delta P^- - \Delta P^+}{\text{Price (0)} \times (\Delta y)^2} \times 100$$

when the duration is decreasing, the convexity is negative. For example, the IO's convexity is initially negative but begins to increase after rates fall by more than 100 basis points; although the duration is still negative at -200 basis points, the positive convexity indicates that the duration is increasing. The peak in the convexity of the IO at a change of -300 basis points indicates that the rate of increase in its duration is greatest at this point, as shown in Exhibit 8–7.

In summary, the prepayment S curve implies that for SMBS collateralized by

- Current or discount pass-throughs, the PO has substantial upside potential and little downside risk, whereas the converse is true for IOs

- Low premiums, there is a somewhat comparable upside potential and downside risk

- High premiums (including the majority of SMBS issued to date), the PO has little upside potential and significant downside risk whereas the reverse is true for IOs

Pricing of SMBS and Option-Adjusted Spreads

The strong dependence of SMBS cash flows on future prepayment rates, combined with the typically asymmetric response of prepayments to interest rate changes, make traditional measures of return such as yield to maturity of limited usefulness in analyzing or pricing SMBS. The most common method of pricing SMBS is with option-adjusted spreads (OAS). OAS analysis uses probabilistic methods to evaluate the security over the full-term range of interest rate paths that may occur over its term. The impact of prepayment variations on the security's cash flows is factored into the analysis. The OAS is the resulting average spread over Treasuries provided by the security.[9] It gives a long-term average value of the security, assuming a market-neutral viewpoint on interest rates.

Exhibit 8–9 shows the use of OAS analysis for FNMA Trust 303 and FNMA Trust 267 and the underlining pass-through collateral. In each case, the price is chosen to give an OAS of 120 basis points at a 15% annual volatility of short-term interest rates. Also shown are the yields to maturity and standard spreads over the WAL Treasury at these prices using a projected prepayment speed.

The OAS at a 0% volatility when mortgage rates stay at current levels, is typically close to the standard Treasury spread in a flat yield curve environment. The difference between the OAS at 0% and 15% volatilities, which we label the *option cost,* is a measure of the impact of prepayment variations on a security for the given level of interest rate volatility. The option cost, to a large extent, does not depend on the pricing level or the absolute level of prepayment projections (although it does depend on the slope, or response, of prepayment projections to interest rate changes). Hence, the option cost is a measure of the intrinsic effect of likely interest rate changes on an SMBS.

---

9. See Chapter 11.

OAS Analysis for FNMA Trust 303 and FNMA Trust 267

		Price	YTM	WAL	SPD/Tsy	0	15	Option Cost
FNMA Trust 303	PO	63–28	6.273	8.4	21	22	120	–98
FN 7.5% Collateral	IO	34–31	10.849	8.4	479	520	120	400
WAM 29–00 years	PT	98–23	7.768	8.4	173	179	120	59
Proj PSA: 161								

		Price	YTM	WAL	SPD/Tsy	0	15	Option Cost
FNMA Trust 267	PO	70–21	6.662	6	50	72	120	–48
FN 8.5% Collateral	IO	32–08	10.523	6	437	426	120	306
WAM 23–03 years	PT	102–27	7.809	6	165	178	120	58
Proj PSA: 215								

Before discussing the option cost in Exhibit 8–9, note that, in general, interest rate and prepayment variations have two effects on an MBS:

1. For any callable security, being called in a low interest rate environment typically has an adverse effect, since a dollar of principal of the security in general would be worth more than the price at which it is being returned. (An exception is a mortgage prepayment resulting from housing turnover, when the call could be uneconomic from the call-holder's point of view.) To put it another way, the principal that is being returned typically has to be reinvested at yields lower than that provided by the existing security.

2. For MBS priced at a discount or a premium, changes in prepayments result in the discount or premium being received sooner or later than anticipated. This may mitigate or reinforce the call effect discussed in (1).

In general, the first effect is much more important than the second; however, for certain deep-discount securities, such as POs, the second effect may at times outweigh the first. The net result of the two effects depends on the position of the collateral on the prepayment curve shown in Exhibit 8–5.

• FNMA Trust 303, shown in Exhibit 8–9, illustrates the characteristics typical of SMBS collateralized by current or discount coupons. For discount or current-coupon collateral, prepayments are unlikely to fall significantly but could increase dramatically if there is a substantial decrease in interest rates. This asymmetry means that the PO is, on average, likely to gain significantly from variations in prepayment speeds. The option cost for the PO is usually negative; that is, the PO *gains* from interest rate volatility indicating that the benefits of faster return of principal outweigh the generic negative effects of being called in low interest rate environments. On the other hand, the underlying collateral tends to have a positive (but usually small in the case of discount collateral) option cost; the negative effect of being called when rates are low outweigh the benefits of faster return of principal. Finally, the IO typically has a large positive option cost; the asymmetric nature of likely prepayment changes, discussed above, means that the IO gains little if interest rates increase (since prepayments will not decrease significantly), whereas a substantial decline in rates is likely to lead to a surge in prepayments and a drop in interest cash flows.

• FNMA Trust 267 is representative of outstanding SMBS with premium collateral. For *premium* collateral, there is, generally speaking, potential for both increases and decreases in prepayments, and the net effect of prepayment variations will depend on the particular coupon and prevailing mortgage rates. Seasoned premiums, for example, will not have potential for substantial increases in speeds and hence, FNMA Trust 267 PO has a less negative option cost. The collateral has a positive option cost for the same reasons.

The importance of likely variations in prepayments makes the standard yield to maturity of very little relevance in pricing SMBS and therefore, they tend to be priced (as in Exhibit 8–9) on an OAS basis.

SUMMARY

POs and IOs offer the investor the opportunity to hedge a portfolio of MBS against interest rate and prepayment risk for short-term holding periods. In addition, an investor can choose to adjust the proportion of the SMBS hedge in the portfolio according to his perception of market direction. The resulting customized portfolio would then offer optimal performance in a market environment that adheres to investor expectations.

CHAPTER 9

COLLATERALIZED MORTGAGE OBLIGATIONS

Mortgage Research Group
Lehman Brothers Inc.

The U.S. mortgage-backed securities (MBS) market has grown significantly in the last 20 years. At the end of 1980, approximately $111 billion MBS were outstanding; by the end of 1999, the amount had grown to more than $2.2 trillion. Much of this growth has come in the form of collateralized mortgage obligations (CMOs) and real estate mortgage investment conduits (REMICs),[1] structures that significantly broadened the investor base for mortgage-backed securities by offering near-U.S. Treasury credit quality, customized performance characteristics, attractive yields across a range of maturities, and a variety of risk/return profiles to fit investors' needs. CMOs currently account for 40% of all fixed-rate mortgage-backed securities outstanding.

Throughout the 1970s and early 1980s, most mortgage-backed securities were issued in pass-through form. Pass-throughs, which are participations in the cash flows from pools of individual home mortgages, have long final maturities and the potential for early partial repayment of principal. These securities primarily appeal to investors willing to accept long and uncertain investment horizons in exchange for relatively high yields and credit quality.

In 1983, a dramatic fall in mortgage rates and a surging housing market caused mortgage originations to double. Much of this production was sold in the capital markets; pass-through issuance jumped from $53 billion in 1982 to $84 billion. To accommodate this surge in supply, financial innovators designed a security that would broaden the existing MBS investor base. In mid-1983, the Federal Home Loan Mortgage Corporation (Freddie Mac, or FHLMC) issued the first CMO, a $1 billion, three-class structure that offered short-, intermediate-, and long-term securities produced from the cash flows of a pool of mortgages. This instrument allowed more investors to become active in the MBS market. For instance, banks could participate in the

---

The original author of this chapter was Chris Ames. The chapter was updated by Jeffrey K. Mudrick, Vice President, Mortgage Research, Lehman Brothers.

1. Although CMOs and REMICs have different tax and regulatory characteristics for issuers, there is little difference between them for the investor. In practice, the market uses the terms interchangeably, and the term CMO is used generically in this chapter. A detailed discussion of the differences between the two is described later in this chapter.

market more efficiently by buying short-term mortgage securities to match their short-term liabilities (deposits).

The CMO market evolved rapidly, growing in size and complexity. Annual issuance of agency CMOs rose steadily, from $5 billion in 1983 to a peak of $324 billion in 1993. CMO issuance fell between 1994 and 1996 for a variety of reasons. Sharply higher mortgage rates curtailed refinancing activity and resulted in lower MBS collateral issuance. With lower prepayment volatility, many mortgage securities investors chose to hold pass-throughs instead of CMOs. At the same time, bank demand for CMOs softened as lending activity finally began to rise after the credit crunch years 1991–1993. Many of the hedge funds that had been buyers of the more high-risk and high-yielding tranches turned to other investments.

Following the 1994–1996 downtrend, investor interest in CMOs rebounded sharply in 1997. Agency CMO issuance jumped from $50 billion in 1996 to $150 billion in 1997 and $200 billion in 1998. The resurgence of demand for CMOs was linked to two primary factors: (1) dealers simplified structures to enhance liquidity, and (2) bank demand surged as interest rates descended to all-time lows. Banks, typically buyers of first-call CMO tranches, faced greater requirements for replacement assets as mortgage paydowns accelerated in the 1997–1998 prepayment wave. Following the liquidity crisis in the fall of 1998, hedge funds have played a more limited role in CMO issuance, while traditional CMO investors like financial institutions, insurance companies and government-sponsored enterprises have remained the primary participants.

Currently, over 40% of all 30-year FHLMC and Federal National Mortgage Association (FNMA) pass-throughs are pledged as collateral for CMOs. More recently, CMOs backed by individual mortgages and issued by nonagency entities (known as whole-loan or private-label CMOs) have become a significant market in their own right, and Lehman Brothers' estimate of the balance of whole-loan CMOs outstanding as of November 1999 is approximately $280 billion.

The thrust in the CMO market has been the development of innovative structures to meet the needs of institutional investors and broaden the investor base for mortgage-backed securities. For example, demand from traditional corporate bond investors for CMO bonds with insulation from prepayment volatility led to the creation of planned amortization classes (PACs) and targeted amortization classes (TACs). Regulatory pressures on banks and thrifts led to the creation of very accurately defined maturity (VADM) bonds that were guaranteed not to extend past a given date. Growing interest from overseas investors gave rise to floating-rate bonds indexed to the London interbank offered rate (LIBOR). Increased investor sophistication and technological breakthroughs have created a large market for derivative securities: interest- and principal-only bonds (IOs, POs), inverse floaters, and others. A broad range of products is now available to suit almost any investor preference.

This chapter explains how CMOs are structured and defines the major types of securities available. It also describes the evolving CMO regulatory environment, PAC band drift, the pricing relationship between CMOs and collateral, some valuation techniques employed by CMO investors, and trading conventions.

PASS-THROUGHS AND WHOLE LOANS: THE BUILDING BLOCKS OF CMOS

In order to develop realistic expectations about the performance of a CMO bond, an investor must first evaluate the underlying collateral, since its performance will determine the timing and size of the cash flows reallocated by the CMO structure. Agency and whole-loan CMOs have distinct collateral, credit, and prepayment characteristics.

Collateral

Individual home mortgages are the underlying collateral and source of cash flow for CMOs. In the case of agency CMOs, these mortgages are already pooled and securitized in pass-through form. The mortgages backing an agency pass-through are of similar size, age, and underwriting quality and have similar rates. All principal and interest cash flows generated by the underlying mortgages, including any prepayments, are channeled to investors, net of a servicing spread (a small portion of each month's interest payment paid to the institution that collects and distributes the mortgage payments). Pass-through investors share in the cash flows on a pro rata basis.

Whole-loan CMO issuers do not take the interim step of creating a pass-through security from a pool of individual mortgages; instead, they create a structure directly based on the cash flows of a group of mortgages. Whole-loan pools, like agency pass-throughs, usually contain mortgages of similar underwriting quality, age, and rate (the range of ages and rates is often somewhat wider for whole-loan pools than for agency pass-throughs). The most common distinguishing characteristic of whole loans is their size. The agencies accept only mortgages below a certain size (currently $252,700 for FNMA and FHLMC and $219,849 for GNMA); larger loans, known as jumbo loans, make up the primary collateral for whole-loan CMOs.

Credit

GNMA is a U.S. government agency, and FHLMC and FNMA are government-sponsored enterprises. All three entities guarantee the full and timely[2] payment of all principal and interest due from pass-throughs issued under their names. GNMA securities, like U.S. Treasury securities, are backed by the full faith and credit of the U.S. government. FNMA and FHLMC, although not government agencies, are federally chartered corporations, and the market assumes an implicit U.S. government guarantee backing the agency guarantee. Securities issued by all three entities are called *agency securities*.

---

2. Early FHLMC pass-throughs, known as 75-day delay pass-throughs, carry a guarantee of full and timely payment of interest and eventual payment of principal (after disposal of the foreclosed property). FHLMC CMOs backed by these securities carry the same guarantee as the underlying pass-throughs.

Although whole loans do not carry agency guarantees against default, they generally adhere to agency underwriting standards for types of documentation required, loan-to-value ratios, and income ratios. In addition, the rating agencies require significant levels of credit enhancement[3] to obtain a triple- or double-A rating. The combination of collateral quality and structural features make it highly unlikely that investors in senior classes of whole-loan CMOs will sustain credit-related losses.

Prepayments

Expected prepayment behavior is a critical factor in evaluating CMO collateral. Three collateral characteristics are necessary for evaluating collateral from a prepayment perspective: issuer or guarantor, gross weighted average coupon (WAC), and weighted average loan age (WALA) or weighted average maturity (WAM). The issuer or guarantor is important because of the details known about borrowers within different programs. For example, GNMAs are backed by loans insured by the Federal Housing Administration (FHA) or guaranteed by the Veterans Administration (VA). Borrowers under these programs tend to be less mobile than non-FHA or VA (conventional[4]) borrowers, and therefore GNMA prepayments have been slower and more stable than conventional prepayments. Whole loans, on the other hand, tend to be larger and therefore represent more wealthy or sophisticated borrowers: in falling-rate environments, they have prepaid approximately 1.5 to 2 times faster than comparable coupon conventionals.

Gross WAC is the average of the interest rates of the mortgages backing a structure before adjusting for the servicing fee. Since the actual mortgage rate determines a borrower's refinancing incentive, gross WAC is a better indicator of prepayment potential than the net coupon of the collateral. Finally, loan age is important in determining short-term prepayments. The best measure of age is WALA, which tracks the age of the underlying mortgages. If WALA is not available, then taking the original term of the mortgages and subtracting the WAM will give an approximation.

CMO STRUCTURES

In a CMO, cash flows from one or more mortgage pass-throughs or a pool of mortgages are reallocated to multiple classes with different priority claims. The CMO is self-supporting, with the cash flows from the collateral always able to meet the cash flow requirements of the CMO classes under any possible prepayment scenario. The CMO creation process is a dynamic one. This chapter describes the most common types of CMO classes, but dealers will frequently tailor bonds to fit investors' specific needs.

---

3. Common whole-loan CMO credit enhancements are senior or subordinated structures and third-party pool insurance. These are described in Chapter 22.
4. A conventional mortgage is any mortgage not FHA-insured or VA-guaranteed. In practice, the market uses the term *conventional* to group loans eligible for securitization under FHLMC and FNMA programs since securities from these agencies are usually backed by non-FHA VA mortgages.

The following general points are important for any discussion of CMO structures:

- CMOs issued by FNMA and FHLMC (known collectively as conventional CMOs) carry the same guarantee as conventional pass-throughs, and CMOs issued by GNMA carry the same guarantee as GNMA pass-throughs. Both FNMA and FHLMC are authorized to issue CMOs with GNMA pass-throughs as collateral. The guarantee for a FNMA- or FHLMC-issued CMO backed by GNMA collateral is the same as that for a conventional CMO. Since credit risk is not an issue for agency CMOs, there is no need for credit enhancements in the structures.

- Whole-loan CMOs do not carry government default guarantees and are therefore usually rated by the bond rating agencies. A variety of credit enhancement techniques are employed so that most or all bonds in a structure receive a AAA rating. The most common technique today is the senior or subordinated structure, with senior bonds generally rated AAA and layers of subordinated bonds receiving lower investment- or non-investment-grade ratings.

- Most CMO classes pay interest monthly, based on the current face amount of the class, even if it is not currently paying down principal.

- Most CMO classes have a principal lockout period during which only interest payments are received. The payment window is the period during which principal payments are received. In most cases, the lockout period and the payment window are not absolute but are affected by prepayments on the underlying collateral.

- CMO classes are structured with specific cash flow profiles and investment terms based on an assumed prepayment rate. This assumed rate, which represents the market's current expectation of future prepayments on the collateral, is known as the pricing speed.

- CMOs can be structured from collateral of any maturity. The examples that follow focus on 30-year collateral, but in the last few years CMOs have been backed by 20- and 15-year fixed-rate and 5- and 7-year balloon collateral, depending on the supply and cost of the collateral and the demand for CMOs with the particular characteristics imparted by the collateral.

CMO structures are of two major types: One provides for the redirection of principal payments only, and the other for redirection of interest as well as principal. Sequential-pay, PAC-companion, and TAC-companion structures redirect principal and are the starting point for all CMOs.

Sequential-Pay Classes

The primary purpose of the first CMOs was to bring a broader range of maturity choices to the MBS market. These CMOs—called sequential-pay, plain vanilla, or clean structures—reallocate collateral principal payments sequentially to a series of bonds. All initial principal amortization and prepayments from the collateral are paid to the shortest maturity class, or tranche, until it is fully retired; then principal

E X H I B I T   9–1

Principal Plows from a Four-Tranche Sequential-Pay Structure*

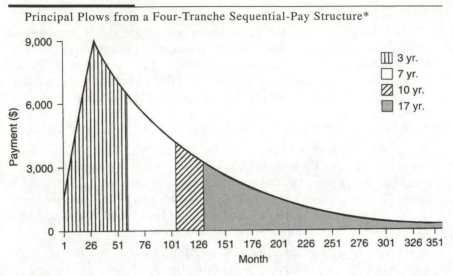

*$1 million 7.5% pool at 185% PSA.

payments are redirected to the next shortest class. This process continues until all classes are paid down. Exhibit 9–1 demonstrates how the principal flows of a $1 million pool of FNMA 7.5s would be distributed in a sequential-pay structure if the collateral prepaid consistently at 185% PSA. In this example, owners of the first class, identified as a 3-year class due to its weighted average life of 3.0 years, receive all principal flows from month 1 until month 64, when their principal balance is $0. Investors who own the second class (the 7-year) receive principal flows from month 65 to month 107. Owners of the 10-year class receive principal from month 108 to month 134, and investors in the final class receive the remaining principal flows. The amount of time that each class is outstanding, as well as the months that principal payments begin and end, vary as actual prepayment experience varies from the assumed prepayment rate.

With the creation of the sequential-pay structure, capital market participants with short investment horizons were able to enter the MBS market because they could buy bonds that more closely matched their desired terms. Investors with long-term horizons also benefited because they were insulated from prepayments during the early years of a pool's life.

Planned Amortization Classes

In 1986, after a period of substantial interest rate declines and the resulting surge of mortgage refinancing activity and prepayments, issuers began producing prepayment-protected bonds called *planned amortization classes* (PACs). These structures offered substantial protection from the reinvestment risk and weighted average-life volatility associated with prepayments.

E X H I B I T   9–2

Determining the PAC Schedule*

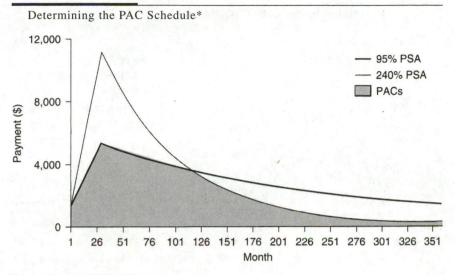

*Principal flows from $1 million 7.5% pool.

     PACs have a principal payment schedule (similar to a sinking fund mechanism) that can be maintained over a range of prepayment rates. This schedule is based on the minimum amount of principal cash flow produced by the collateral at two prepayment rates known as the *PAC bands.* For example, if the PAC bands were 95% PSA and 240% PSA, a PAC principal payment schedule could be constructed equal to the shaded area in Exhibit 9–2. The minimum amount of principal produced in the early months follows the principal payment path of the lower band (95% PSA), and after 116 months (where the two lines on the graph intersect), the schedule is constrained by the upper band (240% PSA) because principal has paid off more quickly under this scenario.

     The total principal flow available under the PAC schedule determines the original amount of PACs in a structure. (In this example, PACs represent 70% of the structure.) If wider bands are chosen, the derived PAC schedule will be smaller; that is, there will be fewer PACs in the structure.

     The PAC schedule is maintained by redirecting cash flow uncertainty to classes called *companions.* In times of fast prepayments, companions support PACs by absorbing principal payments in excess of the PAC schedule. In times of slow prepayments, amortization of the companions is delayed if there is not enough principal for the currently paying PAC. As a result of this support mechanism, faster-than-expected prepayments cause companions to pay off sooner, or contract in weighted average life. Conversely, slower-than-expected prepayments cause companions to remain outstanding longer, or extend. Exhibit 9–3 shows how the companions support the PACs at both ends of the protected prepayment range.

EXHIBIT 9–3

PAC or Companion Profile at PAC Band Limits*

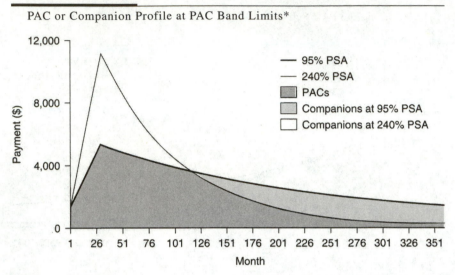

*Principal flows from $1 million 7.5% pool.

EXHIBIT 9–4

PAC or Companion Structure at 185% PSA*

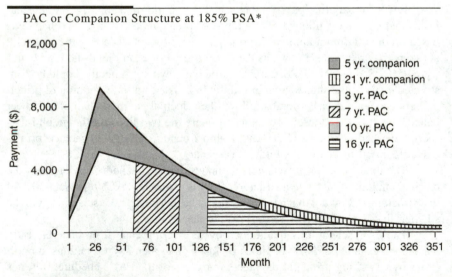

*Principal flows from $1 million 7.5% pool.

Total PAC and companion principal flows can be divided sequentially, much like a sequential-pay structure. Exhibit 9–4 illustrates a possible PAC or companion structure. Exhibit 9–5 shows the WALs of the PACs and companions compared to a sample sequential-pay structure and to the collateral across a range of prepayment rates. In relation to the sequential-pay bonds, the PACs are completely stable

E X H I B I T   9–5

Weighted Average Lives of Alternative CMO Structures Under Selected
Prepayment Assumptions

Backed by 30-year 7.5% pass-throughs
Pricing speed: 185% PSA
PAC bands: 95%–20% PSA

PSA	50%	95%	185%	240%	300%
Pass-through	15.4	12.2	8.3	6.9	5.9
Sequential-pay					
A	6.6	4.5	2.6	2.3	
		3.0			
B	16.0	11.3	7.0	5.7	4.8
C	20.9	15.9	10.0	8.1	6.7
D	26.3	23.3	17.1	14.2	11.9
PAC or companion					
PAC A	4.3	3.0	3.0	3.0	2.9
PAC B	10.4	7.0	7.0	7.0	6.1
PAC C	14.4	10.0	10.0	10.0	8.3
PAC D	19.1	16.2	16.2	16.2	13.6
Companion E	24.6	19.2	5.0	2.8	2.2
Companion F	29.2	28.2	21.5	6.6	4.2

at prepayment rates within the bands and less volatile when prepayments fall outside the bands because the companions continue to provide stability. As a result,
PACs are generally priced at tighter spreads to the Treasury curve, and companion
bonds at wider spreads, than sequential-pay bonds with the same average lives.

Effective PAC bands are important in evaluating PACs. These bands define
the actual range of collateral prepayment rates over which a particular PAC class
can remain on its payment schedule. An example of this distinction can be seen in
the first class of the sample PAC structure. Even though the structure was constructed with bands of 95% to 240% PSA, this class is actually protected from
WAL changes over a broader range of prepayment rates: The effective PAC bands
are 95% to 288% PSA. All the companions in a structure must be paid off before
the WAL of a PAC will shorten, so the earlier PACs in a structure generally have
higher upper effective bands than the later PACs since there are more companions
outstanding. The effective bands of a PAC will change over time, depending on
the prepayment experience of the collateral. As discussed later, most of the time,
this change (drift) is small and gradual.

PACs have been structured with varying protection levels and yield trade-
offs. The most common variants are Type II and Type III PACs and super or subordinate PACs.

EXHIBIT 9-6

PAC or Companion Structure with Type II PACs*

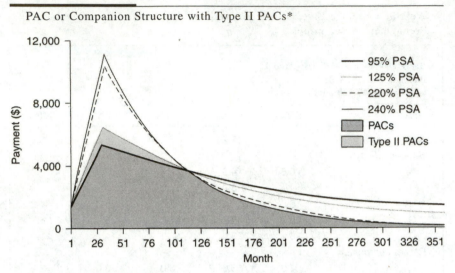

*Principal flows from $1 million 7.5% pool.

Type II and Type III PACs

As the CMO marketplace grew more sophisticated, investors sought bonds that would offer some prepayment protection and earn higher cash flow yields than generic PACs. The resulting innovation was the Type II PAC, structured from companion cash flows in a PAC or companion structure. These bonds have narrower prepayment protection bands than standard PACs, but as long as prepayments stay within the bands, they pay down according to a schedule, much like regular PACs. Because Type II PACs are second in priority to PACs, the remaining companion bonds provide support even if prepayments are outside the bands. If extended periods of high prepayments cause the companions in a structure to be paid off, the remaining Type II PACs become companions to the PACs, with the potential WAL volatility of companion bonds.

Exhibit 9–6 shows the addition of Type II PACs (125% to 220% PSA bands) to the PAC or companion structure illustrated in Exhibit 9–3. The PAC principal flow has not changed, and the Type II PACs are layered on top of the PACs.

Another layer of PACs, with narrower bands, is sometimes created as well. These securities, known as Type III PACs, act as support for PACs and Type II PACs in a structure but retain some stability because of the companions that remain.

Super- and Subordinate-PACs

The prepayment experience of the period 1992–1993 caused many investors to view MBS as more callable than they had previously thought and to demand significantly higher levels of prepayment protection. In early 1993, Lehman Brothers responded by issuing the first super and subordinated PAC structures. In this

EXHIBIT 9–7

PAC or Companion Structure with Super- and Sub-PACs*

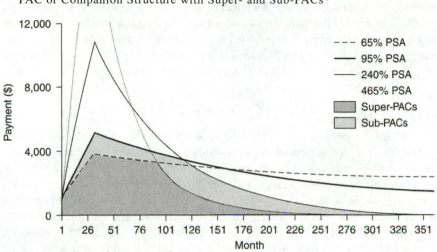

*Principal flows from $1 million 7.5% pool.

setup, standard PACs are divided into super- and subordinate (sub-) PACs. By re-arranging the cash flow priorities within the total PAC class, the super-PACs receive additional prepayment stability from the sub-PACs and therefore have much wider protection bands.

Since both super- and sub-PAC classes are created from the total PAC cash flows and generally have all the structure's companions available to support them, sub-PACs offer more protection from average-life volatility than similar average-life Type II or Type III PACs in the same structure. This relationship can be seen in FHLMC 1499, which has 3-year super-, sub-, and Type III PACs. The effective bands are 70% to 625% PSA on the super-PAC, 100% to 250% PSA on the sub-PAC, and 140% to 220% PSA on the Type III PAC. Sub-PACs trade at higher yields than PACs because they can have more average-life volatility at prepayment rates outside their protection bands.

Exhibit 9–7 shows super- and sub-PACs in the example PAC/companion structure. The combined principal flows of the super- and sub-PACs are equivalent to the original PAC principal flows.

Targeted Amortization Classes

Targeted amortization classes (TACs) were introduced to offer investors a prepayment-protected class at wider spreads than PACs. Like PACs, TACs repay principal according to a schedule as long as prepayments remain within a range. If the principal cash flow from the collateral exceeds the TAC schedule, the excess is allocated to TAC companion classes. Unlike PACs, TACs do not provide protection against WAL extension if prepayments fall below the speed necessary to maintain the TAC schedule. Therefore, the typical TAC can be viewed as a PAC with a lower band equal to the CMO pricing speed and an upper band similar to that of PACs backed by comparable collateral. In falling and low interest rate environments, investors are primarily concerned that increasing prepayments will shorten average life due to increasing prepayments. Many investors are willing to forgo the protection against extension offered by PACs in exchange for the higher yields of TACs.

Companions

Companion is a general term in the CMO market for a class that provides prepayment protection for another class. In evaluating companions (also known as *support classes*), it is important to review the rest of the CMO structure; the behavior of a particular companion class is influenced by the class(es) it supports. For instance, if the companion is supporting a TAC, it will have less extension risk than a PAC companion because the TAC is not protected from extension. In addition, other bonds in the structure may affect the companion's potential performance. For example, the presence of Type II PACs in a structure indicates that part of the original companions is being traded in a more stable form, leaving the remaining companions more volatile. Another important consideration for companions is the collateral backing the CMO. If the pass-throughs have a shorter maturity than 30 years, such as 15-year or balloon MBS, the PACs in the structure will require less extension protection. Therefore, there will be fewer companions in the structure than in a 30-year structure with the same PAC bands, and the companions will have less extension risk. Finally, a class's sensitivity to prepayments should be viewed in a yield or total return context. Because prepayments are paid at par, faster-than-expected prepayments will have a positive effect on a discount bond's yield, and slower-than-expected prepayments will have a positive effect on a premium bond's yield. On a total return basis (see Evaluating CMOs below for details on total return calculation), these generalizations will usually apply as well, although the interaction between prepayments, average life, and reinvestment rate may offset the effects of being repaid at par.

The CMO classes that have been reviewed (sequential-pay, PAC, TAC, and companion) are structures that provide for the redirection of principal payments. The classes that follow address the redirection of interest payments as well. These classes usually rely on one of the above structures to reallocate principal payments.

Z Bonds

The Z bond is a CMO class with a period of principal and interest lockout. It typically takes the place of a coupon-bearing class at or near the end of a CMO structure. When the CMO is originally issued, the Z bond has a face amount significantly lower than it would have if it were an interest-bearing class. Each month that the Z is outstanding, it generates coupon cash flows, like any other bond in the structure; however, as long as the Z class is not paying out principal, this coupon flow is used

E X H I B I T   9–8

Sample Z-Bond Cash Flows in a Sequential-Pay and Z-Bond Structure*

Month	Beginning Balance	Coupon Accretion	Coupon Cash Flow	Amortiz./ Prepay.	Ending Balance	Total Cash Flows
1	118,000.00	737.50	0.00	0.00	118,737.50	0
2	118,737.50	742.11	0.00	0.00	119,479.61	0
3	119,479.61	746.75	0.00	0.00	120,226.36	0
.	.	.	.	.	.	
					0	
.	.	.	.	.	.	
					0	
131	265,245.57	1,657.78	0.00	0.00	266,903.35	0
132	266,903.35	1,668.15	0.00	0.00	268,571.50	0
133	268,571.50	1,678.57	0.00	47.44	270,202.63	47.44
134	270,202.63	0.00	1,688.77	3,131.55	267,071.08	4,820.31
135	267,071.08	0.00	1,669.19	3,099.51	263,971.57	4,768.70

*Backed by 30-year, 7.5% pass-throughs($).

to pay down other classes. The Z gets credit for the forgone interest payments through increases to its principal balance, known as *accretion*. Once the classes preceding the Z bond are fully paid down, it begins to receive principal and interest.

The Z bond in Exhibit 9–8 begins with a face amount of $118,000. The coupon in the first month ($118,000 × 7.5%/12 = $737.50) is paid as a prepayment to the first class in the structure, and the Z bond accretes that amount. The accretion amounts increase as the principal amount (on which coupon cash flows are calculated) grows. In month 133, the final sequential-pay class receives its last principal payment, which includes $1,678.57 from the Z coupon. The collateral has produced an additional $47.44 in principal cash flows that month, and since the Z is the only outstanding class, it receives the principal payment. The Z-bond balance has grown to $270,203. Since the Z is the only remaining class from month 134 on, it receives all principal and interest payments generated by the collateral.

In a simple sequential-pay and Z-bond structure, the Z accelerates the principal repayments of the sequential-pay bonds. As a result, restructuring a sequential-pay bond as a Z allows for larger sequential-pay classes with the same WALs as the original classes. Since a portion of the principal payments of these sequential-pay bonds is coming from the Z-coupon flows (which do not vary until the Z begins amortizing), average life volatility is decreased in the sequential-pay classes. In fact, in the sample structure, all bonds including the Z have less average life volatility when the Z is introduced to the structure (see Exhibit 9–9). The Z's impact is clearest in the scenario where prepayments fall from 185% PSA to 95% PSA: The change in average life is 10% to 23% lower for all bonds than in the basic sequential-pay structure.

EXHIBIT 9–9

Weighted Average Lives of Alternative Sequential-Pay
Structures Under Selected Prepayment Assumptions*

PSA	95%	185%	240%
Sequential-Pay			
A	4.5	3.0	2.6
B	11.3	7.0	5.7
C	15.9	10.0	8.1
D	23.3	17.1	14.2
Sequential-Pay with Z			
A	4.2	3.0	2.6
B	10.1	7.0	5.9
C	13.5	9.9	8.5
Z	21.5	17.0	14.8

*Backed by 30-year, 7.5% pass-throughs; pricing speed: 185% PSA.

EXHIBIT 9–10

Effective Durations of Alternative Sequential-Pay
Structures*

Class	Sequential-Pay	Sequential-Pay with Z
A	1.53 year	1.69 years
B	6.80	6.47
C	8.58	8.16
D or Z	10.19	18.47

*Backed by 30-year, 7.5% pass-throughs.

Although the Z structure appears to have reduced uncertainty across the
board, it is important to look at the effective durations of the bonds as well. Exhibit 9–10 shows that the durations of the first three sequential-pay bonds do not
change substantially when the last class is replaced with a Z. The Z bond, on the
other hand, has almost twice the effective duration of the sequential-pay bond that
it replaced, moving from 10.2 to 18.5 years. The price of the Z is highly sensitive
to interest rate movements and the resulting changes in prepayment rates because
its ultimate principal balance depends on total accretions credited by the time it
begins to pay down. Although WAL volatility has decreased, the price sensitivity
of the last class is increased dramatically by making it a Z.

Z bonds offer much of the appeal of zero-coupon Treasury strips: There is no reinvestment risk during the accretion phase. In addition, Z bonds offer higher yields than comparable WAL Treasury zeros.

Accretion-Directed Classes

In the falling interest rate environment that has characterized most of the CMO era, many structures have been developed to protect investors from higher-than-anticipated prepayments. *Accretion-directed* (AD) bonds are designed to protect against extension in average life if rates rise and prepayments are lower than expected. These bonds, also known as *very accurately defined maturity* (VADM) *bonds,* derive all their cash flows from the interest accretions of a Z class. Because there is no deviation in Z accretions until the Z bond begins to pay down, VADMs do not extend even if there are no prepayments. VADMs are also protected from prepayment increases because the Z bonds that support them tend to be the last classes to begin repaying principal.

Floaters and Inverse Floaters

The first floating-rate CMO class was issued by Shearson Lehman Brothers in 1986. These classes are created by dividing a fixed-rate class into a floater and an inverse floater. The bonds take their principal paydown rules from the underlying fixed-rate class. A floater-inverse combination can be produced from a sequential-pay class, PAC, TAC, companion, or other coupon-bearing class. The coupon of the floater is reset periodically (usually monthly) at a specified spread, or margin, over an index. Typical indices include LIBOR, the Federal Home Loan Bank 11th District Cost of Funds Index (COFI), and various maturities of the constant maturity Treasury (CMT) series. The coupon of the inverse floater moves inversely with the index. Floaters and inverses have caps and floors that set the maximum and minimum coupons allowable on the bonds. These caps and floors may be explicit (e.g., a floater cap of 10%) or implicit (a floater's floor would equal the floater's margin if the underlying index fell to 0%) and may either be constant throughout the life of the bond or may change according to a predetermined schedule.

Floaters are usually designed to be sold at par; their caps and margins are dictated by the option and swap markets and by expectations about the performance of the underlying fixed-rate CMO class. Floaters have many natural buyers, such as banks, which prefer the limited interest rate risk that an adjustable-rate security provides. Since inverse floater coupons move in the opposite direction from their index, investors generally require higher yields for inverses than for floaters or the underlying fixed-rate classes. To increase the yield, cap, and initial coupon, inverses are often structured with multipliers in the coupon formulas that magnify movements in the underlying index.

Exhibit 9–11 shows how a floater and an inverse can be created from a fixed-rate bond. Both floater and inverse have coupon formulas tied to COFI; the floater coupon adjusts at COFI + 65 basis points with a 10% interest rate

E X H I B I T   9–11

Creating a Floater and Inverse

$120MM 5-year, 7.5% companion becomes . . .
$80MM 5-year companion COFI floater (coupon = COFI + 65 bp, 10% cap)
$40MM 5-year companion COFI inverse (coupon = 21.20% − 2 × COFI, 2.50% floor)

| | Coupon | | Wt. Avg. |
COFI Index	Floater	Inverse	Coupon
0.00%	0.65%	21.20%	7.50%
2.00	2.65	17.20	7.50
4.00	4.65	13.20	7.50
6.00	6.65	9.20	7.50
8.00	8.65	5.20	7.50
9.35	10.00	2.50	7.50
10.00	10.00	2.50	7.50
12.00	10.00	2.50	7.50

cap, and the inverse coupon, which has a multiplier of 2, adjusts at $21.20 - 2 \times COFI$ with a 2.50% floor. In this example, the floater class is twice the size of the inverse floater. When a multiplier greater than 1 is used to set the inverse floater's coupon, the face amount of the inverse must be smaller than the floater to keep the weighted average of the two coupons equal to the fixed-rate bond coupon.

Interest- and Principal-Only Strips

Any pool of coupon-bearing collateral can be stripped into interest-only (IO) and principal-only (PO) segments and sold separately. Exhibit 9–12A illustrates the interest cash flows for 7.5% collateral at various prepayment rates. The total amount of interest flow varies, depending on the prepayment rate. Since interest cash flows exist only if principal remains outstanding, IOs benefit from slowing prepayments. POs represent a stream of principal payments purchased at a discount. If prepayments rise, discounted principal flows are received at par earlier than expected, improving the security's performance. Exhibit 9–12B illustrates principal cash flows from the collateral. Here the total flows will always equal the face amount of the collateral, but the prepayment rate affects the timing and value of the flows. IOs are bearish securities and usually have negative durations (their prices rise as rates rise); POs are bullish securities with long, positive durations.

E X H I B I T   9–12

A. Interest flows from $1 million 7.5% pool

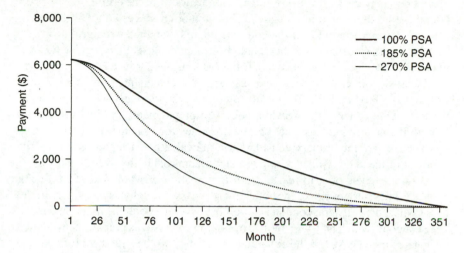

B. Principal flows from $1 million 7.5% pool

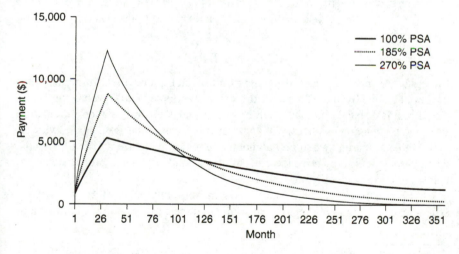

The same principles for stripping pools of collateral can be applied to individual CMO classes or to blocks of classes within a single structure. CMO strips may represent 100% of the interest or principal flows; or, more commonly, only a portion of the interest may be stripped, resulting in an IO and a reduced-coupon fixed-rate bond. For example, if a dealer is structuring a PAC class with a 7.5% coupon but investors are more willing to buy the class if it has a 7% coupon, a 50-bp PAC IO can be stripped from the class and sold separately.[5] Structurers may also strip part of the coupon flows from the entire block of collateral before dividing it into classes. This method produces an "IO-ette" security and is employed to lower the coupons on all bonds in a structure.

Strips made from CMO bonds require more analysis than regular IOs and POs. In the above example, since the IO has been stripped from a PAC class, it will be insulated from cash flow changes as long as prepayments remain within the PAC bands. Only if the PAC begins to pay down principal early will the holder of the PAC IO experience the negative effects of prepayments. An investor should look to the underlying class that defines the rules for principal paydown. Since prepayments are the primary consideration in evaluating stripped securities, the behavior of the underlying class plays a significant role in the overall analysis.

Another type of strip results from the creation of whole-loan CMOs. For agency CMOs, the coupon of the collateral (the pass-throughs) is fixed; for whole-loan CMOs, the collateral coupon is a weighted average of all the individual mortgage coupons (which may vary by 100 bps or more). As loans prepay, the weighted average coupon (WAC) of the collateral can change. To be sure that all fixed-rate bonds in a structure receive their allotted coupons, issuers often split off part of the principal or interest cash flow from individual mortgages in a pool, leaving a block of collateral with a stable WAC. These strips of principal or interest are combined into WAC POs or WAC IOs and trade much like trust POs and IOs.

PAC BAND DRIFT

Effective PAC bands change (drift) over time, even if prepayments remain within the initial bands. Band drift results from the interaction of actual prepayments and the current PAC bands, and the resulting changes in collateral balance and relative PAC and companion balances. The band drift of a particular PAC can be viewed under three scenarios: when prepayments are within the current effective bands, when prepayments are above the current upper band, and when prepayments are below the current lower band.

If prepayments are within the bands, the currently paying PAC will pay on schedule. Any additional prepayments will go to the currently paying companion.

---

5. Until recently, all REMIC IO classes had to be sold with some small amount of principal, called a *nominal balance.* To generate the cash flows for bonds with this structure, the nominal balance is amortized and prepaid according to the type of bond. Since the balance is small, the coupon is extremely large. IOs sold this way tend to have multiple-digit coupons (e.g., 1183%) and high dollar prices (e.g., 3626-12). Alternatively, IOs may be based on a notional balance. Here, the IO tranche has no principal balance and its coupon flows are calculated on the declining balance of the underlying principal-bearing tranche. No principal cash flows are paid to the IO holder. This procedure results in MBS-like coupons (7.5%, 8%, etc.) or in basis-point coupons (e.g., 100 bps) and below-par prices. These two techniques result in equivalent investment amounts and cash flows. The difference in prices (3626-12 versus 18-02, for example) does not denote any relative value difference between IOs priced with one method or the other.

Over time, both upper and lower bands will drift up. This happens because any prepayment within the bands is also lower than the upper band and higher than the lower band. From the point of view of the upper band, prepayments have been slower than expected and more companions are available to absorb high prepayments in the future. Thus, the upper band rises. From the point of view of the lower band, prepayments have been faster than expected and less collateral is outstanding to produce principal flows. If prepayments slow to the original lower band, there may not be enough principal coming in to pay the PACs on schedule, and they will extend. Thus, the lower band rises as well. For most prepayment rates within the bands, the upper band will rise at a faster rate than the lower, so prepayments within the bands tend to cause the bands to widen over time.

If prepayments are above the current upper band, the PAC will continue to pay on schedule until all companions are retired. If the fast prepayments are only temporary, there will probably be little impact on the bands. If prepayments remain above the upper band, however, the upper and lower bands will begin to converge. This happens because there are fewer companions available to absorb fast prepayments and less collateral outstanding to generate principal cash flows if prepayments slow. The bands will converge once all companions have been retired, and the PAC will pay like a sequential-pay class from that point.

If prepayments are below the current lower band, the currently paying PAC will not be able to pay according to its schedule since there will be no other principal flows coming into the structure that can be redirected to the PAC. This is typically a temporary situation because the lower band is usually substantially lower than the base prepayment rate expected from simple housing turnover and because most PACs have priority over all subsequent cash flows until they are back on schedule. Prepayments below the current lower band cause the upper band to rise (more companions are available to absorb faster prepayments in the future) and may cause the lower band to rise slightly (since most PACs have catch-up features, a higher future prepayment rate is necessary to put the PAC back on schedule).

Most band drift is small and gradual. Large changes to PAC bands will occur only if prepayments are significantly outside the bands or if they remain near either of the bands for a long period of time. Effective bands represent the range of prepayment rates that the collateral can experience for its remaining life and still maintain the payment schedule for a specific PAC. Temporary movements outside the bands will not affect PAC cash flows as long as companion cash flows and principal balances are available to support them.

CMO STRUCTURING EXAMPLE

In this section, we follow a structurer through the process of creating a multiclass CMO. Diagrams (not drawn to scale) are included to illustrate the structures.

The structurer begins with a block of collateral—in this case FNMA 7.5s (Exhibit 9–13a). If the market expects interest rates and prepayments to be stable, the structurer may construct a sequential-pay CMO (Exhibit 9–13b). If investors are concerned about rates rising and prepayments slowing (e.g., extension risk),

CMO Structuring Example*

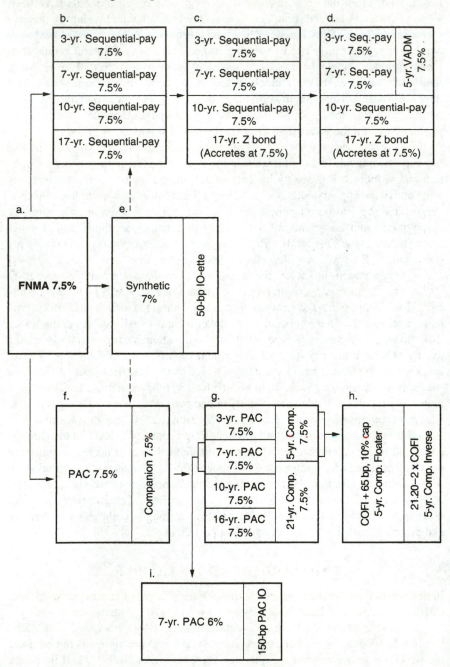

*FNMA 7.5% collateral.

the structurer may produce the last class as a Z bond (Exhibit 9–13c). This allows him to apply the Z-coupon flows as principal payments to the early sequential-pay classes or to create VADMs that offer the strongest extension protection (Exhibit 9–13d). If the collateral is priced at a premium, the structurer may strip some interest cash flows before creating the rest of the classes. This allows the creation of discount or par bonds. Exhibit 9–13e shows the FNMA 7.5s after a 50-bp IO-ette is stripped and sold separately. The remaining collateral now has a 7% coupon and can be structured in any way that the original 7.5s could have been.

If the market expects high interest rate and prepayment volatility, the structurer will likely create PAC-companion or TAC-companion CMOs. Exhibit 9–13f illustrates the initial allocation of cash flows to PACs and companions. Once the amount of principal that can be attributed to PACs or companions is identified, these classes go through the sequential-pay structuring process to create PACs and companions of various average lives (Exhibit 9–13g). Individual classes from any of these structures can be further divided. If a foreign bank wants to purchase a LIBOR-based floater with a relatively high margin and a 5-year average life, for example, the structurer can produce a bond with the desired characteristics from the 5-year companion class (Exhibit 9–13h) that will offer a higher yield than non-companion tranches. At the same time, the structurer will look at the inverse floater market to determine yield and coupon (set by adjusting the multiplier) for the resulting LIBOR inverse floater. On the PAC side, there may be an investor who wants to purchase a 7-year PAC with a 6% coupon (and therefore a lower price) as protection from the risk of high prepayments on premium-priced bonds. If so, the structurer can split the 7-year PAC into a 150-bp PAC IO and a 6% PAC (Exhibit 9–13i). These are a few examples of the flexibility in the structuring process. The customizable nature of many CMO classes is a key to the popularity of these bonds.

REGULATORY DEVELOPMENTS AFFECTING CMOs

When FHLMC issued the first CMO in 1983, multiclass mortgage securities were subject to various regulatory constraints. For example, federal tax law treated payments from a multiclass trust as equity dividends. Unlike debt payments, dividend payments are not tax-deductible. Therefore, the issuer who established a multiclass trust was unable to claim a tax deduction for interest paid to security holders to offset taxes on interest received from the underlying collateral. The resulting double taxation—interest income was taxed at both the trust and investor level—made the transaction economically impractical.

The CMO avoided this problem because it was an offering of collateralized debt. Therefore, tax deductions for interest paid to certificate holders offset the tax liability on interest received from the underlying collateral. However, CMOs were subject to other constraints to ensure that they were treated as debt instead of equity for tax purposes. Issuers had to maintain a portion of residual interests, record CMOs as liabilities in their financial statements, and satisfy minimum capital requirements. Issuers also had to include a call provision, forcing them to price longer maturity bonds at a wider spread to the Treasury curve. In addition, issuers had to structure a mismatch between receipts on the underlying mortgages and payments to the CMO bondholders; generally they passed monthly collateral payments through to bondholders on a quarterly basis. These constraints made it difficult to issue CMOs efficiently.

Toward the end of 1985, issuers overcame some of these obstacles by issuing CMOs through an owner's trust. This mechanism allowed issuers to sell their residual interests and remove the debt from their books. The owner's trust, however, was not conducive to a liquid market because residual buyers became personally liable for the CMO: If the cash flow from the collateral was insufficient to pay regular interest holders, residual owners had to cover the shortage. As a result, issuers could sell residual interests only to investors capable of meeting ongoing net worth tests. Although these tests were different for each transaction, they all effectively limited potential buyers to institutional investors with adequate net worth.

The 1986 Tax Reform Act addressed these problems by defining a new issuance vehicle: the real estate mortgage investment conduit (REMIC). To qualify for REMIC status, a multiclass offering can have multiple classes of regular interests but only one class of residual interest. The legislation defines a regular interest as a fixed principal amount with periodic interest payments or accruals on the outstanding principal balance. Buyers of regular interests are taxed as holders of debt obligations. A residual interest consists entirely of pro rata payments (if any). Buyers of residual interests are taxed based on the taxable income of the REMIC. Taxable income is the excess collateral and reinvestment income over REMIC regular interest and servicing expenses.

REMIC legislation was a milestone in the development of multiclass mortgage securities because it allowed issuers to adopt whatever structure best exploited particular economic, financial, or accounting considerations. For tax purposes, all conduits qualifying for REMIC status are treated equally whether they structure a multiclass mortgage transaction as a borrowing collateralized by mortgages or as a sale of the underlying mortgages. In either case, only the investors and residual holders are subject to tax, not the conduit itself. REMIC legislation also allows issuers to sell the entire residual class, and since 1987 it has permitted issuers to sell floating-rate classes. This flexibility has allowed issuers to develop new products, particularly since repeated interest rate declines since 1982 have led investors to seek products with either improved call protection or higher risk-reward opportunities.

Following a 5-year phaseout of all previous structures that ended in 1991, all issuers of multiclass mortgage securities must now use REMICs. However, from the investor's perspective, there is little difference between CMO and REMIC products; in either case, the investor is buying multiclass mortgage securities. Consequently, the terms *CMO* and *REMIC* are often used interchangeably, even though they are crucially different tax vehicles from the issuer's perspective.

Until 1988, private issuers (primarily investment bankers and home builders) accounted for almost the entire supply of multiclass mortgage securities. These issuers generally used agency collateral to obtain the highest ratings from the nationally recognized rating agencies. However, the credit quality of the issuer was also important insofar as cash flows from the underlying collateral might be insufficient to cover obligations to all bondholders. Therefore, issuers had to take extra measures, such as overcollateralizing the bonds or buying insurance, to obtain high investment-grade credit ratings.

In 1988, FHLMC and FNMA gained full authorization to issue REMICs. Their REMICs automatically obtained government agency status, regardless of the underlying collateral. Therefore, FHLMC and FNMA were not subject to the credit-enhancing constraints imposed on private issuers, giving them a crucial market advantage. Agency CMOs jumped from only 2% of total CMO issuance in 1987 to 33% in 1988 and 83% in 1989. In 1992, agencies issued 85% of CMOs.

By 1988, regulatory and market developments had stimulated demand for multiclass mortgage securities. In July 1988, the Basle Committee on Banking Regulations and Supervisory Practices set forth risk-based capital guidelines to ensure the fiscal stability of the international banking infrastructure by requiring minimum capital levels as a percentage of assets—loans made and securities purchased—weighted according to risk classification. Since agency-issued REMICs offer high yields in relation to their 20% risk weighting, they became increasingly popular with banks and thrifts. Less volatile REMIC products, such as floaters and short and intermediate maturity PACs and TACs, were most appropriate since banks and thrifts needed to match assets with liabilities of similar maturities.

Since about 1988, insurance companies have looked to the REMIC market for assets to offset intermediate- to long-term liabilities. Given the poor performance of real estate holdings and commercial mortgages, insurance companies needed to diversify their portfolios, and REMICs offered an attractive alternative because of their credit quality and spread levels. At year-end 1993, life insurance companies implemented their own risk-based capital requirements, which provided an additional incentive to hold mortgages in securitized form.

EVALUATING CMOs

The most common way to communicate the value and performance expectations of a CMO bond is the yield table, showing cash flow yields under a series of prepayment rate assumptions. Computer models that produce yield tables take price(s) and prepayment rates as inputs (and index levels, in the case of floaters and inverse floaters), and calculate yields and spreads, average lives, durations, and payment windows for each prepayment assumption. With this information, the investor can determine the level of prepayment protection offered by the bond, the average life volatility for given changes in collateral prepayment rates, the impact of prepayments on yields, and the time over which principal is likely to be received. Exhibits 9–14 and 9–15 are yield tables for the 3-year sequential-pay and PAC bonds in the earlier examples. The yield changes for the sequential-pay bond under each prepayment scenario, but the PAC yield is stable from 95% PSA to 285% PSA. The average life and duration of the PAC are more stable at prepayment rates outside the PAC bands as well. The payment windows show when the bonds will begin to pay principal and when the final payment will occur under each prepayment scenario. Finally, a comparison of the two tables

EXHIBIT 9-14

Yield Table for 3-Year Sequential-Pay Class (Price—104-04)

PSA	35%	95%	135%	185%	200%	240%	285%	335%
					Base Case			
Yield (%)/Spread (bp)	6.79/105	6.37/111	6.13/127	5.86/140	5.79/133	5.61/114	5.42/143	5.24/125
Average life (yr.)	7.85	4.54	3.64	3.00	2.86	2.57	2.33	2.13
Moderate duration (yr.)	5.54	3.67	3.06	2.60	2.49	2.27	2.08	1.92
Windows (yr.)	0.1–14.7	0.1–8.6	0.1–6.7	0.1–5.3	0.1–5.1	0.1–4.4	0.1–3.9	0.1–3.5
Benchmark Treasury	7-yr.	5-yr.	4-yr.	3-yr.	3-yr.	3-yr.	2-yr.	2-yr.

EXHIBIT 9-15

Yield Table for 3-Year PAC (Price—106-04)

PSA	35%	95%	135%	185%	200%	240%	285%	335%
					Base Case			
Yield (%)/Spread (bp)	6.04/78	5.31/85	5.18/72	5.18/72	5.18/72	5.18/72	5.18/72	5.13/67
Average life (yr.)	5.07	3.00	3.00	3.00	3.00	3.00	3.00	2.92
Moderate duration (yr.)	4.04	2.62	2.62	2.62	2.62	2.62	2.62	2.56
Windows (yr.)	0.1–9.3	0.1–5.2	0.1–5.2	0.1–5.2	0.1–5.2	0.1–5.2	0.1–5.2	0.1–4.7
Benchmark Treasury	5-yr.	3-yr.	3-yr.	3-yr.	3-yr.	3-yr.	3-yr.	3-yr.

shows that in the base case the sequential-pay bond is being offered at nearly double the spread of the PAC to compensate investors for its additional average life volatility.

Total return scenario analysis may also be used to evaluate CMOs. It addresses two drawbacks of the cash flow yield approach: Many investors do not expect to hold their securities to maturity, and the reinvestment assumption in the cash flow yield analysis—that all cash flows are reinvested at the security's yield—is usually unrealistic. Total return calculations cover a specific investment period and make an assumption about the bond's price at the end of the period (the horizon). They further assume a reinvestment rate and prepayment rate for the period to generate cash flows. Total return is the change in market value of the bond (reflecting price changes and principal paydown) plus the cumulative value of all cash flows and reinvestment proceeds as of the horizon date, divided by the initial market value. Although total return scenario analysis involves several assumptions, it is often a desirable addition to the yield tables, especially if the investment period is expected to be relatively short.

Option-adjusted spread (OAS) analysis is another relative value measurement tool used by fixed income market participants. Based on multiple interest rate simulations and the resulting prepayments predicted by a prepayment model, the cash flows of a callable bond are analyzed to calculate the average spread to the Treasury spot curve implied by the security's current price. Since this process nets out the impact of prepayments (partial calls) of MBS, OAS allows direct comparisons among MBS and other callable and noncallable fixed income securities. Using current OAS to calculate the horizon price of a CMO is a common method in total return analysis. This allows the investor to avoid making a direct horizon price assumption and incorporates more information (such as the shape of the yield curve) into the analysis.

THE CMO-COLLATERAL PRICING RELATIONSHIP

Because of strong investor demand for CMOs, a large percentage of newly issued pass-throughs and jumbo mortgages has gone into CMO structures in recent years. Investor preference for structured mortgage securities has led to a highly efficient pricing relationship between the CMO and collateral sectors.

The source of the CMO-collateral pricing relationship is the interplay between the yield curve and spreads on collateral and CMOs. Exhibit 9–16 shows the projected yields and payment windows of each bond in a four-class sequential-pay CMO and the yield of the collateral. Each bond's yield is quoted as a spread to the on-the-run Treasury with a maturity closest to the bond's average life. In this example, the 3-year CMO class has a lower yield than the collateral. The 7-year yield is about equal to, and the 10- and 17-year yields are higher than, the yield of the collateral. When the yield curve is positively sloped, earlier classes are generally offered at lower yields than later classes. Assuming that spreads remain constant, a steepening of the yield curve results in a greater difference between the yields of shorter and longer classes.

EXHIBIT   9–16

Yields on Collateral and Sequential-Pay CMO Tranches

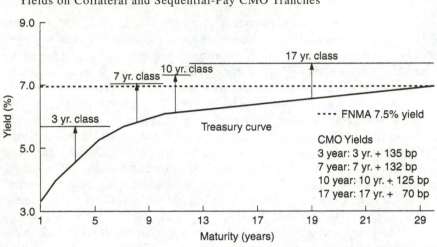

By definition, the price of an individual CMO bond represents the present value of the bond's projected cash flows, using the bond's yield as the discount rate. Therefore, the cash flows of any class with a lower yield than the collateral will be priced using a lower discount rate than the single discount rate used to price all the collateral cash flows. This means that this portion of the pass-through's cash flows will have a higher value when structured as part of a CMO. Likewise, the cash flows of bonds with yields higher than the collateral yield will be priced with a higher discount rate than the collateral, leading to lower valuations in relation to collateral cash flows.

Over time, as CMOs are created using a particular collateral type and coupon, supply and demand forces cause the collateral spread to tighten and/or the spreads of the CMO classes to widen until there is no profit in issuing the CMO. If collateral is too expensive (rich) to make the creation of CMO bonds economically feasible, CMO issuance will slow until pass-through spreads widen and/or CMO spreads tighten. Because of temporary changes in market preference for structured products, collateral can trade at levels too rich to create CMOs. However, in equilibrium, it is rare for CMOs to trade rich to collateral, since collateral spreads will quickly tighten as more CMOs are issued.

CMO TRADING AND CLEARING

Generally, CMO bonds are offered on the basis of a yield (more accurately, a spread over the yield of a benchmark Treasury) and a prepayment assumption. A price is calculated from this information and is agreed upon by both parties to the trade. The CMO market convention is corporate settlement (3 business days after the trade

E X H I B I T   9–17

Payment Delays for CMO Issuers and Collateral Types

CMO Issuer	Collateral Type	Payment Delay
GNMA	GNMA	15 days after the record date
FHLMC	FHLMC 75-day	45 days after the record date[a]
FHLMC	FHLMC Gold	15 days after the record date
FHLMC	GNMA	25 days after the record date
FNMA	FNMA	25 days after the record date
FNMA	GNMA	15 days after the record date
Nonagency	Whole loans	25 days after the record date[b]

[a]Record date is the last calendar day of each month.
[b]May vary by issuer.

date) unless the CMO is a new issue. In the case of a new issue, the settlement date for all the CMO classes is usually 1 to 3 months after the CMO is initially offered for sale. This period allows dealers to accumulate the collateral that will back the CMO. Whether the CMO bond is a new offering or a previously traded security, interest begins accruing on the first day of the settlement month. An exception to this rule is that most floating-rate CMO bonds begin accruing interest on the previous month's payment date so that they more closely resemble floating-rate notes.

Because of their credit quality, most CMOs can be used in repurchase and reverse repurchase agreements.

Most agency CMO trades are cleared through electronic book-entry transfers such as Fedwire, a clearing system maintained by the Federal Reserve. This system also handles monthly principal and interest payments, which are paid to the investor who holds the security on the record date (generally the last calendar day of the month). Whole-loan CMO trades are cleared through physical delivery or electronic book entry, depending on the issuer. Most MBS pay with a delay—the cash flows earned during one month are paid out a fixed number of days after the end of the month to give mortgage servicers time to collect payments. Exhibit 9–17 identifies payment delays for the various combinations of CMO issuers and collateral types.

CONCLUSION

A consistent theme in the CMO market throughout the past decade has been innovation in response to investor needs. As the CMO market has grown more liquid, larger structures have become feasible, providing the flexibility to develop new products. These products have refined the distribution of prepayment uncertainty and risk-reward opportunities to meet the increasingly specialized needs and objectives of investors. The range of options in the CMO market will continue to grow as both originators and investors adapt to a continually changing marketplace.

CHAPTER 10

THE EFFECT OF PAC BOND FEATURES ON PERFORMANCE

Linda Lowell
Senior Vice President
Asset Backed Research
Greenwich Capital Markets, Inc.

Planned amortization class (PAC) bonds represent one of the largest sectors of the CMO market. Among the factors expanding the market for these bonds were widespread defections from the corporate market by investors who were attracted by the high yields and triple-A credit quality and discouraged in their natural habitat by limited supply and tight spreads, as well as by event risk.

Typical PAC buyers tend to be asset-liability matchers such as life insurance companies and commercial banks, but the PAC market appeals as well to investors with active bond management strategies. These investors may have, for instance, opinions about the direction of mortgage-Treasury spreads or mortgage-corporate spreads, they may wish to execute barbell or other strategies designed to take advantage of expectations regarding the shape or direction of the yield curve, or they may be seeking value advantages, either between the PAC and other CMO sectors, or within the PAC sector, among PACs with different features.

The main attraction of PAC bonds lies in the fact that they provide a defined schedule of principal payments (or, similarly, target balances), which is guaranteed as long as prepayment rates remain within a specified range. (Hence the name, planned amortization.) Holders are insulated to a significant degree from the uncertainty regarding the cash flows of most MBS, which arises from the right of mortgage borrowers to prepay their loans at any time. The fact that the prepayment process is interest rate–sensitive—that the tendency of homeowners to move or refinance is inversely related to the direction of interest rates[1]—has a material impact on the average life, duration, and performance of mortgage securities. MBS shorten in rising markets and extend in declining markets. To compensate investors for taking this risk, pass-throughs and other MBS are priced at higher

---

1. See Section IV for a discussion of prepayments.

yields than other, noncallable bonds of similar credit quality (such as agency debt). PAC bonds partake of the incremental yield available in the MBS market while at the same time providing more certain cash flows. In addition to providing guaranteed payments within a range of prepayment behavior, PAC bonds can be further refined to concentrate payments over a shorter period of time or "window." PACs with narrow windows are perceived to be better substitutes for corporate and Treasury bonds with bullet principal payments, and therefore typically trade at tighter spreads than PACs with wider windows.

This chapter is intended to serve both classes of investors—the buy-and-hold PAC buyer, who wants to partake of the attractive yields in the mortgage market but whose liabilities or actuarial requirements necessitate more stable cash flows than either pass-throughs or standard CMOs can provide, and the active portfolio manager. The chapter examines the different features of PAC bonds and their effect on market value and investment performance. Where it is possible to isolate a specific characteristic, an attempt is made to model and examine its impact on the average life and yield behavior of the bond, as well as on its theoretical or option-adjusted value.

THE TERM STRUCTURE OF CMO YIELDS

The yields that investors require for occupying different average life sectors of the PAC market are determined by the same factors that influence other fixed income investors: portfolio objectives and constraints, the current and anticipated shape of the yield curve, expectations regarding the underlying monetary and economic determinants of interest rates, and so forth. In addition, PAC buyers require additional yield as they extend the maturity of their investments to compensate them for the increased risk that the prepayment collars may be broken, as well as the greater average life volatility of the later tranches in a transaction when the prepayment collars are broken. An indication of the average life volatility of PAC tranches of different nominal average lives is provided by Exhibit 10–1. The graph depicts the average lives of a series of PACs from a single CMO issue[2] at two prepayment speeds extreme enough to break both the upper and lower collars of all the PAC bonds. The range between the average lives at the extremes gradually widens for longer expected average lives to its widest point among the intermediate-term PACs.

As a result of investors' demand for greater compensation for holding longer-term PACs, the generic CMO yield curves are more steeply sloped than the Treasury yield curve. Generic yields for current-coupon PACs backed by current-coupon conventional collateral and for on-the-run Treasuries are depicted in Exhibit 10–2. Although a satisfying discussion of the issue is beyond the scope of this chapter, it should be noted that CMO spreads are also influenced by the same factors that affect pass-through spreads—volatility of market yields, prepayment expectations, supply of new product, and so forth. Normally CMO spreads track pass-through spreads, with the relationship enforced by the existence of CMO arbitrage opportunities.

---

2. This example assumes a structure in which PACs have priority to excess principal payments in the order of their scheduled maturities after the companions have been retired.

EXHIBIT 10–1

Extension and Shortening of PAC Bond Average Lives as Prepayments Vary between 0% and 600% PSA

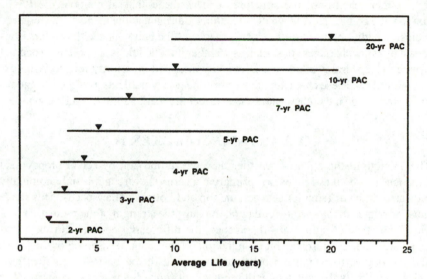

▼Average life at issue. PAC bonds backed by FNMA 9s with prepayment collars of 85-300% PSA.

EXHIBIT 10–2

Treasury and PAC Yield Curves*

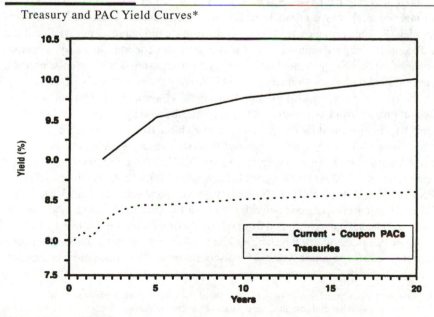

*Pricing date January 29, 1990.

When pass-throughs cheapen relative to CMOs, new transactions are marketed, increasing the supply of CMOs and ultimately allowing CMOs to cheapen relative to pass-throughs, thereby reducing the arbitrage opportunity.

Other features of the structure such as the collateral coupon, the PAC's coupon, the collars, and the window result in additional adjustments to the required yields. In addition, the cash flow performance of the bond outside the collars is affected by other characteristics, such as whether its schedule is supported by accrual from a longer-term Z bond later in the structure, and its priority for receiving excess cash flow. These characteristics determine how volatile its average life and returns are outside the collars, and so also affect the marketability of a PAC bond.

COLLARS AND COLLATERAL

The strength of the collars—whether they will be broken by actual prepayment experience—should be investors' primary concern. The strength is only nominally indicated in the differential between the top and bottom collar speeds. This range must be related to the specific collateral to gauge the strength of the protection provided. The type of collateral—the agency, the differential between current mortgage rates and the mortgage rates on the underlying loans, seasoning of the loans, and the degree to which the pools have prepaid in the past—determines how quickly or slowly the collateral will prepay in different interest rate scenarios. The collars simply define a range of prepayment speeds over which the PAC payments will not vary. When prepayments fall outside the collars, payments to the PAC holders may be either delayed or accelerated (the collars could be broken temporarily without affecting the payment schedule). A given set of PAC collars will provide stronger or weaker protection, depending on the collateral. For example, a top collar of 300% PSA provides greater call protection should interest rates decline if the collateral is a current coupon than if it is a premium coupon. Similarly, a bottom collar of 100% PSA provides better protection from extension if the collateral is a conventional pass-through than if it is a GNMA.

All else being equal, PAC bonds backed by premium-coupon collateral do exhibit greater average life variability than PACs backed by current-coupon collateral. This is illustrated by the comparison in Exhibit 10–3, which displays the average lives at different prepayment speeds of two series of PACs, one backed by FNMA 9s (9.77% weighted average coupon [WAC], 349-month weighted average remaining term [WART]) and scheduled at 85% to 300% PSA, the other backed by FNMA 10½s (11.13% WAC and 347-month WART) and scheduled at 95% to 350% PSA.[3] (Similar comparisons could be made in the case of discount- and current-coupon collateral, but are omitted from this discussion for the sake of brevity.)

Investors recognize the stability lent by discount collateral and will accept a tighter spread for structures backed by discounts when they anticipate prepayments

---

3. These examples were created in January 1990, when 9% coupon pass-throughs were priced below but closest to par, and permitted the creation of tranches with coupons at current market yields across the PAC CMO yield curve.

Impact of Collateral Coupon on the Average Life Variability of PAC Bonds

Average Life (years)

Payment Speed (% PSA)	FNMA 9% Collateral (85%–300% PSA Collars)							FNMA 10.5% Collateral (95%–350% PSA Collars)						
	2-yr.	3-yr.	4-yr.	5-yr.	7-yr.	10-yr.	20-yr.	2-yr.	3-yr.	4-yr.	5-yr.	7-yr.	10-yr.	20-yr.
0	3.20	7.70	11.44	13.74	16.97	20.50	22.75	3.63	8.81	12.78	15.06	18.11	21.01	22.61
50	2.23	3.61	5.25	6.67	9.37	13.49	19.24	2.27	3.79	5.60	7.16	10.06	13.82	19.07
85	2.14	3.05	4.16	5.16	7.13	11.22	19.23	2.16	3.15	4.37	5.45	7.57	11.33	19.07
95	2.14	3.05	4.16	5.16	7.13	11.22	19.23	2.14	3.05	4.16	5.16	7.13	11.22	19.07
300	2.14	3.05	4.16	5.16	7.13	11.22	19.23	2.14	3.05	4.16	5.16	7.13	11.22	19.07
350	2.14	3.05	4.16	4.99	6.29	9.69	17.06	2.14	2.05	4.16	5.16	7.13	11.22	19.07
400	2.14	3.05	3.93	4.40	5.51	8.48	15.09	2.14	3.05	4.16	4.88	6.28	9.81	19.03
450	2.14	2.98	3.52	3.93	4.90	7.52	13.43	2.14	3.04	3.83	4.33	5.56	8.67	15.17
600	2.10	2.38	2.67	2.97	3.67	5.54	9.86	2.14	2.51	2.86	3.22	4.10	6.32	11.11

will accelerate. Similarly, bearish investors require wider spreads for PACs backed by premium collateral than if backed by current-coupon collateral. In markets characterized by bearish sentiment, the relative values can be reversed and investors will pay up for premium coupons and premium-coupon collateral while demanding a concession for discount collateral.

INTERACTION OF COLLARS AND COLLATERAL

Before further examining the contribution of the collar to the PAC's value, it is useful to review the mechanics of defining a collar and creating a payment schedule. Visualizing the cash flows is also helpful in seeking to understand the behavior of the structure in different scenarios. The PAC schedule is defined by projecting the paydowns from the given collateral at a high and a low constant prepayment speed. Those payment amounts that can be satisfied by both sets of projected principal payments (that is, the smaller of the two amounts generated for each date) make up the schedule. This is depicted graphically in Exhibit 10–4. The example depicted was structured from $500 million FNMA 9s with a 9.77% WAC and a 349-month WART[4] on the underlying mortgages, assuming collars of 85% to 300% PSA and a 2-year lockout (the period before the first scheduled principal payment).

---

4. The scheduled amortization for the collateral is determined by the WAC and WART.

E X H I B I T   10–4

Principal Cash Flows at 300% and 85% PSA—FNMA 9% Collateral

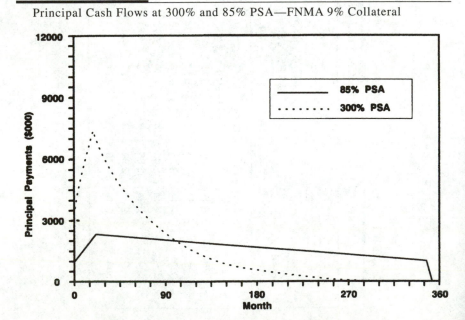

The faster speed results in a cash flow pattern with the bulk of the principal thrown off during the first 5 to 7 years of the issue's life. The slower speed produces a more level set of smaller cash flows extending to the final maturity of the collateral. The intersection of these two sets of payments forms the schedule. In the example, the bottom collar determines the payment amounts during the first 100 or so months of the schedule, and the top collar the amounts in the remaining months.

The graph of *any speed between* those of the top and bottom collars also would contain the area of the schedule below it. The graph of any speed *faster* than the top collar would bunch more principal in the first years and truncate the tail of the schedule in front of the point where the top and bottom collars intersect. Similarly, the graph of any speeds *slower* than the bottom collar would reduce the size of paydowns in the front years. At very slow speeds, most of the principal payments are pushed into the back years.

Once the scheduled principal payments are defined at given collars, the PAC schedule may be further divided into classes with different average lives. The example in Exhibit 10–5 is split into seven tranches. Some of the earlier bonds in the structure have higher *effective top* collars. An effective collar is the highest (or lowest) constant prepayment speed that would satisfy the entire tranche's payments. For instance, many speeds faster than 300% PSA will contain the first tranche in this example. The fastest speed containing all of the first tranche is that bond's effective upper collar. Effective top collars are shown in Exhibit 10–5 for the third and fourth tranches. These effective collars are approximately 370% and 330% PSA, respectively. It should be apparent as well that earlier tranches have still-higher effective collars.

E X H I B I T   10–5

Effective Top PAC Prepayment Collars—FNMA 9% Collateral

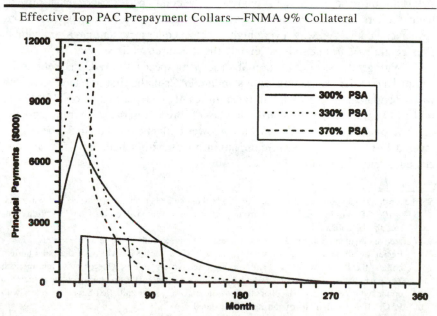

Likewise, the lower collars used to structure the PACs in Exhibits 10–4 and 10–5 do not fully indicate the degree of extension protection that the longer average life bonds, tranches 6 and 7, actually possess. Speeds below 85% PSA throw off principal too slowly to satisfy the scheduled payments in the early PAC tranches, but they provide more cash than needed to meet payments after about month 100, where the upper collar binds the schedule. For example, the effective bottom collar on tranche 7 is 55% PSA. Since tranche 6 begins to pay at the point where the top and bottom collars intersect, its effective collar is the same as the structuring collar.

When PACs first became popular, a wide variety of collar ranges and levels were used to generate the schedules, and even as late as the first quarter of 1989, it was not uncommon still to see some variety in collars on new CMO issues backed by similar collateral. However, the smorgasbord of prepayment collars largely has given way to increasing standardization of the speeds at which PAC schedules are created.

The standard speeds used to create PAC schedules may represent the market's aggregate opinion of what constitutes a "good" collar; however, investors should translate the PSA collars into interest rate collars by using an econometric prepayment model to determine how much interest rates must shift to break the collars. Once the collar speeds are explicitly linked to interest rate shifts, investors can determine if the collar does deliver "good" protection over the scenarios appropriate to the investor's outlook and portfolio.

New-issue PACs may be marketed either at the collars used to create the schedule or at their effective collars, although the trend has been to advertise effective collars. Unless the effective collar is known, the extent of the PAC's protection against shifts in interest rates cannot be determined. Investors, therefore, should insist on this information, as well as analysis of the bond's performance outside the effective collars.[5] By the same token, investors cannot assume that a new-issue short-term average life PAC with a very high effective collar is better than a comparable average life PAC from a series with only the structuring collars indicated.[6]

With greater standardization of structuring speeds, the PAC market has developed a two-tiered structure, with standard PACs in the first tier and PACs with weaker collars in the second, trading significantly cheaper than "good" PACs. In mid-1989, issuers began to issue both types of PACs from the same transaction by layering a second set of PACs with narrower collars over the first. These two-layered PACs are, in essence, companion bonds with schedules. They are discussed at length in Chapter 20.

---

5. The top collar may provide little protection in a bull market, when prepayment speeds are sustained at 100% PSA or higher. In that environment, the bond's value will derive from its stability outside the top collar.

6. If effective collars are indicated, it is usually easy enough to deduce the schedule speeds if information on all the tranches is available. Early PACs in the series will have the same bottom collar—the structuring collar—and varying effective top collars. One or more intermediate PACs will have the structuring collars. Later PACs will show the structuring collar as their top collar and varying effective collars for the bottom. Doing so permits first-cut comparisons with PACs offered with their structuring collars stated.

In the 1991–1994 rally, the practice of carving "super-PACs" out of the first priority PAC schedule became widespread. The PACs which had second priority to the super-PACs still had standard new-issue PAC collars, but they were subject to much greater average life variability outside the collar speeds. As a result, they tended to trade behind standard PACs. As the "prepayment emergency" continued, collars became less important to astute investors who instead scrutinized bond performance across a spectrum of prepayment scenarios.

PAC COLLAR DRIFT

Many investors do not understand that the PAC collars are not fixed for the life of the tranche, but instead change over time with the actual prepayment experience of the collateral. This is evident from the number of investors who seek to evaluate trades in the secondary PAC market by looking at the collars advertised at issue (which could be either structuring or effective collars). Instead, off-the-run PACs should be evaluated by looking at the current effective collars. In most cases, they can be determined by the security dealers or third-party data services that have modeled the structure and know the current bond and collateral balances.

The effective collars simply express the highest and lowest constant prepayment speeds at which the given collateral can continue to meet the scheduled prepayments. Unless the collateral prepays at precisely the collar speed (and then it can match only one, the upper or the lower collar speed), it will have a different balance than was projected when the schedule was defined. Likewise, the amount of companions (and proportion of companions to PACs) will be different. Prepayment rates below the top collar cause the collar to shift upward over time (as there is a greater amount outstanding than anticipated), whereas the collar is lowered if prepayments are higher. Likewise, prepayments above the bottom collar cause it to rise. Short- and intermediate-term PACs are affected differently by speeds below the collar than are long-term PACs at the end or tail of the schedule. Very slow speeds cause the collar to drift up in the earlier tranches, while speeds below the bottom collar can improve the extension protection of long PACs. Prepayment rates somewhere between the top and bottom collars—historically, the common occurrence—cause the effective prepayment protection to widen as the top collar changes more quickly than the bottom collar (unless prepayments are very near the top collar).

WHEN THE PAC BREAKS

Breaking a PAC's schedule and causing it to be partially called or extended are not necessarily negative events for the bond's economic performance. The bond's coupon relative to market yields (or the bond's price relative to parity[7]) determines

---

7. The delay in passing payments through to investors from the mortgage borrowers lowers the yield slightly for any given price because the cash flows are pushed out into the future. Different prepayment speeds do not change the yield if a bond is purchased at the parity price (slightly below 100), which adjusts par for the payment delay.

the effect prepayments outside the collar have on the realized yield or total return. A PAC with a discount coupon may benefit if the upper collar is broken, returning principal at par earlier than anticipated at pricing. Similarly, the extension caused by breaking the lower collar adversely affects the performance of a discount-coupon PAC. In the case of a premium-coupon PAC, it benefits performance when the bottom collar is broken, since the principal remains outstanding longer than anticipated, earning additional coupon interest. And of course, the higher the coupon, the worse the effect of breaking the top collar.

The shape of the yield curve is also a consideration. Extension can be costly in a steep yield curve; discounting a bond's cash flows at a sharply higher yield can offset any value additional coupon income might have. Likewise, the capital gain from rolling down a steep curve can offset the loss of coupon income.

As collars deteriorate and approach a point where they may be broken, the market pays increasing attention to the average life profile. A PAC may no longer have measurable effective collars but may still have a stable average life over a reasonable range of prepayment rates.

WINDOWS

A PAC "window" is the interval over which scheduled principal payments are made to the bondholder. As long as prepayment speeds remain at a constant speed within the upper and lower protection bands, or PAC collars, the dates of the first and last principal payments (and equivalently, the length of the repayment period) are certain. PAC buyers in general prefer tighter windows. To some extent, this preference reflects the practicalities of managing their portfolios. The match between a single liability and a single asset is easier to conceptualize when payments are concentrated over a short period. They also are easier to convert to floating-rate assets with swaps. A shorter window also means fewer and larger repayments. Tighter windows producing a more bulletlike paydown are, conceptually, better substitutes for corporates. The chief benefit of a tight window, however, is the superior roll down the yield curve it provides as it ages. Ideally the average life declines by a year for every year the bond is outstanding (assuming a stable yield and prepayment scenario).

Generally, a tighter window is a greater consideration the longer the average life of the bond. Shorter-term PACs inherently have shorter windows, while the desire for tight windows in the 20-year sector is difficult to satisfy, owing to the "tailish" nature of the cash flows in the later years of the transaction. That is, the principal payments scheduled for the later years are relatively small in any month. This is easily confirmed by glancing at Exhibit 10–4. Carving the "tail" into shorter windows would result in more classes with odd, less marketable average lives.

A "good" window in the 3- and 4-year sectors is 12 to 15 months long. The 5- and 7-year buyers prefer a window of 18 to 24 months; 10-year buyers prefer paydowns over a 24- to 30-month period.

Some investors claim to prefer tight windows because they expect superior average life stability. For example, they may believe a tighter window has less average life variability when prepayments are outside the PAC collars. This hunch is dis-

E X H I B I T   10–6

Impact of Window Size on the Average Life Variability of PAC Bonds

| Payment Speed (% PSA) | Average Life (years) | | | | | |
| | 5-Year PAC | | | 10-Year PAC | | |
	0.5 yr. Window	2.2 yr. Window	4.4 yr. Window	3.2 yr. Window	5.0 yr. Window	7.3 yr. Window
0	13.78	13.69	13.38	20.68	20.61	20.50
50	6.68	6.67	6.65	13.70	13.62	13.49
75	5.49	5.48	5.48	11.42	11.47	11.50
100	5.16	5.16	5.16	11.22	11.22	11.22
300	5.16	5.16	5.16	11.22	11.22	11.22
350	5.01	4.96	4.87	9.68	9.69	9.69
400	4.40	4.41	4.41	8.47	8.48	8.48
450	3.93	3.94	3.96	7.51	7.51	7.52
600	2.97	2.98	3.00	5.53	5.53	5.54

Note: All structures are backed by $500MM FNMA 9s, 9.77 WAC, 349 WAM and have 85% to 300% PSA collars.

proved by experimenting with different window lengths in otherwise identical PACs (same collateral, same average lives). Exhibit 10–6 shows two such experiments manipulating the windows of the 5- and 10-year PACs in a structure containing a complete series of PACs with average lives from 2 to 20 years, backed by $500 million FNMA 9s (9.77% WAC, 349-month WART) and protected between 85% and 300% PSA. Even at fairly extreme prepayment speeds (0% and 600% PSA, for instance), there is little difference in the average lives of otherwise comparable PACs with different windows. *All else equal, as a result of their slightly wider spreads, PACs with average or wide windows should outperform those with tight windows.* This result suggests that investors who do not require a bulletlike repayment of their investment, but rather can accommodate greater payment dispersion, should not discriminate between window sizes, particularly in a flatter yield curve environment. Investors who can adapt to a longer paydown period by such means as modifying their cash management procedures, adopting more sophisticated techniques for modeling and managing their asset-liability positions, initiating or other procedural changes, would also be able to take advantage of the relative cheapness of wide windows.

Tighter windows may improve performance when the PAC is a current pay bond. In this case, a shorter window reduces the likelihood that prepayments can accelerate or decelerate to levels outside the bands before it is fully retired according to schedule.

LOCKOUT

PAC bonds can be "locked out" in two ways. First, the entire PAC schedule can be locked out by adding a portion of the PAC schedule at the very front to the companion

EXHIBIT 10–7

Impact of Lockout Feature on the Average Life Variability of PAC Bonds

| Payment Speed (% PSA) | Average Life (years) | | | | | |
| | No Lockout | | | 2-Year Lockout | | |
	3-yr.	7-yr.	10-yr.	3-yr.	7-yr.	10-yr.
0	11.14	18.98	21.96	7.46	16.57	20.72
50	4.41	10.22	14.36	3.60	9.23	13.75
85	3.05	7.10	11.22	3.05	7.10	11.22
300	3.05	7.10	11.22	3.05	7.10	11.22
355	3.01	6.26	9.70	3.05	6.34	9.68
400	2.84	5.49	8.49	3.02	5.58	8.47
450	2.66	4.89	7.53	2.89	4.96	7.51
600	2.17	3.66	5.55	2.37	3.71	5.53

Note: Both structures are backed by $500MM FNMA 9s, 9.77 WAC, 349 WAM and have 85% to 300% PSA collars.

classes; PAC bonds are locked out for the period over which those principal payments are made instead to companions. Typically this lockout could extend from the first 12 to 24 months of the issue's life. The objective of the lockout is to stabilize the early companion class. This is achieved by paying to the companions the principal cash flows that in effect have the highest effective collars (that is, they will be realized across a very wide range of prepays). These cash flows, which have a high degree of certainty, are used during the lockout to pay the companions. Some market participants, however, speak of the lockout as a PAC bond characteristic or feature; they may be viewing the lockout as a device for narrowing the PAC window. Others may perceive the lockout as somehow detrimental to the PACs in the structure, perhaps assuming that the PACs are somehow hurt to the extent the companions are helped.

Whether any of these assumptions are valid should be apparent from the example in Exhibit 10–7. The table contrasts the volatilities of 3-, 7-, and 10-year average life bonds from a structure without any lockout with those from one with a 2-year lockout. Both structures are backed by the same collateral, FNMA 9s, with a 9.77% WAC and 349-month WART, and use the maximum PAC schedule consistent with collars of 85% to 300% PSA, and, as appropriate, a lockout. The sizes of the bonds compared have been adjusted to match their average lives within two decimal places. (The 20-year bonds are not included in the comparison because their average lives were too different after matching the earlier bonds.)

The lockout, according to the exhibit, benefits the PAC bonds by reducing both call and extension risk. Earlier bonds benefit more than later bonds, with the 10-year classes displaying only marginal reductions in average life volatility. Two effects are at work here. First, the lockout reduces the size of the schedule by removing all payments in the first 2 years. This results automatically in a smaller amount of PAC bonds relative to the companions; conversely, more companions protect the remaining PAC schedule. Since they contain those cash flows from the collateral with the lowest degree of call risk, the companions are much less vulnerable to call risk, and even at very high prepayment speeds a larger proportion of companion bonds remain outstanding to shelter the PAC bonds than would otherwise have been the case. At the same time, these principal amounts are no longer bound to a schedule, meaning that later scheduled payments have a better likelihood of being paid on schedule in event of speeds below the bottom collar.

The second form of lockout is a natural form of call protection common to all types of CMO structures. It refers to the bonds (or principal amount of bonds) that will pay down, in the worst case, before the specific bond begins to pay principal. In a simple sequential structure, all but the shortest average life bond enjoy some lockout while earlier bonds in the structure pay down. PACs enjoy explicit call protection from the companion bonds as well as inherent call protection from any earlier bonds in the schedule. In other words, the longer the average life, the better the bond's inherent call protection. The impact of lockout is particularly apparent when we examine the effect of average life on option costs later in this article.

IS THERE A Z IN THE DEAL?

A Z, or accrual, bond ("Z" standing for zero coupon) is a type of CMO bond structure that pays no interest until it begins to pay principal. Until that time, the interest payments are accrued at the coupon rate and added to the principal amount outstanding. A Z bond is most typically included in a CMO structure as the last bond class to be retired. Of course, the underlying collateral continues to pay coupon interest; the portion that would have gone to the Z-bond holders, had it been structured as a coupon-paying bond, is used instead to retire the earlier classes. In effect, then, the presence of a Z bond permits CMO structurers to increase the size of the earlier classes, since the "accrual" amounts are additional to the projected principal payments from the collateral. More pertinently, the "accrual" helps to stabilize the earlier bonds, since a portion of the cash flow used to retire them is not directly determined by the level of prepayments.

The interaction of Z bonds with earlier classes is discussed in detail in Chapter 19. Readers who are unfamiliar with the Z-bond structure, or are interested in more complex manifestations of the Z structure, should refer to that chapter. The objective of this discussion is to examine the value, if any, that a long-term Z bond contributes to PACs. A related issue also is explored, namely the possibility that accrual from the Z bond is used to stabilize earlier companion bonds and not the PAC bonds, or equivalently, to pay down stated-maturity-type bonds. Such a mechanism might not be explicitly disclosed when the bonds from the structure are traded, and may only be indicated in the prospectus or by careful review of the entire issue.

Two CMO structures were modeled to examine more closely the impact of a Z bond on their performance and relative value, again backed by the same FNMA 9% collateral, and containing the maximum principal amount of PACs given collars of 85% to 300% PSA and the relevant accrual mechanism. The schedule has been divided into a series of bonds with nominal average lives of 2-, 3-, 4-, 5-, 7-, 10-, and 20-years, the average lives of all but the 20-year matching to within two decimal places (as in the lockout example, because the schedules differ significantly in amount, the 20-year bonds are not comparable).

Both structures contain 20-year Z bonds. The first passes accrual to PAC and earlier companion bonds alike, the second to earlier companions only. The average lives of the two PAC series at various prepayment rates are displayed in Exhibit 10–8.

Investors should note the difference in average life performance between the PACs supported by a Z bond and the PACs whose companions alone are supported by the Z bond. The *Z bond stabilizes the PAC bonds when prepayments break the lower collar.* This makes sense—accrual cash flow is generated as long as the Z bond is outstanding. On the other hand, *PAC bonds shorten more sharply* in the structure with the Z bond when the upper collar is broken, because a smaller proportion of companion bonds is outstanding at any time to cushion PACs from high rates of prepayments. In fact, the faster the prepayments, the smaller the principal balance of the Z bond when it begins to absorb excess cash, and the quicker it can be extinguished. This example should warn investors not to assume, however, that because a Z bond is present in the structure, that the PACs will have less extension risk. There is no rule in the marketplace requiring issuers to pay accrual to PAC bonds. In some market environments, diverting accrual to the companions can make them more marketable, and a CMO arbitrage more viable. If this is the case, then issuers will structure their CMOs accordingly. The moral of the story: ask for the priorities in detail and read the prospectus.

Readers also may have noticed that the average life profile of the PACs that receive no accrual in this example is identical to that of the PACs backed by the same collateral in a structure with no Z bond. (See Exhibit 10–3.) In other words, for PAC buyers, diverting accrual to the companions is the same as not including a Z bond in the structure at all. This makes sense: The same aggregate amount of companion bonds is available to support the PAC bonds, with the only difference being that the weight of companion principal payments is shifted forward in time since the payments to the non-Z companions consist in part of interest accrued by the Z bond.

EFFECT OF JUMP-Z AND VADM STRUCTURES ON PAC BONDS

During 1990, structurers began to create a special bond class from the accrual thrown off by a Z bond. Variously called thrift liquidity bonds, VADMs (very accurately determined maturity), or SMAT (stated maturity), these bonds first appealed to savings and loan institutions, who are required by regulation to maintain a portion of their assets in very high quality, short-term investments, and who, accordingly, are willing to pay a premium for instruments that qualify *and* offer yields more attractive than those of, for example, government issues. These bonds appeal to investors such as commercial banks, who are sensitive to the extension risk associated with rising yield environments, so that VADMs with final maturities greater than 2 years have been issued in growing amounts. The size of a VADM class is determined by the amount of accrual (or accrual and principal)

EXHIBIT 10-8

Impact of Z-Bond Accrual on the Average Life Variability of PAC Bonds

Prepayment Speed (% PSA)	Average Life (years)														
	Accrual to PACs and Companions							Accrual to Companions Only							
	2-yr.	3-yr.	4-yr.	5-yr.	7-yr.	10-yr.		2-yr.	3-yr.	4-yr.	5-yr.	7-yr.	10-yr.		
0	2.74	6.03	9.05	11.04	14.01	17.11		3.20	7.70	11.44	13.74	16.97	20.50		
50	2.21	3.53	5.07	6.40	8.85	12.24		2.23	3.61	5.25	6.67	9.37	13.49		
85	2.13	3.05	4.16	5.16	7.13	11.23		2.13	3.05	4.16	5.16	7.13	11.22		
300	2.13	3.05	4.16	5.16	7.13	11.23		2.13	3.05	4.16	5.16	7.13	11.22		
350	2.13	3.00	4.13	4.76	6.19	9.68		2.13	3.05	4.16	4.99	6.29	9.69		
400	2.13	2.82	3.68	4.19	5.93	8.47		2.13	3.05	3.93	4.40	5.51	8.48		
450	2.13	2.21	3.30	3.74	4.83	7.51		2.13	2.95	3.52	3.93	4.90	7.52		
600	1.97	1.82	2.52	2.84	3.62	5.53		2.10	2.38	2.67	2.97	3.67	5.54		

Note: Both structures are backed by $500MM FNMA 9s, 9.77 WAC, 349 WAM and have 85% to 300% PSA collars.

thrown off at a zero-prepayment rate up to the desired final maturity; obviously, faster prepayments will shorten the maturity, but no event can lengthen it. The presence of a VADM has the same effect on the PAC performance as diverting the accrual to the companion classes has in the preceding example.

In a handful of issues, structurers designed the companion Z bonds to convert to a "payer" early, changing their priority among companions for principal from last to current. There are a variety of ways to make a Z "jump"; the chief ones are described in Chapter 19. Once the Z bond converts to the current pay bond and begins to pay coupon interest, its support is no longer available to the PAC classes. The effect on PAC performance is generally the same as in the basic example above. However, the degree to which the PACs lose extension protection is moderated by the amount of time it takes to trigger the conversion, and by whether the jump is a temporary response to some condition (such as a specified prepayment threshold) or permanent (a "sticky" Z). This structuring strategy was more common in the late 1980s and is never seen in the current environment.

PRIORITY TO RECEIVE EXCESS CASH FLOWS

The PAC schedule is protected by the existence of companion classes. The mechanism is simple: In any period the companions absorb all principal in excess of the scheduled payments, and any current-paying PACs have first claim on all principal received. This protection ceases when all the companion classes have been fully retired, an event that occurs if the collateral consistently pays at speeds above the top collar. Once the companions are retired, any principal is distributed to the outstanding PACs, according to priorities defined for the particular CMO issue. Frequently, these priorities pay excess principal to the outstanding PACs in order of final maturity, but this is not always the case. A wholesale examination of CMO prospectuses will unearth numerous examples of structures that paid excess in the reverse of maturity order or otherwise insulated some classes at the expense of others. The impact of such schemes has, as would be expected, a significant effect on the average life volatility of the various PACs.

A simple example contrasting two priority schemes is shown in Exhibit 10–9. This exhibit compares the average lives of two sets of PACs at various prepayment speeds—one receiving excess principal in the maturity order, the other in the reverse maturity order. As the exhibit indicates, reversing the order in which PACs are subjected to prepayments above the top collar drastically alters the average life performance of the PACs, if prepayments are outside the collars. As would be expected, shorter PACs benefit at the expense of the longer. When the excess is paid in reverse, the short- and intermediate-term PACs are more significantly stable; when prepayments increase, longer PACs, with 10- and 20-year average lives, shorten up much more significantly.

THE OPTION COSTS OF PAC FEATURES

Most participants in the PAC market evaluate individual bonds by examining their average life and yield over various constant prepayment scenarios outside the collars, a technique similar to the one used in this chapter to analyze the various PAC

EXHIBIT 10–9

Impact of Excess Payment Order on the Average Life Variability of PAC Bonds

Average Life (years)

Speed (% PSA)	Excess in Order of Maturity							Excess in Reverse Maturity Order						
	2-yr.	3-yr.	4-yr.	5-yr.	7-yr.	10-yr.	20-yr.	2-yr.	3-yr.	4-yr.	5-yr.	7-yr.	10-yr.	20-yr.
0	3.20	7.70	11.44	13.74	16.97	20.50	22.75	3.20	7.70	11.44	13.74	16.97	20.50	22.75
50	2.73	3.61	5.75	6.67	9.37	13.49	19.24	2.73	3.61	5.75	6.67	9.37	13.49	19.24
85	2.14	3.05	4.16	5.16	7.13	11.22	19.23	2.14	3.05	4.16	5.16	7.13	11.22	19.23
300	2.14	3.05	4.16	5.16	7.13	11.22	19.23	2.14	3.05	4.16	5.16	7.13	11.22	19.23
350	2.14	3.05	4.16	4.99	6.29	9.69	17.06	2.14	2.05	4.16	5.16	7.14	11.95	5.42
400	2.14	3.05	3.93	4.40	5.51	8.48	15.09	2.14	3.05	4.16	5.16	7.17	9.65	4.07
450	2.14	2.95	3.52	3.93	4.90	7.52	13.43	2.14	3.04	4.16	5.16	7.26	7.56	3.35
600	2.10	2.38	2.67	2.97	3.67	5.54	9.86	2.14	2.51	4.16	5.16	7.24	3.09	2.27

Note: Both structures are backed by $500MM FNMA 9s, 9.77 WAC, 349 WAM and have 85% to 300% PSA collars.

features. The procedure has recognized disadvantages, some of which can be reduced to the complaint that they use a constant prepayment assumption. Using such tools, investors can devise investment criteria for PACs such as "I will buy 10-year PACs with 4-year windows at 120 off if they don't shorten to less than 8 years average life given an instantaneous 200–basis point (bp) drop in yields." Implicitly, they are using these tools to measure and value the prepayment options embedded in their PAC bonds. However savvy and tough-minded the criteria sound, they are at bottom purely subjective guesses about how much the random exercise of those options will impair or help investment results.

It is possible to measure the impact of prepayment risk on the yields earned by PACs by employing the option pricing models. These models generate spreads, durations (price sensitivity), and convexities (the sensitivity of duration to yield changes) that are explicitly adjusted to account for expected prepayments on a large sample of possible interest rate paths over the life of the PAC. In particular, these models derive an average cost of the prepayment options in the PAC, and determine the expected reduction in total spread caused by interest rate volatility.[8] The model, in simple terms, summarizes hundreds more scenarios than investors can digest looking at price-yield tables. The scenarios, moreover, are more realistic in that they permit interest rates to move randomly at each point along the path.

Option-adjusted spreads (OASs) vary with market conditions. For this reason, a discussion of current OASs is inappropriate here. However, the option costs derived from the analysis are not very sensitive to current market yield levels (although they will vary somewhat with changes in the level of implied volatility), and can be discussed here without becoming hopelessly stale with the next rally or correction in fixed income markets.

As expected, PACs demonstrate low option costs. *Option costs in the current-coupon-backed structures discussed in this chapter generally ranged from 0 to 20 bps for bonds with 3- to 20-year average lives.* By comparison, the collateral (FNMA 9s) had 35 bps of option cost. (Readers should bear in mind that absolute measures of option costs, yields, and so forth are calibrated to a specific option model. PAC and other CMO option-adjusted spreads and costs should always be benchmarked to those demonstrated by the collateral in the same model.) The PAC bonds backed by premium collateral (FNMA 10 1/2s) had demonstrably higher option costs, ranging from 3 to over 40 bps. The collateral had an option cost of 68 bps.

---

8. The model employed in this discussion, like many other OAS models, used Monte Carlo simulation and an econometric prepayment model. A minimum of 200 paths was generated in the analysis. The total spread computed is a total spread to the entire Treasury yield curve (precisely, the forward rates implied by current Treasury yields), as opposed to a single benchmark. It roughly approximates the spread to a particular Treasury quoted in the market, but differs more or less depending on the slope of the yield curve. The total spread is the spread over Treasuries the security would earn given its current market price if there were zero volatility. The option-adjusted spread (OAS) is the average spread earned across a large sample of interest rate scenarios given the market price. The option cost is measured as the difference between total and option-adjusted spread, and captures the reduction in total spread caused by interest rate volatility.

EXHIBIT 10–10

Sensitivity of Option Costs in PACs* to Interest Rate Shifts (Current-Coupon Conventional Collateral)

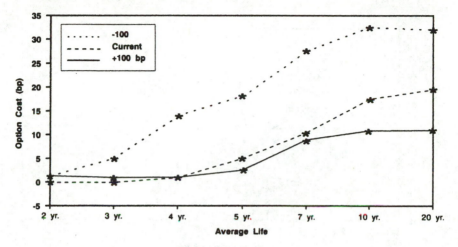

*PACs backed by FNMA 9s; instantaneous interest rate shifts assumed.

The general pattern revealed by the option-pricing model is illustrated in Exhibit 10–10. The option costs are calculated for the series, described in earlier sections, of 2-, 3-, 4-, 5-, 7-, and 20-year average life-PACs backed by FNMA 9s. (See Exhibit 10–3 for the average life profile of these bonds.) The patterns displayed by option costs for premium-backed PACs are shown in Exhibit 10–11. The option costs for these series are analyzed in three scenarios: assuming that the interest rate environment (of January 23, 1990) remains constant and assuming instantaneous parallel shifts in interest rates of up and down 100 bps. Assuming a constant option-adjusted spread, the shifts in the up and down cases are typically large enough to give the tranches, which currently are priced close to par, a discount or premium price. In this way it is possible to draw some conclusions about the sensitivity of the structure to interest rate shocks. Ranging from 3 to over 30 bps, the option costs demonstrated by the current-coupon-backed PACs in the bullish scenario are consistent, as well, with the general magnitude of option costs observed in premium-coupon-backed PACs.

As expected, the option costs rise with the average life of the PAC. This result is expected if only because the probability an option will be exercised is greater the later its expiration date. Comparing the current and bearish cases, the increase in extension risk as interest rates rise results in a slightly higher option cost for 2- and 3-year PACs. Of greater interest is the fact that, going from the 10-year PAC to the 20-year, option costs either decline or increase at a slower rate in every interest rate case. This result holds for the option costs in a similar set of

E X H I B I T   10–11

Sensitivity of Option Costs in PACs* to Interest Rate Shifts (Premium-Coupon Conventional Collateral)

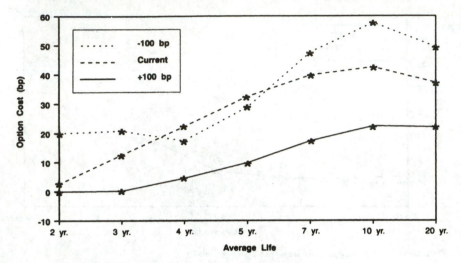

*PACs backed by FNMA 10 1/2s; instantaneous interest rate shifts assumed.

PACs depicted in Exhibit 10–11, backed in this instance by premium coupon collateral (the average life profile is shown in Exhibit 10–3). *The fact that option costs tend to peak with 10-year PACs rather than 20-year PACs should take some market participants by surprise, and suggest to others that the typical incremental spread required by 20-year PAC buyers over 10-year PACs represents extra value.* The result is intuitively appealing as well. It reflects the long lockout imparted by comparisons and shorter PACs in the schedule and the limited room for extension. In addition, the prepayment model used to project prepayments over various interest rate paths correctly reflects the tendency of mortgage pools to "burn out" following sustained periods of fast prepayment rates. As a result, prepayments tend to slow down in the later years of the pool's life.

When the effect of a lockout was examined using average life profiles (Exhibit 10–7), the benefits to the PACs were more pronounced the earlier the bond came in the series. By explicitly valuing the option costs for the same example, a similar effect is observed, as shown in Exhibit 10–12. However, the 7- and 10-year tranches receive no benefit from the lockout on an option-cost basis, whereas their average lives are observed to lengthen less sharply in extremely slow prepayment rate environments. The exhibit also indicates a benefit to the 20-year PAC, except when interest rates drop and the collateral becomes a premium security and subject to faster prepayments. The 20-year PACs were not compared in Exhibit 10–6 since, given a different amount in the schedules, it was not possible to match the average lives of all four bonds (the 20-year in the lockout structure had an aver-

E X H I B I T   10–12

Sensitivity of Option Costs in PACs* to Interest Rate Shifts in Structures With and Without a Lockout

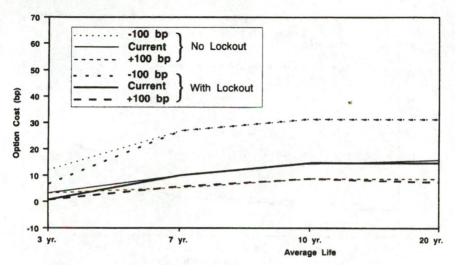

*PACs backed by current-coupon conventional collateral; instantaneous interest rate shifts assumed.

age life close to 16 years). This difference also may account for the lower option cost imputed to the 20-year in the lockout structure.

The impact of various window lengths on 5- and 10-year PACs also was examined, with no increase or diminution of option costs observed, except for the 5-year bonds in the bullish case. Even then, only slight differences, at best 3 bps, were manifested. This reiterates the conclusion, stated earlier, that the length of the window does not significantly affect the average life stability of the bond outside the collars.

Some security analysts and investors resist this result. They believe, for instance, that a tight window lowers the likelihood of breaking the collars during the paydown period. Therefore, they reason, the prepayment options that they effectively hold should be less costly. The time value of the options, however, includes the period prior to the first payment, because the protection implicit in the collars can be damaged or enhanced by prepayment experience in earlier months or years of the structure's life. More than one full interest rate and housing industry *cycle* can occur before a single principal payment is made to a 5- or 7-year PAC, with periods of slower prepayments tending to improve a PAC's call protection and faster prepayments tending to erode it. If prepayments violate the lower collar when earlier PACs are paying, both the call and extension protection of the later PACs can actually improve! When many such possibilities are simulated, the net effect should be small or negligible.[9]

---

9. The first PAC, then, should benefit the most from a tight window. A 2- or 3-year PAC, however, already tends to have a short window and very low option costs, for reasons previously explained.

E X H I B I T   10–13

Sensitivity of Option Costs in PACs* to Interest Rate Shifts When Z Bond Funds Companions Only and When Z Bond Funds Both PACs and Companions*

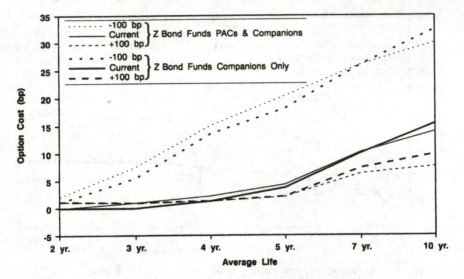

*PACs backed by current-coupon conventional collateral; instantaneous interest rate shifts assumed.

The option costs for two series of PACs in Z-bond structures, one funded by the Z bond and one not, are displayed in Exhibit 10–13. The fact that the Z bond helps reduce the extension risk in the PACs but exposes them to additional call risk is illustrated. The PACs paid down with accrual tend to have higher option costs, except in the bearish case, where prepayments are less likely to retire the Z bond before the PACs have been paid. (The relationship appears to weaken for 20-year bonds, but this most likely reflects the fact that the 20-year bonds have very different average lives as a result of matching the earlier bonds. The 20-year PAC paid by accrual actually has an average life of over 26 years.)

Reversing the priorities when the top collar is broken, so that the last PAC in the schedule is the first to receive excess principal after the companions are retired, has a very large effect on the option costs in the 7-, 10-, and 20-year PACs. This effect is apparent in Exhibit 10–14. The higher the priority, the greater the call risk and the higher the option costs. The impact is, as expected, accentuated as declining yields elevate the risk of prepayment. By contrast, shifting the call risk to the later tranches strips most of the already low option costs from the earlier tranches.

CONCLUSION

The scheduled payments of PACs, protected over a wide range of possible prepayment speeds, appeal primarily to insurance companies and other buy-and-hold investors who are matching specific liabilities. The liquidity, yields, and wide di-

E X H I B I T   10–14

Sensitivity of Option Costs in PACs to Interest Rate Shifts When Excess
Cash Is Paid to PACs in Sequential and Reverse Orders

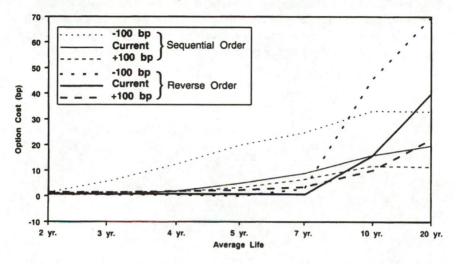

versity of features in the market also attract growing numbers of active bond managers. Misconceptions about the value of certain PAC features can create a number of opportunities for investors in both groups. Most notably, many premium-coupon-backed PACs may be undervalued when their current effective collars are taken into account; the length of the PAC window does not contribute to economic value; lockouts benefit short-term average life PACs as well as companions; and Z bonds can protect earlier PAC bonds from extension risk.

The considerable standardization of the PAC market achieved since 1988 should not distract investors from the need to carefully examine the performance of every bond outside the stated collars. Investors who fail to stress-test PAC investments may overlook the fact that effective collars are significantly different from those stated at issue. Any kink or deviation from sequential order in the prioritization of excess cash flow to the PACs after companion classes are retired must be detected, as it could drastically affect the performance of the longer-term PACs. Although the impact on value is less dramatic, investors should also determine whether a long-term Z bond pays companions or PACs in the structure.

PACs are normally evaluated by examining the yields and average lives of PAC investments over a variety of prepayment scenarios. Such analyses must be carried a step further and linked to possible interest rate scenarios. The soundest way to do this is to employ a prepayment model that explicitly recognizes the determinants of prepayment behavior. Such an analysis can be supplemented and its insights extended by employing option-based pricing methods. The results of explicitly measuring the option costs associated with a variety of PAC features have been summarized in this

chapter, and confirm the general results derived from a price-yield–average life evaluation of the same series of PAC bonds. In some instances, the option-pricing approach differentiated more strongly between the contribution or subtraction to value
made by different PAC features. For example, it was observed that option costs decline or are little higher for 20-year PACs than for 10-year PACs, whereas the required
spreads for 20-year PACs are substantially higher than those of 10-years. This finding suggests valuable opportunities in the 20-year sector.

CHAPTER **11**

Z BONDS

Linda Lowell
Senior Vice President
Asset Backed Research
Greenwich Capital Markets, Inc.

Bruce Mahood

Traditional accrual CMO bonds are long-term bonds structured so that they pay no coupon interest until they begin to pay principal. Instead, the principal balance of an accrual bond is increased by the stated coupon amount on each payment date. Once the earlier classes in the CMO structure have been retired, the accrual bond stops accruing and pays principal and interest as a standard CMO bond. Accrual bonds are commonly called Z bonds because they are zero-coupon bonds during their accrual phase. Bonds created in this way provide investors with long durations, very attractive yields, and protection from reinvestment risk throughout the accrual period. The cash flow pattern produced is suited to matching long-term liabilities, and, as a result, the bonds are sought after by pension fund managers, life insurance companies, and other investors seeking to lengthen the duration of their portfolios and reduce reinvestment risk.

Z bonds have been a staple product of the CMO market since its earliest days. The bulk of the Z bonds currently outstanding are from traditional, sequential-pay CMOs, but the generic structure has adapted well to the PAC-based CMOs favored by the market since the late 1980s, and the inclusion of an accrual bond in the last class continues to be a common practice. At the same time, the Z bond was the focus of innovation in the CMO market, as issuers created a significant amount of intermediate average life Z bonds, a growing number of bonds of various average lives that accrue and pay according to a PAC schedule, and bonds that use various conditions or events to turn the accrual mechanism on or off. These innovations expanded the traditional market for Z buyers by improving the stability of Z-bonds' cash flows, issuing Z bonds in a wider range of average lives, or by creating bonds that perform well in rallies and preserve their high yields better in declines.

The chapter discusses this important sector of the CMO market. We begin with an examination of the mechanics of the traditional Z bond as well as Z bonds issued with PACs, and focus on the behavior of these structures in different prepayment scenarios. We also consider the effect Z bonds have on the other bonds in a CMO, and the relationship between the basic characteristics of the Z bond and its market properties and economic performance. A discussion then follows of the characteristics of more complex Z-bond structures, such as serial Z bonds, Z PACs, and Jump Zs.

THE BASIC ACCRUAL STRUCTURE

Most Z bonds have been issued from traditional, sequential pay CMO structures. Typically, they were the last in a four-class bond issue, and had nominal average lives of 20 years. The principal and interest cash flows for a traditional, sequential-pay CMO containing a Z are diagrammed in Exhibit 11–1. As the graph indicates, the first class pays principal and interest until it is retired, at which time the second class begins to pay down. The coupon-paying bonds, Classes A, B, and C, receive payments of interest at their stated coupon rates on their original principal balances. The Z-bond Class Z, however, receives no payments of interest until the preceding classes are fully retired. Instead, its principal balance increases at a compound rate, in effect guaranteeing the bondholder a reinvestment rate equal to the coupon rate during the accrual period, and insulating the investment from reinvestment risk as long as the earlier classes remain outstanding. The principal balance can triple or quadruple in amount over the accrual period projected at issue. This is graphically depicted in Exhibit 11–2, which indicates the growth

E X H I B I T   11–1

Total Principal and Interest Payments of a Traditional Sequential-Pay CMO with a Z Bond*

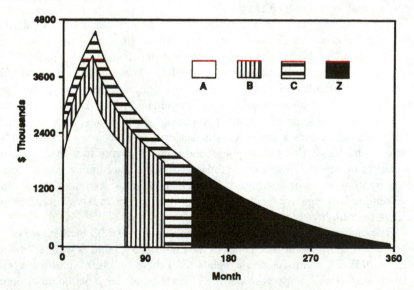

*Prepayments at 165% PSA.

of the principal balance of the Z bond in Exhibit 11–1 over its expected life at an assumed constant prepayment speed of 165% PSA. The principal balance of the tranche at issue is $25 million, and grows to a maximum level of $79.5 million by about the 150th month. From that point, coinciding with the last payment to the preceding tranche, the balance begins to decline as scheduled amortization and prepayments from the collateral are paid to the bondholders.

If actual prepayments occur at a faster rate than 165% PSA, the principal balance of the Z class at the end of the accrual period will be smaller than the $79.5 million shown in the diagram. Since the earlier tranches pay down sooner, the Z bonds accrue over a shorter period of time, and the total amount of accrued interest is lower. Conversely, slower prepayments allow the Z bond to accrue for a longer period, resulting in a larger principal balance at the time when the Z bond begins to generate cash for the bondholders. Principal balances at the end of the accrual period are shown for various constant prepayment speeds in Exhibit 11–3. At the pricing speed of 165% PSA, the balance in this example reaches an amount more than three times the size of the original face amount at issue. At a faster speed of 350% PSA, the original face amount doubles, and at a slower speed, 100% PSA, it quadruples. Likewise, faster prepayments accelerate the receipt of the first payment of principal and interest. In the example, the first payment jumps from halfway into the 12th year at 165% PSA to the beginning of the 9th year at 350%

E X H I B I T   11–2

Principal Balance of a Z Bond Over Time—$25 Million Beginning Balance*

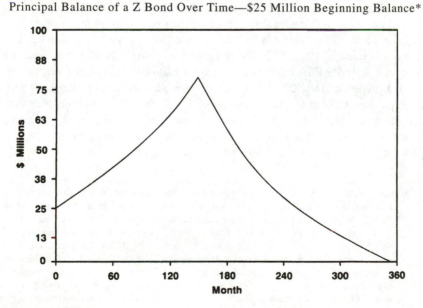

*Prepayments at 165% PSA.

EXHIBIT   11–3

Effect of Prepayment Speed on the Length for the
Accrual Period and the Principal Balance at the End
of the Accrual Period of a $25-Million 20-Year Average
Life Z-Bond Class*

Payment Speed (% PSA)	Principal Balance Outstanding ($MM)	Months from Issue
75	115.4	194
100	102.1	180
125	91.8	166
165	79.5	150
200	71.4	135
250	63.4	119
300	57.2	106
350	52.9	96
425	46.6	80
600	41.1	64

*Total issue $300 million sequential-pay CMO backed by FNMA 9½s.

PSA. If prepayments slow to a constant rate of 100% PSA, the first payment to the Z bond is not made until the beginning of the 16th year after issue.

The effect of faster or slower prepayments on the average life and yield of this same example is shown in Exhibit 11–4, under the heading Z Bond in a Traditional Sequential-Pay CMO. The average life of the Z bond at the pricing assumption of 165% PSA is about 18.5 years; traditional Zs typically have average lives at pricing of 18 to 22 years (and expected accrual periods of 8 to 10 years). If prepayments occur at a constant rate of 100% PSA, the bond lengthens modestly, to an average life of about 22 years. Like other last tranches, the Z has more room to shorten. In this example, the Z shortens to an average life of about 12 years at 350% PSA, and down to about 7.5 years at 600% PSA.[1]

---

1. Average life calculations are intended to measure the weighted average time until receipt of principal payments. Some measures of expected life may include the accrued interest as a cash flow. These increases in the principal balance can enter the calculation as negative weights applied to the elapsed time to early payment dates, and the actual principal payments as positive weights applied to the elapsed time to later payment dates. By placing negative weights on small numbers and positive weights on large numbers, the results can be larger than the remaining term of the underlying collateral (for example, a number of years greater than 30). To avoid this unrealistic result, the convention in the CMO market is to exclude from the calculation all increases in the factor or balance, with the understanding that this method can substantially understate the true interest rate sensitivity of a security.

EXHIBIT 11–4

Yield and Average Life at Various Prepayment Speeds of Comparable CMO and 20-Year Average Life Bonds in Structures With and Without Z Bonds (Pricing Assumption: 165% PSA)

Payment Speed (% PSA)	Coupon-Paying Bond in a Traditional Sequential-Pay CMO		Z Bond in a Traditional Sequential-Pay CMO		Z Bond in a PAC Structure	
	Yield* (%)	Average Life (Years)	Yield[a] (%)	Average Life (Years)	Yield[b] (%)	Average Life (Years)
75	9.97	25.01	9.82	22.91	10.17	22.91
100	9.98	23.25	9.83	21.71	10.20	21.71
125	9.94	21.40	9.83	20.47	10.24	20.47
165	10.00	18.55	9.85	18.55	10.30	18.55
200	10.02	16.41	9.86	17.02	10.35	17.02
250	10.05	13.88	9.89	15.02	10.44	15.02
300	10.08	11.92	9.91	13.37	10.52	13.54
350	10.11	10.38	9.93	11.96	10.69	12.48
425	10.15	8.66	9.98	9.80	11.18	8.38
600	10.27	6.18	10.06	7.61	13.02	3.05

*Price: 96:28.
[a]Price: 96:29.
[b]Price: 90:10.

The yield received on a Z bond is less sensitive to differences in prepayment speeds the closer to par it is priced. At deeper discounts, Z bonds, like other discount mortgage-backed securities, will benefit as their average lives shorten, since principal is returned at par earlier than assumed at pricing. The deeper the discount, the sharper the boost in yield at faster prepayment speeds. Conversely, the yield declines as a function of a slowdown in prepayments and the original discount. Traditional 20-year average life Zs have been issued at original prices as low as 30, but prices above 85 currently are more common. In general, issuers can lower the coupon, achieving a more attractive price, by using discount collateral or by stripping interest into another class.

HOW THE Z INTERACTS WITH OTHER BONDS IN THE STRUCTURE

The interaction of the Z bond with earlier bonds in the CMO structure is a key determinant both of its own behavior and that of the other bonds. By including an accrual bond in the CMO structure, issuers accomplish two purposes: (1) a higher proportion of the total issue can consist of tranches with earlier final maturities than if there were no Z bond in the structure, and (2) the earlier classes have more stable cash flows and average lives across a range of prepayment rates than in a comparable structure without a Z bond. Furthermore, since the timing of cash flows from the Z bond depends on when the earlier tranches are retired, the Z bond itself also is more stable.

An accrual bond supports a larger proportion of early classes because the coupon interest that would have been paid on the outstanding balance of the Z bond is added to the principal payments from the collateral and used to retire the earlier classes. At the same time, the principal amount of Z bonds is increased by the dollar amount of interest diverted. Although at first glance this may look like sleight of hand, the accrual procedure maintains a simple algebraic relationship in which the sum of the principal balances of the outstanding bonds always equals the outstanding principal balance of the collateral. The simple numerical example in Exhibit 11–5 illustrates this relationship. In the example, the collateral pays a 10% coupon and a $100 principal balance in ten equal payments. Both Class A and Class Z have stated coupons of 10%, so that the sum of the interest paid to Class A and either accrued or paid to Class Z is always equal to the interest paid by the collateral. (In an actual CMO, there can be a differential between interest on the collateral and the interest paid to the bondholders, which is then payable to the residual holders.) Notice that Class A is paid down more quickly than it would be if the Z were a coupon-paying bond.

The accrual structure permits issuers to create larger classes with short- and intermediate-term average lives. The effect of an accrual bond on the size of the earlier classes is graphically illustrated in Exhibit 11–6, a diagram of the principal payments only from the CMO in Exhibit 11–1. The discontinuity between the size of principal payments to the Z and those to the earlier tranches reflects the fact that the Z-bond's pro rata share of coupon interest is treated as principal in order to pay down larger earlier tranches (if the last payment to the fourth would be much smaller). This strategy is attractive to issuers when the CMO arbitrage depends primarily on the shape of the yield curve, and larger profits can be made the larger the amount of bonds that can be priced off the front end of the yield curve. In periods when the yield curve is flat or inverted, this strategy helps issuers minimize the proportion of longer average life bonds in the issue. This works because interest payments from the collateral, which would have been paid to holders of the last tranche, are used to support the first tranche. Just how much of an effect an accrual class can have on the allocation of principal to the earlier classes is shown in Exhibit 11–7. The exhibit compares two four-tranche sequential pay CMOs backed by the same collateral, one with a Z and one without. The four tranches in each issue have the same average lives, roughly 3, 7, 10, and 20 years. (The fourth tranches from these examples, all nominally 20-year bonds, are included as well in Exhibit 11–4.) The two structures differ in the way the collateral's principal is distributed among the classes. For example, in the Z-bond structure, a $25 million Z-bond class supports a $136 million 3-year first tranche. The structure without a Z bond has $120 million 3-year bonds in the first class and $79 million 20-year bonds in the fourth tranche.

EXHIBIT 11-5

How a Z Bond Accrues and Pays: A Simplified Example

Collateral: $100 10% loan amortizing in 10 annual payments

CMO: Class A $50 paying 10% coupon
Class Z $50 Z with 10% coupon

| | Collateral | | | Class A | | | Class Z | | |
| | Payments | | | Payments | | | Payments | | |
Payment	Interest ($)	Principal ($)	Balance ($)	Interest ($)	Principal ($)	Balance ($)	Interest ($)	Principal* ($)	Balance ($)
0	0.00	0.00	100.00	0.00	0.00	50.00	0.00	0.00	50.00
1	10.00	10.00	90.00	5.00	15.00	35.00	0.00	(5.00)	55.00
2	9.00	10.00	80.00	3.50	15.50	19.50	0.00	(5.50)	60.50
3	8.00	10.00	70.00	1.95	16.05	3.45	0.00	(6.05)	66.55
4	7.00	10.00	60.00	0.34	3.45	0.00	6.66	6.65[a]	60.00[b]
5	6.00	10.00	50.00	0.00			6.00	10.00	50.00
6	5.00	10.00	40.00	0.00			5.00	10.00	40.00
7	4.00	10.00	30.00	0.00			4.00	10.00	30.00
8	3.00	10.00	20.00	0.00			3.00	10.00	20.00
9	2.00	10.00	10.00	0.00			2.00	10.00	10.00
10	1.00	10.00	0.00	0.00			1.00	10.00	0.00

*Amounts in parentheses are not cash flows but upward adjustments of principal balance.
[a]$6.65 = Principal remaining after Class A retired.
[b]$60 = Previous balance − Principal Paid = $66.55 − $6.65.

227

EXHIBIT 11–6

Total Principal Payments of a Traditional Sequential-Pay CMO with a Z Bond*

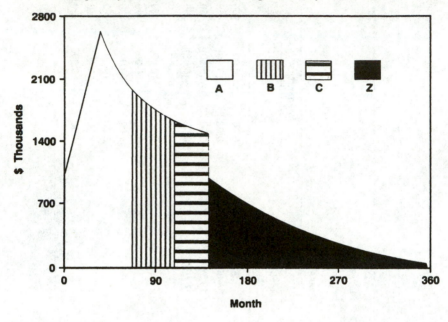

*Prepayments at 165% PSA.

The accrual mechanism imparts greater stability to all the bonds in a typical structure. This is readily apparent in Exhibit 11–8. Each column compares the average life at different prepayment speeds of the different tranches from the sample structures. In each case, the average lives of the tranches are less variable across all scenarios for the structure containing a Z bond than in the structure without.

CMOs WITH PACs AND A Z BOND

The Z bond has a similar effect on earlier bonds in a typical PAC structure. For a given collateral and pricing assumption, accrual from the Z can be used to support a larger amount of PAC and companion bonds in the earlier tranches. The principal and interest payments for a structure containing 3- and 7-year PACs, a 7-year companion, and a 20-year Z are shown in Exhibit 11–9. The yield and average life at various prepayment levels of the Z bond from this structure are included in Exhibit 11–4, and the size and average life of the various classes are shown in Exhibit 11–7. (In fact, the average life of the Z bond is 18.6 years, matching, for the sake of discussion, the average lives of the Z and regular coupon-paying tranches in the other examples.) Funding the earlier classes from the Z-bond's accrual generally creates a much larger portion of available principal, for a given pricing speed, from which to carve PACs, allowing issuers to increase the size of the PAC classes.

EXHIBIT 11-7

Comparison of Various CMO Structures Created With and Without Z Bonds*

Class	Traditional CMO Without Z		Traditional CMO With Z		PAC CMO with Z	
	Original Balance	Average Life	Original Balance	Average Life	Original Balance	Average Life
A	$120,000,000	3.0 Years	$136,000,000	3.0 Years	$ 80,000,000	2.8 Years
B	66,200,000	7.4	84,000,000	7.4	70,000,000	7.0
C	34,500,000	10.9	55,000,000	10.9	125,000,000	7.3
D	79,300,000	18.6				
Z			25,000,000	18.6	25,000,000	18.6
Total	$300,000,000		$300,000,000		$300,000,000	

*Collateral: FNMA 9 1/2s; structured at 165% PSA.

EXHIBIT 11-8

Effect of a Z bond on the Average Life Variability of the Various Classes in a Traditional Sequential-Pay CMO*

	Average Life in Years							
	3-Year Tranche		7-Year Tranche		10-Year Tranche		20-Year Tranche	
Prepayment Speed	No Z Bond	With Z Bond	No Z Bond	With Z Bond	No Z Bond	With Z Bond	Coupon Bond	Z Bond
75% PSA	5.2	4.7	13.2	11.1	18.4	14.9	25.0	22.9
165% PSA	3.0	3.0	7.4	7.4	10.9	10.9	18.6	18.6
425% PSA	1.6	1.7	3.4	3.8	4.8	5.9	8.7	10.3

*Collateral: FNMA 9.5s.

EXHIBIT 11–9

Total Principal and Interest Payments of a CMO with PACs and a Z Bond*

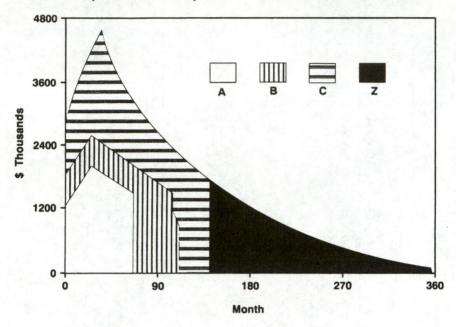

]Prepayments at 165% PSA.

Since companion bonds absorb the prepayment volatility from which the PACs are shielded, the proportion of PACs to companions is an important parameter in determining the degree to which the average lives of the companions will vary over various prepayment scenarios. The presence of a Z bond increases the total amount of principal available at the pricing speed to pay both the PACs and the companions. This means that, all other factors being equal, more PACs may be issued with less negative effect on the stability of the companion bonds. In turn, the length of the accrual period is more stable. Nonetheless, the Z bonds created to support PAC tranches are necessarily more volatile than Z bonds in the traditional CMO issues. The truth of this can be seen by comparing the average life at various prepayment speeds of a Z from a PAC structure to those of a Z from a traditional CMO, as was shown in Exhibit 11–4. As is the case with the fourth tranches in the sample traditional deals, this Z also has an average life of 18.6 years at 165% PSA. As the exhibit indicates, the average life of the Z from a PAC structure would extend more significantly as well, since slow prepayment rates will delay the retirement of the companion bonds, further extending the accrual period for the Zs. (This effect is obscured by oversimplification of the example.)

If the companion tranche(s) in front of a Z are TACs, the Z may be more volatile than if structured with standard companions. When the priorities enforcing the structure require that principal in excess of the TAC (and PAC) payments be paid to the Z, then the Z may begin to receive payments before the companion TAC is retired. This kind of structure produces a Z that is much more volatile in bull markets than a traditional or companion Z bond. Prepayment speeds fast enough to shorten a traditional 20-year Z to a 10-year can shorten this bond to a 1-year. When they carry a low coupon, these bonds are priced to produce generous returns from accelerating prepayments. Indeed, this is one way to create the bullish Z bond known as a "Jump Z." The Jump Z is discussed in greater detail later in this chapter.

PERFORMANCE OF Z BONDS

The variability in the yield of a Z bond over a range of prepayment rates gives at best an imperfect indication of the Z's expected price, and hence, economic performance in different interest rate scenarios. A major drawback of using yield as a measure of a Z-bond's, or for that matter, any mortgage-backed security's expected performance is that the calculation of yield-to-maturity presumes that the amount and timing of cash flows are known with certainty and are reinvested over the life of the investment at a rate equal to the yield. In actuality, mortgage-backed securities are more exposed to reinvestment risk than other common fixed income investments. Most CMOs pay both principal and interest monthly. More importantly, prepayments of principal normally accelerate when market rates decline, just as the yields available on reinvestment opportunities are declining. The opposite occurs as market yields rise; prepayments decline, slowing the receipt of principal just as more attractive reinvestment opportunities appear. Z bonds are protected somewhat from this later source of reinvestment risk, since the reinvestment rate is locked in over the accrual period. They are not fully protected, however. The accrual period is of uncertain length, and when it ends the bonds begin to pay exactly like a coupon-paying CMO bond. For these reasons, yield does not capture the difference in the Z-bond's performance relative to a security with lower reinvestment risk, such as a Treasury bond that pays only coupons until maturity, or one with a fixed accrual period, such as a Treasury zero.

Prepayment risk also exposes investors to call and extension risk, and these have additional consequences for market value. For mortgage-backed securities purchased at prices above par, the early return of principal at par is a negative event, since less interest is earned over the investment horizon. Reflecting the market's perception of these risks, the prices of premium coupon CMOs, including Z bonds, rise more slowly the steeper the decline in interest rates. Investors also are exposed to possible declines in market value when the bond's average life extends and it shifts outward on a positively sloped yield curve. When a bond lengthens in an upwardly sloping yield curve environment, the discount rate applied to the expected cash flow rises, resulting in a lower market value.

Another characteristic that yield calculations cannot reflect is the call provisions established for CMOs. These tend to be more important in the case of older, non-REMIC CMOs, but many REMICs also have significant call provisions. The bonds issued before 1987 used call provisions to insulate the transaction from a more onerous sales tax treatment; some REMIC CMOs have significant call provisions to permit residual holders favorable accounting treatment. Newer issues tend to have minimal clean-up call provisions designed to pay off the bonds when the remaining balance falls below a certain low level. The market considers as fairly favorable terms that permit the bonds to be called at par, 10 or 15 years after issue, when the outstanding balance of the tranche has declined by 10% to 20% of its original amount. These also are the most common. Less favorable terms stipulate a higher remaining balance or a shorter period, or both. A handful of Z bonds currently outstanding could have been called as early as 1990, and a significant number become callable after 1994. Investors are advised to carefully examine the call provisions of Z bonds before trading them.

Z bonds have considerably longer expected durations than coupon payers with similar average lives because the principal balance grows over time. This can be seen by comparing a Z to a coupon payer with the same principal structure (sequential, companion, etc.) and similar average life at the same pricing speed. For example, FHLMC 1727 Z, a companion Z, and FNMA 93-204 J, a companion payer, are both 20-year bonds at 125% PSA (on November 28, 1994) backed by 6.5s. FHLMC 1727 Z has an average life of 20.4 years at 125% PSA, FNMA 93-204 J an average life of 21.5 years. At this speed, the Z bond has a modified duration of 15.4 while the payer has a modified duration of 9.8. At slower prepayment speeds the divergence is even greater: at 90% PSA the Z bond has an average life of 23.4 but a duration of 16.7, the payer an average life of 24.0 and duration of 10.3. Only at speeds which significantly shorten the average lives of these companion structures does the Z-bond's duration converge to that of the comparable payer. At 250% PSA, the Z bond shortens to an average life of 6.1 years, with a modified duration of 3.6 and the payer to an average life of 6.2 years with a duration of 3.5. An option-adjusted analysis produces a similar result: The Z has an expected duration of 15.9, the payer 10.0. Given this pattern of price sensitivity, investors should expect Z bonds on a total return basis to underperform CMO payers and Treasuries with comparable average lives and maturities in bearish scenarios. However, as a result of the accrual mechanism, Z bonds tend to outperform comparable Treasury zeroes in rising rate scenarios. In bullish scenarios, the long duration of the Z bond produces high rates of return, although the Z bond loses its advantage over comparable securities as it shortens dramatically in more sharply declining yield interest rate scenarios.

MORE FUN WITH ACCRUAL BONDS

Some of the CMOs issued since the beginning of 1989 make more creative use of the basic accrual mechanism. The variations on the accrual theme include Z PACs and structures containing an intermediate- as well as long-term Z bond or a series of Z bonds of various average lives. Other structures turn the accrual mechanism on and off, depending on the amount of excess principal available after scheduled payments are met. As complex and exotic as these structures may appear at first glance, the same basic principles at work in traditional Z bonds continue to apply. And in most cases, any additional complexity is accompanied by considerable additional value for investors with particular objectives and investment criteria.

Z PACs

Z PACs combine the cash flow characteristics of a standard Z bond with the greater certainty of a PAC regarding the amount and timing of actual payments. When prepayments occur within the range defined by the PAC collars, the Z PAC will accrue to a scheduled principal balance over a fixed period and make scheduled payments thereafter. As with more familiar, coupon-paying PACs, any excess cash flow is absorbed by companions as long as they are outstanding. Similarly, the coupon interest earned on the Z-PAC's outstanding balance during the accrual period is used to support earlier classes in the structure, and the balance of the Z PAC is increased by an equal amount. For prepayment levels within the PAC collars, the structure eliminates reinvestment risk over a defined accrual period, and then provides predictable payments until maturity. This structure is particularly well suited to matching liabilities. The fact that Z PACs are issued in a range of average lives (typically 5, 7, 10, or 20 years) increases their applicability. Furthermore, the call and extension protection provided by the planned payment schedule means that the duration of the investment is less likely to increase as interest rates rise (or decrease as interest rates decline) than is the duration of a standard or companion Z. That is to say, the Z PACs are less negatively convex than standard or companion Zs. For this reason, active portfolio managers should consider using the Z PAC to lengthen the duration of their portfolios in anticipation of market upswings.

STRUCTURES WITH MORE THAN ONE Z BOND

Although the practice of issuing two or more Zs from a single structure is not new, more of these structures have been created since 1989 than previously. Considerable variety is possible in structuring deals with multiple classes of Z bonds, but two common strategies have been to issue a sequential series of Zs with a range of average lives (5, 7, 10, and 20 years, or 7, 10, 15, and 20 years, for example), or a pair of Z bonds having intermediate- and long-term average lives (5- and 20-year bonds or 10- and 20-year bonds are common examples). In the case of an intermediate- and long-term average life pair, the bonds do not necessarily pay in sequence, but more typically pay down before and after intervening coupon-paying classes. Both strategies have been employed in traditional CMOs as well as in structures containing PAC bonds.

In general, multiple accrual classes in a CMO interact with the rest of the structure in the same way a single traditional Z bond does, supporting the repayment of earlier classes, which themselves may either pay current-coupon interest or accrue it. In a series of Zs, the longer Zs lend stability to the shorter Zs, just as they would to coupon-paying bonds with earlier final maturities. Accrual from the later Zs can be used to retire earlier Zs when they become current-paying bonds, just as if they were coupon-paying bonds.

The cash flows from a sequential-pay CMO containing a series of 5-, 7-, 10-, and 20-year Zs preceded by a 2-year coupon-paying tranche are shown in Exhibit 11–10. This example was constructed using the same collateral and pricing speed

EXHIBIT   11–10

Total Principal and Interest Payments of a Sequential-Pay CMO
with a Series of Z Bonds*

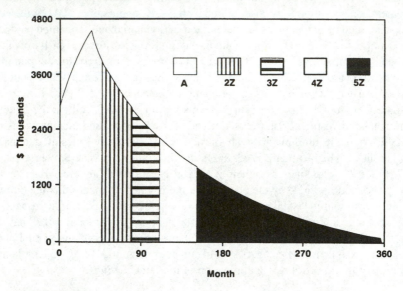

*Prepayments at 165% PSA.

as in the previous examples containing a single Z. The last tranche, 5Z, is the same
size as in the previous example as well, and for this reason has the same average
life at various prepayment speeds. For the sake of discussion, the first tranche is
also the same size as the first tranche in the traditional CMO with a Z bond, $136
million. As indicated in Exhibit 11–11, the large amount of accrual bonds in the
structure has the effect of shortening the average life of this bond from 3 years at
165% PSA in the single Z example, to 2 years in this. (Readers will note that this
example is not necessarily realistic. Structurers would be concerned to issue larger
amounts of short-term average life bonds that can be sold at lower yields for
greater arbitrage profits, manipulating the coupon and offer price, and so forth.)
Exhibit 11–11 lists the average lives of the first five classes at various prepayment
speeds. In general, intermediate-term Zs demonstrate considerable stability. This
is more evident when the 7- and 10-year Zs are compared to the 7- and 10-year
coupon-paying bonds from earlier examples in Exhibit 11–8. The 10-year is supported by a 20-year Z, and is noticeably less variable than one in a CMO without
a Z. As would be expected, given the larger amount of accrual being passed to successively shorter bonds in the current example, the 5-year Z bond is considerably
more stable than a comparable 5-year standard payer supported by a single Z. The
general result is that the shorter Zs in a series of Zs are "cleaner," that is, they have
progressively less average life variability than otherwise comparable coupon-
paying bonds. Intermediate-term average life Zs interspersed among coupon-

E X H I B I T   11–11

Average Lives at Various Prepayment Speeds of the Bonds
in a Sequential-Pay CMO with a Series of Z Bonds

	Average Life (years)				
	A	**2Z**	**3Z**	**4Z**	**5Z**
75% PSA	2.5	6.6	10.1	14.0	22.9
165% PSA	2.0	5.0	7.6	10.5	18.6
425% PSA	1.4	3.1	4.5	6.0	10.3

paying classes in a structure supported by a 20-year Z (the other common strategy) will benefit similarly. They will be more stable than otherwise, and the degree of stability will depend on the size of the Z bond supporting them.

The consequences of multiple-Z strategies are that they produce bonds possessing relatively stable cash flow patterns—not as stable as PACs with decent collars, but more stable than traditional sequential-pay bonds. These stable bonds also possess the partial shield against reinvestment risk that is a chief attraction of traditional Z bonds, and they make it available in any array of expected lives, broadening the appeal of Z bonds to investors with intermediate- rather than long-term horizons.

Tricky Zs

Other innovative approaches to Z bonds appeared in the late 1980s. The common theme of these "trick" Zs involves turning the accrual mechanism on or off under certain conditions. One such condition might be a date; for example, the rule of allocating cash flows between classes might be "accrue until such and such a date" instead of the traditional "accrue until A, B, and C tranches are retired." Or, the decision to accrue the Z bond might depend on the amount of principal available to make payments to the nonaccrual bonds currently paying. The use of such rules results in bonds with performance characteristics that can be very different from the Z bonds discussed previously.

CMO issuers have tinkered with the accrual mechanism of Z bonds to create CMO classes that alternate between paying interest and accruing interest. These special-purpose classes are structured with a set of rules that turn their accrual mechanism on or off according to certain cash flow conditions. These accrual rules are often designed to help preceding classes meet their cash flow schedules and/or expected maturity dates. Beginning in 1988, issuers included these variable-accrual bonds in CMO structures to help earlier classes meet the 5-year maturity requirement for inclusion in thrift liquidity portfolios. These benevolent Zs pay as follows: when cash flows from the mortgage collateral are insufficiently large enough to retire the liquidity bonds according to schedule, their accrual mechanisms are turned on and corresponding coupon from the collateral is applied to the earlier classes; when cash flows are sufficient to retire the liquidity bonds on schedule, their accrual mechanisms are turned off and the bonds act like standard coupon payers. Incorporating a conditional accrual rule into a bond class is an effective way to reduce extension risk on earlier classes. Of course, the extension risk is not eliminated but is instead largely transferred to the benevolent Z and other, later bond classes.

Another wrinkle is to permanently transform Z bonds into coupon-paying bonds when certain cash flow levels are met. An early example of this Z-bond structure was issued as the last of nine classes in FNMA 89-15. This bond was not marketed with any distinguishing label. The other bonds in the structure were a series of PACs and TACs followed by a companion dubbed an "S" bond. The Z bond pays as follows: any excess above the scheduled PAC and TAC payments is distributed to the Z bond as an interest payment; if the amount is lower than the amount that was accrued, the shortfall is accrued; if the amount is greater, the excess is distributed as principal; beginning in the month following the first payment of a complete interest payment, the so-called Z class distributes interest each month. One month of exceptional prepayment experience can trigger the conversion to coupon bond. Thereafter, the average life will be shorter than it would otherwise have been, owing to the fact that a portion of its cash flows is dispersed over what would have been the accrual period. Any protection against reinvestment risk offered by this "chameleon" bond is ephemeral at best. Once converted, the bond behaves like any other companion bond.

Even Z PACs have been subjected to genetic alteration. The first Z PAC issued, the fifth tranche in Ryland Acceptance Corporation Four, Series 88, accrues only until the date of its first scheduled payment or until non-PAC classes in the deal have been retired. Until that date, the Z PAC is the first PAC in line for excess cash flows should the companions be paid down, and after that date, it is last in line. This means it has greater call risk during the accrual period. As a result, its average life is only stable at or below the pricing speed (90% PSA for this deal backed by GNMA 8s). The resultant average life volatility is more typical of a reverse TAC, which does not extend but has considerable call risk.

Jump Zs

Another Z-bond innovation, the jump Z, made its debut in the CMO market during the summer of 1989. Generically, the jump Z is a bullish companion Z bond that is designed to convert to a current payer and to receive excess principal when prepayments accelerate. Under bullish scenarios, this bond "jumps" ahead of other bond classes in the order of priority for receiving principal payments. Once triggered, a jump Z typically receives all excess principal (above scheduled PAC payments) until it is retired. Conceivably, holders of the jump Z could receive these payments early in the expected accrual period. This acceleration of principal can shorten the bond's average life significantly: A Z bond issued with a 20-year average life might shorten to less than 1 year. Since these bonds typically have low coupons and are issued at significant discounts to par (in the eighties), jump-Z holders realized high returns in the 1991–1994 rally. In general, a jump Z priced at a deeper discount traded at a tighter spread, because investors assigned more value to the jump feature. Many investors purchased jump Zs to offset the negative convexity of their other mortgage securities and to enhance the performance of their MBS portfolios in bullish scenarios. Few of these bonds remain outstanding after the 1991–1994 rally, characterized as it was by very high prepayment rates. As the rally continued, the inverse floater became a more popular vehicle for bullish investors and few new jump Zs were issued. The structure reappeared in the late 1990s when underwriters made small jump Zs in order to enhance the profiles of other bonds in the transaction.

Jump-Z bonds have been issued with an extremely diverse set of jump rules. Although apparently lacking uniformity or standardization, these rules have the common objective of increasing the bonds' performance in bullish economic environments. Jumps can be activated by an event associated with a market rally: rising prepayment rates, declining interest rates, or increased cash flow. However, most jump Zs were structured with prepayment triggers: The bonds shortened when prepayment rates on the underlying mortgage collateral rose above a CMO's pricing speed or some other predefined prepayment level. Generally, prepayments above the pricing speed shortened the average life of the jump Z considerably. In structures containing TAC bonds, jump Zs were often designed to shorten when prepayments exceed the speed that defines the TAC schedule. In addition to prepayment triggers, CMO issuers also structured jump Zs with interest rate triggers that were activated when Treasury yields fall below some threshold level. Interest rate triggers eliminated the need for investors to accurately forecast prepayment rates, and ensured that jump-Z holders would benefit even in a market rally that was not accompanied by rising prepayments. In general, the closer the jump trigger is to actual prepayment speeds or current interest rates, the more valuable the jump Z.

Jump-Z bonds can be classified as *cumulative* or *noncumulative,* as well as "sticky" or "nonsticky." A cumulative trigger is activated when since-issuance prepayment rates, or other cumulative measures of prepayment experience, exceed some threshold value. In contrast, a noncumulative trigger only requires prepayments to satisfy the jump condition during a single period. Holders generally prefer noncumulative triggers, since a single month of abnormally high prepayments could force early retirement of their discount security. The adjectives *stick* and *nonstick* indicate whether a jump-Z bond will revert back to its original priority in the CMO structure if jump conditions are no longer met. Once triggered, a sticky Z will continue to receive principal payments, even if prepayments subsequently decline below the threshold value. On the other hand, a nonstick Z can revert back to an accrual bond once its jump rules are no longer satisfied. Holders generally assign the greatest value to jump Zs with noncumulative sticky triggers, because a single increase in monthly prepayment rates could force early retirement of the entire bond class. For jump Zs backed by unseasoned mortgage collateral, a tiny increase in prepayments could trigger a jump: A small increase in CPR can translate into a large PSA spike when prepayments are benchmarked off the early part of the PSA ramp.

The other common approach for creating a jump-Z bond—preceding it with a TAC and other companion bonds in a PAC structure—was described earlier. The jump Z acts like a traditional companion bond and absorbs volatility from both PACs and TACs. Preceded by a TAC, the jump Z receives principal when principal payments from the underlying collateral and Z accrual exceed the amount required to meet the PAC and TAC schedules. The degree to which the bond's average life will shorten depends on its jump rules and the overall deal structure. Jump rules control whether the bond jumps in front of the TAC class when payments break the TAC schedule (sticky Z) or receives only excess payments above the PAC and TAC schedules (nonsticky Z). All else being equal, the average life of a sticky Z is likely to shorten more than a comparable nonsticky Z. Preceded by PACs, TACs, and other support bonds, these jump Zs have a negligible amount of extension risk since they are typically structured as the last companion class in the CMO. In addition to their jump rules, the average life variability of jump Zs is also affected by the features of their preceding PAC bonds. For example, PAC lockouts, typically 1 to 2 years in length, can accentuate the shortening of jump-Z average lives. Since no scheduled principal payments are made during a lockout, there is a much larger amount of cash flow available to pay down a jump Z in the event it is triggered.

This simple form of jump Z (simple to visualize and analyze) does not involve any modification of the standard accrual mechanism: The Z's share of interest is added to principal payments used to pay down earlier bonds according to the schedules and order of priorities established for the deal. Some early jump Zs, however, had modified accrual mechanisms that imposed conditions under which accrual would be turned on or off. These rules can control how coupon interest is paid both before and after the bonds have jumped. Perhaps the most common example of accrual manipulation occurs with jump Zs that pay only a portion of their coupon interest and accrue the shortfall. The exact amount of interest that a jump Z will pay, after being triggered, often depends on the number and size of the companion classes that the bond jumped over. For example, when preceded by both Level I and II PACs, the amount of coupon interest paid to a jump Z bond will depend on whether it jumps over the secondary PACs. If the jump Z remains subordinate to the Level II PACs, then part of the jump-Z's coupon interest can be used to support the second-tier PACs.

CONCLUSION

Z bonds offer investors some of the longest durations and highest yields available in the derivative MBS market, as well as a cash flow pattern well suited to matching long-term liabilities. They also are one of the most liquid varieties of CMO bonds traded in the secondary market. The favorable economics of issuing these bonds will help ensure that a steady supply continues to be produced. Recent innovations have introduced accrual bonds with new and valuable characteristics, including greater stability or accelerated return of principal in rallies, and have widened the availability of intermediate-term Zs. Given the large number of Z bonds outstanding, and the wide familiarity they already enjoy, this trend should continue, creating bonds that meet distinct investor requirements.

CHAPTER 12

COMPANIONS WITH SCHEDULES

Linda Lowell
Senior Vice President
Asset Backed Research
Greenwich Capital Markets Inc.

Collateralized mortgage obligations (CMOs) were first devised to meet two general objectives. The first was to make a better match between a wide range of investors' maturity requirements and the expected cash flows from a pool of mortgages. The second was to redistribute prepayment risk to different classes at levels that many more investors would accept. The initial solution to the problem simply split the returning principal among a series of sequential-pay bonds. Subsequently, this structure has evolved into an array of reduced-risk CMO bond structures, the most heavily issued of which is the planned amortization class (PAC). PACs provide investors with payments scheduled as to payment date and amount, occurring within a defined paydown period (window), and protected over a range of likely prepayment scenarios.

Companion bonds are the natural by-product of creating PAC bonds.[1] In order to protect the schedules of PAC bonds in a CMO issue, a sufficient amount of bond classes must be created to absorb excess principal paydowns and to provide a buffer from which scheduled payments can be made when prepayments are slow. Because companion classes accept additional prepayment volatility, their payments are necessarily more uncertain than either PACs or traditional CMO bonds. As a result, the actual yields or economic returns realized from an investment in companion bonds can vary widely from those projected at the time of investment. Investors recognize this risk, and they demand yields that compensate them accordingly.

Issuers and underwriters also have developed a variety of devices that serve either to reduce the risk of a portion of the companion classes or to create more volatile instruments that reward holders when interest rates (and presumably prepayment

---

1. Other structural devices intended to reduce or transform prepayment risk for some classes in a CMO issue also create support classes. The discussion here should not be presumed to apply to them. Unless clearly indicated, the term "companion" when used in this chapter means PAC companion.

rates) move strongly in a particular direction. Lockouts[2] are among the first group, while super-POs and jump Zs are typical of the second. Another very common strategy is to create companions with floating and inverse floating-rate coupons. One of the oldest and most extensively employed strategies, however, is to give schedules to a portion of the companion cash flows and to provide those schedules with more limited prepayment protection than the primary PAC series receive. This family of reduced-risk companions is the subject of this chapter.

Companions having schedules partake either of the properties of targeted amortization classes (TACs)—so that they are protected against either call or extension risk (a reverse TAC) but not both—or of PAC bonds, so that they have call and extension protection over a range of prepayment scenarios (a Level II PAC). The largest class of these bonds, companion TACs, has been issued since 1988, and is now one of the most liquid of generic CMO classes. Reverse TACs were introduced more in the middle of 1988, but have been marketed explicitly as reverse TACs only since the beginning of 1989. These are more scarce. The concept of Level II PACs took hold during the third quarter of 1989. During the 1990–1994 rally it became common to create several levels of PACs with successively narrower bands of prepayment protection, so that a single transaction could contain PAC Is, IIs and IIIs. In addition, the practice of carving a "super-PAC" schedule out of a primary PAC schedule became popular.

The following discussion explains how companion PAC and TAC bonds are structured and how their structures affect their performance in different prepayment scenarios. The effect of adding a TAC, reverse TAC, or Level II PAC on the behavior of the remaining companion bonds is also explored.

COMPANION BASICS

Companion classes are created from the principal payments remaining after the PAC schedules are defined. In general, companion classes have second claim on excess principal paid down from the collateral after the PAC schedules, and pay sequentially until all the companions are retired. At the pricing prepayment assumption, companion classes pay simultaneously with the PACs. At very slow constant prepayment rates, they must wait to receive principal until the PACs have been retired. At very high speeds, they pay simultaneously with the short-term average life PACs and are quickly retired, after which the PACs themselves must absorb excess paydowns and are retired ahead of schedule.

A simplified example of a standard PAC-companion structure is depicted in Exhibit 12–1. The large unshaded area paying from the first to about the 300th month contains *all* the scheduled payments that would be available to construct PAC bonds, assuming collars of 85% and 300% PSA, and FNMA 9% collateral

---

2. A lockout shifts to a companion bond principal payments that otherwise might be used in a PAC schedule. The effect of a lockout is to push forward the beginning of the first PAC window to a specified date and to stabilize the companion. Lockouts are normally applied to the first PAC for a period of 2 or 3 years, lending stability to the earliest companion class.

E X H I B I T   12–1

PAC with Standard Companion Bonds, 165% PSA

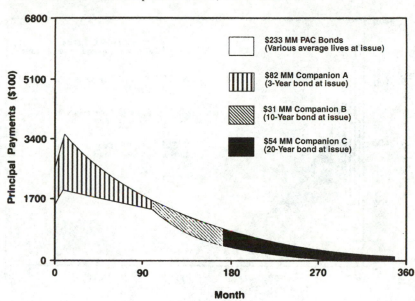

with a WAC of 9.76% and a WAM of 339 months.[3] Normally, structurers would divide this PAC region into a number of PACs with varying average lives. The actual number of PACs created would depend on the demand for particular maturities and windows (the time elapsed between first and last principal payments to the PAC bondholders). For ease of exposition, the PAC region in this and subsequent examples is not divided. The companion bonds are not influenced by the partitioning of a single PAC region into individual bond classes; they are affected, instead, by the size of the entire region in relation to the total size of the companion classes. (In general, the larger the PAC class, given a fixed amount of collateral, the more volatile the companion class is.) The principal payments left over after the PAC region is defined constitute the companion classes. In Exhibit 12–1, these are depicted by the shaded areas. At a pricing prepayment assumption of 165% PSA, the companions pay sequentially over the entire remaining life of the collateral. In this example the companion paydowns at 165% PSA have been divided into three classes with average lives of 3.1, 11.5, and 20.3 years (nominally a series of 3-, 10- and 20-year bonds).

The impact of actual prepayment experience on the size and timing of principal payments to the companion classes is graphically depicted in Exhibits 12–2 and 12–3. When prepayments occur at a constant speed of 300% PSA (the upper

---

3. This is the largest PAC region that could be accommodated by this collateral for the collar given.

EXHIBIT 12–2

PAC with Standard Companion Bonds, 300% PSA

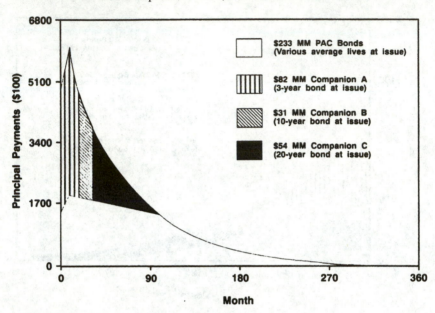

EXHIBIT 12–3

PAC with Standard Companion Bonds, 85% PSA

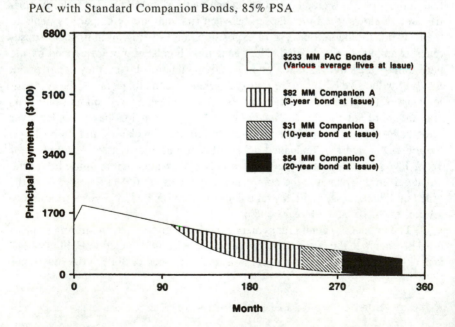

PAC collar), as shown in Exhibit 12–2, the PAC schedule is not disturbed, but the companions shorten dramatically and are all fully retired by the 8th year. By contrast, when prepayments slow to 85% PSA (the lower PAC collar), the first companion does not begin to pay until about the 8th year, as Exhibit 12–3 indicates. The resultant average life volatility is very significant. Bonds with average lives at pricing of 3, 10, and 20 years shorten to 1.0, 2.5, and 5.8 years, respectively, at 300% PSA; and at 85% PSA, the bonds have average lives of 15.0, 21.1, and 25.6 years, respectively.

The average life variability of a companion bond is generally a function of the size of the PAC region relative to the entire issue, the size of the companion relative to the remaining companions, and its average life at the pricing prepayment assumption. A detailed examination of how these characteristics interact to produce the actual behavior of companion bonds in different prepayment scenarios is beyond the scope of this chapter. Still, it is worth outlining the basic relationships between companion structure and behavior because they apply as well to the more complex, schedule-based structures that are the subject of this chapter.

The order in which a companion is scheduled to receive excess cash flows also can profoundly affect its average life behavior. It is normally assumed that companions will be retired in the order of their average lives at issue and that this order of priority does not change over the term of the transaction (indeed, that assumption is made throughout this discussion). This assumption, however, could be altered, generating results that are entirely specific to the transaction in question. Rather than assume that a certain order of priorities is standard, investors should assure themselves that they understand the priorities and other rules on which the structure is based, as well as the conditions under which they may be switched on or off.

There are basically three different ways to vary the relative size of the companions. Lockouts, already mentioned above, are typically employed to improve the stability of payments to the earliest companion class in the issue. Moreover, with two or three years of schedulable paydowns added to its size, the first companion can provide a larger buffer against call and extension for subsequent companions. A similar technique is to pay the later years or "tail" of the PAC schedule to the companions projected to be paying at the same time. Intermediate- or long-term companions can benefit from this technique. The third, tightening the collars, can increase the size of the companions.

Raising the bottom collar increases the principal available for companion classes in the early years (generally the first quarter to first third of the remaining term of the collateral) and lowering the top collar increases principal in later years.

It also should be apparent that the smaller the scheduled PAC payments, the more principal will be available to make payments to companions at any given prepayment speed. This means that extension risk is reduced; call risk is also reduced. The smaller the PAC region, the larger the projected paydowns to the companion in any one period and the smaller the excess principal as a proportion of the projected companion principal payment will be. In other words, excess principal has a proportionally smaller impact on the dollar weights used to compute the companion's average life.

For similar algebraic reasons, changing the proportion of PACs, while holding the average lives about the same, has a bigger impact on the volatility of companions constructed from cash flows at the tail, because smaller dollar weights are applied to later dates. The absolute magnitude of the average life at issue of a companion also determines how much it can lengthen or shorten. This is also very intuitive: The longer the average life at issue, the less room to lengthen and the more room to shorten. Similarly, short-term bonds have less room to shorten, more to lengthen.

The shortening of a CMO bond's average life in a bull market or, conversely, its lengthening in a bear market generally are negative events from the investor's point of view. Two effects are of particular concern. For one, the additional cash flow accelerates or decelerates at the wrong time. As a consequence of the interest rate sensitivity of the prepayment process, reinvestment opportunities are most likely to have declining yields when prepayments are increasing, and rising yields when prepayments are drying up. Second, as average life varies, so too does the bond's duration or price sensitivity. In a bull market, the bond's price appreciates more slowly as market yields decline, generating a lower economic return than a bond of like but stable average life. In a bull market, the companion's value depreciates more quickly as yields rise.[4]

Since companion bonds absorb additional volatility from the protected bonds, changes in expected average life resulting from changes in prepayment experience in the collateral are of heightened concern to investors who hold them. As crucial as an accurate model of the prepayment process is for anticipating the performance of other mortgage-related products in various interest rate scenarios, it is even more valuable in the evaluation of companion bonds. Without appropriate prepayment projections, such as can be derived from an econometric prepayment model, it is not possible to link changes in interest rate levels to meaningful estimates of the yield or total rate of return of a companion.

COMPANION TAC BONDS

Since their introduction in the third quarter of 1988, companion TAC bonds have proved to be a highly marketable innovation. Indeed, since the first TACs were issued, the market has evolved away from TAC-only structures to prefer companion TACs. Clean TAC bonds (from structures without PACs) now are offered less frequently.

A TAC schedule is created by projecting the principal cash flows for the collateral at a single constant prepayment speed. This speed is typically the prepayment speed at which the bonds are priced. In the case of a clean TAC, the projected principal payments define the schedule. In the case of the companion TAC, projected principal remaining after scheduled PAC payments are made defines the schedule. The TACs have first priority after the PACs to principal payments, and their schedules are protected from call risk by the existence of other companion

---

4. Structurers can improve the appeal of volatile securities to some investors by manipulating the coupon so that they are priced as deep discounts to benefit from fast prepayment speeds or as high premiums to benefit from slow prepayments.

E X H I B I T   12–4

PAC with Standard Companion TAC, 300% PSA

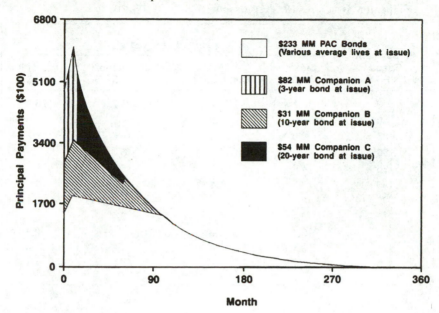

classes that absorb any principal paydowns that exceed both the scheduled PAC and TAC payments in any period. The larger these "support" classes are in relation to the companion TAC, the greater the protection provided to the TAC schedule.

Compared to a clean TAC with similar (in the example they are the same) average life and underlying collateral, the companion TAC necessarily receives less protection, because a larger proportion of the total collateral has already been allocated to high-priority PAC bonds, and a much smaller proportion of principal remains to be allocated to lower-priority support tranches. For this discussion, a simplified example of a companion TAC was created from the 3-year companion in Exhibit 12–1. This was done simply by defining a schedule as the principal payments to the 3-year companion, assuming a constant prepayment speed of 165% PSA. Since it is identical at 165% PSA to the PAC-standard companion example, readers should refer to the cash flow diagram in Exhibit 12–1 to understand this structure. The impact of faster prepayments on this PAC-TAC structure is shown in Exhibit 12–4. At 300% PSA, the higher priority given the TAC schedule forces the 10- and 20-year companions to pay down simultaneously with the TAC (instead of sequentially as in the first example). Readers will note that the shape of the companion TAC at 300% PSA is almost but not entirely identical to its shape at 165%, indicating that the schedule is still well protected at this speed. The size and timing of later payments has been altered slightly at the higher prepayment speed for reasons discussed below.

E X H I B I T   12–5

Average Lives at Various Prepayment Speeds of Different 3-Year PAC-Companion Structures (Pricing Assumption 165% PSA)

Prepayment Speed (% PSA)	Average Life (years)			
	Clean TAC	PAC Companion	Companion TAC	Level II PAC
0	16.7	24.7	24.7	23.3
50	8.0	19.9	19.9	16.8
85	6.0	14.9	14.9	9.5
90	5.2	13.7	13.7	3.1
125	4.0	7.2	7.2	3.1
165	**3.1**	**3.1**	**3.1**	**3.1**
225	3.1	1.6	3.1	3.1
275	3.1	1.2	3.1	2.7
300	3.1	1.0	3.2	2.5
475	3.1	0.6	1.6	1.5
600	3.1	0.5	1.2	1.1

Companion TACs generally have the same properties as clean TACs: They provide a degree of call protection and little extension protection. Many structures actually will first extend, when prepayments slightly exceed the TAC speed, before shortening at higher speeds. The important difference is that companion TACs have significantly less call protection since they must absorb excess principal once the remaining unscheduled companions are retired. This can be seen by examining Exhibit 12–5, in which the average lives of various 3-year CMO bonds at various prepayment speeds are compared. For comparison, a clean TAC with a 3.1-year average life has been constructed from the same collateral used to create the PAC-standard companion and PAC-TAC examples. The clean TAC has unnaturally exceptional call protection (it is protected by $360 million of companion bonds, which comprise the remainder of the structure). The smaller size of the clean TAC also results in its having a lower average life at very low prepayment speeds than the companion TAC does (the clean TAC is small enough for even small paydowns at low speeds to reduce its principal balance significantly in the early years).

The more important comparison, since so few clean TACs are issued at present, is with the 3-year companion from Exhibit 12–1. The companion TAC clearly provides meaningful call protection, requiring speeds in excess of 600% PSA before it shortens as much as the standard companion does at 300% PSA. The two bonds extend identically. This happens because they both have the same priority after the PACs to receive principal paydowns and no companions in front of them (the TAC would have priority over an earlier companion, which would protect it

E X H I B I T   12–6

Average Lives at Various Prepayment Speeds of 20-Year Companions from Different CMO Structures (Pricing Assumption 165% PSA)

Prepayment Speed (% PSA)	Average Life (years)		
	PAC Structure	PAC/TAC Structure	Layered PAC Structure
0	27.7	27.7	27.8
50	26.8	26.8	27.0
90	25.3	25.3	25.6
125	23.3	23.4	23.3
165	**20.3**	**20.3**	**18.2**
190	18.0	18.0	12.5
225	13.6	13.1	5.1
250	10.4	9.2	3.8
275	7.4	5.7	3.1
300	4.8	2.6	2.6
475	2.0	1.0	1.3
600	1.5	0.7	1.0

to a degree from extending, whereas the standard companion would wait until earlier companions were retired, which would cause it to extend).

Notice that at 300% PSA, the companion TAC's average life is about a month longer than at the pricing speed (rounding exaggerates the difference—at several more places of significance the difference is really about 0.08 year). This phenomenon occurs at relatively high speeds, since principal payments become more bunched in the early months and trail off more sharply in later months. Exhibit 12–4, as mentioned above, gives some indication of what is happening at this speed to the principal cash flows thrown off by the collateral. The paydowns become more "tailish" toward the end of the companion's schedule, forcing it to wait as excess payments are, going into the tail, not large enough to meet the schedule.

The other great difference between PAC-TAC structures and both clean TAC and PAC-standard companion structures is how much more volatile the unscheduled companions can be. The presence of additional risk-reduced structures forces the remaining companions to absorb more prepayment volatility. This is demonstrated in Exhibit 12–6, where various 20-year companion structures are compared. At prepayment speeds above 225% PSA, the companion in the PAC-TAC structure begins to shorten much more quickly than the standard companion.

REVERSE TACs

Payment rules and priorities also can be devised that protect a companion bond from extension risk while leaving it more exposed to call risk. These structures fittingly are termed "reverse TACs." Significant amounts of reverse TACs have been issued since the beginning of 1989, stimulated in part by the bearish sentiment prevalent during much of the first half of the year. These structures typically are created as 20-year companion classes. Their long lives make them natural candidates for this treatment, as they have not, in any case, more than six or maybe eight years to extend. Additionally, these structures are priced at significant discounts from par in order to benefit from increases in prepayments.

An example of a reverse TAC was created for this discussion by defining a payment schedule for the fourth tranche of the PAC-companion structure depicted in Exhibits 12–1, 12–2, and 12–3. A cash flow diagram for prepayments at 85% PSA is included in Exhibit 12–7. (At 165% PSA and faster speeds, the PAC-reverse TAC structure, as will be explained, pays exactly like the PAC-standard companion, which is depicted at 165% PSA in Exhibit 12–1 and 300% PSA in Exhibit 12–3.) The schedule was run at 165% PSA, the pricing speed in all these examples, and has priority after the scheduled PAC payments are made. The reverse TAC receives excess cash flow only after the 3- and 10-year companions are retired. These arrangements preserve the schedule at prepayment speeds slower than those used

E X H I B I T   12–7

PAC with Reverse TAC Bond, 85% PSA

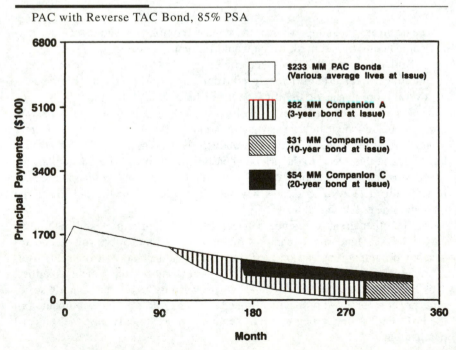

to generate the schedule, but not at faster speeds. The reverse TAC does not begin to extend until prepayments fall below a constant rate of about 70% PSA.

The average life volatility of the reverse TAC is compared to that of other 20-year companion structures in Exhibit 12–8. The reverse TAC in the example has an average life of 20.3 years; in the worst case, that of no prepayments, the bond's average life only extends to 24.5 years. By comparison, the last tranche of the simple structure extends to 27.7 years. The cash flow diagrams in Exhibits 12–3 and 12–7 make it clear why this is so. In the simple PAC-companion structure (Exhibit 12–3), at a speed equal to the upper collar, the companions pay down sequentially after the PAC bonds are retired. In the structure with the reverse TAC (Exhibit 12–7), the 3- and 10-year companions extend to permit the scheduled reverse TAC payments to be met. At 85% PSA, the lower PAC collar, the short- and intermediate-term companions pay simultaneously with the reverse TAC. At slower prepayment speeds, the average lives of both companions exceed that of the reverse TAC.

The reverse TAC imparts considerably more volatility to the other companions when prepayments slow, but it does not cause them to be more volatile in faster prepayment scenarios. This effect can also be seen by comparing the average lives of 3-year companions from both structures listed in Exhibit 12–9. This is a natural consequence of the one-sided protection afforded by targeted amortization structures.

E X H I B I T   12–8

Average Lives at Various Prepayment Speeds of 20-Year PAC Structures (Pricing Assumption 165% PSA)

Prepayment Speed (% PSA)	Average Life (years)		
	PAC Companion	Reverse TAC	Level II PAC
0	27.7	24.5	24.6
50	26.8	20.7	20.3
85	25.6	20.3	18.1
125	23.3	20.3	18.1
165	**20.3**	**20.3**	**18.1**
190	18.0	18.0	18.1
225	13.6	13.6	18.1
250	10.4	10.4	14.7
275	7.4	7.4	
300	4.8	4.8	5.8
350	3.3	3.3	3.7
475	2.0	2.0	2.2
600	1.5	1.5	1.6

EXHIBIT 12–9

Average Lives at Various Prepayment Speeds of 3-Year Companions from Different CMO PAC Structures (Pricing Assumption 165% PSA)

Prepayment Speed (% PSA)	Average Life (years)		
	PAC Structure	PAC/ Reverse TAC Structure	Layered PAC Structure
0	24.7	26.3	26.1
50	19.9	22.7	22.7
85	14.9	16.5	18.3
90	13.7	15.0	17.4
100	11.5	12.4	14.5
125	7.2	7.2	8.7
165	3.1	3.1	3.1
225	1.6	1.6	1.5
275	1.2	1.2	1.1
300	1.0	1.0	1.0
475	0.6	0.9	0.6
600	0.5	0.6	0.5

Schedules can also be applied to intermediate-term companion bonds to protect their average lives from extending in slow prepayment scenarios. At the same time, the structure is "protected" from call risk in moderately fast prepayment scenarios by taking advantage of the natural tendency of TACs to extend slightly as prepayments exceed the pricing speed. The resulting average life profile can be reasonably stable across a significant range of prepayment speeds (for example, extending no more than 2 or 3 years across a range from 50% or 75% PSA to 225% or 250% PSA, assuming a schedule run at 165% PSA). In effect, an intermediate-term companion TAC can be constructed to provide PAC-like stability. A number of such bonds have indeed been issued, some of them with monikers indicating that the payments are stabilized or controlled.

LAYERED PAC BONDS

The value of companion classes also can be enhanced by establishing secondary PAC schedules for a portion of the principal remaining after the primary PAC payments are met. A cash flow diagram for an example of a two-tiered PAC structure, run at a pricing speed of 165% PSA, is shown in Exhibit 12–10. This example uses the same collateral as the previous examples. The same collars—85% to 300% PSA—were used to create the same amount of primary or Level I PACs—$233.0 million of a total original balance of $400 million CMO bonds. Collars for the sec-

EXHIBIT   12–10

Layered PAC Structure, 165% PSA

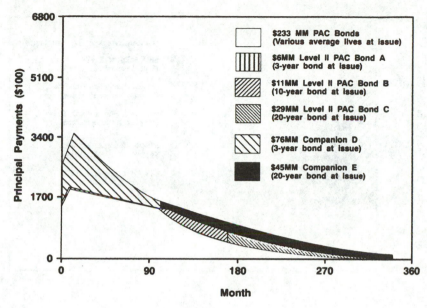

ond tier of PACs were set at 90% to 225% PSA. The second-tier PAC region was further divided into a series of nominally 10- and 20-year bonds and the companions into 3- and 20-year bonds. (In order to match the 3.1-year average lives in the previous examples, it was necessary to let the long-term bonds in the layered PAC example have average lives closer to 18 than to 20 years. This does not vitiate the comparison.) The Level II PACs appear in the figure as a narrow band between the PAC region and the companions: At 165% PSA they pay down simultaneously with the primary PACs in the deal. The size of the second tier of PACs is a function of the collars—the tighter the protection band, the larger the amount of PACs that can be created. In this example, protecting the Level II schedule up to 225% PSA limits the amount of 3-year Level II PACs that can be created to $5.6 million. In total, the second layer of PACs only amount to about 11% of the transaction (58.25% of the transaction is standard, Level I PACs).

The Level II PAC schedule remains intact until prepayment speeds break the primary PAC collars. For example, Exhibit 12–11 shows the principal payments at 300% PSA. At this speed, the primary PAC schedule is not violated, but payments to the Level II PACs are significantly accelerated, shortening to average lives of 2.5, 3.9, and 5.8 years, respectively. Similarly, when prepayments slow to a constant speed of 85% PSA, primary PAC payments are made on schedule, but the payments to Level II PACs are delayed. At 85% PSA, as shown in Exhibit 12–12, the companion PACs have average lives of 9.5, 11.3, and 18.1 years, respectively. As would be expected, the longer Level II PACs are more volatile on

EXHIBIT 12–11

Layered PAC Structure, 300% PSA

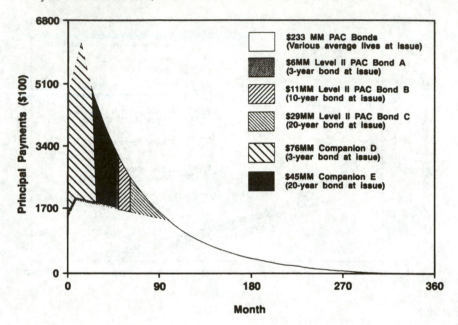

EXHIBIT 12–12

Layered PAC Structure, 85% PSA

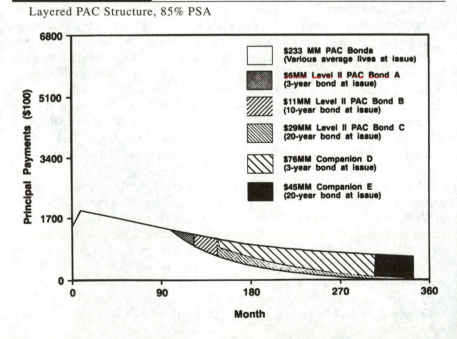

the upside, when prepayments accelerate, and the shorter PACs are more volatile on the downside, when prepayments decelerate. The 3- and 20-year bonds receive no principal until the Level II PACs are paid, extending their average lives to 18.3 years and 25.8 years, respectively.

The average life volatility of Level II PACs is compared to that of companion TACs and 3-year standard companions in Exhibit 12–8. Although not as well protected as primary PACs, Level II PACs do provide modest call protection and decent extension protection. Moreover, these examples demonstrate that they can shorten and extend less vigorously than their TAC and reverse-TAC counterparts when prepayments move outside the appropriate protective boundary. The companions of layered PACs are somewhat more volatile over moderate prepayment shifts. As the comparison in Exhibit 12–6 with a 20-year standard PAC companion and a reverse TAC suggests, the 20-year layered PAC companion shortens faster between 165% and about 250% PSA than either of its counterparts. Similarly, Exhibit 12–9 indicates that the 3-year layered PAC companion lengthens more abruptly than its counterparts at prepayment speeds between 165% and 50% PSA.[5]

CONCLUSION

The average life volatilities of the 3-year companion structures discussed in this chapter are summarized in Exhibit 12–13, as are those of the 20-year companions in Exhibit 12–14. The graphs make plain the differences in call and extension protection that can be provided by furnishing companion classes with TAC or PAC schedules. The Level II PACs have stable average life patterns between the upper and lower collar speeds. (A Level I PAC would have a similar pattern, only it would be stable over a wider range, say 75% to 300% PSA, and owing to the presence of the companions, would shorten or lengthen more moderately outside that range.) By comparison, the standard companions demonstrate steep and continuous changes in average life over the same ranges for which the Level II PACs are protected. The TACs, as would be expected, provide call protection, but no extension protection, while the reverse TACs are stable at slower speeds, but shorten abruptly when prepayments occur at faster constant rates than the prepayment assumption.

---

5. Readers are reminded that all these examples are highly simplified and furnish only a basic understanding of how the structures behave. Actual CMO issues frequently are more complex, containing other structures or variations on those discussed in this chapter. Additional complexity could result in behavior valuably different from that of these examples.

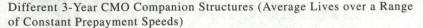

Different 3-Year CMO Companion Structures (Average Lives over a Range of Constant Prepayment Speeds)

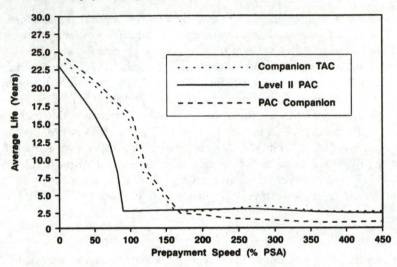

Note: The average lives of the Companion TAC and PAC Companion are the same between 0% and 165% PSA; the lines have been separated for readability.

Different 20-Year CMO Companion Structures (Average Lives over a Range of Constant Prepayment Speeds)

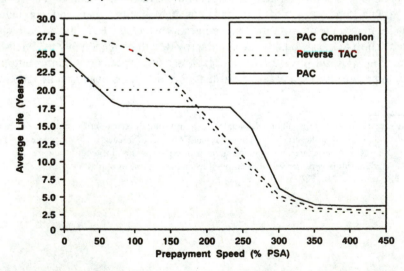

Note: The average lives of the PAC Companion and Reverse TAC are the same at prepayment speeds above 165% PSAs. The lines are separated for readability.

CHAPTER 13

INVERSE FLOATING-RATE CMOs

Errol Mustafa, Ph.D.

Cyrus Mohebbi, Ph.D.
Managing Director
Prudential Securities Inc.
and
Adjunct Professor
New York University

Inverse floating-rate securities are leveraged securities that offer investors a floating-rate coupon that periodically resets off one of several possible index types. In contrast to floating-rate CMOs, the coupon on an inverse floater changes by a specified multiple of the change in the index, decreasing when the index rises and increasing when the index falls. This unusual feature makes inverse floaters unique among mortgage securities. This chapter discusses the structure and investment characteristics of these securities.

STRUCTURAL FEATURES

The investment characteristics of an inverse floater are determined by the nature of the underlying collateral and the structural features associated with the bond (including its multiplier, coupon cap, floor, and index). The impact of the collateral type is primarily prepayment-related and is discussed in the next section. Structural features, however, are key to understanding how the coupon on the bond will respond to interest rate changes.

In typical real estate mortgage investment conduit (REMIC) structures, the cash flows associated with an inverse floater and the corresponding floater tranche each represent a divided interest in the cash flows of a fixed-rate bond. Thus an inverse-floater and floater combination can be structured by carving up the cash flows of what would otherwise be a fixed-rate planned amortization class (PAC), companion, targeted amortization class (TAC), or sequential-pay bond.

One of the simplest examples of a floater and inverse-floater combination is a structure in which the floater and inverse-floater tranches are structured from $100 million of premium fixed-rate collateral (e.g., 8%) and have identical face values (i.e., $50 million). Each tranche would receive the same principal cash flows but with interest allocated as follows: Holders of the floater receive a coupon of

---

Dr. Mustafa was Director of Mortgage Research in the Financial Strategies Group at Prudential Securities Inc. when this chapter was written.

1-month London interbank offered rate (LIBOR) + 65 basis points (bps) with a cap of 16%, whereas holders of the inverse floater receive a coupon given by the formula: 15.35 − 1-month LIBOR. Thus the average of the floater and the inverse-floater coupons is equal to 8% fixed. This simple structure illustrates the important point that the cap on the inverse floater (15.35% = 2 × 8.0% − 0.65%) depends on both the collateral coupon (8%) and the spread specified in the determination of the floater coupon (65 bps). In addition, the inverse-floater coupon in this example has a multiplier of 1.0 and is thus not leveraged. This is a consequence of the fact that the floater and inverse-floater tranches are equal in size. If the inverse-floater class was smaller than the floater class, the coupon multiplier would be greater than unity for the inverse floater.

The relationship between the coupons, caps, floors, and multiplier for an inverse floater and floater can be easily understood using the approach just discussed, that is, allocating "collateral" cash flows between the inverse floater and floater.

The coupon on the floater is usually expressed as a fixed spread S over a specified index subject to some specified cap:

$$\text{Floater coupon} = \text{Index} + S \qquad (13\text{--}1)$$

The inverse-floater's monthly interest cash flow depends on the total interest available from the collateral and the share allocated to the floater:

$$
\begin{aligned}
\text{Inverse-floater interest cash flow} = {} & \text{Collateral-interest cash flow} \\
& - \text{Floater-interest cash flow} \qquad (13\text{--}2)
\end{aligned}
$$

where the monthly cash flow from the fixed-rate collateral coupon C and the monthly cash flow allocated to the floater are

$$\text{Collateral-interest cash flow} = \text{Collateral face value} \times C\,/\,1{,}200 \qquad (13\text{--}3)$$
$$\text{Floater-interest cash flow} = \text{Floater face value} \times (\text{Index} + S)\,/\,1{,}200 \qquad (13\text{--}4)$$

The coupon on the inverse floater depends on the ratio of the inverse-floater's monthly interest cash flow and its face value:

$$\text{Inverse-floater coupon} = 1{,}200 \times \frac{\text{Inverse-floater interest cash flow}}{\text{Inverse-floater face value}} \qquad (13\text{--}5)$$

Equation (13–5) can be rewritten using Equations (13–1), (13–2), (13–3), and (13–4) to give the following expression for the inverse-floater coupon:

$$
\begin{aligned}
\text{Inverse-floater coupon} &= (C\,/\,\text{IFF}) - (\text{Index} + S) \times \frac{\text{Floater face value}}{\text{Inverse-floater face value}} \\
&= (C\,/\,\text{IFF}) - (\text{Index} + S) \times \text{Multiplier} \qquad (13\text{--}6)
\end{aligned}
$$

where

$$\text{IFF} = \text{Inverse-floater fraction} = \frac{\text{Inverse-floater face value}}{\text{Collateral face value}} \qquad (13\text{--}7)$$

It is apparent from Equation (13–6) that the coupon multiplier for an inverse floater is equal to the ratio of the face values of the inverse floater and floater classes:

$$\text{Multiplier} = \frac{\text{Floater face value}}{\text{Inverse-floater face value}} \qquad (13\text{--}8)$$

The cap on a floater's coupon depends on the coupon floor for the inverse floater and the collateral coupon. In a similar way, the floor on both the floater coupon and the inverse-floater cap are dependent on one another. The earlier example of an inverse floater with a multiplier equal to unity demonstrates that the coupon caps on both the floater and inverse floater can exceed the fixed-collateral coupon. In fact, the floater will always hit its cap when the inverse-floater coupon reaches its floor, and vice versa. This is a consequence of dividing an interest cash flow from fixed-coupon collateral between two securities with variable coupons that change in opposite directions. If, for example, it is assumed that the floater has a coupon floor equal to S, that is, index $= 0$ in equation (13–1), then from equation (13–6) it can be seen that the coupon cap on the inverse floater is

$$\text{Inverse-floater cap} = (C/\text{IFF}) - S \times \text{Multiplier} \qquad (13\text{–}9)$$

If it is assumed that the inverse floater has a coupon floor of zero, then, from equation (13–6), the coupon cap on the floater is

$$\text{Floater cap} = (C/\text{IFF}) \times (1/\text{multiplier})$$
$$= C/(1 - \text{IFF}) \qquad (13\text{–}10)$$

Exhibit 13–1 illustrates how coupon cap, multiplier, and inverse-floater coupon vary, depending on the relative sizes of the floater and inverse-floater classes. The exhibit is based on a 1-month LIBOR $100 million floater and inverse floater combination (structured from 7% fixed-rate collateral). For example, the most highly leveraged inverse floater ($10 million face value) has the highest multiplier (9.0) and the highest coupon cap (64.15%), but the associated floater has the lowest coupon cap (7.78%). As the leverage is decreased on the inverse floater, its multiplier and coupon cap also decrease, while the floater coupon cap increases. The least-leveraged inverse floater shown ($80 million face value) has a multiplier of only 0.25 and a coupon cap of 8.59%, but the accompanying floater has the highest coupon cap (35.0%) for any floater shown in the exhibit. As the multiplier on an inverse floater decreases, the bond's cash flows become more heavily weighted toward principal than interest; that is, the bond acquires the bullish characteristics of a PO.

INVESTMENT CHARACTERISTICS

The price behavior of an inverse floater in different interest rate environments is affected by changes in both the coupon, which is tied to a specific part of the yield curve, and in prepayments, which (for fixed-rate collateral) depend on long-term mortgage rates and the long end of the Treasury curve. In addition, the price sensitivity of an inverse floater to changes in prepayments is heavily influenced by how the bond is structured. Inverse floaters that reset off short-term rates, such as 1-month and 3-month LIBOR, are thus dependent on both the short end of the yield curve (coupon sensitivity) and the long end of the yield curve (prepayment sensitivity), whereas those that reset off long-term rates, such as the 10-year or 7-year constant maturity Treasury (CMT), depend only on intermediate- to long-term rates.

EXHIBIT 13–1

Inverse-Floater and Floater Coupon Features*

Floater Face Value ($ Million)	Inverse-Floater Face Value ($ Million)	Inverse-Floater Multiplier	Inverse-Floater Coupon (%)	Inverse-Floater Cap (%)	Floater Cap (%)
90	10	9.00	64.15—9.00 Index	64.15	7.78
80	20	4.00	32.40—4.00 Index	32.40	8.75
50	50	1.00	13.35—1.00 Index	13.35	14.00
40	60	0.67	11.23—0.67 Index	11.23	17.50
20	80	0.25	8.59—0.25 Index	8.59	35.00

*The floater coupon is assumed to be one-month LIBOR + 65.

To illustrate the price behavior of inverse floaters in different interest rate environments, let us consider two types of yield-curve shifts:

Type I   A steepening or flattening of the Treasury curve with the movement occurring in the short- and intermediate-part of the curve (i.e., long end unchanged). Price movements in this scenario isolate the sensitivity of the inverse floater to changes in short- and intermediate-term rates.

Type II   A similar steepening or flattening of the Treasury curve with movement occurring primarily in the long end of the curve (i.e., short-term rates unchanged). In this scenario, the bond's price sensitivity to long-term rates is shown.

Exhibit 13–2 illustrates the price and effective-duration sensitivities of a 1-month LIBOR inverse-floater companion bond, FHLMC 1993-1496 Class PA (FHL31496PA) and a 7-year CMT inverse-floater PAC bond, FHLMC 1992-1388 Class FB (FHL21388FB) across several Type I interest rate scenarios in which short-term rates vary while long term rates remain unchanged. Prices are calculated under the assumption of constant OAS across all scenarios.[1] Variations in prepayments for both bonds will be small because long-term mortgage rates are held constant across the scenarios considered.

It is also assumed in Exhibit 13–2 that the basis spread between LIBOR and Treasuries—Treasury-Eurodollar (TED) spread—is fixed. For FHL31496PA, the 1-month LIBOR bond, this implies that the coupon varies from 18.14% (for a 200-bp downward shift in LIBOR) to 0.0% (for a 578-bp upward shift in LIBOR). As the change in the 7-year CMT across the same scenarios is only 80 bps, the coupon on FHL21388FB varies between 10.42% (7-year CMT unchanged) and 8.76% (an 80-bp upward shift in the 7-year CMT). Given the greater variation in coupon for FHL31496PA, one would expect more price variation in this bond than FHL21388FB across the interest rate scenarios shown—and this is indeed the case. The 1-month LIBOR bond performs much better in a decreasing short-rate environment (i.e., yield curve steepening) than in a rising one.

Effective duration, a measure of price sensitivity to interest rate changes, is almost always positive for an inverse floater. Floaters typically have small positive durations, thus much of the price volatility of the underlying collateral is therefore transferred to the accompanying inverse floater. The second graph in Exhibit 13–2 shows that the effective duration for FHL31496PA decreases as short-term rates increase, since the coupon on this bond is further from hitting its cap as short-term rates increase. The variation in effective duration for FHL21388FB is, by comparison, more stable across the interest rate scenarios considered. This is a reflection of the fact that the variation in the coupon on this bond, which depends on changes in the 7-year CMT rate, is much smaller than the coupon variation of the LIBOR companion bond.

---

1. It should be noted that for extreme flattening or steepening of the yield curve, the constant-OAS assumption used for pricing is, at best, only an approximation.

EXHIBIT 13–2

Price and Effective Duration for FHL31496PA and FHL21388FB Across Different Type I Short-Term-Rate Scenarios

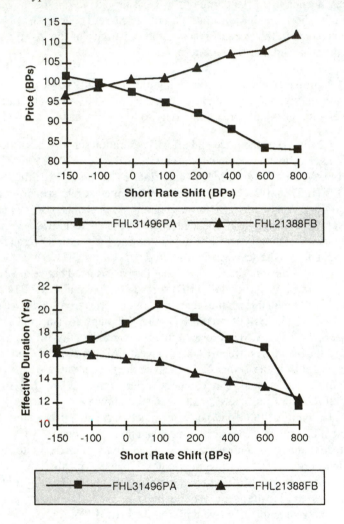

Exhibit 13–3 illustrates the price and effective-duration sensitivities of the same inverse floaters across several Type II interest rate scenarios (long-term rates vary while short-term rates remain unchanged). Prices are again calculated under the assumption of a constant option-adjusted spread (OAS) and fixed-TED spread (for FHL31496PA) across all scenarios. Variations in prepayments for the collateral underlying both bonds is largely dependent on changes in mortgage rates, which range from 4.21% (a 300-bp downward shift in the 10-year Treasury yield) to 10.21% (a 300-bp upward shift in the 10-year Treasury yield).

E X H I B I T   13–3

Price and Effective Duration for FHL31496PA and FHL21388FB Across Different Type II Long-Term-Rate Scenarios

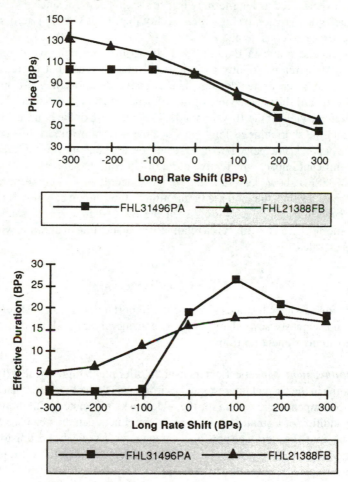

For FHL31496PA, the coupon is 13.48% in each scenario as short-term rates (including 1-month LIBOR) are unchanged across all interest rate scenarios shown. Thus the variation in price for this bond is very similar to that shown for a fixed-rate companion bond structured off the same collateral (FHLMC 7.0% pass-throughs): The average life of the bond lengthens significantly in the rising-rate (yield curve steepening) scenarios and shortens in the lower-rate (yield curve flattening) scenarios. Price appreciation of the bond is limited in the lower-rate scenarios because of the strong negative convexity associated with the acceleration in prepayments as rates decline. (In fact the bond's price begins to decline if rates fall too far). In a rising-rate scenario, the bond price declines, as would be expected for a positive-duration security. FHL21388FB, however, performs better in a lower-rate environment than in a higher one primarily because of the coupon appreciation experienced as long-term rates decline. In addition, since this bond is a PAC, it has much greater average life stability than FHL31496PA across the interest rate scenarios considered.

The second graph in Exhibit 13–3 shows that the effective duration for FHL31496PA increases slightly as long-term rates increase but decreases substantially as long-term rates decline. The effective duration ranges from 0.7 (a 200-bp downward shift in the yield of the 10-year Treasury) to 26.5 (a 100-bp upward shift in the yield of the 10-year bond). The extension of the bond as long rates increase and the shortening as long rates decline is responsible for this behavior. Since the coupon is unchanged in these scenarios, the coupon cap and floor do not have a significant impact on effective duration. In contrast, the effective duration for FHL21388FB shows less variation, but still decreases as long-term rates decline. As rates decline, the increase in duration as the coupon cap moves closer to at-the-money (or in-the-money) is offset by the decrease in duration that occurs as the bond shortens. The net effect is a relatively small decline in duration with long-term interest rates.

CONCLUSION

The above discussion illustrates some of the important characteristics of inverse floaters and suggests several reasons for considering the addition of inverse floaters to an investment portfolio:

Yield Enhancement   Inverse floaters usually offer much higher yields (typically double digits in the current interest rate environment) than other less volatile MBS in order to compensate investors for the added risks associated with these securities. The addition of a small inverse-floater component can thus be used to boost the current yield of a mortgage portfolio. Fund managers may be willing to assume the additional price risk for the inverse floater if they feel that the yield pickup is sufficient compensation for this risk.

Interest Rate Play   Inverse floaters afford the investor with a firm opinion on the direction of interest rates an opportunity to make a leveraged investment based on that opinion. For example, an investor who believes long-term interest rates may decrease while short-term rates will remain stable or rise slightly may wish to consider the purchase of either of the two inverse floaters considered in Exhibit 13–1 or a deep-discount low-multiplier inverse floater that would benefit from an increase in prepayments. An investor with almost the opposite view on interest rates, that is, one who believes that long-term rates may rise while short-term rates will continue to decline, should consider a LIBOR-based inverse IO, which has the characteristics of an IO,[2] but a coupon that increases as LIBOR and other short-term rates decrease. The holder of an inverse IO would benefit both from the decline in prepayments as long-term rates rise and from a high coupon should short-term rates fall further or remain stable.

Floating-Rate Portfolio Hedge   An inverse floater whose coupon is tied a short-term rate, such as a 1-month LIBOR, may be used to hedge some of the interest rate risk of a portfolio of LIBOR floaters, for example. In particular, the dition of inverse floaters to such a portfolio might be used to lengthen duration at the same time, lower the sensitivity of the portfolio to changes in short-term rai This would be an appropriate strategy if the portfolio manager wished to better p sition the portfolio for an anticipated decline in both long- and short-term rates.

---

2. For a discussion of the investment characteristics of IO SMBS, see *Stripped Mortgage-Backed Se curities,* Lakhbir Hayre, Errol Mustafa, Financial Strategies Group, Prudential Securities In corporated, July 1990.

CREDIT-SENSITIVE MORTGAGE-BACKED SECURITIES

CHAPTER 14

NONAGENCY CMOs

Frank J. Fabozzi, Ph.D., CFA
Adjunct Professor of Finance
School of Management
Yale University

Anthony B. Sanders, Ph.D.
Professor of Finance and Galbreath Distinguished Scholar
The Ohio State University

David Yuen, CFA
Portfolio Strategist/Risk Manager
Franklin Templeton Investments

Chuck Ramsey
CEO
Mortgage Risk Assessment Corp.

All the cash flow structures found in agency CMOs are also applicable to non-agency or whole-loan CMO structures. The major additional element in structuring nonagency CMOs is credit enhancement. The investor in a nonagency or whole-loan CMO is exposed to both prepayment risk and credit risk. Other elements include compensating interest payments, weighted average coupon dispersions, and cleanup call provisions. In this chapter, we discuss various credit enhancement structures, compensating interest payments, cleanup call provisions, and the impact of coupon dispersions. In addition, we discuss the PSA standard default assumption benchmark and whole-loan prepayment behavior.

CREDIT ENHANCEMENTS

Three nationally recognized statistical rating organizations rate nonagency CMOs: Standard & Poor's Corporation, Moody's Investors Service, and Fitch. The primary factors these rating organizations consider in assigning a rating are the type of property (single-family residences, condominiums), the type of loan (fixed-rate level payment, adjustable rate, balloon), the term of the loans, the geographical dispersion of the loans, the loan size (conforming loans, jumbo loans), the amount of seasoning of the loan, and the purpose of the loan (purchase or refinancing). Typically, a double-A or triple-A rating is sought for the most senior tranche. The amount of credit enhancement necessary depends on rating agency requirements.

There are two general types of credit enhancement structures: external and internal. We describe each type below.

External Credit Enhancements

External credit enhancements come in the form of third-party guarantees that provide for first-loss protection against losses up to a specified level, for example, 10%. The most common forms of external enhancements are (1) a corporate guarantee, (2) a letter of credit, (3) pool insurance, and (4) bond insurance.

Pool insurance policies cover losses resulting from defaults and foreclosures. Policies are typically written for a dollar amount of coverage that continues in force throughout the life of the pool. However, some policies are written so that the dollar amount of coverage declines as the pool seasons as long as two conditions are met: (1) the credit performance is better than expected, and (2) the rating agencies that rated the issue approve. The three major providers of pool insurance are GEMICO, PMI Mortgage Insurance Corp., and United Guarantee Insurance. Since only defaults and foreclosures are covered, additional insurance must be obtained to cover losses resulting from bankruptcy (i.e., court-mandated modification of mortgage debt), fraud arising in the origination process, and special hazards (i.e., losses resulting from events not covered by a standard homeowner's insurance policy).

Bond insurance provides the same function as in municipal bond structures. The major insurers are FGIC, AMBAC, and MBIA. Typically, bond insurance is not used as primary protection, but to supplement other forms of credit enhancement.

A CMO issue with external credit support is subject to the credit risk of the third-party guarantor. Should the third-party guarantor be downgraded, the CMO issue itself could be subject to downgrade even if the structure is performing as expected. For example, in the early 1990s, mortgage-backed securities issued by Citibank Mortgage Securities Inc. were downgraded when Citibank, the third-party guarantor, was downgraded. This is the chief disadvantage of third-party guarantees. Therefore, it is imperative that investors perform credit analysis on both the collateral (the loans) and the third-party guarantor.

External credit enhancements do not materially alter the cash flow characteristics of a CMO structure except in the form of prepayment. In case of a default resulting in net losses within the guarantee level, investors will receive the principal amount as if a prepayment has occurred. If the net losses exceed the guarantee level, investors will have a shortfall in the cash flow.

Internal Credit Enhancements

Internal credit enhancements come in more complicated forms than external credit enhancements and may alter the cash flow characteristics of the loans even in the absence of defaults. The most common forms of internal credit enhancements are reserve funds (cash reserve funds or excess servicing spread accounts), overcollateralization, and senior-subordinated structures.

Reserve Funds

Reserve funds come in two forms, cash reserve funds and excess servicing spread accounts. Cash reserve funds are straight deposits of cash generated from issuance proceeds. In this case, part of the underwriting profits from the deal are deposited into a hypothecated fund which typically invests in money market instruments. Cash reserve funds are typically used in conjunction with letters of credit or other kinds of external credit enhancements. For example, a CMO may have 10% credit support, 9% of which is provided by a letter of credit and 1% from a cash reserve fund.

Excess-servicing spread accounts involve the allocation of excess spread or cash into a separate reserve account after paying out the net coupon, servicing fee, and all other expenses on a monthly basis. For example, suppose that the gross weighted average coupon (gross WAC) is 7.75%, the servicing and other fees is 0.25%, and the net weighted average coupon (net WAC) is 7.25%. This means that there is excess servicing of 0.25%. The amount in the reserve account will gradually increase and can be used to pay for possible future losses.

The excess spread is analogous to the guarantee fee paid to an agency, except that this is a form of self-insurance. This form of credit enhancement relies on the assumption that defaults occur infrequently in the initial stages of the loans but gradually increase in the following two to five years. This assumption is consistent with the PSA's Standard Default Assumption (SDA) curve that we describe later in the chapter.

Senior-Subordinated Structure

The most widely used internal credit support structure is the senior-subordinated structure. The subordinated class is the first-loss piece absorbing all losses on the underlying collateral, thus protecting the senior class. For example, a $100 million deal can be divided into two classes: a $92.25 million senior class and a $7.75 million subordinated class. The subordination level in this hypothetical structure is 7.75%. The subordinated class will absorb all losses up to $7.75 million, and the senior class will start to experience losses thereafter. So, if there is $5 million in losses, the subordinated class will realize this loss. Thus, it would realize a 64.5% loss ($5/$7.75). If, instead, there is $10 million in losses, the subordinated class will experience $7.75 million of losses or a 100% loss, and the senior class will experience a loss of $2.25 million ($10 million minus $7.75 million) or a 2.4% loss ($2.25/$92.25). Exhibit 14–1 is a loss severity table showing various percentage losses in principal on both senior and subordinated classes at different loss levels.

The subordinated class holder would obviously require a yield premium to take on the greater default risk exposure relative to the senior class. This setup is another form of self-insurance wherein the senior class holder is giving up yield spread to the subordinated class holder. This form of credit enhancement does not affect cash flow characteristics of the senior class except in the form of prepayment. To the extent that losses are within the subordination level, the senior class holder will receive principal as if a prepayment has occurred. Exhibit 14–2 shows

EXHIBIT 14-1

Loss Severity Table: $100 Million Deal, 7.75% Subordination

Loss Amount (millions)	Senior Class	Subordinated Class
$5.00	0.00%	64.50%
$7.75	0.00%	100.00%
$10.00	2.40%	100.00%
$20.00	13.30%	100.00%

EXHIBIT 14-2

Example of a Shifting Interest Structure

Months	Percentages of Prepayments Directed to Senior Class
1–60	100
61–72	70
73–84	60
85–96	40
97–108	20
109+	pro rata

the average life of both classes at 165 PSA before any default assumption for a hypothetical $100 million structure with a 7.75% subordination level.

Almost all existing senior-subordinated structures incorporate a shifting interest structure. A shifting interest structure redirects prepayments disproportionally from the subordinated class to the senior class according to a specified schedule. An example of such a schedule is shown in Exhibit 14-2.

The rationale for the shifting interest structure is to have enough insurance outstanding to cover future losses. Because of the shifting interest structure, the subordination amount may actually grow in time, especially in a low default and fast prepayment environment. This is sometimes referred to as "riding up the credit curve."

Using the same example of our previous $100 million deal with 7.75% initial subordination and assuming a cumulative principal paydown of $16 million ($6 million of regular repayments and $10 million of prepayments) by year 5 and no losses, the subordination will actually increase to 9.5%. The subordinated class principal balance will be reduced by the pro rata share of regular repayments (7.75% of $6 million) and none of the prepayments to $7.29 million. The senior class principal balance will be reduced by the pro rata share of regular repayments (92.25% of $6 million) and all of the $10 million prepayments to $76.71. The new subordination level will increase to 9.5% ($7.29/$76.71). Exhibit 14-3 shows the

EXHIBIT 14–3

Subordination Level: $100-Million Deal, 7.75% Subordination, 5 Years Out
(in millions)

Regular Paydown	Prepayment	Loss	Size of Senior Class	Size of Sub. Class	Sub. Level
$6	$10	$0	$76.71	$7.29	9.50%
$6	$20	$0	$66.71	$7.29	10.93%
$6	$40	$0	$46.71	$7.29	15.61%
$6	$10	$2	$76.71	$5.29	6.90%
$6	$20	$2	$66.71	$5.29	7.93%
$6	$40	$2	$46.71	$5.29	11.33%
$6	$10	$5	$76.71	$2.29	2.99%
$6	$20	$5	$66.71	$2.29	3.43%
$6	$40	$5	$46.71	$2.29	4.90%

EXHIBIT 14–4

Average Life for Senior-Subordinated Structure Assuming
No Defaults and 165 PSA

Structure Gross WAC New WAC WAM (months)	8.13% 7.50% 357	Average Life
No shifting interest		
Senior class	92.25%	8.77
Subordinate class	7.75%	8.77
With shifting interest		
Senior class	92.25%	8.41
Subordinate class	7.75%	13.11
With shifting interest		
Senior class	84.50%	7.98
Subordinate class	15.50%	13.11

new subordination levels, given various combinations of prepayments and losses. Holding net loss at zero, the faster the prepayments, the higher the subordination grows. Even in the case of losses, fast prepayments can sometimes offset the effect of principal losses to maintain the initial subordination.

Although the shifting interest structure is beneficial to the senior class holder from a credit standpoint, it does alter the cash flow characteristics of the senior class even in the absence of defaults. As Exhibit 14–4 indicates, a 7.75% subordination with the shifting interest structure will shorten the average life of the senior class to 8.41 years at the same 165 PSA, assuming no defaults. The size of the subordination also matters. A larger subordinated class redirects a higher proportion of prepayments to the senior class, thereby shortening the average life even further. A 15.5% subordination in the same example shortens the average life to 7.98.

It may be counterintuitive that the size of the subordination should affect the average life and cash flow of the senior class more than the credit quality. This is because the size of the subordination is already factored into the rating. The rating agency typically requires more subordination for lower-credit-quality loans to obtain a triple-A rating and less subordination for better-credit-quality loans. From a credit standpoint, the investor may be indifferent between a 5% subordination on a package of good-quality loans and a 10% subordination on a package of lower-quality loans as long as the rating agency gives them the same rating. However, the quality of the underlying loans will determine the default rate and therefore the timing of the cash flow.

COMPENSATING INTEREST

An additional factor to consider, which is unique to nonagency CMO structures, is compensating interest. Mortgage pass-throughs and CMOs pay principal and interest on a monthly basis (with the exception of some early quarterly-pay CMOs), and principal paydown factors are also calculated only once a month. Although homeowners may prepay their mortgage on any day throughout the month, the agencies guarantee and pay investors a full month of interest as if all the prepayments occur on the last day of the month. Unfortunately, this guarantee does not apply to whole-loan mortgages and, consequently, not to nonagency CMOs. If a homeowner pays off a mortgage on the 10th day of the month, he or she will stop paying interest for the rest of the month. Because of the payment delay (for example, 25 days) and the once-a-month calculation of principal paydown, the investor will receive full principal but only 10 days of interest on the 25th of the following month.

This phenomenon is known as payment *interest shortfall* or *compensating interest* and is handled differently by different issuers and services. Some issuers will only pay up to a specified amount, and some will not pay at all. The economic value of compensating interest depends on the level of prepayment and the types of CMO tranches. Generally, the faster the prepayment and the higher the coupon tranche, the higher the economic value of compensating interest.

WEIGHTED AVERAGE COUPON DISPERSION

The pooling standard on whole loans is looser than that on agency deals. Therefore, most nonagency CMOs have wider gross coupon and maturity dispersions given any WAC and WAM. Although the agency would strip off variable amounts of servicing and guarantee fees to bring the net coupon of a pool down to 50-bp increments, whole loans have fixed servicing fees, and the net coupons can vary. Using Exhibits 14–5 and 14–6 as examples, an agency CMO may contain four pools with gross coupons of 8.7%, 8.6%, 8.5%, and 8.4% to yield a GWAC of 8.55%. Seventy

EXHIBIT 14–5

Agency CMO

Pools	GWAC	Net Coupon	IO-ette (bps)	Stripped-Down Coupon
1	8.70%	8.00%	100	7.00%
2	8.60%	8.00%	100	7.00%
3	8.50%	8.00%	100	7.00%
4	8.40%	8.00%	100	7.00%
Average	8.55%	8.00%	100	7.00%

EXHIBIT 14–6

Nonagency CMO

Pools	GWAC	Servicing (bps)	Net Coupon	WAC IO (bps)	Stripped-Down Coupon
1	8.70%	55	8.15%	115	7.00%
2	8.60%	55	8.05%	105	7.00%
3	8.50%	55	7.95%	95	7.00%
4	8.40%	55	7.85%	85	7.00%
Average	8.55%	55	8.00%	100	7.00%

bps are stripped off the first pool to yield an 8% net coupon. Sixty bps will be stripped off the second pool to also yield an 8% coupon. Fifty bps and forty bps will be stripped off the third and fourth of the fourth pools, respectively. Since all the pools have net coupons of 8%, the weighted average net coupon is also 8%. Conversely, a whole-loan CMO containing four pools with the exact GWACs will have a constant servicing fee of 55 bps. The net coupons on these four pools will then be 8.15%, 8.05%, 7.95%, and 7.85% to yield the same weighted average net coupon of 8%.

To create fixed-rate (e.g., 7% coupon) tranches from the whole-loan CMO regardless of which pool prepays, a weighted average coupon interest-only (WAC IO) tranche must be created to absorb the variability of net coupons on the underlying pools. The WAC IO tranche will receive a weighted average coupon of 100 bps off the whole deal. The WAC IO is equivalent in structure to an IO strip or IO-ette in an agency deal. However, as soon as prepayments start to occur, the WAC IO strip may change. Hypothetically and intuitively, Pools 1 and 2, with the higher WACs, prepay first. Exhibit 14–7 shows that this will leave the WAC IO strip with only 90 bps of coupon, one-tenth less in cash flow going forward. This is extremely important in the analysis of WAC IO since nonagency CMOs tend to have wider WAC dispersion.

Nonagency CMO After Paydown

Pools	GWAC	Servicing (bps)	Net Coupon	WAC IO (bps)	Stripped-Down Coupon
3	8.50%	55	7.95%	95	7.00%
4	8.40%	55	7.85%	85	7.00%
Average	8.45%	55	7.90%	90	7.00%

CLEANUP CALL PROVISIONS

All nonagency CMO structures are issued with a "cleanup" call provision. The cleanup call provides the servicers or the residual holders (typically the issuers) the right, but not the obligation, to call back all the outstanding tranches of the CMO structure when the CMO balance is paid down to a certain percentage of the original principal balance. The servicers typically find it more costly than the servicing fee to service the CMO when the balance is paid down to a small amount. For example, suppose a $100 million CMO was originally issued with a 10% cleanup call. When the entire CMO balance is paid down to $10 million or less, the servicer can exercise the call to pay off all outstanding tranches like a balloon payment, regardless of the percentage balance of the individual tranches.

The call provision, when exercised, shortens the principal payment window and the average life of the back-end tranches of a CMO. This provision is not unique to nonagency CMO structures. It is mandatory, however, for all nonagency CMO structures, whereas agency CMOs may or may not have cleanup calls. Typically, FHLMC CMOs have 1% cleanup calls, and FNMA CMOs do not have cleanup calls.

ASSESSING PREPAYMENT RATES OF NONAGENCY CMOs

Prepayments speeds on nonagency CMOs vary from very sensitive to interest rate changes to independent of interest rates changes. Whole-loan CMOs, such as the Residential Funding Mortgage Securities (RFMSI) 1997-S5, are very sensitive to interest rate changes (see Exhibit 14–8). Home equity loans (such as The Money Store Home Equity Trust 1996-D) tend to be less sensitive to interest rate changes. Shared appreciation mortgage deals (in the United Kingdom) appear to be independent of interest rate changes. Hence, it is impossible to make a blanket statement regarding nonagency CMO prepayment speeds.

To highlight the differences across nonagency CMOs in terms of prepayments, we begin with whole loans. As an example, we use the Residential Fund-

E X H I B I T   14–8

Prepayment Seasoning Curve for Whole Loans

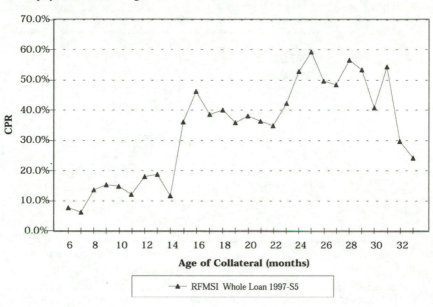

Age of Collateral (months)

RFMSI Whole Loan 1997-S5

Source: Bloomberg Financial.

ing RFMSI 1997-S5 deal (see Exhibit 14–8). Like agency mortgages, whole loans exhibit the same seasonality traits (as can be seen by the seasonal spikes at the beginning of the seasoning curve). After the initial ramp-up occurs, the whole loans are quite sensitive to interest rate changes. After 15 months of loan seasoning, a decline in interest rates sent the CPR from 11% to 37% which lead to a dramatic change in CMO prices.

In contrast to the RFMSI 1997-S5 deal, the home equity loan deal (TMSHE 1996-D) has a considerably different prepayment seasoning curve. The prepayments begin at significantly higher levels and do not exhibit the sensitivity to interest rate changes that the whole loans exhibit. The WAC on the RFMSI 1997-S5 deal is 8.16%, which contracts sharply with the 11.75% WAC on the TMSHE 1996-D home equity loan deal. The weighted average LTV for both the whole-loan and home equity loan deals are approximately the same.

The third deal presented in Exhibit 14–9 is the FirstPlus Financial 125 LTV 97-1. As the name implies, this home equity loan product allows the household to borrow up to 125% of the appraised value of the dwelling. An attractive feature of the 125 LTV loan product is that prepayment speeds should be lower than prepayment speeds on other home equity loans and nonconforming whole loans. One of the reasons for the lower prepayment speeds on the 125 LTV loan is the degree

EXHIBIT 14–9

Prepayment Seasoning Curves for Whole Loans, Home Equity Loans, and
125 LTV Loans

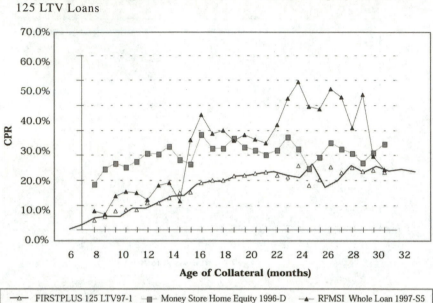

—△— FIRSTPLUS 125 LTV97-1	—■— Money Store Home Equity 1996-D —▲— RFMSI Whole Loan 1997-S5

Source: Bloomberg Financial.

of prepayment protection. Most of the 125 LTV loans have significant prepayments associated with them.

The prepayment speeds on the Residential Funding whole loan portfolio approaches 60% CPR after 2 years. (The dramatic increase in the prepayment speed on the whole loans in month 14 was a sudden decline in mortgage rates.) The Money Store home equity loan portfolio is in the 30% to 40% CPR range after 2 years, whereas the FirstPlus 125 LTV loan portfolio has settled in the low 20% CPR range. Although the historical prepayment speeds on the 125 LTV portfolio are higher than the 14% that some analysts expect after 2 years, the speeds are considerably lower than those of whole loans and traditional home equity loans.

Credit Risk on Alternative Loan Products

As pointed out in the previous section, the 125 LTV loan portfolios have a lower prepayment speed than whole loans and other lower LTV home equity loan products. We would expect that high LTV loan-backed transactions would have the highest default rates and that standard "A-quality" jumbo MBS would have the lowest. Unfortunately, default data are somewhat difficult to obtain for these products; however, we can use historical 90-day delinquencies as a proxy for default.

E X H I B I T   14–10

90-day Delinquencies for Whole Loans, Home Equity Loans, and 125 LTV Loans

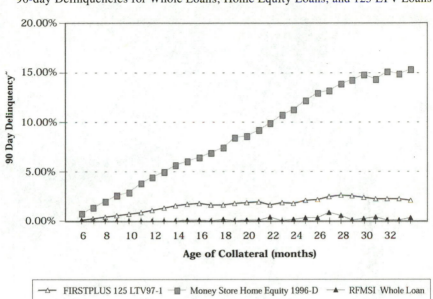

Source: Bloomberg Financial.

In Exhibit 14–10, we compare the historical 90-day delinquencies on whole loans, lower LTV home equity loans, and 125 LTV loans. As expected, the A-quality jumbo delinquencies are very low. What is somewhat surprising is that the lower LTV home equity loans from The Money Store have almost a linear growth in delinquencies that reach 12% after 2 years. The FirstPlus 125 LTV loans have a 90-day delinquency rate that is increasing with time as well; however, it is just above 2% of the portfolio after 2 years, which is substantially lower than the Money Store's experience. This appears to support the wisdom of lending larger amounts to high-quality borrowers, and points out the risks in lending even small amounts at lower LTVs to lesser-quality ones.

PSA STANDARD DEFAULT ASSUMPTION BENCHMARK

With the increase in nonagency CMO issuance, the Public Securities Association introduced a standardized benchmark for default rates. The PSA standard default assumption (SDA) benchmark gives the annual default rate for a mortgage pool as a function of the seasoning of the mortgages. An example of the PSA SDA benchmark, or 100 SDA, is as follows.

1. The default rate in month 1 is 0.02% and increases by 0.02% up to month 30, so that in month 30 the default rate is 0.60%.

EXHIBIT 14–11

PSA Standard Default Assumption Benchmark (100 SDA)

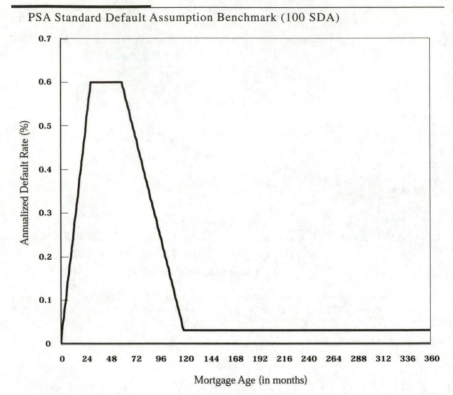

Mortgage Age (in months)

2. From month 30 to month 60, the default rate remains at 0.60%.

3. From month 61 to month 120, the default rate declines linearly from 0.60% to 0.03%.

4. From month 120 on, the default rate remains constant at 0.03%.

This pattern is illustrated in Exhibit 14–11.

As with the PSA prepayment benchmark, multiples of the benchmark are found by multiplying the default rate by the assumed multiple. For example, 200 SDA means the following pattern:

• The default rate in month 1 is 0.04% and increases by 0.04% up to month 30, so that in month 30 the default rate is 1.20%.

• From month 30 to month 60, the default rate remains at 1.20%.

• From month 61 to month 120, the default rate declines from 1.20% to 0.06%.

• From month 120 on, the default rate remains constant at 0.06%.

A zero SDA means that no defaults are assumed.

E X H I B I T   14–12

Historical Foreclosure on REFMSI 1997-S5 Deal

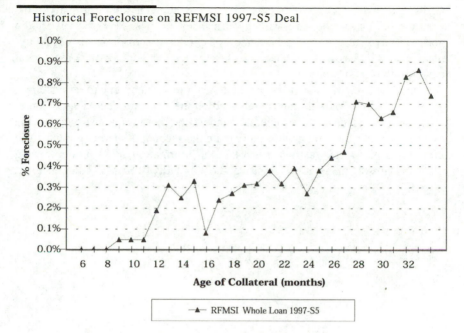

The foreclosure experience for the RFMSI 1997-S5 deal is presented in Exhibit 14–12. As with the PSA SDA standard in Exhibit 14–10, the foreclosure experience for the RFMSI 1997-S5 deal shows a positive ramping from month 8 out to month 33. The SDA speed for this deal is faster than the 100 SDA, with foreclosure rates reaching almost 0.9% in month 32 (while the 100 SDA peaks at 0.6% in month 31). According to history, the foreclosure rate for RFMSI 1997-S5 should flatten out for 30 months and then decline to 0.03% after ten years of total aging.

PREPAYMENT AND DEFAULT RESISTANT MORTGAGES

Thus far, we have examined whole loans, home equity loans, and 125 LTV loans. Each of these mortgages has a different sensitivity for prepayment rate and default. The whole loans are very sensitive to interest rate changes, whereas the home equity loans have the greatest sensitivity to 90-day delinquency risk.

An interesting alternative to these loan products is the shared appreciation mortgage (SAM), which has been issued in the United Kingdom for several years. The UK SAM (originated primarily by Bank of Scotland) has some interesting features that make it resistant to both prepayment and default. To begin with, the UK SAM is usually made to households that are free and clear on their property (or have a substantial equity cushion). For example, consider a household with a dwelling that is currently appraised at $200,000 and has no mortgage outstanding.

The lending institution will give the borrower $50,000 today in exchange for the borrower repaying the $50,000, plus 75% of any appreciation in property value when the borrower sells the dwelling, refinances, or dies. There is no periodic mortgage payment due, so the likelihood of default is zero. In terms of prepayment, there is little risk of refinancing risk (although the likelihood of prepayment due to death is not trivial).

Despite being resistant to both default and prepayment (due to refinancing), very few CMOs or pass-throughs are based on the SAM product. This is somewhat surprising given that consumer demand for the SAM is quite strong. It is the investment banks that are unwilling to create the secondary market product. The primary reason for this resistance is a lack of information about future housing prices. As housing price indices improve, the popularity of SAMs should increase as well.

CHAPTER 15

SECURITIES BACKED BY CLOSED-END HOME EQUITY LOANS

R. Russell Hurst
Director
First Union Securities, Inc.

This chapter provides investors with an understanding of the U.S. home equity loan (HEL) securitization market and the tools that an investor will need to identify and understand the investment opportunities in the HEL market. To gain a firm understanding of HEL asset-backed securities (ABS), an investor must know the fundamental characteristics of the loans, the structure and its characteristics that may affect the credit protection of the security purchased, the credit standing and economic motive of all parties to a transaction, and the legal concepts used to achieve bankruptcy remoteness and sale treatment by the seller-originator.

WHAT IS THE U.S. HOME EQUITY LOAN TODAY?

In the early 1990s, HEL referred to a traditional second lien mortgage with the proceeds primarily used for home improvement, college education, or debt consolidation. Although second mortgage HELs are still originated, more than 95% of the current nonprime HEL product described above is a first lien mortgage product. A simple but important distinction between HEL mortgage products and other similar securitized nonprime nonconforming mortgage products is that the proceeds from an HEL mortgage are not used to purchase a new home but to refinance an existing mortgage. The payment behavior of nonprime purchase money mortgages and home improvement loans (HILs) differ from HELs primarily due to the circumstances of the borrowers. The proceeds of an HEL loan may be used in part to finance home improvements but most likely will not be used in its entirety for

---

This chapter is reprinted with permission from Frank J. Fabozzi (ed.), *Investing in Asset-Backed Securities* (New Hope, PA: Frank J. Fabozzi Associates, 2000).

that purpose. The prepayment behavior of HELs is closely related to the characteristics of the borrower. HELs are typically used to

- Consolidate consumer debt in a lower-rate, tax-deductible form
- Monetize equity in the home
- Reduce a homeowner's monthly mortgage payment by extending the loan's term
- Finance home improvements
- Finance temporary liquidity needs such as for education or medical expenses

The traditional second mortgage is still included in the HEL category, but HELs now commonly refer to first lien mortgages to borrowers with some combination of impaired credit history and/or debt-to-income ratios that exceed agency guidelines. These borrowers are commonly referred to as *nonprime* or *B* and *C borrowers*. The originators of HELs use proprietary credit scoring techniques to grade each borrower on their ability to repay debt with letter gradations from A to D. The criteria vary by company, and each company has made some disclosure of the characteristics of each class of borrower. The nuances of underwriting standards among home equity lenders is useful when trying to differentiate the quality of one pool of collateral from another. The underwriting guidelines by credit class of borrower in Exhibit 15–1 are fairly representative of the collateral in the market.

As the credit profile of the borrower becomes increasingly risky or complex, a greater reliance is placed on the equity in the property mortgaged. This equity improves the chances of fully recovering the full principal value of the loan in foreclosure as well as the foreclosure costs including lost interest. An incrementally higher rate is also charged to financially weaker borrowers, which helps ensure a higher return on a portfolio of nonprime HELs.

The U.S. economy has enjoyed six consecutive years of low inflation, low interest rates and sustained growth, all of which have had a favorable effect on property values in the United States. In addition to contributing to the growth in the HEL market, these factors have reduced the severity of losses in this market. Another, often overlooked, aspect of this market is that bankruptcy law in the United States does not allow a bankruptcy election more than once every 7 years. This places the lender in a powerful position with regard to the borrower and may partly explain why bankruptcies are acceptable to this group of lenders. Thus, bankruptcy law is a great motivator for the borrower to make payments and serves to shorten the foreclosure period, thereby reducing the cost of foreclosure (time value of money).

The most prevalent forms of HELs include the following:

- *Closed-end HELs,* where the loan amount and term to maturity are set at origination and bear a fixed rate, constitute most of the market.

- *Adjustable-rate, closed-end HELs* (HEL ARMs) have a set term to maturity and usually have both periodic and lifetime caps. The loans generally allow for the accretion of interest to the principal while the interest rate is at the cap. The additional principal is repaid from future payments when the interest rate is reset or when the rate recedes from the capped level. If the interest rate remains at the cap

Representative Home Equity Underwriting Guidelines

Grade	Quality	Credit History and Ratios
A	Good	• No late payment on mortgages • Maximum of two or three late payments on revolving credit and no more than three 30-day late payments on installment debt; perhaps one 60-day late payment • Chapter 7 or 13 bankruptcy must be discharged for 1 to 3 years with credit reestablished for 2 years • Maximum debt-to-income ratio of 45% • Maximum loan-to-values ranging from 85% to 95%
B	Satisfactory	• Maximum of three or four 30-day late payments on mortgage payments in the past 12 months • For nonmortgage debt, pattern of 30 delinquencies and limited 60-day delinquencies with isolated 90-day delinquency • Bankruptcies acceptable with 1 to 2 years reestablished credit • Maximum debt-to-income ratio of 50% • Maximum loan-to-value of 85%
C	Fair	• Maximum 210 total days delinquent with limited 60-day and isolated 90-day delinquencies on mortgage debt • Discretionary with cross section of 30-, 60-, and 90-day delinquencies • Bankruptcies acceptable with 1 to 2 years reestablished credit • Maximum debt-to-income ratio of 55% • Maximum loan-to-value of 80%
D	Poor	• No more than 120-day mortgage or rent delinquency in the past 12 months and property not in foreclosure • Delinquent or charged-off receivables • Bankruptcies acceptable if discharged or dismissed • Maximum debt-to-income ratio of 60% • Maximum loan-to-value of 65%

Source: First Union Securities, Inc.

for the life of the loan, there is usually a provision to extend the maturity. The loans are structured in a manner that renders this extension risk as highly improbable.

- *Home equity lines of credit* (HELOCs) are open-end, revolving loans, where the borrower receives an HEL line of credit that can be partially or completely drawn down and partially or completely paid back over time. HELOCs carry floating rates, usually with high lifetime caps and no interim caps. Because of the open-end, revolving structure of the HELOC collateral, which is similar to that of credit cards, these loans are not discussed in this chapter.

BASIC STRUCTURE

HELs are financial assets or receivables originated by a bank, a finance company, or other financial institution. HELs are then sold to a bankruptcy-remote special-purpose vehicle (SPV). Certain conditions must be met to achieve a "true sale," and reputable counsel provides legal opinions that confirm these conditions, such as the arm's length requirement and the transfer of the legal title to the asset, have in fact been met.

HEL issues usually take the form of a real estate mortgage investment conduit (REMIC), which allows cash flows to be redirected to create several tranches of certificates with expected average lives at many points on the yield curve. REMICs were created as a new issuance vehicle by the Tax Reform Act of 1986 to solve many of the problems experienced with collateralized mortgage obligations (CMOs) that used a multiclass trust structure. The first passthrough was issued in 1970, followed by the first CMO in 1983. As the moniker implies, CMOs were technically debt instruments rather than passthrough certificates and were successful in avoiding tax liability to the issuing trust. Issuers had to maintain a portion of residual interests, record CMOs as liabilities in their financial statements, and satisfy minimum capital requirements. The CMO structure also created a mismatch between the monthly receipts on the collateral and the quarterly payments on the bonds. In 1985, use of the owner trust structure solved some of these problems by allowing the sale of the residual interest to others and removal from the issuer's balance sheet. The new residual interest holder then became liable for interest rate shortfalls on any of the owner trust tranches. Buyers for the residuals were scarce and as a result the market for this type of CMO was not liquid.

REMICs changed all this. To qualify for REMIC status, a multiclass offering can have multiple classes of *regular interests* but only one class of *residual interest*. The legislation defines a "regular interest" as a fixed principal amount with periodic interest payments or accruals on the outstanding principal balance. Buyers of regular interests are taxed as holders of debt obligations, and the buyers of the residual interest pay taxes on the earnings, if any, of the trust. Due to its flexibility in meeting investor demand, the CMO and HEL markets have used the REMIC structure almost exclusively since 1991.

Following these guidelines, the trust issues either debt or pass-through certificates (a ratable equity interest in the pool or some portion of the pool), the proceeds of which are used to buy the pool of assets to be securitized. To facilitate the selling of certificates or debt to the market, some combination or variation of the following provides credit enhancement:

- *Excess spread:* Revenue less expenses of the trust.

- *Reserve account:* Excess spread captured and held in the trust as some prede-termined or calculated level to pay any cash flow shortfalls in the trust.

- *Subordinated protection:* The amount by which the collateral value exceeds any class of liability.

- *Senior-subordinated structures:* Certain classes of securities have a senior claim to others on the cash flow of the trust. The purest form of this structure is re-ferred to as *sequential,* where any principal payments received by the trust are used to fully pay down the principal of the most senior class prior to any of the junior classes. All classes receive principal payments sequentially according to their rank of claim to the cash flow of the trust. The lowest-ranking class will be the last to receive a principal payment as well as the last to have its principal fully retired. This is commonly referred to as the *waterfall.* Any amount left over is referred to as the *residual*and flows to the equity holder. A minimal amount of true equity is provided at the formation of the SPV and is necessary to com-ply with certain legal and tax requirements of the trust. The residual can be, and often is, separated from the true equity in the trust and retained by the seller-servicer. Retention of this amount by the seller-servicer provides a primary mo-tivation to maximize the cash flow in the trust (i.e., accelerate collections and minimize losses) so that the value of the residual is realized.

- *Third-party guarantee:* This can take the form of bond insurance, a letter of credit, or a corporate guarantee of all or any class of a securitization. The moti-vations vary, but the result is a better economic execution for the issuer, which may have to provide less collateral to the trust or may achieve a better pricing on insured bonds than an uninsured funding execution. The issuer may not have access to the market by any other means. Firms active in the guaranty of HEL transactions include Capital Markets Assurance Corp. (CapMac), Financial Guaranty Insurance Co. (FGIC), Mortgage Bond Insurance Associates (MBIA), Financial Security Assurance (FSA), and Capital Guaranty Assurance (CGA).

The most important basic feature of an asset-backed security that should not be underemphasized or overlooked when viewing the home equity securitization market for investment purposes is the true sale of the assets into a bankruptcy-remote SPV (the issuer). This issue as it relates to the recent economic hard times and bankruptcy of seller-servicers will be discussed in more detail later. From a pure credit perspective, these structures have survived bankruptcy, minimal degra-dation of servicing cash flow, and there is some evidence that retained residual in-terests are providing the proper motivation, even in bankruptcy, for the seller-servicer to continue servicing and collections in an efficient manner. In this regard, having tested the structure is a positive for the market and should provide an ad-ditional level of comfort to the investor.

EXHIBIT 15-2

HEL Principal Paydown—The Money Store 98-B

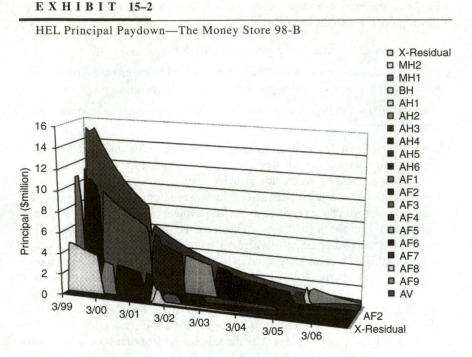

Source: First Union Securities,Inc.

Not surprisingly, because growth in the HEL market followed the growth in the mortgage-backed securities (MBS) market, many of the features are patterned after those used in the MBS market and are aimed at smoothing prepayment volatility such that payment windows for each class are shortened. This will reduce the risk that the investment will experience a shorter or longer average life than expected. The most common structures are discussed below.

- Senior-subordinated with up to 10 fixed-rate senior tranches with different average lives ranging out to 10 years. This is a lesser number of fixed-rate subordinated tranches with different average lives and backed by a fixed-rate pool of HELs. There is also a larger, longer service average life floating-rate tranche backed by a floating-rate pool of HELs.

- Senior-subordinated with some combination of fixed, floating, HEL, and HIL collateral

- Single-class with 100% surety bond

- Senior-subordinated with 100% surety bond on a subordinate piece

Exhibit 15–2 illustrates the principal paydown of The Money Store 98-B home equity securitization and the total collateral cash flow and its allocation to principal payment and the expenses of the program.

E X H I B I T   15-3

The Money Store 98-B HEL Cash Flow

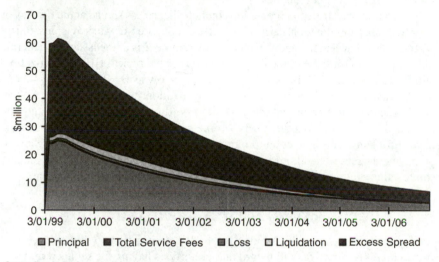

Source: First Union Securities, Inc.

Exhibit 15–3 illustrates the total collateral cash flow of The Money Store 98-B home equity securitization and its allocation to principal payment and the expenses of the program. This exhibit illustrates the excess spread concept.

An increasingly important structural feature for analyzing the cash flow expectations of HEL securitizations is the step-down provision. Due to the senior-subordinated structure, where all excess spread and principal payments are used to repay the senior tranche(s), subordinated tranche protection increases as a percentage of total certificate outstandings. This increased percentage protection is more than necessary to support the rating of the senior tranches. Step-downs were created as a method to redirect some of the excess spread cash flow to the subordinated tranches while protecting the rating on the senior ranking tranches throughout the life of the transaction.

Step-downs allow the redirection of a portion of the excess spread to subordinated tranches as long as the collateral is performing within the parameters described later. If the deal deteriorates due to higher-than-expected losses, the redirection of cash flows, or step-down, would not be allowed until the conditions were met. If step-down conditions are not met and the collateral exceeds the collateral quality triggers, cash flow would be redirected to the senior tranche until the collateral met the predetermined conditions. The step-down is set to occur usually 3 to 4 years from the date the deal was issued and requires that the collateral pool outstandings exceed a certain percentage of the original collateral balance, usually 50%, as well as meet certain asset quality tests as of a certain date. Failure to meet the step-down tests would alter the cash flow assumptions on which the senior, mezzanine, and subordinated tranches were priced, resulting in a shorter average life for the senior and mezzanine tranches and a longer average life for the subordinated tranches. The closer an issue comes to failing the tests should be an uncertainty properly priced into the spread of that issue compared with other issues that clearly will not fail the test.

In summary, structural protections include the excess spread at the first layer of protection, subordination, cash collateral accounts, step-down provisions, third-party credit enhancement, and the bankruptcy remoteness of the issuer. In general, ratings from two or three of the rating agencies for the typical HEL securitization will range from AAA for the senior tranches to as low as B− for the most subordinated tranche. In 1998, 42% of all HEL securitizations were floating rate. All the HEL structures shift credit volatility to the subordinated tranches in varying degrees and ensure in all but the most extreme cases that the senior AAA tranches have sufficient credit protection to remain rated AAA while outstanding. Slower prepayments generate additional credit support. When prepayments slow, the absolute value of the excess servicing spread remains higher for a longer time.

RATING AGENCY APPROACH

Rating agencies assign a AAA rating to an HEL transaction so that an investor, from a credit perspective, will regard that security as having the same credit worthiness as any other AAA at that moment. The rating agencies are looking to achieve a certain rating consistency across all fixed income sectors at all rating grades. Moody's Investors Service, Inc. (Moody's), and Standard and Poor's Corp. (S&P) were the first to rate structured transactions.

S&P's approach to structured finance began with a study of defaults in the Great Depression and resulted in a worst-case economic scenario on which it based its cash flow stress scenarios. If a transaction could withstand a number of iterations of this worst-case scenario and survive simulated depression scenarios, it deserved a AAA rating. The model introduced the concept of default frequency and loss severity. This basic model has been applied in modified form to each class of ABS rated by S&P. The result for all ABS, including the HEL sector, is that a AAA will survive three to five times historical losses. S&P constructs a prime pool for residential mortgages. As the characteristics of the prime pool differ from the pool to be securitized, penalties are assessed to default frequency and loss severity assumptions used in the cash flow scenarios. Lesser-quality pools require a greater amount of credit loss protection for the senior tranche to achieve a AAA rating than that required for the prime pool. Factors considered in analyzing the mortgage pool include historical level of delinquencies, loss severity, lien type, loan type, number of loans, geographical concentration, quality of borrower and step-downs. The IBCA Fitch and the Duff and Phelps models followed an approach similar to that of S&P in developing their cash flow models.

Moody's started out on a somewhat different route toward the same end. By looking at historical defaults for each rating level, Moody's thought that Aaa-structured financial issues should have the same probability of default as a Aaa-corporate and so on for each rating grade. Taking this approach to its logical extreme, Moody's studied the Great Depression as well as other recessions in the twentieth century and observed how the collateral being securitized behaved in

EXHIBIT 15–4

Yield Change Limits for Moody's Rated
HEL Transactions

Rating	Yield Change (bps)
Aaa	0.06
Aa2	1.30
A2	9.00
Baa2	27.00
Ba2	106.00
B2	231.00

Source: Moody's Investor Service, Inc.

stressful economic situations. This resulted in the identification of a positive correlation between collateral performance and economic events, allowing Moody's to use a Monte Carlo model to generate a worst-case loss distribution for the collateral pool. Moody's then quantified the loss protection needed for that pool to achieve Aaa loss protection (approximately three standard deviations from the expected loss). Aa transactions provided enough protection to cover 2.5 standard deviations, and single A covered 2.0 standard deviations. Although Moody's approach is similar, the data available for this type of analysis have greatly improved for each asset class (and for the other forms of derivatives in the structure, such as swaps). This approach is also called the *expected value approach.* Currently, Moody's sets credit enhancement levels so that the annual change in yield on the rated security, due to defaults in the collateral pool and other credit events that would cause a loss of cash flow to the trust, is equivalent to the target levels in Exhibit 15–4.

HEL COLLATERAL PERFORMANCE

Exhibits 15–5 and 15–6, taken from First Union Securities home equity prepayment model, show that collateral performance has been excellent and is well within the worst-case parameters set by the rating agencies. Loss information on HEL product is presented by year of origination (vintage) to avoid any understatement of losses because of new-issue volume. Exhibit 15–5 shows that net losses are low the first year after origination and increase rapidly for the next 2 years. From the peak in the 36th month, the losses recede for 2 years before percentage net losses increase again.

By examining the loss curve of each issue, an investor can decide, on a relative basis, whether the spread received is appropriate for the collateral's risk profile. Loss curves differ by issuer and vintage because of the targeted niche borrower, underwriting guidelines and, in some cases, servicing and collection.

It is particularly useful to look at cumulative HEL collateral losses by year of origination for the entire HEL universe as shown in Exhibit 15–6.

EXHIBIT 15–5

Annualized HEL Net Loss Rate by Vintage

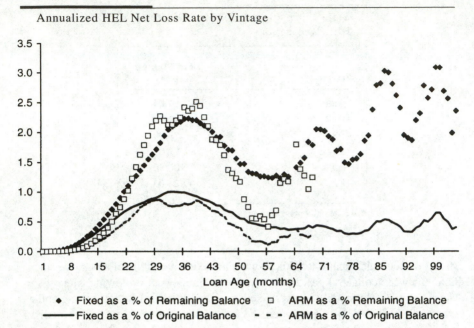

- ◆ Fixed as a % of Remaining Balance   □ ARM as a % Remaining Balance
- —— Fixed as a % of Original Balance   - - - ARM as a % of Original Balance

ARM: Adjustable-rate mortgage.
Source: First Union Securities, Inc.

EXHIBIT 15–6

Cumulative HEL Losses by Vintage

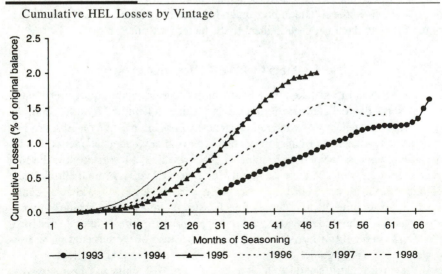

—●— 1993   ······ 1994   —▲— 1995   ······ 1996   —— 1997   – · – 1998

Source: First Union Securities, Inc.

HELs originated in 1993 and 1994 have had significantly better loss experience than the product originated during the period 1995–1998. In all likelihood, this is the result of the increased competition and market growth during the latter period. Lower interest rates and aggressive origination by brokers also explain why a lower-quality product was originated. It is also useful to compare cumulative loss curves by year of origination for the same issuer to see if the loss experiences on collateral pools originated in the same year differ dramatically from each other.

An increase in 60-day delinquencies, sustained for more than a month or two, is a good predictor of increased losses and whether a certain collateral pool is beginning to deteriorate. If the pool is in fact deteriorating, the increase in 60-day delinquencies will be followed by an increase in 90-day delinquencies and finally an increase in losses.

Loss curve analysis of the collateral pool is fundamental to understanding whether the probability of default has increased or decreased since the origination of the transaction. In most cases, the subordinated protection increases as the senior bonds pay down (see Exhibit 15–7).

EXHIBIT 15–7

Seasoned HEL Transaction Comparison

	ContiMortgage 1997-1 A4	Advanta 1993-1 A1	Saxon 1997-3 AF1
Weighted Average Coupon			
Original	11.556	10.340	10.094
Current	11.360	10.092	10.044
Certificate Coupon			
Original	6.680	5.950	5.816
Current	6.680	5.950	5.097
Servicing Fee			
Original	1.500	0.500	0.534
Current	0.500	0.500	0.533
Net Annualized Losses			
Original	0.000	0.000	0.000
Current	1.480	0.440	0.040
Net Excess Spread			
Original	3.376	3.890	3.744
Current	2.700	3.202	4.374
Level of Credit Enhancement Class A			
Original	11.500	100.000	9.230
Current	23.116	100.000	17.474
Original Rating	Aaa	Aaa	Aaa
Current Reading	Aaa	Aaa	Aaa

Note: All numbers are stated as percentages.
Source: First Union Securities, Inc.

There has *not* been a performance downgrade of a public HEL issue since the inception of the asset-backed market. However, variations in collateral performance will cause issues of the same average life to trade at different spreads to the Treasury market. This is also true for insured transactions though to a lesser degree than for senior-subordinated transactions.

HEL PREPAYMENT EXPERIENCE

Prepayments are extremely important in determining the value of any mortgage-backed investment. Exhibit 15–8, from First Union Securities prepayment model, shows the prepayment of the rated universe of HEL product from 1994 to 1998.

The prepayment of HEL product has proved to be much more stable than that of the MBS market and has resulted in securitization with less negative convexity. Investor acceptance of HEL prepayment characteristics contributed to market growth during the period 1997–1998. From a credit perspective, prepayments will accelerate the retirement of the senior-most tranches and increase the subordinated protection available to classes of the same rank when measured as a percentage of current outstandings. Due to B and C borrowers' limited refinancing opportunities, refinancing rates must fall 200 to 300 basis points (bps) to significantly increase prepayments due to refinancing in the HEL market versus the 25 to 50 bps that move the private MBS market. Examination of this data shows that HEL product originated prior to 1997 has had the highest prepayment experience. HELs originated in 1996 and earlier had higher coupons than current HEL prod-

E X H I B I T   15–8

Aggregate Historical CPR Versus Model CPR

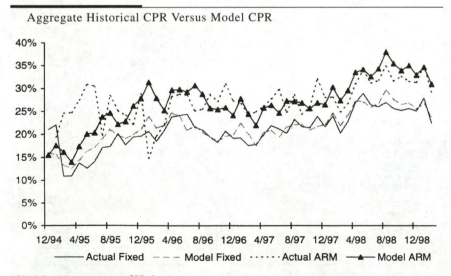

ARM: Adjustable-rate mortgage; CPR: Conditional prepayment rate.
Source: First Union Securities, Inc.

uct. Coupons originated as of this writing are lower because of a lower absolute level of interest rates. Intense competition in the market for product and market share has also accelerated prepayments.[1]

SEPARATING HEL CREDIT RISK FROM THE MARKET PRICING OF THAT RISK

For HEL securitizations, credit risk includes collateral performance, cash flow allocations, asset-quality triggers, access to established reserves, sufficiency of any subordinated tranche protection, credit worthiness of any third-party guarantor or substitute credit provider, legal integrity of the structure, and administrative risk.

The bankruptcy of a servicer does not, as a stand-alone event, increase the credit risk of any particular HEL investment. It does raise the concern that the servicing of the collateral may become less efficient while being transferred to a backup servicer and that collections may be less efficient and result in slower collections due to a significantly pared down servicing operation or the lack of economic incentive if the servicing is allowed to remain with the bankrupt entity while it is reorganized or sold to a third party. This is appropriately referred to as *administrative risk.*

Insured transactions provide solid protection from administrative risk. Insurers become insiders, use covenant protection to a greater degree than for senior-subordinated structures and promise timely payment of principal and interest as scheduled. For an HEL pass-through, interest due on the outstanding principal will be paid to certificate holders when due, and payment of any principal amount after the collateral is fully depleted (the only time principal is "due" in a pass-through). Although there is no promise to pay if collections slow down, the insurers, to protect their own interests, have teams of auditors that continually review collateral performance and the servicing process. The insurers stand ready to take control of collateral if covenants are breached, and the result is to significantly reduce administrative risk in the insured transaction. The insurers are in the business of insuring investment-grade or better transactions and are heavily regulated by the rating agencies as to capital sufficiency. Insured transactions, without the insurance, would result in a senior tranche rating of AA or A and investment grade or better for the subordinated tranches. Insured transactions provide multiple levels of protection to the investor.

Without a fundamental change in credit risk, HEL credit spreads are affected by the market pricing of that risk. Supply and demand drives the market pricing of credit risk between sectors and includes the market's reaction to world events, the health of the U.S. economy, capital flows around the world, or the market's reaction to headline risk within a sector.

---

1. For greater detail on HEL prepayment behavior, see James S. Anderson and Webster Hughes, *Prepayment Models and Home Equity Analysis,* First Union Securities, Inc., Asset-Backed/Quantitative Research, October 1998.

HEADLINE RISK AND HARD TIMES

The public and private asset-backed market has been largely free of event risk. The distinction between event and headline risk is important. *Event risk* in the corporate market represents an event that when announced has immediate credit rating implications for a company's outstanding debt or the debt of an industry, which, in most cases, would result in a downgrade (or an upgrade) of the company or companies affected by the event. The most obvious example would be mergers and acquisitions. *Headline risk* may immediately affect the credit spread of a security but does not have immediate upgrade or downgrade implications. None of the recent bankruptcy announcements by sellers-servicers in the HEL market have resulted in the downgrading of the related HEL securitizations.

Since its inception, the ABS market has had a remarkable track record of credit stability. Exhibit 15–9 shows that over the 5-year period 1994–1998 no asset-backed security rated by Moody's has defaulted in the public or private market at any rating level. In fact, that statement holds true for the asset-backed market since inception. Moody's first downgrade of a public asset-backed security occurred in February 1998, then again in April 1998 when it downgraded the lower-rated B-1 and B-2 tranches of BankAmerica Manufactured Housing Contract 1996-1. Prior to 1997, only three ABS had been downgraded by Moody's. In 1997, Moody's downgraded four tranches of three private nonprime automobile transactions (Aegis, Autoflow, and AJ Acceptance). In 1998, Aegis was downgraded further, as well as a private LSI nonprime auto tranche, and three private securities backed by charged-off credit card accounts issued by Commercial Financial Services (CFS). The undetected fraud in the CFS SMART transactions will result in the first ABS default. Even in this situation, collections on the receivables continue and payments to certificate holders continue. Technically, in a

EXHIBIT 15–9

Credit Stability of ABS Versus Comparable Corporates (as of June 30, 1998)

Original Rating	Average 5-Year Default Rate		Percent Downgraded after 5 Years		Percent Upgraded after 5 Years	
	CORP*	ABS*	CORP*	ABS*	CORP*	ABS*
Aaa	0.10%	0.00%	28.40%	0.00%	0.00%	0.00%
Aa	0.40%	0.00%	28.90%	0.00%	5.50%	12.80%
A	0.50%	0.00%	20.80%	0.70%	10.20%	11.60%
Baa	1.70%	0.00%	17.80%	1.90%	20.90%	4.10%
Ba	11.40%	0.00%	23.50%	5.70%	17.90%	0.00%

*ABS: All public and private asset-backed securities rated by Moody's; CORP: All public corporate bonds rated by Moody's.
Source: Moody's Investors Services, Inc. and First Union Securities, Inc.

senior-subordinated structure, a default will only occur when pass-through payments fail to make a payment while a certificate balance is still outstanding. This can occur only when current pay collateral is fully depleted.

At this juncture, investors have become conditioned to the headline risk present in the HEL market. Some investors regard headline risk spread widening as a buying opportunity. A pattern has emerged whereby announcements have been made by sellers-servicers in financial difficulty that they are either seeking a strategic partner, seeking to restructure or sell certain parts of their operations, plan to reduce growth, or plan to eliminate or decrease their most costly source of loan origination (in most cases, third-party broker originated product). A few months after this announcement, seller-servicers that did not find a partner or alternative sources of financing have announced bankruptcy. Significant headline risk announcements by seller-servicers are summarized in Exhibit 15–10.

These events will affect the liquidity and pricing of all HEL product. Some issues, with strong seller-servicers or those owned by investment-grade parents, and insured issues will recover to a normalized spread more quickly than those with servicers experiencing some form of financial stress. In reality, investors prefer not to own a HEL issue when the servicer files for bankruptcy, not because there is an immediate risk of downgrade or default (there is not), but because the investor prefers not to have to deal with the spread widening that accompanies the announcement (i.e., the headline risk).

For an issue sponsored by a seller-servicer that has just filed for bankruptcy, the spread widening is less severe for insured issues. At this point, the market goes through a discovery period with regard to the affected issues and trading in these issues may be light to nonexistent. For the insured issues, investors are uncertain whether the insurer will require that the servicing be transferred to the backup servicer and whether servicing continues smoothly with no discernible slowdown in collections or confusion surrounding the transfer. Liquidity should return to the market for these issues, albeit at a modestly wider spread.

For senior-subordinated structures, the discovery and return to liquidity in the market will take longer and, in the case of Southern Pacific's senior-subordinated issues, has taken 3 to 6 months. In this case, the bankruptcy court allowed Southern Pacific to retain a substantial amount of its servicing in an effort to maximize the value of residuals held by the bankruptcy estate. Despite pared-down operations, the retention of the residual by the bankruptcy estate has apparently provided the necessary motivation for Southern Pacific to continue servicing the affected issues in an efficient manner. As a result, some investors have returned cautiously to the market for these securities and currently view the available spreads as cheap. The failure of a servicer-seller should worry the investor to the extent it causes a deterioration in the performance of the collateral. This could be the result of a lost economic incentive for diligent collection of payments or rapid resolution of problem loans. This collateral degradation, if sustained, fundamentally changes the credit protection afforded the issuer, and the investor should be compensated for this uncertainty.

E X H I B I T   15–10

1998–1999 Headline Risk Announcements

Aames Financial	Third-quarter 1998 earnings down more than 95%, with much of the reduction attributed to losses on hedging positions. Servicing operation might be sold. Has exited the securitization market.
Amresco	Announced a $50 million–$60 million loss for 1998 and major reorganization and closing of its wholesale and retail operations.
Cityscape	Filed for bankruptcy in October 1998.
ContiFinancial	Made first-quarter 1999 announcement that it is seeking a strategic partner following a large loss in the third quarter of 1998 and announcement of major restructuring.
FirstPlus	Announced $82 million third-quarter 1998 loss. Reduced staff more than 50%. Eliminated wholesale division. Terminated agreement to sell servicing operation to Superior Bank. Proposed merger with Life Financial canceled. Did no securitization in the fourth quarter. Sold U.K. operations and its conforming loan business. Filed for bankruptcy the first week of March 1999.
IMC Mortgage	Third-quarter 1998 earnings down more than 80% from last year. Had severe liquidity problems. Completed previously announced agreement with Greenwich Street Capital Partners to purchase 95% interest in company and assume control in February 1999.
IndyMac	Announced fourth-quarter 1998 loss and laid off 280 employees. Reducing servicing portfolio. Exiting manufactured housing business.
Southern Pacific	Wrote down earnings during the summer. Sought to raise capital through whole-loan sales. Sought strategic partner and then filed for bankruptcy in October 1998.
United Companies	Major reorganization announced in the fourth quarter and announced it was looking for a partner. Filed for bankruptcy the first week of March 1999.

Source: First Union Securities, Inc.

In some senior-subordinated issues, backup servicers were not required and the concept of a special servicer was not contemplated. For most commercial mortgage-backed securities, a special servicer is paid a fee and a success fee for collecting seriously delinquent loans or loans in foreclosure. The documents of an HEL issue do not allow a step-up in servicing fees as an incentive for another servicer to step in and take over servicing. As a result, provisions such as these are now being incorporated into some of the new senior-subordinated deals in the market. The insurers have long used the two-tier fee concept.

In a perverse way, all this has been a positive for the HEL market. The experience of seller-servicer bankruptcy, together with the maintenance of existing ratings, has satisfactorily tested the structural safeguards put in place in HEL transactions and validated the principal tenet of asset securitizations—that the deals are isolated from the insolvency of the issuer. This should result in a higher confidence level in the transactions and in further modification, or fine-tuning, of the documentation used in future transactions.

CHAPTER **16**

SECURITIES BACKED BY MANUFACTURED HOUSING LOANS

James S. Anderson
Managing Director
First Union Securities, Inc.

Kristina L. Clark
Assistant Vice President
First Union Securities, Inc.

This chapter provides investors with an overview of the manufactured housing industry and the collateral underlying manufactured housing asset-backed securities (ABS). For investors already familiar with manufactured housing ABS, we discuss current issues in the industry and their impact on ABS as well as introduce a source of higher-level analytics and surveillance.

The manufactured housing industry has undergone dramatic changes since the late 1970s and early 1980s. Government regulations and advances in home design have greatly improved product quality and safety. Competitive financing and changes in consumer demand have led to a shift in sales from smaller, less expensive single-section homes to larger, more expensive multisection homes (see Exhibit 16–1). New manufactured homes are being designed to resemble more closely traditional site-built homes, offering amenities such as vaulted ceilings, fireplaces, and walk-in closets. Manufacturers have been working with land developers and dealers to change the negative stereotype of "trailer parks" by promoting the construction of "manufactured housing communities," which include swimming pools, clubhouses, and recreational facilities.

As the manufactured housing industry evolved and demand for such accommodations increased, loans providing underlying financing became more common collateral for securitization. As with other ABS classes, manufactured housing ABS are subject to the growing pains of the underlying industry, and although the manufactured housing industry has come a long way, increased competition and a loosening of credit standards pose a continuing challenge to pool performance.

This chapter is reprinted with permission from Frank J. Fabozzi (ed.), *Investing in Asset-Backed Securities* (New Hope, PA: Frank J. Fabozzi Associates, 2000).

E X H I B I T   16–1

Average Size and Sales Price of Manufactured and Site-Built Homes

($)	1992	1993	1994	1995	1996	1997
Manufactured homes						
Total						
Average sales price	28,400	30,500	33,500	36,300	38,400	41,100
Average square footage	1,255	1,295	1,330	1,355	1,380	1,420
Cost per square foot	22.63	23.55	25.19	26.79	27.83	28.94
Single section						
Average sales price	20,600	21,900	23,900	26.700	28,200	29,000
Average square footage	1,035	1,065	1,085	1,115	1,120	1,125
Cost per square foot	19.90	20.56	22.03	23.95	25.18	25.78
Multisection						
Average sales price	37,200	39,600	42.900	45,900	47,300	49,500
Average square footage	1,495	1,525	1,565	1,585	1,600	1,615
Cost per square foot	24.88	25.97	27.41	28.96	29.56	30.65
Site-built homes						
Average sales price	144,100	147,700	154,100	158,700	166,200	176,200
Land price	36,025	36,925	38,525	39,675	41,550	44,050
Price of Structure	108,075	110,775	115,575	119,025	124,650	132.150
Average square footage	2,095	2,095	2,115	2,115	2,125	2,150
Cost per square foot	51.59	52.88	54.65	56.28	58.66	61.47

Source: Manufactured Housing Institute.

Fortunately for investors, the issuers in this industry are not novice securitizers. Companies such as Green Tree (now wholly owned by Conseco, Inc.), Oakwood Homes Corp., Vanderbilt Mortgage and Finance, Inc., and GreenPoint Credit Corp. (with the recent addition of Bank of America Corp.'s manufactured housing operation) have extensive experience securitizing this industry. By the end of 1998, much of the industry had reorganized and refocused. The credit crunch in the third quarter of 1998 and less-than-stellar performance from 1995–1996 collateral pools have forced the industry to change, and the result has been a clearer focus on borrower and collateral quality.

The manufactured housing industry's troubles continued in 1999 and 2000. Shipments dropped dramatically, reflecting an overabundance of inventory, partially due to an increased supply of repossessed homes. In addition, several subordinated tranches of existing ABS were downgraded, primarily due to poorer than expected performance of the underlying collateral pools.

WHAT IS A MANUFACTURED HOUSE?

According to the Department of Housing and Urban Development (HUD), manufactured houses are single-family homes constructed on a chassis at a factory and

E X H I B I T   16–2

Manufactured Housing Loan Characteristics

	Single Section	Multisection	U.S. Average Site Built
Loan rate versus conventional (bps)	338	288	
Average loan term (months)	200	240	360
Average monthly payment ($)	260	406	831

Source: Green Tree Financial Corp.

shipped in one or more sections to a housing site, then installed on a semipermanent foundation. Single-section manufactured homes are typically 12 to 14 feet wide and 40 to 64 feet long. Multisection homes are created by joining two or more single sections along their length or by stacking them to create additional stories.

Manufactured housing is generally less expensive (15%–40%) and smaller than comparable site-built housing. In 1997, the average manufactured home had 1,420 square feet of living space and cost $41,100 compared with the average site-built home (2,150 square feet costing $132,150, excluding land). Although commonly referred to as mobile homes, most manufactured homes are permanent residences. Transporting a manufactured home can cost between $2,000 and $6,000, depending on the size of the home and the location.

There has been a shift in sales from smaller, less expensive single-section homes to larger, more expensive multisection homes (see Exhibit 16–2).

MANUFACTURED HOUSING LOAN PRODUCTS

Manufactured homes can be purchased separately or with land. In a land-and-home purchase, the unit is permanently affixed to the site, and the entire property is taxed as real estate. Loans for land-and-home purchases typically have more financing options and more closely resemble mortgages for traditional site-built homes. The number of land-and-home contracts has increased in recent years along with the growth in popularity of more expensive multisection homes. This trend has had a positive impact on loan pools since historical performance shows that consumers who borrow to purchase the home and the land are more reliable than consumers who borrow to purchase only the home.

Homes purchased separately are typically financed through a retail installment sales contract or a personal property loan. Typically, a UCC filing on the home (similar to the documentation for an automobile loan) takes the place of a deed of trust. These loans are commonly referred to as chattel loans. Historically, terms for a chattel loan were between 15 and 20 years with a 10% down payment. Recently, however, lenders have begun offering terms of 25 to 30 years with as low as a 5% down payment in an effort to increase market share.

E X H I B I T   16–3

Manufactured Housing Borrower Demographics

(%)	Single Section	Multisection
Average age		
18–34	71.0	23.5
35–54	24.2	67.9
55+	4.8	8.6
Average years same job		
0–5	72.3	29.1
5–10	23.4	59.5
10+	3.4	11.4
Family income		
$15,000–$25,000	64.7	12.8
$25,000–$50,000	34.5	84.6
$50,000+	0.8	2.6

Source: Manufactured Housing Institute.

WHO ARE THE BORROWERS?

Although the characteristics of a typical manufactured housing buyer have been changing since the late 1980s and early 1990s, two population segments show particular growth. The first segment consists of retirees and baby boomers. A total of 27% of the heads of manufactured housing households are retired, and occupants older than 70 years account for 21% of all manufactured housing residents (see Exhibit 16–3). Manufactured housing combined with home health care has become for some a favorable alternative to nursing home care.

The second growth segment is Generation X as they move into the first-time home-buying market. Because rents have been rising for the past decade, manufactured housing offers a strong alternative to apartments in addition to substantial cost savings in relation to site-built homes.

For both segments, the average annual income is $21,500 with 21% exceeding $40,000. The average household net worth is $58,000 with 27% exceeding $100,000.

In the late 1980s and the early 1990s, interest rates for manufactured housing loans for lower-income borrowers were as high as 14%. These exorbitant rates negated cost savings from choosing manufactured housing instead of site-built homes, further inhibiting the industry's growth. Finance companies claimed the high rates reflected the greater risk of delinquency and default associated with manufactured housing borrowers, a stereotype plaguing the industry. Reports at that time disproved the claim and illustrated that average delinquencies on manufactured home loans were significantly fewer than delinquencies on comparable mortgages. Finance companies have since realized their prejudice and, during the past few years, rates for manufactured housing loans have fallen closer in line with mortgage rates.

Increases in the popularity and acceptance of multisection homes have exposed the industry to higher-credit borrowers than those that sought a single-section home (see Exhibit 16–3). The typical multisection homeowner is older, has a longer employment history, and has a larger income. In contrast, the traditional single-section borrower is younger, has a shorter employment history, and has a smaller income.

OVERVIEW OF MANUFACTURED HOUSING ABS

Manufactured housing ABS volume has grown dramatically, culminating in a 17% increase in volume from 1997 to 1998 before contracting in 1999 and 2000. The rapid expansion reflected changing characteristics in the industry. Some of the most prevalent changes include the following:

- Increasing demand for low-cost housing alternatives
- Refinancings due to increased industry competition
- Larger loan balances due to increased desire for larger or multisectional homes
- Longer loan terms to help borrowers manage monthly payments
- Maturing of the industry and its key players
- Industry support provided by government agencies such as HUD

The majority of manufactured housing ABS issuance has been in the public market. As of June 22, 1999, issuance volume had reached a level comparable to total issuance in 1995. At this rate, the asset class would have more than doubled in size in only 4 years. The asset class has proved its ability to grow in the face of volatility and unsure market conditions as evidenced by record growth despite the tough third quarter of 1998 experienced by all ABS market participants. Industry conditions, however, have caught up with ABS issuance, as only $11.4 billion came to market in 2000.

Manufactured housing ABS has been a significant portion of total ABS issuance since 1995. Although the aggregate market has seen the emergence of many new asset classes from 1995 to 1998, manufactured housing ABS has remained a consistent 3% to 6% of the total market.

Manufactured housing competition continues to decrease. However, an overwhelming majority of new issuance still comes from key market players such as Green Tree, Oakwood, Vanderbilt and GreenPoint. Green Tree, in particular, consistently appears at the top of the league table.

With $4 billion of total manufactured housing ABS volume in 1995, Green Tree accounted for 62% of the asset class's total new issuance that year. Although still the largest issuer of manufactured housing ABS, Green Tree's share of new issuance fell from 53% in 1997 to 47% in 1998 (Exhibit 16–4).

POOL CHARACTERISTICS

Most loan pools today contain a mixture of single- and multisection manufactured home loans. Placement of the homes also varies with some of the collateral on pri-

EXHIBIT 16–4

Change in Market Share by Key Players

	1996	1997	1998	1999
Green Tree Financial Corp.	63%	53%	47%	1%
Associates	16%	8%	0%	0%
Oakwood Homes Corp.	8%	9%	9%	8%
Vanderbilt Mortgage and Finance, Inc.	5%	10%	8%	11%
Others	5%	12%	11%	0%
BankAmerica Housing Services	3%	8%	13%	0%
Merit	0%	0%	0%	5%
Bombardier Capital Mortgage Securitization Corp.	0%	0%	6%	2%
GreenPoint Credit Corp.	0%	0%	6%	23%

Note: GreenPoint acquired BankAmerica Housing Services on Sept. 30, 1998.
Source: Asset-Backed Alert and First Union Securities, Inc.

vate lots and others in communities. Loans collateralized by larger homes and those supported by land in addition to the home are generally preferred as collateral rather than a loan on a smaller, unattached unit. Historically in pools, there has been a prevalence of multisection homes as collateral, even when single-section home sales exceeded multisection home sales. Multisection homes accounted for 60.9% of total shipments in 1997, whereas single-section home shipments have slipped since 1995. Issuers tend to place higher-credit collateral in their securitization pools to obtain and sustain tranche ratings. By the end of the first quarter of 1999, multisection homes in securitization pools on average were 67.7% of the underlying collateral.

The majority of loans placed in pools are for new property as opposed to used or secondary market collateral. New homes have constituted 76% or more of total loan pools since 1995. Also evident is a steady increase in used homes as a percentage of the total, which is due to the growth of the secondary market. Also spurring used homes as acceptable collateral is the increasing quality of manufactured homes over the past five years. With better quality standards supported by manufactured housing manufacturers and government housing agencies, it is reasonable that the newer homes would last longer and depreciation rates would be lower than those for homes manufactured and sold a few years ago. As manufactured housing increasingly becomes a more acceptable alternative to site-built homes, secondary market activity should increase and thus more used homes should be financed.

To date, collateral on private lots has been more prevalent than properties situated in communities. This aversion to manufactured housing communities is an offshoot of the old trailer park image. As more upscale communities are tailored for manufactured homes, we expect to see an increase of community-based collateral.

The average life of a typical manufactured housing loan currently ranges from 7 to 8 years, but this is lengthening. Due to increased demand for larger or multisection homes, loan balances have also been rising. Concurrent with rising financing amounts, borrowers have been demanding longer loan terms to accommodate budgets and to simulate site-built home mortgages. There has also been a heightening of industry competition to meet the requirements of increased business flow. A relaxation of credit underwriting has plagued the industry of late. This issue is discussed in greater detail later in this chapter.

DRAWING BORROWERS AND THE EFFECT ON SECURITIZATION POOLS

During the mid-1990s, as the demand for manufactured housing increased, retailers and financiers began implementing aggressive lending terms to capture greater market share. Higher advance rates, extended loan terms and buy-down programs were used to attract customers and increase underwriting volume. Traditional 15- to 20-year loan terms were extended to 25 and 30 years and industry standard down payments of 10% to 15% were lowered to 5% in some cases. The increase in more expensive multisection home purchases and the availability of "5% down" financing have led to a greater percentage of loans with loan-to-value (LTV) ranges of 95% and higher. The proportion of high-LTV loans has risen on average from 0% to 5% of the total in 1994 to 30%–40% in 1998 and 1999, depending on the lender.

Not surprisingly, as a result of looser credit standards, defaults and the number of used and repossessed homes on the market has risen and has affected pool performance. To assuage losses, many lenders have switched from wholesale to retail channels to clear repos. In retail disposition, homes are often placed on a consignment basis on a dealer's lots. The dealer receives a commission for the sale of the home and the lender provides financing for the new buyer. Pricing trends suggest that many repossessed homes on consignment are sold at or above their true market price. The problem with using retail disposition as a form of loss mitigation is that lenders run the risk of replacing old bad loans with new bad loans. In fact, statistics show that consumers with a weak credit history are more likely to purchase repossessed manufactured homes.

With new unit shipments leveling off, many lenders have turned to refinancing as a source of increased volume. Larger loan balances, combined with relatively low interest rates, have created an incentive for many borrowers to refinance. Naturally, this trend in loans appeared within securitization pools and resulted in increasing delinquencies, prepayments, and defaults. Although data shows that borrowers in the high advance rate category typically perform better than the average manufactured housing borrower, some have argued that the lack of equity in the home raises the likelihood of default should the borrower run into financial trouble.

In 1997, the manufactured housing financing industry began reorganizing and consolidating. This was accelerated by market volatility in the third quarter of 1998, which hindered many specialty finance companies from securitizing. Reorganization and consolidation have continued as weaker players drop out because of their inability to successfully execute in the market.

What Happened to Green Tree in the Mid-1990s?

Green Tree Financial Corp., the market's top securitizer for manufactured housing, experienced trouble and controversy related to its collateral and use of gain-on-sale accounting. In 1996, the company was forced to take a $150 million cash charge resulting from the miscalculation of assumptions on loans originated in 1995 and 1996. Although the charge was small in relation to the $26 billion in loans under management, the action highlighted the importance of conservatively measuring the gain on sale of securitized assets. Unfortunately for Green Tree, its trouble did not stop there. As a result of similar prepayment miscalculations, the company revised 1996 and 1997 earnings down $400 million. Lawsuits were brought by shareholders who believed that management did not efficiently report troubles in the company. Controversy accelerated when it was revealed that former Chairman Larry Coss' salary was a percentage of reported earnings, an amount that reached $102 million in 1996.

Green Tree has since rebounded from the negative press associated with its gain-on-sale treatment, but an example has been made of the potential problems that can arise from misjudging these calculations.

Buy-Down Programs

In a buy-down program, the lender offers the borrower a rate lower than the prevailing rate by charging the borrower points in exchange for the lower rate. The points are either added to the loan amount or financed by the lender under a separate agreement. Standard practices in the industry are a 1.0 point charge for every 25-bp reduction in rate. Exhibit 16–5 provides an example of buy-down terms for a 20-year $50,000 loan with a base rate of 10%. By reducing monthly payments, buy-down programs enable lenders to offer financing to home buyers

EXHIBIT 16–5

An Example of Buy-Down Terms

Original Loan Amount ($)	Loan Term (years)	Interest Rate	Monthly Payment ($)	Points	Buy-Down Amount ($)
50,000	20	10.00%	482.51	0.0	0
50,000	20	9.75%	474.26	1.0	500
50,000	20	9.50%	466.07	2.0	1,000
50,000	20	9.25%	457.93	3.0	1,500
50,000	20	9.00%	449.86	4.0	2,000
50,000	20	8.75%	441.86	5.0	2,500
50,000	20	8.50%	433.91	6.0	3,000
50,000	20	8.25%	426.02	7.0	3,500
50,000	20	8.00%	418.22	8.0	4,000

Source: First Union Securities, Inc.

who might otherwise not qualify for a manufactured housing loan. The low rate also makes it difficult for competitors to refinance the loan, which decreases the likelihood of prepayment.

Buy-down loans that are securitized result in tighter spreads due to the lower weighted average coupon (WAC). The likelihood of prepayments is less, but this is offset by an increase in potential loss severity. When buy-down loans are sold to a trust, the lender receives the face value of the loan plus any points financed. If a buy-down loan defaults, the sale of the asset must cover the loan amount plus points and liquidation costs. Depending on depreciation and the timing of default, it is likely that the necessary recovery amount will exceed the value of the underlying asset.

ISSUER PROFILES

Throughout late 1998 and 1999, the manufactured housing industry has undergone restructuring and reorganization. Bank of America sold its housing operation to GreenPoint, Green Tree merged with Conseco, Inc., in July 1998, and small players such as United Companies Financial Corp. exited the market. Throughout this process, underwriting standards and dealer networks stood out as keys to industry success. This has brought intense focus on the key industry issuers and how they differentiate themselves.

Green Tree Financial Corp. (Conseco, Inc.)

Green Tree, founded in 1975, is a diversified finance company with nationwide operations serving the consumer and commercial markets. The company has more than 20,000 independent retail dealer relationships and seven business lines with more than 8,000 employees in more than 200 offices nationwide. The company is known for its well-developed dealer network. With finance receivables in excess of $33 billion, Green Tree is the nation's second largest issuer of asset-backed securities, totaling $13.4 billion in 1998. In July 1998, the company merged with Conseco, a specialist in supplemental health insurance, retirement annuities, and universal life insurance.

Green Tree has been and remains the dominant player in the manufactured housing securitization market. In 1998, the company's securitizations totaling $5.5 billion represented roughly 50% of the manufactured housing securitization market. As a result, Green Tree has played a major role in determining market standards for securitization structures and collateral characteristics. Green Tree also leads the market in structural sophistication and has begun to provide a guaranty on subordinated pieces rather than retaining them.

Green Tree's recovery rate on deals from 1995 through 1998 averaged 56.1%, which ranks in the middle of the industry. Green Tree's deals consist primarily of new units on private lots. Average loan size has trended upward, which parallels the industry overall. WACs have fallen as LTVs have increased, again reflecting overall industry trends.

Oakwood Homes Corp.

Oakwood Homes, headquartered in Greensboro, N.C., is one of only a few vertically integrated housing companies. Oakwood engages in the production, sale, financing, and insuring of manufactured housing units. Founded in 1946, Oakwood (NYSE: OH) is the nation's third largest manufacturer of factory-built homes. With 32 nationwide manufacturing plants and 359 company-owned retail sales centers, Oakwood sells more homes each year than any other retail competitor. Furthermore, the company's financial services business unit completes the sale process by providing customer financing as well as insurance coverage. The company markets its retail businesses under the names Oakwood, Freedom, Victory, Golden West, Schult, Crest, Suburban, and Destiny homes.

Since the issuance of the company's first securitization in 1994, Oakwood has significantly increased its manufactured housing securitization program. With a total of $3.7 billion in securitizations, Oakwood is recognized as a quarterly securitizer and maintains a stable presence in the manufactured housing securitization market. According to the rating agencies, the loans in Oakwood's securitizations are typically of lower credit quality as Oakwood liberally uses the 95% LTV program. In addition, Oakwood's securitizations generally have higher credit support levels than others in this market. Although Oakwood has a relatively high default rate, its recovery rate remains well in excess of other market leaders such as Green Tree. This is attributable to Oakwood's strong dealer network, fostered through its vertical integration. This structure allows for increased success with repos, unit trading, secondary market creation, and the avoidance of liquidation through wholesaling, but it may not be enough to sustain collateral troubles over an extended time.

Oakwood announced in mid-June 1999 that earnings for the third quarter, ended June 30, would fall short of analysts' expectations by as much as 50% ($0.55/share). Management also announced a decision to explore strategic alternatives, including a management-led buyout. The earnings shortfall stemmed from "unanticipated softness" in both retail and wholesale sales that, as previously noted, has of late generally affected the industry. Another announcement was made on July 17, 1999, stating that third-quarter earnings would be 65% to 75% below analysts' estimates. The company's Baa3/BBB ratings have been placed on negative watch by both Moody's Investor Services, Inc., and Standard & Poor's Corp. Recent troubles, however, have not hindered Oakwood from continuing to access the securitization market.

Vanderbilt Mortgage and Finance, Inc.

Vanderbilt is the captive finance arm and wholly owned subsidiary of Clayton Homes, Inc. (NYSE: CMH), a vertically integrated manufactured housing company operating in 28 states. Vanderbilt engages in manufacturing, retailing, financing and insuring homes as well as operating manufactured housing communities. As a financial services group, Vanderbilt provides financing and insurance for consumers buying manufactured homes from Clayton-owned retail offices and select independent retail centers. The company's current servicing portfolio contains more than 140,000 loans, totaling more than $3 billion.

Since 1995, Vanderbilt has established itself as a quarterly issuer and has increased its market presence in the manufactured housing securitization market. Historically, the issues have been considered by rating agencies as being at the higher end of the credit spectrum. Average loan maturity is below the norm, reducing depreciation risk, and the company has not been as involved in the 95% LTV program, thus reducing the relative delinquency and loss risk of the pools. In addition, the company does not repurchase defaulted loans from its securitizations, but instead relies on the dealers to perform this task. As a result, losses are absorbed at the dealer level rather than in Vanderbilt's securitizations. In 1998, total issuance of manufactured housing securitizations exceeded $850 million.

Vanderbilt tends to use predominantly community-based loans as opposed to private-lot-based loans in its securitizations. Its weighted average LTVs are lower than Oakwood's, but higher than Green Tree's, reflecting Vanderbilt's middle-of-the-market strategy.

GreenPoint Credit Corp.

GreenPoint Credit, headquartered in San Diego, is a wholly owned subsidiary of GreenPoint Financial Corp. (NYSE: GPT) specializing in the manufactured housing lending industry. It is the second-largest originator and servicer of manufactured housing loans, with annual originations of more than $2.6 billion and a servicing portfolio of more than $10 billion. GreenPoint Credit, with 1,500 employees across a national sales and service network of 45 offices, has relationships with 5,000 dealers.

On November 18, 1998, GreenPoint brought its first manufactured housing securitization to market. The $728 million offering consisted of fixed and floating loans purchased from Bank of America as part of the acquisition of BankAmerica Housing Services. Since the first securitization, GreenPoint has issued two others in 1999 for a total of more than $2.3 billion.

On December 7, 1998, the company announced it had acquired the dealer origination segment of NationsCredit Manufactured Housing Corp.'s manufactured housing business. NationsCredit's business was part of NationsBank prior to its merger with Bank of America. On an annual basis, NationsCredit has originated approximately $400 million through its dealer channel. The purchase provided GreenPoint with access to NationsCredit's dealer business throughout the United States. In addition, the agreement called for a future correspondent relationship in which manufactured housing loans originated through Bank of America's branches will be sold to GreenPoint.

The WAC of the GreenPoint deals is lower than that of its competition's deals. GreenPoint also has had more than 80% of new home collateral for all four deals. Like Vanderbilt, GreenPoint's pool collateral is predominantly located in housing parks or communities as opposed to private lots. This parallels the trend in the manufactured housing industry toward planned communities built with the help of developers and with full recreational equipment for the community and residents.

Bombardier Capital Mortgage Securitization Corp.

Bombardier Capital is the financial services arm of global transportation equipment manufacturer, Bombardier, Inc. An international provider of financial solutions, Bombardier Capital offers a full line of lending, leasing, and asset management services to the consumer, inventory, commercial, and industrial markets. The company employs more than 1,100 people at multiple locations in the United States, Canada, and Europe.

Bombardier Capital has been in the manufactured housing business for more than 10 years. In 1997, the company launched a manufactured housing retail financing business to provide financing services. The business expanded to double its market share in early 1999 with the purchase of NationsCredit Manufactured Housing's manufactured housing inventory finance portfolio.

Bombardier Capital's portfolio prior to the acquisition encompassed $200 million in assets under management and 540 manufactured housing retailers. The purchased portfolio included floor plan financing loans outstanding of $195 million with approximately 290 retailers at the end of 1998.

The company began to securitize in 1998 and, to date, has issued four securitizations totaling $849.3 million. Almost all of Bombardier Capital's collateral consists of new homes, and weighted average LTVs are lower than much of the competition's.

MANUFACTURED HOUSING PREPAYMENT MODELS

The Asset-Backed and Quantitative Research groups at First Union Securities have developed prepayment models for a variety of mortgage and mortgage-related asset types.[1] There are two models reflecting differing origination and underwriting criteria for manufactured housing originators and servicers. We have tested each model against all publicly issued ABS and have determined the best fit for each particular collateral group. Below we highlight some of the findings regarding manufactured housing prepayments.

Exhibits 16–6 and 16–7 show the prepayment and delinquency or loss for the universe of manufactured housing ABS. Though the data goes back to 1990, the bulk of the information is from 1993 onward. Note the high original WACs from 1990 to 1992, as well as the repricing of manufactured housing loans since 1993. It is not surprising the life speed of 1994 production shows a higher rate than subsequent years, given the higher WAC of that year's production. Moreover, the 12-month speeds for 1994 and 1995 vintages are somewhat above the total life speed. This reflected the interest rate environment, turnover, and competition.

The 1995 vintage at 4.26% exhibits the highest cumulative net loss of any year. The loss curves in Exhibit 16–7 are interesting in that there is a peak in Year

---

1. The basic framework of our approach may be found in our October 1998 report *Prepayment Models and Home Equity Analysis*.

EXHIBIT 16-6

Prepayments for the Universe of Manufactured Housing Asset-Backed Securities

Vintage	Historical CPR* by Vintage				Current WAC*	Original WAC*	Current Balance ($000)	Projected CPR* by Vintage Base Case				−100 bps 12 Month	+100 bps 12 Month
	1 Month	3 Month	12 Month	Life				1 Month	3 Month	6 Month	12 Month		
1990 FIX	10.24	10.27	11.31	16.95	14.00	14.23	29,515	10.53	9.33	9.91	10.25	11.23	9.62
1991 FIX	10.22	11.03	12.96	15.20	11.98	12.36	109,880	10.10	8.97	9.50	9.76	10.99	9.00
1992 FIX	10.79	11.00	11.38	13.11	11.67	11.80	263,700	9.90	8.87	9.37	9.54	11.02	8.76
1993 FIX	8.49	8.84	10.03	12.05	10.24	10.28	658,127	9.43	8.52	8.90	9.00	10.17	8.42
1994 FIX	9.89	10.64	11.63	12.92	11.01	11.08	1,652,207	10.97	10.00	10.44	10.58	12.01	9.89
1995 FIX	10.68	11.10	12.81	12.17	10.81	10.98	3,314,602	12.22	11.19	11.68	11.83	13.43	11.07
1996 FIX	9.75	9.90	10.25	10.53	10.29	10.37	4,411,384	12.31	11.36	11.88	12.11	13.67	11.41
1997 FIX	9.11	10.35	10.43	10.82	10.21	10.23	6,182,199	12.20	11.27	11.78	12.08	13.53	11.43
1997 ARM	10.98	11.71	10.95	11.86	10.36	10.66	193,606	16.48	15.30	16.03	16.37	17.94	15.34
1998 FIX	7.96	8.69	8.58	8.26	9.76	9.75	10,764,629	11.47	10.63	11.17	11.48	12.69	10.89
1998 ARM	15.63	14.99	12.97	11.86	10.59	9.07	513,098	15.94	14.85	15.62	15.99	17.79	15.08
1999 FIX	6.86	7.34	6.35	6.57	10.15	9.99	8,511,948	9.91	9.41	10.40	11.27	12.07	10.40
1999 ARM	13.67	14.03	12.82	12.84	11.32	10.19	586,427	14.76	13.77	14.91	15.83	16.98	14.36
2000 FIX	6.85	6.40		6.95	11.35	11.43	4,665,781	6.74	6.58	7.74	9.25	10.01	8.33
2000 ARM	7.15	6.90		6.92	9.82	9.77	673,163	13.34	12.66	14.35	15.68	15.58	12.92

*CPR: Conditional prepayment rate; WAC: Weighted average coupon; FIX:Fixed-rate mortgage; ARM: Adjustable-rate mortgage.
Source: First Union Securities, Inc.

EXHIBIT 16-7

Delinquency or Loss for the Universe of Manufactured Housing Asset-Backed Securities

	Delinquency or Loss by Vintage												
	As % of Remaining Balance									As % of Original Balance			
						Annualized Net Loss Rate				Annualized 1-Month			
Vintage	30 Days	60 Days	90+	REO[a]	1 Month	3 Month	6 Month	12 Month	Net Loss	Cumulative Net Loss	WALA[a]	Factor[b]	No. of Groups
1990 FIX	1.32	0.77	0.00	0.50	3.18	2.17	2.22	2.23	0.35	9.36	123	0.11	2
1991 FIX	1.49	0.49	0.12	0.35	1.07	1.35	1.40	1.45	0.19	5.97	111	0.17	4
1992 FIX	1.48	0.70	0.15	0.36	1.38	1.53	1.32	1.32	0.33	5.18	101	0.24	5
1993 FIX	1.40	1.12	0.00	0.47	1.01	1.36	1.27	1.30	0.32	3.78	88	0.31	4
1994 FIX	1.60	1.14	0.22	0.95	1.75	2.06	1.89	1.87	0.65	5.16	76	0.37	15
1995 FIX	1.96	1.70	0.40	1.90	2.03	2.45	2.42	2.47	0.94	6.14	65	0.46	21
1996 FIX	2.02	1.75	0.59	1.83	2.62	2.92	2.78	2.69	1.54	5.27	54	0.59	22
1997 FIX	2.33	2.04	1.37	2.09	2.56	3.05	2.92	2.82	1.67	4.20	41	0.65	30
1997 ARM	3.80	0.96	1.15	0.21						0.00	41	0.60	4
1998 FIX	2.07	1.66	1.45	2.53	2.20	2.52	2.33	2.05	1.78	2.27	28	0.81	27
1998 ARM	2.33	0.63	1.44	2.04	6.05	5.95	4.86	3.81	4.55	2.67	28	0.75	7
1999 FIX	2.70	2.45	1.25	2.14	1.22	1.49	1.32	0.92	1.11	0.85	18	0.90	15
1999 ARM	4.76	1.15	1.89	1.38	3.08	2.71	2.32	1.57	2.52	0.59	17	0.82	6
2000 FIX	1.67	1.61	0.27	1.00	0.49	0.45	0.32	0.20	0.47	0.14	8	0.96	8
2000 ARM	2.29	0.80	0.85	1.00	1.58	1.36	0.82	0.55	1.49	0.40	9	0.95	5

[a]REO: Real estate owned; WALA: Weighted average loan age; FIX: Fixed-rate mortgage; ARM: adjustable-rate mortgage.
[b]Factor: Remaining balance compared with the original balance.
Source: First Union Securities, Inc.

3, followed by a decline until the loans are seasoned (6–7 years). By this time, the factors (current pool collateral balance) are in the 0.2 to 0.3 range, possibly indicating adverse borrower selection and burnout in seasoned pools.

In Exhibits 16–8 and 16–9, the historical data on Green Tree shows fairly consistent collateral performance, with prepayments over the past two years oscillating in a fairly narrow range around a 12% constant prepayment rate (CPR);

EXHIBIT 16–8

Green Tree Financial Corp. Aggregate Historical CPR* Versus Model CPR

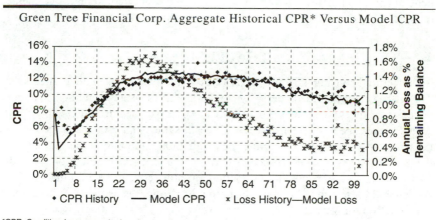

*CPR: Conditional prepayment rate.
Source: First Union Securities, Inc.

EXHIBIT 16–9

Green Tree Financial Corp. Cumulative Losses

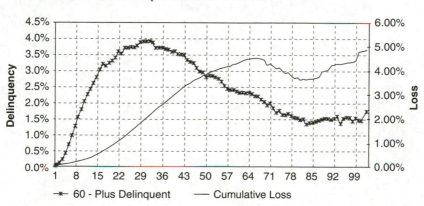

Source: First Union Securities, Inc.

this is consistent with Green Tree's FASB 125 assumption of 200 MHP. The effect of competition and the subsequent rise in prepayments is apparent in Exhibit 16–8. Delinquencies (60+ days) have been between 1.5% and 2.0% over the same time frame, with the peak occurring out about 2.5 years. Annualized net losses peak at Year 3 at just under 2.5%. There is some collateral performance tail risk since cumulative net losses rise after Year 5, though thus far exhibiting a much smaller cumulative net loss than the universe as a whole.

Other issuers show a higher base prepayment rate than Green Tree and the manufactured housing universe in general. It seems as though this asset class in general exhibits fairly stable prepayments and therefore better convexity characteristics than other competing mortgage-backed product.

CONCLUSION

Manufactured housing ABS have been a consistent investment vehicle since 1995. The diverse nature of the underlying collateral allows issuers and underwriters to create securities with favorable convexity characteristics and solid credit support. As with many specialty finance sectors, investors must understand and account for the competitive landscape affecting the origination and ongoing performance of these ABS. The growth of the secondary market, alternative distribution methods, and mortgagelike financing terms continue to draw consumers into this product. As demand for the underlying product remains strong, the asset class should be a viable option for investors.

CHAPTER 17

MORTGAGE CREDIT ANALYSIS

Joel W. Brown, CFA
Mortgage Credit Analyst
Stein, Roe & Farnham, Inc.

William M. Wadden IV
Senior Vice President and Principal
Stein, Roe & Farnham, Inc.

In 1983, the first CMO was introduced and it vastly increased the appeal of residential mortgages to the investment community. CMOs allowed for the tranching of principal and interest payments to fit specific investor profiles. As a result of CMO development, prepayment analysis gained momentum. The sophistication of prepayment analysis grew as fast as computer technology permitted, and Wall Street firms spent millions of dollars in this area of research. During the late-1980s, the securitization of nonagency jumbo whole loans not only utilized time tranching but credit tranching as well. Cash flow payment priority was split between senior and subordinate tranches whereby subordinate investors absorbed credit losses of the underlying mortgage loans. Whereas initial CMO innovation allowed the interest rate risk of agency mortgages to be tranched, subsequent innovation in senior-subordinate structures allowed nonagency whole-loan mortgages to be credit-tranched according to a variety of credit ratings. This permitted investors to adjust the level of mortgage credit risk suitable for their investment mandate. By the mid-1990s, the mortgage and mortgage-related asset-backed market evolved to the point where nonprime collateral had also become a permanent part of the mortgage credit landscape. The nonprime market includes alternative-A quality documentation (Alt-A), home equity loans, home improvement loans, manufactured housing, and 125% high LTV loans.

Mortgage credit analysis has not evolved to the same level of sophistication as prepayment analysis. In fact, highly leveraged credit-sensitive mortgage securities are created without modeling delinquency and loss rates in an equally sophisticated manner as is done for voluntary prepayments. The goal of this chapter

This chapter is reprinted with permission from Frank J. Fabozzi (ed.), *Investing in Asset-Backed Securities* (New Hope, PA: Frank J. Fabozzi Associates, 2000).

E X H I B I T   17–1

Standard Default Assumption Curve

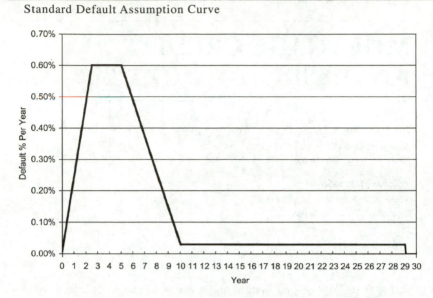

Source: Adaped from Exhibit 1 in Robert I. Gerber, "A User's guide to Buy-Side Bond Trading," Chapter 16 in Frank J. Fabozzi (ed.), *Managing Fixed Income Portfolios* (New Hope, PA: Frank J. Fabozzi, 1997), p. 279.

is to demystify the jargon of mortgage credit analysis as well as to present a preferred approach for forecasting delinquency and loss rates.

THE SDA CURVE

The Public Securities Association introduced the Standard Default Assumption (SDA curve) in 1993.[1] Exhibit 17–1 illustrates the shape of this curve. The SDA curve standardized default projections for prime mortgages, and it is useful for forecasting default rates on nonagency whole-loan REMICs. The SDA curve relates to defaults just as a PSA curve relates to prepayments; it is a forecasted speed for removing loans from a pool. With the SDA curve, default prompts the removal of a mortgage from a loan pool. In the real world of mortgage servicing, however, default is neither a delinquency nor liquidation. Instead, default signifies when foreclosure proceedings commence on a property. In the corporate bond market, default

---

1. Andrew K. Feigenberg and Adam S. Lechner, "A New Default Benchmark for Pricing Nonagency Securities," Salomon Brothers (July 22, 1993).

signifies the inability of a company to meet an interest or principal payment. In the mortgage market, a delinquency signifies the borrower's inability to make a timely payment. Thus, corporate bond credit terminology is not fungible to the mortgage credit market.

The mortgage credit analyst must forecast losses as well as defaults. By itself, the SDA curve is insufficient to forecast losses. Three other assumptions are necessary before obtaining a final loss curve:

1. The liquidation timeline
2. Whether a servicer advances principal and interest on a defaulted loan
3. Loss severity[2]

The liquidation timeline is the number of days required to foreclose and dispose of a property. The disposition might require the lender to acquire the property and hold it in inventory for some time before it can be sold [real estate owned (REO)] or use an alternative foreclosure process such as a deed in lieu of foreclosure.[3] Servicers may advance principal and interest payments to a security holder that a nondefaulted loan would otherwise pay. When the proceeds of a liquidated property do not cover the unpaid principal balance of a mortgage loan, a loss occurs. Loss severity is largely due to an impairment of a home's value, recovery of principal and interest advances, costs to remarket the property (brokers' fees and commissions), and legal fees incurred from the foreclosure process.

CONSTANT DEFAULT RATE APPROACH

Most nonagency mortgage credit analysis relies on the *constant default rate* (CDR) approach to forecast mortgage defaults. CDR is computed as follows:

$$CDR = 100 \times \left[1 - \left(1 - \frac{D_t}{P_{t-1} - S_t} \right)^{12} \right]$$

where

D_t = Defaulted loan balance in month t
P_t = Pool balance in month t
S_t = Scheduled principal payment in month t

---

2. Jerome S. Fons and James Schmidbauer, "Moody's Approach to Rating Residential Mortgage Pass-Through Securities," Moody's Investors Service (November 8, 1996).
3. Jack C. Harris and Jack P. Friedman, *Real Estate Handbook,* 4th ed. (Barrons, 1993).

As the above formula suggests, a CDR is merely a constant annualized rate at which defaulted loans are removed from their pool. A slight modification to the constant loan removal approach is to allow CDRs to gradually ramp upward during the first 12 to 24 months of a pool's life until reaching a plateau. Within the home equity sector, an analyst might fashion a base case assumption that ramps from 0% to 4% CDR over an 18-month period and then remains at 4% CDR for the rest of the transaction. To run a default stress on the transaction, the analyst will incrementally raise the CDR plateau until the first loss occurs.

A NEW APPROACH

We suggest that, by itself, the CDR approach (or its ramped version) is not a complete mortgage credit analysis tool. In the following text, we demonstrate a preferred method of mortgage credit analysis that has three principal improvements over the customary CDR framework:

- Focus on variables that can be measured from actual pool performance
- Focus on estimating loss curves as opposed to default curves
- Model transactions in dollars

Defaults Are Unobservable

Investors have a strong incentive to compare actual defaults versus their own estimated defaults. However, how does an analyst determine actual defaults? In order to properly compute a CDR it is necessary to have (1) a list of newly foreclosed loans, (2) the amount of time it took to liquidate or dispose of the property, (3) the principal and interest advanced, and (4) the gross liquidation proceeds. The effort required to calculate a CDR is not trivial. Market participants must have access to loan-level data obtained from mortgage servicing "tapes" in order to correctly compute an actual CDR. Oftentimes more than one set of tapes is required to track the above variables. Furthermore, it is difficult for investors to gain access to these tapes.

Neither are investors able to observe defaults from monthly remittance reports. The remittance report displays principal and interest payments received by each tranche, fundamental credit trends on the mortgage pool, month-to-month prepayments, and REMIC expenses. CDR, or the data necessary for its calculation, is rarely included in a remittance report. This is peculiar since CDR forecasting has ostensibly become a fundamental part of the forecasting process for nonprime and subordinate mortgages.

To illustrate, Exhibit 17–2 displays the remittance report for Advanta's 1997-1 home equity loan REMIC. The report identifies the stock of delinquencies (30–59, 60–89, and 90+ day), foreclosures, REO, and liquidations. Although this is one of the better remittance reports available, it does not itemize newly foreclosed or liquidated properties. Some remittance reports identify the number and quantity of newly foreclosed loans, but do not contain all the data required for a CDR calculation such as liquidation timelines. Several mortgage companies, notably Citicorp Mortgage, PNC, and RFC, provide access to loan-level information for CDR calculations. However, within the subprime mortgage universe, this level of information usually does not exist.

Liquidations and Losses Are Observable

Although default rates are unobservable, the monthly remittance report does provide figures for liquidated loan amounts and final losses. One of the main purposes of this chapter is to clarify and refine mortgage credit terminology, eliminating confusion among analysts regarding exactly what variables to use as the building blocks of loss forecasting. Instead of using the term CDR, we prefer to define two new terms, which we refer to as the *charge off rate* (COR) and the *loss rate* (LR).

The COR is the annualized rate of loan liquidations. The LR is the product of COR times the loss severity, and represents the annualized rate of losses. Although CDR is usually the core default model in credit-sensitive mortgage securities, in practice, COR actually becomes the monitoring tool. These newly coined terms are mathematically defined by the following formulas:

$$\text{Charge off rate (COR)} = 100 \times \left[1 - \left(1 - \frac{L_t}{P_{t-1} - S_t} \right)^{12} \right]$$

$$\text{Loss severity} = \frac{L - LP}{L}$$

$$\text{Loss rate (LR)} = \text{COR} \times \text{Loss severity}$$

where

L_t = Liquidated loan balance in month t
LP = Liquidation proceeds
P_t = Pool balance in month t
S_t = Scheduled principal payment in month t

Loss severity is 100% when there are no liquidation proceeds, and zero severity occurs when liquidation proceeds equal the liquidated loan balance.

EXHIBIT 17-2

Advanta Mortgage Loan Trust 1997-1 Mortgage Loan—Asset-Backed Certificates Series 1997-1*

Distribution date: December 27, 1999.

Delinquent Loan Information	30–59 days	60–89 days	90+ days (Excluding F/C, REO and Bankruptcy)	Loans in Bankruptcy	Loans in REO	Loans in Foreclosure
Group 1						
Principal balance	3,301,696.44	941,404.09	838,993.29	7,760,042.35	2,822,331.52	5,800,546.82
Percentage of pool balance	2.41%	0.69%	0.61%	5.66%	2.06%	4.23%
Number of loans	64	14	17	142	54	111
Percentage of pool loans	2.67%	0.58%	0.71%	5.92%	2.25%	4.63%
Group 2						
Principal balance	2,354,380.80	434,838.32	500,139.13	6,091,800.19	2,711,702.82	5,150,247.38
Percentage of pool balance	3.84%	0.71%	0.82%	9.95%	4.43%	8.41%
Number of loans	29	4	6	60	28	57
Percentage of pool loans	4.39%	0.61%	0.91%	9.09%	4.24%	8.64%
Combined						
REO book value					7,063,774.27	

General Mortgage Loan Information	Group 1	Group II	Total
Beginning aggregate mortgage loan balance	140,886,676.31	63,121,656.45	204,008,332.76
Principal reduction	3,790,575.73	1,887,296.44	5,677,872.17
Ending aggregate mortgage loan balance	137,096,100.58	61,234,360.01	198,330,460.59
Beginning aggregate mortgage loan count	2,462	676	3,138
Ending aggregate mortgage loan count	2,399	660	3,059
Current weighted average coupon rate	10.65%	11.17%	10.81%
Next weighted average coupon rate	10.64%	11.20%	10.81%

Mortgage Loan Principal Reduction Information

	Group I	Group II	Total
Scheduled principal	245,905.84	33,311.49	279,217.33
Curtailments	0	0	0
Prepayments	2,586,759.04	1,339,677.68	3,926,436.72
Repurchases/Substitutions	0	0	0
Liquidation Proceeds	957,910.85	514,307.27	1,472,218.12
Other principal	0	0	0
Less: Realized losses	504,553.17	135,356.32	639,909.49
Less: Delinquent principal not advanced by servicer	0	0	0
Total principal reduction	3,286,022.56	1,751,940.12	5,037,962.68

Servicer Information

	Group I	Group II	Total
Accrued servicing fee for the current period	39,788.53	14,254.34	54,042.87
Less: Amounts to cover interest shortfalls	598.43	605.69	1,204.12
Less: Delinquent service fees	18,914.25	12,046.35	30,960.60
Collected servicing fees for current period	20,275.85	1,602.30	21,878.15
Advanced principal	33,735.40	8,333.23	42,068.63
Advanced interest	403,698.79	267,499.22	671,198.01

*Statement to certificate holders.

Source: © Copyright 1999 Deutsche Bank.

Losses Are Deducted from Credit Enhancement

In most nonprime mortgage securities, losses are deducted from excess spread. These structures typically use excess spread as the first layer of credit enhancement to cover losses, backed up by overcollateralization and/or subordination. Excess spread is the difference between the mortgage interest collected from borrowers, less the interest payments made to bondholders and any fees paid from the trust. Without explicitly incorporating all the variables influencing ultimate losses, it is impossible for an analyst to determine that a given default rate can be adequately handled by excess spread. Due to the timing difference between a defaulted loan and its ultimate liquidation, it is difficult to determine that a given level of defaults can be absorbed by excess spread without causing deterioration in other forms of credit enhancement.

COR Is Dependent on Voluntary Prepayments and Liquidation Timelines

During 1998 and 1999, some large monoline finance companies failed.[4] One of the prime reasons for failure was due to gain-on-sale accounting assumptions. More specifically, their CDR assumptions broke down. The CDR assumptions failed because voluntary prepayment rates rose and liquidation timelines lengthened. Unexpected changes in voluntary prepayments and liquidation timelines can have a significant impact on the economics of a mortgage securitization.

Exhibits 17–3 and 17–4 illustrate our point. In each of these illustrations, principal payments were calculated using a pool of home equity loans with an 11% gross WAC and 300-month WAM. We also assumed a CDR forecast that ramped from 0% to 4% over 18 months. In Exhibit 17–3, we examine the more minor impact of voluntary prepayment stress on COR calculations. In this example, COR is calculated as a function of two different voluntary CPR vectors. The base case vector ramps from 4% to 25% CPR over 18 months, while the faster vector ramps from 4% to 35% over the same time period. The 10% higher CPR plateau causes the COR calculation to peak at a higher level, 5.9%, versus the base case, which produces a COR of 5.4%. The liquidation timeline pushes a defaulted dollar into the future until it becomes liquidated. Prepayments cause the remaining balance to decline over time. Therefore, a defaulted dollar becomes a larger percentage of the remaining principal balance when it is liquidated. Furthermore, the difference between the CDR and COR increases as prepayments rise. This effect is seen in Exhibit 17–3, where the COR is higher than the CDR when the ramp-up period and liquidation timeline are complete.

The more significant influence occurs when the liquidation timeline lengthens. Exhibit 17–4 shows two COR functions, both created from the same 0% to 4% CDR ramp and 4% to 25% base case voluntary CPR vector. The first COR function is determined using a 12-month liquidation timeline. The second COR func-

---

4. Some of the specialty finance companies that filed for bankruptcy or faced significant reorganization included: AMRESCO (HEL), First Plus Financial (125 LTV), IMC Mortgage (HEL), Southern Pacific Funding (HEL), and UCFC (HEL & MH).

EXHIBIT   17–3

CDR Versus COR Voluntary CPR Stress

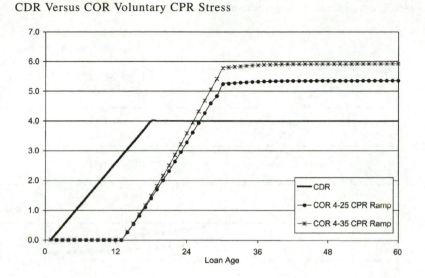

EXHIBIT   17–4

CDR Versus COR Timeline Stress

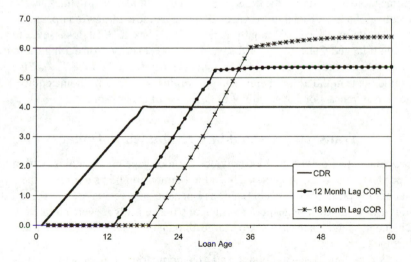

tion represents an 18-month liquidation timeline. Lengthening the liquidation time-line by only 6 months causes the COR to rise to 6.4% from 5.4%. Again, the COR increases as the timeline lengthens, because the remaining loan balance is given a chance to decline further with 6 months additional time. As an aside, loss severity will also rise as the timeline stretches because principal and interest advances

EXHIBIT 17–5

Net Excess Spread Versus Voluntary CPR Stress

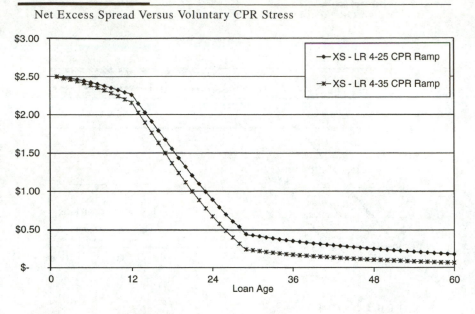

become more expensive to the transaction. Longer liquidation timelines are usually indicative of a less efficient mortgage servicing and loss mitigation operation.

Assuming that a 12-month lagged COR has a 35% loss severity, an 18-month lagged COR might produce a 45% loss severity. Correlating these two factors causes the loss rate (LR) to increase from 1.88% to 2.87%. Such an increase in the liquidation timeline can put serious pressure on a home equity deal, since these transactions have only 2.0% to 2.5% of excess spread.

Transactions Should Be Evaluated in Dollars

Observing actual dollars at work provides the mortgage credit analyst with much deeper insight into a transaction. This added dimension helps eliminate the noise that ongoing principal balance reductions can have on percentage-based credit statistics. For instance, when a pool's principal balance is high, even a relatively low delinquency percentage can lead to a large amount of delinquent loans that are burdensome to the servicer.

Forecasting losses in dollars, and then comparing those losses to credit enhancement levels is the ultimate goal of a mortgage credit analyst. Exhibits 17–5 and 17–6 take the COR vectors previously shown and convert charge-offs into future dollar amounts of losses. These losses are subtracted from excess spread to determine net excess spread. Exhibit 17–5 shows the net dollars of excess spread remaining after losses have been charged off from our hypothetical transaction, assuming the transaction generates 2.5% of excess spread and loss severity is 35%.

EXHIBIT 17–6

Net Excess Spread Versus Timeline Stress

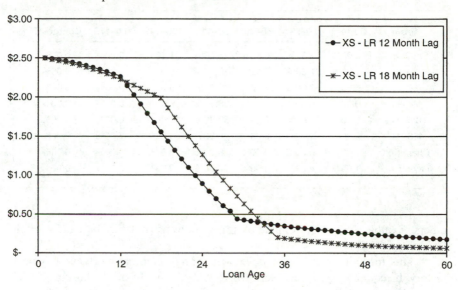

The dollar amount of net excess spread declines as higher voluntary prepayments produce lower amounts of remaining principal balance. A 10% increase in voluntary prepayment cuts the dollar amount of net excess spread virtually in half, causing a real squeeze in credit enhancement.

Exhibit 17–6 demonstrates how a longer liquidation timeline affects the timing of net excess spread. As liquidation timelines increase, losses are lower early on. This delay causes the losses to be applied versus a lower amount of excess spread, thus causing a real squeeze of excess spread later in the transaction. Both graphs show little net excess spread dollars by the third year.

TRANSITION MATRIX APPROACH

Up to now, we have defined more precise terminology for evaluating and measuring mortgage credit risk. Establishing better terminology is just a beginning, because mortgage credit analysts still need better tools to forecast delinquency and loss rates. The use of transition probability matrices offers one promising approach. This procedure measures the probability of a mortgagor "rolling" (or transitioning) from one credit status to another. To imagine how this works, consider a borrower who is 30 to 59 days delinquent. A transition matrix contains the complete set of mathematical probabilities of this borrower rolling from his or her current status to any of the other possible states (1) performing, (2) more severely delinquent (60–89 days), (3) refinanced, or (4) bankrupt. Also contained within the matrix are probabilities of status changes from those states to the remaining

E X H I B I T   17–7

Transition Probability Matrix

From	Current	30–59	60–89	90–119	120–149	150–179	Charge-off
To: Current	96.63%	31.37%	6.15%	6.43%	1.00%	0.00%	0.00%
30–59	1.72%	27.00%	7.12%	0.00%	0.00%	0.00%	0.00%
60–89	0.00%	37.00%	12.00%	10.13%	0.00%	0.00%	0.00%
90–119	0.00%	0.00%	74.73%	26.01%	4.00%	0.00%	0.00%
120–149	0.00%	0.00%	0.00%	57.43%	12.00%	0.00%	0.00%
150–179	0.00%	0.00%	0.00%	0.00%	83.00%	7.00%	0.00%
Charge-off	0.00%	0.00%	0.00%	0.00%	0.00%	93.00%	0.00%
Pay-off	1.65%	4.63%	0.00%	0.00%	0.00%	0.00%	0.00%

others. Exhibit 17–7 is an example of a transition matrix table for a 125% High LTV securitization.

This transition matrix was developed using empirical mortgage payment history. It required loan-level detail, which was obtained from the mortgage servicer's loan tapes. Due to the simplicity of loss mitigation options, 125% high LTV loans are an ideal collateral class to forecast delinquencies and losses with transition matrix technology. This mortgage subsector has no foreclosure or REO process, and the loss mitigation effort is more transparent because of the sequential order of realized delinquency experience. Either delinquent borrowers are cured, or they progressively become more delinquent. Loans are then liquidated after missing seven consecutive payments.

It is not as cut and dry to develop a transition matrix for a pool of first lien mortgages (such as home equity loans). Within the foreclosure bucket, a range of delinquency periods exists, each requiring a different loss mitigation approach. This produces a unique roll rate emanating from each subdelinquency category. To complicate matters further, state laws dictate foreclosure timelines unique to each state.

The graph presented in Exhibit 17–8 uses transition probabilities from Exhibit 17–7. We connected actual delinquency figures to the matrix to develop a forward-looking delinquency forecast measured as a percent of remaining principal balance. CPR and COR forecasts can be developed with this framework, too. Furthermore, it is very easy to observe the effect on delinquency and loss rates by changing any one of the variables in the matrix. The mortgage credit analyst can appreciate the transition matrix framework compared to more simplistic approaches. For instance, some CDR-based models forecast delinquencies as a percentage of defaults. This type of forecast is both backward-looking and unintuitive. Due to the complex delinquency and loss-based trigger and step-up formulas embedded in securitizations, it is imperative that analysts make use of the best possible delinquency forecast.

E X H I B I T   17–8

Delinquency

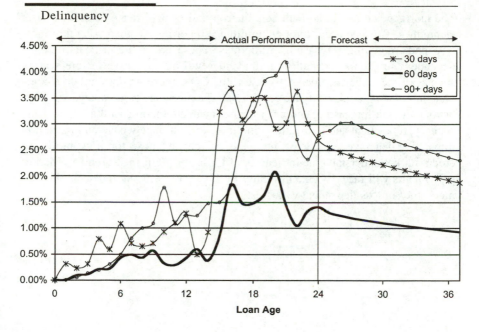

Although the initial motivation for developing a transition matrix is for credit forecasting, there is a hidden benefit in that it can be used to quantitatively compare performance among different servicers. A transition matrix may help identify whether delinquency transition differences are due to unique loan and geographical concentrations or to unique servicing practices. However, if loan attributes are identical, a transition matrix will measure the effectiveness of loss mitigation strategies on roll rates and timeline management among servicers.

Thus far the most sophisticated transition matrix has been developed from Markov chain analysis. This work is very promising, but analysis is limited to only a few servicers and collateral programs. We have uncovered one shortcoming to the transition matrix approach: delinquency, COR, and CPR achieve a level state after several months into the forecast due to constant transition ratios.

We do not think that transition matrix analysis is fully mature today. There is more room for development and sophistication in this area of research. Nonagency mortgage servicers have much more data available to analyze than agency programs, and many of the nonprime mortgage programs have been around long enough from which useful data are available. In the future, we will likely see transition matrices with time-dependent features such as pool seasoning, and geographic factors will influence the foreclosure timelines. The greater number of variables within a transition matrix framework will provide mortgage credit analysts a robust tool for delinquency and loss forecasts.

CONCLUSION

The mortgage credit market will benefit from more sophisticated credit analysis techniques. This can occur through remittance reporting, standardizing terminology, and improving forecasting techniques. These issues are critical for loss-dependent structures and collateral, and they will help improve mature sectors such as prime nonagency deals. By itself, the CDR approach does not do a complete job of evaluating mortgage credit risk. The mortgage credit analyst must go beyond default forecasting and must further evaluate the impact that other risks, such as prepayment and liquidation timelines, will ultimately have on losses. It is imperative that anyone participating in the loss-dependent sector of the mortgage credit market understand the intricacies of CDR and COR measurement. Market participants will face extreme difficulty in this sector without understanding the mechanics of loss-dependent variables.

CHAPTER 18

CREDIT PERFORMANCE OF HIGH LTV LOANS

Thomas Zimmerman
Director
Mortgage Strategy Group
UBS Warburg

Kumar Neelakantan
Vice President
ABS Research
Credit Suisse First Boston

The high loan-to-value (LTV) market (sometimes referred to as the "125 market" because issuers allow LTVs of up to 125%) is still struggling to right itself after the severe credit problems of 1998. As other sectors improve, the high LTV sector continues to lag. There are several reasons why a more complete recovery has not come sooner. Many of the leading issuers were specialty finance companies. When the credit crisis hit, the largest (FirstPlus) was driven into bankruptcy and others were forced to exit the sector or vastly decrease loan production. Even more important, early underwriting standards for this relatively new product proved less stringent than they should have been. The result was that deals from 1996 to early 1997 experienced higher-than-expected defaults. Because of this performance, many investors still perceive the product as a poor credit risk.

However, since the credit crisis of 1998, the high LTV sector has evolved from being dominated by highly leveraged finance companies to being led by well-capitalized companies with strong parents. The participation of RFC as an issuer and the purchase of DiTech by GMAC Mortgage have greatly enhanced the market's credibility and liquidity. The presence of these well-capitalized companies issuing securities should encourage more investors to return to the sector.

Another reason for the slow recovery was a lack of historical data on this sector's performance since it is a relatively new product. We think the study reported in this chapter will go a long way toward filling that information gap. This study is a major reevaluation of the credit performance of the high LTV mortgage sector. The study utilizes a large loan-level database composed of over 340,000 loans from FirstPlus, Empire, Master Financial, and RFC with almost 50,000 loans having at least 3 years of data. The purpose of this study is to incorporate new insights into credit performance and to examine the important role nonquantitative criteria play in predicting defaults.

High LTV Loan-Level Database

The study includes data from 29 deals, including twelve from FirstPlus, eight from Empire, five from Master Financial, and four from RFC (see Exhibit 18–1). Master Financial issued two deals using RFC's shelf, RFMS2 1997 HI-1 and HI-3, and so these are included with Master's performance data, not with RFC's. Note that all the 1996 loan data, the oldest in the study, are from FirstPlus and represent the early underwriting standards that were in place at that time. All the 1999 loan data, the most recent in the study, are from RFC and represent the new underwriting standards. In Exhibit 18–2 we break out the loan-level data used in our study by issuer and by seasoning to show the depth of product currently in our database. Our database consists of 340,336 loans, of which, 224,562 have 24 months of seasoning and 49,524 have 36 months of seasoning. To our knowledge, this database of $10.97 billion in loans is the largest high LTV portfolio reviewed to date.

Average Loan Characteristics

Exhibit 18–3 shows a number of key loan characteristics by issuer and by vintage year. In our study we used vintage years to summarize the results of the analysis. This table highlights some of the improvement in credit quality in the loan characteristics over time. For example, the percentage of FirstPlus loans with FICO scores below 640 went from 29% in 1996 to 4% in 1998, and the percentage of California loans went from over 50% in the early days to a current level of 15% to 20%. On balance, there has been a very noticeable trend toward higher-quality borrowers.

Defaults Versus Losses

Before looking at the actual results of our study, it seems useful to review how high LTV credit analysis differs from the analysis of most other mortgage-related securities.

Since high LTV lending involves a second lien position with the LTV in excess of 100%, in the event of a default, losses approach 100%. (Servicers do, in fact, recover a small percentage on defaulted loans, typically between 5% and 15%.) The deal structure required by the rating agencies charges loans off after 180 days, but the servicer continues to collect on the loans (any collections after the mandatory charge-off flow through the waterfall as excess interest).

This has several ramifications. For one, delinquencies, foreclosures, and REOs do not build as they sometimes do in other housing sectors. Also, with the assumption of 100% loss severity and a 180 day write-off, the terms *default* and *loss* have virtually the same meaning and are often used interchangeably. In contrast, in most other parts of the residential mortgage market, defaults are linked indirectly to losses by recovery rates and loss severities, both of which can differ markedly from company to company. In the high LTV market, loss severity is not a major concern. This is not to suggest that intensive servicing and collection efforts are not important: they are. However, it is generally not economical to trigger a foreclosure on a defaulted high LTV loan. Hence, the issues of loss severity and proper LTV percentage take on a much lower profile than when the foreclosure option is more viable.

EXHIBIT 18–1

Deals Used in High LTV Credit Performance Study

Issuer	Vintage Year	Avg. GWAC[a]	Avg. FICO[b]	FICO <640 (%)	Avg. DI[c]	% DI[c] <1500 (%)	Loans with DI[c] Data (%)	Avg. DTI[d]	Avg. CLTV[e]	Avg. Orig. Bal.	Avg. Orig. Term	CA (%)	Prepay Penalty (%)	Number of Loans
FirstPlus	1996	14.5	664	29	3,115	7	22	37	114	31,263	225	54	63	32,593
	1997	13.8	681	9	3,017	8	17	36	112	36,329	234	33	42	96,384
	1998	13.5	688	4	NA	NA	NA	35	113	37,262	252	15	45	83,426
Empire	1997	14.2	672	17	3,456	4	99	36	115	38,070	240	33	NA	28,609
	1998	13.7	680	8	3,476	3	78	35	117	40,995	228	13	NA	24,044
RFC	1998	13.8	678	10	3,482	4	100	38	116	41,948	223	17	35	17,097
	1999	13.7	691	2	3,310	1	100	39	116	40,303	240	16	57	24,272
Master	1997	14.1	670	18	4,909	2	100	35	114	45,907	244	51	44	19,390
	1998	13.8	677	13	3,487	3	100	39	113	45,919	240	25	41	14,426

[a]GWAC = gross weighted average coupon.
[b]FICO = Fair, Isaac Company.
[c]DI = disposable income.
[d]DTI = debt to income.
[e]CLTV = combined loan to value.

EXHIBIT 18–2

Loans Used in High LTV Credit Performance Study

Loan Age (months)	FirstPlus			Empire			Master			RFC			Aggregate		
	No. of Loans	Bal. ($MM)	Avg. FICO	No. of Loans	Bal. ($MM)	Avg. FICO	No. of Loans	Bal. ($MM)	Avg. FICO	No. of Loans	Bal. ($MM)	Avg. FICO	No. of Loans	Bal. ($MM)	Avg. FICO
1	212,468	6,512.78	682	52,683	1,741.93	676	33,816	1,233.96	673	41,369	1,481.45	686	340,336	10,967.27	681
2	212,465	6,501.50	682	52,681	1,737.79	676	33,816	1,195.75	673	41,369	1,479.33	686	340,331	10,912.00	681
3	212,463	6,484.09	682	52,677	1,732.61	676	33,816	1,181.16	673	41,369	1,476.45	686	340,325	10,872.63	681
4	212,460	6,458.70	682	52,676	1,725.46	676	33,816	1,171.07	673	40,537	1,443.67	686	339,489	10,797.48	681
5	212,455	6,426.52	682	52,674	1,717.88	676	33,816	1,163.57	673	37,491	1,330.91	685	336,436	10,637.69	681
6	212,453	6,388.03	682	52,671	1,709.84	676	33,816	1,156.75	673	33,881	1,197.90	684	332,821	10,451.86	680
7	212,452	6,341.22	682	52,668	1,696.73	676	33,816	1,149.18	673.	30,744	1,083.56	684	329,680	10,270.08	680
8	212,452	6,288.69	682	52,666	1,680.24	676	33,816	1,141.26	673	27,966	977.53	683	326,900	10,087.38	680
9	212,452	6,227.59	682	52,665	1,664.07	676	33,816	1,132.18	673	24,770	859.99	682	323,703	9,883.76	680
10	212,451	6,162.01	682	52,663	1,645.38	676	33,816	1,122.06	673	22,102	761.22	680	321,032	9,690.84	680
11	212,446	6,086.82	682	52,657	1,624.67	676	33,816	1,111.36	673	19,883	681.07	680	318,802	9,504.23	680
12	212,437	5,991.66	682	52,654	1,596.68	676	33,816	1,097.22	673	17,937	609.34	679	316,844	9,295.06	680
13	212,435	5,880.93	682	52,652	1,567.74	676	33,816	1,079.32	673	16,510	552.20	679	315,413	9,080.21	680
14	212,427	5,765.49	682	52,649	1,539.11	676	33,816	1,061.37	673	15,332	505.96	679	314,224	8,872.00	680
15	212,421	5,651.42	682	50,446	1,442.73	676	33,816	1,043.79	673	14,173	462.15	679	310,856	8,600.25	680
16	212,417	5,536.83	682	47,492	1,324.46	675	33,816	1,024.23	673	13,125	418.60	679	306,850	8,304.04	680
17	211,685	5,404.70	682	45,829	1,249.16	675	33,816	1,006.24	673	11,990	373.22	679	303,320	8,033.14	680
18	209,488	5,231.34	682	44,742	1,195.03	675	33,816	986.10	673	10,911	331.78	678	298,957	7,744.07	680
19	204,153	4,972.94	682	42,405	1,107.82	675	33,720	962.94	673	10,103	299.60	678	290,381	7,343.26	679
20	195,951	4,647.85	682	40,034	1,020.43	674	33,069	937.33	673	9,263	267.98	678	278,317	6,873.63	679
21	187,332	4,327.89	681	37,644	934.81	673	31,756	889.72	672	8,259	232.61	678	264,991	6,384.99	679
22	178,691	4,017.29	681	36,025	872.21	673	30,324	830.95	672	7,366	201.77	678	252,406	4,922.30	678
23	171,694	3,760.70	680	34,154	803.20	673	28,529	783.48	672	6,249	167.14	678	240,626	5,514.61	678
24	162,461	3,461.64	680	30,731	697.96	673	26,388	718.05	671	4,982	129.29	678	224,562	5,007.03	678
25	152,458	3,153.75	679	28,111	619.94	673	24,247	643.37	671	3,819	95.87	678	208,635	4,512.93	677
26	140,365	2,808.60	679	25,156	539.38	673	22,048	568.91	671	2,887	69.93	677	190,456	3,986.81	677
27	128,520	2,485.32	678	21,698	453.48	673	20,091	504.34	670	2,109	48.30	676	172,418	3,491.45	676
28	118,006	2,203.06	677	18,021	367.35	673	18,267	442.75	670	1,310	27.96	672	155,604	3,041.14	676

29	107,354	1,933.90	676	13,930	276.25	672	15,834	369.31	670	735	15.15	670	137,853	2,594.60	675
30	96,686	1,683.18	675	10,258	192.38	671	13,214	293.05	671	437	8.49	670	120,595	2,177.10	674
31	87,206	1,469.14	675	7,711	137.13	671	10,633	218.52	670	260	4.86	668	105,810	1,829.66	674
32	76,237	1,242.40	673	5,016	82.87	669	9,098	175.63	670	164	2.87	666	90,515	1,503.77	673
33	66,033	1,033.06	672	2,973	44.45	666	8,178	149.91	670	89	1.58	664	77,273	1,228.99	671
34	57,390	865.56	671	2,182	30.78	663	7,319	126.65	670	28	0.48	676	66,919	1,023.46	670
35	50,105	726.13	669	1,725	23.46	662	6,132	99.45	670	7	0.09	700	57,969	849.14	669
36	43,429	601.10	668	1,215	16.06	659	4,875	71.63	671	5	0.06	695	49,524	688.85	668
37	38,159	501.08	666	933	12.13	657	3,661	46.38	670				42,757	559.64	666
38	31,656	394.49	665	582	6.99	655	2,786	29.67	674				35,027	431.18	665
39	24,679	292.28	663	302	3.17	652	2,143	19.39	677				27,127	314.88	664
40	17,695	197.34	662	72	0.65	633	1,726	13.59	681				19,494	211.61	663
41	11,817	128.29	662	8	0.13	655	1,451	9.42	683				13,277	137.88	663
42	8,209	84.05	661	5	0.12	655	1,350	7.66	684				9,565	91.86	663
43	5,556	53.76	660	3	0.09	664	1,268	653	684				6,828	60.42	663
44	3,225	29.43	660	2	0.07	708	1,180	5.65	686				4,408	35.18	664
45	1,591	13.78	661	2	0.07	708	1,124	4.99	685				2,718	18.87	668
46	727	5.93	657	2	0.07	708	1,079	4.50	684				1,809	10.53	669
47	537	5.22	658	2	0.07	708	1,040	4.02	684				1,580	9.34	670
48	451	4.84	659	2	0.07	7.08	996	3.63	683				1,450	8.56	670
49	410	4.55	659				943	3.19	680				1,356	7.84	669
50	267	3.07	660				898	2.87	678				1,168	6.03	670
51	147	1.52	659				840	2.46	675				990	4.08	672
52	81	0.84	657				785	2.17	670				869	3.11	671
53	60	0.57	656				715	1.82	669				778	2.48	668
54	57	0.53	658				640	1.38	665				700	2.00	668
55	55	0.51	658				559	1.05	660				617	1.65	666
56	54	0.49	658				495	0.81	653				551	1.35	663
57	54	0.44	658				435	0.63	647				491	1.13	660
58	53	0.41	654				383	0.52	640				438	0.99	655
59	51	0.38	654				341	0.44	634				394	0.87	653
60	43	0.28	658				294	0.34	629				339	0.67	653
61	33	0.23	654				247	0.31	627				282	0.59	649
62	24	0.19	656				208	0.30	627				234	0.53	649
63	11	0.12	659				179	0.29	627				192	0.47	649
64	10	0.12	659				149	0.29	627				161	0.46	649

EXHIBIT 18-3

Loan and Borrower Characteristics by Issuer and Vintage Year

Issuer	Vintage Year	Avg. GWAC	Avg. FICO	FICO < 640 (%)	Age. Disp. Inc.	Disp. Inc. < 1500 (%)	Loans with Disp. Inc. Data (%)	Avg. DTI	Avg. CLTV	Avg. Orig. Bal.	Avg. Orig. Term	CA (%)	Prepay Penalty (%)	Number of Loans
FirstPlus	1996	14.5	664	29	3,115	7	22	37	114	31,263	225	54	63	32,593
	1997	13.8	681	9	3,017	8	17	36	112	36,329	234	33	42	96,384
	1998	13.5	688	4	NA	NA	NA	35	113	37,262	252	15	45	83,426
Empire	1997	14.2	672	17	3,456	4	99	36	115	38,070	240	33	NA	28,609
	1998	13.7	680	8	3,476	3	78	35	117	40,995	228	13	NA	24,044
RFC	1998	13.8	678	10	3,482	4	100	38	116	41,948	223	17	35	17,097
	1999	13.7	691	2	3,310	1	100	39	116	40,303	240	16	57	24,272
Master	1997	14.1	670	18	4,909	2	100	35	114	45,907	244	51	44	19,390
	1998	13.8	677	13	3,487	3	100	39	113	45,919	240	25	41	14,426

EXHIBIT   18–4

High LTV Default Curves by Vintage Year—Industry Averages

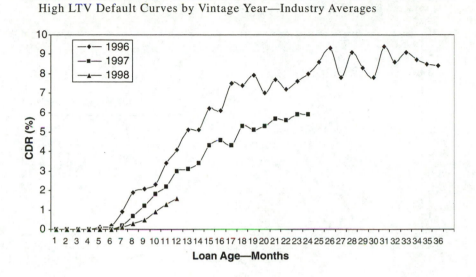

High LTV Default Curve

Exhibit 18–4 shows the default curves derived from our loan-level database as industry averages for the 1996, 1997, and 1998 vintage years. These results are important for several reasons. First, as recently as 6 months ago there was some question as to whether and where the high LTV default curve would level off. Sufficient loans have seasoned that a typical high LTV default curve is beginning to emerge. As seen in Exhibit 18–4, for the first 6 months the curve is zero (no loans are written off for 180 days); it then rises steadily through months 20 to 22 and then levels off. We suspect the default rate will remain at a plateau for around 1½ years, and then begin to decline. We base that estimate on the fact that high LTV delinquency curves appear to be turning down at around 36 months. Defaults should turn down with a lag. The second important point from the exhibit is that the default rate on the later vintage years is much lower than on the earlier years. The trend toward higher credit quality has had a significant and unmistakable impact on the credit performance of this product.

In order to compare the three vintage curves, in Exhibit 18–5 we extrapolated the current default curves from Exhibit 18–4 out to 36 months. It appears that whereas the 1996 loans leveled off at 8%-plus CDR, the 1997 loans are leveling off at around 6%, and the 1998 loans are likely to level off at just over 4%. So when we talk about an improvement in the credit quality of the average high LTV product, we are not just talking about loan and borrower characteristics, but the actual performance of the loans, as well.

EXHIBIT 18–5

Projected High LTV Default Curves—Industry Averages

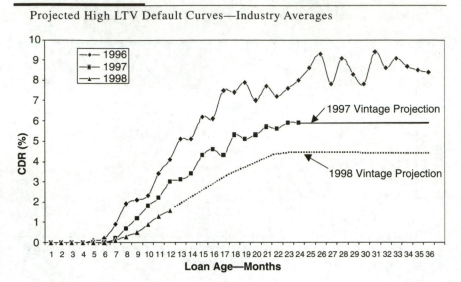

EXHIBIT 18–6

High LTV Cumulative Default Curves by Vintage Year—Industry Averages

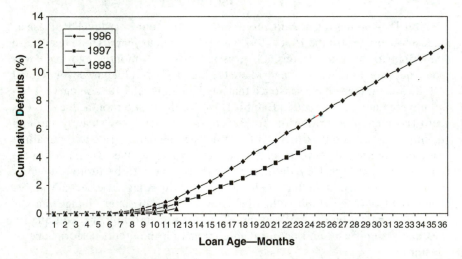

Exhibits 18–4 and 18–5 show credit performance as monthly default rates measured in CDRs. That is, the amount of loan balance defaulted each month is depicted as a percent of the remaining loan balance, at an annual percentage rate (a calculation equivalent to computing a CPR for prepayment speeds). Exhibits 18–6 and 18–7 show the same credit performance in terms of cumulative losses, that is, total balances written off as a percent of the original balance.

EXHIBIT   18–7

Projected High LTV Cumulative Default Curves—Industry Averages

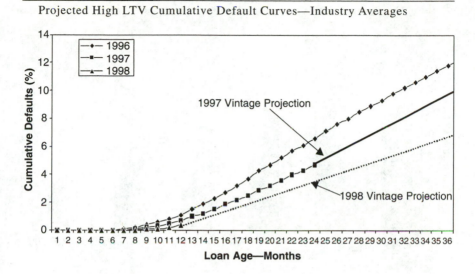

Exhibits 18–6 and 18–7 show the same trends as Exhibits 18–4 and 18–5, but on a cumulative basis. Cumulative losses on the 1996-year loans are approximately 12% at month 36. Our extrapolation in Exhibit 18–7 puts 1997 and 1998 vintage year losses at 10% and 7%, respectively, by the 36th month.

Going one step further, we can project total losses beyond the seasoning shown in Exhibit 18–7, to the end of the average loans life, with the help of an assumed standard default curve. This is a curve that gives the expected distribution of total losses over time. On the basis of that standard curve, the level of defaults shown in Exhibit 18–7, and the expected voluntary prepayment speeds, it appears that total losses on the 1996 loans will approach 20%. In contrast, total losses on the 1998 loans should be closer to 10%. And as we show later, there is reason to believe that the 1999 and 2000 vintage year high LTV product will perform even better.

The total losses discussed above should be viewed in relation to the enhancement on a high LTV securitization. We note that in a typical 1998 high LTV deal, the AAA bonds were protected against losses of up to 40-plus% by excess spread, over-collateralization, and subordination. This high level of enhancement reflected the rating agencies' conservative stance when setting levels for a new asset class. However, even though credit performance has improved dramatically, the rating agencies continue to use their conservative enhancement levels from the early days.

QUANTITATIVE FACTORS THAT DETERMINE DEFAULTS

From the earliest days of the 125 market, issuers were well aware that this product contained more risk than the average residential mortgage loan, because it is essentially unsecured debt. In fact, many feel it should be viewed as a cross between

EXHIBIT 18–8

FICO Versus Cumulative Defaults—Industry Averages

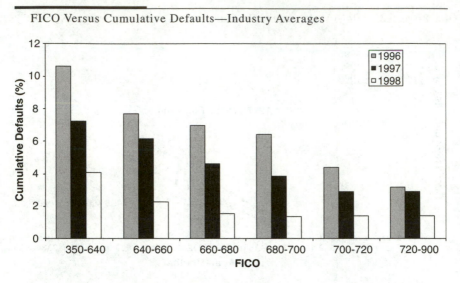

credit card and mortgage debt. High LTV issuers, in general, will only lend to borrowers with good credit, typically someone who could qualify for a conforming mortgage but needs to borrow an amount that takes them beyond the 100% LTV threshold. Since the LTV is above 100% and foreclosure is not as viable as in other mortgage products, there has always been a great deal of attention given to FICO scores and other factors that determine consumer credit. As in other areas of consumer lending, the task is to assess the expected credit losses for various combinations of borrower and loan characteristics and then to price the loans accordingly.

In this section we show the degree to which different attributes such as FICO, disposable income, debt to income (DTI), loan balance, combined loan to value (CLTV), loan term, and state concentration (see the section below on the California percentage) impact default rates. In a later section we take a look at some nonquantitative factors that can have a significant impact on credit performance.

FICO

Exhibit 18–8 shows the well-known relationship between FICO scores and defaults in 125 lending. The graph shows cumulative defaults by vintage year. Notice that the shape of the curve is similar for each vintage, but it becomes more exaggerated over time. Also note that the curves are not linear. As the FICO score declines, the average default rate begins to climb ever faster. For this reason high LTV issuers have always had a specific FICO cutoff. In particular, the industry focuses on reducing the number of loans with a FICO score of 640 or lower. For example, in the 1996 deals from FirstPlus, loans with FICO scores of below 640 accounted for 29% of the total. But by 1998, most deals had few, if any, loans with

FICO scores below 640. The high percentage of low FICO scores clearly contributed to the large losses on older vintage loans.

Exhibit 18–9 shows the impact of FICO score on defaults as loans season (we chose to use the 1997 vintage data since it is representative of several issuers and is more seasoned than later vintage years). The exhibit also shows the contribution of different FICO buckets to the overall default rate. Cumulative defaults in the 600 to 640 bucket exceed 7%, and the cumulative defaults in the 680 to 720 bucket are around 3.5%. The data box at the bottom of Exhibit 18–9 presents average loan characteristics for each FICO bucket. These characteristics can be quite useful in interpreting the loss data in the exhibit. For example, the far-right column shows the number of loans in each bucket. If a particular bucket has a very small percentage of loans, it may not be an accurate representation of the credit performance of that FICO range. In the case of the 1997 vintage loans used in this figure, the 600 to 640 bucket, with 20,208 (14%) of the loans, had a major impact on producing a relatively high overall default rate.

Disposable Income

While FICO has been a well-known predictor of consumer defaults, only a few high LTV lenders focused on disposable income in the early lending days. DiTech was one issuer that always used high disposable income (as well as high FICO scores) as a key underwriting criteria. However, it was only in recent years that high LTV lenders in general began to realize the importance of disposable income. In fact, in some of our earlier studies on high LTV defaults, we did not have sufficient data to analyze this variable properly. We now have enough data, and it indicates that disposable income is nearly as important a predictor of defaults as are FICO scores. Our study included disposable income data for nearly all RFC, Empire, and Master loans and for about 17% of the FirstPlus loans. Exhibit 18–10 shows the relationship between disposable income and defaults.

The reason disposable income is such a good predictor of high LTV defaults is quite simple. If a borrower has a good credit record but very little disposable income, a small change in financial circumstances can lead to a default. A temporary loss of employment or a death in the family can be enough to push a borrower into default. On the other hand, a borrower with exactly the same credit profile but a much higher disposable income will have the excess funds to manage through such problems.

Disposable income is measured by the amount of excess cash flow borrowers have after meeting monthly fixed expenses, including payments on their first mortgage and high LTV loan, as well as credit card debt, auto loans, student loans, and all other consumer installment debt. Most high LTV lenders now impose a cutoff of $1,500 for monthly disposable income. This criteria, along with higher FICO scores, has done much to improve current average credit quality when compared to 1996 and 1997 vintage loans. In a later section we review more completely the changes that have taken place in FICO score and disposable income, and how they interact with each other.

FICO Versus Cumulative Defaults—1997 Industry Averages

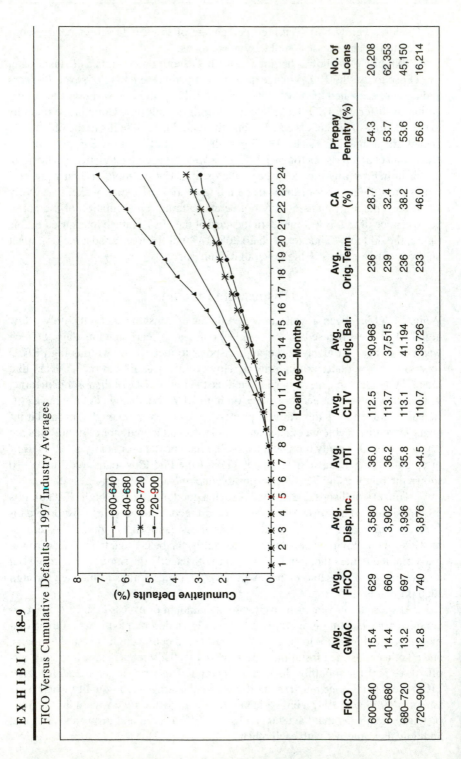

FICO	Avg. GWAC	Avg. FICO	Avg. Disp. Inc.	Avg. DTI	Avg. CLTV	Avg. Orig. Bal.	Avg. Orig. Term	CA (%)	Prepay Penalty (%)	No. of Loans
600–640	15.4	629	3,580	36.0	112.5	30,968	236	28.7	54.3	20,208
640–680	14.4	660	3,902	36.2	113.7	37,515	239	32.4	53.7	62,353
680–720	13.2	697	3,936	35.8	113.1	41.194	236	38.2	53.6	45,150
720–900	12.8	740	3,876	34.5	110.7	39.726	233	46.0	56.6	16,214

EXHIBIT 18-10

Disposable Income Versus Cumulative Defaults—1997 Industry Averages

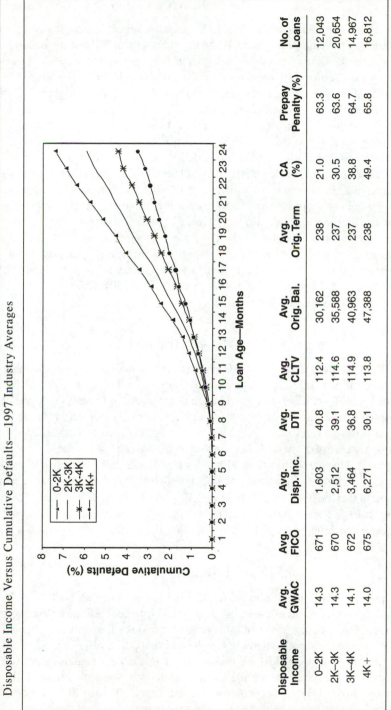

Disposable Income	Avg. GWAC	Avg. FICO	Avg. Disp. Inc.	Avg. DTI	Avg. CLTV	Avg. Orig. Bal.	Avg. Orig. Term	CA (%)	Prepay Penalty (%)	No. of Loans
0–2K	14.3	671	1.603	40.8	112.4	30,162	238	21.0	63.3	12,043
2K–3K	14.3	670	2,512	39.1	114.6	35,588	237	30.5	63.6	20,654
3K–4K	14.1	672	3,464	36.8	114.9	40,963	237	38.8	64.7	14,967
4K+	14.0	675	6,271	30.1	113.8	47,388	238	49.4	65.8	16,812

The California Effect

In our earlier studies of the high LTV market, California was always an enigma. Defaults from that state ran well ahead of defaults in the rest of the country. For instance, the data from both FirstPlus and Empire had shown default rates much higher in California than elsewhere for comparable FICO buckets. We earlier posited that perhaps the laid-back California lifestyle led to a higher level of delinquent borrowers. When we first looked at the RFC data, there was very little difference between California and the rest of the country. Using 1998 RFC loans, the average cumulative loss at 15 months for the non-California loans is 0.26%, whereas for the California loans it is 0.33%. However, if we adjust the FICO and disposable income bucket distributions of the California product to match the non-California distributions, (e.g., if the non-California lowest FICO-disposable income bucket accounts for 5% by balance, assume the same percentage in that bucket for the California product), the California performance would be 0.48%.

The data in Exhibit 18–11 show the difference between California and the rest of the country for 1997 vintage loans (note that there are almost no RFC loans for that period). The cumulative California losses are about 5.7% versus 4.0% for the rest of the country (about 43% greater). Why this differential in credit performance exists is still not known.

Debt to Income

Like FICO, debt to income (DTI) is a well-known determinant of default rates. The relationship of DTI to defaults is shown in Figure 18–12. After 30% DTI, the default rate begins to increase rapidly. Although not apparent in Exhibit 18–12, default rates continue to increase sharply over 45% DTI when all other variables are kept constant. However, all other variables are not held constant. Most issuers require a stronger borrower for DTIs beyond that level. We can use the data in the box at the bottom of the graph to explain why in Exhibit 18–12 defaults decline in the 45 to 50 DTI bucket. As the data show, the FICO score of 684 for the 45 to 50 bucket is quite a bit higher than for the 35 to 40 and 40 to 45 buckets. This reflects the fact that higher FICOs are required for DTIs over 45%, and it is the higher FICO scores and other more stringent requirements that cause the decline in the 45 to 50 bucket.

Original Term

The impact of original term on defaults is illustrated in Exhibit 18–13. There is a clear tendency for longer-term loans to have higher default rates than shorter-term loans. This is common in mortgage lending, since homeowners who are more highly leveraged will often choose the mortgage that offers the lowest monthly payment—which means the longest term available. In addition, however, as shown in the data beneath the graph, the shorter loans also have higher FICO scores, lower DTIs, and much lower loan balances. These other variables all help reduce the default rates on the shorter-term loans.

EXHIBIT 18-11

California and Other Versus Cumulative Defaults—1997 Industry Averages

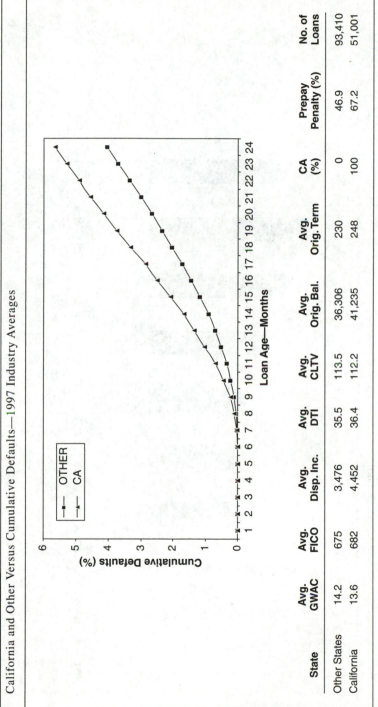

State	Avg. GWAC	Avg. FICO	Avg. Disp. Inc.	Avg. DTI	Avg. CLTV	Avg. Orig. Bal.	Avg. Orig. Term	CA (%)	Prepay Penalty (%)	No. of Loans
Other States	14.2	675	3,476	35.5	113.5	36,306	230	0	46.9	93,410
California	13.6	682	4,452	36.4	112.2	41,235	248	100	67.2	51,001

Debt to Income Versus Cumulative Defaults—1997 Industry Averages

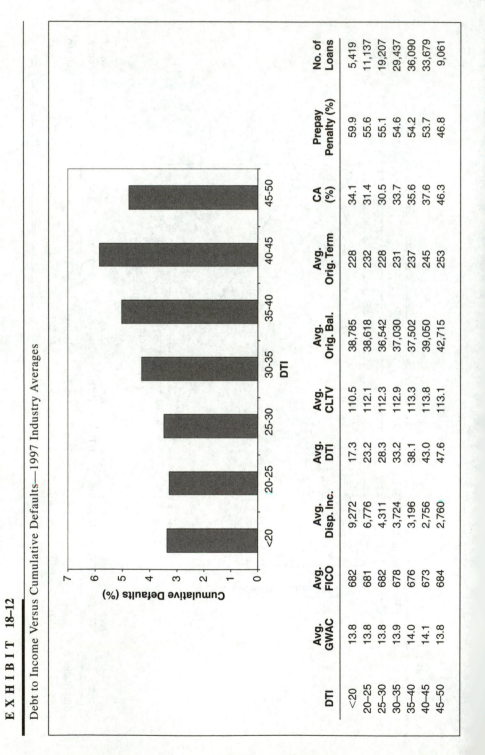

DTI	Avg. GWAC	Avg. FICO	Avg. Disp. Inc.	Avg. DTI	Avg. CLTV	Avg. Orig. Bal.	Avg. Orig. Term	CA (%)	Prepay Penalty (%)	No. of Loans
<20	13.8	682	9,272	17.3	110.5	38,785	228	34.1	59.9	5,419
20–25	13.8	681	6,776	23.2	112.1	38,618	232	31.4	55.6	11,137
25–30	13.8	682	4,311	28.3	112.3	36,542	228	30.5	55.1	19,207
30–35	13.9	678	3,724	33.2	112.9	37,030	231	33.7	54.6	29,437
35–40	14.0	676	3,196	38.1	113.3	37,502	237	35.6	54.2	36,090
40–45	14.1	673	2,756	43.0	113.8	39,050	245	37.6	53.7	33,679
45–50	13.8	684	2,760	47.6	113.1	42,715	253	46.3	46.8	9,061

EXHIBIT 18-13

Original Term Versus Cumulative Defaults—1997 Industry Averages

Orig. Term	Avg. GWAC	Avg. FICO	Avg. Disp. Inc.	Avg. DTI	Avg. CLTV	Avg. Orig. Bal.	Avg. Orig. Term	CA (%)	Prepay Penalty (%)	No. of Loans
30–90	14.0	683	3,751	34.4	105.8	24,591	67	16.5	53.2	3,151
90–150	14.0	680	3,580	34.1	110.7	29,366	120	15.8	45.9	12,006
150–210	13.9	679	3,943	34.8	112.8	35,375	180	30.0	49.6	41,941
210–270	13.9	675	3,723	36.2	113.5	37,495	239	41.4	60.2	37,332
270–330	13.9	678	3,954	36.7	113.5	42,456	300	41.1	55.2	49,951

From Exhibit 18–13, it is clear that defaults are a complex interaction of many variables. In order to sort out the impact of any one variable, we need more powerful statistical tools than these simple graphs. At the end of this section we show the results of an analysis which produces risk multipliers for each variable. Nonetheless, a one-dimensional analysis is a good starting point for isolating the variables that have a significant impact on credit performance.

CLTV

Exhibit 18–14 shows the relationship between CLTV and defaults. When projecting losses on first lien mortgages, LTV is an extremely important variable. In fact, for years the rating agencies relied largely on LTV for estimating losses on whole-loan pools. In high LTV lending, CLTV is less important because a 100% loss severity is assumed. But the relationship from the whole-loan market still holds, as shown in Exhibit 18–14. The lower the CLTV, the lower the default rate. Because CLTVs have proved to be an important credit variable, lenders are beginning to pay more attention to appraisals. Until recently the industry relied on stated values for high LTV loans. However Empire, for example, has already moved away from stated values and uses items such as statistical valuations, actual appraisals, property tax statements, and settlement statements to arrive at a more reliable value. Other issuers are moving in the same direction.

Another reason that CLTVs are related to defaults is that CLTVs are extremely important in determining voluntary prepayment rates in this sector. Further, faster prepayments lead to lower default rates, since many possible defaulters prepay before they run into financial difficulties.

Original Balance

As shown in Exhibit 18–15, original balance has only a modest impact on defaults, and its influence is often overwhelmed by other variables. For example, the highest original balance bucket also has the highest FICO scores (see the data box in the exhibit) and the lowest default rates. The one bucket that has the lowest default rate is the one with the smallest loans; and one reason those loans perform so well is that they have fast voluntary prepayments. The average default rate for the best and worst performing buckets differ by only 1.30% CDR. Some of the more important variables have differentials of 4.00% to 5.00% CDR between the lowest and highest buckets.

Risk Multipliers

We calculated risk multipliers for each of the quantitative variables discussed in this section using a multivariate logistic regression model. This type of analysis is a powerful statistical technique for determining the impact of individual factors when numerous independent variables contribute to a performance measure, such as the default rate. The results of this approach are presented in Exhibit 18–16. The risk

EXHIBIT 18-14

CLTV Versus Cumulative Defaults—1997 Industry Averages

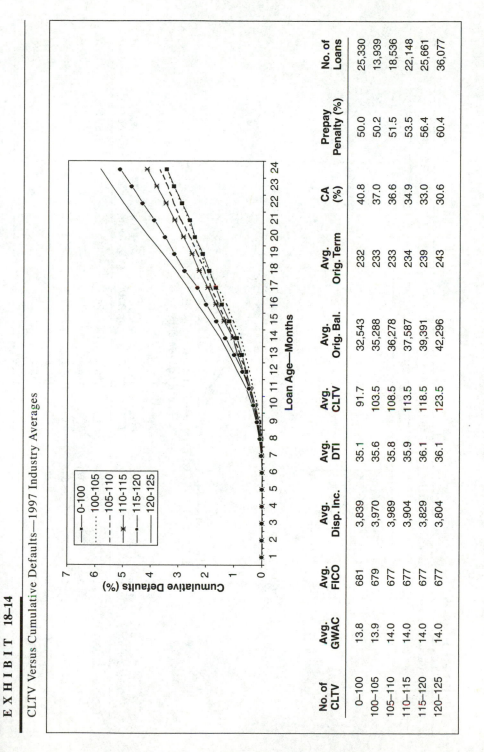

No. of CLTV	Avg. GWAC	Avg. FICO	Avg. Disp. Inc.	Avg. DTI	Avg. CLTV	Avg. Orig. Bal.	Avg. Orig. Term	CA (%)	Prepay Penalty (%)	No. of Loans
0-100	13.8	681	3,839	35.1	91.7	32,543	232	40.8	50.0	25,330
100-105	13.9	679	3,970	35.6	103.5	35,288	233	37.0	50.2	13,939
105-110	14.0	677	3,989	35.8	108.5	36,278	233	36.6	51.5	18,536
110-115	14.0	677	3,904	35.9	113.5	37,587	234	34.9	53.5	22,148
115-120	14.0	677	3,829	36.1	118.5	39,391	239	33.0	56.4	25,661
120-125	14.0	677	3,804	36.1	123.5	42,296	243	30.6	60.4	36,077

EXHIBIT 18-15

Original Balance Versus Cumulative Defaults—1997 Industry Averages

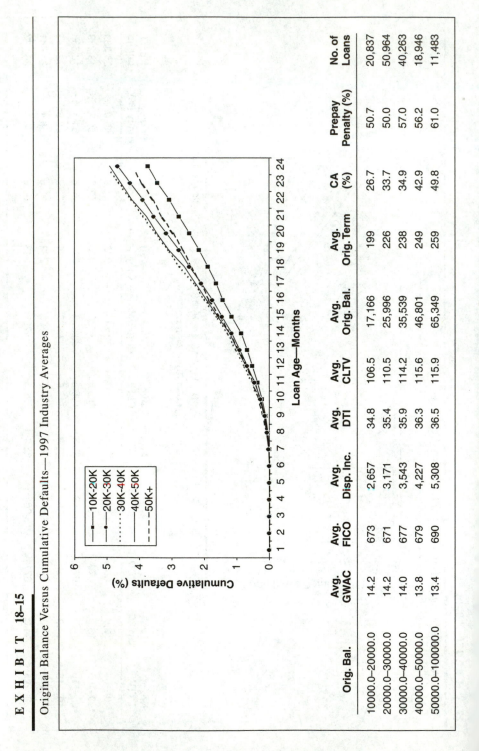

Orig. Bal.	Avg. GWAC	Avg. FICO	Avg. Disp. Inc.	Avg. DTI	Avg. CLTV	Avg. Orig. Bal.	Avg. Orig. Term	CA (%)	Prepay Penalty (%)	No. of Loans
10000.0–20000.0	14.2	673	2,657	34.8	106.5	17,166	199	26.7	50.7	20,837
20000.0–30000.0	14.2	671	3,171	35.4	110.5	25,996	226	33.7	50.0	50,964
30000.0–40000.0	14.0	677	3,543	35.9	114.2	35,539	238	34.9	57.0	40,263
40000.0–50000.0	13.8	679	4,227	36.3	115.6	46,801	249	42.9	56.2	18,946
50000.0–100000.0	13.4	690	5,308	36.5	115.9	65,349	259	49.8	61.0	11,483

EXHIBIT 18-16

Risk Multipliers by Issuer

Empire

	Baseline	Shift	Shift (%)	Default Risk Multiplier
California	0	1	N/A	1.44
Avg. FICO	675	10	1.48	0.89
Avg. DTI	36	5	13.89	1.02
Avg. CLTV	116	10	8.62	*
Avg. Orig. Bal.	39,500	5,000	12.66	1.08
Avg. Orig. Term	235	60	25.53	1.31
Avg. Disp. Inc.	3,475	500	14.39	0.92

RFC

	Baseline	Shift	Shift (%)	Default Risk Multiplier
California	0	1	N/A	1.46
Avg. FICO	678	10	1.47	0.80
Avg. DTI	38	5	13.16	1.08
Avg. CLTV	115	10	8.70	*
Avg. Orig. Bal.	42,000	5,000	11.90	1.18
Avg. Orig. Term	223	60	26.91	1.47
Avg. Disp. Inc.	3,500	500	14.29	0.72

FirstPlus

	Baseline	Shift	Shift (%)	Default Risk Multiplier
California	0	1	N/A	1.26
Avg. FICO	685	10	1.46	0.88
Avg. DTI	35	5	14.29	1.09
Avg. CLTV	115	10	8.70	*
Avg. Orig. Bal.	36,000	5,000	13.89	1.06
Avg. Orig. Term	240	60	25.00	1.30
Avg. Disp. Inc.	N/A	N/A	N/A	N/A

Master Financial

	Baseline	Shift	Shift (%)	Default Risk Multiplier
California	0	1	N/A	1.18
Avg. FICO	675	10	1.48	0.92
Avg. DTI	37	5	13.51	1.12
Avg. CLTV	114	10	8.77	*
Avg. Orig. Bal.	45,900	5,000	10.89	1.02
Avg. Orig. Term	242	60	24.79	1.42
Avg. Disp. Inc.	4,200	500	11.90	0.97

*Not statistically significant.

multipliers show how much of a change in the default rate is caused by a change in one particular variable. The baseline for each risk multiplier is the average of the variable (run for each issuer). The amount of change for each variable from that baseline is shown in the column marked Shift. The risk multiplier presented in column 5 shows the change that would result in the default rate as a consequence of changing that one variable by the specified shift, assuming all other variables are held constant. For example, for Empire, increasing the average FICO score from 675 to 685 would decrease defaults by 11%; that is, the risk multiplier is 0.89. Note that the risk multiplier for the same variable differs from issuer to issuer, but they are all similar in sign and pretty close in magnitude, as well. The risk multipliers for RFC show a slightly greater sensitivity. This is largely due to the fact that RFC's default rate is significantly lower than other issuers, and a change in a variable has a greater proportionate impact on defaults even though the absolute impact may be small.

Since this analysis is measuring human behavior, there is a fair amount of statistical variation, but the results can help forecast default levels for a pool of loans, given any set of loan and borrower characteristics. It is perhaps more useful for estimating the change that might occur if an issuer with a long track record and a large amount of historical data wants to modify a single variable in its underwriting criteria. However, one would not want to rely exclusively on such a statistical approach. As we show in a later section, nonquantitative underwriting criteria can also play an important role in overall credit performance.

IMPROVEMENTS IN QUANTITATIVE FACTORS

In the previous section we discussed the importance of various loan and borrower characteristics in determining high LTV defaults. The analysis we have made parallels the efforts undertaken by the leading issuers. As more data became available, the issuers adjusted their underwriting standards to incorporate the new information. It should come as no surprise that over time the underwriting specifications on this product tightened significantly. In this section we illustrate the extent to which this tightening has taken place.

FICO Scores Lower Than 640

Early on it became apparent that high LTV loans with low FICO scores accounted for a disproportionate share of defaults. Hence, there was a consistent effort to reduce the percentage of borrowers with low scores. As discussed earlier, the relationship between FICO and defaults is not linear. As the FICO score declines, defaults increase at an ever-increasing rate. Hence, by cutting off, say 10%, of the lowest FICO scores, defaults can be reduced by more than 10%. However, as in all areas of consumer lending, volume is also important. Most issuers at the time settled on 640 as a lower acceptable FICO score and worked to reduce that section of their borrower base. The success of this endeavor can be seen from the downtrend in the percentage of loans securitized with FICO scores below 640. In 1996 that percentage was almost 30%, while today, virtually no loans are underwritten with FICO scores below 640. DiTech was unique in its emphasis on not lending to homeowners with low FICO scores. The percentage of borrowers with FICO scores below 640 for their 1997 and 1998 transactions was 6.6% and 0.43%, respectively. These were much lower than industry standards at the time.

Disposable Income Greater Than $1,500

Just as issuers found that FICO scores below 640 were lethal in terms of credit performance, they also found that disposable incomes below $1,500 per month produced an inordinate amount of defaults. Consequently, they began to focus more on this variable, and some placed a $1,500 limit on their high LTV lending programs. The trend of originating fewer loans with disposable incomes below $1,500 was evident from our analysis of the data. DiTech focused on this issue in 1997 and originated a smaller percentage of high LTV loans with low disposable incomes than other issuers.

California Percentage

Just as in the case of low FICO scores, FirstPlus and Empire discovered early on that California loans were experiencing much higher default rates than loans from the rest of the country. Initially, FirstPlus believed that the higher defaults might be the result of aggressive broker or corresponding operations in California. However, when they began to originate a large percentage of their loans through their own direct marketing efforts, the California effect was still present.

Because of this poor performance, both FirstPlus and Empire began to reduce the percentage of loans originated in California. Also, as the product became more national in scope, brokers and correspondents around the country ramped up production and the percentage of California loans declined. Today, the California percentage, at around 15%, is simply representative of California's share of the national housing market. But this is a considerable change from 1996 and has, along with higher FICO scores and disposable income levels, contributed to improved credit performance. Exhibit 18–17 shows the concentration of California loans by issuer and vintage year. Empire has chosen to limit California loans to borrowers with minimum disposable incomes of $3,000 in order to improve credit performance from this state.

The FICO–Disposable Income Mix

The interactive nature of the variables that determine default rates is apparent from our discussion to this point. The paragraph on risk multipliers was an attempt to isolate the influence of individual factors because they are so interdependent. In this part of the study we examine the interaction of two of the most important variables, FICO and disposable income, and show how the improvement in both these variables has significantly improved expected performance.

Exhibit 18–18 shows cumulative defaults by joint FICO–disposable income buckets for 1997 vintage year loans. As one would expect, the largest losses occur in the bucket with the lowest FICO scores (600–640) and the lowest disposable incomes (0–$2,000). Cumulative losses in that bucket reached 11.30%

EXHIBIT 18–17

Percentage of California Loans

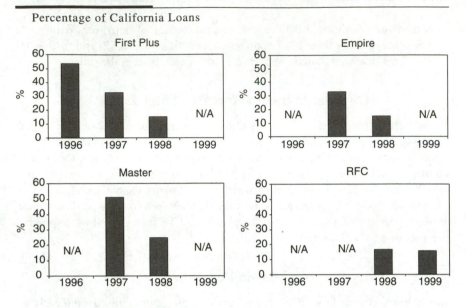

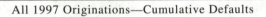

EXHIBIT 18–18

All 1997 Originations—Cumulative Defaults

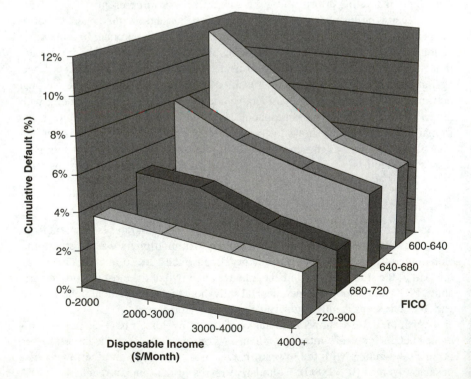

after 24 months. Contrast that with the best bucket, at FICO scores of 720 to 900 and disposable incomes of $4,000-plus, where losses only reached 2.50%.

An obvious way of improving performance would be to shift originations away from the worst-performing buckets. That trend is illustrated in Exhibit 18–19. For each vintage year the exhibit shows the distribution of loans by FICO–disposable income bucket. Note that the worst bucket (600–640/0–$2,000) represented 4.43% of all loans in 1996. The percentage in that bucket declined to 2.71% in 1997 and was down to 0.34% in 1999. At the same time, the percentages increased in the better-performing buckets.

Also shown in Exhibit 18–19 for each vintage year are projected total losses at 24 months based on the FICO–disposable income distributions in the exhibit (for each year) and the cumulative losses actually experienced by the 1997 loan cohort. To obtain the projected total loss numbers, we first multiplied the percentage in each bucket in Exhibit 18–19 by the loss for that bucket shown in Exhibit 18–18. This produced an expected loss for each bucket for a given year. By summing across all buckets we obtained an estimate of total losses (not actual losses) at 24 months for that vintage year. The projected number for 1996 was 5.45%. By 1999 that number had declined to 4.34%, a reduction of 20.3%.

Nonquantitative Underwriting Guidelines

Halfway through our loan-level study we ran into a relationship that did not fit the model we had constructed for high LTV defaults. As a result, we became aware that beyond FICO scores, DTI ratios, and disposable income minimums originators can alter their credit performance a great deal by adhering to tough, nonquantitative underwriting criteria.

Underwriting and Servicing Differences

In the course of investigating individual issuer performance, it became clear that certain issuers were performing better than others. Historically, research reports have used FirstPlus as the benchmark for industry performance because FirstPlus's volume of outstanding high LTV loans is by far the largest. In Exhibit 18–20 we compare performance from 1998 when the two largest issuers, FirstPlus (over $6.5 billion) and RFC (over $2.8 billion as of December 31, 1999) were active in the market. At 12 months, the RFC loans had cumulative losses of 0.16% compared to 0.36% for FirstPlus.

We assumed when we examined the RFC quantitative underwriting criteria—such as FICO, DTI, and disposable income—that RFC would show a better mix. After all, the statistical analysis that we described earlier in this chapter showed a very strong correlation between FICO, DTI, disposable income, and defaults. To our surprise, the distribution of FICO and disposable income for RFC in 1998 was similar to that of the other issuers used in the study. The FICO and disposable income distributions for the 1998 vintage year for the issuers is presented in Exhibit 18–21.

EXHIBIT 18-19

Distribution of Loans by FICO and Disposable Income Buckets and Projected Losses

	0–$2,000	$2,000–$3,000	$3,000–$4,000	$4,000+	Projected Losses*	Curr. Yr. Change	Total Change from 1996
All 1999					4.34%	9.8%	20.3%
720–900	1.81%	4.95%	3.65%	6.94%			
680–720	5.49%	16.25%	11.55%	11.35%			
640–680	5.33%	14.27%	8.94%	7.32%			
600–640	0.34%	0.81%	0.48%	0.50%			
All 1998					4.81%	3.5%	11.7%
720–900	1.58%	3.20%	2.59%	3.05%			
680–720	4.89%	10.67%	9.15%	10.06%			
640–680	7.15%	14.96%	11.95%	11.59%			
600–640	1.54%	3.26%	2.40%	1.94%			
All 1997					4.99%	8.5%	8.5%
720–900	1.23%	2.40%	2.01%	2.99%			
680–720	3.90%	8.19%	7.28%	9.98%			
640–680	6.54%	13.68%	11.40%	14.34%			
600–640	2.71%	5.23%	3.86%	4.27%			
All 1996					5.45%		
720–900	1.47%	2.16%	1.87%	1.86%			
680–720	4.26%	8.31%	6.78%	6.47%			
640–680	8.14%	14.73%	11.57%	9.86%			
600–640	4.43%	8.14%	5.99%	3.97%			

*Total projected loss at 24 months.

EXHIBIT 18-20

1998 Cumulative Defaults–RFC Versus FirstPlus

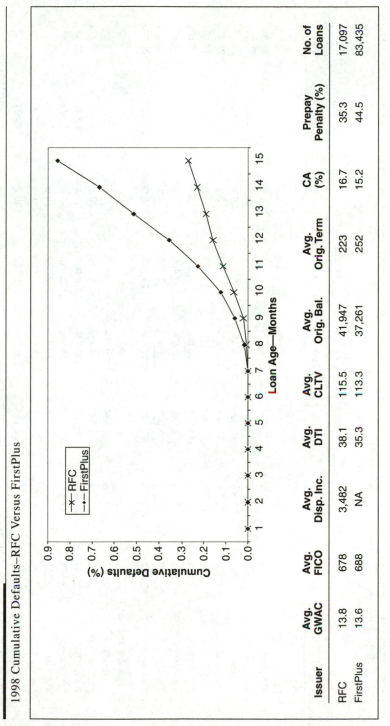

Issuer	Avg. GWAC	Avg. FICO	Avg. Disp. Inc.	Avg. DTI	Avg. CLTV	Avg. Orig. Bal.	Avg. Orig. Term	CA (%)	Prepay Penalty (%)	No. of Loans
RFC	13.8	678	3,482	38.1	115.5	41,947	223	16.7	35.3	17,097
FirstPlus	13.6	688	NA	35.3	113.3	37,261	252	15.2	44.5	83,435

EXHIBIT 18–21

1998 Loans—FICO and Disposable Income Distributions

	RFC 1998		FirstPlus 1998		Empire 1998		Master 1998	
	No. of Loans	Percent	No. of Loans	Percent	No. of Loans	Percent	No. of Loans	Percent
FICO								
350–600	—	0.0%	12	0.0%	2	0.0%	17	0.1%
600–620	44	0.3%	194	0.2%	54	0.2%	191	1.3%
620–640	1,985	11.6%	3,604	4.3%	2,127	8.8%	2,003	13.9%
640–660	3,898	22.8%	15,323	18.4%	5,873	24.4%	2,975	20.6%
660–680	4,055	23.7%	19,384	23.2%	5,590	23.2%	3,089	21.4%
680–700	3,398	19.9%	17,851	21.4%	4,691	19.5%	2,633	18.3%
700–720	2,132	12.5%	14,175	17.0%	3,155	13.1%	1,727	12.0%
720–740	985	5.8%	7,520	9.0%	1,465	6.1%	926	6.4%
740<	600	3.5%	5,372	6.4%	1,116	4.6%	864	6.0%
Total	17,097	100.0%	83,435	100.0%	24,073	100.0%	14,425	100.0%
Disposable income								
0–1500	1,009	5.9%	984	9.7%	854	4.5%	721	5.0%
1500–2500	5,159	30.2%	3,505	34.7%	5,625	29.8%	4,407	30.6%
2500–3500	5,441	31.8%	3,122	30.9%	5,916	31.4%	4,492	31.1%
3500–4500	2,978	17.4%	1,577	15.6%	3,632	19.3%	2,527	17.5%
4500–8000	2,333	13.7%	926	9.2%	2,632	14.0%	2,084	14.5%
8000–25000	171	1.0%	1	0.0%	203	1.1%	190	1.3%
Total	17,091	100.0%	10,115	100.0%	18,862	100.0%	14,421	100.0%
Sample (%)*	100.0%		12.1%		78.4%		100.0%	

*Percent of loans with disposable income data.

Note that there are only marginal differences between issuers. It was apparent from this comparison that we needed additional variables to account for RFC's stronger performance.

In discussing the RFC performance with RFC and other industry members, it became clear that even though RFC's quantitative criteria were similar to other issuers, their "nonquantitative" underwriting standards were more stringent. These criteria included such things as the number of 30-day mortgage late payments, the length of time since prior bankruptcy, and simultaneous close on first and second mortgage. Exhibits 18–22 to 18–26 present the industry standards for a number of these variables as they were in 1998 (at that point, all the issuers listed in the table were actively originating loans). In virtually every area RFC had the toughest standards. Now RFC is the dominant issuer and uses a set of guidelines that are more stringent than those shown in the Exhibits 18–22 to 18–26.

Below we discuss in greater detail several of the nonquantitative criteria that we feel contribute to RFC's low default rates.

- *Time since bankruptcy*—RFC requires a minimum of 7 years from bankruptcy (generally as far back as the credit agencies track it). Most other issuers required 3 or 4 years as a bankruptcy cutoff point. This may be one of the most important reasons for RFC's stronger performance. Since bankruptcies account for roughly 50% of all high LTV defaults, homeowners who previously have allowed their financial condition to deteriorate to the point of bankruptcy would naturally be a higher risk than those who had always maintained better credit history.

- *Number of 30-day mortgage lates payments*—Most issuers allowed one or two late mortgage payments for the previous 12 months for their lower-grade (higher-rate) loans. RFC's underwriting guidelines do not allow any late mortgage payments, even for its lowest-grade loan.

- *Simultaneous close of first and second mortgages*—Most originators historically allowed the simultaneous closing of a first and second mortgage. The authors believe that a borrower who is required to close the first lien and has the funds to essentially hold the second lien until the second lien is issued (could be the next day) is a less leveraged borrower. To our knowledge, RFC is the only originator that would not allow simultaneous closings.

- *Homeownership*—RFC requires that borrowers be homeowners for at least a year before they take out a high LTV loan. This means they have had at least 12 months of mortgage history.

- *Servicing*—RFC had the luxury (and capital) to add a high LTV component to their already large servicing platform. Having vast resources to tap when developing this platform provided many benefits. These included a tested servicing system, a significant legal department, a knowledge of the broker and correspondent channels, and a sophisticated data warehouse and analytical capability. The latter allowed RFC to develop a comprehensive loan-borrower database that provided crucial insight into the credit performance of this new product.

Some other issuers recognize many of these criteria as important but, rather than impose a lower or more stringent cutoff point, prefer to increase the loan rate to account for these risk factors.

EXHIBIT 18–22

Credit Score Minimums, Score Averages, and Number of Reports on Recent Deals by Issuer—Early 1998

	FirstPlus Financial	Empire Funding	Master Financial	DiTech Funding	PSB Lending	Mego Mortgage	RFC
Minimum credit score	630	620	620	640	580	620	630
Recent wtg. avg. FICO and deal	685 1998-1	677 1998-1	674 1998-1	699 1998-1	669 1997-4	671 1997-4	678 1998-2
Minimum number of credit reports required	One	One	One	Three	One	One	Two

EXHIBIT 18–23

Credit Grades and Number of 30-day Late Payments Allowed by Issuer—Early 1998

Borrower Grade by Credit Score and Number of Late Mortgage Payments

	FirstPlus Financial	Empire Funding	Master Financial	DiTech Funding	PSB Lending	Mego Mortgage	RFC
Maximum Number of Mortgage Late Payments in Last 12 Months							
Best grade 0 × 30	630+	700+	700+	640+	700+	680+	630+
Middle grade 1 × 30	630+	<700	680–699	NA	660–699	<680	NA
Lower grade 2 × 30	NA	NA	650–679	NA	<660	NA	NA
Lowest grade 3 × 30	NA	NA	620–649	NA	NA	NA	NA

EXHIBIT 18–24

Loan Size by Credit Score and Issuer—Early 1998

Credit Bucket	FirstPlus Financial	Empire Funding	Master Financial	Di Tech Funding	PSB Lending	Mego Mortgage	RFC
720+	75,000	100,000	100,000	150,000	100,000	100,000	75,000
700–719	65,000	100,000	100,000	150,000	100,000	100,000	75,000
680–699	55,000	75,000	100,000	125,000	85,000	75,000	75,000
670–679	50,000	65,000	75,000	85,000	75,000	65,000	50,000
660–669	50,000	65,000	75,000	85,000	75,000	65,000	50,000
650–659	40,000	45,000	75,000	50,000	55,000	45,000	50,000
640–649	40,000	45,000	50,000	50,000	55,000	45,000	35,000
630–639	30,000	30,000	50,000	NA	45,000	35,000	35,000
620–629	NA	30,000	50,000	NA	45,000	35,000	NA
600–619	NA	NA	NA	NA	35,000	NA	NA
580–599	NA	NA	NA	NA	35,000	NA	NA
Min. Loan Size	Unknown	Unknown	Unknown	15,000	Unknown	Unknown	10,000

E X H I B I T 18-25

Maximum Cash-out Allowed by Credit Score and Issuer—Early 1998

Credit Bucket	FirstPlus Financial	Empire Funding	Master Financial	Di Tech Funding	PSB Lending	Mego Mortgage	RFC
720+	40,000	35,000	25,000	150,000	35,000	35,000	15,000
700–719	35,000	35,000	25,000	150,000	35,000	35,000	15,000
680–699	30,000	25,000	25,000	125,000	25,000	25,000	15,000
670–679	25,000	15,000	15,000	85,000	15,000	15,000	10,000
660–669	25,000	15,000	15,000	85,000	15,000	15,000	10,000
650–659	20,000	5,000	15,000	10,000	10,000	10,000	10,000
640–649	20,000	5,000	5,000	10,000	10,000	10,000	7,000
630–639	15,000	2,500	5,000	NA	5,000	5,000	7,000
620–629	NA	2,500	5,000	NA	5,000	5,000	NA
600–619	NA	NA	NA	NA	—	NA	NA
580–599	NA	NA	NA	NA	—	NA	NA

*Technically, RFC limits cash-out to 20% of the loan balance as does Di Tech for borrowers with low credit score 640–660).

Maximum Debt Ratios Allowed by Credit Score and Issuer—Early 1998

Credit Bucket	FirstPlus Financial	Empire Funding	Master Financial	Di Tech Funding	PSB Lending[a]	Mego Mortgage[b]	RFC
720+	50[c]/1,250	40/1,000	50/1,500	50/1,500	50	50	50/3,000
700–719		45/1,500	45 otherwise	45 otherwise			45 otherwise
680–699		50/2,000[e]	45 otherwise	45			
670–679							
660–669	45%[d]/1,250	40/1,000					
650–659		45/1,500	45		45	45	
640–649							
630–639	36%/1,250	40/1,000		NA		40	
620–629	NA	NA	NA	NA			NA
600–619	NA	NA	NA	NA		NA	NA
580–599	NA	NA	NA	NA		NA	NA

[a]Minimum disposable income is $1,000 and jumps to $1,500 for debt ratios over 45%.
[b]Minimum disposable income is $1,000 for individuals and $1,500 if two or more people are in the household.
[c]40% on loans over $50,000 and 45% on loans between $35,000 and $50,000.
[d]40% on loans over $50,000
[e]45% for loans over $50,000.

RISK ADJUSTMENTS

In this chapter we have discussed both quantitative and nonquantitative variables that effect the performance of high LTV product. The last, but equally as important item to address, is risk pricing and adjusting. There are really two ways to account for the risk in a pool of loans. Either (1) charge a high-enough rate so that the coupon will cover both the losses and the all-in funding rate and provide enough excess to compensate for the risk of lending, or (2) don't originate the loan.

Some issuers, such as Empire, adjust loan coupons based on disposable income, in addition to the FICO score and payment-consumer history, or require higher disposable incomes in areas they find risky, such as California. In another example, RFC's minimum disposable income increases from $1,500 to $2,000 for a DTI above 45%.

Whether by increasing the coupon or by not originating high-risk loans with certain characteristics, originators now have the data to determine more effectively the performance of their pools.

SUMMARY

In this chapter we discussed the results of a study that demonstrate the key role played by FICO scores, disposable incomes, and other quantitative factors in determining default levels. We also showed that these variables have improved dramatically since 1998 and that this improvement has already lead to noticeably lower default rates. In addition, we examined the important role played by non-quantitative variables in lowering default rates.

Based upon the current underwriting standards, the strong servicing, and the involvement and commitment of well-capitalized finance companies, we believe that the high LTV loan sector will become an increasingly important component of the home equity securitization market.

SECTION **IV**

PREPAYMENT MODELING

CHAPTER 19

OVERVIEW OF RECENT PREPAYMENT BEHAVIOR AND ADVANCES IN ITS MODELING

Michael Bykhovsky
President and CEO
Applied Financial Technology, Inc.

In recent years some new approaches have been developed in modeling the refinancing behavior of mortgage loans. Significantly, some of them were successful with both back testing and out-of-sample testing. What makes these new approaches work is their focus on modeling borrower behavior and the reasons for changes in that behavior.

Older types of models were constructed with an emphasis on their tenability within the existing statistical machinery. The number of variables was minimized and the structures simplified in order to achieve a statistically satisfactory separation of variables and tight confidence intervals, given the history of prepayment behavior. This approach to model building had to make certain presumptions about the properties of the historical data and of the model structure. In order to apply available statistical machinery, errors in the historical fit had to be treated as random and normally distributed, even though most commonly they were neither (which rendered the results suspect at best). In addition, many aspects of the behaviors that were known to exist a priori were not modeled due to the difficulty of separating the variables, given the historical data set. Basically, the approach was to create a model that the statistical tools permitted. A much richer understanding of the underlying phenomenon had to be sacrificed for the sake of satisfying the available mathematical methods.

Not surprisingly, this class of models performed poorly under the fairly volatile market conditions of the period from 1990 to 1999. Most models of the older type dramatically underprojected the 1992–1993 refinancing wave. The model's creators explained that the refinancing process had become much more efficient and they refit the same models to the new data. These models then dramatically *overprojected* the 1996–1997 slowdown in refinancings, followed by a claim that the world had become much *less* efficient. The models were again refit to the new data, only to dramatically underproject 1998–1999 refinancings, followed by a claim that once again the refinancing process had become *more* efficient.

The efficiency of the exercise of the refinancing option *did* increase somewhat between 1987 and 1992 as the aggressive correspondent network became a dominant factor in the refinancing wave. But that efficiency has remained mostly unchanged from then until now. Homeowners received dozens of refinancing solicitations back then, and they still do. In addition, the costs for title searches, appraisals, and title insurance have changed very little over time, keeping up with or exceeding the CPI. The internet may have reduced the costs of paper processing, but paper processing was never a major cost contributor anyway. Moreover, changes in average points paid are just camouflaged modifiers to the stated coupon rates, since points can be readily changed to effect different coupons. Therefore, in reality, the time-varying efficiency argument is mostly a way of explaining a model's inadequacy in representing the underlying phenomenon.

Since the goal of any prepayment model is to make a valid connection between *projected* mortgage rates and *projected* prepayments, we should also examine whether we can expect the mortgage market to remain essentially the same as it is now, or what, if any, changes we can expect in the future. That understanding will allow us to ascertain the extent to which the historical data is applicable for the purposes of constructing a prepayment model.

TECHNOLOGY EFFECTS

The effect of the internet and of improved computer technology on the increase in the efficiency of the exercise of the refinancing option has been widely publicized in the professional press and deserves a numeric estimate. Generally, technology improvements affect either the efficiency of the bank's internal processes, like the cost of servicing, internal costs of mortgage origination, and so on, or they affect the consumer directly, like the efficiency of refinancing solicitations, ease of the process, costs charged by the brokers, and paper processing costs.

Improvements in the efficiency of the banking system, if passed along to the consumer, would result in the long-term tightening of the spreads between the effective mortgage rate (the rate that takes into account points paid at origination as well as the stated coupon) and a risk-free rate (like a U.S. Treasury). Mortgage market participants, though, will readily recognize that the spread volatility is also closely related to interest rate volatility, liquidity issues, varying risk preferences, and a host of other phenomena that will most likely either largely mask the potential long-term spread tightening or erase it altogether. Nevertheless, one could make a ballpark estimate of the extent of the technology-related spread-tightening potential. The data on the average physical costs of servicing a mortgage is hard to come by, and it is even harder to ascertain how these costs are divided between what is susceptible to increasing efficiencies and what is not. Generally, though, market participants assume that total servicing costs are on the order of 15 to 20 basis points (bps), varying greatly as a function of mortgage type. A large share of these costs is related to administration of nonperforming mortgages like the legal and collection costs, which are not greatly amenable to reduction within the U.S. legal system. The other part of the cost is the regular loan administration. This process has been largely computerized already. It is probably safe to assume that the total cost reduction potential in the servicing component of the system is no greater than 5 bps. There is also a potential for increased profitability with the various comarketing programs that mortgage servicers run, thus making servicing rights more attractive and tightening mortgage spreads. These programs have been in place for a long time, and it is not clear at all that there exists a significant technology-related potential for the expansion of their profitability.

The potential for cost reduction due to the increasing efficiency of the loan origination process is probably greater than that of the servicing process. The common brokerage commission currently and historically paid by the originators is on the order of 1% of the loan amount. One could imagine that with wider use of the internet, and given the potential ability of large internet brokers to process a volume of loan applications efficiently, the average commission paid for loan origination could drop by ½%. Points can be translated to mortgage rates by using the modified duration of the current-coupon mortgages, which is approximately 5 years. Under that assumption, there is a potential for a 10-bp spread tightening due to the internet-related efficiencies. Therefore, the total potential of effective mortgage rate spread tightening due to possible increases in the processing efficiency is on the order of 15 bps.

Notice that the efficiency consideration of the previous two paragraphs would result only in a spread tightening of the effective mortgage rate. Since prepayment models receive mortgage rates as an input, these considerations would not affect the model's performance at all. Mortgage market participants will have to make independent judgments on whether they believe that there will indeed be a long-term spread tightening of the magnitude described above, given all other exogenous influences not affected by processing efficiency considerations.

The other component of technological improvements may affect the consumer, and thus has the potential of introducing errors in the models that are constructed to reflect the current reality of the mortgage markets. The most commonly cited effect is the increased awareness of consumers of the available refinancing options. It is hard to imagine how that awareness could be increased any further though, given the dozens of refinancing solicitations that home owners receive now. It is possible that with the projected increased use of the internet, these options will somehow be easier to decipher, away from the clutter of mortgage brokers. Nevertheless, the argument of internet-related increased awareness remains tenuous at best.

The other effect of technology on consumers would be to ease the process and reduce paper processing costs. Currently, out of an approximately $2,500 of closing costs that consumers generally pay, about $400 are paper processing–related. Under the most aggressive assumptions, one could imagine these costs dropping by $200— not a significant portion of the overall costs. Regarding the potential for increasing the ease of application process, there is not that much room to make it any easier. Currently, mortgage brokers commonly send forms by FedEx and the consumer only has to sign at the bottom line, attaching supporting documents.

Therefore, generally, one can assume that technology may have some, though most likely a limited, effect on the consumer response to the refinancing incentive. That effect will probably be dwarfed by the effect of varying economic conditions, even for similar rate incentives.

PURPOSE AND USES OF A PREPAYMENT MODEL

The purpose of constructing a prepayment model is *not* to project prepayments: It is impossible to project prepayments, since future mortgage rates are not known. The purpose of a model is to define a relationship between projected mortgage rates and the resulting rates of prepayment activity, given all available information regarding the mortgage, the mortgage holder, the current state of the economy, and so forth. If this relationship were well-modeled, it would in turn allow one to answer all the questions that one may ask as a holder of a mortgage-backed security—questions such as the value of the option to refinance, the average advantage of owning a mortgage versus owning other instruments, the comparison of a mortgage to a collection of bonds and short positions in interest rate derivatives.

One of the more common ways of expressing that relationship is to state long-term projected prepayment speeds under the scenarios of mortgage rates going up or down instantaneously and staying unchanged thereafter. That method has many flaws. It does not capture the differences between short-term projections and long-term projections. Projected speeds that are very high and then drop precipitously may have the same average long-term value as constant projected speeds, but their effect on a security valuation may vary greatly. The method does not demonstrate sensitivity to the "whiplash" effect—changes in the model behavior if interest rates go up and then down versus the opposite sequence. The overall value of this method is to vaguely demonstrate the sensitivity of the model to interest rate changes and not much else, and it should not be relied upon for security valuation. Given the limitations of the method, it is quite surprising that many market participants continue using it—often with devastating results.

An appropriate use of the model would be to utilize its *month-by-month* projections of prepayments, given interest rate scenarios, when calculating cash flows of securities and/or of a portfolio. The set of interest rate scenarios should be great enough to cover most of the likely ones, as in an option-adjusted spread (OAS) framework, or a manually selected set of possibilities, as in risk control applications.

GENERAL THOUGHTS ON MODEL CONSTRUCTION

The overall effect of the above considerations on model construction is to allow one to assume that the structure of the mortgage market will remain largely similar to the current one, with some small potential for refinancing efficiency increases. Thus, fitting the model to history should yield reasonably good projections, if the model reflects completely and accurately the structure of the current mortgage market and of the consumer response. One could also choose to slightly overproject the history, if one believes that the efficiency of the refinancing option exercise is greater than before.

There probably will always be unexpected events that temporarily, but not greatly, confound a well-constructed model. The most common one would be the changing relationship between economic activity and mortgage rates. We experienced an exceptional economy in the late 1990s and into 2000 when interest rates in general, and mortgage rates in particular, were quite low by historical standards. The rate of existing home sales in the United States is normally around 4.1-million units per year, being a function of population mobility, generational, and wealth formation factors. It jumped by more than 25% from the end of 1997 to the middle of 1998. That increase cannot be accounted for by anything other than exceptional wealth formation conditions. So the extra 1-million units per year rate of existing home sales does not correspond to anything observed before. One of the effects of an exceptional home sales rate is some contraction in the aging process of the current-coupon collateral originated in the latter half of 1998. The extra existing home sales correspond to the unusual wealth formation rate, and are not as affected by the normal mortgage-aging process, thus leading to a shortening of the normal aging curve. Models constructed with the knowledge of this phenomenon can incorporate that effect. A more distant example would be the 1987 stock market crash. Housing sales and refinancing activity took an unexpected and temporary dip at a time of falling mortgage rates.

MODERN MODEL CONSTRUCTION

A well-constructed model should incorporate all known factors that affect a mortgage holder's inclination to move or to refinance, as well as the overall state of the U.S. housing market. The factors that a well-constructed model should take into account will be discussed below. The focus will be on a 30-year fixed-rate pool-level model using Applied Financial Technology's prepayment model. The parameters of this model were set in 1996 and remain essentially unchanged since then. Loan-level models, ARMs, home equity models, and all others will be discussed later as variations on the theme.

Modeling the Housing Turnover Component of Prepayments

Every prepayment related to housing turnover is a result of an existing home sale in the United States. Thus, it is crucial to model changes in the rate of projected existing home sales as a function of changes in interest rates. When interest rates go up, generally, existing home sales should slow down and vice versa. Nevertheless, since the long-term rate of existing home sales is a function of socioeconomic variables and not of interest rates, some mean reversion of the home sales to a "normal" level over a long period of time should be expected. There are seasonal variations in housing sales with the peak in housing turnover occurring during the late summer months and the trough in prepayment activity taking place during the months of January and February, as the tendency of home owners to move is affected by the school calendar and other seasonal factors. The relationship between housing sales and mortgage rates is a fairly stable one. It is possible to project 1998 U.S. housing sales data based on 1977 mortgage rates and housing sales data.

EXHIBIT   19–1

Existing Home Sales (Monthly)

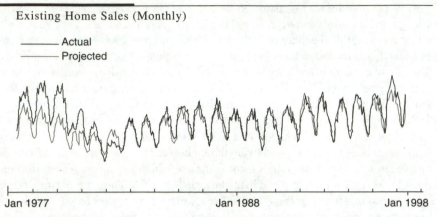

Jan 1977   Jan 1988   Jan 1998

As shown in Exhibit 19–1, the only time the model's projections of the U.S. housing sales diverged significantly from the actual was between 1978 and 1981. The model projected a drop in housing sales during the period 1980–1981, but both mortgage rates *and* housing sales went up due to real interest rates becoming negative during that period.

All existing home sales result in prepayments. A model should then assign these sales to different types of collateral. There is an aging process in the mortgage holder's propensity to move. Home owners who have just purchased property are less likely to move than others who have inhabited their homes for a longer period of time. In addition, they are even less likely to move if the prevailing mortgage rates are considerably higher than the rate they are currently paying. That disincentive should diminish over time, as inflation and regular amortization decrease the real value of the mortgage and the disincentive to move.

Before 1987, almost all the mortgages originated had either 30- or 15-year terms. After 1991, mortgage holders had a greater variety of terms to choose from. Post-1991, home owners who selected a 30-year mortgage were a self-selected group relative to pre-1987 home owners, and post-1991 mortgage pools experienced lower rates of housing turnover than comparable pre-1987 pools. Generically, every indication of self-selection in a particular mortgage cohort should be identified and modeled, be it the number of points paid, the mortgage rates at the time of origination, and so on.

The last factor affecting housing turnover is geographics. We know that some regions occasionally experience faster or slower rates of housing turnover due to differing rates of economic growth. Even though the differences are not generally sustainable over the long term, models should take these differences into account to improve short-term projections.

Projecting the rate of prepayments related to housing turnover has been a fairly easy job for well-constructed models. As shown in Exhibit 19–2, for most collateral types our model has come within a fraction of the conditional prepayment rate (CPR) versus actual for collateral experiencing only housing turnover–related prepayments.

Housing Turnover Component of Prepayments

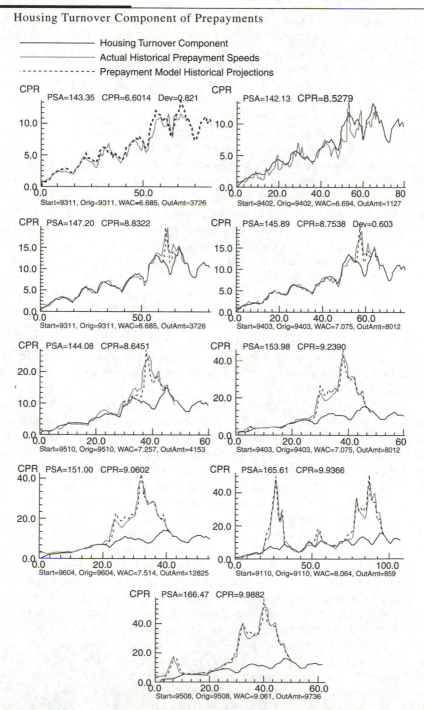

——————— Housing Turnover Component
⋯⋯⋯⋯⋯ Actual Historical Prepayment Speeds
·------------· Prepayment Model Historical Projections

Modeling the Refinancing Component of Prepayments

The evaluation of refinancing-related prepayments is by far the more crucial component in the valuation of mortgage-backed securities. This component is the most volatile and contributes the most to the value of the prepayment option. Refinancing occurs when mortgage holders prepay their mortgages by taking out another loan, most frequently at a lower rate or with other financially advantageous term(s). This is the component that has proved to be the most challenging for older types of models. A successful approach to modeling this refinancing behavior has been similar to modeling the housing turnover component, which is to create a complete and accurate model of the underlying phenomenon.

Prepayment models usually start by assuming that the refinancing incentive is measured as either the difference or the ratio between a loan coupon rate and an effective mortgage rate. The effective mortgage rate takes into account the stated mortgage commitment rate as well as average points paid—points being just a way of modifying the stated commitment rate. As an example, the average points paid at the end of 1992 were 1.7. At the end of 1998, average points paid were about 0.95. The effective mortgage rate used in 1998 would be lower than the effective mortgage rate used in 1992 even if the stated mortgage commitment rate were the same.

Additionally, there are slight seasonal effects in the refinancing response. These effects are most closely tied to the number of effective days in a month.

High premium-originated collateral tends to be more sluggish in response to refinancing incentives versus current coupon originated collateral because there usually is a reason for the high-premium originated. The reason could be related to credit quality or loan size; in either case the subsequent response to refinancing incentive tends to be diminished.

In Exhibit 19–3, the charts show three sets of pools issued only months apart. The charts where the green line is horizontal are normally originated pools, and those with a sloping green line are premium-originated. On the right scale the green line shows the extent to which our model depresses the refinancing component of prepayments due to the fact that the loan was originated at a premium. The graphs demonstrate that there are significant differences in the response to refinancing incentive between mortgages originated only months apart when one was premium-originated and the other not.

Another effect that a model should capture is the effect of the shape of the yield curve. A steep yield curve can provide an opportunity for some mortgage borrowers to "roll down the curve" and refinance into shorter-term mortgages. This is especially true when refinance transaction costs are low. The yield curve impact is most pronounced for 30-year mortgages and, as expected, is less so for 15-year mortgages.

Where new models differ significantly from the older generation of models is in the way they model burnout. Burnout occurs when, as a result of exposure to refinancing opportunity, mortgage holders most prone to refinance do so, leaving a remaining population of more "sluggish" borrowers. Older methods of calculating the burnout involve measuring accumulated exposure to refinancing opportunity and depressing the entire refinancing response of the model as a function of that measure. The problem with this approach is that a loan that has been exposed to a

EXHIBIT 19-3

High-Premium Originated Collateral Behavior

——————— Refinancing Rate Suppression Due to Premium Origination
——————— Actual historical Prepayment Speeds
------------- Prepayment Model Historical Projections

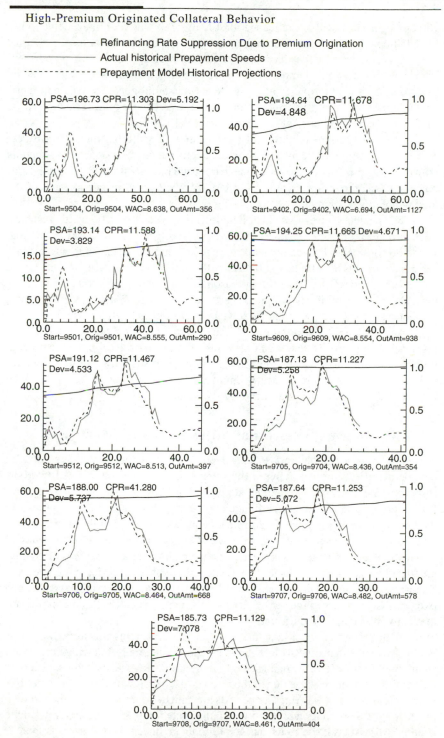

150-bp opportunity will not refinance for 100 bps, but will very much come to life for a 250-bp opportunity, confounding the model's projections under most scenarios.

This phenomenon has lead some modelers to state that there is no burnout. This is of course a logical impossibility since the only way that statement could be true would be if the mortgage holders were entirely homogeneous. We know a priori that this is not the case, since if they were, everyone would refinance at the same time—and this does not happen.

The new class of prepayment models simulates the burnout effect by assuming that the pool of loans is not homogeneous but consists of several subpools with differing propensities to refinance. After each refinancing exposure, the composition of the remaining pool is modified, and the overall responsiveness of the total population is changed.

When interest rates reach historical lows, the pattern of refinancing response goes through a dramatic change. The overall sensitivity is increased, pools that would be considered burned out start refinancing, and the refinancing curve experiences changes. This effect is variously called either the "publicity effect" or the "*USA Today*" effect. The underlying reason is that when interest rates reach their lows, the resulting publicity prompts otherwise-complacent borrowers to refinance, and borrowers that were waiting for lows in interest rates "pull the trigger."

Accumulated inflation from the time of loan origination tends to depress the refinancing response as the real dollar value of the loan drops. On the other hand, it somewhat diminishes accumulated burnout. In other words, as equity in a house increases, the ability to refinance is improved, but as the real dollar value of the loan decreases, there are fewer reasons to do that.

Refinancing Behavior of Adjustable-Rate Mortgages

Generally, borrowers that choose ARMs are a self-selected group. They usually have less expectation of staying in the same house as opposed to fixed-rate borrowers. Some are financially stretched, requiring a lower "teaser" rate to qualify for a mortgage; others are more financially astute, choosing an ARM product in the hope of refinancing into a fixed-rate mortgage when the conditions are advantageous. The above self-selection has several effects on the prepayment behavior of ARMs. The housing turnover–related prepayment rate for an ARM is often double that of a fixed-rate mortgage. The greatest share of ARM refinancing goes into fixed-rate mortgages. The composition of ARM borrowers seems to have changed over the last six years as the sensitivity to refinancing incentive has increased dramatically over that period of time.

A model can safely assume that most of the refinancing incentive for ARMs is into fixed-rate loans. ARM into ARM spread-tightening refinancings are a very small fraction of all refinancings, and ARM into ARM refinancings generally makes little economic sense due to the fixed costs. "Teaser surfing"—as repetitive refinancings into new ARM teaser periods are called—does not exist much in reality since excess origination points often compensate for most of the teaser discount. If an ARM WAC is close to its cap, the refinancing incentive is lower, as there is less risk to borrowers that their mortgage rates will go up. If the 30-year mortgage rate drops compared to what it was at the ARM's origination, borrowers may refinance into a 30-year mortgage just because that was their initial preference anyway. Most ARM refinancings happen between plus and minus a 50-bp incentive. Under conditions of publicity (when interest rates reach their lows) the refinancing response gets modified even more drastically for ARMs than for fixed-rate loans.

Projecting ARM prepayments has been considered an extremely difficult and, according to some, an essentially impossible task. We find that ARMs, although somewhat more volatile than fixed-rate loans, are quite tenable within the paradigm of the new prepayment model. The graphs in Exhibit 19–4 were selected as a cross section of WACs and origination years for GNMA ARMs and, as can be seen, most projections are within an acceptable range of actual prepayments.

Uses of Loan-Level Information

When loan-level information is available, as in mortgage servicing or whole-loan applications, it should be used to amend the generic prepayment model response. The additional variables available may be the loan's current LTV; its balance; whether the loan was full documentation; single-family; primary residence; and whether the last refinancing (if any) was "cash-out" or not.

The values of the above variables affect the expected housing turnover and the refinancing response of the collateral to differing degrees, and that effect should be modeled properly. For example, larger loan balances create a greater incentive to refinance, but the housing turnover component is lower due to a lower rate of "trade-up" activity. Lower current LTV would generally lead to both a greater refinancing propensity and a higher rate of housing turnover. It is possible to separate the effects of each of the variables and to estimate their separate contribution.

Lower-credit loans demand another extension of the generic prepayment model. Credit-impaired collateral experiences, in addition to prepayments related to housing turnover and interest rate, some "credit-driven" refinancings. These refinancings occur due to a number of credit-related activities, such as loan term extension, credit improvement–related refinancings, loan consolidation, etc. The extent of these activities are all related to credit quality. One can estimate the credit quality from the spread between the WAC and mortgage rates at the time of origination. Other measures of credit quality differ by originator and are not directly comparable to one another. The spread between the WAC and mortgage rates, being an economic measure, is more reliable. Generally, shorter-term lower-credit loans tend to experience higher rates of refinancings related to credit quality. It should be noted that publicity has a profound effect on the behavior of credit-impaired collateral.

Most of the variability of the prepayment response between issuers can be explained by the variability of their collateral. For example, different issues may have different LTVs, loan amounts, or quality. Nonetheless, even accounting for these differences, some residual differences still remain in the behavior of the collateral of the different issuers.

EXHIBIT 19-4

Projected versus Actual Prepayment Speeds for GNMA ARMs

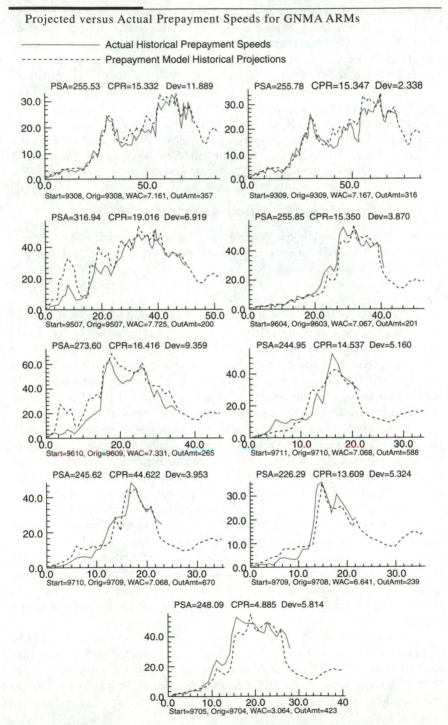

————— Actual Historical Prepayment Speeds
------------- Prepayment Model Historical Projections

PSA=255.53   CPR=15.332   Dev=11.889
Start=9308, Orig=9308, WAC=7.161, OutAmt=357

PSA=255.78   CPR=15.347   Dev=2.338
Start=9309, Orig=9309, WAC=7.167, OutAmt=316

PSA=316.94   CPR=19.016   Dev=6.919
Start=9507, Orig=9507, WAC=7.725, OutAmt=200

PSA=255.85   CPR=15.350   Dev=3.870
Start=9604, Orig=9603, WAC=7.067, OutAmt=201

PSA=273.60   CPR=16.416   Dev=9.359
Start=9610, Orig=9609, WAC=7.331, OutAmt=265

PSA=244.95   CPR=14.537   Dev=5.160
Start=9711, Orig=9710, WAC=7.068, OutAmt=588

PSA=245.62   CPR=44.622   Dev=3.953
Start=9710, Orig=9709, WAC=7.068, OutAmt=670

PSA=226.29   CPR=13.609   Dev=5.324
Start=9709, Orig=9708, WAC=6.641, OutAmt=239

PSA=248.09   CPR=4.885   Dev=5.814
Start=9705, Orig=9704, WAC=3.064, OutAmt=423

MODELING RELIABILITY AND ACCURACY

Judging the validity of a prepayment model is always difficult. As discussed at the beginning of the chapter, it is fairly easy to create a model that would fit history well and still have zero predictive power, by using a mathematical technique known as the Fourier series. While a good fit to history is not a sufficient condition, a reasonable fit is definitely a necessary one. A more reliable evaluation of a model should involve an out-of-sample testing procedure. This type of testing is difficult to perform since the process of fitting parameters to a limited data set is extremely laborious. The process cannot be machine-driven given the current state of computer technology (see the discussion in the beginning of the chapter), and so it falls to the modeler to fit the patterns of the response. Nevertheless, an excellent way of analyzing a model's performance would be to track its performance through time, using a constant set of parameters. A satisfactory performance through time and a good fit to history are indications of the robustness of the model. In Exhibit 19–5, the projected and actual prepayments are graphed as of late 1999 and are based on parameters calculated in 1996.

A wide range of coupons and origination years was selected for the demonstration. As can be seen, the same parameters fit the 1992–1993 prepayment data as well as the 1998–1999 data. This demonstrates that the efficiency of the refinancing response changes very slowly. It is the relative stability of the refinancing response that enables one to model the underlying process. That is not to say that some components of the response for certain collateral types could not undergo a rapid change (as we saw with the ARM's response), but it is the general level of response that is fairly stable.

CONCLUSION

Every aspect of a "good" prepayment model must be designed to reflect people's behavior. History should be used, but only as an indication of what the parameters should be. And, if there is not enough history to set the value of certain parameters that we know exist in the real world, it is better to set them to some reasonable value than not set them at all and have them *implied* by other parameters (since the implied value may not be a reasonable one). The quality of a model depends *only* on the *accuracy and completeness* of the representation of the underlying phenomena that we know exists in the real world.

Performance Accuracy of the Model over Time

———————————— Actual Historical Prepayment Speeds
- - - - - - - - - - - - - - Prepayment Model Historical Projections

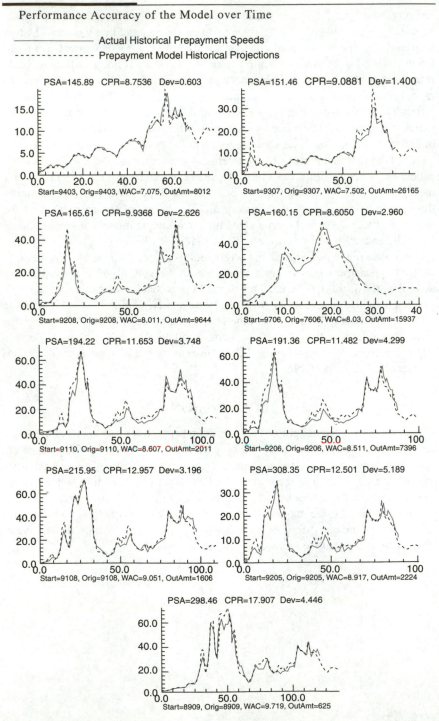

CHAPTER **20**

GNMA ARM PREPAYMENT MODEL

Satish M. Mansukhani
Managing Director
Bear, Stearns & Co. Inc.

V.S. Srinivasan
Associate Director
Bear, Stearns & Co. Inc.

The prepayment and convexity profile of GNMA adjustable-rate mortgages (ARMs) is different from traditional fixed-rate mortgages. Until recently, however, our ability to evaluate GNMA ARMs was limited by data that did not cover several crucial aspects of prepayment behavior. For example, the rate environment during the last three years has for the first time provided observations on the prepayment behavior of GNMA ARM borrowers during a deep in-the-money exposure to a sustained refinancing incentive. As shown in Exhibit 20–1, prepayment observations until mid-1997 failed to reveal the true refinancing sensitivity of GNMA ARM borrowers

With this recent experience, the quantity and quality of information available to the analyst has improved dramatically. Furthermore, a substantial number of pools issued in the mid-1990s with high gross margins have now faced multiple resets and are exhibiting the effects of burnout. Armed with this new information and more accurate prepayment analytics, investors can now perform a more rigorous analysis of the performance characteristics of GNMA ARM securities. In this chapter we explore the results of a study of GNMA ARM prepayment behavior.

THE GNMA ARM BORROWER

Understanding GNMA ARM loan and borrower characteristics provides the key to isolating the determinants of GNMA ARM prepayments. Most GNMA ARM borrowers use an ARM to qualify for a larger loan than they might otherwise be able to obtain using fixed-rate financing. This is evident from the larger loan balances on GNMA ARMs versus GNMA FRMs, which respectively stand at $115,000 and $98,000 based on the 1999 vintage.

Although the popularity of the GNMA ARM mortgage as a financing vehicle is contingent on curve steepness and the level of interest rates, the GNMA

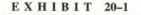

E X H I B I T   20–1

Prepayment Exposure of the GNMA ARM Sector

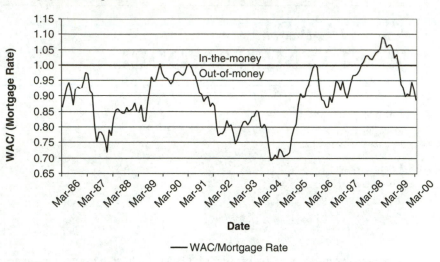

Date

—— WAC/Mortgage Rate

Source: Bear, Stearns & Co. Inc.

ARM has been offered at a consistent rate discount of approximately 160 basis
points (bps) to fixed-rate mortgages (see Exhibit 20–2).

Offsetting the benefits of lower borrowing costs is the higher interest rate
uncertainty assumed by the ARM borrower. Thus, the GNMA ARM borrower ex-
tracts a rate discount at the cost of facing a potentially higher mortgage payment
at the time of the first reset (generally this is between 13 to 15 months after origination). As such, ARM prepayments depend not only on refinancing incentives,
but also on borrower expectations about future interest rates and the degree of borrower risk aversion. Optimizing the trade-off between the current rate discount
and future rate uncertainty drives ARM prepayment behavior.

The prepayment profile of GNMA ARMs is also different from that of conventional annually adjusting ARMs and hybrid ARMs. Although the GNMA ARM
borrower is affordability-constrained (loan-to-value ratios on FHA-insured mortgages are approximately 95%), the conventional ARM borrower is attracted by either deep teaser rates (annually adjusting conventional ARMs) or by a rate advantage to 30-year FRM for a period that matches the anticipated financing term
(hybrid ARMs). The prospect of these incentives being eliminated at reset is often
the catalyst for prepayment activity.

THE SEASONING OF GNMA ARM PREPAYMENTS

The GNMA ARM current-coupon rate is closely linked to the level of 30-year
fixed mortgage rates. Irrespective of curve shape and the level of interest rates, the
weighted average mortgage coupon of newly originated GNMA ARMs has aver-

EXHIBIT 20–2

Thirty-Year FRM and ARM Rates

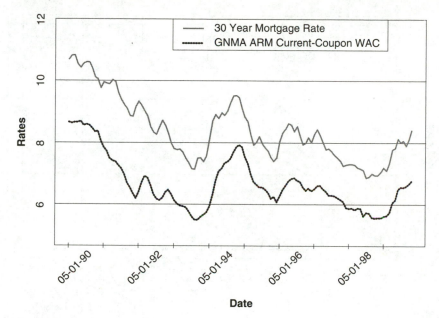

Source: Bear, Stearns & Co. Inc.

aged 160 bps lower than fixed mortgage rates. This constant rate differential suggests that the origination community is unwilling to attract borrowers to the sector by offering deeply teased rates. Therefore, we believe that the borrower seeking GNMA ARM financing does so primarily for affordability reasons.

The prepayment experience of current-coupon GNMA ARM borrowers shows that baseline prepayments increase to approximately 5% conditional prepayment rate (CPR) during the first 12 to 15 months reaching 10% CPR by month 40 and a steady-state level of 14% CPR in 10 years (see Exhibit 20–3). The seasoning ramp is reflective of the impact of housing turnover on GNMA ARM prepayments. Influencing this seasoning ramp are the combined effects of pure aging, interest rate lock-in and assumability. In Exhibit 20–3, we plot the seasoning ramp for both current-coupon and teased GNMA ARMs. Actual prepayment speeds overlay the impact of seasonal factors, rate resets, and refinancing incentives over this seasoning curve.

In general, not only do prepayments increase due to turnover as a loan ages, but the affordability-constrained borrower underlying a GNMA ARM pool is also less likely than a traditional fixed-rate borrower to move soon after incurring the costs of purchasing a new home. We also find that lock-in dampens prepayment speeds during the first few years after loan origination. Borrowers who use an ARM to finance the purchase of a home will have difficulty trading up to another home until they have realized some equity or income growth. This difficulty is further

E X H I B I T   20–3

The GNMA ARM Seasoning Curve

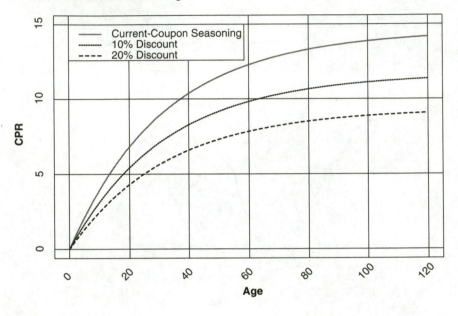

compounded by the high loan-to-value (LTV) ratios on GNMA ARMs versus conventional fixed-rate mortgages. Over time, however, as the borrower's economic situation improves, there is an increasing likelihood that the borrower relocates or "trades up." Therefore, ARM borrowers demonstrate a propensity to be "locked into" their existing mortgage during the initial period after origination.

Assumability on FHA mortgages lengthens the seasoning curve relative to "due-on-sale" conventional mortgages. Even if a borrower sells the home, there is a strong incentive for the new borrower to "assume" the existing loan, thereby preventing a prepayment. The assumability incentive weakens over time due to amortization and home price appreciation (the new borrower has to pay up the difference between the property value and the remaining outstanding balance on the loan).

SEASONAL FACTORS

Seasonality has a universal impact on all home owners. Housing turnover prepayments are linked to the weather, vacation schedules, and the school year. Home owners are much more likely to move in the summer when the weather is warm and their children are out of school than in the winter when the opposite is true. The seasonal patterns observed in GNMA ARMs are consistent with the seasonal adjustments reported by the National Association of Realtors (NAR). Prepayments related to housing turnovers usually peak in the late spring and summer at levels that are 20% faster than the annual average and bottom out in February at 26% slower than the annual average.

EXHIBIT 20-4

The GNMA ARM Refinancing Profile

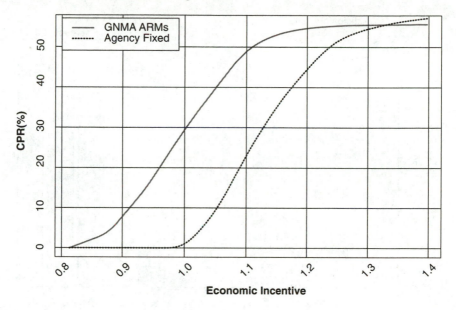

REFINANCING SENSITIVITY

Our baseline GNMA ARM refinancing profile (see Exhibit 20–4) depicts the projected prepayment rate for a GNMA ARM borrower across a wide spectrum of refinancing incentives. A refinancing incentive of 1.0 means that the mortgage rate on the ARM is the same as that on a 30-year fixed mortgage. At this level, borrowers are able to refinance into an FRM without facing a change in their monthly mortgage payment. Even though this refinancing decision is not accompanied by an immediate economic advantage, borrowers are able to avoid future rate uncertainty by switching to fixed-rate financing. In fact, ARM borrowers that qualify for fixed-rate financing switch even if they face a slightly higher monthly mortgage payment. Hence, ARM prepayments due to refinancing pick up even when the economic incentive is less than 1.0.

The impact of certainty considerations on refinancing decisions is unique to the ARM borrower. Refinancing activity on fixed-rate mortgages picks up when market rates move below the borrower's mortgage rate (i.e., a refinancing incentive of 1.0 or greater). The ARM refinancing function is similar to the FRM function (i.e., flat when the economic incentive is less than 1.0) when the ARM lifetime caps are struck. In this case, the rate-certainty trade-off favors ARM borrowers since the lifetime caps protect them from paying the market rate. Consequently, borrowers start to explore refinancing alternatives as the market rate falls toward the ARM borrower's current mortgage rate. This shifts the refinancing profile to the right starting from an incentive level of 1.

E X H I B I T   20–5

Impact of Rate Resets on Refinancing Profile

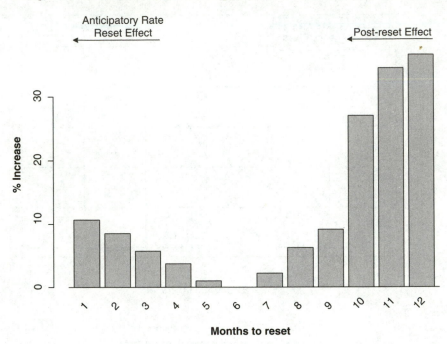

Since ARM borrowers are forward-looking prior to a rate reset, the borrower's refinancing decision is a function of the difference between the current mortgage rate and the expected rate upon reset. To capture this, we fine-tune the refinancing incentive calculation by expressing the ARM WAC as a linear weighting of the mortgage rate today and the expected mortgage rate on the reset date, weighted by the months to reset. Thus, for a GNMA ARM with a 6% mortgage rate and 12 months to reset, assuming a future mortgage rate of 7%, the WAC used in our economic incentive calculation is 6.5% 6 months from today, and 6.75% 9 months from today.

Rate shock also impacts the refinancing profile of GNMA ARM borrowers. We find that the effect of a rate reset is felt in speeds almost immediately after occurrence. Thus, speeds during the first 3 months after reset tend to increase by 25% to 35%. The effect of the rate reset wears off gradually during months 4 to 9. Even before reset occurs we find that anticipatory rate shock increases speeds by 5% to 10% during the 3 months prior to the adjustment (see Exhibit 20–5).

EXHIBIT 20–6

All Aggregate GNMA ARMs: 1995 and Later Originations

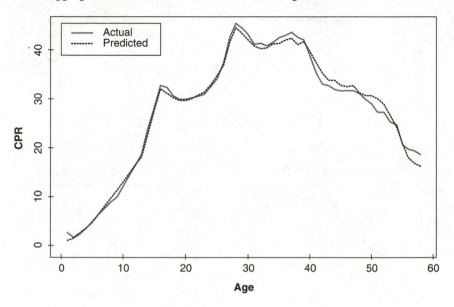

Finally, we study the impact of burnout on GNMA ARM prepayments. Similar factors influence burnout in ARMs and FRMs, namely, the strength of past refinancing incentives and the length of exposure to such opportunities. However, as adjustable-rate mortgages eventually index toward market rates, the cumulative burnout levels reached are smaller than in the case of fixed-rate mortgages. For example, a borrower paying a fixed mortgage rate at a premium to market rates is continuously exposed to a refinancing incentive. In contrast, ARM financing will result in the borrower rate's resetting toward market rates, limiting the extent of the refinancing exposure and thereby limiting burnout.

THE PREDICTIVE POWER OF OUR MODEL

Putting all the pieces together we find that our GNMA ARM prepayment model provides robust prepayment projections across different interest rate and economic environments. To validate the model, we examine actual versus predicted prepayments using three different test criteria: aggregate pools, loan age, and selected data panels. In all cases the model fits the data extremely well. We focus on the 1995 and later vintages given the uniform increase in the weighted average gross margins (WAGM) on all originations since 1995. The results are shown in Exhibits 20–6 to 20–8.

E X H I B I T   20–7

Aggregate GNMA ARMs, Conditional on Loan Age: 1995 and Later Originations

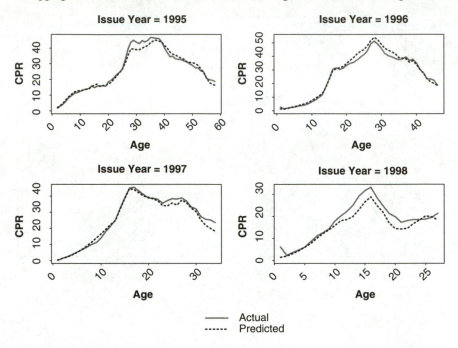

RELATIVE VALUE IMPLICATIONS

The unique factors impacting GNMA ARM prepayments result in a prepayment profile that is substantially different from that of fixed-rate mortgages. Based on our analysis, we specifically draw attention to the short-duration, front-loaded cash flows of GNMA ARMs versus FRMs. In addition, we find that GNMA ARMs are substantially less negatively convex than FRMs.

Our study of GNMA ARM prepayments has revealed that changing refinancing alternatives allows borrowers to reduce the weight of their mortgage debt load and/or reduce their exposure to future changes in rates. Hence, one would expect acceleration in prepayment speeds when either or both of these objectives can be met. In contrast, borrowers backing fixed-rate mortgages are more comfortable with the carrying costs of their mortgages and are more opportunistic when acting on a refinancing opportunity.

Actual Versus Predicted Prepayments for the 1995 Vintage, by Original Coupon

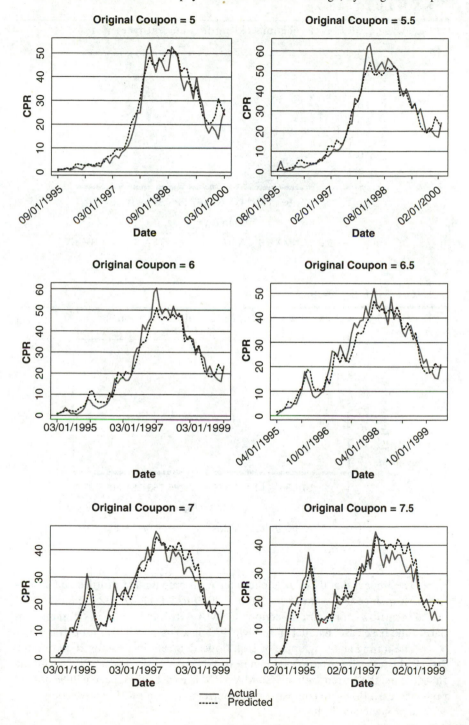

E X H I B I T   20–9

Base Case Cash Flow Projections ($1 million current face)

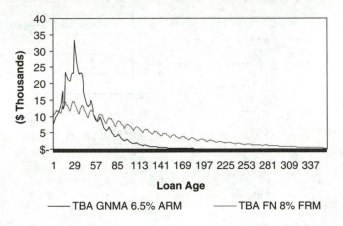

— TBA GNMA 6.5% ARM   — TBA FN 8% FRM

E X H I B I T   20–10

Down 100 Case Cash Flow Projections ($1 million current face)

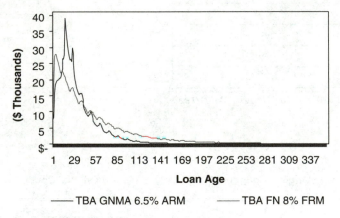

— TBA GNMA 6.5% ARM   — TBA FN 8% FRM

The impact that these differences have on prepayment profiles and securities performance is illustrated in Exhibits 20–9 to 20–11 where we plot the projected cash flows for a current-coupon GNMA ARM and for FRMs in three scenarios: the base case, parallel shift down 100 bps, and parallel shift up 100 bps.

The timing and magnitude of cash flows depicted in Exhibits 20–9 through 20–11 illustrate the front-loaded nature of GNMA ARM cash flows. During the first 5 years, the current-coupon GNMA ARM is expected to receive 78% of total projected cash flows. In comparison, the current-coupon FRM receives only 41% of total projected cash flows.

E X H I B I T   20–11

Up 100 Case Cash Flow Projections ($1 million current face)

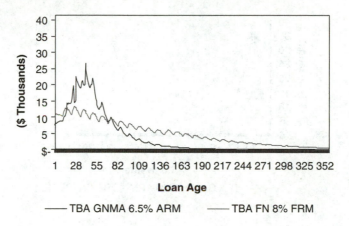

— TBA GNMA 6.5% ARM   —— TBA FN 8% FRM

E X H I B I T 20–12

Percentage of Cash Flows Received in First 5 Years, Base Case,
Up/Down 100 bps

Security	Base Case	Down 100 bps	Up 100 bps
GNMA ARM	78%	87%	67%
FNMA FRM	41%	69%	36%

Stressing each of these securities to a parallel up and down shift in interest rates reveals the symmetrical impact on the cash flows of GNMA ARMs. We observe that changes to the cash flow distribution on GNMA ARMs is much more symmetrical than the changes observed on a FRM. Thus, using 5 years as the cutoff, we observe that in both scenarios, investors in GNMA ARMs face a 9% to an 11% shift in the cash flow distribution; cash flows received in the first 5 years jump from 78% to 87% when rates rally and decrease from 78% to 67% when rates back up (see Exhibit 20–12). In comparison, changes to the FRM cash flow distribution is asymmetrical, with cash flows received in the first 5 years jumping by 28% when rates rally, and declining by 5% in the backup scenario.

One important objective of our study is to capture the factors that trigger a GNMA ARM refinance. Analysis to date has focused on trying to separate the impact of curve shape from the impact of rate levels on prepayment behavior. In our study, we find that borrowers will refinance *whenever* presented with an opportunity to reduce carrying costs and increase certainty.

E X H I B I T   20–13

One-year Treasury Up 100 Cash Flow Projections ($1 million current face)

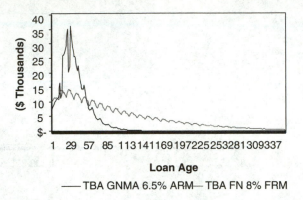

Loan Age

——— TBA GNMA 6.5% ARM— TBA FN 8% FRM

E X H I B I T   20–14

One-year Treasury Down 100 Cash Flow Projections ($1 million current face)

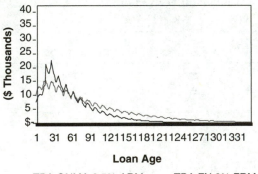

Loan Age

——— TBA GNMA 6.5% ARM   ——— TBA FN 8% FRM

This is best illustrated by subjecting the current-coupon ARM and FRM securities to two additional scenarios: 1-year CMT rates up or down 100 bps (see Exhibits 20–13 and 20–14). In Exhibit 20–15 we present the impact these scenarios have on the cash flow distribution of each security. We observe that the impact of this change on the FRM security is minimal (small differences are due to the residual impact on mortgage rates introduced by shifting only one point on the curve). In comparison, the impact of these scenarios on ARM cash flow distributions is comparable to the impact of a parallel up or down shift of the entire curve. Hence, in the scenario where 1-year CMT rates move up 100 bps, pushing ARM mortgage rates higher, 87% of total cash flows are received during the first 5 years. Similarly, 61% of cash flows are received in the scenario where 1- year CMT rates drop by 100 bps.

EXHIBIT 20–15

Percentage of Cash Flows Received in First 5 Years, Base Case, 1-Year CMT
Up and Down 100 bps

Security	Base Case	Up 100 bps	Down 100 bps
GNMA ARM	78%	87%	61%
FNMA FRM	41%	40%	45%

EXHIBIT 20–16

GNMA ARM Projected Cash Flows, by Original Coupon ($1 million
current face)

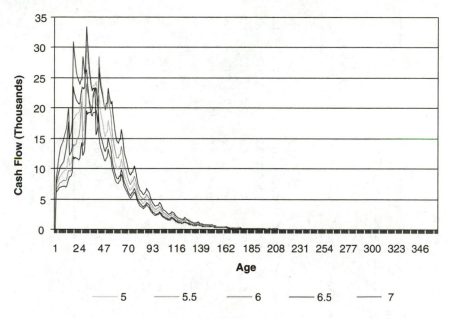

The concentration of cash flows during the first few years after origination
and little fluctuation to this distribution as rates change make ARMs positively
convex relative to FRMs. The front-loaded cash flows across all ARMs, irrespective of coupon, cause little variation in the convexity levels across the coupon
spectrum (see Exhibit 20–16). As shown in Exhibit 20–17, the absolute convexity
levels and convexity costs of GNMA ARMs vary by small amounts across the
coupon spectrum. In contrast, in the case of FRMs, convexity costs almost double
as one moves up the coupon curve. As such, investors in FRMs are forced to make
a yield-convexity trade-off. In the case of GNMA ARMs, however, a similar move

EXHIBIT 20-17

Valuation of GNMA ARMs and FRMs

	Coupon	WAM[a]	Price[b]	Yield	WAL[c]	Life CPR[d]	Zero Volatility OAS	OAS	Convexity Cost	LIBOR OAS	Duration	Convexity
GNMA FRM												
TBA GN 6.00% I 30 yr	6	2029	91:30+	7.27	11.2	5.3	134	120	13	−16	6.70	−0.196
TBA GN 6.50% I 30 yr	6.5	2029	94:24	7.37	10.9	5.7	144	123	22	−12	6.30	−0.479
TBA GN 7.00% I 30 yr	7	2029	97:5+	7.52	10.3	6.6	157	126	30	−5	5.78	−0.955
TBA GN 7.50% I 30 yr	7.5	2030	99:8+	7.70	9.6	7.6	170	130	40	4	5.14	−1.365
TBA GN 8.00% I 30 yr	8	2030	101:1	7.88	8.6	9.0	183	134	49	13	4.37	−1.698
TBA GN 8.50% I 30 yr	8.5	2030	102:7	8.12	7.5	10.9	196	144	53	29	3.60	−2.061
TBA GN 9.00% I 30 yr	9	2028	103:10	8.25	6.0	13.9	196	154	42	46	2.83	−1.636
GNMA ARM												
GNMA 5.0 07/01	5	2030	96:7+	7.48	4.7	18.1	111	86	25	−26	3.14	−0.674
GNMA 5.5 07/01	5.5	2030	97:14	7.46	4.4	19.4	111	86	25	−23	2.80	−0.606
GNMA 6.0 07/01	6	2030	98:15+	7.42	4.1	20.9	105	87	17	−20	2.50	−0.880
GNMA 6.5 07/01	6.5	2030	99:18	7.34	3.8	22.4	97	83	14	−21	2.12	−0.823
GNMA 7.0 07/01	7	2030	100:11	7.26	3.5	24.1	98	83	15	−18	1.78	−0.640

[a]WAM = weighted average maturity.
[b]Valuation date: April 12, 2000, for April settlement. Effective duration and convexity based on LIBOR curve.
[c]WAL = weighted average life.
[d]CPR = conditional prepayment rate.

EXHIBIT   20–18

Projected 12-Month Rate of Return Profiles of TBA GNMA ARMs

Security	Down 100 bps	Base Case	Up 100 bps
GNMA 5.0	9.459	**7.593**	4.916
GNMA 5.5	9.133	**7.695**	5.365
GNMA 6.0	8.645	**7.773**	5.800
GNMA 6.5	7.992	**7.790**	6.231
GNMA 7.0	7.509	**7.671**	6.682

up the coupon curve is essentially a repositioning in duration with a minimal change to convexity. We find that nominal yields on higher-coupon ARM securities are lower than those offered on lower-coupon securities as investors are willing to accept lower yields on shorter-duration securities especially when the cash flows are not accompanied by greater negative convexity. Based on current pricing, we recommend GNMA ARM 7s based on their wider London interbank offered rate (LIBOR) option-adjusted spread (OAS) and lower negative convexity.

In general, we also favor GNMA 6s, 6.5s, and 7s based on the projected rate of return profiles of to-be-announced (TBA) ARM securities (see Exhibit 20–18). These are all projected to offer higher 12-month rates of return in the base case than longer–duration GNMA 5s and 5.5s.

As GNMA ARM borrowers season, the effects of rate shock and resets diminish. Borrowers remaining in a pool, particularly after being exposed to refinancing opportunities, demonstrate the presence of limiting factors such as the inability to qualify for a fixed-rate loan. These factors dampen the prepayment response at the pool level to future refinancing events. Over time, as additional mortgage options open up to these borrowers through income growth and/or accumulation of savings, pool level prepayments reach a steady-state level. Based on current pricing, however, we believe that TBA securities offer better relative value than seasoned GNMA ARMs. At similar dollar prices and approximately the same durations as TBA 7s, seasoned securities are priced at similar yields but are significantly more negatively convex (see Exhibit 20–19). Lower rates of return in the base case and down-100-bp scenario versus TBA 7s further point to value in the latter (see Exhibit 20–20). Higher rates of return in the up-100-bp scenario, however, point to the sensitivity of returns on seasoned securities to reset date (July 2000, for the example securities).

---

1. We extend the definition of seasoned GNMA ARMs to all securities that bear a fully-indexed servicing rate reflective of the WAGM. Prior to this, seasoned GNMA ARMs referred to securities originated prior to 1995 when a uniform shift in origination practices resulted in the adoption of a 275 basis points WAGM standard.

EXHIBIT 20–19

Valuation of Seasoned GNMA ARMs

Vintage	Coupon[a]	WAM	Price[b]	Yield	WAL	Life CPR	Zero Volatility OAS	OAS	Convexity Cost	LIBOR OAS	Duration	Convexity
1993	6.375	2022	100:14	7.400	5.2	15.2	122	112	16	−2	1.58	−1.955
1994	6.375	2024	100:11	7.397	4.6	17.5	121	111	18	−1	1.57	−1.942
1995	6.375	2025	100:08+	7.288	2.9	28.1	105	95	22	−3	1.35	−1.599
1996	6.375	2026	100:06+	7.296	2.8	29.7	106	97	22	−1	1.36	−1.641
1997	6.375	2027	100:03+	7.342	2.8	29.4	111	102	23	3	1.39	−1.672
1998	6.375	2027	100:01+	7.373	2.8	29.1	115	105	24	4	1.41	−1.774
1999	6.000	2029	99:09	7.561	3.3	25.8	134	117	31	11	1.94	−1.050

[a]Valuation Date: April 12, 2000, for April settlement. Effective duration and convexity based on LIBOR curve.
[b]July 2000, reset date.

E X H I B I T   20–20

Projected 12-Month Rate-of-Return Profiles of Seasoned GNMA ARMs

Vintage	Down 100 bps	Base Case	Up 100 bps
1993	7.032	**7.585**	6.968
1994	6.989	**7.578**	6.979
1995	6.754	**7.409**	7.061
1996	6.750	**7.421**	7.070
1997	6.812	**7.472**	7.088
1998	6.828	**7.516**	7.096
1999	7.532	**7.898**	6.775

CONCLUSION

The prepayment experience during the latter half of the 1990s has led investors to question the prepayment profile of GNMA ARM borrowers. By incorporating the latest information available on the prepayment behavior of GNMA ARM borrowers, the results our study reported in this chapter bring to investors a new valuation tool that can be used to accurately model portfolio cash flows, make informed cross-sector relative value decisions, and enhance hedging capabilities.

CHAPTER 21

THE NEXT GENERATION OF PREPAYMENT MODELS TO VALUE NONAGENCY MBS

Dale Westhoff
Senior Managing Director
Bear, Stearns & Co. Inc.

V.S. Srinivasan
Associate Director
Bear, Stearns & Co. Inc.

The rapid evolution of the nonagency mortgage market has necessitated the development of a new breed of mortgage prepayment model that accommodates a much wider range of loan and borrower attributes than we have seen historically. In just the last few years the nonagency sector has grown from a single market dominated by jumbo[1] loans with fairly uniform characteristics to one with several subsectors predicated on diverse loan features that fall outside the scope of agency underwriting guidelines. Existing nonagency prepayment models have not kept pace with these developments, in part because of a lack of historical prepayment data on these new subsectors. Furthermore, despite access to a rich database of property level information in the nonagency sector, technology constraints have prevented modelers from bringing the full value of this data to investors. Today, however, three factors are serving to change the face of nonagency valuation models going forward.

1. The technology now exists to handle the massive computational requirements involved in implementing a prepayment model entirely at the property level.

2. The refinancing events in the first and fourth quarters of 1998 filled critical information voids in our alternative-A and jumbo prepayment databases.

3. The availability of detailed loan-level information in the nonagency sector allows us to examine this recent refinancing experience in extensive detail.

---

1. Loans that exceed GSE loan size limits.

This chapter is reprinted with permission from Frank J. Fabozzi (ed.), *The Handbook of Nonagency Mortgage-Backed Securities* (New Hope, PA: Frank J. Fabozzi Associates, 2000).

Taken together these factors represent the foundation for what we believe will be a new era in nonagency mortgage valuation technology. For the first time we believe that the precision and accuracy of these models will far surpass what is available in the agency sector where there is no disclosure of property level information. It is in this context that we introduce our new nonagency prepayment model that incorporates this new data while delivering uncompromised, loan-level parametrics to the nonagency mortgage investor.

INNOVATIVE FEATURES:
A TRUE LOAN-LEVEL IMPLEMENTATION

The most unique aspect of our new model is that it is implemented entirely at the property level[2] despite enormous computational requirements. In general, the precision of first generation loan-level prepayment models was compromised by the need to aggregate data at run time to reduce computational load and turnaround time. This resulted in a loss of information and precision. A full loan-level implementation implies that when evaluating a particular security for a given interest rate assumption, the model preserves all loan-level information by amortizing each loan individually rather than aggregating loans together. To do this, a unique vector of single monthly mortality (SMM) rates is generated for each loan in a deal conditional on the interest rate path and specific loan and borrower characteristics. Until recently, the drawback to this approach was its processing demand, particularly in an option-adjusted spread (OAS) framework where hundreds of randomly generated interest rate scenarios are evaluated in the calculation of a single OAS. For example, for a nonagency deal backed by 2,000 loans the prepayment function is invoked 648 million times to compute the option-adjusted duration of a single bond.[3] To overcome these tremendous computational requirements, we employ state-of-the-art multiprocessor technology in a distributed computing user environment to deliver timely run-time executions.

Our return from this investment in technology is a level of precision in cash flow projections that was previously unattainable. This comes at a time when there is a growing demand from mortgage investors for more rigorous valuation models that address increasingly disparate loan and borrower features. It is imperative that nonagency investors have the ability to quantify the performance implications of wide distributions in loan size, coupon, and loan-to-value (LTV). Furthermore, models must be able to differentiate along secondary loan characteristics such as property type, occupancy status, loan purpose, documentation level, and borrower credit quality.

Beyond the added precision of a loan-level implementation, our second generation nonagency prepayment model incorporates several unique and innovative features:

1. *Borrower specific home equity levels calculated:* A borrower's current equity position in the home is a key determinant of both refinancing and hous-

---

2. No run-time aggregation is performed.
3. (2,000 loans) × (360 amortization months) × (300 interest rate paths) × (3 scenarios) = 648 million model evaluations.

ing turnover prepayment behavior. Since LTV changes as home prices rise or fall in a particular region, we update the LTV of over 350,000 loans in our nonagency database every month using Mortgage Risk Assessment Corporation (MRAC) zip code level home price indices.

2. *Incorporation of 1998 refinancing data:* 1998 provided invaluable nonagency prepayment data, particularly in the alternative-A sector. Our model incorporates this new data without sacrificing its fit to pre-1998 data.

3. *Borrower self-selection and burnout:* One of the intrinsic benefits of a loan-level prepayment model is that it replicates the borrower self-selection or "burnout" that occurs as borrowers prepay their mortgages. By amortizing each loan individually our forecast always reflects the characteristics of the surviving population of borrowers in a pool or deal.

4. *Unique loan sectors addressed:* In addition to the standard residential mortgage types (30-year, 15-year amortization loans) our model handles several less traditional mortgage types, including: relocation mortgages, Community Reinvestment Act (CRA) loans, and prepayment penalty mortgages.

THE BEAR STEARNS NONAGENCY PREPAYMENT DATABASE

Central to the development of a robust loan-level prepayment model is having access to prepayment data that cover a wide range of interest rate environments over a diverse set of loan and borrower attributes. Our nonagency models were estimated from over 350,000 jumbo and alternative-A nonagency loans collected from six major issuers and originated between 1990 and 1998. Actual prepayment observations cover 1990 to 1998, a period marked by a 400-basis-point (bp) range in long-term interest rates and punctuated by four major refinancing events. These data represent over 70% of the outstanding nonagency mortgage-backed securities (MBS) universe. The alternative-A subuniverse of loans in our database is generally characterized by conforming balances but other nonstandard features that prevent agency purchase. The unique characteristics of these loans will be discussed in a subsequent section.

It is important to note that most of the loans coming from the major conduits are actually purchased from broker-correspondents. Therefore, the data tend to represent a fairly diverse group of originators. This is one reason why we elected not to use issuer-specific parameters in our model estimation. Issuer-specific prepayment models run the risk that a change in an issuer's broker-correspondent purchasing patterns or a change in originator underwriting guidelines will disrupt historical prepayment patterns at the issuer level. That weakness also calls into question the cross-issuer applicability of models developed from a single issuer's data set. Instead, we chose to specify our model by identifying long-term relationships in loan and borrower attributes from a multiple issuer data set. We believe this approach delivers a model with the broadest application while leveraging on the richness of loan-level detail.

THE IMPACT OF THE AGENCIES ON NONAGENCY PREPAYMENT BEHAVIOR

Changes in agency underwriting guidelines directly impact the prepayment behavior of nonagency securities. By definition, the nonagency sector contains loans above the agency loan size limits or outside of other underwriting criteria established by Fannie Mae and Freddie Mac. Nearly every year, agency loan size limits are adjusted higher, based on the observed increase in national home prices over the year.[4] In addition to changes in loan size limits, the successful implementation of automated underwriting systems has allowed the agencies to price credit risk more effectively and expand underwriting criteria to accommodate less traditional mortgagors with impaired credit or nonstandard features. Clearly, the portion of the existing nonagency universe that qualifies under expanded agency guidelines is at greater risk of prepayment since borrowers can usually obtain much lower financing rates in the conforming market.

These guideline changes can sometimes wreak havoc on short-term prepayment rates in the nonagency sector. For example, at the end of 1997 the agencies raised their loan limits from $214,600 to $227,150, increasing the refinancing incentive on existing jumbo loans with balances between these levels (since they qualified for agency purchase). By isolating the post-change prepayment rates of the loans that fell between the old and new limits, we can see a clear structural increase in speeds beginning in 1998 as these borrowers started to refinance into conforming loans. As Exhibit 21–1 illustrates, the "between limit" loans prepaid systematically faster than identical loans with balances just above the new limit. To an uninformed investor, this would seem counterintuitive since we would normally expect smaller balance loans to pay slower than their large balance equivalent.

Fortunately, access to loan-level information in the nonagency sector allows us to identify the nonagency mortgage population affected by such a change and adjust our models accordingly before the change is implemented.

Expanded agency underwriting criteria also impact the conforming sector where loan disclosure is limited to pool level statistics. As the agencies stretch their guidelines to accommodate less traditional mortgagors that currently fall under the alternative-A, home equity, or B/C umbrellas, to-be-announced (TBA) pools become increasingly heterogeneous and less predictable. Without disclosure of property level information or a separate pool prefix to identify these loans, we currently have no mechanism at the agency pool level to model the impact of increased dispersion in loan characteristics. This puts agency prepayment models at a significant disadvantage versus their nonagency counterparts. Exhibit 21–2 summarizes the disclosure deficit that currently exists between the agency and nonagency sectors.

---

4. So far this has always been an upward revision (or the level has remained flat) since aggregate home prices have not declined.

EXHIBIT 21–1

Impact of Increase in FNMA/FHLMC Loan Size Limit on the Nonagency Sector (GWAC* = 8.25)

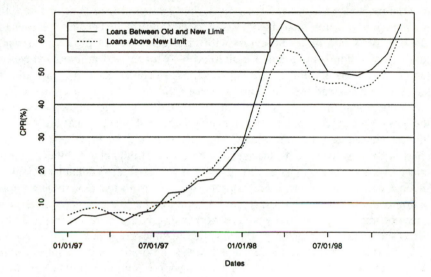

*GWAC = gross weighted average coupon.

EXHIBIT 21–2

Disclosure Deficit Between the Agency and Nonagency Sectors

	Agency (Pool Level)	Nonagency
Loan age	Weighted average plus FHLMC quartiles	Loan level
Loan maturity	Weighted average	Loan level
Location	State level	Zip code level
Loan size	Weighted average + FHMLC quartiles	Loan level
LTV	None	Loan level (original and current)
FICO	None	Loan level
Occupancy	None	Investor/owner
Purpose	None	Purchase/cash-out/ refinancing
Documentation	None	Limited/EZ/full
Rate premium	None	Loan level

DEFINING THE SUBSECTORS
WITHIN THE NONAGENCY MARKET

The importance of loan size and its impact on prepayment behavior in the residential mortgage sector has been well studied and empirically documented. In the nonagency sector, loan size takes on added importance because it serves to classify loans into three subsectors with different levels of prepayment risk: jumbo loans, conforming balance alternative-A loans, and jumbo balance alternative-A loans. Exhibit 21–3 compares the loan characteristics of these three subsector classifications. The jumbo sector represents the most creditworthy and prepayment-sensitive group of borrowers in the mortgage market. Loans in the jumbo sector do not qualify for agency purchase almost exclusively because the loan size exceeds the conforming limit. In contrast, the alternative-A sector is characterized by loans below the agency-conforming limit but with other features that prevent agency purchase. This usually involves limited documentation/no income verification loans, investor properties, cash-out loans or some combination of these characteristics. It should be noted that the alternative-A sector does not imply a substantially weaker borrower credit profile as evidenced by FICO scores that average only 10 points below the average jumbo FICO score.

In 1998, a hybrid sector developed consisting of alternative-A loans above the agency loan size limit. This sector has a lower concentration of investor properties and a heavier concentration of limited documentation loans than the traditional alternative-A sector. A key distinction between the jumbo, conforming alternative-A, and jumbo alternative-A sectors is the rate premium paid by the borrowers over the prevailing prime jumbo rate. Alternative-A borrowers face a rate premium of between 20 and 150 bps, depending on their nonstandard loan characteristics. A further blurring of definitions occurs between the home equity and alternative-A sectors where the key to differentiation often lies in the lower credit quality of home equity borrowers.

We can think of the nonagency sector as a continuum of borrowers who face a range of transaction costs. At one end of the spectrum we find the jumbo borrower who is characterized by a large balance, superior credit, no rate premium, and few barriers to refinancing. At the other end of the spectrum we find small balance alternative-A borrowers with nonstandard features, high rate premiums, and significant barriers to refinancing. One important advantage of our loan-level approach is that it allows us to focus entirely on the loan and borrower attributes that determine the level of transaction costs faced by individual borrowers. The model is impervious to classification distinctions such as alternative-A, home equity, and jumbo.

In this framework our forecast is determined by where a particular loan is positioned on the nonagency borrower-transaction cost continuum. For example, a loan labeled as "alternative-A" but with a jumbo balance, standard loan features, and a small rate premium will be treated as a standard jumbo loan.

E X H I B I T 21-3

Collateral Profiles in the Nonagency Sector 1997 and 1998 Deals

Product	Average Balance	LTV	FICO	Rate Premium	Documentation		Purpose			Occupancy		
					Full	Other	Purchase	Cash-out	Refinance	Owner	Investor	Other
Alt-A	$96,646	74.7%	716	0.92	58.3%	41.7%	58.7%	25.6%	15.7%	51.7%	43.1%	5.2%
Jumbo alt-A	$330,129	73.9%	714	0.65	53.3%	46.7%	44.3%	26.5%	29.2%	87.9%	6.8%	5.3%
Jumbo	$312,072	73.8%	725	0.09	80.1%	19.9%	54.2%	11.7%	34.1%	97.5%	0.0%	2.5%

DECONSTRUCTING OUR NONAGENCY PREPAYMENT FORECAST

Mortgage prepayments occur for five reasons.

1. The borrower elects to sell the home and relocate.

2. The borrower refinances the existing mortgage to lower interest costs and/or cash out equity.

3. The borrower pays more than the scheduled monthly principal and interest payment (partial prepayment or curtailment).

4. The borrower elects to pay off the entire mortgage ahead of schedule.

5. The borrower is unable or unwilling to make scheduled payments and defaults on the mortgage.

Although identifying the reasons for a mortgage prepayment is straightforward, modeling the probability that a prepayment will occur in any particular month is a complex process that requires understanding a myriad of forces—both internal and external to the borrower—that influence the prepayment decision. The more insight we have into a borrower's current circumstances, the more likely we will be able to understand and model his behavior. Indeed, in our study of property level information in the nonagency sector, we find that what frequently appears to be an "inefficient" exercise of the prepayment option can often be explained by sound underlying economic factors that affect a borrower's transaction costs and ability to refinance.

By far, the most important type of prepayment is the refinance transaction. It is the only class of prepayment where a large number of borrowers respond, more or less in unison, to an external event (lower mortgage rates). This can drive annualized prepayment rates from below 10% CPR to above 60% CPR in just two or three months time. Equally important from the mortgage investor's perspective is that refinancing events almost always serve to negatively impact performance; that is, they shorten the duration of mortgage securities in a low interest rate environment (refinancing increases) and extend the duration of mortgage securities in a high rate environment (refinancing declines). In contrast, the other types of prepayment events tend to be much less volatile and more spread out, driven more by long-term housing fundamentals and/or a borrower's current economic situation than by interest rates.

For example, although prepayments from home resale activity account for about 10% CPR for fully seasoned jumbo securities, it is highly unlikely that a surge in activity would cause this level to change by more than just a few percent. Default and partial prepayments are even less volatile components of the overall prepayment mix, accounting for less than 1.5% CPR on a combined annual basis.[5] Since refinancing accounts for much of the volatility and negative convexity observed in historical prepayments, we begin our discussion with the refinancing component of our model.

---

5. During the initial 5 years of the seasoning process.

EXHIBIT 21–4

Baseline Refinancing Profiles

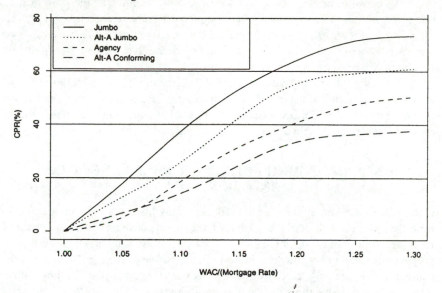

DEFINING THE BASELINE NONAGENCY
REFINANCING PROFILE

Our refinancing submodel is contingent on the complex interaction of multiple variables defined at the property level. To present our findings in a way that is both intuitive and transparent to the reader, we first define a baseline refinancing profile for
a representative nonagency jumbo and alternative-A borrower and then measure the
relative change in this profile for different permutations of loan-level characteristics.
Our baseline jumbo profile (see Exhibit 21–4) depicts the projected prepayment
rate[6] for an average jumbo borrower across a wide spectrum of refinancing incentives. For purposes of this analysis we assume that our baseline jumbo loan has the
following characteristics: it is a new, full documentation, purchase loan; single-
family detached home, owner-occupied property, with a $300,000 loan balance,
75% LTV, and no rate premium.[7] For our alternative-A baseline we modify the
jumbo profile in the following way: $150,000 loan balance, limited documentation,
and 90-bp rate premium. In addition, we choose a representative refinancing environment by assuming that mortgage rates are at a 3-year low and that the 2- to 10-
year yield curve slope is 80 bps. For comparative purposes, Exhibit 21–4 also shows
the baseline profiles for the agency and jumbo alternative-A borrowers.

To understand the many nuances of refinancing behavior it is critical that we
have access to historical refinancing data in a wide range of interest rate environments.

---

6. Expressed in terms of an annualized prepayment (CPR).
7. The rate premium is the spread above the prevailing prime jumbo mortgage rate.

Fortunately for the nonagency sector much of this important refinancing data was collected in 1998.

We chose to model a borrower's refinancing incentive as the ratio of loan rate to prevailing mortgage rate (rather than the difference) since it best approximates the dollar cost savings of the refinancing transaction. We first address two critical aspects of refinancing behavior that are a function of the historical path and absolute level of mortgage rates.

The first of these "path-dependent" behaviors is often referred to as "burnout" and occurs at the pool level as borrowers selectively prepay their mortgages. The second effect occurs at the loan level as borrowers respond with increased intensity to certain absolute levels in the prevailing mortgage rate.

UNDERSTANDING BORROWER SELF-SELECTION AND "BURNOUT"

One of the first observations we can make regarding historical refinancing behavior is that we rarely observe the same refinancing response from the same pool of mortgagors through two different interest rate cycles. As a general rule, pool level prepayments tend to become less interest rate–sensitive over time. This occurs because of the refinancing self-selection in borrowers that takes place as they prepay their mortgages. If we think of a pool of mortgages as a continuum of borrowers with various refinancing transaction costs, then over time we would expect the borrowers with the lowest costs to refinance first, leaving the borrowers with the higher costs and slower prepayment speeds behind. In nearly all situations, the surviving borrower population at any point in time will have fundamentally different prepayment characteristics than the original pool.

We find that refinancing self-selection or burnout has both permanent and transitory components. Since the largest loans with the highest rates tend to refinance first in the jumbo sector, both the loan size distribution and coupon distribution tend to shift downward, reducing the expected level and volatility of future prepayments. These are permanent structural changes at the pool or deal level that have long-term implications for our prepayment forecast. However, self-selection also takes place based on more transitory properties associated with an individual's financial status. The most common financial barriers arise from either a lack of equity in the home (caused by declining home values) or a weak credit history. Clearly, these factors are more temporary in nature as depressed home values usually recover with cyclical housing market expansions and credit status improves with stable or rising personal incomes. Although initially a powerful component of burnout, there is substantial empirical evidence to support the diminution of credit- and equity-related refinancing barriers over time. The most recent example of a dramatic shift in the transaction cost structure of a population of borrowers occurred in Southern California, where a recovery in home prices has unlocked significant pentup refinancing demand as previously equity-impaired borrowers take full advantage of lower financing costs. We discuss the California situation in more detail in a subsequent section on LTV.

Traditional agency prepayment models are at a tremendous disadvantage when it comes to modeling the complex forces that cause burnout. Having access to pool level information only, agency models have no mechanism available to them to model the actual change in borrower composition or the actual change in surviving borrower transaction costs. Instead, modelers are left to develop artificial proxies for this behavior such as a cumulative measure of historical refinancing incentives and/or prepayments or assumed distributions of fast/slow prepayment buckets. Many of these approaches are predicated on the assumption that borrower self-selection is a cumulative and permanent process, that is, there is no diminution of refinancing constraints over time.[8]

One of the most powerful aspects of a model estimated and implemented entirely at the property level is that it replicates the changing composition of a pool over time. In a property level framework we process and amortize each loan separately, ensuring that our composite forecast for a pool of mortgages reflects the characteristics of the surviving borrowers. Each forward month forecast is contingent on the distribution of loan characteristics of the previous month's surviving population. We add further precision to this forecast by monitoring and dynamically updating each surviving borrower's monthly equity position using zip code level home price indices. This captures the most transitory component in an individual's financial profile that could inhibit or aid a refinancing transaction.

The profound impact that prepayments have on the distribution of loan attributes is best illustrated with an example. In Exhibit 21–5 we summarize the loan attributes of 1992 jumbo originations before and after the severe 1993 refinancing event. To demonstrate the ability of our model to replicate this process, we also

---

8. However, some models assume a decay constant in the definition of the burnout function.

E X H I B I T   21–5

Loan Attribute Distributions Before and After the 1993 Refinancing Event (1992 Jumbo Originations)

Loan Characteristics	Actual		Model Projected May 1994
	Jan 1993	May 1994	
WAC*	8.66	8.54	8.53
Avg. loan size	$326,753	$300,556	$300,195
Loan size > 300K	46.52%	38.82%	39.20%
LTV	71.29%	73.01%	72.23%
LTV > 80	9.9%	12.4%	11.8%
Limited documentation	35.7%	43.5%	41.5%
Cash-out	16.3%	17.0%	16.8%

*WAC = weighted average coupon.

provide the same attribute statistics based only on our model projected prepayment rates over the period. Approximately 48% of the loans refinanced during this time. As Exhibit 21–5 clearly illustrates, the loan attribute distributions were substantially altered by the refinancing wave as borrowers with high loan rates, large loan balances, and high levels of equity refinanced out of the deal. Secondary loan attributes also shifted toward the less refinance sensitive characteristics such as limited documentation and nonpurchase loans. Our model projected change in attributes mirrors the actual change that occurred.

MODELING BORROWER REFINANCING INTENSITY

Even after carefully controlling for all loan characteristics, including refinancing incentive, loan age, and loan size, substantial differences emerge in refinancing behavior through different refinancing events. Consider the refinancing patterns of new conventional conforming loans in three different interest rate cycles: the fourth quarter of 1993, the first quarter of 1996, and the first quarter of 1998, as shown in Exhibit 21–6. In each case, whether we look at agency or nonagency prepayment data, the intensity of the borrower response to the refinancing opportunity is substantially different. Although some of these differences can be explained by structural efficiency gains in the refinancing process itself, we are still left with a funda-

E X H I B I T   21–6

Actual Agency Prepayment Curves

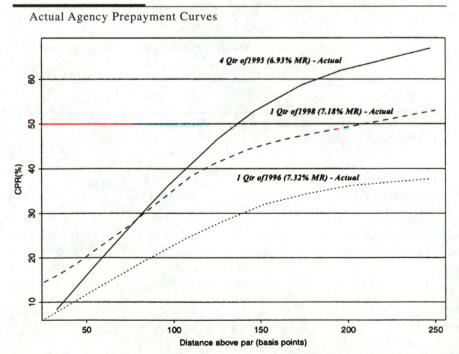

mentally different borrower response in each period, particularly in 1996. Why do borrowers with nearly identical loan attributes and identical refinancing incentives sometimes exhibit very different refinancing behavior? How we reconcile this behavior is one of the most important challenges facing prepayment modelers today.

What is clear from empirical analysis is that borrowers time their refinancing transactions to lock in a perceived low point in the mortgage rate cycle. Borrower perceptions of the relative attractiveness of the prevailing mortgage rate play a crucial role in determining the timing and intensity of a lock-in event. Panel studies suggest that these perceptions are shaped by the recent path of mortgage rates as well as the absolute level of today's rate. For example, if we are in a declining interest rate environment and similar refinancing opportunities have existed in the recent past, borrowers will often refrain from refinancing on the expectation that rates will continue to decline in the future. However, the propensity of a borrower to refinance increases sharply as the rally pushes the absolute level of mortgage rates through previous historical low points. This is usually accompanied by increasing media attention, raising the consciousness of the entire mortgage universe. The condition that ultimately triggers a simultaneous rate lock by borrowers is usually a sudden backup in interest rates, as was the case in the fourth quarter of 1993, or when rates match a historically significant threshold, as in the first quarter of 1998.

To model this behavior we have defined a "lookback" function that compares today's mortgage rate to all previous historical levels. This function is sensitive to both the absolute level of rates and the time since equivalent refinancing opportunities existed in the past. In this way it takes on increasing significance as the mortgage rate matches previous historical lows in rates, for example, a 1-year low in rates takes on less significance than a 5-year low in rates. The function achieves its maximum value when mortgage rates reach an all-time low as in 1993 and the fourth quarter of 1998. This framework is logical and intuitive in that it captures the pentup demand that results when a long period of time elapses between equivalent opportunities. It also matches the data extremely well. By viewing prior refinancing events in this context the observed discrepancies in 1993, 1996, and 1998 come into focus:

- The 1996 refinancing wave was very muted because the market had experienced equivalent or better opportunities in the recent past (the fourth quarter of 1993 and the first quarter of 1994).

- The first quarter of 1998 refinancing episode was triggered when mortgage rates fell below 1996 levels, making it the best opportunity to refinance in over four years. This event was still less intense than the 1993 episode, which represented a 30-year low.

- The fourth quarter of 1998 spike in new issue prepayments almost equaled 1993 as mortgage rates approached a lifetime low.

It should be noted that this function serves to steepen the refinancing profile for all mortgage products including very seasoned and burned-out issues (although the relative magnitude of prepayments between new and seasoned issues

E X H I B I T   21–7

Projected Baseline Jumbo Refinancing Profiles

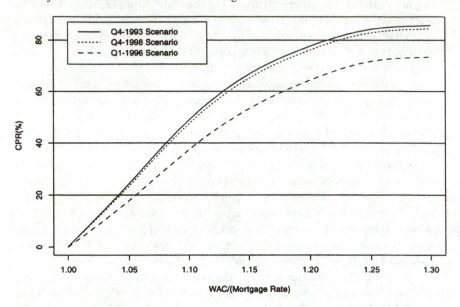

WAC/(Mortgage Rate)

is maintained). This is consistent with recent data showing that even seasoned borrowers respond to a historical low in mortgage rates despite having passed up
nearly similar opportunities in the recent past. Exhibit 21–7 provides our projected
baseline jumbo refinancing profiles if we replicate the conditions that existed in
1993, 1996, and 1998. Note that the relative magnitude of the curves is consistent
with actual experience.

THE IMPACT OF LOAN SIZE ON NONAGENCY REFINANCING BEHAVIOR

Apart from refinancing incentive, loan size is the most important determinant of
prepayment behavior in the nonagency sector. A small loan balance reduces the
economic incentive to refinance assuming fixed transaction costs. Even if small
balance borrowers amortize these costs in a "no-point" option, they still face
higher effective mortgage rates since the costs are a larger percentage of the loan
balance. Jumbo borrowers, on the other hand, have an increased economic incentive to refinance and are more likely to be aggressively solicited by mortgage brokers (broker commissions are commensurate with loan size).

The opposite is true in a rising rate environment, when jumbo borrowers have
a greater disincentive to prepay their below market mortgage rate relative to con-

EXHIBIT 21–8

Prepayment Profile Comparison

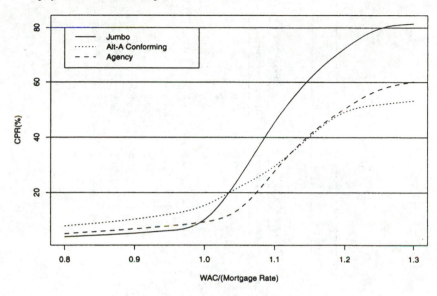

forming balance borrowers. Rising rates also make "trading up" in homes less attractive, forcing some borrowers to postpone a planned move. This behavior is responsible for the increased "negative convexity" often associated with the nonagency jumbo mortgage market. This is clearly evident in Exhibit 21–8 which contrasts the prepayment profile of our baseline jumbo borrower (average balance of $300,000) to the much flatter profiles of agency borrowers (average balance $110,000) and conforming balance alternative-A borrowers (average balance $96,646).

Beyond the refinancing economics, borrowers with small loan balances typically represent a lower income and demographic segment of the population given that personal income is the key underwriting criteria that originators use to size a mortgage. Exhibit 21–9 summarizes jumbo and alternative-A loan characteristics by loan size quartile. In general, we observe that there is a positive correlation between loan size and a borrower's income level and credit rating. Furthermore, we observe that small balance borrowers tend to pay a higher rate premium (spread over the prime jumbo rate) than large balance borrowers. In the alternative-A sector, we also find that investor properties make up over 40% of the loans with balances below the conforming limit. As we will show, all these characteristics are linked to less efficient refinancing behavior in the small balance universe.

It is important to note that these findings are consistent in both the agency and nonagency sectors even though we cannot observe loan-level attributes directly in the agency sector. We can, however, examine actual agency prepayment speeds conditional on the average loan size of a pool. For example,

EXHIBIT 21-9

Jumbo and Alternative-A Loan Characteristics by Loan Size Quartile

Product	Quartile	Avg. Bal. ($)	Avg. Prem.	LTV* (%)	Documentation (%)		Purpose (%)			Occupancy (%)		
					Full	Other	Purchase	Cash-out	Refinance	Owner	Investor	Other
Jumbo	25%	521,776	0.04	7.15	91.7	8.3	47.8	12.4	39.8	96.9	0.0	3.1
	50%	311,523	0.05	74.4	93.1	6.9	52.5	11.5	35.9	97.8	0.0	2.2
	75%	259,058	0.08	76.2	93.6	6.4	55.9	9.8	34.3	98.0	0.0	2.0
	100%	163,904	0.21	73.0	62.1	37.9	60.3	13.2	26.5	97.2	0.0	2.7
Alt-A	25%	293,087	0.68	74.1	50.4	49.6	46.2	26.6	27.3	85.8	9.1	5.1
	50%	132,909	0.85	75.8	50.8	49.2	56.2	24.6	19.2	66.4	28.1	5.5
	75%	82,471	0.93	74.3	58.8	41.2	58.2	27.0	14.9	49.2	45.2	5.5
	100%	45,235	1.06	74.0	71.1	28.9	64.4	24.7	10.8	29.5	66.0	4.6

*LTV = loan-to-value.

E X H I B I T   21–10

1998 FHLMC LLB Actual Prepayments (CPR) (Post-1993 Originations)

Coupon	Universe (CPR)[a]	LLB[b] (CPR)[a]	% Slower
7.0	17.6	8.3	−53
7.5	29.5	17.0	−42
8.0	37.3	23.9	−36
8.5	40.0	30.0	−25

[a]CPR = conditional prepayment rate.
[b]LLB = low loan balance.

E X H I B I T   21–11

Loan Size Effect—Jumbo Sector

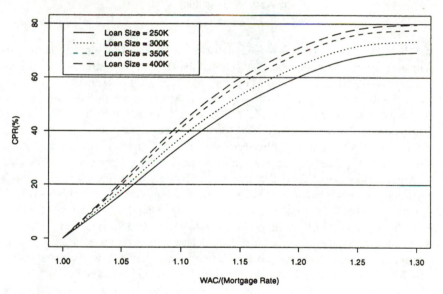

Exhibit 21–10 compares the 1998 prepayment speeds of FHLMC pools with average loan sizes less than or equal to $70,000 to their equivalent TBA counterparts. The low balance pools paid 25% to 53% slower than otherwise-equivalent TBA pools during a period dominated by refinancing activity. The jumbo universe shows a similar separation in speeds by loan size category up to approximately the $400,000 loan balance (see Exhibit 21–11). Above this level there is little additional increase in prepayment sensitivity.

Another important aspect of loan size that is not fully captured by traditional prepayment models is the substantial risk associated with loan size dispersion at the deal level. Exhibit 21–12 shows the distribution of loan sizes by balance in the jumbo

E X H I B I T   21–12

Jumbo Versus Alt-A Loan Size Distribution (balance weighted)

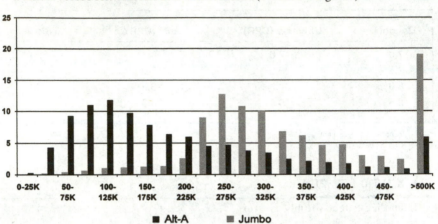

and alternative-A sectors for deals issued in 1997 and 1998. Although the alternative-A distribution is lower and more concentrated than the jumbo distribution, both sectors have substantial exposure to a high-balance "tail" in the distribution. For example, on a balance-weighted basis approximately one third of the loans in the alternative-A sector are above the $200,000 mark whereas nearly 20% of the jumbo distribution is above $500,000.[9] This tends to make nonagency cash flows very "front-loaded" since the largest balance loans refinance first, generating proportionally larger prepayment rates (a large balance loan is a bigger percentage of the total outstanding principal of a pool/deal than a small balance loan). Therefore, a pool with a wide distribution is much more likely to exhibit a high level of prepayment volatility early in its life than a pool with the same average loan size but a narrow distribution. The additional prepayment sensitivity caused by a wide distribution in loan sizes is the primary reason that most nonagency deals are priced to a significantly faster prepayment assumption than equivalent agency deals; that is, most nonagency deals have a portion of this distribution that is in the "refinancing window."

However, as pools are exposed to multiple refinancing opportunities, the distribution of loan sizes migrates rapidly toward smaller balances as the large balance portion of the deal pays off. The dramatic shift that takes place in the loan size distribution is best illustrated by an actual example. Consider PHMSC 9501, a $205-million jumbo deal issued in 1995 with an original average loan size of $249,000 (38% of the loans had balances above $300,000) and a GWAC of 8.85%.

As Exhibit 21–13 shows, PHMSC 9501 experienced two major refinancing events: one at the beginning of 1996 and the another at the beginning of 1998.

---

9. On a frequency basis these numbers would be much lower. For example, the percentage of jumbo loans exceeding $500,000 drops to 6% based on frequency of occurrence.

PHMSC 9501 Loan Size and WAC Migration

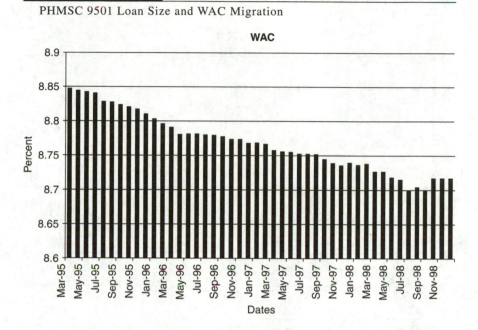

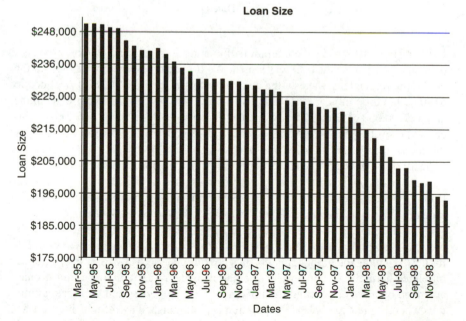

Continued

EXHIBIT 21–13

Continued

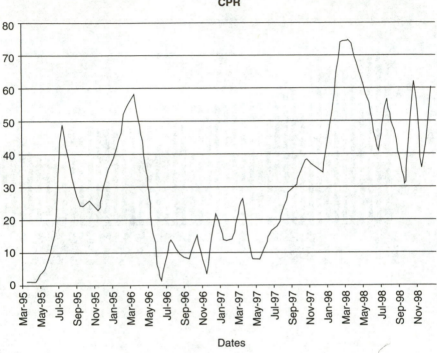

Exhibit 21–13 also tracks the migration of average loan size and weighted average coupon (WAC) since the deal was issued. We find that by December 1998—at the end of the refinancing waves—the average loan size of PHMSC 9501 declined to $190,000 (a drop of nearly $60,000) with only 24% of the remaining loans in the above $300,000 category. Meanwhile the percentage of loans below $200,000 increased from 10% to 26% while the WAC decreased from 8.85% to 8.72%. Clearly the prepayment characteristics and our forecast for PHMSC 9501 have changed radically since its issue. The key to accurately modeling the powerful effects of loan size and loan coupon dispersion and the front-loaded nature of the resulting cash flows is through loan-level processing. Since our model amortizes each loan individually, it predicts the migration of loan size and coupon distributions.

In the alternative-A sector, despite very disparate loan and borrower attributes, we also find that loan size plays a central role in refinancing behavior. Exhibit 21–14 plots the refinancing profiles conditional on loan size category for our baseline alternative-A borrower. The small balance universe in this sector is characterized by a heavy concentration of investment properties and large rate premiums whereas the large balance population is distinguished by refinancing transactions, owner-occupied properties, and low rate premiums. Although the overall interest rate sensitivity of this sector is lower than in the jumbo or agency sector,

EXHIBIT 21–14

Loan Size Effect—Alternative-A Sector

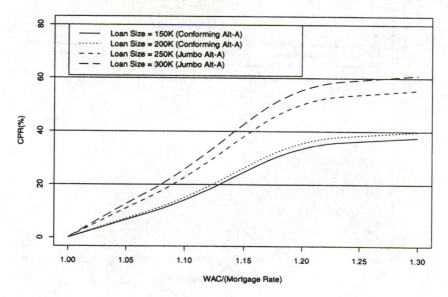

the familiar pattern of increasing refinancing sensitivity with increasing loan balances is clearly evident in the data. Note also the clear separation in speeds above and below the agency conforming limit of $240,000.

The distinction between the alternative-A and jumbo sectors blurs at loan balances above the agency conforming limit. With minimal differences in credit quality, it is the nonstandard features of jumbo balance alternative-A loans that tend to increase the transaction and "hassle" costs associated with refinancing. This is evidenced by an average rate premium of 65 bps paid by jumbo alternative-A borrowers versus 0 to 5 bps for regular jumbo borrowers. Over time, we would expect a large percentage of the alternative-A jumbo borrowers to qualify for standard financing as they establish consistent income patterns or fall within the expanded loan limits established by FNMA/FHLMC. A comparison of the refinancing profiles of our baseline jumbo borrower to an equivalent loan size alternative-A borrower is shown in Exhibit 21–15. As we previously stated, our model forecast is completely independent of the alternative-A or jumbo sector designation. The model relies solely on the type of nonstandard features and the relationship of these features to historical prepayments to determine a specific loan's refinancing sensitivity.

CREDIT QUALITY

Borrowers with weak credit typically receive less attractive financing rates than borrowers with strong credit because originators must compensate for the greater likelihood of default. As a result, weak credit can substantially alter prepayment

E X H I B I T   21–15

Traditional Jumbo Versus Alternative-A Jumbo Refinancing Profiles

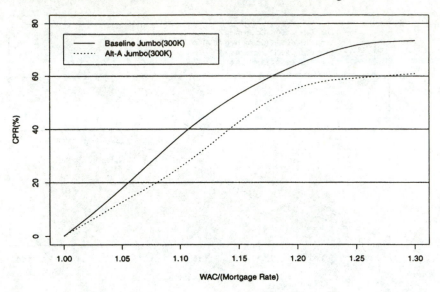

behavior since, to a large extent, the borrower's evolving credit status—not inter-est rates—governs the prepayment decision. This accounts for the well-recognized "credit cure" effect that accelerates prepayments in the B/C home equity market as borrowers in a low credit tier improve their credit and qualify for a lower financing rate in a higher credit tier.

In general, jumbo and alternative-A residential borrowers do not exhibit credit curing since they represent the highest end of the credit spectrum (average FICO scores in both sectors usually exceed 675). Very few nonagency loans are below the agency FICO "floor" of 620. Therefore, we feel that credit does not present a sig-nificant barrier to refinancing in the nonagency sector unless there is substantial ero-sion in credit status after a loan is originated. However, we find this to be the ex-ception and not the rule given that credit quality usually improves as personal incomes and property values increase over time. Exhibit 21–16 compares the jumbo and alternative-A FICO distributions collected from several recently issued nona-gency deals.

Within the jumbo and alternative-A sectors we do find a weak but intuitive correlation between FICO and other loan attributes. Exhibit 21–17 provides sum-mary FICO quartile statistics in the alternative-A and jumbo sectors. In both sec-tors a lower FICO is associated with a higher average rate premium, a higher LTV, and a bigger percentage of cash-out refinance transactions (lower percentage of purchase transactions). Not surprisingly, in the jumbo sector we find that the largest balances are associated with the highest FICO score. Finally, although the average alternative-A borrower has a slightly lower FICO score than the average jumbo borrower by about 10 bps, these findings confirm the fact that circum-

EXHIBIT 21–16

FICO Distribution (Jumbo avg. = 725, alt-A avg. = 715)

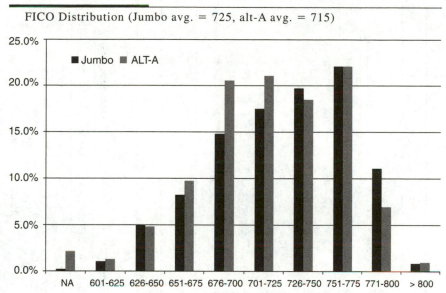

stances other than credit prevent agency purchase of alternative-A loans. FICO alone did not produce statistically significant results as an explanatory variable in our nonagency prepayment model.

RATE PREMIUM

We found that an objective measure of a borrower's underwriting status could be obtained by calculating the amount of spread or "rate premium" that the individual pays above the prevailing prime jumbo rate at origination.[10] Loans with the highest rate premium tend to represent borrowers with the least standard loan characteristics, the smallest loan balances, and the lowest credit quality as measured by FICO score. Therefore, although high rate premium loans may be nominally more "in-the-money," they are intrinsically less refinanceable than low rate premium loans. This is confirmed in Exhibit 21–18 which shows that as the rate premium increases, the concentration of high-LTV nonowner occupied properties increases while loan size decreases.

This suggests that the prepayment behavior of the high rate premium borrowers is likely to be closely associated with a change in their particular situation and less correlated to a change in interest rates. Often their need for alternative financing diminishes over time as they establish sufficient income history, as property values increase, or as they qualify under expanded agency underwriting policies. Once an alternative-A borrower qualifies under agency guidelines there is an immediate and significant refinancing incentive that is usually in excess of 75 bps.

---

10. Given that we know when every loan in our nonagency prepayment database was originated, we can estimate its rate premium.

EXHIBIT 21-17

Loan Characteristics by FICO Score Quartile

Product	FICO	Quartile	Avg. Bal. ($)	Avg. Prem.	LTV (%)	Documentation (%)		Purpose (%)			Occupancy (%)		
						Full	Other	Purchase	Cash-out	Refinance	Owner	Investor	Other
Jumbo	666	25%	304,092	0.27	75.6	91.6	8.4	39.8	13.9	46.3	99.2	0.0	0.8
	713	50%	309,807	0.19	74.5	87.4	12.6	40.5	12.3	47.2	98.9	0.0	1.1
	746	75%	325,544	0.16	72.7	89.4	10.6	43.7	10.6	45.8	99.2	0.0	0.8
	777	100%	325,760	0.13	72.2	92.7	7.3	49.2	10.4	40.4	99.3	0.0	0.7
Alt-A	664	25%	139,956	0.97	79.4	71.0	29.0	47.5	32.1	20.4	56.4	41.6	2.0
	702	50%	138,609	0.93	77.2	53.0	47.0	50.8	27.6	21.6	57.7	39.0	3.4
	732	75%	135,393	0.91	77.0	54.7	45.3	55.7	24.5	19.8	54.5	43.5	2.0
	770	100%	132,980	0.86	76.3	57.4	42.6	64.3	20.1	15.6	50.7	46.1	3.2

EXHIBIT 21-18

Alternative-A Loan Characteristics by Rate Premium Quartile

Rate Prem.	Quartile	Avg. Bal ($)	LTV (%)	Documentation (%)		Purpose (%)			Occupancy (%)		
				Full	Other	Purchase	Cash-out	Refinance	Owner	Investor	Other
0.19	25%	177,236	70.5	53.2	46.8	47.1	26.7	26.3	80.1	15.5	4.3
0.71	50%	150,980	73.0	49.1	50.9	52.1	27.9	20.1	70.0	24.5	5.5
1.05	75%	125,244	75.4	56.2	43.8	57.4	27.0	15.5	53.8	40.7	5.5
1.52	100%	103,938	79.4	71.2	28.8	67.6	21.6	10.8	29.3	65.2	5.5

E X H I B I T   21–19

Fourth Quarter 1998 Prepayment Comparison (1997 Originations)

Alt-A-Gross WAC	Alt-A RALI[a] (CPR)	Alt-A RAST[b] (CPR)	Equiv. Jumbo (CPR)	Equiv. FNMA (CPR)
7.50%	22	30	12	10
8.00%	29	34	37	25
8.50%	30	34	52	38

[a]RALI = Residential Accredit Loans, Inc.
[b]RAST = Residential Asset Securitization Trust.

As a result, a pattern develops that is similar to "credit curing" in the B/C home equity sector: a high base level of prepayments is established by "situation curing" as former alternative-A borrowers refinance into conforming mortgages. However, existing alternative-A borrowers still exhibit less sensitivity to interest rates since they continue to face higher transaction costs. This was indeed the case during the major fourth quarter 1998 refinancing event summarized in Exhibit 21–19. The exhibit compares the actual fourth quarter prepayments of alternative-A borrowers (all of whom paid a significant rate premium) to equivalent, rate-adjusted jumbo and agency prepayments. The alternative-A sector exhibited very little differentiation in speed across coupons whereas a 100-bp differential in coupon in the jumbo and agency sector resulted in a 40 CPR and 28 CPR separation in speed, respectively. Exhibit 21–20 shows the impact of a 20-bp differential in rate premium on our baseline alternative-A refinancing profile.

One consequence of the expanded underwriting criteria implemented by both FNMA and FHLMC that specifically targets the alternative-A and/or credit-impaired borrower is that more agency pools are likely to be issued with a rate premium. We believe these self-selected pools will exhibit a more stable prepayment profile than equivalent WAC non–rate premium pools. In fact, we can isolate preexisting cohorts of rate premium pools in our agency database to support this expectation. For example, Exhibit 21–21 compares the recent prepayment experience of 8.75% to 9.0% gross WAC FNMA pools issued in 1996 to those issued in 1994. Since mortgage rates never exceeded 8.50% in 1996, we know that these borrowers paid a substantial rate premium, whereas mortgage rates averaged 8.75% in 1994 indicating that these borrowers did not pay a rate premium. Under normal circumstances, we would expect the more burned-out 1994 pools to prepay slower than the 1996 pools. However, as Exhibit 21–21 clearly shows, the rate premium effect has produced exactly the opposite results.

E X H I B I T 21–20

Alternative-A Rate Premium Effect

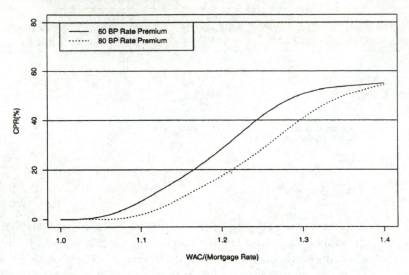

E X H I B I T 21–21

Agency "Rate Premium" Effect 1994 Versus 1996 Origination 8.75% Gross WAC FNMA MBS

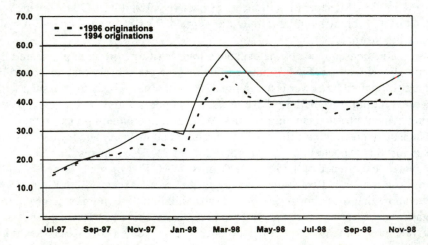

SECONDARY REFINANCING EFFECTS: DOCUMENTATION, LOAN PURPOSE, OCCUPANCY STATUS

The jumbo nonagency sector represents the most homogeneous group of borrowers in the residential mortgage market. As Exhibit 21–3 showed, the vast majority of jumbo mortgage transactions are characterized by borrowers with excellent credit histories, full documentation, owner-occupied properties, and less than 80% LTVs. Consequently, most of the historically observed jumbo prepayment behavior can be explained by the level of mortgage rates and the interaction of four loan attributes: WAC, age, loan size, and LTV. We feel that the biggest risk to investors in jumbo transactions is the implicit "front-loaded" nature of the cash flows owing to the powerful effects of coupon and loan size dispersion. As previously discussed, we believe that our loan-level implementation replicates the evolution of loan size and coupon distributions.

In contrast, the hallmark of the alternative-A sector is its heterogeneous loan and borrower composition. In this sector, secondary loan characteristics play a key role in defining the ability of a borrower to refinance today and offer insight into whether a borrower will be able to qualify for agency financing in the future. We have identified three of these attributes that, when observed in isolation, significantly alter prepayment behavior in the alternative-A sector. They are documentation level, loan purpose, and occupancy status.

Limited Documentation Versus Full Documentation

Limited documentation loans typically are obtained by borrowers who want financing without verification of income or employment. These programs are often structured so that only "stated income" levels are necessary. Many borrowers who qualify under these options are self-employed or work on commission and do not have a steady income or employment history. Under these programs, underwriting criteria highlight a borrower's credit history and ability to pay, while limiting the maximum-allowable LTV. Limited documentation loans make up nearly 50% of the alternative-A universe and often have other factors that preclude agency purchase. The higher transaction and "hassle" costs associated with qualifying under limited documentation programs have historically reduced the refinancing efficiency exhibited by these borrowers.

Exhibit 21–22 compares our baseline alternative-A refinancing profiles for full and limited documentation borrowers. To the extent that a borrower establishes a consistent income pattern in the future or qualifies under expanded streamlined documentation programs implemented by FNMA and FHLMC, these barriers to prepayment may be eliminated over time. Therefore, we view limited documentation in itself as having only a moderate and transitory effect on prepayment speeds.

E X H I B I T   21–22

Alternative-A Documentation Effect

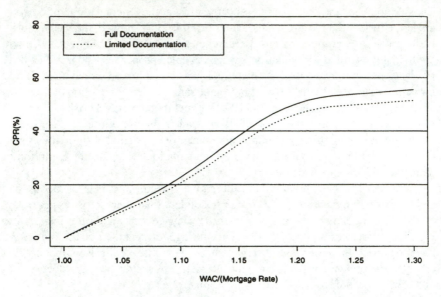

WAC/(Mortgage Rate)

Investor Versus Owner-Occupied Properties

Investor properties make up approximately 36% of the total alternative-A universe with some issuers originating much heavier concentrations than others. Investor properties typically have smaller loan balances, higher rate premiums, and somewhat higher LTVs than owner-occupied properties. Prepayments differ from owner occupied properties in two important respects:

1. Housing turnover prepayments tend to be higher than in owner-occupied properties.

2. Investors tend to refinance less optimally than owner-occupied properties.

In the first case, we find that investors are more likely to take advantage of a housing market expansion by selling the property and locking in profits than are owner-occupied properties. In the second case, investors typically face greater documentation scrutiny, increasing the hassle factor when refinancing. More importantly, investors tend to view their financial situation in a different context than the owner-occupied population; that is, maintaining positive cash flow on a property is often more important than optimizing financing. Exhibit 21–23 contrasts our baseline refinancing profile for owner-occupied properties to that of investor properties in the alternative-A sector.

We observe that existing investor properties with LTVs in the 70% to 80% range are the most vulnerable to the recent expansion in agency underwriting guidelines (although it is not yet evident in actual data). To the extent that these

EXHIBIT 21–23

Alternative-A Investor Versus Owner

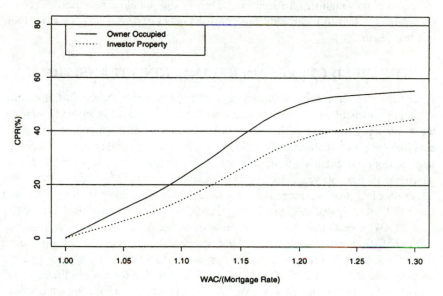

borrowers now qualify under agency guidelines, we would expect a structural shift to faster prepayments in this segment of the alternative-A universe as borrowers take advantage of lower agency financing rates.

Loan Purpose: Cash-Out Refinance, Rate or Term Refinance, Purchase

We find very little difference in the overall prepayment characteristics of loans originated as rate or term refinance transactions versus loans originated to purchase a home. We suspect that there may be a minor appraisal bias associated with refinancing transactions that is responsible for a slight LTV offset in our findings. For example, we observe that a 75% LTV refinancing transaction is similar to an 80% purchase transaction in terms of refinancing sensitivity. We believe the average purchase appraisal is likely to be more rigorous and conservative than the average refinancing appraisal.

Cash-out loans exhibit about 5% less sensitivity to interest rates than either rate or term refinance or purchase loans. A cash-out transaction may be indicative of a borrower with less financial capacity than other borrowers. This view is supported by our finding that FICO score is negatively correlated to cash-out levels (see Exhibit 21–17). Although cash-out borrowers may be predisposed to another cash-out transaction once equity levels increase sufficiently, this decision tends to be influenced more by home price appreciation and amortization than by interest rates.

In every loan purpose category, we observe a period of 6 to 8 months after a loan is originated where borrowers exhibit a strong aversion to refinancing despite sometimes significant incentives. During this window new borrowers are probably reluctant to incur additional out-of-pocket expenses so soon after their last transaction.

THE YIELD CURVE AND REFINANCING TRANSITIONS

After the 1993 refinancing wave some market participants attributed the record-setting prepayment speeds, in part, to a steep yield curve since it served to increase the refinancing incentive of 30-year mortgage holders into shorter maturity products like ARMs and balloons. By 1998, however, it was clear that some of the original assumptions made about the impact of the yield curve were overstated. Prepayments of new 30-year MBS in 1998 reached record levels across the entire spectrum of refinancing incentives despite a 150-bp flattening in the yield curve since 1993. A review of 1993 and 1998 FHLMC refinancing transition data (see Exhibit 21–24) reveals that there was remarkably little difference in the refinancing choices of 30-year borrowers between the two periods. The most notable difference was a 9.0% transition rate from 30-year product into ARMs and balloons in 1993 compared to just 1% in 1998. We speculate, however, that for most of these "term" transition borrowers, the yield curve does not preclude a refinance transaction; rather, it serves to change the optimal transition product. The important point is that in most cases a full prepayment occurs whether the yield curve is flat or steep.

We also note that the 30- to 15-year transitions were actually higher in 1998 (29%) than in 1993 (26%) despite the fact that the 30- to 15-year mortgage rate spread declined from 48 bps in 1993 to 33 bps in 1998. Here again the absolute yield curve effect is secondary to the borrower's desire to optimize his transition mortgage.

In view of these findings, we think a strong argument can be made that a steep yield curve has a localized effect on prepayment behavior that is limited to the marginal refinancer at the cusp who may not otherwise have an opportunity to refinance when the yield curve is flat. Borrowers well "in the money," on the other hand, are likely to refinance in either situation (although it may be into different products). Exhibit 21–25 shows projected refinancing prepayments conditional on the slope of the yield curve for our baseline jumbo borrower with a marginal refinancing incentive.

E X H I B I T   21–24

FHLMC 30-Year Mortgage Refinance Transitions

| | New Transition Product | | | | | |
	30-Year	20-Year	15-Year	ARM	5-Year Balloon	7-Year Balloon
1993 Q4	58%	7%	26%	5%	2%	2%
1998 Q1	62%	7%	29%	0%	0%	1%

E X H I B I T   21–25

Refinancing Conditional on Yield Curve Slope (borrowers with marginal incentive WAC/MR = 1.05)

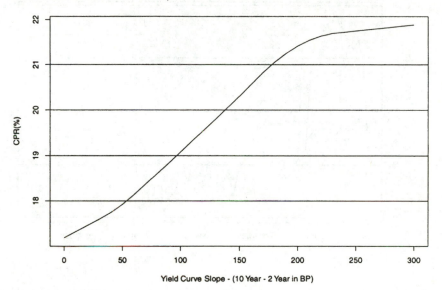

Yield Curve Slope - (10 Year - 2 Year in BP)

THE VALUE OF UPDATED LTV INFORMATION

A borrower's equity position in the home as measured by the LTV ratio is a key determinant of both refinancing and housing turnover prepayments. One of the unique aspects of our modeling platform is that it incorporates real-time LTV information updated every month on over 350,000 nonagency loans in our database. This is accomplished by using zip code level home price data to compute current property values across the country. Equity plays a crucial role in a borrower's financial decision-making process. Rising property values increase the likelihood that a borrower will "trade up" to a bigger home or monetize the gain in value through an equity take-out refinance. Increasing equity also lowers a borrower's financing costs by reducing default risk to the lender and reducing or eliminating private mortgage insurance costs. Finally, it provides borrowers with financial leverage when evaluating alternative sources of financing. A high-LTV ratio, on the other hand, increases refinancing transaction costs, reduces the likelihood of a cash-out transaction, and limits the ability of a borrower to trade up.

A recent example of a dramatic shift in the transaction cost structure of a population of borrowers occurred in Southern California where jumbo borrowers experienced home price declines of up to 40% at the bottom of the California real estate cycle in 1996. In this situation, the loss of equity and rising LTVs served to increase refinancing transaction costs and slow prepayments on a large segment of our nonagency database. As a result, the impact of the housing recession in California is

E X H I B I T   21–26

PHMSC 9204 Actual Versus Projected Prepayments

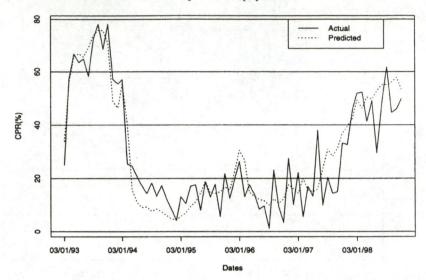

clearly evident in the historical prepayment behavior of nearly every seasoned jumbo deal (the typical jumbo deal has a 45% California concentration), particularly those issued in the early 1990s at the peak of the California housing market.

Consider, for example, PHMSC 9204, a 9.09% gross WAC jumbo deal issued in 1992 with a 70% California concentration and a $261,000 average loan size. Exhibit 21–26 plots a time series of actual prepayments for PHMSC 9204 since 1993. What is extraordinary about Exhibit 21–26 is the contrast between prepayments in the first quarter of 1996 and the first quarter of 1998. In 1996, despite a 130-bp refinancing incentive, PHMSC 9204 borrowers showed virtually no reaction to the refinancing opportunity. In contrast, during the first quarter of 1998 PHMSC 9204 speeds spiked to 50 CPR despite 6 years of seasoning and only a marginally better refinancing incentive than in 1996. At this point most prepayment models would predict significant burnout in these loans.

What has changed since 1996 that would increase the prepayment speeds of this deal? Upon closer inspection we find that the percentage of loans with LTVs above 80% increased from 9.6% at deal issue to 46% in 1996 (70% of the loans backing PHMSC 9204 were from California). Refinancing had become prohibitively expensive for many of the PHMSC 9204 borrowers. By 1998, however, a home price recovery in California plus two additional years of amortization pushed equity levels into positive territory for the first time in 6 years, unlocking an explosive surge in pent-up refinancing demand.

In addition to the historical prepayments of PHMSC 9204 shown in Exhibit 21–26, we also provide our model projections for the deal incorporating monthly updated LTV information for each of the surviving loans in the deal. The close fit

LTV Effect—Alternative-A Sector (purchase loans)

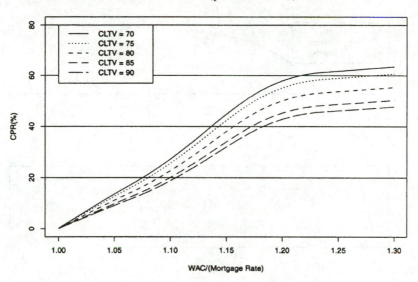

of our projected deal prepayments to actual experience confirms the value of incorporating current LTV information into our model specification. LTV explained the inability of borrowers to respond to a strong nominal refinancing incentive in 1996 and the subsequent release of that pent-up demand in 1998.

Exhibit 21–26 also demonstrates the ability of current LTV to capture the impact of regional economic activity on prepayments; for example, a weak regional economy will be reflected in a contracting housing market, declining real estate values, and increasing LTVs (this would tend to slow our projected prepayments for loans located in that region). Thus, LTV eliminates the need to incorporate other regional economic variables to explain this behavior. Exhibit 21–27 illustrates the impact of a change in LTV on our baseline alternative-A refinancing profile for purchase loans.

HOUSING TURNOVER PREPAYMENTS: SEASONING AND LOCK-IN

Housing turnover prepayments tend to increase as a loan ages—a reflection of the natural life cycle of homeownership. New homeowners are less likely to move since, by definition, the property fulfills their current housing demands. Moreover, borrowers are less willing to incur moving expenses so soon after the original relocation. However, over time there is an increasing probability that a borrower will relocate, "trade up" in homes, or monetize equity gains as real estate values increase, their financial situation improves, housing demands increase, or job status changes. In addition, there is an increasing probability that a noneconomic prepayment event

E X H I B I T   21–28

Seasoning Function

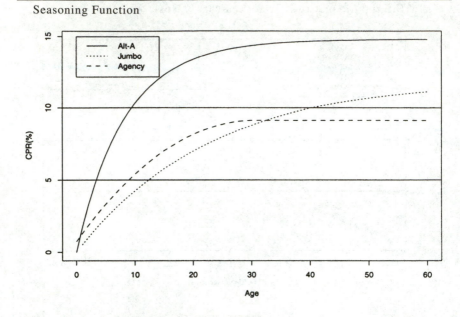

Age

will occur from other factors such as divorce or death. The unique baseline seasoning pattern for each of the sectors is shown in Exhibit 21–28 (it plots current-coupon
prepayments conditional on loan age).

For jumbo loans, we find that this baseline seasoning process takes about 5
years. Jumbo seasoning starts out slower than that found in the agency sector but
eventually overtakes agency seasoning after about 2.5 years. In the alternative-A
sector there is an added dimension to the seasoning process caused by "situation
curing" (previously discussed in the Rate Premium section). Over time, there is a
greater likelihood that an alternative-A borrower will qualify for more attractive
conventional financing. As shown in Exhibit 21–28, this accelerates the baseline
seasoning function to 15 CPR over approximately 20 months, well above that
found in both the agency and nonagency sectors.

Two other exogenous factors affect the seasoning process:

1. *Home values.* As previously discussed, rising home values increase the
   probability that a borrower will "trade up" to a larger home or cash-out the
   gain in equity. Exhibit 21–29 illustrates the impact that a change in real estate values has on the baseline seasoning curve in the jumbo sector.

2. *The level of interest rates.* Just as borrowers have an economic incentive to
   prepay an above market rate mortgage, they have a financial disincentive to
   prepay a below market rate mortgage. This disincentive or "lock-in" effect
   is proportional to loan size and, consequently, has the greatest effect on the
   jumbo mortgage seasoning profile. Given their current funding advantage

Jumbo Seasoning Function—LTV Effect

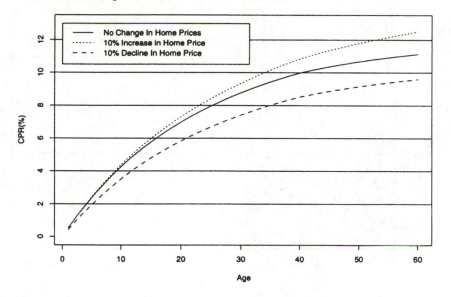

and less attractive housing affordability levels at prevailing market rates, borrowers with below market mortgages are less likely to move or cash-out equity. Exhibit 21–30 plots the baseline jumbo aging profile conditional on various levels of lock-in.

SEASONALITY

It has long been recognized that housing turnover prepayments are linked to the weather, vacation schedules, and the school year. Homeowners are much more likely to move in the summer when the weather is warm and their children are out of school than in the winter when the opposite is true. The seasonal patterns observed in our nonagency prepayment data (shown in Exhibit 21–31) are very consistent with the seasonal adjustments reported by the National Association of Realtors (NAR) and with that found in the agency sector. Prepayments related to housing turnovers usually peak in late spring and summer at levels that are 20% faster than the annual average and bottom in February at 26% slower than the annual average. This results in an absolute prepayment difference of approximately 5% CPR from the fastest to the slowest month for a fully seasoned, near-current-coupon jumbo mortgage security. Absolute seasonal variations will be proportionally less than this for newer issues. Actual versus model projected plots for low coupon jumbo loans originated in 1993 are shown in Exhibit 21–32. Note that the strong seasonal patterns in housing turnover were evident even when the loans were very new.

EXHIBIT 21–30

Jumbo Seasoning Function—Lock-in Effect

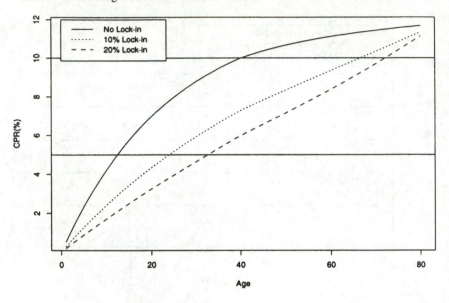

EXHIBIT 21–31

Nonagency Seasonal Adjustments

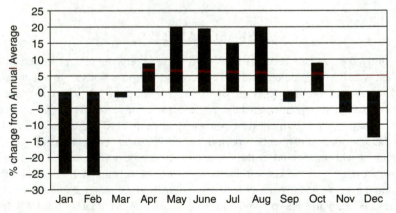

E X H I B I T   21–32

Actual Versus Model Projected Seasonal Prepayments

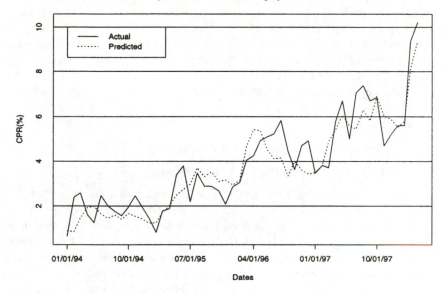

ADVERSE SELECTION IN HOUSING
TURNOVER PREPAYMENTS

The model also captures a more subtle version of borrower self-selection that takes place on a regional basis from housing turnover prepayments. As properties located in high growth areas prepay out of a pool, we are left with an increasing share of properties in areas of the country experiencing lower growth rates or a housing contraction. The key difference between refinancing and housing turnover adverse selection is the time it takes to develop. In general, it takes several years for housing turnover prepayments to significantly alter the composition of a pool versus just several months for a refinancing cycle. In addition, the adverse selection in LTV is often wiped out by amortization and the general trend of rising home prices across the country. Nevertheless, we capture all forms of burnout in an identical way: by modeling the evolution in the distribution of loan attributes over time.

This discussion highlights our previous observation that the vast majority of the prepayment volatility and negative convexity observed in the mortgage market comes from refinancing activity rather than housing resale activity. Indeed, because housing resale prepayments occur throughout the year and are more correlated to where an individual is in the homeownership cycle than to interest rates, we will never see a refinancing-like spike take place because of an increase in housing activity. Consequently, MBS valuation results based on simulated interest rates tend to be dominated by the refinancing component in economic prepayment models.

INVOLUNTARY PREPAYMENTS AND CURTAILMENTS

Two other types of prepayments that affect the observed seasoning patterns in all mortgage-backed securities are involuntary prepayments (defaults) and curtailments. In the nonagency universe the combined contribution of these two components occurs at a rate that is usually less than 1.5% CPR during the first 5 years of the seasoning process; however, both types of prepayments tend to increase as a loan seasons after origination.

The foreclosure and liquidation of a property (default) always results in a full prepayment of the mortgage. We find that the probability of default is influenced by two factors:

1. The level of equity a borrower has in a property

2. An individual's ability to meet debt obligations

We find that it is usually a combination of events rather than a single factor that triggers a default. For example, declining real estate values accompanied by sudden financial distress (e.g., job loss, income disruption, or unexpected debt) greatly increases the likelihood of a default. Consequently, current LTV and FICO scores are often used contemporaneously to explain the propensity of a borrower to default. Since nonagency borrowers represent the top of the FICO spectrum and the low end of the LTV spectrum, defaults have historically played a relatively minor role in the seasoning process (see Exhibit 21–33).

E X H I B I T   21–33

Jumbo Defaults Conditional on Loan Age

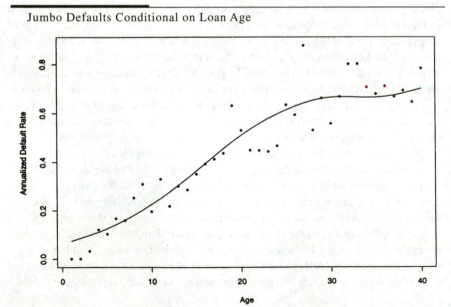

EXHIBIT   21-34

Jumbo Curtailments Conditional on Loan Age

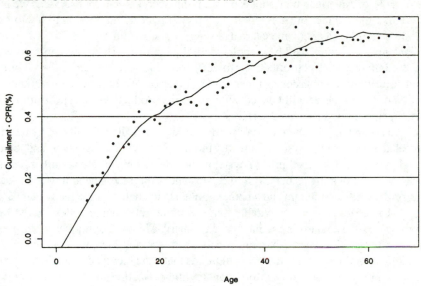

A similar profile emerges when we isolate curtailments or partial prepayments as a function of loan age. Borrowers often send in payments that exceed scheduled principal and interest as a way to increase their equity position in a property and reduce the time it takes to pay off their mortgage debt. As a loan seasons and a borrower's financial status improves over time, partial prepayments tend to increase. In addition, when a loan amortizes to a very small balance, borrowers will often increase their curtailment rate to accelerate retirement of the debt and avoid the fixed transaction costs associated with a refinance transaction. Exhibit 21-34 plots partial prepayments conditional on loan age in the jumbo sector.

REFINANCING EFFICIENCY: THE NEXT FRONTIER

We believe that the next frontier for efficiency gains in the refinancing process is likely to come from the internet as mortgage service providers work toward a vertically integrated origination process. It is clear that the internet is changing the way Americans refinance their mortgages. Although it is estimated that less than 10% of the refinance transactions in 1998 were executed over the internet, a far greater number of borrowers used it to shop for competitive rates. Furthermore, the success of internet-based mortgage companies such as E-loan, Homeshark, and Keystone plus a proliferation of sites from virtually every major originator is a testament to the viability of the internet as a delivery mechanism for mortgage services.

The burgeoning use of the internet is resulting in a democratization in mortgage service providers, as smaller lenders find that they can compete and market effectively on the internet. However, further automation and integration of the origination process is needed, particularly in the area of title search processing. With 50% of American households now having access to internet services we believe that the number of transactions completed over the internet is likely to explode in coming years (some estimates suggest that within 5 years 75% of all refinancing transactions will be completed on the internet). The remarkable growth of E-commerce in 1998 reflects a growing consumer confidence in the viability and security of the internet as a means of commerce. We believe the natural evolution of E-commerce will take consumers up the product-service spectrum leading them to mortgage-related services.

This end-to-end integration of mortgage services will be facilitated by the automated underwriting systems already put in place by the agencies and other venders. These risk-based pricing systems include automated credit and appraisal evaluations, providing lenders with a near-instantaneous assessment of where a loan fits on the credit continuum and whether or not a loan qualifies for agency purchase.

Therefore, it seems inevitable that electronic refinancing is destined to become the gold standard in the mortgage industry. This will continue to put pressure on transaction costs, shorten processing times, and increase the number of "marginal" refinance transactions—all trends that were clearly evident in the 1998 refinancing prepayment data. More than anything else, this sweeping transformation in refinancing behavior will minimize the "hassle costs" involved with refinancing, allowing borrowers to respond more "efficiently" and frequently to refinancing opportunities. Consequently, we would expect the refinancing elbow to shift even lower in the future.

MODELING THE MORTGAGE RATE PROCESS

Since 1993, the spread between jumbo and conforming mortgage rates has been as narrow as 10 bps and as wide as 50 bps. This has important implications in terms of the relative prepayment risk faced by agency and nonagency securities. For example, as Exhibit 21–35 clearly illustrates, there was a convergence in prepayment speeds between the jumbo and conforming sectors in 1998—jumbo prepayment speeds were the same or slower in 1998 than in 1993, whereas the opposite was true for agency prepayments.[11] We attribute most of this convergence to the widening spread between jumbo and conforming mortgage rates.

In general, jumbo borrowers found much less attractive refinancing opportunities as jumbo rates lagged the rally in conforming rates. This occurred because global credit events caused subordinate spreads to widen dramatically (doubling spreads in many cases), making the economics of securitization much less attractive to issuers (which in turn negatively impacted conduit pricing of mortgage purchases). In addition, the flat yield curve mitigated the additional arbitrage gained from faster prepayment assumptions on jumbo product. In contrast, nearly opposite conditions

---

11. Burnout also played a role in slowing high-premium jumbo prepayments in 1998.

Convergence Trend Between Jumbo and Conforming Prepayments

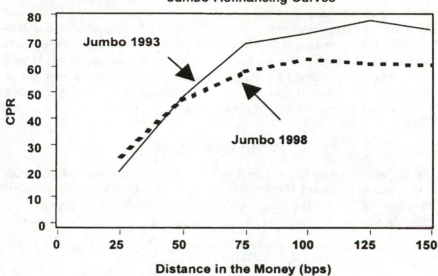

Jumbo Refinancing Curves

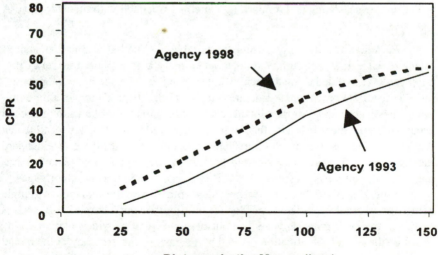

Agency Refinancing Curves

prevailed in 1993 as a steep yield curve and fast prepayment assumptions improved deal arbitrage. At the same time subordinate pricing remained competitive. All these factors served to compress the jumbo to conforming mortgage rate spread in 1993.

To calculate current nonagency mortgage rates in our modeling framework, we closely monitor mortgage rate spreads between the conforming, jumbo, and alternative-A sectors. For jumbos we add the appropriate spread to our conforming rate consistent with today's pricing of jumbo mortgages. Since there is very little uniformity in the alternative-A sector, we must calculate an appropriate spread for each individual loan, and apply this spread to our current prime jumbo rate. To the extent that today's jumbo to conforming spread is above or below historical averages, we allow for a mean reversion in this spread when forecasting.

MODEL TESTING

The production version of our nonagency prepayment model was evaluated using both in-sample and out-of-sample testing to assess forecast error. It was particularly important that the model explain certain key aspects of the data that we felt provided unusually valuable insights into nonagency prepayment behavior. These include

- The muted refinancing response of new issues during the first quarter of 1996 despite substantial economic incentives to refinance

- The impact of the contraction and expansion phases of the California housing cycle from 1990 to 1998

- The relative magnitude of the refinancing spikes in 1993, 1996, the first quarter of 1998, and the fourth quarter of 1998

- The unique seasoning and refinancing patterns associated with the alternative-A sector

We relied heavily on deterministic variables defined at origination such as loan size, LTV, rate premium, and documentation type to explain nonagency prepayments. We avoided using artificially constructed variables that, although correlated to historical prepayment data, are often less reliable predictors of future prepayment behavior. It was important that each model variable explain a fundamental aspect of prepayment behavior that could be observed consistently over time and that would likely persist in the future. The model also handles three less standard mortgage types that are not addressed in this chapter: prepayment penalty mortgages, Community Reinvestment Act (CRA) loans,[12] and relocation mortgages.

Appendix A of this chapter provides both in-sample and out-of-sample actual-versus-model predicted results for the jumbo and alternative-A sectors across all major origination years. An out-of-sample test provides a "real world" check on the model specification given that it measures the accuracy of the model against data that was not part of the estimation. In our test, we first estimated on

---

12. See Chapter 10.

data through June of 1998 and then measured the accuracy of our model forecast versus post-June 1998 data (the out-of-sample test) as well as pre-June 1998 data (the in-sample test). Of course the production version of our model was estimated from the complete data set. The representative deals shown in Appendix A were selected on the basis of deal size (to minimize the noise in the data) and collateral profile.

Appendix A is intended to be only a representative sample of our results, not an exhaustive review of the fits (a comprehensive series of both in-sample and out-of-sample model fits is available upon request). The results demonstrate that the model explains much of the monthly variation observed in nonagency prepayment data since 1990. Moreover, we believe the results satisfy our "key aspects" criteria outlined above.

Nevertheless, a good fit to the data is only the first step in the successful implementation of a model. We must be cognizant of potential structural changes in the nonagency market that could erode model performance going forward. These may include additional modifications to current agency underwriting guidelines, the introduction of an alternative or competing mortgage product, or a significant change in transaction costs.

CONCLUSION

We have presented a new and innovative prepayment model for the valuation of nonagency mortgage-backed securities. We believe the union of new processing technology, new prepayment information, and the availability of extensive property level data will usher in a new generation of nonagency prepayment models whose accuracy and precision will surpass that of existing agency models where no loan-level data are available. Central to our effort is a full property level implementation of the model that captures the powerful effects of WAC and loan size dispersion on the expected future prepayments of nonagency issues. Also unique to our model is the incorporation of current housing price and LTV data as key determinants of both refinancing and housing turnover prepayments. In addition, the model accounts for the influence of secondary loan characteristics such as loan purpose, occupancy status, documentation type, and rate premium. We find that this specification performs well in rigorous in-sample and out-of-sample tests on actual deal level prepayments in both the jumbo and alternative-A mortgage sectors. The end result is a model that, we believe, provides nonagency mortgage investors with a powerful new valuation tool that can be used to accurately model portfolio cash flows, make informed cross-sector relative value decisions, and enhance hedging capabilities.

Model Projected Versus Actual Results for Representative Deals

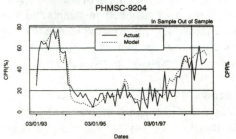

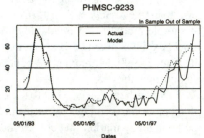

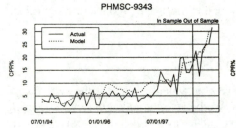

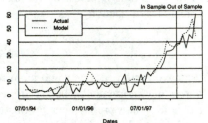

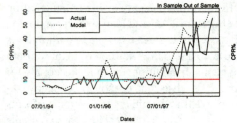

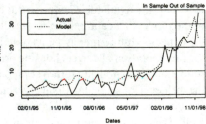

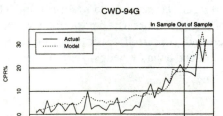

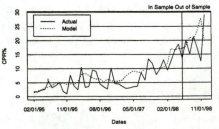

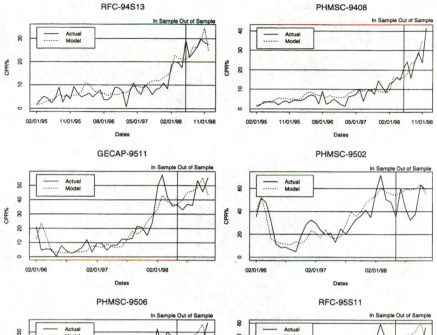

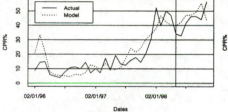

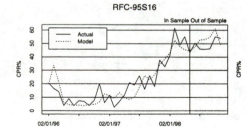

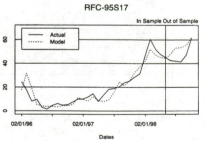

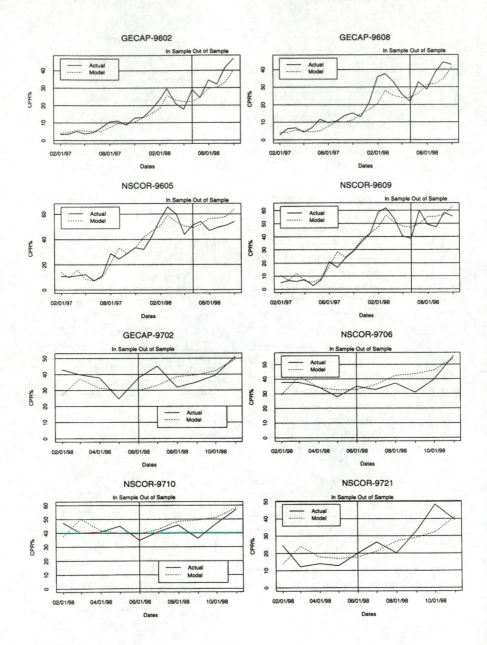

442

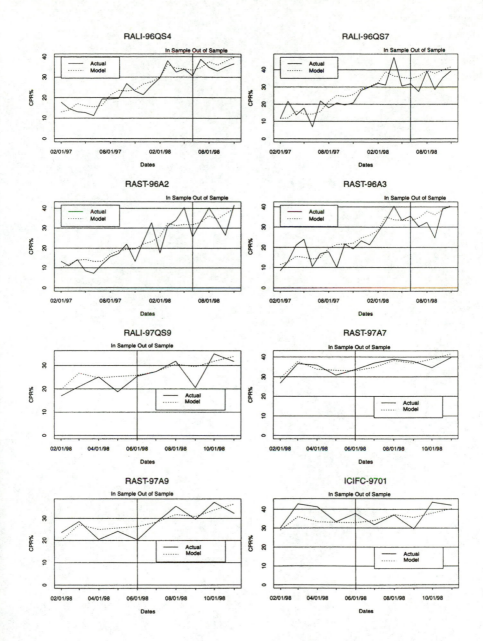

CHAPTER 22

PREPAYMENT INSIGHT: SAXON MORTGAGE HOME EQUITY PORTFOLIO

Glenn Schultz, CFA
Director, Senior Research Analyst
Banc One Capital Markets

Alessandro Pagani
Director, Research Analyst
Banc One Capital Markets

Accurate modeling of the prepayment rate of home equity loans is of paramount importance for investors and issuers alike. For the investor, the proper modeling of prepayment rates is crucial in estimating the value of the embedded option due to borrower refinancing. Furthermore, the strength of an issuer's balance sheet and future financial flexibility also depend on the prepayment assumptions used for its gain-on-sale accounting. Consequently, investors need accurate estimates of future prepayment variability to assess the likelihood of a disruption of servicing due to financial distress brought about by potential write-downs on the retained interest in securitized assets.

Issuers depend on accurate prepayment estimates for similar reasons, albeit from an opposite perspective. First, greater investor confidence regarding the pricing speed will improve execution costs in the term ABS market. Second, the use of accurate prepayment estimates for gain-on-sale accounting improves the perceived financial strength and flexibility of the issuer. Finally, accurate prepayment assumptions improve the issuer's ability to monetize the full value of the servicing portfolio through a net interest margin transaction.

Home equity loans, unlike agency mortgages, do not represent a homogeneous loan class. Rather, borrower profiles and underwriting practices can differ greatly from issuer to issuer. These differences are largely due to the efforts of lenders to find profitable lending niches and may result in pools of collateral with different prepayment characteristics. Most prepayment studies have attempted to create models from large data samples, and then to apply the results to all issuers. Although theoretically justifiable, this approach tends to ignore the unique underwriting practices of each issuer. Alternatively, loan-level issuer-specific analysis represents a better approach to the modeling of home equity loans, because of its ability to capture the unique characteristics of an issuer's loan production. To this end, in this chapter we present our analysis of the Saxon Mortgage, Inc., home equity loan portfolio.

COMPANY OVERVIEW

Since 1996 Saxon Mortgage has issued twelve transactions totaling over $6.0 billion. In 1996 Saxon issued two transactions totaling about $684,000, which represented 1.7% of the total home equity loan securitizations for the year. Saxon's share of public home equity issuance increased to 2.4% in 1997 and 2.9% in 1998. Saxon's 1999 securitization totaled $2.49 billion, accounting for 4% of public year-to-date home equity issuance. This made Saxon the sixth largest issuer of home equity loans, up from eleventh place in 1998.

Saxon Mortgage is a subsidiary of Dominion Capital, Incorporated. Dominion Capital, Inc., was organized in 1985 as the first nonutility subsidiary of Dominion Resources, which is the parent of Virginia Power. Saxon mortgage, based in Richmond, Virginia, originates home equity loans to individuals through its national broker, correspondent, and retail network. Saxon's wholesale lending business consists of 2,800 brokers with approximately 400 active brokers and over 100 account executives throughout the United States. The wholesale lending operation originates about $80 million of nonprime mortgages per month. The correspondent lending business originates a range of A- through D-quality loans. Exhibit 22–1 provides an organization chart summarizing the relationship between Saxon and Dominion Resources, Inc.

E X H I B I T   22–1

Organizational Structure

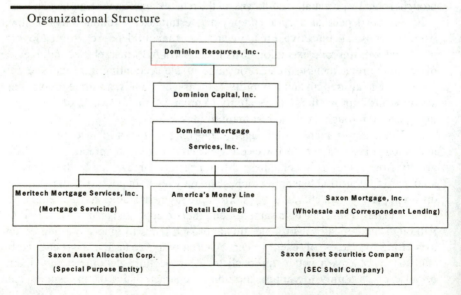

As of this date Dominion Resources has agreed that it will merge with Consolidated Natural Gas.[1] Dominion Resources will become a public utility holding company that will register under the Public Utility Holding Company Act of 1935. The 1935 Act "limits the ability of registered holding companies to engage in activities unrelated to their utility operations and regulates holding company system service companies and the rendering of services by holding company affiliates to other companies in their system." Therefore, Dominion Resources intends to divest Dominion Capital, Inc. We expect the divestiture to proceed after the necessary, Securities Exchange Commission (SEC) approval, the timing of which remains uncertain.[2]

UNDERWRITING AND SERVICING PRACTICES

Saxon Mortgage approves and purchases loans that represent a reasonable and prudent risk by analyzing the likely performance of the loan based on both the collateral and credit characteristics. Appendix A shows Saxon's underwriting guidelines. Saxon Mortgage underwrites loans across the credit spectrum, and the primary underwriting objectives are to

- Determine the borrower's ability and willingness to repay a loan according to its terms
- Determine that the property securing the loan provides sufficient value to recover the lender's investment if the loan defaults

To determine the borrower's ability and willingness to repay, Saxon evaluates the borrower's credit history and performs a collateral overview with special emphasis on type and value of property. In addition, Saxon requires verified, stable, and sufficient income as well as employment verification. In the case of a loan purchase, Saxon requires complete and accurate information from the seller of the mortgage loan. Compensating factors used to evaluate exceptions include loan-to-value, mortgage payment history, employment stability and years at residence, property type, and debt-to-income analysis.

In order to determine that the property securing the loan provides sufficient value to recover Saxon's investment in the event of loan default, special emphasis is placed on both the type and value of the property. In addition, Saxon maintains a bad appraiser list and conducts continual reviews of the property appraisals.

Saxon's loans are serviced by Meritech, a subsidiary of Dominion Capital, Inc. Meritech has been in business since 1960. Saxon's relationship with Meritech

---

1. "Dominion Resources and Consolidated Natural Gas entered into an amended and restated merger agreement as of May 11, 1999. Shareholder approvals have been obtained, but the transaction remains subject to a number of regulatory approvals." Saxon Mortgage Loan Asset Backed Certificates Series 1999-3—Prospectus Supplement dated August 6, 1999, page S-9.
2. "Although CNG and Dominion Resources believe that Commission approval of the transaction under the 1935 Act on terms acceptable to both parties will be obtained, it is not possible to predict with certainty the timing of such approval and whether the approval will be on terms acceptable to them." Saxon Mortgage Loan Asset Backed Certificates Series 1993-3—Prospectus Supplement dated August 6, 1999, page S-9.

EXHIBIT 22-2

Saxon's Servicing Portfolio by Credit Quality

Description	No. of Loans	Original Balance	Percent Original Balance	Current Balance	Percent Current Balance
A+	1,980	$ 332,068,846	7.9	$ 126,755,305	4.6
A	9,046	1,077,101,639	25.7	710,363,894	25.7
A-	15,993	1,805,219,101	43.1	1,226,866,913	44.5
B	5,781	561,869,946	13.4	407,936,856	14.8
C	3,504	312,034,427	7.5	220,429,678	8.0
D	1,213	97,294,908	2.3	66,792,203	2.4
Total	37,517	$4,185,588,866	100.0%	$2,759,144,849	100.0%

is a critical success factor, given that efficient servicing is a key element in a successful home equity lending program. Meritech has implemented systems and processes to establish itself as a leader in the nonprime servicing industry. Some of its key abilities include

- Monthly billing statement preparation
- In-house payment processing
- Default management system
- Imaging technology

THE SERVICING PORTFOLIO

Exhibit 22–2 provides a breakdown of the credit quality of Saxon's servicing portfolio. The exhibit shows that 74.8% of the portfolio is rated A- or better. Loans rated B comprise 14.8% of the portfolio, and C and D loans 10.4% of the portfolio. This represents a slight migration down the credit spectrum from the firm's last analysis, which examined the servicing portfolio as of March 1998.[3] Specifically, A- and better loans declined 2.5%, B loans increased 1.8%, and C and D loans increased 0.8%.

Exhibit 22–3 graphically illustrates the credit migration in each of Saxon's outstanding securitizations through 1998. The exhibit shows that Saxon's exposure to the highest quality of the subprime market has steadily declined over time. Concurrently, Saxon's exposure to the middle- and low-middle-quality borrowers of the sub-prime market has increased. Despite the migration down

---

3. Glenn Schultz and Alessandro Pagani, *Prepayment Insight: An Analysis of Saxon Home Equity Loan Portfolio,* Banc One Capital Markets, Inc., November 12, 1998.

E X H I B I T   22–3

Saxon's Credit Migration by Transaction

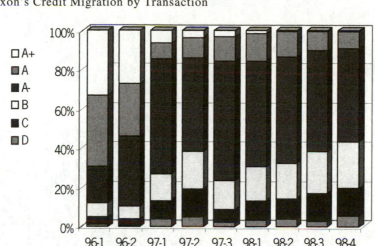

the credit spectrum, Saxon's losses and delinquencies have remained low relative to its peers.[4]

Saxon underwrites both fixed- and adjustable-rate home equity loans. Exhibit 22–4 provides a breakdown by loan type of Saxon's servicing portfolio as of February 1999. The exhibit shows that 43.6% of the loans originated, measured as a percent of the original balance, are fixed-rate loans. This is a 5.5% increase over March 1998's servicing portfolio. The increase in fixed-rate origination was due to an increase in balloon and 15-year mortgages. The concentration of balloon mortgages increased to 10.2% from 6% and the concentration of 15-year mortgages increased to 4.5% from 4%.

The remainder, 56.4% of the original balance, consists of adjustable-rate loans indexed to 6-month London interbank offered rate (LIBOR) for 1-year constant maturity Treasury (CMT). Six-month LIBOR-indexed ARMs account for 87% and 1-year CMT ARMs account for 13% of the total adjustable-rate mortgage origination. This report will focus on the prepayment behavior of both Saxon's fixed- and adjustable-rate loan portfolios. Our analysis of the fixed-rate collateral is based on 19,741 loans with an original balance of $1,822,872,460. The adjustable-rate analysis is based on 17,776 loans with an original balance of $2,362,716,406. In all, we examined 37,517 loans with an original balance of $4,185,588,866. The analysis begins in August 1996 and runs through February 1999.

---

4. For a detailed discussion see Glenn Schultz, *"Balancing Act: Saxon Experiences Stable Prepayments with High Quality Obligors,"* Banc One Capital Markets, Inc., April 14, 1999.

EXHIBIT 22–4

Saxon's Servicing Portfolio by Loan Type

Description	No. of Loans	Original Balance	Percent Original Balance	Current Balance	Percent Current Balance
2/28 ARM	7,631	$ 940,916,021	22.5	$ 748,826,477	27.1
LIBOR	7,543	1,020,334,387	24.4	369,709,914	13.4
1-year Treasury (ARM)	1,758	297,444,846	7.1	134,490,420	4.9
3/27 ARM	758	94,448,699	2.3	61,759,355	2.2
Other	86	9,572,453	0.2	5,878,701	0.2
Subtotal	**17,776**	**$2,362,716,406**	**56.4%**	**$1,320,664,866**	**47.9%**
30-year fixed	11,151	$1,168,475,418	27.9	904,718,357	32.8
Balloons	4,521	426,185,911	10.2	355,280,054	12.9
15-year fixed	3,276	186,499,588	4.5	143,901,170	5.2
20- and 25-year fixed	554	33,249,107	0.8	27,910,360	1.0
10- and 12-year fixed	239	8,462,436	0.2	6,670,041	0.2
Subtotal	**19,741**	**$1,822,872,460**	**43.6%**	**$1,438,479,982**	**52.1%**
Total	**37,517**	**$4,185,588,866**	**100.0%**	**$2,759,144,849**	**100.0%**

450

FIXED-RATE LOANS PREPAYMENT ANALYSIS
Portfolio Stratification

Exhibits 22–5 and 22–6 give a stratification of Saxon's fixed-rate portfolio by region and loan type. The tables highlight the following points regarding the portfolio.

- The loans are geographically diverse. The largest concentrations are in the west and south Atlantic accounting for 27.5% and 24.8% of the loan portfolio, respectively. The largest state concentrations are in California and Florida, representing 18.4% and 8.7%, respectively.

- The largest average original balance is in the West ($124,764) followed by New England ($101,049). The lowest average balances are in the West South Central ($71,426) and East South Central ($74,586). Thus, based on average original loan balance, the West and New England regions should exhibit faster prepayment rates and the West South Central and East South Central regions should exhibit slower prepayment rates.

- The weighted average combined loan-to-value (CLTV) ratio of the fixed-rate portfolio is 77%. The highest CLTV is 80.3% in the West North Central region and the lowest is 75.5% in the West region. We expect lower CLTV loans to prepay faster than higher CLTV loans. This is due to the fact that lower CLTV borrowers have a greater amount of equity in their home and are in a better position to take advantage of refinancing opportunities.

- The fixed-rate portfolio consists of 96.1% first lien mortgages and 3.9% second lien mortgages. The high percentage of first lien mortgages is not unusual given the low interest rate environment that has prevailed over the past three years; when interest rates are low, home equity borrowers are inclined to consolidate all their debt into a first lien. Conversely, when interest rates are high, borrowers are inclined to preserve their low-rate first mortgage. The most important difference between first and second lien mortgages is that second lien mortgages bear the full prepayment risk of the underlying first lien mortgages. In addition, very little information is available regarding the characteristics of the first lien mortgage. Consequently, second lien prepayment risk is often vague. Thus, the primary benefit of first lien home equity loans is that investors have complete information with which to determine prepayment risk.

- Despite Saxon's recent migration down the credit spectrum, the fixed-rate portfolio remains underwritten to high credit standards, with 82.9% A-quality borrowers. For a given decline in interest rates, higher-credit-quality borrowers are more likely to refinance than lower-credit-quality borrowers. Therefore, the high concentration of A-quality borrowers suggests that default risk is low, but refinancing risk is high.

Stratification by Region

Region	Total Current Balance (%)[a]	Average Original Balance	Average Current Balance[a]	Weighted Average CLTV[b] (%)	Weighted Average Original Term (Mos.)	Weighted Average Loan Age (Mos.)	Weighted Average Coupon (%)
East North Central	8.4	$ 75,663	$56,898	78.1	336	11	9.9
East South Central	4.4	74,586	58,410	79.2	318	12	10.0
Middle Atlantic	9.6	90,690	72,932	77.1	335	14	10.0
Mountain	11.5	97,067	69,642	76.6	344	13	9.7
New England	2.0	101,049	85,171	76.9	338	13	10.0
South Atlantic	24.8	86,228	68,688	79.0	336	13	9.9
West	27.5	124,764	99,346	75.5	346	13	9.5
West North Central	3.9	76,083	60,934	80.3	341	10	10.1
West South Central	8.0	71,426	62,219	77.6	325	11	10.2
Total	**100.0**	**$ 92,339**	**$72,868**	**77.4**	**338**	**13**	**9.8**

Region	First Mortgages Current Balance (%)	A Obligors Current Balance (%)	Purchase Current Balance (%)	Refinance Current Balance (%)	Single-Family Detached Current Balance (%)	Full Documentation Current Balance (%)	Primary Owners Current Balance (%)
East North Central	98.5	79.7	21.7	78.3	86.2	74.7	90.0
East South Central	99.1	81.2	24.8	75.2	89.0	74.0	93.8
Middle Atlantic	97.0	79.9	34.3	65.7	77.2	64.6	90.6
Mountain	95.5	86.6	21.9	78.1	80.3	65.4	89.7
New England	95.2	83.2	34.0	66.0	72.8	63.9	78.5
South Atlantic	96.5	84.5	33.4	66.6	80.4	70.0	92.6
West	93.5	83.8	19.3	80.7	83.4	64.8	91.8
West North Central	98.4	80.1	27.9	72.1	90.3	77.4	94.8
West South Central	97.3	78.4	37.5	62.5	87.6	68.7	95.3
Portfolio weighted average	**96.1**	**82.9**	**27.1**	**72.9**	**82.6**	**68.2**	**91.7**

Top Ten States

State	No. of Loans	Original Balance	Original Balance (%)	Current Balance	Current Balance (%)
California	4,373	$ 859,612,905	36.4	$ 432,555,278	32.8
Washington	1,092	138,316,846	5.9	102,256,142	7.7
Colorado	1,115	133,069,106	5.6	56,336,750	4.3
Utah	1,115	132,831,974	5.6	83,844,441	6.3
Oregon	814	95,712,170	4.1	59,544,719	4.5
Illinois	778	93,302,532	3.9	42,910,893	3.2
Arizona	512	65,158,683	2.8	38,412,889	2.9
Virginia	389	64,344,684	2.7	31,227,234	2.4
Florida	589	61,863,551	2.6	40,460,583	3.1
Texas	498	55,529,692	2.4	38,890,157	2.9
Other states	6,501	662,974,264	28.1	394,225,781	29.9
Total	**17,776**	**$2,362,716,406**	**100.0**	**$1,320,664,866**	**100.0**

[a]As of February 1999.
[b]CLTV = Combined loan-to-value

453

EXHIBIT 22–6

Stratification by Loan Type

Loan Type	Original Balance (%)	Current Balance (%)[a]	Class A Credit Quality Current Balance (%)	Second Lien Current Balance (%)	WAOT[b] (Mos.)	WALA[c] (Mos.)	WAC[d] (%)	WACLTV[e] (%)
30-year fixed	64.1	62.9	85.4	0.05	360	14	9.7	77.4
Balloons	23.4	24.7	77.4	7.1	360	10	10.1	79.6
15-year fixed	10.2	10.0	82.3	15.8	180	13	9.8	72.6
20- and 25-year fixed	1.8	1.9	77.9	21.3	243	12	10.2	77.2
10- and 12-year fixed	0.5	0.5	74.6	21.1	122	10	10.3	68.3
5- and 7-year fixed	0.03	0.02	70.9	53.2	63	7	11.7	55.8
Total	100.0	100.0	82.9	3.9	338	13	9.8	77.4

[a]As of February 1999.
[b]WAOT   = weighted average original term.
[c]WALA   = weighted average loan age.
[d]WAC   = weighted average coupon.
[e]WACLTV = weighted average combined loan-to-value.

- Purchase money mortgages constitute 27.1% of the fixed-rate portfolio and the balance of the portfolio is refinancing and cash-out refinancing. We expect cash-out refinancing to prepay faster because borrowers who have refinanced in the past are more likely to refinance again if conditions permit. In the case of B and C purchase money mortgages, the credit curing effect will result in early prepayments, absent prepayment penalties, as the borrower's credit profile improves.

- A comparison of loan type by original and current balance indicates that the 30-year loan product accounts for the greatest percentage, 64.1%, of Saxon's fixed-rate portfolio. The 15-year and balloon products account for 10.2% and 23.4% of the fixed-rate portfolio, respectively. Exhibit 22–6 also shows that the weighted average coupon of the 15-year and of the balloon loans is 10 and 40 basis points (bps), respectively, above that of the 30-year loan. At first blush, this seems counterintuitive, given standard mortgage pricing conventions. However, closer inspection of Exhibit 22–6 shows that 15.8% of the 15-year loans and 7.1% of the balloon loans are second liens, whereas only 0.05% of the 30-year loans are second liens. Given that second lien loans are generally perceived as riskier, the pricing relationship in Exhibit 22–6 seems appropriate.

Observed Prepayment Behavior

Exhibit 22–7 displays the monthly prepayment rate of selected Saxon transactions. The exhibit shows that Saxon's fixed-rate portfolio has prepaid faster than expected at the time of pricing. Saxon has responded by increasing the pricing speed from 18% CPR to 24% CPR since the pricing of the 1997-2 transaction.

Exhibit 22–8 illustrates the results of our loan-level prepayment analysis of Saxon's fixed-rate portfolio. The collateral demonstrates a prepayment ramp that begins at 0.4% CPR in the first month and increases 2.5% CPR per month for 13 months to a peak of 33% CPR in month 14.

Effect of Prepayment Penalties

Saxon uses prepayment penalties that range from 12 to 60 months. Exhibit 22–9 provides a breakdown of prepayment penalties by loan type. The exhibit shows that as a percentage of the original balance, 34% of the 30-year loans, 31% of the 15-year loans, and 46% of the balloon loans carry prepayment penalties.

EXHIBIT 22–7

Monthly CPR of Select Saxon Deals

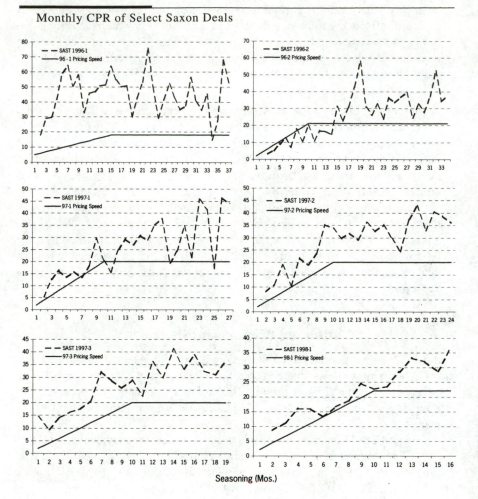

Seasoning (Mos.)

Saxon Fixed-Rate HEP Curve

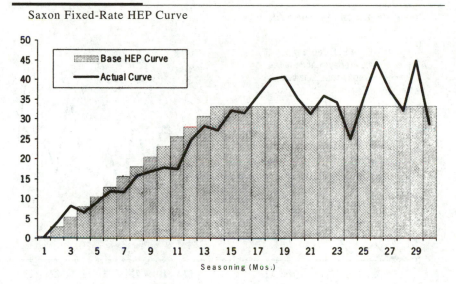

Prepayment Penalties by Loan Type

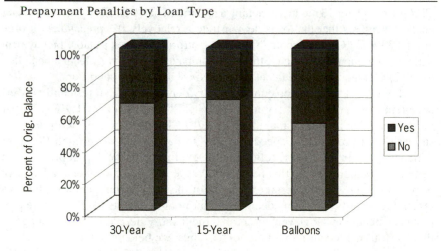

E X H I B I T   22–10

Prepayment Penalty Analysis

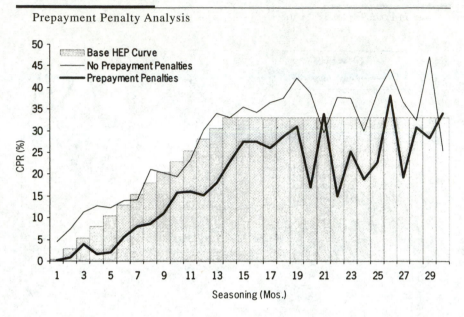

Exhibit 22–10 graphically illustrates the effect of prepayment penalties on the fixed-rate portfolio. The exhibit shows that loans with no prepayment penalties demonstrate a ramp that begins at 5% CPR in the first month and increases 2.5% CPR per month for 13 months, reaching a maximum of 34% CPR by month 14. Our analysis suggests that the loans demonstrate a relatively flat prepayment profile around 33% CPR out to month 30. It is not surprising to see a stable prepayment pattern out to month 30 because the above prepayment ramp results in a bond factor of 30% in month 42, the factor at which most agree burnout occurs.

Loans that carry a prepayment penalty demonstrate a significantly different prepayment ramp that begins at 0.2% CPR and increases 1.9% CPR per month for 14 months to a maximum of 27% CPR by month 15. Our analysis suggests that prepayment speeds decline from months 19 through 26, after which they begin to increase following the expiration of the 2-year prepayment penalties. We believe that this pattern will repeat as borrowers take advantage of refinancing opportunities at expiration of the prepayment penalties, but to a lesser degree as bond factors decline and burnout manifests itself in future prepayment behavior. However, the prepayment ramp described above suggests that burnout will occur around month 53. Thus, we believe that the presence of prepayment penalties will most likely hold prepayment rates below 30% CPR going forward.

E X H I B I T   22–11

The 30-Year Loan Prepayment Curve

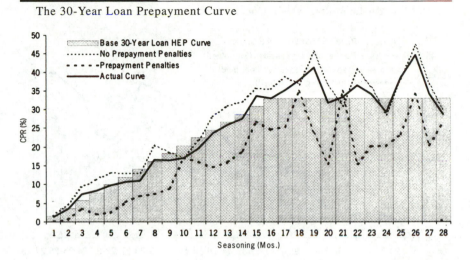

Loan Type Analysis

The 30-year loan type accounts for 62.9% of Saxon's fixed-rate portfolio and 32.8% of the total servicing portfolio. Exhibit 22–11 shows that the 30-year loan type exhibits a prepayment curve that begins at 1.5% CPR and increases about 2.1% CPR per month for 15 months to a maximum of 33% CPR by month 16. Loans that carry a prepayment penalty have a prepayment ramp that begins at 0.1% CPR and peaks at 25% CPR during month 16. Loans that do not carry a prepayment penalty have a prepayment ramp that begins at 1.8% CPR, reaching a peak prepayment rate of 35% CPR during month 16. The analysis shows that in the case of the 30-year loan type, prepayment penalties are effective in reducing the borrower's incentive to refinance.

The 15-year loan type accounts for 10.0% of Saxon's fixed-rate portfolio and 5.2% of the total servicing portfolio. Exhibit 22–12 shows that this loan type exhibits a prepayment curve that begins at 0.3% CPR and increases about 2.0% CPR per month for 17 months to a maximum of 35% CPR by month 18. Loans with shorter maturities are expected to have faster prepayment rates than those with longer maturities. For this pool, the peak prepayment rate is maintained at a relatively low level because its average original balance is particularly low (about $35,000 less than the average original balance of the overall fixed-rate portfolio). We will show later in our analysis (Exhibit 22–15) that loans with a smaller balance

EXHIBIT 22–12

The 15-Year Loan Prepayment Curve

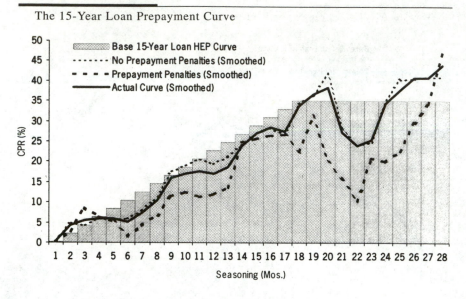

Seasoning (Mos.)

have a markedly slower prepayment speed. The beginning CPR rate for loans with and without prepayment penalties is 0.3% and 0.4% CPR, respectively. The prepayment rate increases for 17 months, reaching a peak in month 18, at which time loans with prepayment penalties peak at 22% CPR while loans without prepayment penalties peak at 34% CPR.

The origination of balloon loans has increased during the last year. They now account for 24.7% of the fixed-rate portfolio and 12.9% of the total servicing portfolio. Exhibit 22–13 shows that the balloon prepayment ramp is shorter and begins at a higher level than the one for the 30- and 15-year loan types. In particular, the balloon loan type prepayment curve begins at 8.0% CPR and increases about 2.1% CPR per month for 13 months to a maximum of 33% CPR by month 14. Loans with a prepayment penalty have a prepayment ramp that begins at 0.1% CPR in the first month, increasing for 13 months to a maximum of 27% CPR during month 14. Loans without a prepayment penalty have a prepayment ramp that begins at 13% CPR and increases for 13 months to a peak of 41% CPR during month 14.

Despite small variations in the length and steepness of the ramps, we can conclude that the base prepayment profiles of these three loan types are very similar. Hence, we do not find it useful to analyze each loan type separately. Because the large majority of the pool is composed of 30-year loans, we continue to analyze this loan type. The reader should bear in mind that the same conclusions could be extended to both the 15-year and balloon loan types.

E X H I B I T   22–13

Balloon Loan Prepayment Curve

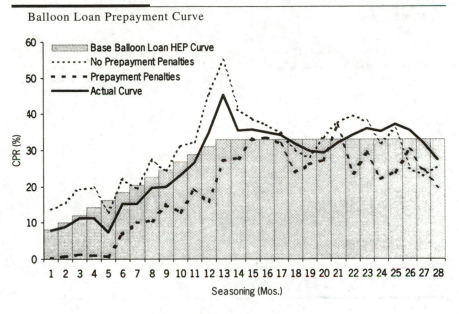

Seasoning (Mos.)

Prepayment Variables

During the development of our fixed-rate prepayment model, we have examined the following variables: property type, loan balance, credit quality, loan purpose, combined loan-to-value ratio, and interest rate sensitivity.

- Single-family loans account for 82.5% of the 30-year loan portfolio. As a result, the prepayment curve of the single-family property type closely resembles that of the aggregate 30-year loan type. As shown in Exhibit 22–14, the non-single-family property type indicates a prepayment curve that begins at 0.5% CPR in the first month and increases 2.09% CPR per month for 13 months, peaking at 27% CPR in month 14.

- The loan balance has a significant effect on both the seasoning ramp and the peak prepayment rate. Borrowers who can afford higher-priced homes generally have higher incomes and superior credit profiles compared to those who carry lower loan balances, all other things being equal. Consequently, higher balance loans demonstrate a higher tendency to turn over, either through refinancings or trading up. Exhibit 22–15 provides a graphic illustration of the prepayment curves for loan balances lower than $60,000 and greater than $120,000. The exhibit shows that smaller balance loans tend to prepay significantly more slowly than larger loans, with the former having a seasoning ramp that peaks in month 14 at 23% CPR while the latter shows a peak CPR rate of 35% in month 16.

E X H I B I T   22–14

Non-Single-Family Loan

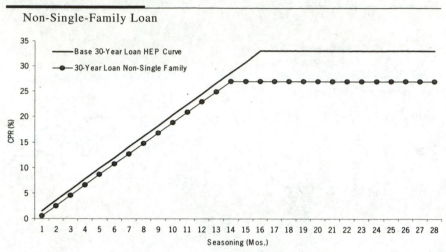

E X H I B I T   22–15

Loan Balances

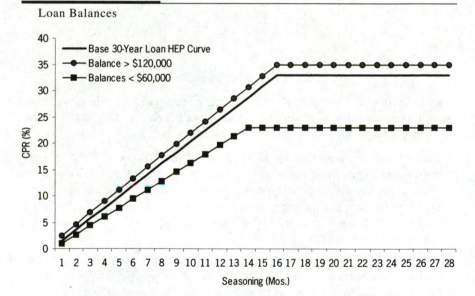

- The fixed-rate portfolio consists of 82.9% A-quality borrowers and 17.1% B/C and D-quality borrowers. Exhibit 22–16 compares the seasoning curve for both credit types relative to the base prepayment curve. B/C and D loans exhibit a slightly steeper seasoning ramp, peaking at 42% CPR in month 15. However, following the peak, the prepayment rate falls to 26% CPR in month 18, after which it begins to increase and peaks again at 54% in month 22. The presence

EXHIBIT   22–16

Credit Quality

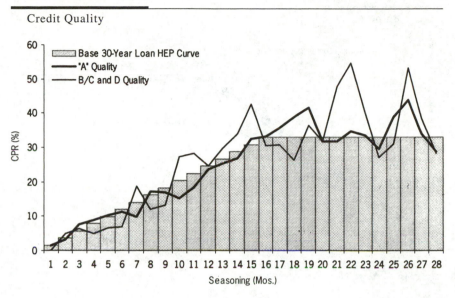

Seasoning (Mos.)

of prepayment penalties increases the cost of refinancing and partially offsets the incentive to refinance due to the credit curing effect. The credit curing effect occurs when the borrower's credit profile improves, thereby making the borrower eligible for a lower-rate loan. This phenomenon translates into B/C and D loans normally exhibiting a steeper prepayment curve than A borrowers.

- Loan purpose also has an effect on prepayments. Exhibit 22–17 compares the seasoning curve for cash-out refinance, refinance, and purchase mortgages. The exhibit shows that purchase money mortgages exhibit a steeper seasoning ramp than either cash-out refinance or refinance. The prepayment curve for purchase money loans begins at 5% CPR in the first month and increases 2.3% CPR per month, up to a peak of 35% CPR in month 14. Alternatively, cash-out refinancing and refinancing loans exhibit prepayment curves that begin at 2.5% and 1% CPR in the first month and peak at 32% and 23% CPR, respectively, in month 15. The findings by loan type are somewhat counterintuitive. Specifically, cash-out refinancing loans tend to peak higher than those of purchase money loans. However, in this case a greater percentage of the cash-out refinancing loans carry prepayment penalties than do purchase loans, 37% versus 26%. The presence of prepayment penalties alters the commonly accepted wisdom regarding the prepayment pattern of cash-out refinancing loans relative to purchase money loans, and in this case reverses the relationship.

- Combined loan-to-value (CLTV), as shown in Exhibit 22–18, also affects the prepayment behavior of Saxon's loans. Although the lower CLTV loans reduce the probability of default, they tend to prepay faster than higher CLTV loans. In

EXHIBIT 22–17

Loan Purpose

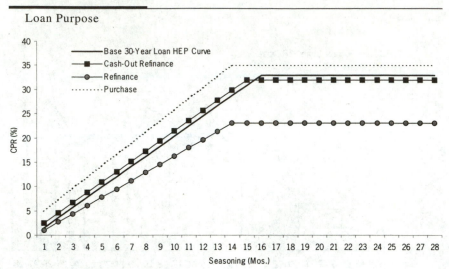

EXHIBIT 22–18

Combined Loan-to-Value (CLTV)

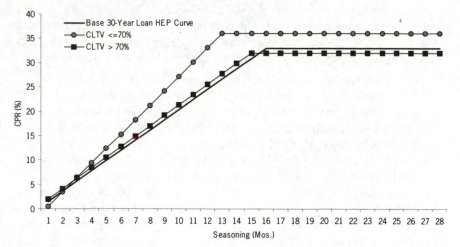

fact, lower CLTV loans display a greater tendency to refinance or exit the pool due to the homeowner's trading up to a larger, more expensive home. The greater propensity to refinance is due to the borrower's superior credit position, resulting from the significant equity in the home. Consequently, the potentially slower prepayment rates due to lower default rates are offset by the above factors.

E X H I B I T   22–19

Interest Rate Sensitivity

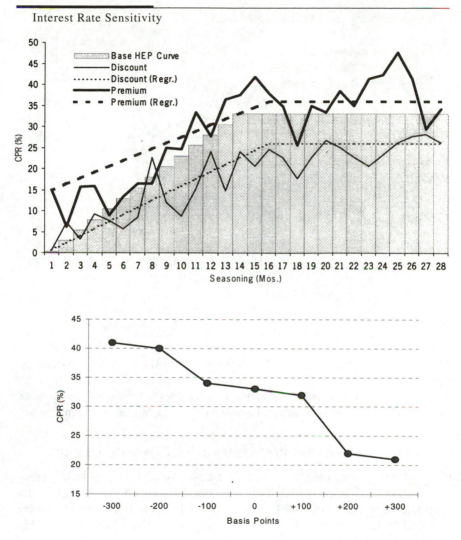

Interest Rate Sensitivity

Exhibit 22–19 provides a comparison between the premium and the discount loan seasoning ramps. The exhibit shows that fully seasoned discount loans have a minimum prepayment rate of 21% CPR whereas premium loans have a peak prepayment rate of 40% CPR. The premium loan's peak prepayment rates coincide with the expiration of the 1- and the 2-year prepayment penalties. The analysis confirms the notion that prepayment penalties dampen interest rate–induced refinancing activity and reduce the slope of the prepayment curve.

E X H I B I T   22–20

Impact of Prepayment Penalties on Credit Curing

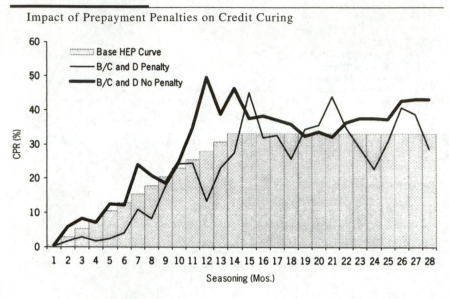

Seasoning (Mos.)

The servicing portfolio has low interest rate sensitivity, with a refinancing threshold at about 150 to 200 bps. This interest rate insensitivity, a hallmark of home equity loans, further supports our contention that despite the higher-than-average credit quality of the portfolio, Saxon's loans behave like traditional home equity loans.

Conclusions About Prepayments for Fixed-Rate Loans

Our analysis has identified three trends in Saxon's fixed-rate underwriting practice: first, a migration down the credit spectrum from the highest quality of the subprime market into B/C and D lending; second, a greater use of prepayment penalties; third, a continued diversification away from 30-year loans into both 15-year and balloon loans.

Typically, a migration down the credit spectrum would result in a steeper seasoning ramp and a higher-peak CPR due to the credit curing effect. However, the presence of prepayment penalties in the B/C and D loans increases the cost of refinancing and offsets the credit curing effect resulting in lower prepayment rates. Exhibit 22–20 illustrates that B/C and D loans with a prepayment penalty demonstrate a prepayment curve that begins at 0% CPR in the first month and remains below the A-quality prepayment ramp up to month 14. During month 15, loans experience a prepayment spike around 45% CPR and then decline below 30% CPR. Prepayment spikes are also evident in months 21 and 25, coinciding with the expiration of longer-dated prepayment penalties.

The fixed-rate portfolio seasons over a 14-month period. The prepayment ramp begins at 0.4% CPR in the first month and increases 2.5% CPR per month for 13 months, reaching a peak of 33% CPR in month 14. The 30-year loan type exhibits a prepayment curve that begins at 1.5% CPR in the first month, reaching a peak of 33% CPR in month 16. The 15-year loan type exhibits a prepayment curve that begins at 0.3% CPR in the first month, reaching a peak of 35% CPR in month 18. Finally, the balloon loan type prepayment curve begins at 8% CPR in the first month, reaching a peak of 33% in month 13.

Throughout our analysis we have shown that prepayment penalties are remarkably effective in both controlling and modifying the prepayment characteristics of home equity loans. This leads us to believe that the increased use of prepayment penalties in newly originated loans, combined with the burnout of older loans, will result in an overall slower rate of prepayment going forward.

ADJUSTABLE-RATE LOANS PREPAYMENT ANALYSIS

Portfolio Stratification

Exhibits 22–21 and 22–22 give a stratification of Saxon's adjustable-rate portfolio by region and loan type. The tables highlight the following points regarding Saxon's adjustable-rate portfolio:

- The loans are geographically diverse. The largest regional concentrations are in the West and Mountain regions, which account for 45.5% and 16.8% of the loan portfolio, respectively. The largest state concentrations are California and Washington, which account for 32.8% and 7.7% of the loan portfolio.

- The largest average original loan balance is in the West region ($174,538), followed by the South Atlantic region ($130,290). The lowest average loan balances were in the West North Central ($83,536), followed by the East South Central ($88,233). Thus, based on average loan balance, the South Atlantic and West regions should exhibit faster prepayment rates and the West North Central and East South Central should exhibit slower prepayment rates.

- The weighted average loan-to-value (WALTV) is 77.4%. The highest WALTV is 80.5% in the East South Central region and the lowest WALTV is 75.8% in the New England region. We expect lower LTV borrowers to prepay faster than the higher LTV borrowers. This is because lower LTV borrowers have a superior credit position vis-à-vis their greater equity position and are able to take advantage of refinancing opportunities.

- The adjustable-rate portfolio is 100% first lien loans. This is not unusual given the low interest rate environment that has prevailed over the last three years and the fact that adjustable-rate mortgage rates are set below fixed-mortgage rates at inception. The lower relative adjustable mortgage rate provides an incentive for borrowers to consolidate all their debt into a first lien mortgage. The most important difference between first and second lien mortgages is that second lien mortgages bear the full prepayment risk of the underlying first lien mortgages.

E X H I B I T 22-21

Stratification by Region

Region	Total Current Balance (%)	Average Original Balance	Average Current Balance*	Weighted Average Remaining Term (Mo)	Weighted Average Gross Margin (%)	Weighted Average Life Cap (%)	Weighted Average LTV (%)
East North Central	9.4	$ 95,516	$52,173	343	6.0	16.3	76.5
East South Central	1.7	88,233	49,819	340	5.9	16.2	80.5
Middle Atlantic	4.5	102,953	62,236	336	6.1	16.5	76.0
Mountain	16.8	118,463	65,759	344	6.0	16.0	77.0
New England	3.3	125,342	83,020	343	6.0	16.5	75.8
South Atlantic	12.1	130,290	75,212	341	5.7	16.0	79.1
West	45.5	174,538	95,228	344	5.9	15.8	77.4
West North Central	2.9	83,536	40,285	334	6.0	16.4	77.9
West South Central	3.7	104,687	71,049	343	6.0	16.5	78.0
Total	**100.0**	**$113,729**	**66,087**	**343**	**5.9**	**16.0**	**77.4**

Region	Purchase Current Balance (%)	Refinance Current Balance (%)	A Obligors Current Balance (%)	B, C, D Obligors Current Balance (%)	Single-Family Detached Current Balance (%)	Full Documentation Current Balance (%)	Primary Owners Current Balance (%)
East North Central	21.2	78.8	57.5	42.5	86.3	72.8	95.4
East South Central	34.8	65.2	66.5	33.5	92.5	85.0	94.1
Middle Atlantic	34.0	66.0	56.8	43.2	83.5	76.2	93.5
Mountain	23.6	76.4	66.1	33.9	86.8	69.1	93.4
New England	36.3	63.7	62.8	37.2	83.7	64.4	93.2
South Atlantic	47.1	52.9	72.0	28.0	82.5	70.9	95.3
West	33.2	66.8	67.7	32.3	83.8	68.7	92.1
West North Central	30.4	69.6	61.8	38.2	86.9	75.8	94.8
West South Central	64.0	36.0	63.5	36.5	85.3	71.8	92.0
Portfolio weighted average	**33.4**	**66.6**	**66.0**	**34.0**	**84.6**	**70.2**	**93.2**

Top Ten States

State	No. of Loans	Original Balance	Original Balance (%)	Current Balance	Current Balance (%)
California	4,373	$ 859,612,905	36.4	$ 432,555,278	32.8
Washington	1,092	138,316,846	5.9	102,256,142	7.7
Colorado	1,115	133,069,106	5.6	56,336,750	4.3
Utah	1,115	132,831,974	5.6	83,844,441	6.3
Oregon	814	95,712,170	4.1	59,544,719	4.5
Illinois	778	93,302,532	3.9	42,910,893	3.2
Arizona	512	65,158,683	2.8	38,412,889	2.9
Virginia	389	64,344,684	2.7	31,227,234	2.4
Florida	589	61,863,551	2.6	40,460,583	3.1
Texas	498	55,529,692	2.4	38,890,157	2.9
Other states	6,501	662,974,264	28.1	394,225,781	29.9
Total	17,776	$2,362,716,406	100.0	$1,320,664,866	100.0

*As of February 1999.

EXHIBIT 22-22

Stratification by Loan Type

Loan Type	ARM Portfolio Original Balance (%)*	ARM Portfolio Current Balance (%)*	Nonconvertible Current Balance (%)	6-Mo. Rate Adj. Current Balance (%)	Weighted Average Periodic Cap Current Balance (%)	Weighted Average Life Cap Current Balance (%)	Weighted Average Gross Margin Balance (%)
1-year Treasury (ARM)	12.6	10.2	9.6	0.0	2.0	15.7	5.6
2/28 ARM	39.8	56.7	56.6	56.7	1.3	16.3	6.1
3/27 ARM	4.0	4.7	4.7	4.7	1.1	16.5	5.7
LIBOR	43.2	28.0	27.7	28.0	1.0	15.4	5.6
Other	0.4	0.4	0.4	0.4	1.6	15.8	5.9
Total	**100.0**	**100.0**	**99.1**	**89.7**	**1.3**	**16.0**	**5.9**

*As of February 1999.

In addition, very little information is available regarding the characteristics of the first lien mortgage. Consequently, second lien prepayment risk is often vague. Thus, the primary benefit of first lien home equity loans is that investors have complete information to determine prepayment risk.

- The portfolio consists of 66% A-quality borrowers. For a given decline in interest rates, higher credit quality borrowers are more likely to refinance than lower credit quality borrowers. Therefore, the percentage of A-quality borrowers suggests that the default risk is low but refinancing risk is high.

- Purchase money mortgages constitute 33.4% of the adjustable-rate portfolio, and the balance of the portfolio is cash-out refinancings. We expect the cash-out refinancings to prepay faster because borrowers who have refinanced in the past are more likely to refinance again if conditions permit. In the case of B and C purchase money mortgages, the credit curing effect will result in early prepayments, absent prepayment penalties, as the borrower's credit profile improves.

- The majority of loans, 89.8%, are 6-month reset loans and the balance, 10.2%, are annual resets indexed to 1-year CMT. The weighted average periodic cap rate is 1.3%. The highest periodic cap rate, 2.0%, is found in the 1-year CMT loan and the lowest periodic cap rate, 1.0%, is found in the 6-month LIBOR loans. The weighted average life cap is 16.0%. The distribution of the life cap is relatively narrow across loan types. The weighted average gross margin is 5.9%, and the distribution of the gross margin is narrow across loan types.

- A comparison of loan type by original and current balance indicates that LIBOR-indexed products account for the greatest percentage, 43.2%, of Saxon's origination. However, 2/28 ARM product accounts for the greatest percentage, 56.7%, of Saxon's servicing portfolio. This implies that LIBOR-indexed ARMs prepay at a faster rate than 2/28 ARMs, thus increasing the servicing portfolio's exposure to 2/28 ARMs over time.

Roll Rate Analysis

As of February 1999, 41.6% of the ARM portfolio adjusts on an annual or semi-annual basis. The balance, 58.4%, is composed of hybrid ARMs, either 2/28 or 3/27, with fixed rates between March 1999 and November 2001.

Exhibit 22–23 provides an analysis of the roll rates for each loan type individually and in aggregate for the ARM component of the servicing portfolio that is in the reset window. The exhibit shows that the bulk of the 1-year CMT ARM adjustments occur between May and July. The hybrid ARM 2/28 and 3/27 adjustment dates are concentrated in the January/July and February/August roll schedule. However, because only 5% of the hybrid ARMs have entered the reset period, the percentage of hybrids rolling is low relative to the total hybrid portfolio. The 6-month LIBOR ARM resets are concentrated in the February/August, March/September, and April/October roll schedule.

EXHIBIT 22–23

Roll Rate Analysis

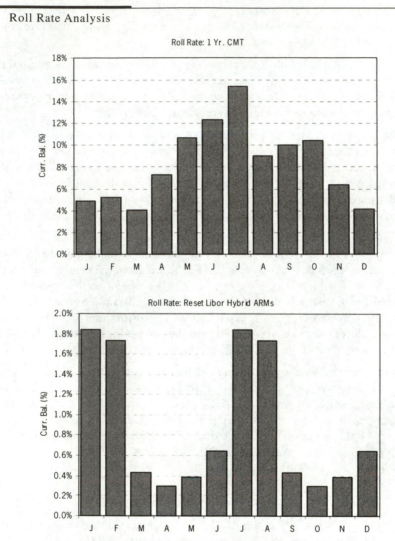

The above roll schedules combine to give a slightly humped roll rate distribution, closely resembling that of the 6-month Libor ARMs. Consequently, we expect prepayment spikes to occur in those months as borrowers react to rate resets, payment adjustments, and refinancing alternatives.

Finally, it is important to note that 58% of the servicing portfolio as of February 1999 consists of hybrid ARMs that have not hit the first reset date. This means that a significant percentage of the portfolio faces prepayment risk due to rate resets. Exhibit 22–24 provides a quarterly analysis of the hybrid ARM conversion schedule. The exhibit shows that about 75% of the hybrid ARMs will reach the first reset date between the third quarter of 1999 and the third quarter of 2000.

EXHIBIT 22–23

Continued

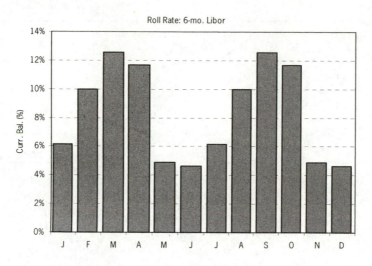

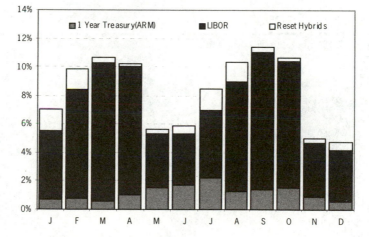

Our analysis suggests that the first reset will result in a brief prepayment spike up to the area of 70% to 75% CPR as borrowers react to the ARM reset. We expect the initial spike to persist for about four months. After the initial borrower response, we believe that the remaining loans will prepay very similarly to seasoned 6-month LIBOR ARMs.

Observed Prepayment Behavior

Exhibit 22–25 displays the monthly prepayment rate of select Saxon transactions. The exhibit shows that Saxon's adjustable-rate portfolio has prepaid faster than

Hybrid ARM First Reset Date (Quarterly)

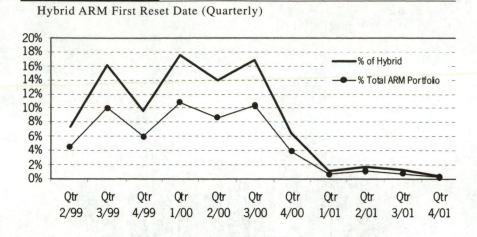

E X H I B I T   22–25

Monthly CPR of Select Saxon Deals

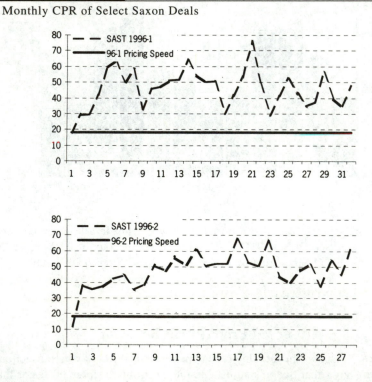

Continued

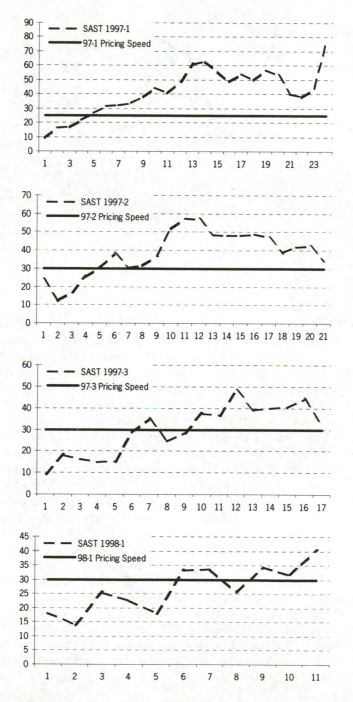

E X H I B I T   22–26

Saxon Adjustable-Rate HEP Curve

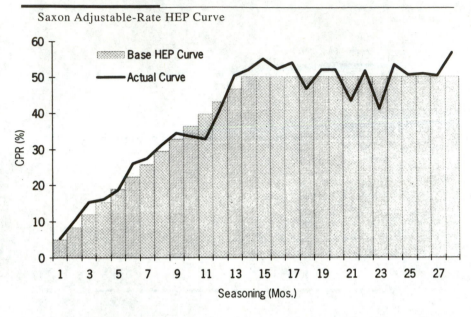

expected at the time of pricing. Saxon has responded to this by increasing the pricing assumption from 18% to 30% CPR since the pricing of the 1997-2 transaction.

Exhibit 22–26 shows that Saxon's adjustable-rate portfolio demonstrates a prepayment curve that begins at 5% CPR in the first month and increases 3.46% CPR per month for 13 months to a maximum of 50% CPR in month 14. The high peak CPR speed to date is partly due to the relatively flat yield curve environment that has persisted over the last three years. From January 1996 to present, the spread between the 1-year bill and the 10-year Treasury has averaged 52 bps. The maximum and minimum spread over the period were 122 and −1.2 bps, respectively.

We believe that adjustable-rate prepayment speeds are likely to slow going forward. First, we demonstrate that the prepayment profile of each loan type can differ significantly from the aggregate curve presented in Exhibit 22–26 and, as a result, the evolution of the servicing portfolio by loan type will alter the prepayment profile going forward. Second, the interaction of rate resets and prepayment penalties significantly alters the prepayment profile of the loans, creating prepayment spikes on coincident anniversary dates that have masked the burnout effect.

In developing our adjustable-rate prepayment model, we examined the following variables: property type, loan balance, credit quality, loan purpose, loan-to-value ratio, and gross margin. Because Saxon's adjustable-rate mortgage portfolio consists of three distinct loan types (1-year CMT ARMs, 6-month LIBOR ARMs, and hybrid 2/28 and 3/27 ARMs), the balance of the analysis will focus on decomposing the prepayment profile of each of the principal components listed above for each loan type.

E X H I B I T   22–27

Prepayment Penalties by Loan Type

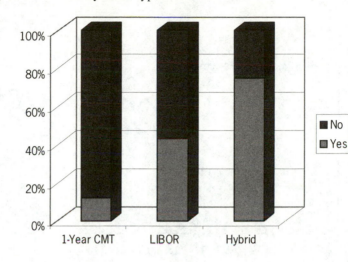

Effect of Prepayment Penalties

Saxon uses prepayment penalties that range from 12 to 60 months. Exhibit 22–27 provides a breakdown of prepayment penalties by loan type. The exhibit shows that less than 15% of the 1-year CMT loans have prepayment penalties. As a result, the 1-year CMT prepayment curve is not significantly affected by the presence of prepayment penalties. By contrast, over 40% of the 6-month LIBOR and close to 75% of the hybrid loan types have prepayment penalties in place. As a result, there is a distinct difference between the loans with and without prepayment penalties.

Exhibit 22–28 graphically illustrates the effect of prepayment penalties on Saxon's adjustable-rate servicing portfolio. The exhibit shows that loans without prepayment penalties demonstrate a ramp that begins at 7% CPR in the first month and increases 4.7% CPR per month for 12 months to a maximum of 60% CPR in month 13. Our analysis suggests that speeds remain around 60% CPR for the next 10 months and then decline to about 45% CPR around month 25. The observed prepayment behavior is consistent with the early stages of burnout. In fact, the actual prepayment behavior of the loans without penalties illustrated in Exhibit 22–28 results in a bond factor of 29%, the point at which most agree burnout occurs, in month 22.

Finally, loans that carry prepayment penalties demonstrate a significantly different ramp that begins at 1% CPR in the first month and increases 3.5% CPR per month for 14 months to a maximum of 50% CPR in month 15. At first blush, it seems counterintuitive that the maximum prepayment rate for loans with penalties would match that of the base curve. However, the peak CPR rate is a function of the expiration of the 1-year penalties and reflects pent-up refinancing demand, evidenced by the lower prepayment rates witnessed during the ramping period.

E X H I B I T   22–28

Prepayment Penalty Analysis

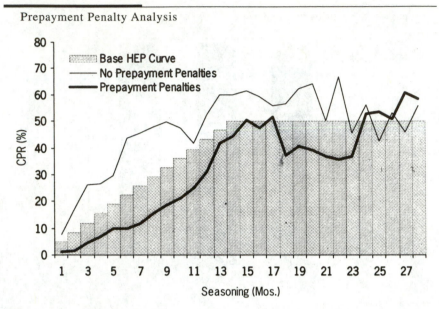

Our analysis suggests that speeds remain around 50% CPR for 4 to 5 months and then decline to almost 35% CPR before climbing again in response to the expiration of 2-year penalties. The actual prepayment behavior of the loans with penalties illustrated in Exhibit 22–28 result in a bond factor of 37% in month 28. Consequently, we expect this pattern to repeat once more as the 3-year penalties expire, but to a lesser degree due to the influence of burnout.

One-Year CMT Loan

One-year CMT ARMs account for 10.2% of Saxon's adjustable-rate portfolio and 4.9% of the total servicing portfolio. Exhibit 22–29 illustrates the 1-year CMT prepayment curve. The 1-year CMT loan type exhibits a prepayment curve that begins at 4% CPR and increases 4.31% CPR per month for 13 months to a maximum of 60% CPR in month 14. Prepayment rates remain around 60% CPR to month 25 and then begin to decline to about 35% CPR. The actual monthly prepayment rates presented in Exhibit 22–29 result in a bond factor of 30% in month 23. Thus, we believe that the 1-year CMT loan type begins to demonstrate burnout beginning around months 23 to 25.

- Single-family loans account for 84.3% of the 1-year CMT loan. As a result, the prepayment curve for this property type closely approximates the aggregate 1-year CMT prepayment curve. However, non-single-family property types demonstrate a shorter seasoning ramp and lower peak CPR rate. Exhibit 22–30 illustrates

EXHIBIT 22–29

The 1-Year CMT Prepayment Curve

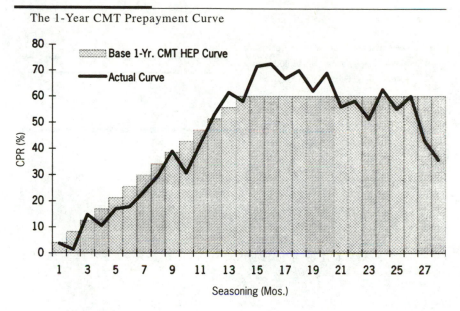

EXHIBIT 22–30

The 1-Year CMT Property Type: Non-Single-Family Loan

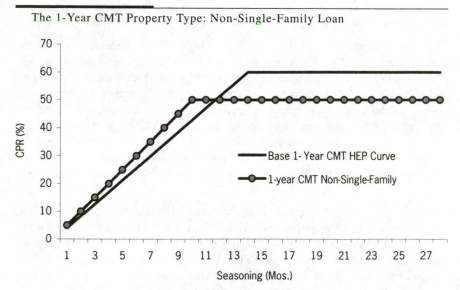

E X H I B I T   22–31

The 1-Year CMT Loan Balance

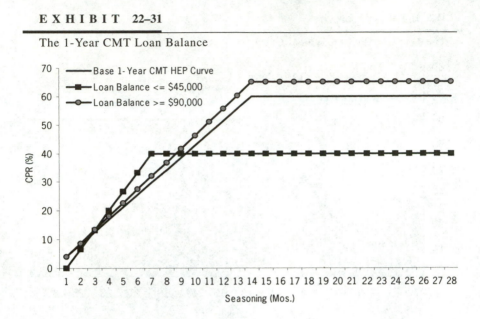

Seasoning (Mos.)

Saxon's 1-year CMT non-single-family prepayment curve. In the case of non-single-family 1-year CMT loans, prepayments begin at 5% CPR and increase by 5% CPR per month for 9 months to a maximum of 50% CPR.

- The loan balance has a significant effect on both the seasoning ramp and peak prepayment rate. This is because home owners who can afford higher-priced homes generally exhibit higher incomes and superior credit profiles than those who carry lower loan balances, all other things equal. Consequently, higher loan balance loans tend to turn over faster, either through trading up or refinancing. Exhibit 22–31 provides an illustration of the 1-year CMT prepayment curve for loan balances less than or equal to $45,000 and loan balances greater than or equal to $90,000. The exhibit shows that lower loan balance loans tend to season faster, peaking at 40% CPR in 7 months. Conversely, higher loan balance loans peak at 65% CPR in 14 months.

- Saxon's adjustable-rate portfolio is underwritten to a high credit quality. Exhibit 22–32 compares the prepayment curve for A-quality loans to the B-, C-, and D-quality loans. The exhibit shows that the B, C, and D loans season to a higher peak CPR rate, 75% CPR, relative to the A-quality loans, 55% CPR. The higher peak CPR rate of the B, C, and D loans is due to the credit curing effect. The credit curing effect results in refinancing activity in the B, C, and D credit domain

E X H I B I T   22–32

The 1-Year CMT Loan Quality

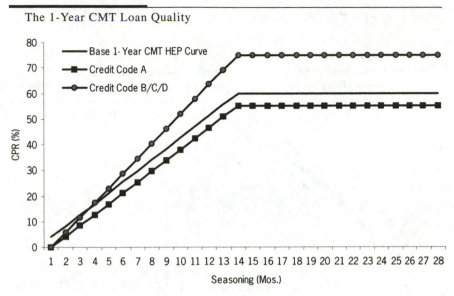

Seasoning (Mos.)

as the lower-quality borrowers' credit improves over time and they ultimately refinance out of the pool.

- The loan purpose also exerts an influence on prepayment behavior. Exhibit 22–33 provides a detailed analysis of the effect of loan purpose on the 1-year CMT ARM portfolio. Purchase money ARMs demonstrate a prepayment curve that peaks slightly below the base curve at 55% CPR. However, refinancing and cash-out refinancing loans demonstrate peak prepayment rates of 65% CPR and 70% CPR, respectively. Two factors contribute to the higher-peak CPR rate of both types of loans. First, borrowers who have refinanced in the past are likely to refinance again given the incentive. Second, the loan stratification by purpose and credit quality shows that a higher percentage of the B, C, and D borrowers take cash-out loans, whereas a higher percentage of A borrowers take purchase money mortgages.

- The LTV also affects the observed prepayment behavior of the 1-year CMT ARMs. Although a lower LTV reduces the probability of default, it also increases the probability of prepayment, either through refinancing or turnover. The greater propensity to refinance is due to the borrower's superior credit position vis-à-vis the significant equity in the home. Consequently, the potentially slower prepayment rates due to lower default rates

E X H I B I T   22–33

The 1-Year CMT Loan Purpose

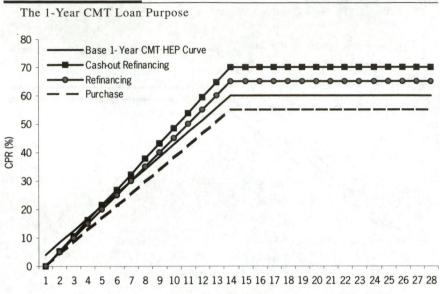

	Loan Purpose by Credit Quality			
	Class A (%)	Classes B, C, and D (%)	Current Balance ($)	Percent
Cash-out refinancing	37.6	47.5	$ 53,261,763	39.6
Purchase	46.1	33.7	58,582,023	43.6
Refinancing	16.3	18.8	22,646,635	16.8
Total	**100.0**	**100.0**	**$134,490,420**	**100.0**

are offset by the above factors. Exhibit 22–34 shows that loans with an LTV lower than 70% reach a peak prepayment rate of 75% CPR. Conversely, higher LTV loans, greater than or equal to 70%, reach a peak prepayment rate of 55% CPR.

The 6-Month LIBOR Loan

The 6-month LIBOR ARMs constitute 28% of the adjustable-rate portfolio. Exhibit 22–35 illustrates the 6-month LIBOR prepayment curve. The 6-month LIBOR loan exhibits a prepayment curve that begins at 5% CPR in the first month and increases 3.8% CPR per month for 13 months to a maximum of 55% CPR in month 14. Observation of the actual prepayments suggests that prepayment rates

The 1-Year CMT Loan-to-Value

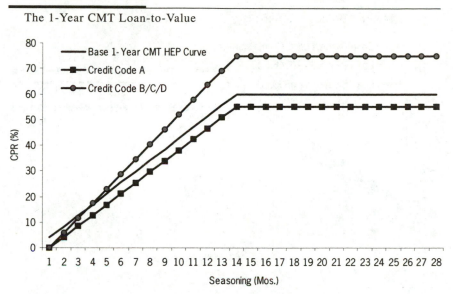

The 6-Month LIBOR Prepayment Curve

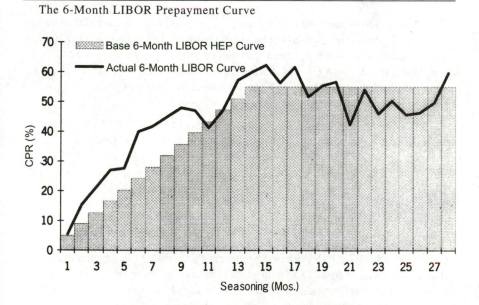

EXHIBIT 22–36

EXHIBIT 22–36

The 6-Month LIBOR Loan Balance

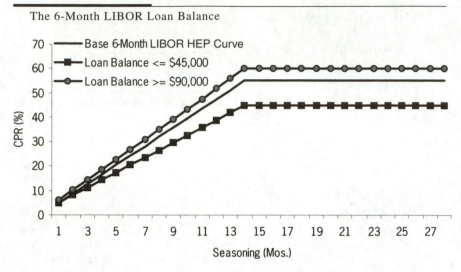

decline somewhat around month 20. We believe that this is in fact the case; however, the loan count drops below 1,000 after the month 24 and as a result, statistical confirmation of the decline beyond the third reset will require another 6 to 12 months of seasoning.

- Single-family loans account for 84.3% of the 6-month LIBOR portfolio. As a result, the single-family property type prepayment closely resembles the aggregate 6-month LIBOR prepayment curve. The non-single-family property type prepayment curve also reflects the aggregate 6-month LIBOR curve. Thus, in the case of the 6-month LIBOR loan, we do not believe that property type exerts a significant influence on prepayment behavior.

- The loan balance does influence the prepayment behavior of the 6-month LIBOR loan types. Exhibit 22–36 shows that loans with a balance equal to or below $45,000 demonstrate a prepayment curve that begins at 5% CPR in the first month and increases 3.1% CPR each month, peaking at 45% CPR in month 14. Loans with a balance over $90,000 demonstrate a steeper seasoning ramp. The prepayment curve begins at 6% CPR and increases 4.1% CPR each month, peaking at 60% CPR in month 14.

- Our analysis suggests that loan quality does have an effect on the prepayment curve of 6-month LIBOR ARMs. The effect of loan quality is prominent during the ramp-up period from 1 to 14 months. However, we believe that loan quality exerts very little influence on the peak CPR realized by 6-month LIBOR ARMs once the loans are fully seasoned. Exhibit 22–37 provides a graphic illustration of actual A and B/C/D prepayment curves relative to the 6-month LIBOR HEP

E X H I B I T   22–37

The 6-Month LIBOR Loan Quality

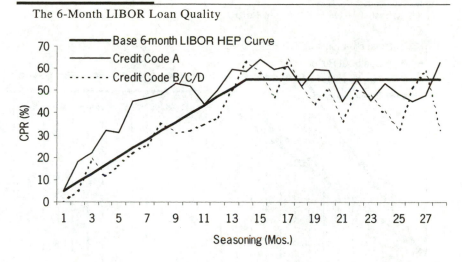

curve. We choose to illustrate actual versus HEP curves for both loan classes in this case because our findings are counter to traditional wisdom. Traditional wisdom suggests that the credit curing effect will result in B, C, and D loans seasoning to a higher peak CPR rate than A loans. Our findings suggest that both loan groups demonstrate a seasoning ramp of 14 months. However, A loans start at 6% CPR and increase 3.7% CPR each month to 55% CPR, and B/C/D loans begin at 0% CPR and increase 3.9% CPR each month to a peak CPR rate of 55%. Thus, our analysis suggests that while B/C/D 6-month LIBOR ARMs demonstrate a steeper seasoning ramp, they do not demonstrate a higher peak CPR relative to A loans.

- Loan purpose exerts a significant influence on the prepayment of 6-month LIBOR ARMs. Once again our findings, shown in Exhibit 22–38, are somewhat contrary to conventional wisdom. Our analysis suggests that the cash-out refinancing 6-month LIBOR ARM prepayment curve begins at 5% CPR and increases 3.4% CPR each month to a peak of 50% CPR in month 14. Normally, we expect to see cash-out refinancing loans season to a higher peak CPR rate than either refinancing or purchase money loans. Exhibit 22–38 shows that 56.8% of B/C/D borrowers take cash-out refinancing loans. Consequently, we believe the findings presented above regarding the effect of loan quality support our findings regarding loan purpose. Loans taken for refinancing demonstrate a steeper and higher prepayment curve. Their prepayment curve begins at 5% CPR and increases 6.8% CPR each month to a peak of 60% CPR in month 9. Finally, purchase money loans follow the general prepayment curve for the 6-month LIBOR loan type.

E X H I B I T   22–38

The 6-Month LIBOR ARM Loan Purpose

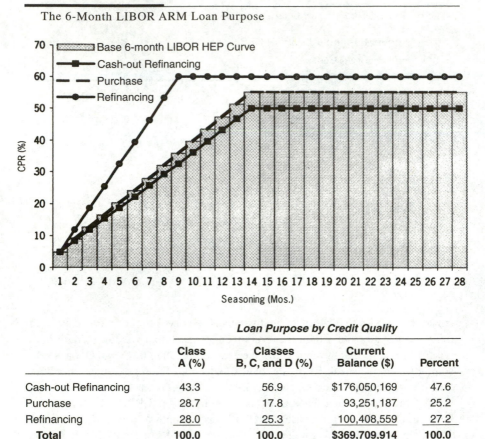

	Loan Purpose by Credit Quality			
	Class A (%)	Classes B, C, and D (%)	Current Balance ($)	Percent
Cash-out Refinancing	43.3	56.9	$176,050,169	47.6
Purchase	28.7	17.8	93,251,187	25.2
Refinancing	28.0	25.3	100,408,559	27.2
Total	**100.0**	**100.0**	**$369,709,914**	**100.0**

- Loan-to-value also affects the prepayment curve for 6-month LIBOR ARMs. Exhibit 22–39 demonstrates that the prepayment curve for loans with an LTV lower than 70% begins at 0% CPR and increases 13% CPR each month for 5 months to a peak of 65% CPR. Loans with an LTV greater than or equal to 70% begin at 5% CPR in the first month and increase 3.4% CPR per month to a peak of 50% CPR in month 14.

- Exhibit 22–40 graphically illustrates the effect of prepayment penalties on the 6-month LIBOR loan type. The exhibit shows that loans without prepayment penalties demonstrate a ramp that begins at 8% CPR in the first month and increases 8.6% CPR per month for 6 months to a maximum of 60% CPR in month 7. Our analysis suggests that speeds remain around 60% CPR for the next 13 months and then begin to decline to around 40% CPR. Once again the observed prepayment behavior is consistent with the early stages of burnout. The actual prepayment behavior of the loans without penalties results in a bond factor of 30% in month 19.

E X H I B I T   22–39

The 6-Month LIBOR ARM Loan-to-Value

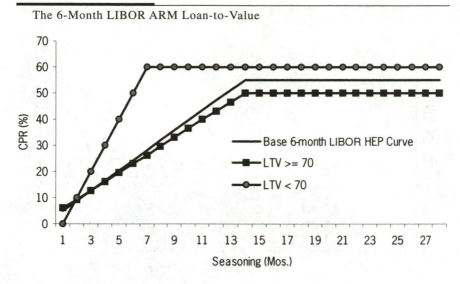

E X H I B I T   22–40

Prepayment Penalty Analysis

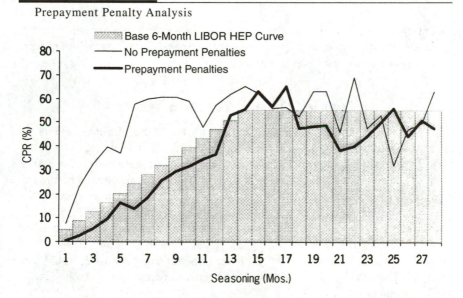

• Loans that carry prepayment penalties demonstrate a significantly different ramp that begins at 1% CPR in the first month and increases 4.2% CPR per month for 14 months to a maximum of 60% CPR in month 15. Our analysis suggests that speeds remain around 60% CPR for about 2 months and then begin to decline to around 40% CPR. A second peak occurs in month 24, reflecting the

E X H I B I T   22–41

Hybrid Loan Type

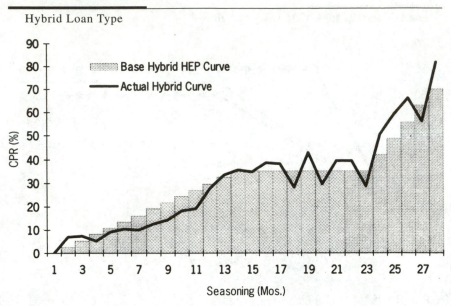

expiration of the 2-year prepayment penalties. We expect this pattern to repeat to a lesser extent when the 3-year prepayment penalties expire, with an even lower peak due to the effects of burnout.

Hybrid 2/28 and 3/27 Loan Types

Hybrid ARMs, types 2/28 and 3/27, account for 61% of the adjustable-rate portfolio. However, hybrid ARMs that have not reached the first reset date account for 58% of the adjustable-rate portfolio. The roll rate analysis presented earlier in this chapter indicates that another 12 to 18 months of seasoning are required before we can directly observe the prepayment behavior of the hybrids and make statistically solid conclusions regarding the prepayment curve beyond 24 months. Exhibit 22–41 provides the prepayment curve to date for the hybrid loan type. The exhibit shows that the hybrids demonstrate a prepayment curve that begins at 0% CPR in the first month and increases 2.7% CPR each month to a peak of 35% CPR in month 14. Thus, the hybrid ARMs appear to behave very much like Saxon's fixed-rate home equity loans.

Principal component analysis showed that prepayment curves by property type, loan balance, credit quality, loan purpose, and loan-to-value ratio demonstrated very little variance from the base prepayment curve. This implies that the first reset date dominates the hybrid prepayment curve for the first 24 months. We believe that the hybrids will assume a prepayment personality similar to the 6-month LIBOR ARMs after the first reset date.

EXHIBIT   22–42

Prepayment Penalty Analysis

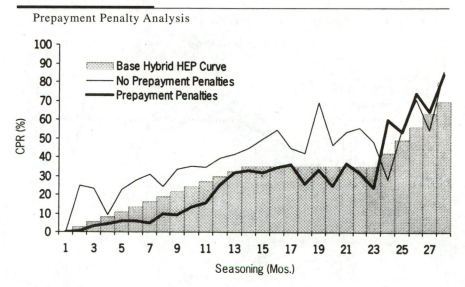

Exhibit 22–42 illustrates the effect of prepayment penalties on the hybrid ARM portfolio. The exhibit shows that loans without prepayment penalties demonstrate a ramp that begins at 0% CPR in the first month and increases 3.66% per month for 15 months to a maximum of 55% CPR in month 16. Prepayment spikes occur between months 19 and 24 as well as in month 28. The prepayment spikes are largely a result of the resets in months 24 and 36.

Loans that carry prepayment penalties demonstrate a significantly different ramp that begins at 0% CPR in the first month and increases 2.30% CPR per month for 13 months to a maximum of 30% CPR in month 14. Prepayment speeds remain around 30% to 35% CPR for 3 to 4 months as prepayment penalties expire and then begin to decline to around 20% to 25% CPR. A prepayment spike is evident starting in month 24. This is most likely due to the expiration of prepayment penalties. We expect this pattern to repeat itself around month 36 as well. Following the reset anniversary for 3-year hybrids and the expiration of 3-year prepayment penalties, we expect the hybrid portfolio to demonstrate a prepayment profile similar to that of the 6-month LIBOR ARMs. Specifically, our expectation is for speeds to decline to around a 35% to 40% CPR.

Gross Margin Analysis

The average gross margin of the ARM portfolio is 5.9%. We stratified the loan portfolio at a gross margin lower than or equal to 4.9%, discount, and greater than or equal to 6.9%, premium, to examine the effect of gross margin on the

EXHIBIT 22–43

Adjustable-Rate Portfolio Gross Margin Analysis

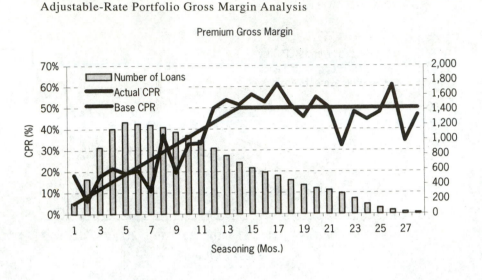

Premium Gross Margin

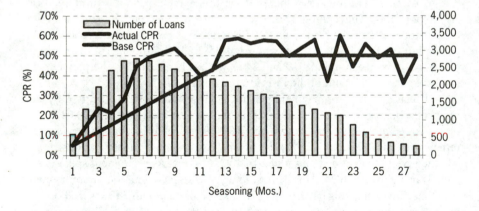

Discount Gross Margin

prepayment curve. Our findings are presented in Exhibit 22–43. Our analysis suggests that the gross margin has a minimal impact on the peak CPR rate. However, the gross margin does influence the slope of the prepayment ramp. Discount gross margins demonstrate a steeper prepayment ramp, peaking at 50% CPR in month 9, whereas premium loan portfolios demonstrate a flatter prepayment ramp, peaking at 50% CPR in month 14.

E X H I B I T   22–44

Loan Type Migration

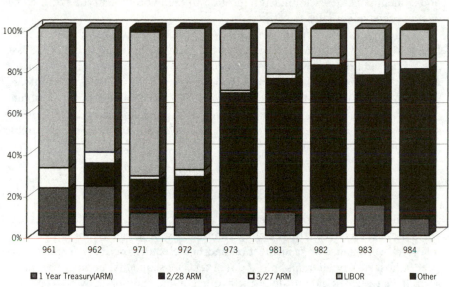

| | 1 Year Treasury(ARM) | | 2/28 ARM | | 3/27 ARM | | LIBOR | | Other |

Conclusions About Prepayments for ARMs

Our analysis suggests that Saxon's adjustable-rate portfolio seasons over a 14-month period, reaching a peak CPR rate of 50%. This is faster than the 30% CPR currently used to price Saxon's adjustable-rate transactions. However, we believe that going forward, the prepayment rates will decline for the following reasons:

First, prepayment penalties do suppress refinancing activity while they are in force. The trade-off to prepayment penalties is a delayed burnout effect. As a result, we expect prepayment spikes to occur around months 12, 24, and 36 after which we expect a full burnout leading to lower prepayment rates on the existing portfolio.

Second, we believe that hybrid ARMs, which account for 61% of the current balance of the existing ARM portfolio, will demonstrate a prepayment profile similar to the 6-month LIBOR loan after the first reset. Consequently, we expect prepayment spikes to occur centered on months 24 and 36, which correspond with both rate resets and the expiration of prepayment penalties. Following these anniversary dates, we expect burnout to decrease the hybrid prepayment rates to about 35% to 40% CPR. Exhibit 22–44 breaks down each transaction by loan type. The exhibit shows that Saxon's product mix has steadily migrated to hybrid ARMs, which carry a high percentage of loans with prepayment penalties. Continued migration to the hybrid loan type will reduce overall prepayment rates.

Finally, when evaluating the prepayment behavior of Saxon's adjustable-rate portfolio, investors must factor in the flat yield curve environment of the last 3 years. In addition, absolute rates have been relatively low as well. From January 1996 to the present, the 10-year Treasury has averaged 5.91%. The maximum rate was 7.01% and the minimum rate was 4.28%. The combination of low absolute rates and a flat yield curve is conducive to ARM prepayments because it offers ARM borrowers the opportunity to refinance into fixed-rate mortgages, thereby locking into cheap long-term financing.

SUMMARY

The home equity market has experienced dramatic changes over the last several years. Lenders have benefited from greater access to the capital markets due to investors' acceptance of securitization and home equity products. This has enticed a host of new entrants into the market. Consequently, competitive pressures have reshaped the profile of the average home equity borrower. The most notable changes are higher average loan balances, higher average credit quality, higher percentage of purchase money mortgages, and lower CLTV ratios. The combination of these factors had led many investors to conclude that both absolute prepayment rates and interest rate sensitivity had increased. The investors' perception was due to the fact that home equity loans began to take on characteristics similar to those of traditional or alt-A mortgages and that pricing speeds appeared to be systemically low. Indeed, Saxon's portfolio, like those of most other issuers, has experienced historical prepayment rates higher than expected at the time of origination.

Saxon Mortgage has responded to these changes by altering its origination practices in the following ways:

• Increased use of prepayment penalties

• Diversification of loan product types for both fixed- and adjustable-rate loans

• Migration away from the highest quality of the subprime market into B, C, and D lending

The cumulative effect of Saxon's underwriting practices will reduce the overall prepayment rate of newly originated loans. Specifically, the increased use of prepayment penalties reduces the interest rate sensitivity of the portfolio and offsets the credit curing effect. In addition, we believe that burnout will result in slower prepayment rates of seasoned transactions. Thus, the overall prepayment rate on both new and seasoned transactions will be slower going forward due to the combination of burnout and the changes in Saxon's underwriting practices.

Also, we have shown Saxon's consistent migration down the credit spectrum into B, C, and D lending. The overall high credit quality of the servicing portfolio is due in large part to earlier lending practices targeted to higher-quality borrowers.

In summary, we believe that the analysis presented clearly shows that Saxon Mortgage has completed its transition from a jumbo loan lender to a home equity lender.

Underwriting Guidelines

	A+	A	A−	B	C	D
Mortgage history	No late payments	No late payments	Maximum of two 30-day late payments in the last 12 months (maximum of one 30-day late payment if the LTV is greater than 85%)	Maximum of four 30-day late payments or two 30-day and one 60-day late payments in the last 12 months	Maximum of five 30-day and one 60-day late payments or four 30-day and one 90-day late payments in the last 12 months	Maximum of six 30-day, two 60-day and one 90-day late payments
Secondary credit	Maximum of two 30-day late payments on revolving credit; one 30-day late payment on installment credit	Maximum of three 30-day late payments on revolving credit; three 30-day late payments on installment credit	Maximum of three 30-day late payments on revolving credit; three 30-day late payments on installment credit (isolated 60-day late payments acceptable)	Maximum of three 30-day late and one 60-day late payments on revolving credit; three 30-day and one 60-day late payments on installment credit (isolated 90-day late payments acceptable)	Discretionary	Discretionary

Bankruptcy filings	Chapters 7 and 13 must be discharged 3 years prior to closing (reestablished credit since the discharge)	Chapter 7 must be discharged 2 years prior to closing; Chapter 13 must be discharged 1 year prior to closing (reestablished credit since discharge)	Chapter 7 must be discharged 2 years prior to closing; Chapter 13 must be discharged 1 year prior to closing (reestablished credit since discharge)	Chapter 7 must be discharged 2 years prior to closing; Chapter 13 must be discharged 1 year prior to closing (good credit since discharge)	Chapter 7 must be discharged 2 years prior to closing; Chapter 13 must be discharged 1 year prior to closing (fair credit since discharge)	Chapter 7 must be discharged 2 years prior to closing; Chapter 13 must be discharged 1 year prior to closing (fair to good credit since discharge)
Debt-to-income ratio	28%–38%	Less than or equal to 80% LTV = 38% to 40%; greater than 80% LTV = 33% to 38%	45%	50%	55%	60%
Maximum loan-to-value	95%	95%	90%	85%	80%	65%

VALUATION TECHNIQUES, RELATIVE VALUE ANALYSIS, AND PORTFOLIO STRATEGIES

CHAPTER 23

VALUATION OF MORTGAGE-BACKED SECURITIES

Frank J. Fabozzi, Ph.D., CFA
Adjunct Professor of Finance
School of Management
Yale University

Scott F. Richard, DBA
Portfolio Manager
Miller, Anderson & Sherrerd

David S. Horowitz, CFA
Portfolio Manager
Miller, Anderson & Sherrerd

The traditional approach to the valuation of fixed income securities is to calculate yield—the yield to maturity, the yield to call for a callable bond, and the cash flow yield for a mortgage-backed security. A superior approach is the option-adjusted spread (OAS) method. Our objective in this chapter is to describe the OAS method as applied to mortgage-backed securities. At the end of the chapter, we apply the method to three collateralized mortgage obligation (CMO) deals.

In this chapter, we describe the theoretical foundations of this technique, the input and assumptions that go into the development of an OAS model, and the output of an OAS model, which in addition to the OAS value includes the option-adjusted duration and option-adjusted convexity. Because the user of an OAS model is exposed to *modeling risk,* it is necessary to test the sensitivity of these numbers to changes in the assumptions.

Valuation modeling for CMOs is similar to valuation modeling for pass-throughs, although the difficulties are amplified because the issuer has sliced and diced both the prepayment risk and the interest rate risk into smaller pieces called *tranches.* The sensitivity of the pass-through securities from which the CMO is created to these two risks is not transmitted equally to every tranche. Some of the tranches wind up more sensitive to prepayment risk and interest rate risk than the collateral, whereas others are much less sensitive.

This chapter is adapted from Chapter 6 in Frank J. Fabozzi (ed.), *Advances in the Valuation and Management of Mortgage-Backed Securities* (New Hope, PA: Frank J. Fabozzi Associates, 1998).

The objective of the money manager is to figure out how the OAS of the collateral, or, equivalently, the value of the collateral, gets transmitted to the CMO tranches. More specifically, the objective is to find out where the value goes and where the risk goes so that the money manager can identify the tranches with low risk and high value: the ones he or she wants to buy. The good news is that this combination usually exists in every deal. The bad news is that in every deal there are usually tranches with low OAS, low value, and high risk.

STATIC VALUATION

The yield on any financial instrument is the interest rate that makes the present value of the expected cash flow equal to its market price plus accrued interest. For mortgage-backed securities, the yield calculated is called a *cash flow yield*. The problem in calculating the cash flow yield of a mortgage-backed security (MBS) is that because of prepayments (voluntary and involuntary) the cash flow is unknown. Consequently, to determine a cash flow yield, some assumption about the prepayment rate must be made.

The cash flow for an MBS is typically monthly. The convention is to compare the yield on the MBS to that of a Treasury coupon security or an alternative benchmark by calculating the MBS's bond-equivalent yield. The bond-equivalent yield for a Treasury coupon security is found by doubling the semiannual yield. However, it is incorrect to follow that convention for an MBS because the investor has the opportunity to generate greater interest by reinvesting the more frequent cash flows. The market practice or convention is to calculate a yield so as to make it comparable to the yield to maturity on a bond-equivalent yield basis. The formula for annualizing the monthly cash flow yield for a mortgage-backed security is as follows.

$$\text{Bond-equivalent yield} = 2[(1 + i_M)^6 - 1]$$

where i_M is the monthly interest rate that will equate the present value of the projected monthly cash flow to the market price (plus accrued interest) of the security.

All yield measures suffer from problems that limit their use in assessing a security's potential return. The yield to maturity has two major shortcomings as a measure of a bond's potential return. To realize the stated yield to maturity, the investor must (1) reinvest the coupon payments at a rate equal to the yield to maturity and (2) hold the bond to the maturity date. The reinvestment of the coupon payments is critical and for long-term bonds can be as much as 80% of the bond's return. The risk of having to reinvest the interest payments at less than the computed yield is called *reinvestment risk*. The risk associated with having to sell the security prior to the maturity date is called *interest rate risk*.

These shortcomings are equally applicable to the cash flow yield measure: (1) the projected cash flows are assumed to be reinvested at the cash flow yield and (2) the security is assumed to be held until the final payout based on some prepayment assumption. The importance of reinvestment risk, the risk that the cash flow will have to be reinvested at a rate lower than the cash flow yield, is particularly important for MBS because payments are monthly and both interest and principal (regularly scheduled repayments and prepayments) must be reinvested. Moreover, an additional assumption is that the projected cash flow is actually realized. If the prepayment experience is different from the prepayment rate assumed, the cash flow yield will not be realized.

Average Life

The *average life* of a mortgage-backed security is the weighted average time to receipt of principal payments (scheduled payments and projected prepayments). The formula for the average life is

$$\frac{1(\text{Principal at time } 1) + \cdots + T(\text{Principal at time } T)}{12(\text{Total principal received})}$$

where T is the number of months.

In order to calculate average life, an investor must either assume a prepayment rate for the mortgage security being analyzed or use a prepayment model. By calculating the average life at various prepayment rates, the investor can gain some feeling for the stability of the security's cash flows. For example, a planned amortization class (PAC) bond's average life will not change within the PAC bands, but may shorten significantly if the prepayment rate exceeds the upper band. By examining the average life at prepayment rates greater than the upper band, an investor can judge some of the PAC's risks. With a prepayment model available, the average life of a mortgage security can be calculated by changing the mortgage refinancing rate. As the refinancing rate rises, the prepayment model will slow the prepayment rate and thus cause the bond's average life to extend. Conversely, if the refinancing rate is lowered, the model will cause prepayments to rise and shorten the average life.

Nominal Spread

Given the computed cash flow yield and the average life for an MBS based on some prepayment assumption, the next step is to compare the yield to the yield for a comparable Treasury security. *Comparable* is typically defined as a Treasury security or equivalent benchmark with the same maturity as the average life of the security. The difference between the cash flow yield and the yield on a comparable benchmark security is called a *nominal spread*.

Unfortunately, it is the nominal spread that some investors will use as a measure of relative value. However, this spread masks the fact that a portion of the nominal spread is compensation for accepting prepayment risk. For example, CMO support tranches were offered at large nominal spreads. However, the spread embodied the substantial prepayment risk associated with support tranches. An investor who bought solely on the basis of nominal spread—dubbed a "yield hog"—failed to determine whether that nominal spread offered potential compensation given the substantial prepayment risk faced by the holder of a support tranche.

Instead of nominal spread, investors need a measure that indicates the potential compensation after adjusting for prepayment risk. This is the OAS that is described later.

Static Spread

The nominal spread is found by spreading the yield to the average life of an interpolated Treasury yield curve or other benchmark. This practice is improper for an amortizing security even in the absence of interest rate volatility because each cash flow should be discounted at its own unique interest rate (i.e., the theoretical spot rate).

What should be done instead is to calculate what is called the *static spread*, or *zero volatility spread*, (Z spread). This is the yield spread in a static scenario (i.e., no volatility of interest rates) of the bond over the entire theoretical Treasury spot rate curve, not a single point on the Treasury yield curve. The magnitude of the difference between the nominal spread and the static yield depends on the steepness of the yield curve: The steeper the curve, the greater the difference between the two values. In a relatively flat interest rate environment, the difference between the nominal spread and the static spread will be small.

There are two ways to compute the static spread. One way is to use today's yield curve to discount future cash flows and keep the mortgage refinancing rate fixed at today's mortgage rate. Since the mortgage refinancing rate is fixed, the investor can usually specify a reasonable prepayment rate for the life of the security. Using this prepayment rate, the bond's future cash flow can be estimated. Use of this approach to calculate the static spread recognizes different prices today of dollars to be delivered at future dates. This results in the proper discounting of cash flows while keeping the mortgage rate fixed. Effectively, today's prices indicate what the future discount rates will be, but the best estimates of future rates are today's rates.

The second way to calculate the static spread allows the mortgage rate to go up the curve as implied by the forward interest rates. This procedure is sometimes called the *zero volatility OAS*. In this case a prepayment model is needed to determine the vector of future prepayment rates implied by the vector of future refinancing rates. A money manager using static spread should determine which approach is used in the calculation.

DYNAMIC VALUATION MODELING

A technique known as *simulation* is used to value complex securities such as mortgage-backed securities. Simulation is used because the monthly cash flows are path-dependent. This means that the cash flows received this month are determined not only by the current and future interest rate levels, but also by the path that interest rates took to get to the current level.

There are typically two sources of path dependency in a CMO tranche's cash flows. First, collateral prepayments are path-dependent because this month's prepayment rate depends on whether there have been prior opportunities to refinance since the underlying mortgages were issued. Second, the cash flow to be received this month by a CMO tranche depends on the outstanding balances of the other tranches in the deal. We need the history of prepayments to calculate these balances.

Conceptually, the valuation of pass-through securities using the simulation method is simple. In practice, however, it is very complex. The simulation involves generating a set of cash flows based on simulated future mortgage refinancing rates, which in turn imply simulated prepayment rates.

The typical model that Wall Street firms and commercial vendors use to generate these random interest rate paths takes as input today's term structure of interest rates and a volatility assumption. The term structure of interest rates is the theoretical spot rate (or zero coupon) curve implied by today's Treasury securities. The volatility assumption determines the dispersion of future interest rates in the simulation. The simulations should be normalized so that the average simulated price of a zero-coupon Treasury bond equals today's actual price.

Each OAS model has its own model of the evolution of future interest rates and its own volatility assumptions. Until recently, there have been few significant differences in the interest rate models of dealer firms and OAS vendors, although their volatility assumptions can be significantly different.

The random paths of interest rates should be generated from an arbitrage-free model of the future term structure of interest rates. *Arbitrage-free* means that the model replicates today's term structure of interest rates, an input of the model and that for all future dates there is no possible arbitrage within the model.[1]

The simulation works by generating many scenarios of future interest rate paths. In each month of the scenario, a monthly interest rate and a mortgage refinancing rate are generated. The monthly interest rates are used to discount the projected cash flows in the scenario. The mortgage refinancing rate is needed to determine the cash flow because it represents the opportunity cost the mortgagor is facing at that time.

If the refinancing rates are high relative to the mortgagor's original coupon rate, the mortgagor will have less incentive to refinance, or even a disincentive (i.e., the home owner will avoid moving in order to avoid refinancing). If the refinancing rate is low relative to the mortgagor's original coupon rate, the mortgagor has an incentive to refinance.

Prepayments are projected by feeding the refinancing rate and loan characteristics, such as age, into a prepayment model. Given the projected prepayments, the cash flow along an interest rate path can be determined.

To make this more concrete, consider a newly issued mortgage pass-through security with a maturity of 360 months. Exhibit 23–1 shows N simulated interest rate path scenarios. Each scenario consists of a path of 360 simulated 1-month future interest rates. Just how many paths should be generated is explained later. Exhibit 23–2 shows the paths of simulated mortgage refinancing rate corresponding

---

1. A risk-neutral, arbitrage-free model of Treasury yields means that at all future dates the price of any long-term bond equals the expected value of rolling short-term to maturity. For more details, see Fischer Black, Emmanuel Derman, and William Toy, "A One-Factor Model of Interest Rates and Its Application to Treasury Bond Options," *Financial Analysts Journals* (January/February 1990), pp. 33–39.

E X H I B I T   23–1

Simulated Paths of 1-Month Future Interest Rates

	Interest Rate Path Number					
Month	1	2	3	...	n	N
1	$f_1(1)$	$f_1(2)$	$f_1(3)$	...	$f_1(n)$	...	$f_1(N)$
2	$f_2(1)$	$f_2(2)$	$f_2(3)$	...	$f_2(n)$	...	$f_2(N)$
3	$f_3(1)$	$f_3(2)$	$f_3(3)$	...	$f_3(n)$	...	$f_3(N)$
t	$f_t(1)$	$f_t(2)$	$f_t(3)$	...	$f_t(n)$	...	$f_t(N)$
358	$f_{358}(1)$	$f_{358}(2)$	$f_{358}(3)$	...	$f_{358}(n)$	...	$f_{358}(N)$
359	$f_{359}(1)$	$f_{359}(2)$	$f_{359}(3)$	...	$f_{359}(n)$	...	$f_{359}(N)$
360	$f_{360}(1)$	$f_{360}(2)$	$f_{360}(3)$	...	$f_{360}(n)$	...	$f_{360}(N)$

Notation: $f_t(n)$ = one-month future interest rate for month t on path n.
   N = total number of interest rate paths.

E X H I B I T   23–2

Simulated Paths of Mortgage Refinancing Rates

	Interest Rate Path Number					
Month	1	2	3	...	n	N
1	$r_1(1)$	$r_1(2)$	$r_1(3)$	...	$r_1(n)$	...	$r_1(N)$
2	$r_2(1)$	$r_2(2)$	$r_2(3)$	...	$r_2(n)$	...	$r_2(N)$
3	$r_3(1)$	$r_3(2)$	$r_3(3)$	...	$r_3(n)$	...	$r_3(N)$
t	$r_t(1)$	$r_t(2)$	$r_t(3)$	...	$r_t(n)$	...	$r_t(N)$
358	$r_{358}(1)$	$r_{358}(2)$	$r_{358}(3)$	...	$r_{358}(n)$	...	$r_{358}(N)$
359	$r_{359}(1)$	$r_{359}(2)$	$r_{359}(3)$	...	$r_{359}(n)$	...	$r_{359}(N)$
360	$r_{360}(1)$	$r_{360}(2)$	$r_{360}(3)$	...	$r_{360}(n)$	...	$r_{360}(N)$

Notation: $r_t(n)$ = mortgage refinancing rate for month t on path n.
   N = total number of interest rate paths.

to the scenarios shown in Exhibit 23–1. Assuming these mortgage refinancing rates, the cash flow for each scenario path is shown in Exhibit 23–3.

Calculating the Present Value for a Scenario Interest Rate Path

Given the cash flow on an interest rate path, its present value can be calculated. The discount rate for determining the present value is the simulated spot rate for each month on the interest rate path plus an appropriate spread. The spot rate on a path can be determined from the simulated future monthly rates. The relationship

EXHIBIT 23-3

Simulated Cash Flow on Each of the Interest Rate Paths

			Interest Rate Path Number			
Month	1	2	3	...	n	N
1	$C_1(1)$	$C_1(2)$	$C_1(3)$	...	$C_1(n)$	...	$C_1(N)$
2	$C_2(1)$	$C_2(2)$	$C_2(3)$	...	$C_2(n)$	...	$C_2(N)$
3	$C_3(1)$	$C_3(2)$	$C_3(3)$	...	$C_3(n)$	...	$C_3(N)$
t	$C_t(1)$	$C_t(2)$	$C_t(3)$	...	$C_t(n)$	...	$C_t(N)$
358	$C_{358}(1)$	$C_{358}(2)$	$C_{358}(3)$	...	$C_{358}(n)$	...	$C_{358}(N)$
359	$C_{359}(1)$	$C_{359}(2)$	$C_{359}(3)$	...	$C_{359}(n)$	...	$C_{359}(N)$
360	$C_{360}(1)$	$C_{360}(2)$	$C_{360}(3)$	...	$C_{360}(n)$	...	$C_{360}(N)$

Notation: $C_t(n)$ = cash flow for month t on path n.
N = total number of interest rate paths.

that holds between the simulated spot rate for month T on path n and the simulated future 1-month rates is

$$z_T(n) = \{[1 + f_1(n)][1 + f_2(n)] \ldots [1 + f_{2T}(n)]\}^{1/T} - 1$$

where

$z_T(n)$ = simulated spot rate for month T on path n
$f_j(n)$ = simulated future 1-month rate for month j on path n

Consequently, the interest rate path for the simulated future 1-month rates can be converted to the interest rate path for the simulated monthly spot rates as shown in Exhibit 23–4. Therefore, the present value of the cash flow for month T on interest rate path n discounted at the simulated spot rate for month T plus some spread is

$$\text{PV}[C_T(n)] = \frac{C_T(n)}{[1 + z_T(n) + K]^{1/T}}$$

where

$\text{PV}[C_T(n)]$ = present value of cash flow for month T on path n
$C_T(n)$ = cash flow for month T on path n
$Z_T(n)$ = spot rate for month T on path n
K = spread

The present value for path n is the sum of the present value of the cash flow for each month on path n. That is,

$$\text{PV}[\text{Path}(n)] = \text{PV}[C_1(n)] + \text{PV}[C_2(n)] + \cdots + \text{PV}[C_{360}(n)]$$

where $\text{PV}[\text{Path}(n)]$ is the present value of interest rate path n.

EXHIBIT 23-4

Simulated Paths of Monthly Spot Rates

Month				Interest Rate Path Number			
	1	2	3	...	n	...	N
1	$z_1(1)$	$z_1(2)$	$z_1(3)$	...	$z_1(n)$	...	$z_1(N)$
2	$z_2(1)$	$z_2(2)$	$z_2(3)$	...	$z_2(n)$	...	$z_2(N)$
3	$z_3(1)$	$z_3(2)$	$z_3(3)$	...	$z_3(n)$	...	$z_3(N)$
t	$z_t(1)$	$z_t(2)$	$z_t(3)$	...	$z_t(n)$	...	$z_t(N)$
358	$z_{358}(1)$	$z_{358}(2)$	$z_{358}(3)$	...	$z_{358}(n)$	...	$z_{358}(N)$
359	$z_{359}(1)$	$z_{359}(2)$	$z_{359}(3)$	...	$z_{359}(n)$	...	$z_{359}(N)$
360	$z_{360}(1)$	$z_{360}(2)$	$z_{360}(3)$	...	$z_{360}(n)$	...	$z_{360}(N)$

Notation: $z_t(n)$ = spot rate for month t on path n.
          N = total number of interest rate paths.

The *option-adjusted spread* is the spread, K, that when added to all the spot rates on all interest rate paths will make the average present value of the paths equal to the observed market price (plus accrued interest). Mathematically, OAS is the spread K that will satisfy the following condition.

$$\text{Market price} = \frac{\text{PV}[\text{Path}(1)] + \text{PV}[\text{Path}(2)] + \cdots + \text{PV}[\text{Path}(N)]}{N}$$

where N is the number of interest rate paths.

This procedure for valuing a pass-through is also followed for a CMO tranche. The cash flow for each month on each interest rate path is found according to the principal repayment and interest distribution rules of the deal. In order to do this, a CMO structuring model is needed. In an analysis of CMOs, a structuring model is needed.

Selecting the Number of Interest Rate Paths

Let's now address the question of the number of scenario paths or repetitions, N, needed to value a mortgage-backed security. A typical OAS run will be done for 512 to 1,024 interest rate paths. The scenarios generated using the simulation method look very realistic and furthermore reproduce today's Treasury curve. By employing this technique, the money manager is effectively saying that Treasuries are fairly priced today and that the objective is to determine whether a specific tranche is rich or cheap relative to Treasuries.

The number of interest rate paths determines how "good" the estimate is, not relative to the truth but relative to the OAS model used. The more paths, the more average spread tends to settle down. It is a statistical sampling problem.

Most OAS models employ some form of *variance reduction* to cut down on the number of sample paths necessary to get a good statistical sample.[2] Variance reduction techniques allow us to obtain price estimates within a tick. By this we mean that if the OAS model is used to generate more scenarios, price estimates from the model will not change by more than a tick. So, for example, if 1,024 paths are used to obtain the estimated price for a tranche, there is little more information to be had from the OAS model by generating more than that number of paths. (For some very sensitive CMO tranches, more paths may be needed to estimate prices within one tick.)

Interpretation of the OAS

The procedure for determining the OAS is straightforward, although time-consuming. The next question, then, is how to interpret the OAS. Basically, the OAS is used to reconcile value with market price. On the left-hand side of the last equation is the market's statement: the price of an MBS or mortgage derivative. The average present value over all the paths on the right-hand side of the equation is the model's output, which we refer to as value.

What a money manager seeks to do is to buy securities whose value is greater than their price. A valuation model such as the one described above allows a money manager to estimate the value of a security, which at this point would be sufficient to determine whether to buy a security. That is, the money manager can say that this bond is 1 point cheap or 2 points cheap, and so on. The model does not stop here, however. Instead, it converts the divergence between price and value into a yield spread measure, as most market participants find it more convenient to think about yield spread than about price differences.

The OAS was developed as a measure of the yield spread that can be used to reconcile dollar differences between value and price. But what is it a "spread" over? In describing the model above, we can see that the OAS is measuring the average spread over the Treasury spot rate curve, not the Treasury yield curve. It is an average spread because the OAS is found by averaging over the interest rate paths for the possible spot rate curves.

Option Cost

The implied cost of the option embedded in any MBS can be obtained by calculating the difference between the OAS at the assumed volatility of interest rates and the static spread. That is,

$$\text{Option cost} = \text{Static spread} - \text{Option-adjusted spread}$$

The reason that the option cost is measured in this way is as follows. In an environment of no interest rate changes, the investor would earn the static spread. When future interest rates are uncertain, the spread is less, however, because of the

---

2. For a discussion of variance reduction, see Phelim P. Boyle, "Options: A Monte Carlo Approach," *Journal of Financial Economics* 4 (1977), pp. 323–338.

home-owner's option to prepay; the OAS reflects the spread after adjusting for this option. Therefore, the option cost is the difference between the spread that would be earned in a static interest rate environment (the static spread) and the spread after adjusting for the home-owner's option.

In general, a tranche's option cost is more stable than its OAS in the face of market movements. This interesting feature is useful in reducing the computational expensive costs of calculating the OAS as the market moves. For small market moves, the OAS of a tranche may be approximated by recalculating the static spread (which is relatively cheap and easy to calculate) and subtracting its option cost.

Other Products of the OAS Models

Other products of the valuation model are effective duration, effective convexity, and simulated average life.

Effective Duration

In general, duration measures the price sensitivity of a bond to a small change in interest rates. Duration can be interpreted as the approximate percentage change in price for a 100-basis point (bp) parallel shift in the yield curve. For example, if a bond's duration is 4, this means a 100-bp increase in interest rates will result in a price decrease of approximately 4%. A 50-bp increase in yields will decrease the price by approximately 2%. The smaller the change in basis points, the better the approximated change in price will be.

The duration for any security can be approximated as follows.

$$\text{Duration} = \frac{P_- - P_+}{2P_0 \Delta y}$$

where
P_- = price if yield is decreased (per \$100 of par value) by Δy
P_+ = price if yield is increased (per \$100 of par value) by Δy
P_0 = initial price (per \$100 of par value)
Δy = number of basis points change used to calculate P_- and P_+

The standard measure of duration is *modified duration*. The limitation of modified duration is that it assumes that if interest rates change, the cash flow does not change. Although modified duration is fine for option-free securities such as Treasury bonds, it is inappropriate for MBS, because projected cash flows change as interest rates and prepayments change. When prices in the duration formula are calculated assuming that the cash flow changes when interest rates change, the resulting duration is called *effective duration*.

Effective duration can be computed using an OAS model as follows. First the bond's OAS is found using the current term structure of interest rates. Next the bond is repriced holding OAS constant, but shifting the term structure. Two shifts are used; in one yields are increased, and in the second they are decreased. This produces the two prices, P_- and P_+, used in the above formula. Effective duration calculated in this way is also referred to as *option-adjusted duration* or *OAS duration*.

The assumption in using modified or effective duration to project the percentage price change is that all interest rates change by the same number of basis points; that is, there is a parallel shift in the yield curve. If the term structure does not change by a parallel shift, then effective duration will not correctly predict the change in a bond's price.

Effective Convexity

The convexity measure of a security is the approximate change in price not explained by duration. *Positive convexity* means that if yields change by a given number of basis points, the percentage increase in price will be greater than the percentage decrease in price. *Negative convexity* means that if yield changes by a given number of basis points, the percentage increase in price will be less than the percentage decrease in price. That is, for a 100-bp change in yield,

Type of Convexity	Increase in Price	Decrease in Price
Positive convexity	X%	Less than X%
Negative convexity	X%	More than X%

Obviously, positive convexity is a desirable property of a bond. A pass-through security can exhibit either positive or negative convexity, depending on the prevailing mortgage rate relative to the rate on the underlying mortgage loans. When the prevailing mortgage rate is much higher than the mortgage rate on the underlying mortgage loans, the pass-through usually exhibits positive convexity. It usually exhibits negative convexity when the underlying coupon rate is near or above prevailing mortgage refinancing rates.

The convexity of any bond can be approximated using the formula

$$\frac{P_+ + P_- - 2(P_0)}{2P_0(\Delta y)^2}$$

When the prices used in this formula assume that the cash flows do not change when yields change, the resulting convexity is a good approximation of the standard convexity for an option-free bond. When the prices used in the formula are derived by changing the cash flows (by changing prepayment rates) when yields change, the resulting convexity is called *effective convexity*. Once again, when an OAS model is used to obtain the prices, the resulting value is referred to as the *option-adjusted convexity,* or *OAS convexity.*

Simulated Average Life

The average life reported in an OAS model is the average of the average lives along the interest rate paths. That is, for each interest rate path, there is an average life. The average of these average lives is the average life reported in an OAS model.

Additional information is conveyed by the distribution of the average life. The greater the range and standard deviation of the average life, the more the uncertainty about the tranche's average life.

EXHIBIT 23–5

Diagram of Principal Allocation Structure of FHLMC 1915

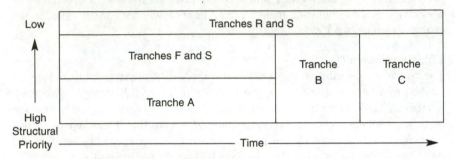

ILLUSTRATIONS

We use three deals to show how CMOs can be analyzed using the OAS methodology: a plain vanilla structure, a PAC-support structure, and a reverse pay structure.

Plain Vanilla Structure

The plain vanilla sequential-pay CMO bond structure in our illustration is FHLMC 1915. A diagram of the principal allocation structure is given in Exhibit 23–5. The structure includes eight tranches, A, B, C, D, E, F, G, and S, and two residual classes. Tranche F is a floating-rate bond, and tranche S is an inverse floating-rate interest-only (IO) bond. Tranches D, E, and G are special "exchangeable bonds" which allow for the combination of tranches F and S. The focus of our analysis is on tranches A, B, and C.

The top panel of Exhibit 23–6 shows the OAS and the option cost for the collateral and the five classes in the CMO structure. The OAS for the collateral is 51 bps. Since the option cost is 67 bps, the static spread is 118 bps (51 bps plus 67 bps). The weighted-average OAS of all the classes (including the residual) is equal to the OAS of the collateral.

At the time this analysis was performed, March 10, 1998, the Treasury yield curve was not steep. As we noted earlier, in such a yield curve environment the static spread will not differ significantly from the traditionally computed yield spread (i.e., the nominal spread). Thus, for the three tranches shown in Exhibit 23–6, the static spread is 83 for A, 115 for B, and 116 for C.

Notice that the classes did not share the OAS equally. The same is true for the option cost. The value tended to go toward the longer bonds, something that occurs in the typical deal. Both the static spread and the option cost increase as the maturity increases. The only tranches where there appears to be a bit of a bargain is tranche C. A money manager contemplating the purchase of this last cash flow

E X H I B I T   23-6

OAS Analysis of FHLMC 1915 Classes A, B, and C*

	Base Case (assumes 13% interest rate volatility)		
	OAS (in bps)	Option Cost (in bps)	Effective Duration
Collateral	51	67	1.2
Class			
A	32	51	0.9
B	33	82	2.9
C	46	70	6.7

	Prepayments at 80% and 120% of Prepayment Model (assumes 13% interest rate volatility)					
	New OAS (in bps)		Change in Price per $100 Par (holding OAS constant)		Effective Duration	
	80%	120%	80%	120%	80%	120%
Collateral	63	40	$0.45	−$0.32	2.0	0.6
Class						
A	40	23	0.17	−0.13	0.9	0.9
B	43	22	0.54	−0.43	3.3	2.7
C	58	36	0.97	−0.63	7.4	6.0

	Interest Rate Volatility of 9% and 17%					
	New OAS (in bps)		Change in Price per $100 Par (holding OAS constant)		Effective Duration	
	9%	17%	9%	17%	9%	17%
Collateral	79	21	$1.03	−$0.94	1.4	1.1
Class						
A	52	10	0.37	−0.37	0.9	0.9
B	66	−3	1.63	−1.50	3.1	2.7
C	77	15	2.44	−2.08	6.8	6.5

*As of March 10, 1998.

tranche can see that C offers a higher OAS than B and appears to bear less of the risk, as measured by the option cost. The problem money managers may face is that they might not be able to go out as long on the yield curve as the C tranche because of duration, maturity, and average life constraints.

Now let's look at modeling risk. Examination of the sensitivity of the tranches to changes in prepayments and interest rate volatility will help us understand the interaction of the tranches in the structure and who is bearing the risk.

We begin with prepayments. Specifically, we keep the same interest rate paths as those used to get the OAS in the base case (the top panel of Exhibit 23–6), but reduce the prepayment rate on each interest rate path to 80% of the projected rate.

As can be seen in the second panel of Exhibit 23–6, slowing down prepayments increases the OAS and price for the collateral. This is because the collateral is trading above par. Tranches created by this collateral will typically behave the same way. However, if a tranche was created with a lower coupon, allowing it to trade below par, then it may behave in the opposite fashion. The exhibit reports two results of the sensitivity analysis. First, it indicates the change in the OAS. Second, it indicates the change in the price, holding the OAS constant at the base case.

To see how a money manager can use the information in the second panel, consider tranche A. At 80% of the prepayment speed, the OAS for this class increases from 32 to 40 bps. If the OAS is held constant, the panel indicates that the buyer of tranche A would gain $0.17 per $100 par value.

Notice that for all of the tranches reported in Exhibit 23–6 there is a gain from a slowdown in prepayments. This is because all of the sequential tranches in this deal are priced over par. If the F and S tranches were larger, then the coupon on tranche A would have been smaller. This coupon could have been made small enough for tranche A to trade at a discount to par, which would have caused the bond to lose in a prepayment slowdown. Also notice that, although the changes in OAS are about the same for the different tranches, the changes in price are quite different. This arises because the shorter tranches have less duration. Therefore, their prices do not move as much from a change in OAS as a longer tranche. A money manager who is willing to go to the long end of the curve, such as tranche C, would realize the most benefit from the slowdown in prepayments.

Also shown in the second panel of the exhibit is the second part of our experiments to test the sensitivity of prepayments: the prepayment rate is assumed to be 120% of the base case. The collateral loses money in this scenario because it is trading above par. This is reflected in the OAS of the collateral which declines from 51 to 40 bps.

Now look at the four tranches. They all lost money. Additionally, the S tranche, which is not shown in the exhibit, also loses in an increase in prepayments. The S tranche is an IO tranche, and, in general, IO types of tranches will be adversely affected by an increase in prepayments.

Now let's look at the sensitivity to the interest rate volatility assumption, 13% in the base case. Two experiments are performed: reducing the volatility assumption to 9% and increasing it to 17%. These results are reported in the third panel of Exhibit 23–6.

Reducing the volatility to 9% increases the dollar price of the collateral by $1.03 and increases the OAS from 51 in the base case to 79 bps. This $1.03 increase in the price of the collateral is not equally distributed, however, between the four tranches. Most of the increase in value is realized by the longer tranches. The OAS gain for each of the tranches follows more or less the durations of those tranches. This makes sense, because the longer the duration, the greater the interest rate risk, and when volatility declines, the reward is greater for the accepted risk.

At the higher level of assumed interest rate volatility of 17%, the collateral is severely affected. The collateral's loss is distributed among the tranches in the expected manner: the longer the duration, the greater the loss. In this case, tranche F and the residual are less affected.

Using the OAS methodology, a fair conclusion that can be made about this simple plain vanilla structure is: What you see is what you get. The only surprise in this structure is the lower option cost in tranche C. In general, however, a money manager willing to extend duration gets paid for that risk in a plain vanilla structure.

PAC and Support Bond Structure

Now let's look at how to apply the OAS methodology to a more complicated CMO structure, FHLMC Series 1706. The collateral for this structure is Freddie Mac 7s. A summary of the deal is provided in Exhibit 23–7. A diagram of the principal allocation is given in Exhibit 23–8.

Although this deal is more complicated than the previous one, it is still relatively simple compared to some deals that have been printed. Nonetheless, it brings out all the key points about application of OAS analysis, specifically, the fact that most deals include cheap bonds, expensive bonds, and fairly priced bonds. The OAS analysis helps a money manager identify how a tranche should be classified.

There are 19 classes in this structure: ten PAC bonds (including one PAC IO bond), three scheduled (SCH) bonds, two TAC support bonds, a floating-rate support bond, an inverse floating-rate support bond, and two residual bonds. This deal contains no principal-only (PO) tranches.

The deal also includes an IO tranche, IA, which is structured such that the underlying collateral's interest not allocated to the PAC bonds is paid to the IO bond, which causes the PAC bonds to have discount coupons (as shown by the lower coupons of the front PACs in Exhibit 23–7). Unlike a typical MBS backed by deep discount collateral, prepayments for the front tranches will be faster because the underlying collateral is Freddie Mac 7s, which was premium collateral at the time this analysis was computed. Thus, with PAC C, the investor realizes a low coupon rate but a much higher prepayment rate than would be experienced by such a low coupon mortgage bond.

Tranches A and B had already paid off all their principal when this analysis was performed. The other PAC bonds are still available. Tranche IA is a PAC IO. The prepayment protection for the PAC bonds is provided by the support or companion bonds. The support bonds in this deal are tranches LA, LB, M, O, OA, PF, and PS. LA is the shortest tranche (an SCH bond), while the floating-rate bonds, PF and PS, are the longest. SCH bonds, as represented by tranches LA and LB, have PSA bands similar to a PAC bond, but they typically have a narrower window of speeds. Also, they are often much less protected from prepayment surprises when the bands are exceeded. The LB tranche, for example, is essentially a support bond, once the PSA bands are broken.

The top panel of Exhibit 23–9 shows the base case OAS as the option cost for the collateral and all but the residual classes. The collateral OAS is 60 bps, and

EXHIBIT 23–7

Summary of Federal Home Loan Mortgage Corporation—Multiclass
Mortgage Participation Certificates (Guaranteed), Series 1706

Total issue:	$300,000,000	Original settlement date:	3/30/94	
Issue date:	2/18/94	Days delay:	30	
Structure type:	REMIC CMO	Payment frequency:	Monthly;	
Issuer Class:	Agency		15th day of month	
Dated date:	3/14/94			

Tranche	Original Balance ($)	Coupon (%)	Stated Maturity	*Original Issue Pricing (225% PSA Assumed)* Average Life (yrs)	Expected Maturity
A (PAC bond)	24,600,000	4.50	10/15/06	1.3	6/15/96
B (PAC bond)	11,100,000	5.00	9/15/09	2.5	1/15/97
C (PAC bond)	25,500,000	5.25	4/15/14	3.5	6/15/98
D (PAC bond)	9,150,000	5.65	8/15/15	4.5	1/15/99
E (PAC bond)	31,650,000	6.00	1/15/19	5.8	1/15/91
G (PAC bond)	30,750,000	6.25	8/15/21	7.9	5/15/03
H (PAC bond)	27,450,000	6.50	6/15/23	10.9	10/15/07
J (PAC bond)	5,220,000	7.00	10/15/23	14.4	9/15/09
K (PAC bond)	7,612,000	7.00	3/15/24	18.8	5/15/09
LA (SCH bond)	26,673,000	7.00	11/15/21	3.5	3/15/02
LB (SCH bond)	36,087,000	7.00	6/15/23	3.5	9/15/02
M (SCH bond)	18,738,000	7.00	3/15/24	11.2	10/15/08
O (TAC bond)	13,348,000	7.00	2/15/24	2.5	1/15/08
OA (TAC bond)	3,600,000	7.00	3/15/24	7.2	4/15/09
IA (IO, PAC bond)	30,246,000	7.00	10/15/23	7.1	9/15/09
PF (FLTR, support bond)	21,016,000	6.75	3/15/24	17.5	5/15/19
PS (INV FLTR, support bond)	7,506,000	7.70	3/15/24	17.5	5/15/19
R (Residual)	—	0.00	3/15/24		
RS (Residual)	—	0.00	3/15/24		

Structural Features

Prepayment Guarantee: None

Assumed Reinvestment Rate: 0%

EXHIBIT 23–7

Continued

Cash flow allocation:	Excess cash flow is not anticipated; in the event that proceeds remain after the payment of the bonds, however, the Class R and RS bonds will receive them. Commencing on the first principal payment date of the Class A bonds, principal equal to the amount specified in the prospectus will be applied to the Class A, B, C, D, E, G, H, J, K, LA, LB, M, O, OA, PF, and PS bonds. After all other classes have been retired, any remaining principal will be used to retire the Class O, OA, LA, LB, M, A, B, C, D, E, G, H, J, and K bonds. The Notional Class IA bond will have its notional principal amount retired along with the PAC bonds.
Redemption provisions:	Nuisance provision for all classes: Issuer may redeem the bonds, in while but not in part, on any payment date when the outstanding principal balance declines to less than 1% of the original amount.
Other:	The PAC range is 95% to 300% PSA for the A–K bonds, 190% to 250% PSA for the LA, LB, and M bonds, and 225% PSA for the O and OA bonds.

EXHIBIT 23–8

Diagram of Principal Allocation Structure of FHLMC 1706*

*As of March 10, 1998.

E X H I B I T 23-9

OAS Analysis of FHLMC 1706*

| | Base Case (assumes 13% interest rate volatility) | | |
	OAS (in bps)	Option Cost (in bps)	Effective Duration
Collateral	60	44	2.6
Class			
C (PAC)	15	0	0.2
D (PAC)	16	4	0.6
E (PAC)	26	4	1.7
G (PAC)	42	8	3.3
H (PAC)	50	12	4.9
J (PAC)	56	14	6.8
K (PAC)	57	11	8.6
LA (SCH)	39	12	1.4
LB (SCH)	29	74	1.2
M (SCH)	72	53	4.9
O (TAC)	70	72	3.8
OA (TAC)	68	68	5.4
PF (Support Floater)	17	58	1.5
PS (Support Inverse Floater)	54	137	17.3
IA (PAC IO)	50	131	0.5

Prepayments of 80% and 120% of Prepayment Model (assumes 13% interest rate volatility)

	Base Case OAS	New OAS (in bps)		Change in Price per $100 par (holding OAS constant)		Effective Duration	
		80%	120%	80%	120%	80%	120%
Collateral	60	63	57	$0.17	−$0.11	3.0	2.4
Class							
C (PAC)	15	15	15	0.00	0.00	0.2	0.2
D (PAC)	16	16	16	0.00	0.00	0.6	0.6
E (PAC)	26	27	26	0.01	−0.01	1.7	1.6
G (PAC)	42	44	40	0.08	−0.08	3.5	3.1
H (PAC)	50	55	44	0.29	−0.27	5.5	4.7
J (PAC)	56	63	50	0.50	−0.47	7.3	6.4
K (PAC)	57	65	49	0.77	−0.76	9.1	8.1
LA (SCH)	39	31	39	−0.12	0.00	1.5	1.2
LB (SCH)	29	39	18	0.38	−0.19	1.3	1.1
M (SCH)	72	71	76	−0.07	0.18	5.9	4.2
O (TAC)	70	69	72	−0.06	0.10	4.0	3.6
OA (TAC)	68	69	71	0.07	0.15	5.8	5.3
PF (Support Floater)	17	26	7	0.75	−0.69	1.8	1.3
PS (Support Inverse Floater)	54	75	49	1.37	−0.27	17.6	17.2
IA (PAC IO)	50	144	−32	0.39	−0.32	1.0	−1.2

Continued

*As of March 10, 1998.

EXHIBIT 23-9

Continued

	Base Case OAS	New OAS (in bps)		Change in Price per $100 par (holding OAS constant)		Effective Duration	
		9%	17%	9%	17%	9%	17%
Collateral	60	81	35	$0.96	−$0.94	2.9	2.5
Class							
C (PAC)	15	15	15	0.00	0.00	0.2	0.2
D (PAC)	16	16	16	0.00	0.00	0.6	0.6
E (PAC)	26	27	24	0.02	−0.04	1.7	1.7
G (PAC)	42	48	34	0.21	−0.27	3.3	3.3
H (PAC)	50	58	35	0.48	−0.72	5.1	4.9
J (PAC)	56	66	41	0.70	−1.05	7.1	6.6
K (PAC)	57	66	44	0.82	−1.19	8.9	8.4
LA (SCH)	39	47	24	0.09	−0.18	1.3	1.4
LB (SCH)	29	58	−4	0.80	−0.82	1.1	1.2
M (SCH)	72	100	41	1.80	−1.72	5.4	4.7
O (TAC)	70	103	30	2.03	−1.74	3.9	3.8
AO (TAC)	68	103	30	2.40	−1.98	5.8	5.4
PF (Support Floater)	17	51	−27	3.11	−2.92	1.0	2.1
PS (Support Inverse Floater)	54	123	−5	4.85	−2.85	20.7	15.6
IA (PAC IO)	50	158	−70	0.45	−0.48	0.8	0.2

Interest Rate Volatility of 9% and 17%

the option cost is 44 bps. The static spread of the collateral to the Treasury spot curve is 104 bps.

The 60 bps of OAS did not get equally distributed among the tranches, as was the case with the plain vanilla structure. Tranche LB, the scheduled support, did not realize a good OAS allocation, only 29 bps, and had an extremely high option cost. Given the prepayment uncertainly associated with this bond, its OAS would be expected to be higher. The reason for the low OAS is that this tranche was priced so that its cash flow yield is high. Using the static spread as a proxy for the spread over the Treasury yield curve, the 103-bp spread for tranche LB is high given that this appears to be a short-term tranche. Consequently, "yield buyers" probably bid aggressively for this tranche and thereby drove down its OAS, trading off "yield" for OAS. From a total return perspective, however, tranche LB should be avoided. It is a rich, or expensive, bond. The three longer supports did not get treated as badly as tranche LB; the OAS for tranches M, O, and OA are 72, 70, and 68 bps, respectively.

It should be apparent from the results of the base case OAS analysis reported in the first panel of Exhibit 23–9 where the cheap bonds in the deal are. They are the long PACs, which have a high OAS, a low option cost, and can be positively convex. These are well-protected cash flows.

Notice that the option cost for tranches IA and PS are extremely high. These two tranches are primarily IOs. An investor who purchases an IO has effectively sold an option, and this explains the large option cost. As long as volatility is low, the owner of the IO will be able to collect the premium, because the realized option cost will be lower than that implied by the model.

The next two panels in Exhibit 23–9 show the sensitivity of the OAS and the price (holding OAS constant at the base case) to changes in the prepayment speed (80% and 120% of the base case) and to changes in volatility (9% and 17%). This analysis shows that the change in the prepayment speed does not affect the collateral significantly, while the change in the OAS (holding the price constant) and price (holding OAS constant) for each tranche can be significant. For example, a faster prepayment speed, which decreases the time period over which a PAC IO bondholder is receiving a coupon, significantly reduces the OAS and price. The opposite effect results if prepayments are slower than the base case.

Tranche H, a premium-priced medium-term PAC, benefits from a slowing in prepayments, as the bondholder will receive the coupon for a longer time. Faster prepayments represent an adverse scenario. The PAC bonds are quite well-protected. The long PACs will actually benefit from a reduced prepayment rate because they will earn the higher coupon interest longer. So, on an OAS basis, our earlier conclusion that the long PACs were allocated a good part of the deal's value holds up under our first stress test.

A slowdown in prepayments helps the support tranche LB and a speedup hurts this tranche. A somewhat surprising result involves the effect that the change in prepayments has on the TAC bond OA. Notice that whether the prepayment speeds are slower or faster, the OAS and the price increases. This result arises from the structure of the bond. The prepayment risk of this bond is more prevalent when

E X H I B I T   23–10

Summary of Bear Stearns 88-5 Reverse-Pay Deal

Tranche (type)	Coupon (%)	Average Live (years)	Balance (millions)
A (PAC)	9.125	2.4	$28.7
B (PAC)	9.250	5.9	30.1
C (PAC)	9.625	10.9	44.4
D (PAC)	9.800	19.7	29.8
E (Support TAC)	9.450	1.1	5.3
F (Support TAC)	9.500	5.9	35.6
G (Support)	9.750	22.2	26.1

prepayments increase sharply, and then soon return to the base speed. This phenomenon, known as a "whipsaw," would adversely affect the OA tranche. Without the use of an OAS framework, this would not be intuitively obvious.

The sensitivity of the collateral and the tranches to changes in volatility are shown in the third panel of Exhibit 23–9. A lower volatility increases the value of the collateral, and a higher volatility reduces its value. Similarly, but in a more pronounced fashion, lower volatility increases the value of IO instruments, and higher volatility decreases their value. This effect can be seen on the PAC IO tranche IA in Exhibit 23–9.

The long PACs continue to be fairly well protected, whether the volatility is lower or higher. In the two volatility scenarios they continue to get a good OAS, although not as much as in the base case if volatility is higher (but the OAS still looks like a reasonable value in this scenario). This reinforces our earlier conclusion concerning the investment merit of the long PACs in this deal.

Reverse-PAC Deal

We have stressed that the OAS analysis helps the money manager avoid the traps inherent in examination of a deal on a static basis. The next deal we look at is the Bear Stearns 88-5 deal, a reverse-pay deal. Although it is an old deal, it highlights this point. The deal is summarized in Exhibit 23–10. It has four PACs and three support bonds, two of which are TACs. The principal allocation diagram is shown in Exhibit 23–11.

Our focus here is on the PAC bonds. According to the average life reported in Exhibit 23–10, PAC D is the longest bond with an average life of 19.7 years. The next-to-the-longest PAC is PAC C with an average of 10.9 years.

How good is the average life as a proxy for the price sensitivity of a bond? Since the average life is a static measure, it does not take into consideration inter-

E X H I B I T   23–11

Principal Allocation Diagram of Bear Stearns 88-5 Reverse-Pay Deal

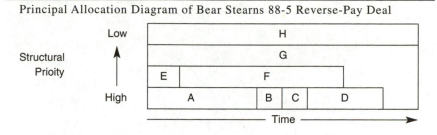

est rate volatility. The effective duration and convexity of PAC C and PAC D are as follows:

	Average Life	Effective Duration	Effective Convexity
PAC C	10.9	6.3	−0.22
PAC D	19.7	5.9	0.04

PAC C actually has a longer duration than the PAC that follows it because it is a reverse-pay structure. OAS and effective duration would show the money manager immediately where the risk is. Moreover, it can be seen that PAC C is a negatively convex tranche.

SUMMARY

Mortgage-backed securities are complex instruments. The valuation model described in this chapter is a sophisticated analytical tool available to analyze MBS. The product of this valuation model is the option-adjusted spread. The results of this model should be stress-tested for modeling risk: alternative prepayment and volatility assumptions.

OAS analysis helps the money manager to understand where the risks are in a CMO deal and to identify which tranches are cheap, rich, and fairly priced. Compared to a sophisticated analytical tool such as OAS analysis, traditional static analysis can lead to very different conclusions about the relative value of the tranches in a deal. This may lead a money manager to buy the expensive tranches and miss the opportunity to invest in cheap tranches.

CHAPTER **24**

ARMs ANALYSIS

Richard Gordon
Director
First Union Securities, Inc.

In this chapter, we outline a seven-step process by which to understand and evaluate adjustable-rate mortgage (ARM) securities. These thoughts are certainly not all-inclusive; there are many other valid methods for evaluating ARMs. However, we believe this methodology provides a sound and consistent framework for the analysis of these relatively complex securities.

STEP 1: IDENTIFY THE BOND

The first step is to identify the salient features of the security. These features include the issuer; the index and coupon formula, or net margin; the underlying collateral's weighted average maturity (WAM); any lifetime caps and periodic caps and floors; and the time to the next coupon reset, or months to roll (MTR).

Issuer

Securitized ARMs are issued by the Federal National Mortgage Association (Fannie Mae), the Federal Home Loan Mortgage Corp. (Freddie Mac) and the Government National Mortgage Association (Ginnie Mae). Although Fannie Mae and Freddie Mac have issued a number of different types and structures, the vast majority have lifetime caps on the coupon that can be paid to the underlying security holder. The flip side is that the rate on the mortgage paid by the mortgagor can never be higher than the life cap. Also, Fannie Mae and Freddie Mac ARMs usually have 2% periodic caps and floors. Therefore the most the coupon can adjust in 1 year is 200 basis points (bps) up or down. Ginnie Mae ARMs have lifetime caps similar to those of conventional ARMs but always have 1% periodic caps and floors. This 1% periodic cap makes a Ginnie Mae ARM a longer-duration security than a conventional ARM with the same coupon. Ginnie Mae ARMs are therefore considered a "bullish" investment among ARM buyers.

Indexes and Net Margin

The index and net margin determine the nominal coupon rate that will ultimately be paid on the security after it is fully indexed. Indexes are based on various types of short-duration money market indicators. The vast majority of ARMs are written using one of three indexes:

- The 1-year constant maturity Treasury (CMT) is the most commonly used index. Approximately 60% of the ARMs outstanding in the marketplace reset off of the 1-year CMT. This rate represents the average yield of an amalgamation of the 1-year government Treasury bills currently trading in the market. Because the Treasury market is highly liquid and yields immediately respond to current news and events, the 1-year CMT index is considered highly responsive, or rate-sensitive. A rate-sensitive index is preferred by bearish investors, who want the coupon to respond quickly to increases in market yields on short-term Treasuries.

- The London interbank offered rate (LIBOR) is also considered a rate-sensitive index. Because LIBOR is a European interbank lending rate similar to the federal funds rate in the United States, it is highly responsive to movements in interest rates. However, few LIBOR ARMs exist. Less than 3% of the outstanding universe of ARMs are indexed off LIBOR.

- The Cost-of-Funds Index (COFI), once widely used, has sharply declined in popularity. Only a few large institutions in the western United States still originate mortgages using COFI. The index's level is determined by averaging the cost of funds at certain banks and savings and loans in the western United States. COFI is a "sticky" index, which means it is far less responsive to movements in interest rates than are the CMT and LIBOR. There are two reasons for this. First, most financial institutions have liabilities for which the average life is a year or longer because savings accounts, checking accounts, and certificates of deposit (CDs) of 1 year or longer constitute a significant portion of the funding side of many financial institutions' balance sheets. Also, financial institutions reprice liabilities slowly and reluctantly when rates rise, relying on their franchise value to retain customers and slow the cost growth of their liabilities in a rising-rate environment. As a result, COFI is a lagging index, and COFI ARMs perform as a cross between an adjustable-rate and a fixed-rate product.

After the index is identified, the margin is added to the index to determine the coupon that the security will pay after it is fully indexed. For example, a 1-year CMT ARM with a margin of 2.25%—or 225 bps—will eventually pay a coupon of 6.92%. This is calculated by taking the 1-year CMT rate (4.67% as of May 4, 1999) and adding 2.25%.

STEP 2: DETERMINE WHETHER THE ARM IS IN A TEASER PERIOD

Many ARMs have low coupons during the first 12 months after origination. This is known as the *teaser period,* and the fact the initial coupon is well below that of alternative fixed-rate mortgages is the incentive for the mortgagor to choose the ARM instead of a fixed-rate mortgage. During this period, prepayments are normally low because the underlying mortgagor has little economic incentive to refinance. Prepayments on ARMs tend to increase sharply as the end of the teaser period draws near and the reset date approaches. Fast prepayments continue for some months after the reset date because mortgagors become aware of the higher rate and seek lower-coupon alternatives. Unless there has been a violent decline in interest rates during the teaser period, the coupon almost always resets higher after the reset period expires. If the teaser coupon is low enough, it may be the case that the periodic cap keeps the security's coupon from resetting to the fully indexed rate. In this event, it would take two reset periods for the security's coupon to become fully indexed. An ARM buyer must be aware of the depth of the teaser and the length of the teaser period, together with any periodic cap restrictions. These factors affect the interest rate risk (duration) of the security.

Hybrid ARMs have the longest duration of any 2% periodic cap conventional ARMs because they have an extended time to the first reset. Hybrids are usually in the form of 3/1, 5/1, 7/1 or 10/1. This means the coupon is fixed for a period of time—for example, in the case of a 3/1 for 36 months. After the initial reset, the coupon adjusts every 12 months thereafter, the same as any other 1-year CMT conventional ARM.

STEP 3: PRICE THE BOND

ARMs are priced at a bond-equivalent effective margin (BEEM), at a conditional prepayment rate (CPR) or at a constant dollar price. The BEEM is simply the yield on the security, assuming a certain CPR, minus the index. For example, we use Fannie Mae pool 342050. This bond has a dollar price of 102–130 and a coupon of 6.81%. Assuming a CPR rate of 20, the yield is 5.65% and the BEEM is 98 bps. The BEEM is determined by the formula: yield minus index—or 5.65% − 4.67% = 98 bps. Whether the bond is offered at price or at BEEM, investors should determine one from the other to fully understand the security being offered and the level of the offering.

STEP 4: USE VECTOR ANALYSIS TO CREATE THE MOST REALISTIC OUTCOME

Vector analysis is used to reflect the dynamic nature of prepayment patterns. Prepayments on ARMs tend to accelerate rapidly before and just after the first coupon reset date. Prepayments then decline gradually as the bond "seasons." Eventually, enough of the underlying pool of mortgages has refinanced that the cash flow variability of the pool has been reduced. Exhibit 24–1, gives an example of the vector we use to analyze 1-year CMT conventional ARMs.

The prepayment assumptions are based on empirical data available in the marketplace. The vector represents a best guess of the most likely pattern of prepayments over time (Exhibit 24–2). The data from which Exhibit 24–1 is drawn is shown in Exhibit 24–2.

The 1-Year CMT ARM Prepayment Vector

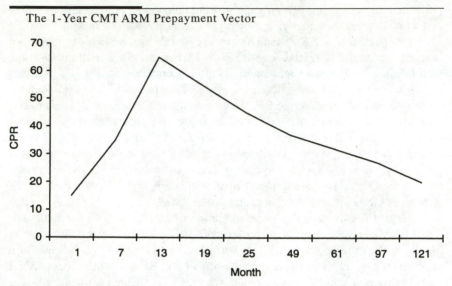

CPR = constant prepayment rate.
Source: First Union Capital Markets Corp.

The 1-Year CMT ARM
Prepayment Vector

Month	CPR
1	15
7	35
13	65
19	55
25	45
49	37
61	32
97	27
121	20

Source: First Union Capital Markets Corp.

To determine the prepayment speed for months that are not shown, we linearly interpolate. For example, the prepayment rate in month 16 is assumed to be 60 CPR. Vectors can also be done without linear interpolation. The vector function on Bloomberg on the yield analysis (YA) screen does not allow for linear interpolation. However, even with these limitations, vector analysis can provide analysts with a more accurate assessment of the inherent value in a given ARM structure.

The WAM of the ARM will determine the point at which the ARM enters the prepayment vector. The 1-year CMT ARM in our example—Fannie Mae 342050, which has a WAM of 255—would be assumed to prepay at 25 CPR next month, based on the prepayment vector.

Applying these principles to this ARM, the BEEM at the vectored prepayment assumption is 93 bps, a level that most income-oriented, short-duration investors would consider acceptable. A savvy investor will determine BEEMs at the offering speed, a vectored speed, and the BEEM at the historical 1-month, 3-month, 6-month and 1-year CPR rates.

STEP 5: USE OAS ANALYSIS TO VALUE
THE CAPS AND FLOORS

ARMs contain embedded options, which must be evaluated to understand the risk or return attributes of the security. The prepayment option should be evaluated using vector analysis. The holder of an ARM security is also "short" a series of periodic interest rate caps and a life cap. The holder is "long" a series of periodic floors. By running Monte Carlo analysis (Exhibit 24–3), the value of these caps and floors can be determined assuming market levels of volatility for pricing. In the case of Fannie Mae 342050, the short-options position adds up to an "options cost" to the bondholder of 6 bps, assuming a volatility of 17%, which is the approximate pricing volatility on caps of moderate expiry (as of May 5, 1999). Thus the cost of hedging the cap risk in the security is approximately 6 bps (note that few investors fully hedge the option risk in the security). A short recap of the results of the Monte Carlo analysis on this security follows.

EXHIBIT   24–3

Fannie Mae Pool 342050

Static spread	93 bps
Option cost	6 bps
OAS (option-adjusted spread)	87 bps

Note: Analysis was run on derivative solutions. Option-adjusted spread (OAS) analysis assumes 17% volatility and the conventional prepayment vector described in the text.
Source: First Union Capital Markets Corp.

The key number in this analysis is the cap-adjusted spread. It indicates the spread investors are most likely to receive over the duration-matched Treasury after evaluation of the various options risks inherent in the adjustable-rate structure. The vector attempts to value the prepayment option, and the Monte Carlo analysis evaluates the caps and floors. Taken together, investors can quickly determine if the level of return is commensurate with the risk profile. By looking at many different securities and structures in this way, over a period of time investors develop a feel for whether securities are "rich" or "cheap" at any given time.

STEP 6: ANALYZE THE CASH FLOW OF THE ARM VERSUS LIBOR

During the volatility in the world markets during 1998 and 1999, investors became well aware of the potential basis risk between the Treasury curve and LIBOR. Because most ARMs are indexed off the 1-year CMT, these securities are especially sensitive to the relationship between short-term Treasuries and LIBOR. Because ARMs—especially fully indexed conventionals—have short durations, they make excellent "carry" vehicles for leveraged investors such as mortgage-backed securities (MBS), Wall Street trading desks, real estate investment trusts (REITs), hedge funds and federal agencies such as the Federal Home Loan Bank. The carry on the position is determined by the spread between the level at which leveraged investors fund the position and the yield investors earn on the asset on a monthly basis. Most leveraged positions are funded off LIBOR, or a rate closely tied to LIBOR. Therefore, the relationship between the realized and expected future yield on the ARM and LIBOR is a critical determinant to the overall market demand for ARM securities.

For these reasons, we look at the spreads over LIBOR that investors would receive given both historical levels of prepayments, as well as expected levels of prepayments. The ARM we have been using as an example is Fannie Mae 342050. Exhibit 24–4 shows the yield on the security at various prepayment assumptions, as well as the carry assuming monthly funding at LIBOR.

In the case of Fannie Mae 342050, the LIBOR analysis shows a favorable profile and trend. Prepayments have been slowing because of the 9-month trend of rising interest rates and the further seasoning of the collateral. The carry on the security is a full 64 bps over LIBOR at the last month's prepayment speed. At the 12-month speed, the carry would actually be below LIBOR. In 1998 when prepayments were fast, many investors experienced negative carry on their ARM positions because of the rapid premium erosion of their holdings. As speeds have slowed, positive carry has returned, as have leveraged investors. Not surprisingly, ARMs have been "bid up," although they are still far cheaper than they were during the first part of 1998.

The final measure we look at is a cap-adjusted spread analysis run using the LIBOR curve instead of the Treasury curve. In the LIBOR curve, the 3-month, 6-month and 1-year spots are given by the yields on LIBOR implied from the price of Eurodollar contracts. The 2-year and out spots are given by the swaps curve. For example, 2-year LIBOR is simply the 2-year Treasury yield plus the

EXHIBIT 24-4

Yield on the Security at Various Prepayment Assumptions

	Yield	Carry over LIBOR[a]
Assuming		
1-Month historical CPR[b]	5.70%	64 bps
3-Month historical CPR	5.34%	28 bps
6-Month historical CPR	5.11%	5 bps
12-Month historical CPR	5.02%	−4 bps
Yield using prepayment vector	5.61%	53 bps

[a]This analysis was run on May 4, 1999. On that day, 1-month LIBOR was 4.91%. LIBOR is quoted on an actual/360 basis. As a source of funding (a liability), 1-month LIBOR is paid on a monthly basis. Therefore, two conversions are necessary to convert the quoted rate on 1-month LIBOR to a bond-equivalent yield (BEY) basis to be directly comparable with the convention used on securities. First, the actual/360 basis must be converted to a 30/360 basis. Next, monthly pay must be converted to semiannual pay to match with bond-equivalent convention. These conversions are worth approximately 15 bps. Therefore, a 1-month LIBOR rate of 4.91% converts to approximately 5.06% in bond convention.
[b]CPR = Constant prepayment rate.
Source: First Union Capital Markets Corp.

swap spread. A LIBOR cap-adjusted spread analysis shows what is "left over" after the cash flow of the security is hedged using a series of interest rate swaps. The caps are "bought back," again assuming cash flow from our prepayment vector. The LIBOR cap-adjusted spread is the remuneration investors can expect to receive over LIBOR after the duration and negative convexity of the ARM security have been neutralized—duration brought to almost zero and convexity flat. When we ran this analysis on our system, the LIBOR cap-adjusted spread on the security was 22 bps. This is comfortably positive over LIBOR and gives some room if prepayments deviate slightly from the assumed vector. Most investors in ARMs go through this or other similar analytical exercises but tend to accept or only partially hedge the embedded optionality in the ARM, preferring to take the carry and accept some of the prepayment and cap risk, as well as the basis risk between LIBOR and CMT. When the risks begin to escalate, they decrease their exposure to the product.

STEP 7: LOOK AT ARMs VERSUS OTHER SHORT-DURATION ALTERNATIVES

Because ARM investors typically manage short-duration portfolios, they must be aware of the relative value of ARMs securities against competing short-duration alternatives. The most common alternatives are short collateralized mortgage obligation (CMO) sequentials and short callable agencies. We can apply the principles outlined in this chapter to compare the relative values of these competing alternatives. At pricing the spread on the CMO was 107-bps/curve at 321 PSA. The pricing spread on the 3NC1 was 56 bps, priced at par. Volatility was assumed at 15%.

E X H I B I T   24–5

Comparison of Short Duration Alternatives

	FNR 93-23 PJ (1.5-year sequential)	FN 342050 (1-year CMT ARM)*	3NC1 (agency)
Yield at			
1-Month spread	5.08%	5.70%	5.58%
3-Month spread	5.14%	5.34%	5.58%
6-Month spread	4.87%	5.11%	5.58%
1-Year spread	5.19%	5.02%	5.58%
Yield at vector speed		5.61%	
Static spread	97 bps	93 bps	56 bps
Options cost	23 bps	6 bps	32 bps
Option-adjusted spread	74 bps	87 bps	24 bps
Effective duration	0.80	0.66	1.93
Effective convexity	−1.20	−0.08	−0.65

*ARM = adjustable-rate mortgage; CMT = constant maturity Treasury.
Note: Analysis completed on May 4, 1999.
Source: First Union Capital Markets Corp.

Exhibit 24–5 shows why short-duration buyers returned to the ARMs market during the first 4 months of 1999. The decline in speeds, coupled with the downward adjustment in dollar prices on higher-coupon ARMs compared with 12 months ago, again rendered this sector of the ARMs market the highest-yielding and the highest OAS short-duration asset. This ARM appears to have value against the short sequential with which it is compared. It also shows a yield assuming a prepayment vector roughly comparable with that of the 3NC1 year agency, but with a far-shorter duration and a higher OAS. This is because of the highly efficient nature of the call option in the agency bond, which drives the OAS of the callable bond lower and creates effective sub-LIBOR funding for the agencies. Agency callables can be used as a shelter from periods of fast prepayments on short-amortizing MBS products because investors can maintain yield by avoiding the rapid premium erosion caused by faster-than-expected prepayment levels. This was the case in the third and fourth quarters of 1998, during which some total-return investors who had previously not been involved in the callable agency market used them as a proxy for MBS to maintain yield while avoiding the prepayment wave caused by the market rally.

CHAPTER 25

TOWARD A NEW APPROACH TO MEASURING MORTGAGE DURATION

Bennett W. Golub, Ph.D.
Managing Director
BlackRock, Inc.

Measuring the duration of mortgage-backed securities (MBS) has been one of the most challenging analytical problems faced by investors in recent years. Reasonable measures of mortgage durations are critical to fixed income investors given the growing size of the mortgage market and the volatility of monthly mortgage total rate of returns (TRRs). In Exhibit 25–1, a histogram of GNMA 8.5 monthly TRRs shows a standard deviation of 130 basis points (bps). Considering that mortgage pass-throughs are among the least volatile part of a mortgage universe populated by interest-only and principal-only investments, support bonds, and inverse floaters, the need for viable risk management techniques should be apparent.

A tremendous amount of effort has been devoted to developing various mortgage risk management techniques, with varying degrees of success. However, given current approaches, even with good duration estimates,[1] mortgage returns will exhibit a significant amount of unpredictability, as seen in Exhibit 25–2. For GNMAs, monthly residuals have a standard deviation of 68 bps! Thus, consistent portfolio management requires continual evaluation of the accuracy of approaches relative to new analytical developments and to changes in mortgage market behavior.

In this chapter, some of the different approaches to solving this problem are reviewed and some possible future directions are explored. First, existing approaches to mortgage durations are reviewed. Then, promising new directions are briefly discussed. Finally, implications for fixed income investors are drawn.

---

1. "Good" estimates are defined later in this chapter.

EXHIBIT 25–1

Distribution of Monthly Total Returns for GNMA 8.5s*

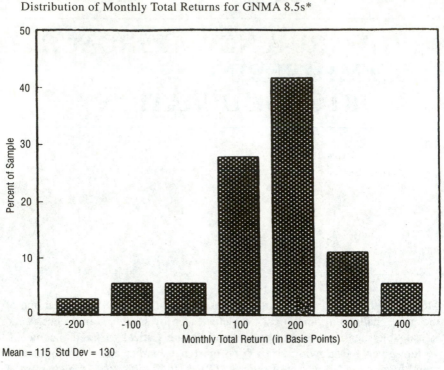

Mean = 115 Std Dev = 130

*April 1990 to April 1993.

EXISTING APPROACHES TO MORTGAGE DURATIONS

As almost all fixed income professionals know, Macaulay is recognized as the first person who thought about explicitly measuring the price risk of a portfolio of bonds. His measure, known as the duration of a bond, is now referred to as the *Macaulay duration* (or adjusted or unmodified duration). Macaulay's simple formula calculates the time-weighted present value of a bond's cash flows. It measures the change in the value of a bond as the discount factor changes 1% (i.e., $1 + r$), meaning that if the yield of a bond with a Macaulay duration of 10 and currently yielding 10% rose 1.1% to 11.1%, its price would drop 10%.

Modified Duration

Most practitioners prefer to think about the price risk of bonds directly in terms of changes in yields (i.e., changes in r, not $1 + r$).[2] Thus, when most people talk

---

2. Robert Kopprasch, "Understanding Duration and Convexity," Chapter 5 in Frank J. Fabozzi and Irving Pollack (eds.), *The Handbook of Fixed Income Securities* (Homewood, IL: Dow Jones–Irwin, 1987).

EXHIBIT 25–2

Distribution of Residuals from Coupon Curve Duration Model for GNMA 8.5s*

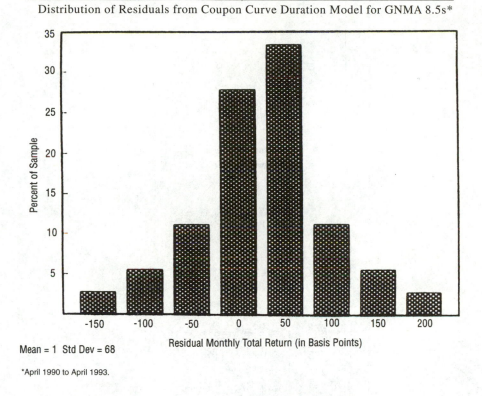

Mean = 1   Std Dev = 68

*April 1990 to April 1993.

about duration, they are talking about modified duration (in units of years). This requires a small modification to Macauley's formula. Whichever methodology is chosen to compute a duration (see below and Exhibit 25–3), the results are almost always interpreted as meaning that a bond with a (modified) "duration" of 10 years would be expected to drop in price 10% if the yield of the bond rose 1%.

For MBS, modified duration is usually computed using an assumed prepayment rate. The prepayment assumption reduces the modified duration that would be computed assuming 30 years of level payments. For example, on October 4, 1993, a 30-year FHLMC Gold 7 would have been projected to have a modified duration of 4.78 years. The same FHLMC Gold 7, if no prepayments were assumed, would have had a modified duration of 10.13 years! As shown in Exhibit 25–3, the modified durations of FHLMC Golds drop dramatically as their coupons increase until the cash flows projected by the prepayment model "burn out." Thus, the lowest modified duration of 1.64 years is found for FHLMC Gold 9s. The modified durations then increase somewhat for 9.5s and 10s.

E X H I B I T 25–3

Alternative Measures of Mortgage Duration

Mortgage Type	Coupon	WAM[a]	Price[b]	Nominal Yield	OAS[c]	Up 50-pp Change in OAS	Down 50-pp Change in OAS	Modified Duration	Pop[d] Duration	OAD[e]	Implied Duration	CCD[f]
FHLMC Gold	6.50%	355	101–17	6.29%	48	–7	18	6.33	4.68	5.14	2.18	3.79
FHLMC Gold	7.00%	350	102–30	6.43%	66	–18	26	5.85	2.79	4.26	3.70	2.37
FHLMC Gold	7.50%	359	103–31	6.49%	92	–26	–15	4.78	1.83	3.96	2.68	1.62
FHLMC Gold	8.00%	343	104–20	5.91%	77	15	–28	3.85	0.42	2.13	1.52	1.02
FHLMC Gold	8.50%	336	105–01	5.15%	49	28	–35	2.32	0.19	1.20	0.73	1.67
FHLMC Gold	9.00%	335	106–12	5.43%	84	–35	14	1.64	0.65	1.52	0.61	2.64
FHLMC Gold	9.50%	325	107–27	5.56%	98	–14	3	1.93	1.06	1.67	0.34	3.10
FHLMC Gold	10.00%	323	109–23	5.58%	101	–3	33	2.14	1.48	1.80	–0.04	2.56

[a] WAM = weighted average coupon.
[b] Price as of October 4, 1993.
[c] OAS = option-adjusted spread.
[d] POP = percent of price.
[e] OAD = option-adjusted duration.
[f] CCD = coupon curve duration.

As is also well known, standard modified duration formulas are not as useful for bonds with embedded options. Macaulay's formulas don't apply when the value of the bond changes because of both changes in the time value of money and changes in the amount and timing of the bond's cash flows in response to changes in interest rates.

To deal with this limitation, four general approaches for determining the duration of MBS have been tried with varying degrees of success. The first approach (and the approach most akin to the spirit of modified durations) is to generate base, up, and down present values (say plus and minus 50 bps) of the MBS cash flows using different prepayment speeds and discount rates. The prepayment rate used would be the one appropriate for the assumed interest rate environment. Given these present values, a *percent of price* (POP) *duration* can be computed.[3] This method is computationally simple, but does not necessarily properly capture the full optionality of MBS and CMOs. Clever CMO structurers quickly learned how to create bonds which had radically different risk profiles outside the modest interest rate shifts used to compute POP durations. POP durations can also be biased to be a little long relative to observed price performance because they implicitly assume that MBS have constant yield spreads as interest rates change. The same 30-year FHLMC Gold 7 would have a POP duration of 2.79 years. As seen in Exhibit 25–3, the POP durations decline very rapidly with increasing coupon until "burnout" occurs. In all cases, they are markedly lower than the modified duration for their respective coupons.

Option-Adjusted Durations

Option-adjusted durations (OADs) were developed to eliminate the first disadvantage of POP durations by explicitly modeling the embedded options in a bond and simulating their expected behavior in different interest rate environments. In the mortgage market, OADs are typically inferred from Monte Carlo type models, which actually subject MBS to a large number of different interest rate paths.[4] First, an option-adjusted spread (OAS) must be computed. In each of many (i.e., 500–1,000) scenarios, a prepayment model is used to project future cash flows. Given these cash flows and discount rates, different spreads can be tested to see what current price they imply. The OAS is the single discounting spread over the appropriate future interest rates of each scenario which is consistent with the current market price of the MBS. Given the OAS, two other yield curves are created, up and down, say 50 bps of parallel shifts. For each of these yield curves, another set of scenarios (i.e., interest rate paths and cash flows) is created and then discounted using the OAS. These option-adjusted values (OAVs) are then taken to be estimates of the price of the MBS in the up and down yield curve cases. The OADs (and option-adjusted convexity) are then computed using these OAVs and the current market price.

---

3. Blaine Roberts of Bear Stearns coined the term POP.
4. David Jacob and Alden Toevs, *An Analysis of the New Valuation, Duration and Convexity Models for Mortgage-Backed Securities* (New York: Morgan Stanley, January 1987).

As seen in Exhibit 25–3, our FHLMC Gold 7 would have had an OAD of 4.26 years. The OADs decline as coupon increases until the 9s. The OADs are longer than the POP durations but shorter than the modified durations for all coupons.

The advantages of OADs are that

1. They explicitly model the embedded options so they are ideal for structured securities like CMOs (where all other methods fail)

2. They do not require price histories that may not exist or do not reflect current market conditions

3. They lend themselves to other types of scenario analyses (such as nonparallel yield curve shifts)

4. At least until recently, they were relatively accurate predictors of future price sensitivity

The disadvantages of OADs are that

1. They are computationally difficult and time-consuming to calculate

2. They are extremely sensitive to the prepayment models used (which are themselves often inaccurate)

3. Recently they have tended to be longer than actual market prices and performance would justify

Implied Durations

A totally different approach to calculating duration, usually called *implied durations,* uses actual historical price data to statistically estimate the price sensitivity to interest rates *actually exhibited* by MBS.[5] Regressions are generally run with historical percentage changes in prices as the dependent variable and changes in the appropriate Treasury yield as the independent variable. The coefficient of the change in Treasury yield is the implied duration.

Our FHLMC Gold 7s would have had an implied duration of 3.7 years measured over the last 6 months. It is difficult to determine a consistent pattern of the implied durations shown in Exhibit 25–3 with respect to both the coupon of the MBS and the other duration measures.

The advantages of implied durations are that

1. These estimates of interest rate risk do not rely upon any theoretical formulas or analytical assumptions

2. They are very simple to compute

3. All they require are some reasonably accurate price series

---

5. See Paul DeRosa, Laurie Goodman, and Mike Zazzarino, "Duration Estimates of Mortgage-Backed Securities," *Journal of Portfolio Management* (Winter 1993), pp. 32–38.

The disadvantages of implied durations are that

1. Good price data is not always available, either because of thin markets or because investors often purchase and then hold fixed income securities directly purchased from the primary market

2. Without imposing some information about the structure of the options embedded in a bond, an implied duration may significantly differ from the actual prospective price risk of the bond

3. Price history may lag current market conditions, especially after there has been a sharp and sustained shock to interest rates

4. Spread volatility can cloud the impact of interest rates on changes in bond prices

Coupon Curve Durations

Coupon curve durations (CCDs) represent yet another completely different approach to measuring duration.[6] They are perhaps the simplest durations to calculate. All they require is the coupon curve of prices for similar MBS. Roughly speaking, if interest rates decrease 50 bps, the market price of a GNMA 7 should rally to the current price of a GNMA 7.5. Similarly, if rates rise 50 bps, the price of a GNMA 7 should decline to the current price of a GNMA 6.5. Thus, the CCD (and coupon curve convexity) for similarly aged MBS can be determined.

Our FHLMC Gold 7 had a CCD of 2.37 years. The CCDs in Exhibit 25–3 are shorter for the lower-coupon MBS than the OADs but longer for the higher coupons.

The advantages of CCDs are that

1. They are simple

2. Based upon BlackRock's testing, they are relatively accurate

3. They reflect the market's current expectations

The disadvantages of CCDs are that

1. They can only be applied to fairly generic MBS that are well-priced (technically speaking, they only make sense for MBS with similar WAMs)

2. The approach cannot be extended to CMOs since no two tranches can be easily compared to each other

---

6. The only published reference to CCDs found by the author is Douglas Breeden, "Risk, Return, and Hedging of Fixed-Rate Mortgages," *Journal of Fixed Income* (September 1991). He called them "roll-up, roll-down elasticities" and performed analyses of the accuracy of the approach over the sample period January 1979 to December 1990.

EXHIBIT 25–4

Durations for GNMA 8.5s

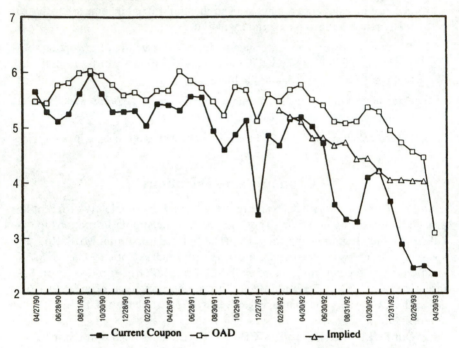

— Current Coupon   —□— OAD   —△— Implied

Historical Stability

These methods diverge at a fixed point in time, as shown in Exhibit 25–3. As shown in Exhibit 25–4, the relationship between these different approaches to measuring duration has itself been quite volatile. OADs and CCDs closely tracked each other from April 1990 through October 1991, with CCDs generally being slightly lower. CCDs then began to fall rather dramatically. At one point in the fall of 1993, the CCD was over 2 years shorter than the OAD. Implied durations, which appear in Exhibit 25–4 after February 1992, tended to run between the OAD and CCD.

FUTURE APPROACHES TO MORTGAGE DURATIONS

Since all the above approaches have both advantages and disadvantages, investors continue to search for a better way. A better way will be accurate, easy, extensible to new issues or to securities which are difficult to price, and reflective of current conditions in the marketplace.

Currently, at least three alternative approaches to estimating mortgage durations are being explored by practitioners: (1) market-implied corrections to existing prepayment models,[7] (2) market-implied prepayment models, and (3) estimation of the relationships between OAS and the characteristics of an MBS in different interest rate scenarios.[8] Unfortunately, it is unrealistic to assume that an approach that solves all the problems of existing methods will be easy.

Market-Implied Corrections

Empirical tests tell us that the CCDs are quite accurate when they are available. Suppose we could somehow adjust our prepayment model so that it better fits the CCDs when run through the simulation model used to compute OADs? If this could be done, the model would be better calibrated so that it would properly predict the duration for generic MBS and, therefore, do a better job of predicting the duration of CMOs. This calibration would be similar in spirit to the procedures currently used to make sure that callable bond models correctly reprice Treasury bonds.

Market-Implied Prepayment Models

If we take the above market-implied corrections approach to its logical extreme, the entire prepayment function might be implied from the marketplace. Other than imposing a basic structure on the "market-implied prepayment model" that would include reasonably stable elements such as seasonality, prepayments that are not sensitive to interest rate changes, a flexible "S-curve" structure for refinancings, and a plausibly shaped burnout function, market prices could tell us what the market is assuming about future prepayments. With this approach, it might not even be necessary to worry about "spreads" because cash flows could be valued based upon their underlying credit. Assuming that decent market prices are available for a range of coupons and WAMs, there should be adequate information available to infer the implied prepayment model.

Estimation of OAS Functions

A less radical approach to improving OADs might be to try to somehow estimate a relationship between OAS and interest rates for a given security. Traditional OAD calculations assume that OAS remains constant in the up and down cases. This is often inconsistent with the marketplace. In October 1993, OAS increased with pass-through coupon, then fell, and then rose again. Exhibit 25–3 shows the OAS changes implied by the current market prices in the up-50-bp and down-50-bp cases for each coupon. In November 1994, the pattern reversed with OASs falling with coupon and then rising with the high coupons.

Moreover, although this approach might be workable for pass-throughs, it would require quite a bit of subtlety to be extensible to CMOs. Since CCDs can

7. Richard Klotz and A. Shapiro, *Dealing with Streamlined Refinanced: A New Implied Prepayment Model* (New York: Merrill Lynch, 1994).
8. Ravi Sobti, *What Is the "Correct" Duration for MBS?* (New York: Donaldson, Lukfin & Jenrette, 1994).

already be computed for pass-throughs, this approach will make sense only if a reasonable method can be found to extend it to CMOs.

IMPLICATIONS FOR INVESTORS

Given this saga of mortgage durations, how should investors respond to the above strengths and weaknesses of existing approaches and new future directions? Is the problem unsolvable or are more sophisticated solutions within reach that will better tame mortgage risk? The prudent answer is for investors and investment managers to proceed forward cautiously with an active program of reconciling predicted performance with actual performance. Even the best methods will be imperfect and subject to future revision.

Efforts are under way to implement these concepts to create newer and better tools for managing these risks. Keeping pace with changes in the mortgage market will be critical to achieving portfolio objectives. Investors today know a tremendous amount about mortgage securities and continue to improve their techniques. Going forward, actual performance versus projected performance needs to be carefully monitored so that large discrepancies can be quickly identified and portfolios restructured in a timely fashion.

CHAPTER **26**

DURATION AND CONVEXITY DRIFT OF CMOs

David P. Jacob
Managing Director and Head of Research and Structuring
Nomura Securities International, Inc.

Sean Gallop

Joshua R. Phillips
Vice President
Nomura Securities International, Inc.

Duration and convexity are the standard measures of the price sensitivity of fixed income instruments. They are used to compare the relative risk of bonds and portfolios and to help investors look for relative value by enabling them to classify bonds with similar risk profiles. Total rate of return managers often use duration to position their portfolios relative to the major bond indices, and asset-liability managers use these measures to control risk by matching the duration and convexity characteristics of their assets to those of their liabilities.

Duration and convexity are, of course, only summary measures of a security's sensitivity to instantaneous changes in interest rates. They do not provide insight into how a bond's characteristics will change over time. It is important, however, for both the asset-liability manager and the total rate of return manager to know in advance how a security's characteristics can evolve.

For example, an insurance company might use duration and convexity to set up a portfolio of mortgage-backed securities or corporate bonds to back its GIC portfolio. The insurer would like to remain matched so as to minimize the need to rebalance, which would result in increased transaction costs and potential negative impact on surplus. However, simply being matched at the onset does not ensure that the book remains matched. In fact, unless the manager perfectly matches the cash flows of the assets and liabilities at the beginning for all future interest rate environments, the duration of the assets and liabilities will inevitably drift apart. The question is how much and how quickly this drift or mismatch will arise. Knowing this beforehand is important for proper management. As we will see, for CMOs, the evolution of the characteristics are sometimes not so obvious.

Alternatively, consider the case of the total rate of return manager who matches the duration, and, perhaps, the convexity of her portfolio with that of

---

Sean Gallop was employed at Nomura Securities International when he coauthored this chapter.

some index, and attempts to outperform the index by loading up with bonds that appear to offer substantial up-front yield. If, at the end of the performance measurement period, the price sensitivity characteristics of these bonds have changed substantially (for example, their duration has increased and they are more negatively convex), the market will likely price these bonds at wider spreads, and thus hurt the performance of these securities. For Treasury securities and noncallable corporates this is not a problem, since the duration of bonds with periodic, non-interest-sensitive cash flows, for the most part, decline in a well-defined and predictable manner as time passes. As a result, experienced portfolio managers either intuitively know or can readily calculate how the duration and convexity of these types of bonds change as time passes.

Unlike Treasuries, however, mortgage-backed securities (MBS) and their derivatives can exhibit very different, and at first, often nonintuitive price sensitivity characteristics at the performance horizon. Moreover, for many MBS, the horizon characteristics will be a function of not just the ending interest rate environment, but of what occurs during the holding period as well. For the asset-liability manager, this could necessitate unexpected portfolio rebalancing, and for the total rate of return manager, inferior performance under certain scenarios. For MBS, the degree to which price sensitivity characteristics improve or deteriorate over time is determined by such factors as prepayment assumptions, yield curve shapes and levels, and liquidity, and for CMOs, structural considerations.

The major conclusion reached in this chapter is that using current price sensitivity characteristics such as duration and convexity as a basis for estimating performance or anticipating the cash flow characteristics of MBS can be misleading. Investors must assess the current performance characteristics as well as how these characteristics change over time. They should not rely on their intuition derived from traditional bonds. We believe that by using an analytic framework that anticipates a security's horizon characteristics, the investor can more readily distinguish between bonds that appear to offer good value from ones that actually do.

REVIEW OF DURATION AND CONVEXITY FOR TREASURIES

Before discussing the unusual evolution of the duration and convexity of CMO bonds, we first quickly review this evolution for an ordinary Treasury note.

Consider the 5.00 of February 15, 2011, which, on March 6, 2001, was offered at 100-6+ to yield 4.973%. Its modified duration was computed to be 7.74 years. One year forward, assuming the same yield, its duration is 7.12 years. In fact, for a 100–basis point (bp) shift up or down in the horizon yield, the duration will vary by no more than 0.11 years. Similar stability would be computed for the convexity. Thus, an asset-liability manager can readily tell how this bond's price sensitivity characteristics change, and therefore anticipate the potential drift between the duration of this bond and that of a liability payment due 7.7 years. Similarly, a manager interested in computing horizon returns can do so easily because he knows that the bond at the horizon will be 1 year shorter in maturity and roughly half a year shorter in duration. Thus, the horizon price can be computed using an appropriate yield.

EVOLUTION OF DURATION AND CONVEXITY FOR CMOs

Consider instead the bonds shown in Exhibit 26–1, which were selected from a recently issued CMO. In this FNMA deal the collateral was 9.5%, and the pricing speed was 165 PSA. Exhibit 26–1 contains the usual information supplied to the portfolio manager by a dealer, or which might have been obtained from an information service.

Both bonds are planned amortization class (PAC) bonds with average lives (at the pricing speed of 165) of approximately three years. As a result, they are priced at spreads off the 3-year Treasury. The first bond is a standard 3-year PAC bond, whereas the second is a PAC II, since its average life is protected for a tighter range of PSA and its principal amortization is junior to that of the first bond. The second column shows the spread off the 3-year Treasury. The next two columns show the first and last principal payment dates. The following column shows the PSA bands for which the average life is constant. The PAC is protected from 90 to 380 PSA, whereas the PAC II is only protected from 140 to 250 PSA. Since the collateral to date has been prepaying at 125 PSA, we show the average life at some speeds below the original pricing speed of 165 PSA. The last three columns in Exhibit 26–1 show that even at the slower speeds, the average lives remain the same for the first bond. This is because 105 PSA and 125 PSA are still within its PAC band. However, the average life of the second bond, at 125 PSA, extends to 4.6 years and, at 105 PSA, it extends to 7.6 years. Since these slower speeds are outside the lower band, the extension in average life is expected.

Most managers stop at this point and try to decide whether the extra 54 bps provided by the PAC II is sufficient to compensate them for the potential adverse average life variability (i.e., negative convexity). We return to this point later. At this juncture we would like to analyze what happens to the average life, and the average life sensitivity as time passes.

Exhibit 26–2 describes how this evolution takes place for the simplest scenario. The exhibit shows the expected average life and sensitivity for each bond at pricing as well as 1 year forward and 2 years forward. The first row repeats the numbers from Exhibit 26–1. For example, at pricing, the 3-year PAC has a 2.8-year

E X H I B I T   26–1

The 3-Year PAC Bonds

		First Pay (Month)	Last Pay (Month)	PAC Band	Average Life at PSA*		
	Spread				105	125	165
PAC	66 bp	15	27	90–380	2.8	2.8	2.8
PAC	120 bp	1	162	140–250	7.6	4.6	3.1

*Public Securities Associations.

EXHIBIT 26–2

Evolution of Average Life and Average Life Sensitivity

	The 3-Year PAC		
	PSA 105	PSA 125	PSA 165
Current	2.8	2.8	2.8
One Year forward	1.8	1.8	1.8
Two Years forward	0.8	0.8	0.8
	Level 2 PAC		
	PSA 105	PSA 125	PSA 165
Current	7.6	4.6	3.1
One Year forward	8.9	5.2	3.1
Two Years forward	9.5	5.7	3.3

average life at each of the three PSA speeds listed. In the second row we show the average life and how it varies at the end of the first year, assuming that for the first year the collateral paid at 125 PSA and thereafter at 105, 125, or 165 PSA. For the 3-year PAC, we see that after 1 year has passed the average life has shrunk by 1 year from 2.8 years to 1.8 years. This is as expected, since, as indicated in Exhibit 26–1, principal does not begin paying until month 15. Moreover, even if from the end of the first year forward the speed changes up to 165 PSA or down to 105 PSA, the expected average life would still be 1.8 years.

However, the PAC II paints a different picture. As before, the second row shows the average life and how it varies 1 year out, assuming that during the first year the collateral pays at a 125 PSA. The surprising result is that not only does the average life increase from 4.6 years to 5.2 years, but the sensitivity increases as well. Now, the average life can increase by 3.7 years if speeds decrease to 105 PSA, and can decrease by 2.1 years if speeds increase to 165 PSA. The third row shows the situation 2 years out, assuming 125 PSA for the first 2 years. The average life and average life sensitivity continue to increase. Since higher prepayment speeds are usually associated with lower interest rates, this security has not only increased in duration as time has passed, it has also become more negatively convex!

Exhibit 26–3 shows how the average life evolves for each of the bonds for their entire lives for level 105, 125, and 165 PSA scenarios. For example, from the graph in the foreground one can see how the average life under a 105 PSA scenario first increases and then decreases for the PAC II, whereas for the PAC, the decline is linear.

E X H I B I T   26–3

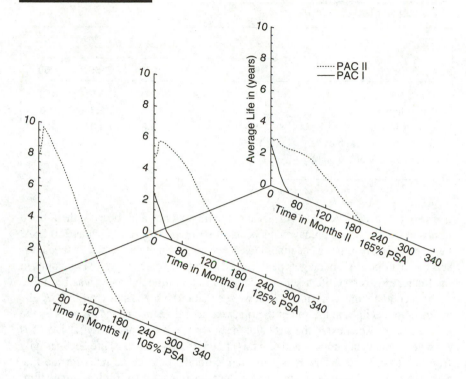

Before we examine why such behavior occurs, we note that this example demonstrates how unexpectedly average life can change given a very simple tranche from a very simple deal under a very simple scenario. One can expect even more dramatic effects as the complexity of the deal and realism of the analysis increase. For example, it is entirely possible to find a bond, which for two different scenarios, has two radically different durations and convexities.

As an example, consider a support bond from another recent deal. This deal contains a Z bond[1] that jumps in front of the support bond if the speed on the FNMA 9.0% collateral exceeds the pricing speed of 155 PSA. The first row of Exhibit 26–4 shows the average life at pricing for speeds ranging from 90 to 200 PSA. Since this bond is a support and is thus junior to the PACs in the deal, its expected average life at pricing declines from 9.5 to 3.0 years as speeds increase

---

1. A *Z bond* is one that accrues rather than pays its interest until other bonds in the deal have been retired. A *jump Z* is one that, based on some event, stops accruing and begins paying interest and principal.

E X H I B I T   26–4

Evolution of Average Life

	PSA				
	90	**125**	**155**	**165**	**200**
Current	9.5	4.9	3.0	3.5	2.5
1 year forward	8.8	4.2	2.3	2.8	1.8
5 years forward	8.4	4.1	2.2	4.0	2.2
5 years forward (with spike to 165 PSA for 1 month)	12.6	8.2	4.7	4.0	2.2

from 90 to 155 PSA. At 165 PSA, its average life extends a bit because the Z bond jumps in front of it. As prepayments occur at still higher speeds such as 200 PSA, the average life resumes its decline. This is because ultimately the higher speed offsets the fact that the Z bond gets paid first. The other rows show, at several points in the future, the average life assuming that prior to that time the speed was 125 PSA. In the second column of Exhibit 26–4, we see that if the speed stays at 125 PSA, the average life declines at the end of the first year to 4.2 years, and to 4.1 years by the end of 5 years. The next to the last column shows that if the speed stays at 125 PSA for 5 years and then jumps to and remains at 165 PSA, the average life declines only from 4.9 to 4.0 years. This is because the Z bond's balance accretes for the first 5 years, so that when it does jump it has a greater impact than if it had jumped immediately. As a result, the effect of the jump offsets the higher speeds.

Now suppose, instead of the relatively simple scenarios shown in the first three rows of Exhibit 26–4, the speed starts at 125 PSA, remains there for 5 years, then jumps for 1 month to 165 PSA, and finally returns to either 90, 125, 155, 165, or 200 PSA. The expected average life at that point becomes 12.6, 8.2, 4.7, 4.0, or 2.2 years, respectively. It is incredible that this 1-month jump could cause this bond's horizon average life and average life sensitivity to be so radically different from that at the beginning or from that 5 years out, where there was no 1-month spike to 165 PSA. Most analyses ignore the horizon characteristics, particularly for complicated scenarios. All the investor is likely to have seen would be the initial average life table and/or price yield table, neither of which inform her of the possibility of this behavior, let alone explaining why it could happen.

IMPLICATIONS FOR PERFORMANCE AND RISK MANAGEMENT

Given that the price sensitivity of a bond affects the spread at which it trades, one can imagine that the implications for performance and risk management can be substantial. Price sensitivity characteristics of a bond affect the spread at which it trades. Typically, for the same average life, spreads widen as negative convexity increases. Also, everything else equal, the greater the average life, the wider the

E X H I B I T   26–5

Current Generic CMO Spreads

	2 Year	3 Year	4 Year	5 Year	7 Year	10 Year	20 Year
PAC	115	125	130	135	155	160	143
Sequential	153	160	165	174	178	180	152
PAC II	190	195	200	210	200	195	170

E X H I B I T   26–6

Yield and Average Life at Different PSA Speeds for 3-year PAC and PAC II Bonds

			Yield and Average Life					
	Price	Coupon	105 PSA	125 PSA	165 PSA	OAS	Duration	Convexity
PAC	103–14	9.375	7.82/2.8	7.82/2.8	7.82/2.8	62	2.5	7
PAC II	102–12	9.500	9.14/7.6	8.69/4.6	8.35/3.1	52	2.7	−69

	Theoretical CMO Spreads and Treasury Yield Curve						
	2 Year	3 Year	4 Year	5 Year	7 Year	10 Year	20 Year
PAC	59	66	76	84	87	93	105
PAC II	110	120	124	130	134	139	143
Treasury yields	6.84	7.15	7.36	7.75	7.98	8.11	8.20

spread. Exhibit 26–5 shows recent generic CMO spreads for PAC bonds, Sequential bonds, and PAC II's at increasing average lives. One can see that, in general, the bonds that are the shortest and have the most protection, such as the 2-year PACs, trade at the tightest spreads, and the longer, more negatively convex bonds, such as the 20-year PAC II's trade at the widest spreads.

Consider again the first example, in which we compare a 3-year PAC with a 3-year PAC II. In Exhibit 26–6 we show some of the pricing information on these bonds based on the theoretical spreads and yield curve in the same exhibit. We intentionally utilize both a steeper yield curve and higher current coupon collateral for illustrative purposes than are the current market levels (as of mid-March 2001). This allows the effect of both the rolling up/down the curve and the extension/shortening of the average lives to be more pronounced. Investors must decide between the prepayment protection of the level 1 tranche and the extra yield of the level 2. From an OAS standpoint, in this case, the PAC looks like the slightly better value. However, since many assumptions go into an OAS evaluation and OAS does not give a complete picture of prospective performance, most managers will want to perform a total return analysis.

EXHIBIT 26–7

Performance Results of 3-Year PAC Bonds

| | Initial Price | Yield at 125 PSA | Spread Adjustment | | | | Horizon Price | One-Year Total Return |
			Treasury	CMO	Quality	Total		
PAC	103–14	7.82	−31	−7	0	−38	102–21	8.54
PAC II	102–12	8.69	+39	+6	+4	+49	101–00	7.44

In order to compute the expected total return for a year, we need to compute the terminal prices, but, as we have seen, yield spreads, which determine prices, are a function of the average life and sensitivity of the security.

Consider first the regular 3-year PAC. At the end of 1 year, we found in Exhibit 26–2 that this bond's average life moved from 2.8 to 1.8 years. The difference between the 2-year and 3-year Treasury is negative 31 bps, and the difference between the 2- and 3-year PACs is −7 bps. No adjustment is made for change in quality, since the bond remains well-protected at the horizon. In total, the horizon yield of 7.44% is 38 bps tighter than the starting yield of 7.82%. This results in an ending price of 102-21, which translates into a total return of 8.54%.

Now consider the PAC II. At the end of the first year, its average life has risen from 4.6 to 5.2 years, assuming a 125 PSA. The difference between the 4-year and the 5-year Treasury is 39 bps (*this bond has rolled up the yield curve*), and the difference between 4- and 5-year PAC II's is 6 bps.

As we noted previously in Exhibit 26–2, not only has this bond gotten longer, but its quality has deteriorated, since its average life is more adversely sensitive (i.e., it extends when speeds slow down and rates rise, and contracts when speeds increase and rates fall). As a result we will penalize this bond by an additional 4 bps.[2] Thus, the horizon yield is 49 bps greater than at the original yield. The computed terminal price is 101-00, which produces a total return of 7.44%. These results are summarized in Exhibit 26–7.

The total return of the PAC (8.54%) is considerably higher than its yield of 7.82% at a 125 PSA. On the other hand, the PAC II's total return of 7.44% is not only lower than its expected yield of 8.69%, but it is also lower than the expected yield of the PAC.

In Exhibit 26–8 we show the 1-year returns for the two bonds for the base case, assuming shifts of 100 bps up and down, where, as before, we have made adjustments to the horizon spread where appropriate. The PAC II underperforms the PAC in all three scenarios. Since the PAC II was initially more negatively convex than the PAC,

---

2. For the purposes of this chapter, we arbitrarily used a penalty of 4 bps. To be more precise, one needs to look more closely at breakeven returns at the market assessment of the value of the additional negative convexity.

EXHIBIT 26–8

One-Year Total Returns

	Shift in Rates (bps)		
	−100	**0**	**+100**
PAC	10.07	8.54	7.03
PAC II	9.07	7.44	3.07
PSA	165	125	105

it is not surprising that its relative performance suffers as rates move up or down. This is particularly true in the up-100-bp scenario, because the average life of the PAC II extends considerably. What is unusual in this example is that even in the no-change-in-rates scenario, the PAC II performs so poorly. This occurs because again the bond's performance characteristics have weakened over the holding period.

Of course, one could debate the various spread adjustments used in this example, but the notion that the terminal characteristics of a bond are important in analyzing performance is indisputable. Although we chose a straightforward PAC structure to demonstrate the effect on performance, this impact will be still greater for more complicated bonds under more realistic scenarios.

Although the initial OAS differential provides a hint of the prospective performance profile, it is not sufficient to quantify the scenario analysis. Some analysts perform what is known as constant OAS total returns. In this framework the ending price in each scenario is computed by adding the initial OAS to the horizon yield curve in each scenario, and then computing the expected discounted value of projected cash flows. This analysis skirts the issue of the security's ending characteristics, because the methodology directly incorporates the terminal sensitivity of the cash flow. We believe that this type of analysis is a good start, and is far better than computing returns based on constant yield spread analysis. Nevertheless, it is still deficient, because the market tends to price instruments with different durations and convexities at different OAS levels. The difference is sometimes market-directional. For example, when the market is bullish, the demand for interest-only (IOs) strips from mortgage securities declines. Although the decline may be justified, it is often dramatic and the OAS for IOs widens greatly during the initial stages of a bullish environment, as the durations become more negative.

Another reason that constant OAS total return is insufficient for the practitioner is that the analysis does not provide insight into the reasons for unusual performance patterns. In order for the investor to be able to distinguish between genuinely attractive opportunities and ones that only appear as such, he needs to know what causes the behavior and how to anticipate it.

The starting point for analyzing these bonds, as with any, should be a thorough understanding of the cash flows. Exhibit 26–9 shows the monthly principal payments for the PAC and the PAC II that were discussed in the first example. The three diagrams

E X H I B I T   26–9

Monthly Principal Payments for PAC and PAC II

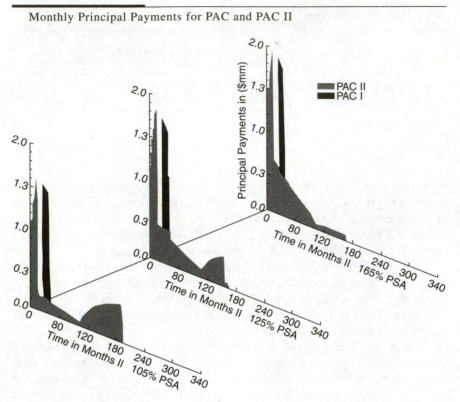

show the monthly principal payments for level 105 PSA, 125 PSA, and 165 PSA scenarios. In each diagram the horizontal axis represents time in months, and the vertical axis represents the principal payment in millions of dollars. The dark set of flows are from the PAC. The combination of the separate diagrams when read laterally shows that the "shape" of the PAC cash flow is invariant to changes in prepayment.

The lightly shaded region shows the paydown of the PAC II. Under each of the scenarios, we see a significant paydown in principal in the first year, and then it begins to tail off. In the 105 PSA scenario the principal paydown is initially high, then drops, and finally begins to pick up toward the end of the bond's life. Looking at this picture, it is no wonder that the average life increases after the first year. The early payments—from a vantage point of time 0—reduce the expected average life. After they are paid down, however, the remaining average life is longer.

The extreme case of this would be a portfolio consisting of two zero-coupon bonds of similar balances but different maturity. One zero matures in 1 year, and the other in 10 years. The initial average life of this portfolio is 5.5 years. One year later, however, the average life of the portfolio has risen to 9 years assuming that the investor does not reinvest the proceeds of his short zero. Indeed, it is true that

E X H I B I T   26–10

Monthly Principal Payments for Jump Z and PAC Support

the investor could rebalance his portfolio at the end of a year. Such a strategy, however, generates larger transaction costs and greater reinvestment risk.

The diagrams in Exhibit 26–9 make clear how it is possible that the average life increases. However, these diagrams represent only simple, level PSA scenarios. They do not show how average life sensitivity can vary. In order to do this, one needs to be able to project forward the cash flows for varying PSA scenarios. As we will show, this is crucial in the next example.

The cash flow patterns of the second example are more complicated because the jump Z leads to highly path-dependent cash flow patterns. As a result, it is very important to analyze the flows of all the bonds in such a deal under a variety of nonlevel PSA scenarios. Exhibit 26–10 shows the monthly principal cash flow at 90 PSA, 125 PSA, 155 PSA, and 165 PSA for the support bond and jump Z that were discussed in the second example. For the level 90 PSA scenario, a principal cash flow pattern similar to that of the PAC II from the first example emerges. At 125 PSA, the principal cash flow compresses considerably. Mentally combining these two diagrams allows one to understand why, if the collateral paid at 125 PSA for 5 years and then paid at 90 PSA for the rest of its life, it

EXHIBIT 26–11

Principal Payments Corresponding to Scenarios in Last Row of Exhibit 26–4

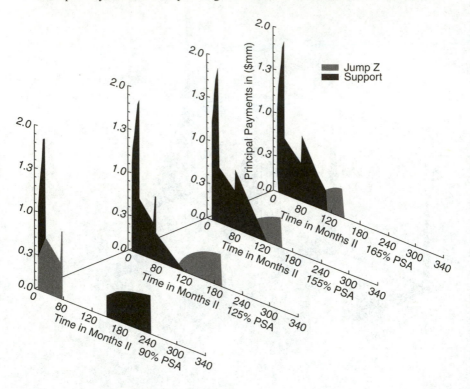

extends from 4.9 to 8.2 years (see Exhibit 26–4). Under the 90 PSA, 125 PSA, and 155 PSA scenarios, the Z bond does not begin paying for many years. However, recall that the Z bond jumps when prepayments rise above 155 PSA. As a result, the jump-Z bond moves in front of the support bond, thereby causing the extension one observes in the average life table of this deal at pricing.

This exhibit, however, tells only a small part of the story, since, with level scenarios, the Z bond either jumps in the beginning or not, and is therefore not given the opportunity to have its balance increase via accretion. In order to assess the impact of this, consider Exhibit 26–11. In these diagrams we show the cash flow that corresponds to the scenarios in the last row of Exhibit 26–4. In that scenario, the collateral pays at 125 PSA for 5 years, then spurts to 165 PSA for 1 month (recall that this causes the Z bond to jump), and then pays at either 90 PSA, 125 PSA, 155 PSA, or 165 PSA. This 1 month of 165 PSA causes the principal cash flows of the support bond to split apart. In the 90 PSA scenario there is a 90-month hiatus during which the support bond receives no principal. It is for this reason that the average life after 5 years extends from 4.9 years at pricing to 12.6 years in this scenario. We feel that these diagrams are invaluable for understanding and therefore for anticipating the nature of the bonds under consideration.

CONCLUSION

CMO tranches have cash flow patterns that often do not resemble those of more intuitive fixed income securities. Moreover, the cash flow is not static. It is interest-sensitive and path-dependent. Therefore, as time passes and interest rates and prepayment scenarios unfold, some bond classes undergo radical changes in their price sensitivity characteristics. Pricing at the horizon will reflect these altered sensitivities. For the total return account, this can have significant impact on performance. In order to discern value and anticipate the potential decline in quality, the manager should analyze the cash flow carefully. The asset-liability manager must assess the impact of a CMO's changing cash flow on the exposure of his book.

Clearly, some investor several years from now will hold the bonds that are created today. Duration and convexity do not tell the whole story, since they are summary instantaneous measures. In order to understand how a bond's characteristics can change, investors need to analyze the performance of their securities and picture their cash flows.

CHAPTER **27**

UNDERSTANDING INVERSE FLOATER PRICING

Michael L. Winchell

Michael Levine
Senior Managing Director
Mortgage Trading
Bear, Stearns & Co. Inc.

THE COMMON MISTAKE

Many investors mistakenly expect the price of an inverse floater to increase with a decline in short-term rates. In fact, changes in short-term rates alone could have little to no impact on the price of an inverse floater.

Inverse floaters are characterized by a coupon rate designed to reset inversely with changes in an index, most often that of a short-term rate such as London interbank offered rate (LIBOR). Some inverse floaters have coupon rates that change four, five, or six times as much as the change in the rate index, a multiplicative effect often described as the coupon leverage of the inverse floater. For an inverse floater with high coupon leverage, any drop in the short-term rates causes a large increase in its coupon rate, and thus a sharp increase in the income to the investor in the payment period. It is not surprising, therefore, that many investors expect a drop in short-term rates to cause a price increase in the inverse floater.

However, the expectation that changes in short-term rates have a great impact on the price of inverse floaters does not recognize the direct relation between inverse floaters and the fixed-rate bonds from which they are derived.

Inverse floaters are almost always carved out of an underlying fixed-rate tranche or MBS collateral, in conjunction with the creation of a floating-rate tranche. It may be difficult to "see" the fixed-rate tranche behind a floater and its inverse, but it is there nonetheless.

Since the floater and its inverse constitute the entire underlying fixed-rate bond when combined, there must be a "conservation" of market value. A simple observation is that the typical floater remains unchanged in price given changes in

---

Michael Winchell was employed at Bear, Stearns & Co. when he coauthored this chapter.

both short- and long-term yields. Its market value remains more or less constant. Thus, any change in the market value of an inverse floater must be primarily the result of a change in the value of the underlying fixed-rate bond, and any change in the market price of the underlying fixed-rate bond must cause a change in the value of the inverse floater.

VIEWING THE INVERSE FLOATER AS A LEVERAGED PURCHASE OF THE FIXED-RATE BOND

Many investors fail to recognize the similarity between the cash flows of an inverse floater and the cash flows generated by financing, at a floating rate, a fixed-rate bond similar to the underlying fixed-rate bond. The cash flows of an inverse floater resemble the cash flows available if the investor had purchased the underlying fixed-rate bond from which the inverse was derived, and then financed most of the purchase at the short-term rate used as the index for the floater and the inverse.

If an investor were willing to buy a fixed-rate bond and finance it at short-term rates, then the inverse floater represents a similar opportunity to earn a net interest margin in a steep yield curve environment.

ADVANTAGES OF INVERSE FLOATERS AS LEVERAGE VEHICLES

The allure of inverse floaters is the ability to profit from a steep yield curve through leverage and a significant interest margin. The greater the leverage available to the investor, the higher the potential return on capital, and, accordingly, the greater the risk. Thus, the purchase of an inverse floater in many ways resembles the leveraged funding of mortgage assets at short-term rates via the dollar roll or repurchase market.

What differentiates the inverse floater from typical financing vehicles is that the inverse floater buyer obtains an amortizing and prepay-sensitive cap on the financing rate (*through the cap on the floater*), and locks in access to funding over the term of the underlying fixed-rate bond without needing to reserve capital for potential margin calls. Neither of these two safety features are readily available in the mortgage market today, outside of the inverse floater.

An interest rate cap is an option that pays the investor if the reference rate rises above a strike rate. Inverse floaters have embedded interest rate caps. Coupon rates can never go below 0%, and some are structured with caps that limit coupon declines at relatively high coupon levels.

This is not to say that the buyer of fixed-rate bonds cannot also buy a cap to provide insurance for a financing arrangement. The advantages of the prepay sensitivity and matched amortization of the inverse floater's embedded cap position, however, would be difficult to replicate in the derivative market. Compared to non-prepay sensitive derivatives, the embedded cap of the inverse becomes more valuable in bearish scenarios as it extends and becomes more in the money. This increased cap value offsets some of the reduced value of the underlying fixed rate bond from which the inverse is derived. In bullish scenarios, the cap is losing value and shortens. This reduced cap value, however, is being offset by increases in the value of the underlying fixed rate bond. In other words, the long cap position of the inverse floater acts like a natural hedge to the price variability of the underlying fixed rate bond from which the inverse is derived.

Another advantage is that, unlike other funding sources, an inverse floater represents a locked in source of financing. The spread to LIBOR (or other reference interest rate) of the funding source does not change and there are no margin calls to offset changes in market values of the underlying fixed rate bond. Not only can the inverse potentially provide a competitive financing level compared to other financing vehicles (especially for institutions with low credit ratings), but also the advantage of locked in leverage in times of illiquidity or tight credit shouldn't be minimized.

A SIMPLE METHOD FOR EVALUATION
OF INVERSE FLOATERS

A simple technique to arrive at fair value is to ascertain the value on two pieces of the puzzle, and arrive at the third by addition or subtraction.

To value the inverse floater tranche, one need only calculate the total market value of the underlying fixed-rate bond from which it is derived, and then subtract the total market value of the floater that accords the inverse both its cap and its leverage.

Assuming that a floater always remains priced at par, we can see that all the change in value of an inverse floater tranche must be the result of a change in the value of the underlying fixed-rate bonds.

Therefore, if $50 million in inverse floaters are derived from $100 million in underlying fixed-rate bonds, and if the floater remains priced at par, the price change of the inverse floaters will be *twice* the price change of the underlying fixed-rate bonds. If only $20 million in inverse floaters are derived from $100 million in the underlying fixed-rate bonds, then given no change in the floater price, the inverse will change in price *five* times more than the underlying fixed-rate tranche.

Floaters, however, do not always remain at par, because the value of the embedded interest rate caps often changes. The spread over LIBOR offered by the floater may at times be more than enough compensation for the short cap position, and at other other times, not enough.

HOW THE LEVEL OF THE SHORT-TERM RATE AFFECTS
THE VALUE OF INVERSE FLOATERS THROUGH THE CAP

In a steep yield curve environment, a reasonably creditworthy buyer of a 5-year Treasury note could probably finance 98% to 99% of the proceeds at a monthly or overnight rate well below the yield of the 5-year note. The steeper the curve, the higher the spread and the greater the income.

We would not, however, expect the price of the 5-year note to change with the level of overnight repo rates, even though the net interest margin between the assets and the funding costs increases. We expect the price of the 5-year note to change only when 5-year yields change.

So too is it with inverse floaters. We should expect a change in the price of an inverse floater when market conditions (*yields and prepayment assumptions,* for example) cause a change in price of the underlying bond and similar bonds.

Where the level of short-term rates correctly enters into the valuation process for inverse floaters is through the evaluation of the cap on financing provided by the cap on the floater. This embedded interest rate cap has a value that is commonly determined by reference to the implied forward rate curve, and, since the interest rate cap agreement is an option agreement, by the volatility of short-term rates.

Fixed income analysts often refer to the *implied forward rate curve* when inverse floaters are analyzed to describe how the coupon rate of the security is expected to change through time. In essence, the market's expectation of future short-term rates is defined by the shape of the yield curve. To explain a steep yield curve, for instance, it must be the case that investors are willing to accept the low yields of short-term securities today because they expect rates to rise in the future.

The implied forward curve is derived in such a way as to make the continuous rollover of an investment at the short-term rate for 5 years, for example, equivalent to the realized compound yield (total return) of a 5-year note. The most common implied forward rate curve used by the market is a Eurobond curve. Some of the curve is derived directly from the Eurodollar futures market, the rest from the swap curve, or swap spreads and the Treasury curve extrapolated for 30 years.

To properly value the cap embedded in the inverse floater properly, one needs the implied forward rate curve and an estimate regarding rate volatility to value the cap. One could use these parameters within an option pricing method such as the option-adjusted spread (OAS) model. However, this supposes we "know" what the right OAS for an inverse floater is.

As an alternative to an OAS model, the investor can approximate the market value of the cap by pricing non-prepay-sensitive, amortizing, over-the-counter caps. To do this, the investor could choose upper and lower bounds for the range of expected prepayments and specify a number of other prepayment estimates. The investor would price different amortizing cap agreements, each based on the outstanding balance of the floater at various prepayment assumptions, but all having a strike rate given by the cap on the floater. The investor would then calculate an average price for the embedded mortgage security interest rate cap, given a weight for each of the prices of the over-the-counter cap agreements.

Note that we use the amortization of the floater to determine the total market value of the cap agreements outstanding. This is because the floater, as the financing arrangement, defines the number of caps available.

WHAT DOES A YIELD SENSITIVITY MATRIX REVEAL?

Yield, as an internal rate of return, assumes the investors put up a certain amount of cash today to receive cash flows in the future. Yield measures the rate of return on a fully paid investment over the life of the security, ignoring reinvested cash flows.

The typical yield sensitivity matrix of an inverse floating-rate tranche essentially reveals the rate of return generated by fixed-rate bonds that have been financed by the issuance of floating-rate debt. As in any financing of fixed income assets, the total return depends on the ultimate net interest margin. As in any mortgage financing, the total return can be affected by the rate of prepayment.

The cash flows of a financed purchase of fixed-rate bonds could be expressed as a rate of return on capital assuming various levels of financing rates. We could examine the "yield" of any fixed-rate bond in this fashion.

An Example Comparing an Inverse Floater to the Financing of the Underlying Fixed-Rate Bond

Below we show the similarity between a yield sensitivity matrix for a LIBOR inverse floater tranche carved from a REMIC PAC tranche to the return on equity of the same PAC tranche financed at LIBOR.

Consider the PAC tranche shown in Exhibit 27–1, similar to many available in the mortgage market priced at 100.10604 to yield 8.09%.[1] The tranche is backed by new FNMA 9.00% MBS pass-throughs.

---

[1]This analysis was based on 1989 market levels when this chapter was first published. Its usefullness, however, still applies today.

E X H I B I T 27–1

Fixed-Rate PAC Tranche

Coupon rate		7.9750%	
Maturity date		06-25-21	
Projected average life		7.95 years	
Prepay assumption		165% PSA	
PAC range		90% to 250% PSA	
Face amount		42,108,000	
Price		100.10604	

PSA*	50%	165%	300%
Average life	**10.21**	**7.95**	**7.12**
Yield	8.09%	8.09%	8.09%

*Public Securities Association.

E X H I B I T   27–2

LIBOR Floating-Rate PAC Tranche

Initial coupon rate	6.0875%
Coupon rate cap	10.750%
Maturity date	06-25-21
Projected average life	7.95 years
Prepay assumption	165% PSA
PAC range	90% to 250% PSA
Face amount	31,238,260
Price	100.0000

PSA Average Life	50% 10.21	165% 7.95	300% 7.12	LIBOR
Yield	5.79%	5.79%	5.79%	5.3125
Yield	8.84%	8.84%	8.83%	8.3125
Yield	10.93%	10.92%	10.92%	11.3125
Yield	10.93%	10.92%	10.92%	14.3125

Before we calculate the returns of a leveraged purchase of the PAC tranche, examine the alternative. Instead of issuing the PAC tranche above, a floating-rate tranche and an inverse floating-rate tranche could have been issued using LIBOR as the index rate to reset the coupon on each. The cash flows that would otherwise be paid to the PAC tranche are instead divided between the floater and the inverse floater.

The first step in the process is to carve out a floater tranche. Suppose we want to issue a floating-rate tranche priced at par. Market conditions require that a monthly floater, having this type of amortization schedule and average life, pay 40 bps over 1-month LIBOR and be subject to a coupon rate cap no lower than 10.75%. If we want to issue the maximum amount of floater bonds to achieve the greatest leverage, we will allocate the principal between the floater and the inverse in such a way as to exhaust all available interest from the underlying fixed-rate cash flows at the level of LIBOR at which the floater caps out. This results in a floater tranche face amount of $31,238,260.

The inverse floater is allocated the remaining principal, and both tranches return principal pro rata. The face amount of the inverse floater is $10,869,740.

Assume that the level of 1-month LIBOR equals 5.6375% on the pricing date. The descriptions of the two tranches that could have been issued, along with the familiar yield sensitivity tables, are shown in Exhibit 27–2 and 27–3. The floating-rate tranche now provides built-in financing at 40 bps over LIBOR, capped at 10.750%, with matched amortization and no counterparty credit risk. We can think of the 40-bp spread over LIBOR as the market's current evaluation of the embedded interest rate cap.

E X H I B I T   27–3

LIBOR Inverse Floating-Rate Tranche

Initial coupon rate	7.9750%	
Coupon rate cap	29.750%	
Maturity date	06-25-21	
Projected average life	7.95 years	
Prepay assumption	165% PSA	
PAC range	90% to 250% PSA	
Face amount	10,869,740	
Price	100.410773	

PSA Average Life	50% 10.21	165% 7.95	300% 7.12	LIBOR
Yield	14.82%	14.81%	14.81%	5.3125
Yield	5.96%	5.96%	5.97%	8.3125
Yield	0.07%	0.09%	0.10%	11.3125
Yield	0.07%	0.09%	0.10%	14.3125

The inverse floating-rate tranche benefits from the leverage provided by the floater tranche. That is, the investor is able to capture the net interest margin of approximately $42 million in fixed-rate PAC bonds financed at LIBOR up 40 bps, with a cap at a cost of $10,914,390.

The structure shown in Exhibit 27–3 represents the opportunity to buy a leveraged position in the underlying fixed-rate PAC tranche through the inverse floater. The investor could execute a similar strategy by financing the PAC tranche directly. What differs is the financing rate, the presence of a prepay-sensitive interest rate cap, and the absence of counterparty credit risk and margin calls.

Exhibits 27–4, 27–5, and 27–6 display the return on capital of financing the underlying PAC tranche given similar leverage, that is, similar capital invested. In the first example (see Exhibit 27–4), no cap is purchased, as is evident from the negative returns given high LIBOR levels. In the second example (see Exhibit 27–5), a cap is purchased that amortizes coincident with the outstanding balance of the PAC tranche at the pricing prepayment assumption of 165% PSA. The third example, shown in Exhibit 27–6, reveals the returns if a cap is purchased to provide protection on a balance equivalent to 50% PSA. Just as is the case for an inverse floater, the rate of return is a function of the level of LIBOR (*assumed to be constant at the indicated rate over the life of the financing arrangement*) and the prepayments that occur.

In the three financing arrangements presented in Exhibits 27–4, 27–5, and 27–6, the market value of the PAC tranche is assumed constant over the term to maturity. Accordingly, there would be no margin calls that would require additional capital.

EXHIBIT 27–4

Short-Term Financing of a Fixed-Rate PAC Tranche, No Interest Rate
Cap Agreement

	Interest rate cap strike	None		
	Interest rate cap cost	None		
	Financing rate	LIBOR flat		
	Total capital invested	$10,914,390		
	Initial amount financed	$31,238,261		
PSA	**50%**	**165%**	**300%**	**LIBOR**
ROE*	16.04%	16.03%	16.02%	5.3125
ROE	7.14%	7.14%	7.15%	8.3125
ROE	−1.53%	−1.50%	−1.49%	11.3125
ROE	−9.93%	−9.89%	−9.87%	14.3125

*ROE = Return on equity.

EXHIBIT 27–5

Short-Term Financing of a Fixed-Rate PAC Tranche, Interest Rate Cap
Agreement Matched at 165% PSA

	Interest rate cap strike	10.750%		
	Interest rate cap cost	$440,675		
	Financing rate	LIBOR flat		
	Total capital invested	$11,355,065		
	Initial amount financed	$31,238,261		
PSA	**50%**	**165%**	**300%**	**LIBOR**
ROE*	15.22%	15.11%	15.04%	5.3125
ROE	6.58%	6.47%	6.42%	8.3125
ROE	−0.67%	−0.40%	−0.26%	11.3125
ROE	−2.78%	−0.40%	0.69%	14.3125

*ROE = Return on equity.

The embedded cap of the inverse floater distinguishes the two strategies
most. The investor in an inverse floater pays for the cap in the spread over LIBOR
paid on the floater. This may be more or less than the direct cost of an interest rate
cap agreement. Consider too, that many floaters and inverse floaters are carved out
of fixed-rate REMIC tranches having average lives of 15 years or longer. An amortizing, prepay-sensitive cap of such a long term would be difficult (potentially impossible) to replicate as efficiently in the derivative market.

E X H I B I T 27–6

Short-Term Financing of a Fixed-Rate PAC Tranche, Interest Rate Cap
Agreement Matched at 50% PSA

	Interest rate cap strike	10.750%		
	Interest rate cap cost	$718,480		
	Financing rate	LIBOR flat		
	Total capital invested	$11,632,870		
	Initial amount financed	$31,238,261		

PSA	50%	165%	300%	LIBOR
ROE*	14.73%	14.55%	14.46%	5.3125
ROE	6.24%	6.07%	5.97%	8.3125
ROE	−0.55%	−0.26%	−0.11%	11.3125
ROE	−0.55%	1.86%	−2.93%	14.3125

*ROE = Return on equity.

SUMMARY

Investors need to compare the relative cost of financing a fixed-rate tranche or MBS directly to the implied financing rate of the inverse floater, taking into consideration the relative value of the interest rate cap embedded in the inverse floater, the secure nature of the funding agreement, and the absence of margin calls.

Investors must recognize that the value of inverse floaters depends both on the value of the underlying fixed-rate cash flows and on the value of the floater that provides the inverse with its leverage and its cap. Short-term rates will only impact the value of an inverse floater to the extent they affect the floater and its cap, or the underlying fixed-rate cash flows. Otherwise, the value of an inverse floater and its price movements can be compared to that of the underlying fixed-rate tranche.

CHAPTER 28

UNCOVERING VALUE IN ROTATING PSA ENVIRONMENTS

Lang Gibson
Vice President
Fixed Income Research
First Union Securities, Inc.

When rate cycles are approaching their turning, or rotating, points, there are often significant pricing inefficiencies in mortgage-backed securities (MBS) as prepayment assumptions become increasingly uncertain. For example, in a low PSA environment, investors able to take advantage of these pricing inefficiencies stand to benefit greatly as they buy discounts priced at unrealistically low PSAs or premiums priced at unrealistically high PSAs. This chapter focuses on opportunities available during the period mortgage rates were rising between late 1998 and mid-2000 and the period mortgage rates were falling between early 1995 and late 1998. Drawing on this prepayment history of coupons between 7% and 9% since 1988, analogies to detect relative value are drawn between these periods and similar periods historically. Further, we look at relative value tools such as LIBOR OAS and LIBOR spread/implied volatility ratios that are useful in rotating prepayment environments when volatility and spreads are particularly uncertain.

Rising mortgage yields between late 1998 and mid-2000 took their toll on mortgage portfolios, particularly bonds or loans purchased at discounts, due to extension pressure. However, in the terminal PSA environment, in which prepayments converged toward a 100 PSA floor, during the year 2000, it was possible to find value in discounts (particularly high WAC) priced at deflated PSA levels. Many factors, other than refinancing opportunities, such as relocation, equity buildup, salaries and employment (earning power), drive prepayments. Therefore, in rising interest rate environments, when the option to refinance is well out of the money, it is typical for prepayments to slow significantly. However, there is a definite floor for lower coupons due to non-interest-rate-related prepayment factors. Discount mortgages priced without fully taking this floor into account offer value, as the discount will be returned faster to the investor. In other words, the more deeply discounted the mortgage, the more positive convexity embedded in the asset. Support and principal-only (PO) bonds offer a particularly high degree of positive convexity in terminal PSA environments. These mortgages and high WAC discounts benefit most as the interest rate cycle reverses and prepayments increase. At some point, prepayments are so slow they can only increase from their floor.

Falling mortgage yields between early-1995 and late 1998 caused mortgage portfolios, particularly bonds or loans purchased at premiums, to be negatively impacted by ever-increasing prepayments. This period witnessed a terminal PSA environment in which prepayments converged upwards towards a cap. Only for short periods of time did PSAs exceed 1,200% as the prepayment option held by the borrower has historically been exercised inefficiently. However, as we will show, borrowers have become increasingly smarter about their refinancing options. In a falling interest rate environment, premiums mortgages purchased at unrealistically high prepayment speeds stand to benefit as prepayments slow with the turning interest rate cycle.

In this chapter, we present a number of tools that investors can use to uncover relative value in MBS. These relative value tools are particularly useful in a rotating PSA environment when PSAs approach their terminal PSA caps and floors:

- Evaluation of prepayment speeds in terminal PSA environments
- LIBOR option-adjusted spread (OAS) analysis
- LIBOR spread/implied volatility ratios

Exhibit 28–1 demonstrates the upside potential for discounts in the turning interest rate cycle of mid-2000 where the Fed was believed to be near the end of its rate hikes and the eventual rotation of its policy to once again lowering rates. The Bloomberg median PSA forecasts show increasing prepayments with falling rates. In this chart and other charts in this chapter, we have divided 30-year mortgages into the following sectors:

- Discounts as represented by Fannie Mae (FNMA) 7% unseasoned collateral (FNCL 7 N)

E X H I B I T   28–1

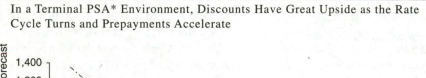

In a Terminal PSA* Environment, Discounts Have Great Upside as the Rate Cycle Turns and Prepayments Accelerate

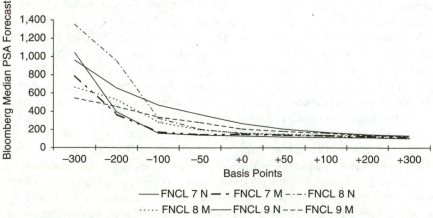

*PSA = Public Securities Association.
Source: First Union Securities, Inc.

- Discounts as represented by FNMA 7% moderately seasoned collateral (FNCL 7 M)

- Current coupons as represented by FNMA 8% unseasoned collateral (FNCL 8 N)

- Current coupons as represented by FNMA 8% moderately seasoned collateral (FNCL 8 M)

- Premiums as represented by FNMA 9% unseasoned collateral (FNCL 9 N)

- Premiums as represented by FNMA 9% moderately seasoned collateral (FNCL 9 M)

Unseasoned collateral is defined as weighted average maturities (WAMs) of 330–360 months, and moderately seasoned collateral is defined as WAMs of 300–330 months. Whereas prepayments on lower WAC discounts, as represented by FNMA 7% collateral, were not forecast by the Street to significantly accelerate until rates declined 100 bps, prepayments on higher WAC discount paper, as represented by coupons of 7%–8%, were forecast to significantly accelerate as rates fell as little as 50 bps. After a 100 bps rate decline, all discount paper was forecast by the Street to sharply accelerate in prepayments. Once the rate cycle turned, discount paper was expected to appreciate in value with any decline in rates as these faster prepayments are priced into the collateral. For investors able to purchase discount collateral at speeds unrepresentative of this upside from falling rates, there was particularly good value. At this point in the rate cycle, a downside scenario would have been speeds falling further from current pricing at the time, a risk closely examined in the following section.

EVALUATION OF PREPAYMENT SPEEDS IN TERMINAL PSA ENVIRONMENTS

For all six sectors analyzed—7%, 8% and 9% coupons, both unseasoned and moderately seasoned—prepayments had slowed at speeds lower than those of mid-2000 over prolonged terminal PSA periods and at similar yield levels. Therefore, if history is any indicator of the future, we could imagine a scenario where prepayments slow more than the mid-2000 levels. Exhibits 28–2 and 28–4 show actual prepayments for the six sectors since 1988 plotted against 30-year mortgage yields.

7% Collateral

The 1994–1995 Fed rate hikes pushed 7% collateral into a terminal PSA environment that was prolonged through 1998 (Exhibit 28–2). At the onset of this period, seasoned and moderately seasoned collateral prepaid at speeds below 100 PSA. Speeds then remained range-bound at 100 PSA–200 PSA until the end of this period despite rising mortgage yields in late 1996. In mid-2000, FNCL 7 Ns had speeds just inside 200 PSA, whereas FNCL 7 Ms had speeds close to 150 PSA. The reason unseasoned collateral prepays at higher speeds than moderately seasoned collateral is that newer production is relatively more sensitive to interest rates. With both sectors forecasted to prepay by the Street at 130 PSA–150 PSA for rates unchanged, there was significant upside if the rate cycle reversed.

The 1989–1993 bull market in fixed income saw little impact to 7% collateral, as mortgage yields never fell below 7% until early 1993. Only in late 1993

EXHIBIT 28–2

7% Coupon MBS* in Terminal PSA Environments

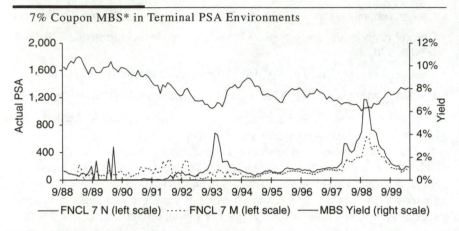

*MBS = Mortgage-backed securities; PSA = Public Securities Association.
Source: First Union Securities, Inc.

did unseasoned 7% collateral spike to about 700 PSA as borrowers took advantage of the refinancing opportunity. In the post-1994 bull market, unseasoned 7% collateral barely touched 1,200% as mortgage yields fell to 6%, which translated into a 150 bps lower rate for borrowers in 7% coupon collateral pools, which typically have a gross WAC upwards of 7.5%. However, moderately seasoned collateral barely approached 500 PSA.

8% Collateral

In Exhibit 28–3, which shows actual PSAs for 8% collateral, we see much higher terminal PSAs in rising rate environments. However, in response to the 1994–1995 Fed rate hikes, both unseasoned and moderately seasoned 8% collateral prepaid at 100 PSA levels for a few months. In mid-1995, unseasoned 8% collateral speeded up substantially to 950 PSA in the face of declining yields in late 1996 before falling again to levels more in line with moderately seasoned collateral. Over this period, moderately seasoned collateral barely budged above 200 PSA except for a few months during the late 1996 rate increase. As of mid-2000, unseasoned 8% collateral was still prepaying at approximately 700 PSA, although the Street's forecast was down at 160 PSA for rates unchanged. On the other hand, moderately seasoned 8% collateral speeds had fallen below the 200 PSA level. Of the two, this collateral was the most likely to slow toward 100 PSA if yields continued to rise. Otherwise, purchased at a discount, moderately seasoned 7.5%–8.0% collateral, which was priced by the Street at approximately 160 PSA, had substantial upside if the rate cycle reversed.

The 1989–1993 bull market in mortgage yields witnessed the largest spike in prepayments for 8% collateral at the onset of 1993 when yields fell below 7% to a low of approximately 6.25%. Seasoned 8% collateral rose above 1,200% for a few months, whereas moderately seasoned collateral came close but short of

E X H I B I T   28–3

8% Coupon MBS* in Terminal PSA Environments

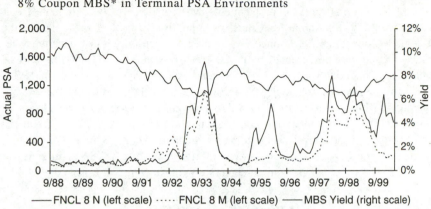

——— FNCL 8 N (left scale) ····· FNCL 8 M (left scale) ——— MBS Yield (right scale)

*MBS = Mortgage-backed securities; PSA = Public Securities Association.
Source: First Union Securities, Inc.

E X H I B I T   28–4

9% Coupon MBS* in Terminal PSA Environments

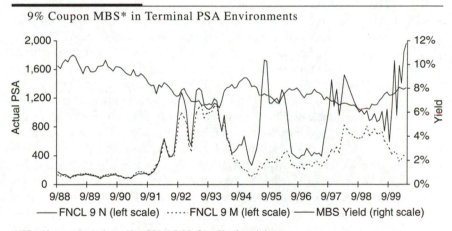

——— FNCL 9 N (left scale) ····· FNCL 9 M (left scale) ——— MBS Yield (right scale)

*MBS = Mortgage-backed securities; PSA = Public Securities Association.
Source: First Union Securities, Inc.

1,200 PSA. In the post-1994 bull market, 8% collateral PSAs spiked twice. Only seasoned 8% collateral spiked to 900 PSA when yields approached 6.5% in late-1995. Both seasoned and unseasoned 8% collateral had the largest spike as rates approached 6%, with seasoned collateral hitting its cap of 1,200% for one month.

9% Collateral

Exhibit 28–4 shows substantially higher historical prepayments for FNCL 9 N and FNCL 9 M as mortgage yields had not risen above 9% for nine years between mid-1991 and mid-2000. Early in the 1994–1995 Fed rate hike cycle, 9% collateral prepayments began to slow sharply. As rates began to fall again in early 1995, seasoned 9% collateral spiked in prepayments, whereas moderately seasoned 9% collateral went into a terminal PSA state for approximately six months. Despite the 1999–2000 rate hikes, unseasoned 9% collateral, which is the most sensitive to refinancing opportunities, prepaid in mid-2000 at levels well above 1,400 PSA. On the other hand, moderately seasoned 9% collateral was hovering around only 400 PSA.

In low rate environments, the 1,200 PSA cap rule is irrelevant for 9% collateral, which has historically been well in-the-money for the borrower. However, the period from late 1999 to mid-2000, when mortgage yields were rising, showed unseasoned 9% collateral accelerating in prepayments for the first time. This anomaly of positive correlation between mortgage yields and PSA is reflective of mortgage borrower's increasing understanding of the valuable option they hold.

LIBOR OAS ANALYSIS

Although LIBOR OAS is an important relative value tool in any prepayment environment, it is particularly important in a rotating, or terminal, PSA environment when we are approaching a turning point in the interest rate cycle and volatility is unstable.

OAS has always been the standard for measuring relative value in MBS. OAS is simply the spread to a benchmark less the option cost. With the option cost quantified in basis points subtracted from the spread, the adjusted spread can be compared with fixed income securities without optionality or securities with the same option adjustment. Due to the dwindling Treasury supply and its sensitivity to technical gyrations, the benchmark for our analysis is LIBOR, or the swap curve. For MBS, the option cost is calculated using Monte Carlo simulation, which runs hundreds of paths of interest rates to estimate possible prepayment patterns. The best known OAS models, Andrew Davidson and Espiel, are available on Bloomberg. The most critical input into these OAS simulation models is volatility, which in large part drives the results. Therefore, it is important to use actual volatility as implied by the market.

Exhibit 28–5 plots LIBOR OAS against swaption volatility between January 1997 and mid-2000. One can observe a declining LIBOR OAS for current-coupon 30-year FNMA collateral between the 1998 market contagion period and mid-2000. The OAS data comes from Bloomberg (MOAS FNCL <Index> Go). To convert Bloomberg's Treasury OAS to LIBOR OAS, we subtract the appropriate swap spread from the treasury OAS. At the time, we had little historical data on true LIBOR OAS, which requires simulation on swap rates instead of Treasury rates, as this was a new phenomenon. At first glance, a declining LIBOR OAS trend indicates poor relative value in MBS versus its benchmark, LIBOR. Although spreads in general had declined since the contagion period, the largest driver in this OAS calculation, option cost, biased the OAS results to the downside.Bloomberg's historical OAS assumes a constant 15% volatility. Because market-implied volatility, as represented here by 3×10 swaption volatility, has declined from 18.2% to 12.0% in the most recent one-year period, a 15% constant volatility assumption was largely responsible for the two-year decline in LIBOR OAS. Indeed, we could observe a significantly positive correlation between swaption volatility and Bloomberg OAS (Exhibit 28–5).

EXHIBIT 28-5

Bloomberg Current-Coupon LIBOR OAS* Has Tightened Significantly Due in Large Part to the Constant Volatility Assumption

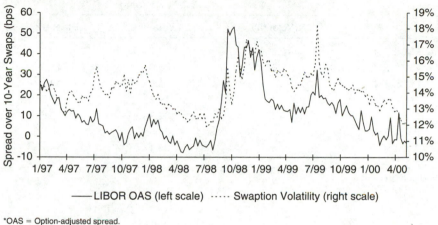

——— LIBOR OAS (left scale) ····· Swaption Volatility (right scale)

*OAS = Option-adjusted spread.
Source: First Union Securities, Inc.

EXHIBIT 28-6

Bloomberg Current-Coupon Option Cost Has Risen Despite Declining Volatility Due to the Constant Volatility Assumption

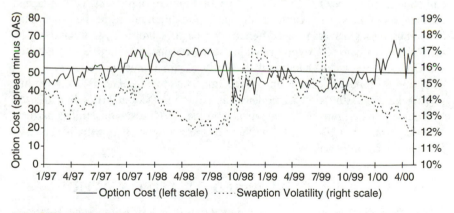

——— Option Cost (left scale) ····· Swaption Volatility (right scale)

OAS = Option-adjusted spread.
Source: First Union Securities, Inc.

Exhibit 28–6 plots swaption volatility versus the Bloomberg-implied option cost and shows option cost rising during the most recent year over the 3.5 year look-back period just as swaption volatility had declined. A similar negative correlation pattern can be observed in past periods. This negative correlation can be attributed to the constant volatility assumption in the Bloomberg calculation.

EXHIBIT 28-7

Constant Versus Actual Volatility LIBOR OAS*

	LIBOR OAS (bps)		
	15% Volatility	12% Volatility	Difference
FNCL 7 N	0.5	12.7	12.2
FNCL 7 M	12.6	23.6	11.0
FNCL 8 N	−2.5	15.5	18.0
FNCL 8 M	3.3	19.3	16.0
FNCL 9 N	16.1	31.7	15.6
FNCL 9 M	20.3	35.5	15.2
Average	8.4	23.1	14.7

*OAS = Option-adjusted spread.
Source: First Union Securities, Inc.

To see the difference as of June 1, 2000, using different volatility assumptions, we show the LIBOR OAS for our six 30-year MBS sectors (Exhibit 28–7). In this example, we price OAS using Bloomberg's default Andrew Davidson model at the default 15% volatility and at the true market implied volatility of 12% at June 1, 2000. For instance, FNCL 8 N was priced at an OAS of negative 2.6 bps under the 15% constant volatility assumption and 15.5 bps under the market-implied 12% volatility assumption, a difference of 18 bps. The Cuspier of the three coupons, 8% collateral, had the highest option cost and consequently the largest difference using the two volatility assumptions. On average, the difference for our six sectors was approximately 15 bps, which is significant when evaluating relative value opportunities. Essentially, this OAS sensitivity to a change in the volatility assumption is known as vega.

In a terminal PSA environment, it is important to have a realistic market implied volatility assumption when detecting value in discount MBS. Because the best value in rising rate environments is in higher WAC discounts, this is particularly important, as LIBOR OAS on these cuspier coupons is especially sensitive to volatility assumptions.

LIBOR SPREAD/IMPLIED VOLATILITY RATIO

In any prepayment environment, risk-adjusted return analysis is important. However, in a rotating, or terminal PSA environment, where risk and return are so volatile, it is particularly important to constantly measure the changes in the risk/return relationship.

Implied volatility, which is forward-looking, is a better predictor than historical volatility for determining risk-adjusted value opportunities. In the previous section, we showed how swaption volatility had declined from a high of 18.2% to a low of 12.0% in the period between mid-1999 and mid-2000. The decline was due to the rise in mortgage yields and the related decline in Fannie Mae and Freddie Mac portfolio growth. Likewise, over this same period, the implied price

EXHIBIT 28–8

LIBOR Spread-Implied MBS* OTC Price Volatility Ratio

	Ratio	Current-Coupon Implied Volatility	Current-Coupon LIBOR Spread
June 6, 2000	17.53	3.6%	0.63
One-Year Statistics			
Mean	13.65	4.6%	0.60
Maximum	21.50	6.3%	0.74
Minimum	8.25	3.1%	0.47

*MBS = Mortgage-backed securities.
Source: First Union Securities, Inc.

EXHIBIT 28–9

LIBOR Spread-Implied Swaption Yield Volatility Ratio

	Ratio	Swaption Implied Volatility	Current-Coupon LIBOR Spread
June 5, 2000	5.00	12.7%	0.63
One-Year Statistics			
Mean	4.29	14.1%	0.60
Maximum	5.33	18.2%	0.74
Minimum	2.97	12.0%	0.47

Source: First Union Securities, Inc.

volatility for current-coupon MBS OTC options declined from 6.3% to 3.6%. As LIBOR spreads had yet to narrow in response to this volatility shift downward, we expected outperformance in the near term, as of June 6.

A useful relative value tool for the MBS markets is the LIBOR spread/ implied volatility ratio. Similar to other risk-adjusted return measures, higher ratios imply higher risk-adjusted value. Furthermore, we would expect declining volatility to lead to falling spreads as the risk premium (e.g., option cost) declines. Lower volatility implies lower option cost and thus, lower spreads. The LIBOR spread/implied volatility ratio shows mean reverting characteristics over time as spreads step back in line with waning volatility.

Exhibits 28–8 and 28–9 show two ratios. The numerator in our ratios uses current-coupon spread to swaps. The denominator uses two different implied volatility measures relevant for the MBS market: swaption yield volatility and current-coupon MBS OTC price volatility. We show statistics for these ratios only over the period between mid-1999 and mid-2000, as this is the period over which we had maintained a database for the latter volatility. Both measures indicated risk-adjusted value in current-coupon MBS as of June 6, 2000.

E X H I B I T   28–10

MBS LIBOR Spread-Implied MBS* OTC Price Volatility Ratio: July 1999 to June 2000

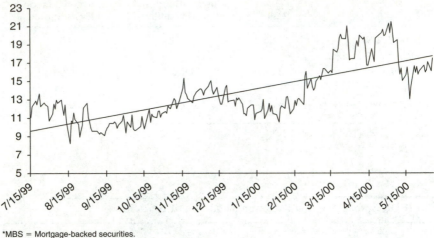

*MBS = Mortgage-backed securities.
Source: First Union Securities, Inc.

The June 6 MBS OTC price volatility ratio of 17.53 was well above its one-year mean of 13.65 (Exhibit 28–8). This difference was due to the denominator—3.6% volatility—being well below its one-year mean of 4.6%. Furthermore, the LIBOR spread of 63 bps was 3 bps above its mean of 60 bps. We would expect MBS LIBOR spreads to narrow to catch up with the downward movement in volatility. However, spread movement often lags implied volatility trends. Consequently, narrowing so far had been delayed.

Exhibit 28–9 shows similar value for current-coupon MBS when we look at swaption volatility instead of MBS OTC option volatility. The June 6 ratio of 5.00 was well above its 1-year mean of 4.29. Again, this difference was due to swaption volatility being 1.4% below its one-year mean, whereas LIBOR spreads were higher than the mean.

Exhibits 28–10 and 28–11 show an upward trend for both ratios over the period between mid-1999 and mid-2000. We expected this upward trend to flatten in the medium term, as market spreads priced in declining option implied volatility and uncertainty in the general fixed income environment started to subside. Exhibit 28–12 demonstrates the mean reverting tendency of the swaption-based ratio over longer periods of time. As we have swaption volatility dating back to January 1997, we can see a flattening trend over a 3.5-year period starting at this time versus a rising trend over the year between mid-1999 and mid-2000. Although we have only shown these ratios for current-coupon MBS to limit this chapter to a reasonable length, this ratio is useful for detecting risk-adjusted value over the range of coupons offering opportunities in a rotating, or terminal, PSA environment.

E X H I B I T   28–11

MBS* LIBOR Spread-Implied Swaption Yield Volatility Ratio: July 1999 to June 2000

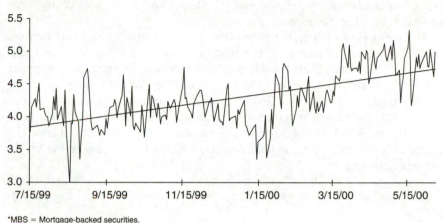

*MBS = Mortgage-backed securities.
Source: First Union Securities, Inc.

E X H I B I T   28–12

MBS LIBOR Spread-Implied Swaption Yield Volatility Ratio: January 1997 to June 2000

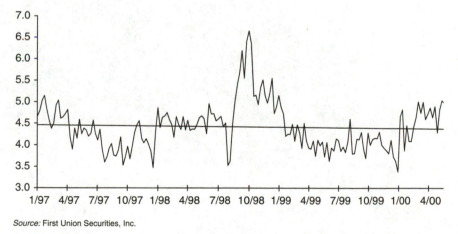

Source: First Union Securities, Inc.

CONCLUSION

As we approach a turning point in the interest rate cycle, there is increasing un-certainty about where interest rates and, by extension, prepayments may go in the short and medium terms. If rates continue to rise before the turn of the cycle, his-torical precedent indicates prepayments have further to fall before hitting their floor, or terminal PSA level. Otherwise, if rates stabilize and then start falling again, market pricing for prepayments may be too slow. Consequently, discount MBS may outperform as the discount is returned to the investor faster than pricing indicates. The relative value tools in this chapter are useful for detecting value in such a rising rate environment.

Likewise, in a falling rate environment, there is some point where prepayment assumptions for premium MBS may be too high. In this scenario, relative value tools as presented here could be used to detect value for purchasing premium MBS priced at PSAs above realistic levels. Slowing prepayments on premium bonds would result in the premium being paid by the investor over a longer period, which would result in outperformance in premium MBS.

The OAS and risk-adjusted return measures presented in this chapter are particularly important in turning interest rate cycles when spreads and volatility are especially erratic.

CHAPTER 29

ANALYSIS OF LOW LOAN BALANCE MBS

Anand K. Bhattacharya, Ph.D.
Executive Vice President
Countrywide Capital Markets Inc.

As one of the major drivers in the valuation of mortgage backed securities (MBS), the prepayment behavior of the underlying mortgages is a heavily researched and highly debated issue. Over the years, as the field matured and as additional data became available, the traditional prepayment paradigm of interest rates, demographics, defaults, housing turnovers, and curtailments broadened to include various attributes of the borrower and distinguishing characteristics of the loan. With more information available, ongoing developments led to an expanded form of prepayment modeling and forecasting that included the evaluation of microlevel loan variables as additional explanatory factors. Instead of using the traditional macrolevel prepayment paradigm of rate, refinancing, death, divorce, and demographics, the scope of investigation extended to include pool-specific variables that consider the unique attributes of loans, underlying real estate, and the borrowers themselves as independent variables in the forecast. In step with these current developments, this chapter focuses on the efficacy of using the loan balance as an explanatory factor in the determination of prepayments and hence the relative value of low loan balance (LLB) MBS.

The issue of using microvariables in analyzing prepayment behavior was brought to the forefront of MBS evaluation during the prepayment wave of 1993 when interest rates reached historic lows. At this time, the debate centered on the idea of using loan seasoning as a driver of prepayment behavior. As this argument became accepted in the marketplace and as actual speed behavior provided empirical evidence validating the hypothesis, seasoned pools were priced at a premium to newly issued mortgages. The premise was that as the loan seasoned, the

---

Computational and research assistance with this chapter by Esther Chang and Nick Trosper is gratefully acknowledged.

prepayment behavior of the mortgage would be dampened, especially if the mortgagor had been exposed to a regime of lower interest rates. Additionally, for lower coupons where the refinancing incentive was minimal, the prepayment behavior would likely be further affected, with the underlying speeds being directly correlated to the age of the loan. For premium coupons, this argument was cast as being determined by a higher degree of burnout.

In recent years, another attribute of mortgage loans, namely the loan size, has been used as a determinant of prepayment behavior. The thought here is that low balance pools are likely to prepay slower than higher balance pools, ceteris paribus for an equivalent move in interest rates. The theoretical arguments for slower speeds of low balance pools include such factors as higher refinancing thresholds for the borrowers and reduced monetary incentives to originators with LLB refinancing. However, it has been suggested that LLB pools have a lower proportion of mortgages originating in higher cost states, such as New York and California, thereby resulting in pools that were not geographically diverse, but concentrated in lower-cost states. Consequently the argument holds that these pools are affected by housing turnover, especially during periods of robust real estate appreciation and may not exhibit slow prepayment behavior.

In this chapter we evaluate these arguments and, by using loan-level information from our proprietary databases, find that current- and premium-coupon LLB pools prepay more slowly than generic pools, irrespective of vintage and geographical locations. However, discount-coupon low balance pools pay at a slightly faster rate than equivalent generic pools. Note that despite this finding, the aggregate prepayment behavior of discount LLBs is slower than generics. Although the LLB pools on which this chapter is based did include a lower percentage of mortgages that originated in higher-cost states than are included in generic pools, the effect of this reduced concentration is not significant to cause any divergence in prepayment behavior for current- and premium-coupon pools. At the same time, this "adverse selection" of low balance mortgages in lower-cost states may actually be a driver of faster (than generic) prepayment rates for discount-priced mortgages as a result of the effects of housing turnover and trade-up home purchases stemming from lower housing costs. In addition, using prepayment models developed from our databases to capture the drivers of LLB pool prepayments, we also offer our thoughts on the superior relative value characteristics of these types of mortgages. Our findings[1] are significant in that the conclusions are derived based on loan-level data and are therefore distinguished from similar studies that rely upon average loan balances obtained from pool-level information. In view of these findings, it is also our conclusion that true LLB pools exhibit an improved convexity profile over similar-coupon higher balance pools and justify a premium based on the dampened prepayment behavior. With respect to these "payups," it is also our opinion that the market payup for both discount- and current-coupon pools is fairly underpriced.

---

1. This data are taken from loans originated and sourced by Countrywide Home Loans.

THE ARGUMENTS FOR SLOWER PREPAYMENT BEHAVIOR OF LLB POOLS

Several arguments have been advanced for the slower prepayment pattern of LLB pools based on such factors as higher refinancing thresholds and reduced refinancing incentives on the part of the servicer. The reduced sensitivity of LLB mortgages stems from the fact that a large move in interest rates is necessary to create a meaningful reduction in the mortgagor's monthly payment or to overcome the fixed costs of financing. Moreover, the lower the mortgage loan balance, the lower the monthly savings for an equivalent drop in interest rates. Despite the discussions in the popular financial media about "no-cost refinancing," the dynamics of this phenomenon are different for LLBs. Given a fixed cost of originating a loan, the amount of which is invariant with the size of the loan, the refinancing threshold for LLB is higher. This occurs because the rate equivalent of the fixed up-front costs of originating a small loan is greater than a higher balance loan. For instance, consider the case of two loans, a higher balance loan of $200,000 and a lower balance loan of $50,000, where the fixed costs of originating the loan are $2,500 per loan. In this case, the fixed cost is 1.25% of the higher balance loan and 5% of the lower balance loan. Assuming that the mortgage option under consideration is a no-cost refinance, the interest rate equivalent of 5% of the loan amount is higher than 1.25% of the loan amount. Hence, the low balance mortgagor is less sensitive to refinancings despite the no-cost option. By the same token, LLB mortgages also have a higher threshold with respect to solicited refinancing activity because the costs of such activity may not justify the benefits of such solicitations—primarily due to the size of the component mortgages as well as due to the lower commissions.

THE ARGUMENTS AGAINST SLOWER PREPAYMENT BEHAVIOR OF LLB POOLS

Although such theoretical arguments are intuitively appealing, the low balance debate has been colored by ideas suggesting that because of demographics and housing turnover, LLB pools may not exhibit a significant degree of dampened prepayment behavior. The crux of this argument arises from the fact that self-selection occurs in the creation of LLB pools. Since LLB mortgages are directly related to the cost of the underlying real estate, such pools do not include a significant number of mortgages that originated in high-cost areas, such as New York and California. Therefore, LLB pools are most likely comprised of mortgages located mainly in low-cost states. Due to this self-selection, the argument suggests that in periods of high real estate appreciation, the turnover of such mortgages may serve to counteract the prepayment dampening effect associated with LLB pools. This appreciation-generated turnover may be manifested in trade-up buying or "cashout" refinancing due to the buildup of equity. As a result, the prepayment advantage of LLB pools is not universally accepted. As noted above, our research suggests that the possibility of this phenomenon is actually a positive feature since the impact is most pronounced with discount-coupon mortgages. Since discount

LLB mortgages prepay just as fast—if not faster than generic mortgages—our findings also cast doubts on the commonly held belief that discount LLB mortgages have a higher degree of extension risk. Although a higher balance mortgagor has no incentive to refinance in a higher interest rate environment, low balance mortgagors may not be quite as "locked" in to the note rate due to trade-up buying and the effect of real estate appreciation, especially in low-cost areas. In other words, ceteris paribus, due to the lower balance, especially if there is a buildup of some degree of equity, LLBs are more likely to refinance than higher balance loans in the face of noneconomic considerations such as demographics even when the refinancing option is "out of the money."

The Data Are the Vindicating Factor

In most situations where theoretical arguments have intuitive appeal, evaluation of the empirical data usually provides the supporting evidence for testing the various hypotheses. Using loan-level information from our proprietary databases, our analysis involved the evaluation of historical trends of generic cohorts versus low balance cohorts using various criteria such as vintage, coupon, and geography as the stratification factors. This analysis was conducted for FHA and VA loans where low balance mortgages were defined as loans with maximum original loan size of $65,000. Our comparisons use Government National Mortgage Association (GNMA) "generic" prepayments obtained from agency pool factor tapes. Similar comparisons were conducted for conventional mortgages, where low balance mortgages were defined as loans with a maximum original loan size of $80,000.[2] In this

---

2. As a reference point, using FNMA conventional loan data, the average loan size for various coupons with the maximum amount outstanding (as of February 28, 1999) in the various vintages is as follows:

Coupon	Current Outstanding (in millions of dollars)	Mean (in thousands of dollars)	Fifth Percentile	Ninety-fifth Percentile	Range
6.0	91,153.3	129.7	76.9	162.1	85.2
6.5	195,597.6	117.1	67.1	151.7	84.6
7.0	132,163.8	101.3	62.5	139.0	76.5
7.5	66,519.6	90.2	55.0	131.0	76.0
8.0	32,372.8	73.9	33.7	125.2	91.5

Note that for higher coupons, the average loan balance approaches our upper limit for low balance loans, whereas the range of the loan sizes in the cohort is fairly high, suggesting the incidence of higher (than our upper limits) balance mortgages in the pools.

Similar data for FHA- and VA-insured pools are not available for the period under study. It is only recently that GNMA has decided to release loan-level information on insured mortgages. As noted in "Ginnie Joins Loan-Level Parade," *Mortgage-Backed Securities Letter* (May 10, 1999), these disclosures are expected to include the percentage of loans by state. Additionally, the information is expected to include the insurance program (FHA or VA) and loan amount. It is expected that information on existing pools will be updated on a quarterly basis and new pool information may be revised on a monthly basis.

subset of the analysis, conventional low balance prepayment speeds were compared to an index of conventional cohort generic speeds, composed of a weighted average of speeds for Federal Home Loan Mortgage Corporation (FHLMC) and Federal National Mortgage Association (FNMA) conventional programs.

Regarding the data, note that our evaluations use actual loan-level information, where the maximum upper limit is predefined and based upon the original mortgage balance. This point is relevant, as our upper limits in the analysis are not averages obtained from pool-level information. At the same time, since our evaluation is based upon original balance, the analysis captures the true low balance effect as opposed to an "artificial" low balance effect, which may occur through the observation of paid-down current mortgage balance. Similarly, our method introduces a high degree of homogeneity in the analysis, thereby creating tighter loan size dispersion within the pools under investigation and therefore antiseptic prepayment behavior. In our opinion, herein lies the reason for the divergence in opinion regarding the prepayment behavior of low balance pools.

The use of average pool balance as the guiding criteria for determining low balance pools is fraught with the discrepancies involved in deriving conclusions from averaged data. Conclusions drawn from such sources may not accurately reflect the true prepayment behavior of LLB pools since they actually reflect prepayments of higher as opposed to lower balance mortgages from the averaging process. For example, in a hypothetical pool composed of two mortgage loans, an upper limit of $60,000 by definition restricts the mortgages in the pool to an amount no greater than the limit. However, in a similar pool where the average balance is used as the stratification element, a $60,000 average balance could be obtained by including a $100,000 loan with a $20,000 mortgage or a $110,000 loan with a $10,000 loan—or any other permutation and combination of loan balance. In the former case, where the pool balance serves as the upper bound on the mortgage loan balance, the observed prepayment behavior truly reflects the effect of the lower mortgage balance. This may not necessarily be true in the prepayment behavior of LLB pools where faster prepayments may be caused by higher (than average balance) mortgages in the pool. In view of this observation, it is not difficult to recognize the caution of our approach in controlling for the loan balance effect by using the original loan balance.

Results of Our Evaluation

Our results show consistently slower prepayment patterns for current- and premium-coupon LLBs, irrespective of vintage and geographical origin, both for FHA or VA and conventional loans. However, for discount-coupon mortgages for which faster prepayment rates have been tallied for both government-insured and conventional loans, the evidence is not quite as conclusive. As noted below, this counterintuitive behavior stems from a higher degree of turnover associated with lower balance pools, which leads to an improved total rate of return profile.

The Aggregate Evidence

As noted in Exhibit 29–1, the prepayment curves—as represented by the 3-month conditional prepayment rate (CPR) for 30-year FHA and VA LLB mortgages (original balance equal to or less than $65,000) for current- and premium-coupon classes—are consistently slower than generic GNMA speeds for all coupon classes for the period ending February 28, 1999. However, for discounts, the

E X H I B I T   29–1

Comparison of FHA and VA LLBs with GNMA Generics by Aggregate Coupon Class

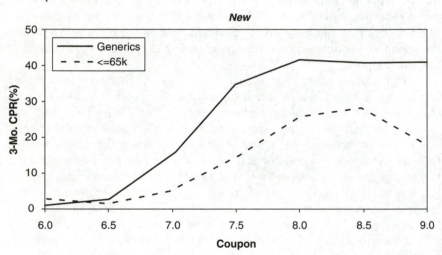

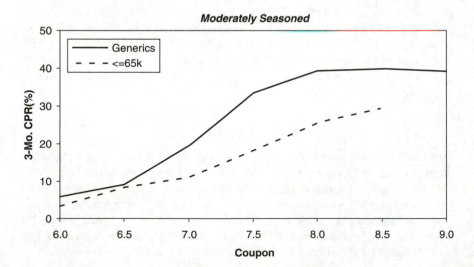

E X H I B I T   29–1

Continued

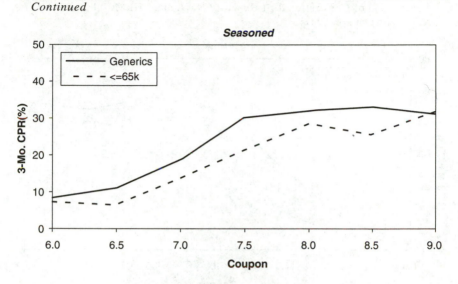

Source: Countrywide Home Loans and Countrywide Securities Corporation as of February 28, 1999.

speeds are in some instances, slightly faster than generics. A similar pattern is observed for conventional loans (original balance equal to or less than $80,000) vis-à-vis FNMA and FHLMC generic speeds for various coupons in Exhibit 29–2. It is interesting to note that these prepayment differences are maintained across the entire universe as well as for different gradations of seasoning. For our purposes, loans with ages between 30 and 60 months were defined as "moderately seasoned," whereas any loan with over an age of 5 years was defined as "seasoned." With respect to new loans, the speed differences are minor for discounts. However, as the loan becomes a premium, the speed differences increase. Notably, the speed difference is an increasing function of the premium coupon. Contrarily, moderately seasoned and seasoned low balance loans exhibit a consistently slower prepayment pattern across the board in comparison to the respective benchmarks (generic GNMAs for FHA and VA loans and FNMA and FHLMC generics for conventional loans).

Comparison of Conventional LLBs with FNMA and FHLMC Generics by
Aggregate Coupon Class

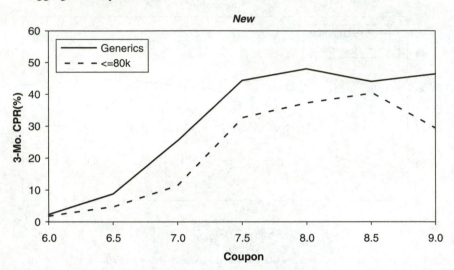

E X H I B I T   29–2

Continued

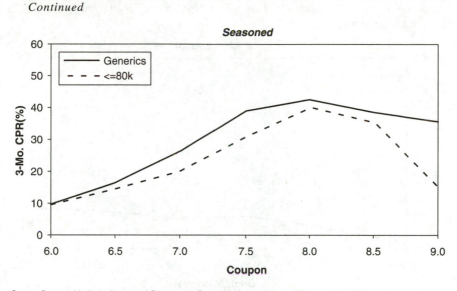

Source: Countrywide Home Loans and Countrywide Securities Corporation as of February 28, 1999.

Evidence by Coupon Class and Vintage

Consistent with the evidence seen with the aggregate-coupon class, results for LLB prepayments within each coupon class are strikingly similar for all vintages (1993 to 1998), with the exception of discount coupons. As noted in Exhibit 29–3, FHA and VA current and premium low balance loans prepay slower than generic GNMAs for all origination years, ranging from 1993 to 1998. The comparisons of the LLB conventional pools (maximum mortgage balance of $80,000) versus FNMA and FHLMC generic pools are detailed in Exhibit 29–4. The findings for the different vintages in conventional pools are similar to the results obtained for the government-guaranteed mortgages. The prepayment behavior of both current and premium LLBs is slower than that of generics, whereas the prepayment behavior of discount loans is equivalent to that of generic cohorts.

The Effect of Geographic Dispersion

One of the major issues of debate in the low balance prepayment discussion is related to the geographic origin of the loan. The argument here stems from the contention that LLBs which originated in areas of high real estate appreciation can refinance even in a regime of higher rates as a result of trade-up buying due to the resultant buildup of equity.

Comparison of FHA and VA LLBs with GNMA Generics by Coupon
and Origination

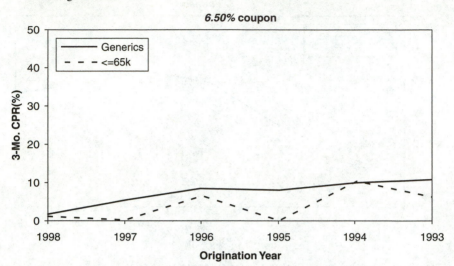

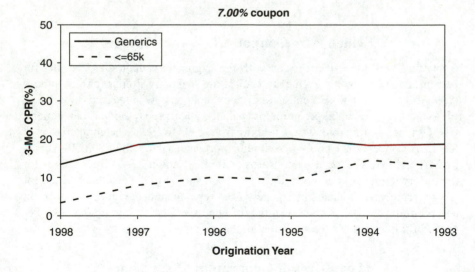

EXHIBIT 29–3

Continued

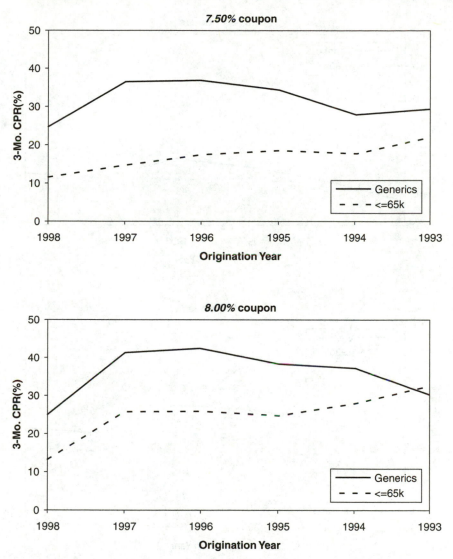

7.50% coupon

8.00% coupon

Source: Countrywide Home Loans and Countrywide Securities Corporation as of February 28, 1999.

Conventional Prepayments by Coupon and Origination—LLBs Versus Generics

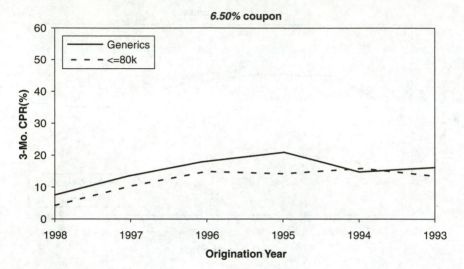

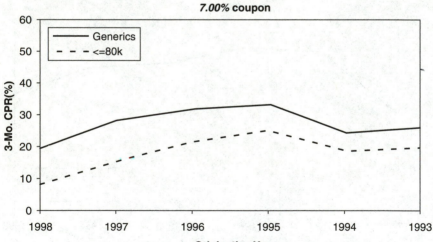

EXHIBIT 29–4

Continued

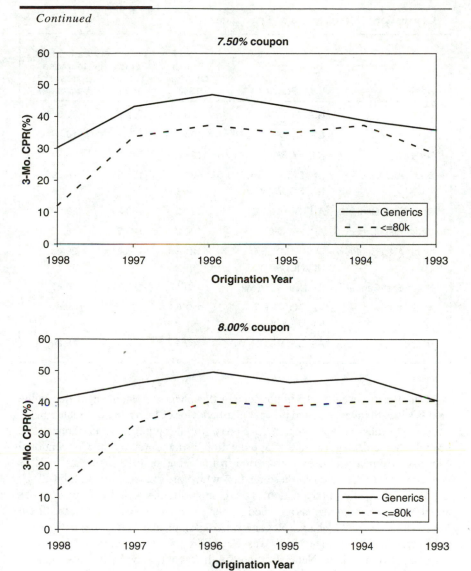

Source: Countrywide Home Loans and Countrywide Securities Corporation as of February 28, 1999.

EXHIBIT   29–5

Conventional Mortgage Home Price Index

Region	States	Fourth Quarter 1993	Fourth Quarter 1998	Percent of Increase (Percent of Decrease)
US	N.A.	129.4	157.7	21.87%
New England	CT, MA, ME, NH, RI, VT	104.4	121.6	16.48
Mid-Atlantic	NJ, NY, PA	128.0	142.0	10.94
South Atlantic	DC, DE, FL, GA, MD, NC, SC, VA, WV	130.1	154.8	18.99
South East Central	AL, KY, MS, TN	124.5	160.7	29.08
South West Central	AR, LA, OK, TX	104.3	123.3	18.22
North West Central	IA, KS, MN, MO, ND, NE, SD	121.6	156.2	28.45
North East Central	IL, IN, MI, OH, WI	143.1	186.7	30.47
Mountain	AZ, CO, ID, MT, NM, NV, UT, WY	121.6	161.5	32.81
Pacific	AK, CA, HI, OR, WA	152.1	176.8	16.24

In order to evaluate the importance of this phenomenon, the next step in the analysis was to investigate the prepayment behavior of loans that originated in areas of high real estate appreciation. As a proxy for the aggregate level of real estate growth, the percentage change of appreciation, as measured by the Conventional Mortgage Home Price Index for a period from the end of 1993 to the end of 1998 was compared.[3] As noted in these results, which are presented in Exhibit 29–5, although appreciation in the nation as a whole during the period investigated was about 21.87%, certain regions recorded higher growth rates. In particular, the South East Central region (Alabama, Kentucky, Mississippi, and Tennessee) exhibited a growth rate of 29.08%. The North West Central region (Iowa, Kansas, Minnesota, Missouri, North Dakota, Nebraska, and South Dakota) grew by 28.45%, and the North East Central region (Illinois, Indiana, Michigan, Ohio, and Wisconsin) recorded real estate appreciation of 30.47%. During the same period, the Mountain region (Arizona, Colorado, Idaho, Montana, New Mexico, Nevada, Utah, and Wyoming) enjoyed growth of approximately 32.81%. In the event that the turnover argument applies to the case of low loan balances, it stands to reason that these regions should exhibit prepayment patterns faster than the aggregate low

3. The source for the Conventional Mortgage Home Price Index data is Bloomberg. This index is a 20-year quarterly index series covering 4.5 million repeat home sales or appraisals as identified through the purchase activity of FHLMC and FNMA.

EXHIBIT 29–6

Countrywide 30-Year Conventional Prepayments by Aggregate Coupon
Class—LLBs Versus Conventional Generics

Coupon	Aggregate Class	Category	Life Percent CPR
		Generic	2.0
6.0	Total	LLB	2.0
		LLB-NEC, NWC, SEC, M	1.9
		Generic	6.3
6.5	Total	LLB	3.9
		LLB-NEC, NWC, SEC, M	4.1
		Generic	13.4
7.0	Total	LLB	8.1
		LLB-NEC, NWC, SEC, M	9.2
		Generic	20.3
7.5	Total	LLB	14.6
		LLB-NEC, NWC, SEC, M	17.9
		Generic	23.2
8.0	Total	LLB	18.7
		LLB-NEC, NWC, SEC, M	22.4
		Generic	24.0
8.5	Total	LLB	21.6
		LLB-NEC, NWC, SEC, M	24.9

Note: NEC = North East Central (IL, IN, MI, OH, WI); NWC = North West Central (IA, KS, MN, MO, ND, NE, SD); SEC = South East Central (AL, KY, MS, TN); M = Mountain (AZ, CO, ID, MT, NM, NV, UT, WY).
Source: Countrywide Home Loans and Countrywide Securities Corporation as of February 28, 1999.

balance population. The results of this analysis, which describes the prepayment patterns of conventional loans originated in states comprising the different geographical regions listed above, are detailed in Exhibit 29–6.

In Exhibit 29–6, prepayment speeds, as represented by lifetime CPRs of low balance loans originated in states with real estate appreciation higher than that of the national average, were compared with equivalent speeds for the low loan balance population and generic conventional cohorts. Our evaluation shows several interesting results. First, speeds of loans originating in higher real estate growth areas were faster than speeds of generic LLBs. This suggests the incidence of some degree of cash-out refinancing activity due to equity buildup in the properties, part of which may also be manifested in trade-up buying. However, in all cases, with the exception of 8.5% coupons, speeds of the low balance loans in these states were still lower than speeds of the generic cohorts. Even in the case of 8.5% conventional coupons, the prepayment difference is relatively minor and can be explained by turnover. Alternatively, it is equally likely that the burnout effect in this coupon is counterbalanced by the effect of equity buildup that may lead to a higher rate of prepayment activity. The crux of this analysis is that despite the effect of real estate appreciation generated refinancing activity, the prepayment advantage of low loan balances over conventional generics is still maintained over the majority of the universe. At the same time, due to the effect of real estate appreciation, discount LLBs in these geographic areas are likely to prepay faster than generics due to the effects of turnover. It would also stand to reason that in the absence of real estate growth, the speeds of such loans would revert to average speeds for LLBs.

The Culprit Is Turnover

As noted earlier, in our analysis of LLB mortgages, current and premium coupons prepay slower than generics, regardless of the loan type (conventionals versus governments) and vintage. At the same time, discount low balance coupons exhibit a tendency to prepay slightly faster than equivalent coupon generics. An alternative way of describing this phenomenon is that LLB mortgages prepay slower than generics in an up market (lower rates and positive refinancing incentive) and faster than generics in a down market (higher rates and negative refinancing incentive). Although the former result is acceptable, the latter results in terms of the behavior of discount low balance coupons that are counterintuitive. Why do mortgagors who have no interest rate incentive to refinance prepay their mortgages in an environment of rising interest rates?

In our opinion, the driving force behind this phenomenon is turnover. Recall that in the low balance debate, the geographic origin of the mortgage loan is an issue of some discussion. The onset of this issue rests in the argument that the creation process of LLB pools is colored to some extent by a degree of self-selection. This refers to the argument that the concept of LLB pools excludes mortgages originating in high-cost states like New York and California—an observation that is confirmed by our empirical results. A corollary of this argument suggests that since most LLB pools are composed of mortgages originating in lower-cost states, the prepayment behavior of these pools may be faster due to the influence of turnover caused by a higher rate of housing appreciation. Additionally, low balance mortgagors tend to be first-time home buyers and may need to upgrade housing in the face of changing demographic conditions, such as increased family size. It could also be argued that trade-up buyers in the LLB category might not be quite as sensitive to higher interest rates because of the lower principal amount of the loan. At the same time, in this environment of higher interest rates, home owners with "regular" balance mortgages are likely to be "locked" in to the existing loan as opposed to taking out a new loan with a higher note rate, unless there is a significant amount of real estate appreciation.

Probing further into this phenomenon, we used a two-pronged approach. The first part of the approach was an attempt to evaluate the relative sensitivity of LLBs in different refinancing regimes. Upon confirmation of the fact that LLBs exhibited a faster prepayment pattern in negative refinancing incentive scenarios, the second part of the analysis was an attempt to isolate the effect of turnover. In this stage of the analysis, the prepayment behavior of LLBs of various seasonings was tested in different disincentive refinancing scenarios. By focusing on the prepayment pattern in disincentive scenarios, the effect of interest rate–related prepayment behavior was thereby controlled.

In order to assess the relative prepayment sensitivity of LLB mortgages, data sets were created to correlate the prepayment behavior of such loans in various refinancing scenarios. The results of these analyses are detailed in Exhibits 29–7 and 29–8 for FHA and VA insured and conventional loans, respectively. In these exhibits, the refinancing incentive was obtained by subtracting the note rate of the mortgage from the FHLMC survey mortgage rate prevalent during that time period. In other words, if the loan under question had a note rate of 7% and the existing

E X H I B I T   29–7

FHA and VA 30-Year Fixed-Rate Refinancing* Curves—LLBs Versus Generics

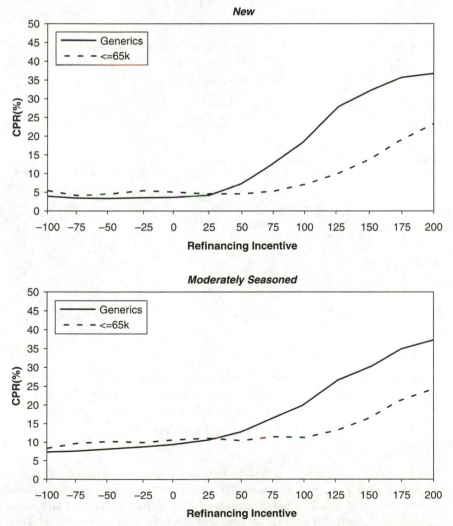

(continued)

E X H I B I T   29–7

Continued

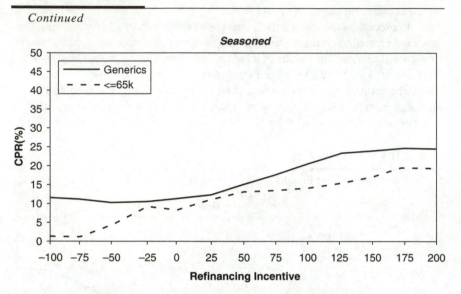

Seasoned

*Refinancing incentive measured is the difference between note rate and the prevailing mortgage rate.
Source:* Countrywide Home Loans and Countrywide Securities Corporation as of February 28, 1999.

E X H I B I T   29–8

Conventional 30-Year Fixed-Rate Refinancing* Curves—LLBs Versus Generics

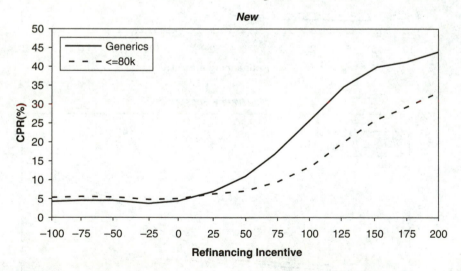

New

FHLMC survey rate was 7.5%, then the refinancing incentive would be labeled as "Negative 50 basis points." As noted in these exhibits, for both government-insured and conventional loans, new and seasoned LLBs prepaid faster than equivalent generics in negative refinancing incentive regimes when interest rates were higher.

EXHIBIT 29–8

Continued

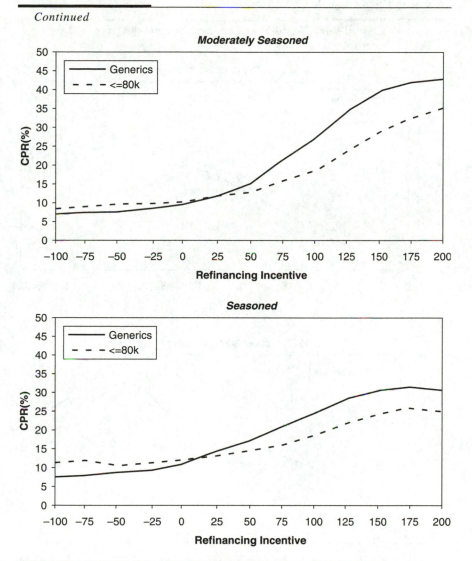

*Refinancing incentive measured is the difference between note rate and the prevailing mortgage rate.
Source: Countrywide Home Loans and Countrywide Securities Corporation as of February 28, 1999.

Yet at the same time, when interest rates were lower, LLBs prepaid slower than those of generic cohorts. For seasoned loans, although conventionals exhibited the same prepayment pattern as other vintages, the government-insured loans were consistently slower than the generic cohorts. There may be several possible reasons for this behavior including, but not limited to, lower loan size, higher LTV ratios, and absence of demographic factors driving the higher turnover.

EXHIBIT   29–9

Countrywide FHA and VA 30-Year Empirical Seasoning Curve—LLBs
Versus Generics

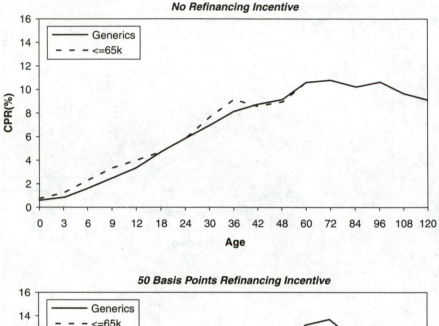

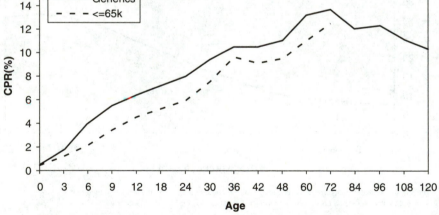

The results of the above analysis provide additional evidence that show discount LLBs prepay faster than equivalent generics, as well as that they are faster than generic cohorts in a negative refinancing environment. Since the determinant of this phenomenon is likely to be faster housing turnover, our analysis focused on further investigating the prepayment behavior of mortgages in various financing incentive scenarios. The results of these analyses are presented in Exhibits 29–9 and 29–10 for both FHA- and VA-insured and conventional loans, respectively.

EXHIBIT 29–9

Continued

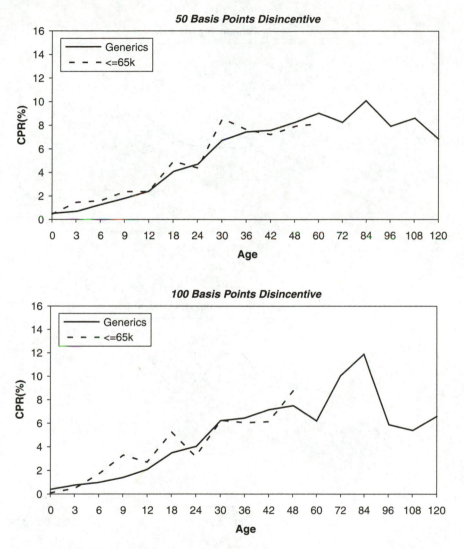

Source: Countrywide Securities Corporation as of February 28, 1999.

Exhibits 29–9 and 29–10 describe the prepayment behavior of the LLBs in various refinancing incentive schemes for different degrees of seasoning. In fact, the emphasis in this analysis was on understanding the prepayment behavior in different refinancing disincentives to control for the effect of interest rate–related refinancing component. In these exhibits, holding refinancing incentive constant,

E X H I B I T   29–10

Countrywide Conventional 30-Year Empirical Seasoning Curve—LLBs
Versus Generics

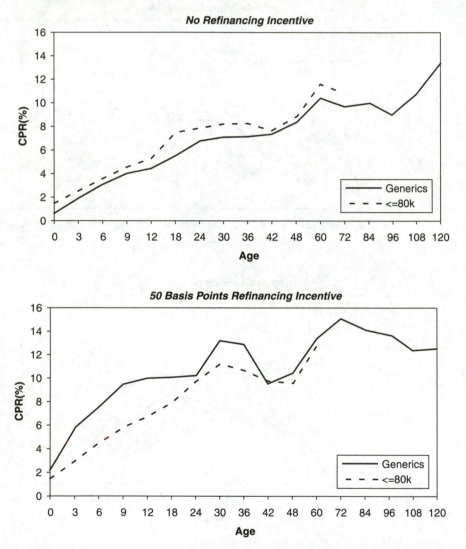

the prepayment behavior of LLBs is compared to generic cohorts with varying degrees of seasoning. In the "No Refinance Incentive" case, the prepayment behavior of mortgages, where the note rate of the underlying mortgages is equal to the FHLMC survey rate is compared to that of generic cohorts. Similarly, the prepayment patterns of MBS, whose note rate is 50 bps higher than the corresponding

E X H I B I T   29–10

Continued

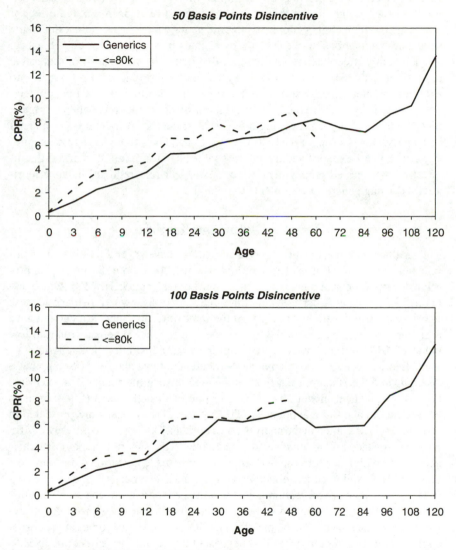

Source: Countrywide Securities Corporation as of February 28, 1999.

FHLMC survey rate are evaluated in the "50 basis points Disincentive" case. Note that for both government-insured and conventional mortgages, prepayments are faster for LLBs. Since this prepayment behavior is recorded during periods of refinancing disincentives, the driver of these prepayments is housing turnovers caused by such factors as trade-up buying and real estate appreciation. Consistent with our earlier hypotheses and related findings, LLBs begin to prepay slower than generic benchmarks when the refinancing incentive becomes positive. In such instances, the note rate of the underlying mortgages is higher than the FHLMC survey rate during this period. As interest rates decrease, the effect of rate-related refinancing becomes stronger in generic mortgages mainly due to the savings in payments that occur from lower rates on a higher mortgage balance. Arguably, this effect becomes exponentially greater during periods of real estate appreciation, as higher valuations may cause the mortgagor to refinance into shorter-term mortgages or to take out a higher balance loan due to the appreciation of the equity in the real estate. In sum, during down markets, when mortgage rates are lower than the prevailing interest rates, the turnover-related component of prepayments is stronger for LLB mortgages and leads to higher aggregate prepayments. On the other hand, as interest rates decrease in an up market, the interest rate–generated prepayment effect is stronger for "regular" balance mortgages, causing generic prepayments to be higher.

Relative Value Implications

The results of our analysis of prepayment patterns have several relative value implications. First of all, it is clear that low balance MBS, both discounts and premiums, have a superior convexity profile than equivalent generic MBS. Since discount LLBs prepay faster (slower) than generics in a down (up) market, these loans have lesser negative convexity. At the same time, discount LLBs do not have a higher degree of extension risk than generic discounts, whereas premium low balance MBS exhibit a lower degree of prepayment sensitivity than generics.

In order to assess the relative value inherent in low balance MBS, our analysis compared the "theoretical value" embedded in such mortgages using our low balance prepayment model on a constant option-adjusted spread (OAS) basis to equivalent-coupon to-be-announced (TBA) prices. These results are presented in Exhibit 29–11. As noted in the analysis, on a constant OAS basis, low balance MBS have an embedded relative value advantage due to the superior prepayment characteristics. With respect to the performance attributes, conventional discount low balance MBS exhibit a lower effective duration and a lower degree of negative convexity profile than generic cohorts. On the other hand, premium conventionals display a slightly longer duration and slightly less positive convex profile. With respect to FHA and VA LLBs, the pickup in additional convexity comes at the cost of slightly longer duration profile. This suggests that the turnover effect on GNMAs is not quite as strong as that of conventionals and may be explained by the differences in credit quality between FHA-VA and conventional borrowers. Nonetheless, the convexity profile of government LLBs is superior to that of GNMA generics.

It is clear from the analysis above that LLBs have an embedded relative value, mostly superior convexity characteristics, without exhibiting any degree of significant duration extension. Although market participants may not completely agree on the benefits of LLB pools, the current pricing scheme in the market prices the premium over generic securities (TBA) as an increasing function of the coupon. Representative "payups" for various coupons over TBA prices are described in Exhibit 29–12. Implicit in the market evaluation of these pay-ups for LLBs is that higher coupon loans prepay slower than lower coupon loans. The comparison between the market-determined payups and the embedded theoretical value for various coupons is also described in Exhibit 29–12. This metric may be more adequately described as the relative value embedded in LLBs after adjusting for the market-determined payups. The higher this metric, the greater is the magnitude of embedded relative value. As noted in the analysis, with respect to conventional loans, this measure of embedded relative value is an indirect function of the market payup. In other words, discount and current loans have the maximum degree of this embedded value. With respect to government loans, the maximum amount of this value rests in the middle of the coupon stack (6.5%s through 7.5%s).

CONCLUSION

Using the expanded methodological framework that includes loan-level information and the associated obligor and property characteristics, our analysis focused on the efficacy of loan balance as an explanatory variable in prepayment behavior. Intuitively, it is not difficult to fathom the reasons for slower prepayments, such as higher refinancing thresholds and the lack of incentives on the part of efficient servicers to solicit such loans. However, since such loans are located in lower-cost areas, LLB pools could exhibit faster prepayment behavior, due to the effects of turnover, especially in a regime of high real estate appreciation. Although our results confirm the existence of this effect, LLB speeds are still slower than those of equivalent conventional generic cohorts. Using loan-level information, our results also indicate that current and premium LLBs exhibit slower prepayment behavior than generic higher balance loans, though counter-intuitively, discount loans exhibit slightly faster prepayments than generics in a regime where there are disincentives to refinance. In our opinion, these results are caused by a higher degree of turnover stemming from trade-up buying and demographic features such as expanded family size. Therefore, the phenomenon of turnover-driven prepayments, which has been used to negate the slow prepayment characteristic of LLBs, actually turns out to be a positive and desirable feature as the impact is mostly on discount loans. In view of these findings, low balance MBS have desirable convexity characteristics without the attendant issues of significant additional extension risk. As much as such results have merit for the relative value of MBS, these findings also have implications for the creation of structured products, such as collateralized mortgage obligations,[4] to exploit the specific prepayment characteristics of LLBs. Although the benefits of the low balance pools may not be universally accepted, the results of our analyses also suggest a certain degree of mispricing in the payups for such pools. The payups for such pools are priced as an increasing function of coupon, with the lowest payups accorded to discount MBS. Yet, given our results, it appears that the discount and current LLBs have the most desirable total return and convexity profiles indicating a higher degree of embedded relative value in these coupons.

---

4. Freddie Mac Series 1980 (Bloomberg ID: FHR 1980) and Freddie Mac Series 2019 are examples of structured deals collateralized by low balance pools.

E X H I B I T 29–11

Relative Value of LLBs

Coupon: 30 Year	Price	OAS	Effective Duration	Effective Convexity	Theoretical Value	Difference in Effective Duration	Difference in Effective Convexity
FNMA 6.0	93-10	82.9	6.01	-0.37	17	-0.19	0.09
FNMA 6.0 (LLB)	93-27		5.83	-0.28			
FNMA 6.5	95-29+	83.9	5.38	-0.61	14+	-0.13	0.10
FNMA 6.5 (LLB)	96-12		5.25	-0.51			
FNMA 7.0	98-11+	84.9	4.67	-0.99	13+	-0.04	0.19
FNMA 7.0 (LLB)	98-25		4.63	-0.80			
FNMA 7.5	100-19+	85.9	3.88	-1.23	14+	0.06	0.07
FNMA 7.5 (LLB)	101-02		3.94	-1.16			
FNMA 8.0	102-12	86.9	3.25	-1.22	8	0.00	0.06
FNMA 8.0 (LLB)	102-20		3.25	-1.16			
Gold 6.0	93-14	87.9	5.99	-0.38	17	-0.18	0.09
Gold 6.0 (LLB)	93-31		5.81	-0.29			
Gold 6.5	96-00+	88.9	5.36	-0.61	14+	-0.13	0.10
Gold 6.5 LLB	96-15		5.23	-0.51			
Gold 7.0	98-15	89.9	4.65	-0.98	13	-0.04	0.18
Gold 7.0 (LLB)	98-28		4.61	-0.80			
Gold 7.5	100-22+	90.9	3.89	-1.21	14+	0.05	0.05
Gold 7.5 (LLB)	101-05		3.94	-1.16			
Gold 8.0	102-14	91.9	3.24	-1.22	7	0.00	0.07
Gold 8.0 (LLB)	102-21		3.24	-1.15			

GNMA 6.0	92-26		7.19	−0.29	5+	0.07	0.16
GNMA 6.0 (LLB)	92-31+	92.9	7.26	−0.13			
GNMA 6.5	95-18+		6.23	−0.83	7+	0.24	0.23
GNMA 6.5 LLB	95-26	93.9	6.47	−0.60			
GNMA 7.0	98-04		5.23	−0.96	8	0.18	0.09
GNMA 7.0 LLB	98-12	94.9	5.41	−0.87			
GNMA 7.5	100-16+		4.27	−1.11	9+	0.21	0.09
GNMA 7.5 LLB	100-26	95.9	4.48	−1.02			
GNMA 8.0	102-17		3.46	−1.30	10	0.31	0.08
GNMA 8.0 (LLB)	102-27	96.9	3.77	−1.22			

Source: Countrywide Securities Corporation as of June 28, 1999.

Market Payup Adjusted Value of LLBs

		Conventionals			
Coupon	Market Payup	Theoretical Payup		Market Payup—Adjusted Relative Value	
		FNMA	FHLMC	FNMA	FHLMC
6.0	0	17	17	17	17
6.5	0	14+	14+	14+	14+
7.0	1	13+	13	12+	12
7.5	3+	14+	14+	11	11
8.0	5+	8	7	2+	1+

		Governments	
Coupon	Market Payup	Theoretical Payup	Market Payup—Adjusted Relative Value
6.0	0	5+	5+
6.5	0	7+	7+
7.0	+	8	7+
7.5	3	9+	6+
8.0	5	10	5

Source: Countrywide Securities Corporation as of June 28, 1999.

CHAPTER 30

ANALYSIS OF LOW-WAC MBS

Anand K. Bhattacharya, Ph.D.
Executive Vice President
Countrywide Capital Markets Inc.

Due to innovation on the part of originators of mortgages and government-sponsored enterprises (GSEs), the field of mortgage-backed securities (MBS) is becoming increasingly diverse. Although some of these products are created as a result of stratification along certain obligor, property, or mortgage characteristics such as loan balance or prepayment penalties, other types of MBS are created as a corollary of efficient and flexible pooling practices. In understanding such securities, evaluation of the structural issues involved in the creation of these pools can be important in the prepayment behavior of the underlying mortgages. One such product is the low-weighted average coupon pool, labeled in industry parlance as "low-WAC." The purpose of this chapter is to present the process by which low-WAC pools are created, to evaluate the prepayment behavior of such pools, and to discuss the associated relative valuation issues.

Low-WAC pools consist of loans with note rates (or gross WAC) between a quarter to three-eighths of the pass-through rate for a given MBS coupon. The typical pool is created with mortgage loans where the note rate varies by increments of one half of 1%. Prior to the advent of the FNMA alternative pricing service (FNMA ASC) program, originators were required to maintain a minimum servicing fee (typically 25 basis points for fixed-rate MBS and 37.5 basis points for adjustable-rate mortgages). With the development of the ASC program, originators are able to retain less than this minimum requirement when pooling conventional loans. Due to the paucity of historical data available on FNMA ASC securities, primarily because of the recent nature of the program, this chapter focuses on the traditional forms of low-WAC pools, which involve the retention of the minimum mandated servicing amount.

Research and computational assistance by Jeremy Burdick, Esther Chang, and Nick Trosper is gratefully acknowledged.

THE CREATION OF LOW-WAC POOLS

Low-WAC pools are created as a corollary of efficient and flexible pooling practices. From the nonbank mortgage originator's perspective, one issue of concern in the secondary marketing of mortgages is obtaining the most efficient execution, which usually translates into the highest cash proceeds. The creation of mortgages into conventional MBS guaranteed by either the Federal National Mortgage Loan Association (FNMA) or Federal Home Loan Mortgage Corporation (FHLMC) involves the following formulation:

$$\text{MBS pass-through rate} = \text{Mortgage note rate} - \text{minimum required servicing fee}$$
$$- \text{ guaranty fee} - \text{excess servicing} \qquad (30\text{--}1)$$

In Equation (30–1) unless the pools are securitized under the FNMA ASC program, the minimum required servicing fee is specified by the agencies, whereas the guaranty fee is negotiated with the agencies as a function of volume, market share, loss and foreclosure experience, and credit underwriting policies.

At first blush the mathematics of the loan securitization process appears fairly straightforward. However, in practice, the process is subject to certain constraints. First, MBS pass-through coupons are typically created in increments of 50 basis points, although quarter coupons have also been issued. However, because the typical coupon is in 0.5% increments, the creation of alternative coupons (quarters or eighths) is usually associated with a lack of liquidity in after-market trading. In the creation of pass-through securities the strict application of the formulation specified in Equation (30–1) leads to the generation of excess servicing.

As an illustration of these issues, consider the following example of a 30-year conventional mortgage:

Mortgage rate	7.875%	7.625%
Less		
Minimum servicing fee	0.250	0.250
Guaranty fee	0.200	0.200
Excess servicing	0.425	0.175
Equals pass-through rate	7.000%	7.000%

In this example the originator is left with an excess servicing asset, which varies in magnitude as a function of the note rate. At the same time the cash proceeds from securitization have not been maximized. In the event the originator does not have an appetite for the excess servicing asset, it could also be argued that the execution was inefficient in both cases.

In order to maximize the proceeds from the securitization of loans, originators rely on the usage of the "buy-down" and "buy-up" mechanism. Recall from the previous discussion that the minimum servicing fee is a fixed amount based on the type of mortgage loan under consideration. However, in order to maximize the sale proceeds, the guaranty fee can be bought up or bought down. In the first example the guaranty fee could be bought down to 12.5 basis points in exchange for a one time fixed fee to the guarantor. Additionally, as part of this process, the excess servicing asset of 42.5 basis points is monetized and the 7.875% note can be delivered into a higher pass-through rate of 7.5%, thereby resulting in a higher price. Applied in this manner, the buy-down of the guarantee fee allows the originator to monetize the excess servicing asset as well as to obtain a higher price by securitizing the loan into a higher pass-through rate. In the second example where the excess servicing asset is 17.5 basis points, the mortgage originator could buy-up the guaranty fee to 37.5 basis points and receive a one time cash payment. Similar to the buy-down fee that is paid by the originator to obtain a higher pass-through rate and to monetize the value of the excess servicing, the amount of the buy-up fee is also determined by a multiple that is determined by the agencies. As a reference point the guaranty fee can be bought down to zero while the maximum amount of the buy-up is 20 basis points.

Assuming that this method of execution was used in the pass-through process, the mathematics of the securitization would be as follows:

Mortgage rate	7.875%	7.625%
Less		
Minimum servicing fee	0.250	0.250
Guaranty fee	0.125	0.375
Excess servicing	0.000	0.000
Equals Pass-through rate	7.50%	7.000%
Buy-down amount	7.5 bps	N/A
Buy-down multiple	4×	N/A
Buy-down fee (paid by originator)	0.30%	N/A
Buy-up amount	N/A	17.5 bp
Buy-up multiple	N/A	3.0×
Buy-up fee (received by originator)	N/A	0.525%

In the first case the originator pays a fee of 0.30% (buy-down guaranty fee amount of 7.5 basis points multiplied by 4) to extinguish the excess servicing asset. Additionally, the originator also obtains a higher price by securitizing the loan as a 7.5% coupon as opposed to a 7.0% coupon, which would have been the case without the buy-down provision. In the second case the originator receives a fee of 0.525% (excess guaranty fee amount of 17.5 basis points multiplied by 3) to liquefy the excess servicing asset of 17.5 basis points. Note, however, in this case the pass-through rate of the security remains at 7.0%. Therefore, buy-downs and buy-ups are mechanisms by which originators are allowed to maximize the proceeds from securitization while simultaneously eliminating the excess servicing asset from the balance sheet.

It is the process of the "buy-down" of the guaranty fees that leads to the creation of low-WAC pools. In our example the low-WAC nature of the MBS stems from the fact that the resultant security has a coupon rate of 7.5% with an underlying mortgage note rate of 7.875%, as opposed to a 7% note rate in the case of a "regular" WAC MBS. Therefore, pools of low-WAC loans have tighter loan dispersion and obviously a lower gross WAC than equivalent coupon MBS.

Analytically, this process of buy-ups and buy-downs is very similar to the trading of interest-only (IO) securities. Assuming that the cash flow pattern of the excess servicing asset is similar to that of IO securities,[1] in the case of buy-downs, where the originator pays an up-front fee to buy-down the guaranty fee, the originator has bought an IO security. The cost of this security is then subsidized by the higher cash proceeds from the sale of the securities. Conversely, in the case of buy-ups, where the originator receives a fee for the value of the excess servicing asset, the originator has sold an IO security. The price received for this security enhances the value of the cash proceeds received from the sale of the lower coupon loan. Note that the multiple for the buy-down is higher than the equivalent multiple for the same coupon for a buy-up. All other factors being equal, this implies that for an equivalent amount of the guaranty fee, the buy-down fee will be higher than the buy-up fee. In theory this is no different from the bid-offer spread in the securities market. Therefore, in this process of buy-ups and buy-downs the role of the agencies is similar to that of MBS trading desks. The buy-up of the guaranty fee by the originator (sale of the IO) where the agencies are buying the IO from the originator is similar to the bid side of the securities market and, hence, trades wider (lower multiple), resulting in lesser proceeds. The buy-down of the guaranty fee by the originator (purchase of the IO) where the agency is selling the IO to the originator is equivalent to the offer side of the securities market and thereby trades tighter (higher multiple), leading to higher proceeds.

Based on this observation, most low-WAC pools are likely to be created during periods when interest rates are expected to decline. Although our objective is not to discuss the originators' strategic considerations for retaining servicing, it is fair to state that originators are less likely to retain excess servicing in a declining rate environment. In addition to the fact that such declines in interest rates lead to impairment of the servicing portfolio, it is also likely that in this environment income from refinancing activity will be higher, possibly resulting in reduced corporate appetite for additional servicing assets. Additionally, during such times the buy-down multiple is likely to be lower, resulting in reduced up-front payment for the buy-down of the guaranty fee. This observation is important because it shows that the average age of low-WAC pools are lower than comparable generics, and as noted subsequently, serves as an explanatory variable in the evaluation of the prepayment behavior of low-WAC pools.

In addition, during such times of interest rate declines, due to the sheer volume of refinancing activity, it is also highly possible that a large share of the refi-

---

1. While the cash flow pattern of agency IOs is affected mainly by prepayments and that of nonagency guaranteed IOs by defaults, prepayments, and structural characteristics of the loans, such as lockouts and yield maintenance, there are several factors that affect excess servicing cash flows. In addition to prepayments and defaults, variables, such as the cost of servicing, interest earned on escrow balances, and frequency of tax payments and costs of foreclosure have an impact on excess servicing cash flows.

nancing volume will be handled by independent brokers. Although this phenomenon is likely to be stronger during periods of high demand, a large percentage of mortgages are originated by independent brokers. As a reference point, according to industry research conducted by Wholesale Access, the estimated number of mortgage brokerages multiplied exponentially to about 36,000 at the end of 1998—up from about 7,000 about a decade ago. Furthermore, these entities handled about 70% of the estimated $1.7 trillion worth of mortgages originated in 1998 versus about 20% in 1987.[2] As a general observation, for certain companies, the mortgage-brokered origination rate tends to be higher due to the costs of broker intermediation. In view of this observation, to the extent that the mortgagor pays a higher rate, there is a greater possibility that such loans do not end up in low-WAC pools. Since loans originated in retail channels and loans with higher discount points are the most likely to end up in low-WAC pools, MBS collateralized by such loans tend to prepay slower than generic cohorts.

CONVENTIONAL VERSUS GOVERNMENT INSURED LOW-WAC MBS

Low-WAC pools are usually created with conventional mortgages. The Government National Mortgage Association (GNMA) does not have a comparable program to the FNMA/FHLMC buy-up/buy-down option that allows originators to use these techniques to extinguish the value of the excess servicing. With respect to Federal Housing Administration (FHA) and Veterans Administration (VA) loans that are insured by GNMA, any "odd" note rates are securitized under the aegis of the GNMA II program. Since the gross WAC in GNMA I program is exactly 50 basis points higher than the net coupon, there is no WAC dispersion in such pools. However, since GNMA II pools can include mortgages with note rates ranging from 50 to 150 basis points higher than the net coupon, the WAC dispersion of these pools is higher.

Recently FNMA started securitizing FHA/VA loans that are not originated in note rate increments of 0.5 or 1% under the label of "Fannie One™" securities or FNGL (Fannie Mae Government Level) pools.[3] Depending on the circumstances at hand, FNGL execution may be more efficient for mortgage note rates that are not in increments of 50 basis points than GNMA IIs due to lower required servicing fees (25 basis points for FNMA versus 44 basis points or greater for GNMA IIs). Along this vein, it is also important to distinguish between the "new" and "old" FNMA GL programs. Prior to 1998 FNGL pools primarily included FHA/VA loans that could not be pooled as GNMA Is or IIs mainly because of age restrictions (the maximum age for inclusion in GNMA pools is 48 months) and certain documentation deficiencies. However, although the FNGL program does not preclude the inclusion of such loans, issuance

---

2. As reported in Michael D. Larson, "Mortgage Brokers Multiply, but Their Deals Are Not Always a Bargain," *Bloomberg*, September 23, 1999.
3. The first FNGL MBS was issued in July 1998 with loans originated by Countrywide Home Loans, whereas the first multistandard major pool was issued in January 1999.

E X H I B I T   30-1

FNMA GL Issuance

Coupon	No. of Pools	Total GL Current Outstanding*	Total Current GNSF Origination*	% of GL in Total GNSF Origination
		Pre-1998 Issued FNMA GL		
5.5	15	20.8	969.8	2.14
6.0	28	51.5	25,580.6	0.20
6.5	79	163.0	88,544.3	0.18
7.0	18	129.5	103,148.7	0.13
7.5	71	258.4	60,878.3	0.42
8.0	138	534.8	40,991.0	1.30
8.5	29	104.6	13,652.6	0.77
		Post-1998 Issued FNMA GL		
6.0	4	10.8	25,580.6	0.04
6.5	6	468.1	88,544.3	0.53
7.0	7	1277.6	103,148.7	1.24
7.5	2	244.0	60,878.3	0.40
8.0	2	16.1	40,991.0	0.04

Source: CHL and Countrywide Securities Corp. as of July 1999 (in $ millions).

trends seem to show that the primary efficacy of the FNGL program is through the usage of an alternative execution vehicle for the creation of low-WAC securities collateralized by FHA/VA loans.

As shown in Exhibit 30–1, FNGL issuance prior to 1998 was fairly insignificant as compared to overall GNMA production.

PREPAYMENT BEHAVIOR OF CONVENTIONAL LOW-WAC MBS

In general, within a given coupon class low-WAC pools are likely to prepay slower than "half" coupon pools. This is due to the fact that note rates of mortgage loans in low-WAC pools will be lower than in "half" coupon pools, and hence will be less sensitive to interest rates because of a higher refinancing threshold. It should be noted at the outset that in the absence of other explanatory variables, the slow prepayment pattern of low-WAC pools is a by-product of efficient pooling practices by creative originators rather than some inherent "slow-pay" characteristics of the underlying loans. At the same time, to the extent that obligors in low-WAC pools obtain lower rates through a combination of superior credit attributes and higher discount points, there are possibly factors that result in a different refinancing threshold for such borrowers in addition to the constraints imposed by the lower mortgage rate.[4] In view of these considerations our investigation followed a sequential approach whereby the first part of the analysis involved the evaluation of pool data from publicly available sources. The findings from this part of the analysis were compared with loan level data obtained from our proprietary databases to obtain additional insights into any obligor attributes that may serve to highlight other possible explanatory variables in the prepayment behavior of low-WAC pools.

In the first part of the analysis, since low-WAC pools do not exist as a readily identifiable class, these securities were identified using FNMA pool level data for various origination years by stratifying securities for each origination year within a particular coupon class. In segmenting these securities, low-WAC MBS were defined as those with gross WACs of between a quarter to three-eighths of the pass-through rate for a given coupon class. The performance of these low-WAC conventional MBS was then compared to that of generic coupons. The results of our analysis are summarized in Exhibit 30–2, which describes the prepayment experience, represented by 3-month CPRs for conventional low-WAC and generic securities of different vintages. Our findings are stated as follows:

- With respect to data at the pool level low-WAC conventional MBS consistently prepay slower than generic securities, irrespective of the origination year of the coupon.

- For higher coupon MBS, especially 8%s and 8.5%s, there is evidence to indicate that speeds for low-WAC securities converge with generic speeds. These findings suggest that the burnout factor for generics is faster than that for low-WAC pools, and as a result, speeds for low-WAC pools have the tendency to approach generic speeds once the underlying loans are sufficiently "in the money." As a reference point this result is found to be consistent with the observed behavior of most prepayment "protected" collateral. In the absence of structural considerations, such as penalties and lockouts, observed speeds for such collateral eventually converge with generic speeds. This occurs because of the combined effect of burnout on generic collateral and the steeper prepayment elbow of the prepayment protected loans due to the higher refinancing threshold. However, due to variation in the magnitude of the underlying prepayment drivers, this convergence may not be attained at the same level for different collateral types.

Our results for loan level data show that where low-WAC conventional loans, segmented using a similar methodology for pool level analysis, are compared with generic cohorts, they are strikingly similar.[5] Prepayment speeds, represented by lifetime and 3-month CPRs for various coupon low-WAC MBS, created by using loan

---

4. At the outset we dismiss the role of volatility in interest rates as a universal reason for lower note rates for certain mortgagors. While we do not rule out the contributing influence of this factor, reliance upon interest rate changes, as the major reason for lower note rates does not explain the behavior of low-WAC prepayments during a period of muted volatility.

5. The data for this analysis are composed of mortgage loans originated or serviced by Countrywide Home Loans.

EXHIBIT 30-2

Conventional 30-Year Prepayments by Aggregate-Coupon Class—Generic Versus Low-WAC

Origination Year	Generic	Low-WAC	Difference*
6.5			
1998	7.55	4.83	−2.72
1997	10.31	7.68	−2.63
1996	14.13	11.02	−3.11
1995	14.79	7.43	−7.36
1994	13.05	8.21	−4.84
1993	13.74	12.01	−1.73
7.0			
1998	12.82	10.68	−2.14
1997	15.64	12.10	−3.54
1996	17.88	15.60	−2.28
1995	19.34	17.13	−2.21
1994	16.74	15.07	−1.67
1993	17.19	15.60	−1.59
7.5			
1998	26.72	21.45	−5.27
1997	24.15	18.19	−5.96
1996	27.72	20.48	−7.24
1995	26.90	21.23	−5.67
1994	24.03	20.54	−3.49
1993	22.67	19.91	−2.76
8.0			
1998	46.48	46.14	−0.34
1997	30.24	27.33	−2.91
1996	32.36	31.24	−1.12
1995	33.06	31.25	−1.81
1994	31.87	28.10	−3.77
1993	29.03	27.82	−1.21
8.5			
1998	N/A	N/A	N/A
1997	36.09	33.24	−2.85
1996	35.80	35.22	−0.58
1995	37.42	34.30	−3.12
1994	35.15	33.90	−1.25
1993	28.90	25.05	−3.85

*Difference is the generic value subtracted from low-WAC value.
Source: CHL and Countrywide Securities Corp. as of July 31, 1999.

EXHIBIT 30–3

Comparison of Countrywide 30-Year Low-WAC Conventional Prepayments by Coupon Class Versus Generics (Life CPR)

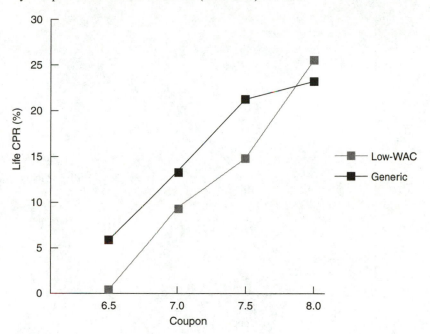

Source: CHL and Countrywide Securities Corp. as of July 31, 1999.

level information versus equivalent speeds for conventional generics, are presented in Exhibit 30–3. As noted from this analysis, low-WAC conventional speeds are significantly slower than equivalent coupon discount and current coupons. For premium coupons low-WAC speeds have a tendency to converge with generic speeds.

RELATIVE VALUE CONSIDERATIONS

Given that conventional low-WAC MBS prepay slower than generics in a negative refinancing environment with speeds converging for high premiums, it appears that such securities have a superior convexity profile than generics. Additionally, as a general rule low-WAC securities provide a higher level of prepayment protection for an equivalent pass-through coupon. In order to demonstrate the embedded value in low-WAC MBS, their descriptive characteristics were compared with generic cohorts, using constant option-adjusted spread analysis.

The results of this analysis are presented in Exhibit 30–4. As noted from these results, low-WAC MBS exhibit a lower degree of negative convexity in comparison to generic securities. However, due to the slower prepayment characteristics of these securities, the effective duration of low-WAC MBS, especially discounts, is

E X H I B I T   30–4

Comparison of Countrywide 30-Year Low-WAC Conventional Prepayments by Coupon Class Versus Generics (3-Month CPR)

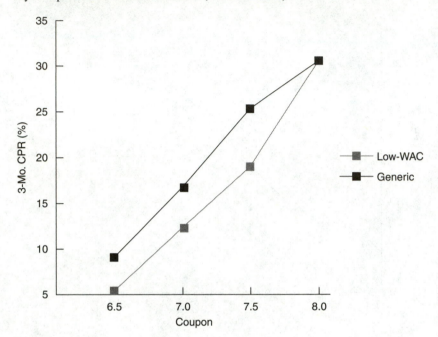

Source: CHL and Countrywide Securities Corp. as of July 31, 1999.

marginally longer. For higher coupons, as prepayment speeds converge toward generic speeds, the duration differences also decrease. With respect to embedded value our evaluation focused on comparing the price of generic coupons with the theoretical prices of equivalent coupon low-WAC MBS. In these computations the theoretical price of low-WAC securities was calculated using constant option-adjusted spread (OAS) analysis and our proprietary prepayment model that adjusts for WAC differences (See Exhibit 30–5). Using this difference as an indicator of value, it appears that most of the embedded value in low-WAC securities resides in the slight discounts, currents, and slight premiums. At the higher end of the premium scale, as low-WAC speeds converge with generic speeds, the value difference declines. Nonetheless, despite the convergence of speeds, higher premium low-WAC securities still exhibit a relative value advantage over generic securities.

CONCLUSIONS

The usage of buy-downs and buy-ups in the context of guaranty fees allows originators a higher degree of flexibility in the pooling process for conventional loans. As part of this process originators are able to monetize the value of any excess

EXHIBIT 30–5

Relative Value Comparison of Conventional Low-WAC Versus Generic Securities

Coupon	Type	Price	Difference	Yield	OAS	OA Dur	OA Cvx	Option Cost
6.5	Low-WAC	95–28	+6	7.17	105	5.75	-0.59	20
	TBA	95–22		7.21		5.54	-0.60	24
7.0	Low-WAC	98–14	+9	7.28	105	5.06	-0.86	31
	TBA	98–05		7.33		4.86	-0.92	36
7.5	Low-WAC	100–21	+12	7.43	104	4.24	-1.24	46
	TBA	100–09		7.49		4.05	-1.18	52
8.0	Low-WAC	102–11	+6	7.50	103	3.27	-1.33	62
	TBA	102–05		7.46		3.17	-1.33	59
8.5	Low-WAC	103–30	+2	7.54	120	3.00	-1.15	51
	TBA	103–28		7.53		2.98	-1.10	50

Source: Countrywide Securities Corp. as of August 24, 1999.

servicing. Low-WAC pools, where the note rate of the pool is within a quarter to three-eighths of the pass-through rate, are created as a direct corollary of the usage of buy-downs in the pooling process. In addition, a greater likelihood exists that such loans are created in periods of interest rate declines resulting in lower age. At the same time there is also a stronger possibility that such loans were originated in the retail rather than the wholesale channel, resulting in slower prepayments until the option was sufficiently in the money.

From the perspective of MBS investors low-WAC pools provide a higher coupon with a greater degree of prepayment protection due to the lower gross WAC and WAC dispersion of the underlying pool within each coupon class. Our research based on loan level information indicates that low-WAC pools tend to prepay slower than generic securities for most coupon classes, irrespective of the vintage. At the extreme end of the coupon stack low-WAC prepayment speeds have a tendency to converge with generic speeds. This occurs due to the combined effect of burnout on the generic coupons and a higher refinancing threshold for borrowers in low-WAC buckets. Our analysis also suggests that low-WAC borrowers exhibit a superior credit profile and a lower loan age than generics, where we observe that the maximum amount of embedded value found as a result of higher coupon and muted prepayment behavior is in slight discounts, currents, and slight premium low-WAC securities.

CHAPTER 31

THE COMBINED EFFECTS OF LOW WAC AND LOW BALANCE ON MBS VALUATION

Anand K. Bhattacharya, Ph.D.
Executive Vice President
Countrywide Capital Markets Inc.

As the traditional mortgage-backed securities (MBS) market becomes increasingly mature and efficient, the valuation of such securities becomes increasingly dependent upon the descriptive characteristics of the underlying collateral. Implicit in this chain of thought is the belief that the evaluation of specific obligor, loan, and property characteristics helps identify various drivers of value and hence uncovers desirable valuation characteristics that may not be readily visible on an aggregated basis. Since some of these variables have varying effects on the valuation of the underlying MBS, it is also important to assess the degree of associated interaction, since such interplay may lead to dampening or enhancing the valuation attributes in various refinancing incentives. In this chapter we extend our analysis and investigate the combined effects of balance and mortgage coupon on the prepayment behavior of the underlying MBS, and discuss the associated relative valuation issues. Our motivation for embarking upon this analysis stems from conclusions drawn from our research which suggests that the effects of these parameters can serve to enhance or dampen the convexity characteristics of MBS collateralized by loans with such attributes.

THE LOW BALANCE EFFECT

Loan balance is relevant as an explanatory variable for determining prepayment behavior since low loan balance (LLB) pools are likely to prepay more slowly than higher balance pools for equivalent moves in interest rates. Slower speeds for LLB

Research and computational assistance by Jeremy Burdick, Esther Chang, and Nick Trosper is gratefully acknowledged.

pools arise from the fact that mortgagors with lower balances have higher refinancing thresholds due to the fixed up-front costs of refinancing. However, low balance mortgages that originated in states with high real estate appreciation may exhibit higher prepayment rates during periods of high real estate appreciation. Despite this possibility, low balance loans do not prepay any faster than generic cohorts. Using loan-level information from our proprietary databases, where FHA- and VA-insured and conventional low balance loans were defined as loans with original balances of equal to or less than $60,000 and $85,000, respectively, our investigation led to the following conclusions[1]:

- Current- and premium-coupon low balance loans exhibit slower prepayment patterns, irrespective of vintage and geographical origin, both for FHA- or VA-insured and conventional loans.

- Low balance loans in areas of high real estate appreciation exhibit faster prepayment speeds than equivalent speeds for the low balance population as a whole, indicating some degree of cash-out refinancing activity and trade-up buying behavior. However, these speeds are still slower than generic speeds for conventional cohorts.

- Discount LLBs exhibit faster prepayments in negative refinancing regimes than generics. This counterintuitive behavior is due to the higher turnover associated with trade-up buying and demographic features, such as expanded family size. In view of this finding, our results also question the commonly held belief that discount low balance pools exhibit a higher degree of extension risk.

- Discount low balance MBS prepay faster than generics in a bearish market environment leading to lesser negative convexity and an improved total rate-of-return profile. At the same time, low balance premiums prepay more slowly than generics leading to an improved performance profile over generic cohorts.

- Pricing for LLB MBS as a premium over generic securities is directly correlated to the coupon, with discounts exacting the lowest premiums. As a result, market payups for the desirable convexity features of LLBs appear underpriced for discounts and currents while payups for premiums were at fair value.

THE LOW-WAC FACTOR

Although the causal factor in the prepayment protection afforded by LLBs stems from the lower balance of the loan, low-WAC pools are created as a direct corollary of efficient pooling practices by originators. Specifically, low-WAC pools are originated with loans in which the guaranty fee has been bought down in a related effort to monetize the value of excess servicing. Such pools consist of loans with note rates (or gross WACs) between one-quarter to three-eighths of the pass-

---

1. See "Low-Balance MBSs—Pay-ups Are Underpriced," Fixed Income Research, Countrywide Securities Corporation (August 1999).

through rate, and are distinguished from typical pools where the note rate varies by increments of one-half of 1 percent.

Using pooled and loan-level data, our research as discussed in the previous chapter leads to the following conclusions:

- Discount, current, and slight premium low-WAC securities consistently prepay slower than generic securities. At the extreme end of the coupon stack, low-WAC speeds have a tendency to converge with generic speeds.

- Obligors in low-WAC buckets have a higher refinancing threshold due to the lower mortgage note rate, higher discount origination points, and, generally, lower age. At the same time, since such loans are more likely to be originated in the retail rather than the wholesale channel, such loans have a certain degree of built-in prepayment protection due to the lower note rates characteristically prevalent in the retail channel.

- Although discount low-WAC MBS exhibit a superior convexity profile over generics, it is attained at the expense of marginally higher effective durations. Within the coupon stack, the maximum degree of embedded value stemming from the higher coupon with lower prepayment exposure resides in currents and discounts. Despite the convergence in speeds for the higher-premium coupons, the relative value advantage over generics is maintained.

INTERACTION BETWEEN LOW BALANCE AND LOW WAC

Given that the effects of loan balance and lower note rates on prepayment behavior are not similar, an interesting valuation question is whether the combined impact of these effects on valuation is additive or exponential. From a macroevaluation point of view, it appears that both low balance loans and low-WAC loans have desirable characteristics that could hasten (dampen) the prepayment behavior of discounts (premiums) and hence, improve the performance characteristics of the underlying securities. In this respect, a couple of interesting valuation issues to consider is whether the slower prepayment characteristics of low-WAC discounts could be counterbalanced by including faster-paying low balance loans, especially from areas of high real estate appreciation in the underlying mortgage pool, or whether including low balance seasoned loans in the MBS pool could dampen the faster-paying characteristics of low-WAC premiums.

As a starting point in this analysis, we used loan-level information and stratified the data using attributes such as loan balance, low-gross WAC and a combination of loan balance and low-gross WAC.[2] In this stratification scheme, conventional LLBs were defined as loans with original (as opposed to current) balance of less than or equal to $85,000[3] and low-WAC loans were defined as

---

2. The data for this analysis is composed of mortgage loans originated or serviced by Countrywide Home Loans, Inc.
3. Since low-WAC MBS collateralized by FHA and VA mortgages do not exist as a readily identifiable class, this analysis was restricted to conventional loan programs.

loans where the note rate was between one-quarter to three-eighths of the pass-through rate. Loans that met both criteria were segmented within the low balance–low-WAC bucket, and the performance characteristics of these strata were compared with those of conventional generic cohorts.

The prepayment behavior of the various strata, as represented by 3-month and life conditional prepayment rates (CPRs) for new and moderately seasoned loans is presented in Exhibits 31–1 and 31–2, respectively.[4] An evaluation of the prepayment history leads to the following results:

- Within the discount-coupon category, LLBs prepay faster than loans in low-WAC buckets. The prepayment behavior of both categories of loans is slower than that of generic cohorts, but the speed behavior of discount moderately seasoned loans is faster than that of generics. These results are consistent with our previous research which indicates that although higher balance loans are subject to the "lock-in" effect in negative refinancing regimes, lower balance loans, especially seasoned loans, could prepay faster due to the combined effects of trade-up buying and home price appreciation. At the same time, consistent with expectations, since loans pooled in lower-WAC buckets have lower note rates and have a higher probability of being originated in the retail channel where rates are typically lower, such loans exhibit slower prepayment experience than generics in a negative refinancing regime. The combined effect of these attributes, as seen from the prepayment behavior of the low-WAC LLB bucket is to dampen the prepayment profile of low balance loans and enhance the profile for low-WAC loans.

- In the case of current and premium coupons, as the refinancing incentive becomes successively more positive, the prepayment patterns exhibit a reversal. As noted earlier, as interest rates decline, the rate of change of speeds for loans in the low-WAC category begins to increase, leading to a higher probability in the exercise of the prepayment option. This occurs as the economic effects of lower rates become greater than the dampening effect of higher up-front discount points. Nonetheless, such loans continue to maintain a prepayment advantage over generics. At the extreme end of the coupon stack for higher premiums, the speed behavior of loans in low-WAC buckets begins to approximate that of generics, as both categories of loans attain burnout; but generics, having higher note rates, attain this state at a faster pace. At the same time, as rates decrease, the interest rate–generated prepayment effect becomes stronger for "regular" balance mortgages leading to divergence in prepayment behavior between generics and LLBs. Since new loans are least likely to have been exposed to previous refinancing opportunities, divergence in prepayment behavior is the strongest for this category and less pronounced for moderately seasoned loans.

---

4. In this analysis, new loans are defined as loans with ages of fewer than 30 months and moderately seasoned loans are defined as loans with ages between 30 and 60 months. Due to the relatively small size of the "low balance–low-gross WAC" seasoned classification in some of the coupon categories, this analysis was not conducted for seasoned loans.

EXHIBIT 31–1

Countrywide 30-Year Conventional Prepayments by Aggregate-Coupon Class*

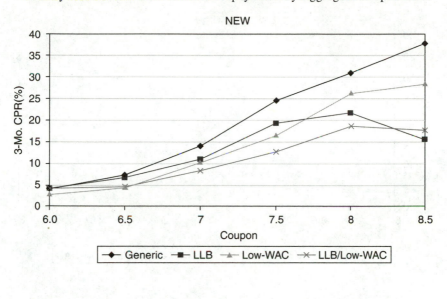

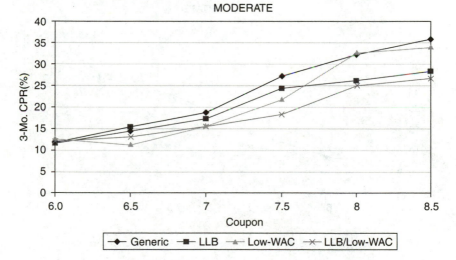

*Low-WAC LLB, low WAC, and LLB versus conventional generic in 3-month CPR (%).

Countrywide 30-Year Conventional Prepayments by Aggregate-Coupon Class*

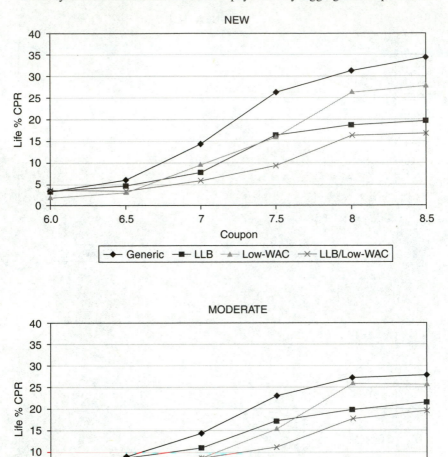

*Low-WAC LLB, low WAC, and LLB versus conventional generic in life CPR (%).
Source: Countrywide Home Loan and Countrywide Securities Corporation as of July 31, 1999.

RELATIVE VALUE IMPLICATIONS

The effect of loan balance and lower note rates on prepayments has several relative value implications. In order to identify the effect of these attributes on valuation, the performance characteristics, such as duration and convexity of the various types of MBS were compared. In addition, the embedded value within these securities, as determined on a constant option-adjusted spread price differential to generic MBS, was also computed. These results are presented in Exhibit 31–3, and the following inferences can be made:

- Within the discount-coupon category (6%s and 6.5%s), the low-WAC LLB combination provides the maximum degree of embedded value. On an individualized basis, low balance MBS provide a greater degree of value than low-WAC securities in this category. This is likely due to the fact that the speeds of low-WAC securities in a negative refinancing environment are slower than that of equivalent low balance MBS. Consequently, the effective duration of low-WAC MBS is the longest, with that of low balance MBS being the shortest. However, low-WAC low balance MBS have the lowest degree of negative effective convexity. Additionally, the effects of the low balance and low-WAC attributes with respect to embedded value are not additive for discount coupons. This is primarily due to the divergence in prepayment speeds for the low-WAC and low balance MBS, as the speeds for low-WAC MBS are significantly lower than that of LLBs.

- Within the slight discount- and current-coupon category (7%s and 7.5%s), the low-WAC LLB combination continues to indicate the highest degree of embedded value within the various strata. Additionally, this category provides the lowest degree of negative convexity within the comparisons. Within this category, although low-WAC MBS have the longest effective duration owing to the comparatively slower speeds, the duration differences between the various categories begin to diminish as prepayment speeds start converging within a narrower band.

- Within the premium category, the effects of both low balance and low WAC start to become additive as the slower speeds resulting from the effects of both attributes begin to enhance value. As the refinancing incentive becomes successively more positive, the low balance effect results in a slowdown of speeds. This effect, as noted in Exhibits 31–1 and 31–2, is more pronounced for newly originated premium LLBs, where the divergence between generic and low balance speeds increases in positive refinancing regimes. This occurs primarily due to the greater economic incentives for refinancing generic loans. At the same time, speeds of low-WAC collateral begin to approximate speeds for generic collateral, resulting in further muting of the prepayment behavior of the low-WAC LLB combination. Although the low-WAC LLB combination continues to exhibit the lowest degree of negative convexity at the lower end of the premium stack, the convexity advantages begin to diminish at the higher end of the premium spectrum. Within the individual categories, our analysis indicates a higher degree of embedded relative value associated with low balance MBS in comparison to low-WAC MBS.

EXHIBIT 31-3

Conventional Coupon	Embedded Value				Convexity				Duration			
	TBA[a] OAS[b]	Low WAC	LLB w/TBA[a] WAC Payup	LLB/ LW[c]	TBA	LLB	Low WAC	LLB/ LW[c]	TBA	LLB	Low WAC	LLB/ LW[c]
6.0	89.5	+6	+17	+20	−0.40	−0.26	−0.18	−0.14	6.13	5.95	6.43	6.14
6.5	92.9	+8	+15	+19	−0.65	−0.57	−0.62	−0.53	5.53	5.42	5.79	5.57
7.0	97.4	+11	+14	+19	−0.92	−0.79	−0.82	−0.74	4.89	4.85	5.12	4.97
7.5	98.4	+15+	+14+	+22+	−1.18	−1.14	−1.24	−1.11	4.05	4.07	4.30	4.22
8.0	98.6	+10+	+16+	+26+	−1.41	−1.41	−1.52	−1.36	3.30	3.37	3.41	3.53
8.5	130.2	+2	+5	+7	−1.11	−1.04	−1.17	−1.08	3.19	3.15	3.21	3.18

[a]TBA = to be announced.
[b]OAS = option-adjusted spread.
[c]LW = low WAC.
Source: Countrywide Home Loan and Countrywide Securities Corporation as of September 28, 1999.

CONCLUSION

In seeking to identify drivers of prepayment behavior as explained by the different property and obligor characteristics, we have explored the effect of loan balance and low WAC on valuation. Our motivation stemmed from the fact that both loan balance and loans pooled in low-WAC MBS have characteristics that lead to dampened prepayment behavior under different refinancing regimes. The interaction between the effects of these variables indicates that in negative refinancing regimes, the combination leads to a smoother prepayment profile where the low balance effect serves to enhance the slower prepayment profile of low-WAC loans. In positive refinancing regimes, the slower prepayment profile of the LLB serves to dampen the faster profile of the low-WAC loans as the latter speeds converge with generic speeds. The effect of these interactions leads to a higher degree of embedded value and a lower degree of negative convexity than the otherwise-desirable isolated effects of these variables.

CHAPTER 32

HEDGING MORTGAGES WITH SWAPS AND AGENCIES

Laurie Goodman, Ph.D.
Managing Director and Head
Mortgage Strategy Group
UBS Warburg

Jeffrey Ho
Director
Mortgage Strategy Group
UBS Warburg

With the Treasury universe shrinking so dramatically since mid-1998, all spread product has experienced higher absolute spreads versus Treasuries, and the correlation of spreads among spread product is also higher. This has lead market participants to conclude that hedging mortgages with Treasuries is useless, since the tracking error is sizable. However, many investors believe that tracking error can be reduced to near zero if they hedge mortgages with agency debentures or with swaps.

In this article, we examine the effectiveness of hedging mortgages with Treasuries, swaps, and agency debentures. We show that hedging mortgages with Treasuries is much less effective than it was prior to mid-1998. By contrast, the tracking error of mortgages versus other spread product is now very similar to what it was compared with Treasuries prior to the summer of 1998.

A WHOLE NEW BALL GAME

After years of budget deficits, the United States is now in surplus. As a matter of fact, 1998 and 1999 were the first back-to-back budget surpluses since 1956 and 1957. Because of these surpluses, the need for Treasury borrowings has been decreased and Treasury debt is actually being paid down. As a result of the Treasury surpluses and the net reduction in Treasury debt, the debt world is a very different place. Treasury securities now constitute a much smaller proportion of the fixed-income universe than they used to. Consequently, spreads on all spread products are wider than they used to be, as scarcity has driven up Treasury prices. Spreads

This chapter is reprinted with permission from Frank J. Fabozzi (ed.), *Professional Perspectives on Fixed Income Portfolio Management,* vol. 2 (New Hope, PA: Frank J. Fabozzi Associates, 2001).

on spread product are also much more volatile than before—top that off with all spread product being much more highly correlated.

Exhibit 32–1 shows average spreads on spread product for four periods: November 1, 1995 to June 30, 1998, July 1, 1998 to March 14, 2000, September 1, 1999 to March 14, 2000, and November 1, 1995 to March 14, 2000. The first period (November 1, 1995 to June 30, 1998) is the period before Treasury scarcity became an issue. We refer to this as "the earlier period." The second period reflects the period in which Treasury scarcity was a problem. We refer to this as "the later period." The third period is the most recent subset of the second period, a period in which mortgages are believed to have traded more closely with swaps and with agency debentures. We refer to this as "the last 6 months" or as "the most recent period." It takes out the spread widenings of October 1998 and August 1999. The final period used for this analysis is the entire period November 1, 1995 to June 30, 1998 (referred to as "the whole period").

As a proxy for the mortgage universe, we used the perfect current-coupon FNMA (the mortgage selling at par for corporate settlement). To characterize agency product, we employed the 10-year benchmark FNMA issue. For swaps, we applied data provided by Telerate. Exhibit 32–2 shows that spreads on all spread product are higher in the later period than they were in the earlier period. For example, mortgage spreads (the spread between the current-coupon mortgage and the 10-year Treasury) averaged 110 basis points (bps) in the earlier period but 147 bps in the later period. Swap spreads averaged 41 bps in the earlier period, then doubled to 81 bps.

The exhibit also evidences that not only are swap spreads higher, they are also more volatile. We display the detrended standard deviation of spreads for each of the two periods. The standard deviation of mortgage spreads averaged 6 bps in the earlier period, then expanded to 20 bps in the second period. Swap spreads and spreads on agency debentures show a more extreme change. The standard deviation on agency debentures was 2 bps in the earlier period, and then it blew out to 10 bps.

Note that average spreads between mortgages and agencies, mortgages and swaps, and swaps and agencies are all roughly the same between the two periods. For example, mortgage-agency spreads averaged 82 bps from November 1, 1995 to June 30, 1998, and 85 bps during the period July 1, 1998 to March 14, 2000. However, the detrended standard deviation of the later period is much higher—5 bps from November 1, 1995 to June 30, 1998, then out to 13 bps during the period July 1, 1998 to March 14, 2000. However, when looking at standard deviations of spreads between mortgage and agency debentures, the last 6 months were approximately as volatile as was the November 1995–January 1998 period—4 bps from September 1, 1999 to March 14, 2000, versus 5 bps between November 1, 1995 and June 30, 1998. Mortgage-agency and mortgage-swap spreads are now, at best, as volatile as mortgage-Treasury spreads used to be.

Higher Spread Correlations

Exhibit 32–2 shows that not only are all spreads more volatile versus Treasury securities, but that spread product is also more highly correlated with other spread

Volatility of Selected Spreads

Begin	End	Mortgage-Treasury	Agency-Treasury	Swap-Treasury	Mortgage-Agency	Mortgage-Swap	Swap-Agency
				Average Spreads			
11/1/95	6/30/98	110	28	41	82	69	13
7/1/98	3/14/00	147	61	81	85	66	19
9/1/99	3/14/00	144	67	85	77	58	19
11/1/95	3/14/00	123	40	56	83	68	15
				Standard Deviation of Spreads (bps)			
11/1/95	6/30/98	6	2	3	5	5	2
7/1/98	3/14/00	20	10	12	13	11	4
9/1/99	3/14/00	13	11	12	4	4	1
11/1/95	3/14/00	13	7	8	9	8	3

Note: Six-month moving average detrended standard deviation of spread level.

EXHIBIT 32–2

Correlation of Selected Yields and Spreads

Correlation Among Spreads

Begin	End	Corporate-Mortgage	Agency-Mortgage	Swap-Mortgage	Agency-Swap	Corporate-Swap	Agency-Corporate
11/1/95	6/30/98	8.1%	14.8%	18.4%	29.8%	22.9%	20.0%
7/1/98	3/14/00	51.5	70.0	69.4	84.7	62.3	60.3
9/1/99	3/14/00	63.7	76.8	76.3	97.5	92.3	89.1
11/1/95	3/14/00	40.6	53.0	53.5	67.4	52.0	50.1

Correlation Among Yields

Begin	End	Mortgage-Treasury	Mortgage-Agency	Mortgage-Swap	Mortgage-Corporate	Agency-Swap	Corporate-Treasury	Agency-Treasury	Swap-Treasury
11/1/95	6/30/98	97.4%	99.6%	99.3%	99.5%	99.2%	99.5%	99.6%	99.3%
7/1/98	3/14/00	85.2	95.1	93.7	90.0	97.9	90.0	95.1	93.7
9/1/99	3/14/00	76.5	90.1	89.2	87.6	99.5	87.6	90.1	89.2
11/1/95	3/14/00	91.2	97.2	96.4	94.6	98.6	94.6	97.2	96.4

product than ever before. The top panel of Exhibit 32–2 illustrates that during the November 1, 1995–June 30, 1998 period, correlation between agencies and mortgages rose from 14.8% to 70%, whereas that between swaps and mortgages increased from 18.4% to 69.4% (exactly the pattern that would be expected!)

The bottom panel of Exhibit 32–2 shows correlation among yields. Here we find results that many will consider surprising. Note that in the earlier period, correlation of the mortgage-Treasury yield was 97.4%; then in the later period it slipped to 85.2%, which is in line with intuition. However, correlation between mortgage and agency yields also dropped, albeit by less (from 99.6% to 95.1%). Note that the correlations between mortgage-agency yields and mortgage-swap yields (95.1% and 93.7%, respectively) are weaker in the later period than the mortgage-Treasury yield correlation was during the earlier period (97.4%). Increased spread volatility outweighs the higher spread correlations, and yield correlations have actually dropped.

Now, it's naturally tough to "see" yield correlations, since they are inherently unintuitive for most of us. Moreover, the doubting Thomases are apt to murmur that this analysis has been "rigged" by our use of the perfect current-coupon mortgage, rather than a real-world mortgage-backed security. So in the next section, we look at how much hedging real-world to-be-announced (TBA) mortgages with swaps and agency debentures actually improves hedge effectiveness as opposed to hedging with Treasuries.

Our Method

Our goal is to determine the hedge effectiveness of hedging mortgages with various alternative securities. Therefore, we hedge FNMA TBAs couponed from 6.5 to 8.5% with each of the following: the 10-year Treasury, the 10-year swap, and the 10-year benchmark note. We used the following method:

1. Calculate the empirical hedge ratios for a given mortgage using 20 days of empirical data. This allows us to set up a position in which we are long $100 of mortgages and short ($100 times the empirical hedge ratio) of Treasuries, agencies, or swaps. The empirical hedge ratio will be different for each instrument.

2. Rebalance our hedge each successive 20-day period. We close out the prior position and tabulate long mortgage position performance versus our short position of the hedging instrument. We assume that all mortgage securities are rolled. Treasury shorts get funded at the 10-year Treasury repurchase rate, which is usually on special. The 10-year agency debentures are assumed to be funded at general collateral levels. The new position is derived from the then-current 20-day hedge ratios.

3. We then look at measures of hedging effectiveness. Our favorite measure is cumulative absolute performance (annualized). Under that view, absolute hedging errors are aggregated and then annualized according to Equation (32–1).

$$\text{CAPA} = \frac{\sum_{i=1}^{n} |x_i|}{\text{yrs}} \qquad (32\text{–}1)$$

where

yrs = number of years in the measurement period

$$x_i = \Delta \text{Mtg } Px_i - \text{B} \times \Delta \text{Hedge } Px_i$$

We also show the annualized variance of performance, which uses the square of the absolute errors. Hence a series with many small errors tracks better than one with several very large errors. This variance measure is calculated as shown in Equation (32–2).

$$\text{AVP} = \frac{\sum_{i=1}^{n} (x_i - \bar{x})^2}{n} \times \frac{260}{t} \qquad (32\text{–}2)$$

where

t = number of trade days in holding period

4. We also used shorter (10- and 5-day) holding periods following the same procedure as in steps 1 to 3 above, (i.e., allowing for more frequent rebalancing). We continued to use 20-day empirical hedge ratios to set the size of the short position, since that length was needed to provide sufficient data to be meaningful.

The Results

Our analysis for 20-day holding periods is shown in Exhibit 32–3. The top part of the exhibit shows hedging with Treasuries; the middle part shows "what if" we hedged with swaps; and the bottom section depicts agency hedges.

Focus on the first section, the top part of which includes cumulative absolute performance. During the November 1, 1995–June 30, 1998 period, cumulative absolute performance was $2.04 per year for FNMA 7s. It more than doubled, to $4.46/year, between mid-1998 and the present. The annualized variance of performance confirms this doubling. Performance variance in the earlier period was $0.46 per year (annualized), versus $2.98 per year during the later period. Thus the intuitive conclusion that it is much more difficult to hedge mortgages with Treasury securities than it used to be.

The bottom section of Exhibit 32–3 hedges mortgages with 10-year agency debentures. For FNMA 7s, the annualized sum of absolute performance was $2.32 in the earlier period, and $2.74 in the later period. The annualized variance of performance results confirms the fact that agency debentures actually provided a better hedge in terms of hedging effectiveness in the earlier period ($0.61 versus $1.26).

Now the punch line: In the earlier period, the 10-year Treasury actually provided a better hedge than did either agency debentures or swaps. Note that

E X H I B I T   32–3

Hedging over 20-Day Holding Periods

Begin	End	6.5%	7.0%	7.5%	8.0%	8.5%
		Mortgages Hedged with Treasuries				
Cumulative Absolute Performance Annualized						
11/1/95	6/30/98	$1.85	$2.04	$2.04	$2.18	$2.44
7/1/98	3/14/00	5.19	4.46	4.02	3.43	3.17
11/1/95	3/14/00	3.15	2.98	2.81	2.66	2.72
Annualized Variance of Performance						
11/1/95	6/30/98	0.37	0.46	0.50	0.54	0.70
7/1/98	3/14/00	3.61	2.98	2.47	1.56	1.25
11/1/95	3/14/00	1.64	1.46	1.30	0.96	0.93
		Mortgages Hedged with Swaps				
Cumulative Absolute Performance Annualized						
11/1/95	6/30/98	$2.11	$2.33	$2.49	$2.50	$2.52
7/1/98	3/14/00	2.57	2.75	2.66	2.30	2.55
11/1/95	3/14/00	2.29	2.49	2.55	2.42	2.53
Annualized Variance of Performance						
11/1/95	6/30/98	0.47	0.52	0.62	0.63	0.74
7/1/98	3/14/00	0.89	1.06	1.05	0.67	0.75
11/1/95	3/14/00	0.63	0.74	0.81	0.67	0.76
		Mortgages Hedged with Agency Debentures				
Cumulative Absolute Performance Annualized						
11/1/95	6/30/98	$2.18	$2.32	$2.32	$2.30	$2.48
7/1/98	3/14/00	2.51	2.74	2.70	2.36	2.47
11/1/95	3/14/00	2.31	2.48	2.47	2.32	2.48
Annualized Variance of Performance						
11/1/95	6/30/98	0.58	0.61	0.62	0.60	0.70
7/1/98	3/14/00	1.11	1.26	1.12	0.72	0.74
11/1/95	3/14/00	0.79	0.88	0.84	0.67	0.74

for hedging FNMA 7s, the cumulative absolute performance (annualized) was $2.04 for the 10-year Treasury versus $2.33 for swaps and $2.32 for 10-year agency debentures. In the later period, Treasury securities had deteriorated so badly as a hedging instrument that both swaps and agency debentures performed much better ($4.46 for Treasury securities versus $2.75 for swaps and $2.74 for agencies). However, even the best hedge during that later period performed more poorly than did the poorest hedge in the earlier period. These results had been foreshadowed by standard deviations in Exhibit 32–1 and the correlations in Exhibit 32–2. We showed that the standard deviations of mortgage-agency and mortgage-swap spreads in the later period were comparable to or actually higher than those on mortgage-Treasury spreads in the earlier period. Moreover, yield correlations between mortgages-swaps and mortgages-agencies were weaker than yield correlations between Treasuries and mortgages used to be.

Many investors will be surprised by the order of magnitude of the annualized sum of absolute performance. Recall from the discussion above that mortgages hedged with the 10-year Treasury have an annualized absolute error of $4.46 versus $2.74 and 2.75 for agency debentures and swaps, respectively. That's 62% as much (or a 38% reduction in risk).

Exhibit 32–4 shows results for an analysis notched down to 10-day holding periods. Note that all numbers are larger than in Exhibit 32–3, because there is less scope for "natural" netting. If a hedged position loses $1.00 in one 10-day period and makes $1.10 the next, Exhibit 32–3 (using the 20-day yardstick) would have only picked $0.10 net, whereas Exhibit 32–4 picks up an absolute error of $2.10. Note also that we have added one more 6-month period (from September 1, 1999 to March 14, 2000). This was again meant to capture the recent period in which market participants believe that the correlation between mortgages versus agencies and swaps has risen. We wanted to test the extent to which that has occurred. (This period could not have been included for 20-day holding periods, as there were too few observations.)

The 10-day holding period results are, by and large, very similar to those for 20-day periods in Exhibit 32–3. In the early period, swap and agency hedges for 10-day holding periods were about as effective as Treasury hedges; in the later period, they were more effective. However, the order of magnitude of risk reduction is less than many would have thought. As an example, look at hedging FNMA 7s. There is a $4.15 annualized cumulative error on swaps and agency debentures as opposed to $6.03 for Treasury securities (69% as much, for a 31% risk reduction).

Now let's look at the September 1, 1999–March 14, 2000 period. Treasuries, swaps, and agency debentures were all more effective hedges during that latest 6-month period than for the entire July 1, 1998–March 14, 1999 period. This is because (as shown in Exhibit 32–5) mortgages held up very poorly in the late 1998 period versus all alternatives—Treasuries, swaps, and agency debentures.

However, note that even over the September 1, 1999–March 14, 2000 period, there was quite a bit of residual risk. The absolute cumulative error (annualized basis) for hedging FNMA 7s is $3.59 for swaps, $2.74 for agencies and $5.21 for Treasuries. Moreover, over the last six months, agency debentures were a better hedge for mortgages couponed 7.5% or below. For the FNMA 8 and 8.5% securities, swaps and agency debentures performed equally well. Bottom line: Clearly, hedging became slightly easier during that 6-month period, a time in which agency debentures surpassed swaps for hedging effectiveness.

Hedging over 10-Day Holding Periods

Begin	End	6.5%	7.0%	7.5%	8.0%	8.5%
		Mortgages Hedged with Treasuries				
Cumulative Absolute Performance Annualized						
11/1/95	6/30/98	$3.53	$3.57	$3.90	$3.94	$3.69
7/1/98	3/14/00	6.24	6.03	5.56	4.66	4.25
9/1/99	3/14/00	5.30	5.21	5.25	4.97	5.83
11/1/95	3/14/00	4.58	4.53	4.55	4.22	3.91
Annualized Variance of Performance						
11/1/95	6/30/98	0.86	0.79	0.88	0.88	0.84
7/1/98	3/14/00	3.07	2.82	2.48	1.62	1.29
9/1/99	3/14/00	2.33	2.36	2.34	1.66	2.02
11/1/95	3/14/00	1.74	1.60	1.52	1.18	1.02
		Mortgages Hedged with Swaps				
Cumulative Absolute Performance Annualized						
11/1/95	6/30/98	$3.49	$3.46	$3.93	$3.97	$3.82
7/1/98	3/14/00	4.35	4.15	3.60	3.00	3.17
9/1/99	3/14/00	3.83	3.59	2.88	2.28	3.78
11/1/95	3/14/00	3.82	3.73	3.80	3.59	3.57
Annualized Variance of Performance						
11/1/95	6/30/98	0.91	0.78	0.90	0.89	0.83
7/1/98	3/14/00	1.12	1.12	1.08	0.66	0.64
9/1/99	3/14/00	0.73	0.65	0.52	0.27	0.83
11/1/95	3/14/00	0.99	0.92	0.98	0.81	0.76
		Mortgages Hedged with Agency Debentures				
Cumulative Absolute Performance Annualized						
11/1/95	6/30/98	$3.73	$3.67	$3.98	$4.03	$3.80
7/1/98	3/14/00	4.34	4.15	3.77	3.08	3.11
9/1/99	3/14/00	2.98	2.74	2.69	2.27	3.74
11/1/95	3/14/00	3.96	3.85	3.89	3.66	3.53
Annualized Variance of Performance						
11/1/95	6/30/98	1.04	0.90	0.94	0.90	0.85
7/1/98	3/14/00	1.26	1.21	1.13	0.67	0.68
9/1/99	3/14/00	0.49	0.49	0.44	0.26	0.86
11/1/95	3/14/00	1.12	1.03	1.02	0.82	0.79

E X H I B I T   32–5

Mortgage Spreads

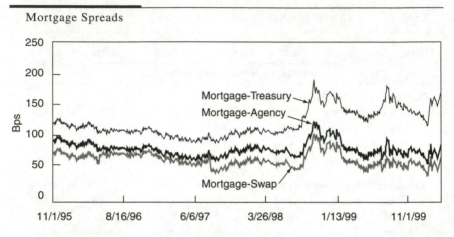

Exhibit 32–6 is very similar to Exhibit 32–4, except that we once more notch down our holding periods, this time to 5-day segments. Errors are larger, since there's simply less time for netting. Note that agency debentures were again the best hedge for FNMA 7s over that 6-month period; the agency debentures carry only 46% of the risk of hedging with Treasuries ($5.69/$12.34).

Some market participants are very surprised by our results. They make the point that it appears that the option-adjusted spreads (OAS) of collateral to the London interbank offered rate (LIBOR) curve have been very stable. Yes, that is certainly the case. We confirmed that using FNMA 7.5 collateral, as shown in Exhibit 32–7. Note that the Treasury curve has no bearing at all on the LIBOR OAS results. The Monte Carlo paths are centered on forward LIBOR rates, and the cash flows are discounted at current LIBOR rates. Moreover, we at UBS Warburg (along with most other major mortgage dealers) have recast our OAS model to allow mortgage rates to be driven by the swap curve. Following that revamping, we have back-filled 3 years of LIBOR OAS data, the results of which are reflected for 30-year FNMA 7.5s in Exhibit 32–7.

Focus on the results for the past 6-month period beginning September 1, 1999. Since then, average LIBOR OAS on FNMA 7.5 collateral has been 2 bps, with a standard deviation of 3 bps. Compare that to a standard deviation of 9 bps on the Treasury OAS over the same time period. Note that the low standard deviation on the LIBOR OAS reflects the fact that LIBOR OAS takes into account changes in the shape of the curve and changes in volatility. It is important to realize that although many investors rely on OAS, few investors strive to completely hedge out the shape of the curve and changes in volatility.

Caveats are in order. First, note that only over the most recent period (September 1, 1999–March 14, 2000) has the LIBOR OAS had a lower standard deviation than the Treasury OAS. For both of the longer subperiods (January 1997–June 1998, and July 1998–March 14, 2000), the LIBOR OAS was higher

Hedging over 5-Day Holding Periods

Begin	End	6.5%	7.0%	7.5%	8.0%	8.5%
		Mortgages Hedged with Treasuries				
Cumulative Absolute Performance Annualized						
11/1/95	6/30/98	$ 4.63	$ 4.63	$ 5.01	$ 5.07	$ 5.06
7/1/98	3/14/00	11.58	10.48	9.82	8.17	6.56
9/1/99	3/14/00	12.46	12.34	12.31	11.52	9.79
11/1/95	3/14/00	7.34	6.90	6.88	6.27	5.64
Annualized Variance of Performance						
11/1/95	6/30/98	0.74	0.67	0.79	0.89	0.84
7/1/98	3/14/00	5.20	4.57	4.21	3.23	2.39
9/1/99	3/14/00	5.97	5.98	5.88	4.89	4.46
11/1/95	3/14/00	2.48	2.20	2.12	1.81	1.45
		Mortgages Hedged with Swaps				
Cumulative Absolute Performance Annualized						
11/1/95	6/30/98	$ 5.05	$ 4.78	$ 5.13	$ 5.24	$ 5.08
7/1/98	3/14/00	6.96	6.50	6.52	5.85	5.54
9/1/99	3/14/00	5.84	6.28	6.45	6.71	7.15
11/1/95	3/14/00	5.79	5.45	5.67	5.47	5.25
Annualized Variance of Performance						
11/1/95	6/30/98	0.85	0.74	0.86	0.95	0.86
7/1/98	3/14/00	1.93	1.57	1.63	1.41	1.33
9/1/99	3/14/00	1.12	1.24	1.31	1.22	1.87
11/1/95	3/14/00	1.27	1.07	1.16	1.13	1.04
		Mortgages Hedged with Agency Debentures				
Cumulative Absolute Performance Annualized						
11/1/95	6/30/98	$ 5.15	$ 4.98	$ 5.16	$ 5.11	$ 5.08
7/1/98	3/14/00	7.17	6.78	6.45	5.67	5.34
9/1/99	3/14/00	5.27	5.69	5.89	6.10	6.68
11/1/95	3/14/00	5.93	5.68	5.66	5.32	5.18
Annualized Variance of Performance						
11/1/95	6/30/98	0.89	0.78	0.84	0.92	0.84
7/1/98	3/14/00	1.81	1.62	1.63	1.33	1.29
9/1/99	3/14/00	0.88	0.99	1.06	1.01	1.81
11/1/95	3/14/00	1.25	1.11	1.15	1.08	1.02

E X H I B I T   32–7

OAS on FNMA 7.5% Collateral

	LIBOR OAS		Treasury OAS	
Period	Average	Standard Deviation	Average	Standard Deviation
1/1/97–6/30/98	8	6	30	5
7/1/98–Present	15	18	56	13
9/1/99–Present	2	3	54	9

than the Treasury OAS. Second, during periods of low interest rates, mortgages tend to behave very differently from their OAS duration. They tend to widen in rallies and tighten in sell-offs, which increases volatility (clearly seen from the numbers). Thus, even though LIBOR OAS performed well in measuring value in collateral during the period September 1, 1999–March 14, 2000, it has clearly not always had that exemplary role.

CONCLUSION

There is no question that 10-year swaps and 10-year agency debentures now provide a better hedge for mortgages than do 10-year Treasuries. However, the hedge improvement is not nearly as dramatic as most market participants expect. There is a substantial amount of basis risk which does not get hedged out when using swaps or agency debentures. In this environment there is also a substantial amount of curve risk and volatility risk. These risks are not being hedged in using a simple agency or swap hedge.

Our bottom line is as follows. Don't be lulled into a false sense of security with a Roberto Benigni energy level approach (that life would be beautiful if you had only used agency debentures or swaps to hedge mortgages). Although reality may be simplified on the silver screen, in the very real world of mortgages, it is not.

CHAPTER 33

HEDGE EFFECTIVENESS: A STUDY BY PRICE BUCKET

Laurie Goodman, Ph.D.
Managing Director and Head
Mortgage Strategy Group
UBS Warburg

Jeffrey Ho
Director
Mortgage Strategy Group
UBS Warburg

Over the past few years, index-based mortgage portfolio managers have increased their reliance on mortgage pass-throughs and have decreased their dependency on structured mortgage products. This has been the inevitable result of liquidity concerns. As a result, we are now seeing more emphasis than ever on three types of trades: (1) the basis trade (mortgages versus Treasuries and mortgages versus agencies), (2) pass-through trades within the mortgage market (up in coupon, down in coupon, GNMA versus FNMA, FNMA versus Gold, 15-year versus 30-year), and finally (3) seasoned versus to-be-announced (TBA) pass-throughs. Of these three types of trades, a mortgage sector underweight or overweight is the most important contributor to outperformance or underperformance versus a fixed-rate index. With the mortgage market itself becoming more efficient, inter-coupon trades within the mortgage market are less rewarding than they used to be.

With any mortgage overweight or underweight, the duration and hedgeability of securities becomes more important. From the perspective of a total rate-of-return money manager, mortgages are not actually being hedged. However, a mortgage overweight at the expense of Treasuries, agency debentures, or corporates will generally be undertaken only when a manager is comfortable that he is "counting" the duration correctly, and believes the mortgage is apt to outperform the security it is being substituted for. Similarly if mortgages are underweighted, the total rate-of-return portfolio manager must make sure that the securities that are substituted for mortgages have similar performance characteristics. Thus we find investors making coupon choices based in part on their perceptions of how hedgeable collateral of the various coupons are.

Traditional wisdom has historically held that it is much easier to hedge discount mortgages than current-coupon or premium mortgages. However, as we watched the market over the past few years, we began to question that traditional wisdom. We have observed that higher-coupon mortgages have been very hedge-able versus Treasuries, albeit with lower hedge ratios. In this chapter, we system-atically look at hedgeability of mortgages by price bucket. We find that tradition-ally the discounts have been easier to hedge, regardless of vehicle used (Treasury securities, swaps, or agency debentures). However, since mid-1998, higher-priced securities have actually been easier to hedge with Treasuries than have been their lower-priced counterparts. We speculate that this reflects higher spread volatility and lower spread duration of higher-priced mortgages. Hedging results using swaps and agency debentures are more mixed, depending on the holding period. The differences between hedging with Treasury securities and hedging with agen-cies and swaps reflects the far greater volatility of the mortgage-Treasury spread than the mortgage-agency or mortgage-swap spread.

OUR METHODS

We paved the way to this analysis using FNMA mortgages having coupons of 6.5% to 8.5%. First,

1. We calculated empirical hedge ratios for a given mortgage using 20 days of empirical data. This allowed us to establish a position of long $100 of mort-gages and short ($100 times the empirical hedge ratios) of Treasuries, agen-cies, or swaps. The empirical hedge ratio was different for each instrument.

2. We rebalanced our hedge each successive 20-day period. We closed out the prior position and tabulated long mortgage performance versus our short of the hedging instrument. All mortgage securities are assumed to be rolled. Treasury shorts are funded at the 10-year Treasury repurchase (repo) rate, which is usually on special. The 10-year agency debentures are assumed funded at general collateral levels. The new position is derived from then-current 20-day hedge ratios.

3. We then divided the results into price buckets, depending on mortgage price at the beginning of the 20-day period. We used four price buckets: 92-98, 98-100, 100-102, and 102-104. Note that lower-priced securities have a larger bucket (i.e., all securities priced between 92 and 98) rather than the otherwise-standard $2 price ranges. This is our attempt to accommodate scarcity of data.

4. We developed and examined measures of hedging effectiveness. Our fa-vorite measure was cumulate absolute performance (annualized). Under that view, absolute hedging errors are aggregated and then annualized. [Thus, if we have 40 observations in a bucket (with each for a 20-day pe-riod), and a cumulative error of $6.00, our annualized error is 6.00/ (800/260) or $1.95.] We also showed the annualized variance of perform-ance, which uses the square of the absolute errors. Hence a series with a lot of small errors tracks better than one with several very large errors.

5. We also used shorter (10- and 5-day) holding periods, following the same method used in steps 1 to 4. This allowed for more frequent rebalancing. We continued to use 20-day empirical hedge ratios to set the size of the short, since that length was needed to provide sufficient data to be meaningful.

HOW TREASURY HEDGES MEASURED UP

The results using the 20-day hedge ratios are shown in Exhibit 33–1. The analysis is broken down into three periods—the early period (November 1, 1995–June 30, 1998), the later period (July 1, 1998–April 14, 2000), and the entire period (November 1, 1995–April 14, 2000). Note that in the earlier period, the best instrument for hedging with Treasury securities (as measured both

E X H I B I T   33–1

Hedging Effectiveness by Price—20-Day Holding Periods

Minimum Price	Maximum Price	No. of Obs.[a]	Treasury Hedge		Swap Hedge		Agency Hedge	
			CAPA[b]	AVP[c]	CAPA[b]	AVP[c]	CAPA[b]	AVP[c]
Early Period (November 1, 1995–June 30, 1998)								
$ 92	$ 98	36	$1.82	0.32	$2.13	0.41	$2.18	0.52
98	100	33	1.99	0.41	2.46	0.57	2.39	0.59
100	102	33	2.34	0.49	2.73	0.58	2.59	0.58
102	104	50	2.55	0.69	2.70	0.72	2.60	0.70
92	104	152	2.21	0.50	2.52	0.58	2.45	0.61
Later Period (July 1, 1998–April 14, 2000)								
$ 92	$ 98	20	$5.52	4.18	$2.83	1.02	$2.96	1.56
98	100	16	4.67	3.23	2.27	0.91	2.43	1.24
100	102	30	4.45	2.33	2.47	0.90	2.62	1.00
102	104	35	3.41	1.27	2.98	0.95	2.85	0.89
92	104	101	4.34	2.48	2.69	0.91	2.74	1.08
Entire Period (November 1, 1995–April 14, 2000)								
$ 92	$ 98	56	$3.14	1.80	$2.38	0.63	$2.46	0.88
98	100	49	2.86	1.36	2.40	0.70	2.40	0.81
100	102	63	3.34	1.37	2.61	0.77	2.61	0.80
102	104	85	2.91	0.94	2.82	0.83	2.70	0.79
92	104	253	3.06	1.33	2.59	0.74	2.57	0.82

[a]Obs = observations.
[b]CAPA = cumulative absolute performance annualized.
[c]AVP = annualized variance of performance.

E X H I B I T   33–2

Mortgage Spread Volatility as a Percentage of Mortgage Yield Volatility

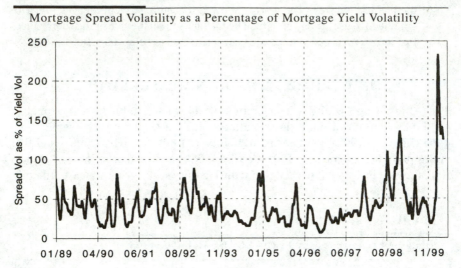

by cumulative absolute performance annualized and the variance) was lower-priced mortgages. The *cumulative absolute performance annualized (CAPA)* was $1.82 for mortgages with a 92-98 dollar price, versus $2.34 for mortgages with a 100-102 dollar price.

In the later period (July 1, 1998–April 14, 2000), the best hedging results using Treasuries were among higher dollar–priced mortgages. Exhibit 33–1 shows the CAPA for the 102-104 price bucket at $3.41, versus $5.52 for the 92-98 price bucket. These results are so strong that over the entire period there was little difference in the hedgeability of lower- and higher-priced buckets.

We speculate that this reflects greater spread volatility of spread product after the middle of 1998, when scarcity considerations forced a decoupling of Treasury securities from the rest of the fixed income universe. Exhibit 33–2 graphically depicts mortgage spread volatility as a percentage of mortgage yield volatility. To eliminate day-to-day noise, we defined volatility as the 20-day moving average of 20-day spread or yield changes. Note that prior to the middle of 1998, spread volatility was generally 25% to 50% of yield volatility: It averaged 41%. During the first half of 2000, it has been well over 100%!

SWAP AND AGENCY DEBENTURE HEDGES

In the earlier period, swaps and agency debentures provided a better hedge for lower dollar–priced mortgages than they did for higher-priced mortgages. This is shown in Exhibit 33–1 in the top right-hand columns. For example, the CAPA with swaps was $2.13 for 92-98 dollar priced mortgages, $2.70 for 102-104 prices. Similar results were obtained for agency debentures.

In the later period, swaps and agency debentures actually produced the smallest CAPA for the 98-100 and 100-102 coupon buckets. For example, CAPA on the 92-98 bucket was $2.83, versus $2.47 for the 100-102 bucket, and $2.98 for the 102-104 bucket. The results, expressed in term of annualized variance of performance (AVP), are similar. Hedging errors were larger for lower-duration mortgages (due to their greater spread duration) and for the very high dollar–priced mortgages.

Finally, note from Exhibit 33–1 that the results of this analysis are very consistent with the results shown in Chapter 32, Hedging Mortgages with Swaps and Agencies. In that chapter, we showed that in the earlier period, the hedging error with swaps and agency debentures was slightly larger than that from using Treasury securities. Exhibit 33–1 showed that the CAPA on the 98-100 coupon bucket was $1.99 with Treasury securities, and $2.46 with swaps. By contrast in the later period, swap and agency hedges served the purpose much better than did Treasury hedges—$2.27 is the CAPA on the swap hedge for the 98-100 bucket, versus $4.67 for the Treasury hedge. Even so, hedging with swaps and agencies in the later period was actually somewhat more fraught with error than hedging with Treasuries in the earlier period.

RESULTS FROM MORE FREQUENT REBALANCING?

Exhibit 33–3 shows our analysis tested by 10-day holding periods. We rebalance the position every 10 days, resetting the empirical hedge ratios using 20 days of data. Note the four time periods in this table—the early period (November 1, 1995–June 30, 1998), the later period (July 1, 1998–April 14, 2000), the last 7.5 months (September 1, 1999–April 14, 2000), and the entire period (November 1, 1995–April 14, 2000). The last 7.5 months (the most recent period) were meant to correspond to the period in which the market had mostly made adjustments to hedging mortgages with other spread product. Note that all CAPAs and AVPs are higher using 10-day holding periods than 20-day holding periods because there is less scope for netting. For example, if the hedged position makes $0.50 in the first 10 days and loses $0.60 in the next 10 days, the 20-day holding periods would pick up the $0.10 net. The 10-day holding periods would pick up an absolute hedging error of $1.10.

In the earlier period (November 1, 1995–June 30, 1998), the easiest mortgages to hedge were those with the lowest dollar price—the 92-98 price bucket. Hedging difficulties monotonically increased as the dollar price of the mortgage increased. This was true regardless of whether the hedge was a Treasury hedge, a swap hedge, or an agency hedge.

In the later period (July 1, 1998–April 14, 2000), higher-coupon mortgages were actually easier to hedge using Treasury securities. The CAPA for the 92-98 price bucket is $7.78 versus $6.58 for the 100-102 price bucket and $4.75 for the 102-104 price bucket. Results are more mixed when using swaps and agency debentures, with little difference between the 92-98, 98-100, and 100-102 coupon buckets. The 102-104 price bucket appears the easiest to hedge.

E X H I B I T   33-3

Hedging Effectiveness by Price—10-Day Holding Periods

Minimum Price	Maximum Price	No. of Obs[a]	Treasury Hedge CAPA[b]	AVP[c]	Swap Hedge CAPA[b]	AVP[c]	Agency Hedge CAPA[b]	AVP[c]
Early Period (November 1, 1995–June 30, 1998)								
$ 92	$ 98	74	$3.49	0.74	$3.25	0.66	$3.32	0.74
98	100	65	3.77	0.83	3.98	0.93	4.04	1.02
100	102	68	3.86	0.77	3.85	0.82	4.12	0.87
102	104	96	4.15	0.91	4.18	0.91	4.29	0.96
92	104	303	3.84	0.82	3.83	0.83	3.97	0.90
Later Period (July 1, 1998–April 14, 2000)								
$ 92	$ 98	40	$7.78	4.17	$4.26	1.08	$4.23	1.30
98	100	32	6.88	3.67	4.26	1.20	4.24	1.27
100	102	58	6.58	2.85	4.59	1.49	4.38	1.30
102	104	73	4.75	1.47	3.73	0.97	3.64	0.87
92	104	203	6.24	2.77	4.18	1.17	4.07	1.13
Last 7.5 Months (September 1, 1999–April 14, 2000)								
$ 92	$ 98	31	$5.90	2.61	$3.82	0.80	$3.13	0.55
98	100	15	6.36	3.07	3.68	0.77	3.23	0.55
100	102	19	7.47	3.84	5.05	1.89	4.06	1.12
102	104	17	6.11	1.79	4.09	0.90	3.60	0.68
92	104	82	6.49	2.87	4.18	1.07	3.46	0.71
Entire Period (November 1, 1995–April 14, 2000)								
$ 92	$ 98	114	$4.99	1.97	$3.60	0.80	$3.64	0.93
98	100	97	4.80	1.78	4.07	1.02	4.11	1.10
100	102	126	5.11	1.75	4.19	1.15	4.24	1.09
102	104	169	4.41	1.15	3.99	0.94	4.01	0.92
92	104	506	4.80	1.62	3.97	0.97	4.01	1.00

[a]Obs = observations.
[b]CAPA = cumulative absolute performance annualized.
[c]AVP = annualized variance of performance.

Exhibit 33–4 shows results of the analysis using 5-day holding periods. These are consistent with those for the 10-day holding periods. In the earlier period, all three hedging vehicles (Treasuries, swaps, and agency debentures) are the most effective for lower-priced securities, but less so for higher-priced securities. In the later period, Treasury hedges are the most effective on higher coupons and

E X H I B I T   33–4

Hedging Effectiveness by Price—5-Day Holding Periods

Minimum Price	Maximum Price	No. of Obs[a]	Treasury Hedge		Swap Hedge		Agency Hedge	
			CAPA[b]	AVP[c]	CAPA[b]	AVP[c]	CAPA[b]	AVP[c]
Early Period (November 1, 1995–June 30, 1998)								
$ 92	$ 98	152	$4.47	0.64	$4.78	0.72	$4.99	0.75
98	100	126	4.87	0.69	5.19	0.80	5.29	0.81
100	102	142	5.16	0.77	5.30	0.84	5.36	0.84
102	104	191	5.69	0.95	5.68	0.97	5.65	0.97
92	104	611	5.11	0.78	5.28	0.85	5.35	0.85
Later Period (July 1, 1998–April 14, 2000)								
$ 92	$ 98	78	$15.14	7.68	$7.09	1.57	$7.07	1.55
98	100	63	12.50	5.63	7.29	1.69	7.42	1.75
100	102	113	10.63	4.02	7.85	2.28	7.57	2.03
102	104	140	7.81	2.62	6.70	1.79	6.54	1.65
92	104	394	10.80	4.51	7.14	1.82	7.04	1.73
Last 7.5 Months (September 1, 1999–April 14, 2000)								
$ 92	$ 98	61	$13.92	6.93	$6.48	1.31	$6.02	1.07
98	100	30	12.73	5.23	7.13	1.44	6.19	1.11
100	102	35	11.84	4.48	8.12	1.82	6.69	1.29
102	104	31	10.03	3.46	7.74	1.94	7.29	1.77
92	104	157	12.47	5.37	7.22	1.56	6.44	1.25
Entire Period (November 1, 1995–April 14, 2000)								
$ 92	$ 98	230	$8.09	3.04	$5.56	1.01	$5.69	1.02
98	100	189	7.42	2.33	5.89	1.09	6.00	1.12
100	102	255	7.59	2.22	6.43	1.50	6.34	1.38
102	104	331	6.58	1.65	6.11	1.31	6.03	1.25
92	104	1,005	7.34	2.25	6.01	1.23	6.01	1.20

[a]Obs = observations.
[b]CAPA = cumulative absolute performance annualized.
[c]AVP = annualized variance of performance.

least effective on lower coupons. Swap and agency hedges in the later period show mixed results. Over this time period, it appears that the swap and agency hedges are the most effective for the 102-104 dollar price bucket.

These results hold up using only the most recent 7.5 months of data (since September 1, 1999–April 14, 2000). The CAPA on Treasury hedges is highest for the lowest-priced securities ($13.92 for the 92-98 price bucket) and lowest for the highest-priced securities ($10.03 for the 102-104 price bucket). Variance numbers follow the same pattern. For the swap and agency hedges, the results over the past 7.5-month period of September 1, 1999–April 14, 2000 are more mixed, as well. However, lower-price buckets (92-98 and 98-100) have lower hedging errors than higher-price buckets (100-102 and 102-104). This is at odds with the results for the entire July 1, 1998–April 14, 2000 period. It is clear the relative effectiveness of swap and agency hedging depends very clearly on one's measurement and holding period.

CONCLUSION

It used to be the case that lower-priced mortgages were the easiest to hedge, regardless of choice of hedging instrument. This has all changed in our brave new world (in which spread volatility has been nearly as pronounced as yield volatility). Higher-priced mortgages are now actually easier to hedge with Treasuries than their lower-priced counterparts, as they have lower spread duration. Hedging with swaps and agencies delivers more mixed results, depending on choice of holding period and measurement period.

CHAPTER 34

HEDGING IOs AND MORTGAGE SERVICING

Laurie Goodman, Ph.D.
Managing Director and Head
Mortgage Strategy Group
UBS Warburg

Jeffrey Ho
Director
Mortgage Strategy Group
UBS Warburg

Hedging mortgage servicing has become far more difficult over the past few years, owing to both the increased negative convexity of mortgage product as well as the decoupling of Treasury instruments from spread product. In this chapter we present some preliminary results on the effectiveness of various instruments for hedging mortgage servicing rights.

HEDGING SERVICING

A considerable amount of consolidation has taken place in the mortgage origination and mortgage servicing industry. This is shown very clearly in Exhibit 34–1. In 1989, the top 25 servicers had a 17% market share, whereas in 1999 the top 25 controlled 55.9% of the market. Concentration was actually even greater than that slicing indicates. In 1989, the top 10 mortgage servicers had a 10.7% market share, which is now up to 40.6%. Thus the "top 10" nearly quadrupled market share, whereas the shares of servicers 11 through 25 did little more than double (from 6.3% [17−10.7] to 15.3% [55.9−40.6]).

This represents an extremely large structural change over a single decade. Servicing used to be a small part of everyone's business. Now it's a very large part of business for the largest originators, which thus makes hedging a far more important issue.

Meanwhile, hedging mortgage servicing became more difficult due to the increase in the negative convexity of mortgage product, as well as the decoupling of Treasury instruments from spread product. Let's review each of these points.

EXHIBIT 34–1

Increased Consolidation in Mortgage Servicing

	Percent of Market Share	
Year	Top 10	Top 25
1999	40.6	55.9
1998	36.4	50.8
1997	30.9	46.8
1996	27.7	41.8
1995	24.7	39.5
1994	21.2	34.8
1993	17.2	30.0
1992	15.2	27.0
1991	13.2	22.5
1990	12.0	20.2
1989	10.7	17.0

Increased Negative Convexity of Mortgages

The greater negative convexity of mortgages stems from the fact that it has become increasingly easier and cheaper to refinance a mortgage. The costs of refinancing will continue to fall, due to growth of the internet as an origination avenue. As a result, it takes less incentive than ever for home owners to refinance their mortgages. We saw this very distinctly in the 1998 wave.

Exhibit 34–2 shows FNMA prepays (1-month CPRs) in December 1993 and December 1998 as a function of the relative weighted average coupon (WAC) of the mortgage. We chose these dates since they represented the peak refinancing speeds for their respective cycles. The relative WAC of the mortgage is the difference between the gross rate a home owner pays and the rate on a new loan. (Note that this is a proxy for measuring refinancing incentive.) It is important to realize that generating 15% CPR in December of 1993 took a refinancing incentive of 135 basis points (bps), whereas in 1998 it took 75 bps. In the next wave of refinancing it should take even less.

The impact of the narrower refinancing trigger can be seen quite clearly in Exhibit 34–3, which illustrates the speed on new 30-year FNMA 6.5s, 7.0s, 7.5s, and 8.0s. Note that new FNMA 7.5s and 8.0s paid very similarly during both the 1993 rally and the 1998 rally. The 7.5s were a little faster in 1998, and the 8s a bit slower, but those differences were marginal. However, behavior of the lower coupons was very different. In 1993, new FNMA 7s never broke 10% CPR, whereas in 1998 they were printing in excess of 30% CPR. In 1993 new 6.5s showed no signs of refinancing activity, but in the 1998 rally these securities hit peak speeds of 12 to 14% CPR.

E X H I B I T   34–2

FNMA Prepayments*

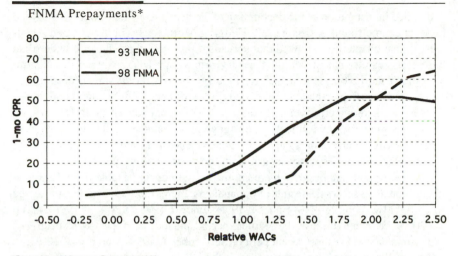

*December 1993 versus December 1998.

E X H I B I T   34–3

New 30-Year FNMA 6.5%, 7.0%, 7.5%, and 8.0%*

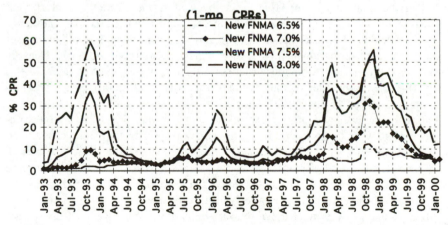

*One-month CPRs.

This increased sensitivity of the prepayment function should, over time, make it more important to hedge servicing with principal-only (PO) products. That is, the increased responsiveness of home owners to their refinancing opportunities is a large minus for interest-only (IOs) products or mortgage servicing rights. It is more difficult to hedge with any vehicle that doesn't provide an offset to this increased sensitivity.

The Decoupling of Treasuries

A detailed investigation of the decoupling of Treasury securities from other spread product can be found in Chapter 32, Hedging Mortgages with Swaps and Agencies. In that chapter, we showed that spreads on all spread product are wider than before, as scarcity has driven up Treasury prices. Spreads on spread product are also much more volatile than before. Finally, spreads on all spread product are much more highly correlated. Thus, hedging with agency debentures and swaps does reduce hedging error versus hedging with Treasury securities. But it does not reduce hedging error by as much as mortgage participants would have thought. In fact, the hedging errors on swaps and agency debentures are now comparable to those we had versus Treasury securities in the period before mid-1998.

These points are best hammered home by reproducing a table from that chapter. Exhibit 34–4 shows the results of our analysis. In this table we examine mortgage spreads for two periods—November 1, 1995–June 30, 1998 and July 1, 1998–March 14, 2000. We refer to these as the "earlier" period and the "later" period, respectively. We also looked at the most recent period (September 1, 1999–March 14, 2000) as a distinct separate period, since this period is the one in which mortgages are believed to have traded more closely with agencies and swaps. Finally, we showed results for the entire period (November 1, 1995–March 14, 2000).

As a proxy for the mortgage universe, we used the perfect current-coupon FNMA (the mortgage selling exactly at par for corporate settlement). For our Treasury proxy, we used the on-the-run 10-year security. For agencies, we used the FNMA benchmark 10-year issue as far back as it was available, and 10-year medium term notes prior to that. For swaps, we similarly used the 10-year tenor.

Note that all spreads are, on average, much higher as opposed to Treasury securities in the later period than they were in the earlier period. Mortgage-Treasury spreads averaged 110 bps in the earlier period (November 1, 1995–June 30, 1998) and 147 bps in the later period (July 1, 1998–March 14, 2000). Swap-Treasury spreads averaged 41 bps in the earlier period and 81 bps in the later period. Note that mortgage-agency, mortgage-swap, and agency-swap spreads were largely unchanged between the two periods. Mortgage-swap spreads, for example, averaged 69 bps in the earlier period, and came in almost evenly at 66 bps in the later period.

Not only are all spreads higher, but spreads have also become much more volatile versus Treasury securities (as shown in the bottom section of Exhibit 34–4). By contrast, spread variability between various spread products has increased somewhat, but not nearly as much as has the variability of the mortgage-Treasury spread. For example, the standard deviation of the mortgage-Treasury spread was 6 bps in the earlier period, and the standard deviation of the mortgage-agency spread was 5 bps in this period. Thus, there was little advantage to hedging mortgages with swaps or agencies over hedging them with Treasuries. By contrast, the standard deviation of the mortgage-Treasury spread was 20 bps in the later period, whereas the standard deviation of the mortgage-agency spread was 13 bps. Thus, in the later period, swaps and agencies provided more effective hedging vehicles. Hedging results for mortgages of different coupons were broadly consistent with these results.

EXHIBIT 34-4

Volatility of Selected Spreads

Begin	End	Mortgage-Treasury	Agency-Treasury	Swap-Treasury	Mortgage-Agency	Mortgage-Swap	Swap-Agency
Average Spreads (bps)*							
11/1/95	6/30/98	110	28	41	82	69	13
7/1/98	3/14/00	147	61	81	85	66	19
9/1/99	3/14/00	144	67	85	77	58	19
11/1/95	3/14/00	123	40	56	83	68	15
Standard Deviation of Spread (bps)*							
11/1/95	6/30/98	6	2	3	5	5	2
7/1/98	3/14/00	20	10	12	13	11	4
9/1/99	3/14/00	13	11	12	4	4	1
11/1/95	3/14/00	13	7	8	9	8	3

*bps = basis points.

HEDGING MORTGAGE SERVICING—CORRELATIONS

Now that you've fallen asleep over the background and backup details—we finally get to the meat of this chapter—hedging IOs and mortgage servicing rights. We do use IOs as a proxy for mortgage servicing, and yes, we fully recognize that it is an imperfect one. We realize that IOs do not take into account any of the income or costs associated with the servicing activity. The big benefit of being in the servicing business is to be able to take advantage of the substantial fee income associated with servicing rights, including late charges, escrow income, prepay float, and any other tie-in services that can be exploited. On the expense side, IOs also fail to take into account the marginal costs of servicing, or the delinquency costs. So by using IOs as a proxy, we are assuming a largely constant relationship between servicing income and expenses. (However, this seems to be a reasonable assumption.)

Exhibit 34–5 shows the correlations between IOs and various hedging instruments. We used four different IOs for this analysis: FNS 249 (backed by seasoned 6.5s), FNS 240 (backed by seasoned 7s), FNS 254 (backed by seasoned 7.5s), and FNS 251 (backed by seasoned 8s). The correlations are derived by comparing daily price changes on these IOs with price changes on the 10-year Treasury, 10-year swaps, 10-year agencies, 6.5% collateral, 7.5% collateral, FNS 249 PO, and FNS 254 PO.

Although Exhibit 34–5 is laid out differently from Exhibit 34–4, the time periods are identical. The block of numbers in the upper left hand corner of Exhibit 34–5 shows the correlations of each of the IOs with its hedging instruments for the November 1, 1995–June 30, 1998 period. The block of numbers on the bottom left hand section covers the July 1, 1998–March 14, 2000 period. The top right hand section covers the period September 1, 1999–March 14, 1999, whereas the bottom section covers the entire period.

There are a number of very interesting results from our simple analysis and comparison. First, the PO hedges are the most effective, as would be expected. For example, hedging FNS 240 IO with FNS 249 PO gave a correlation of 92.7% in the November 1, 1995–June 30, 1998 period (Exhibit 34–5, top left), and a correlation of 95.8% in the July 1, 1998–March 14, 2000 period (Exhibit 34–5, bottom left). However, the second most effective hedge, as measured by correlation, actually turns out to be the Treasury hedge. For example, for the entire period November 1, 1995–March 14, 2000 (Exhibit 34–5, bottom right), the correlation between FNS 240 and the 10-year Treasury was 88.9%, which was lower than either of the PO hedges, but higher than everything else.

Second, there is very little difference in the hedging effectiveness of the 10-year Treasury note, 10-year swaps, or 10-year agencies between the two periods shown on the left-hand side of Exhibit 34–5. That is, the correlations are very similar in the earlier period (November 1, 1995–June 30, 1998) and the later period (July 1, 1998–March 14, 2000). By contrast, FNMA 6.5% collateral was a slightly less effective hedge in the later period (the correlation dropped from 81.4% to 76.6%) and FNMA 7.5% collateral was a much less effective hedge in the later period (that correlation dropped from 73.5% to 52.9%).

E X H I B I T 34-5

Correlation of IOs with Their Hedges (%)

November 1, 1995–	IOs			
June 30, 1998	FNS 249	FNS 240	FNS 254	FNS 251
10-Year Treasury	−83.8	−89.5	−92.2	−92.5
10-Year swap	−82.4	−88.1	−90.9	−91.2
10-Year agency	−82.7	−88.3	−91.1	−91.5
6.5% Collateral	−75.8	−81.4	−84.8	−86.7
7.5% Collateral	−67.6	−73.5	−77.7	−80.7
FNS 249 PO	−92.4	−92.7	−93.2	−92.7
FNS 254 PO	−86.5	−92.2	−96.6	−94.2

July 1, 1998–	IOs			
March 14, 2000	FNS 249	FNS 240	FNS 254	FNS 251
10-Year Treasury	−87.7	−89.2	−91.0	−92.2
10-Year swap	−83.7	−85.2	−87.3	−88.8
10-Year agency	−85.8	−86.8	−89.0	−89.4
6.5% Collateral	−74.2	−76.6	−80.4	−84.1
7.5% Collateral	−49.7	−52.9	−59.6	−65.8
FNS 249 PO	−96.2	−95.8	−95.6	−94.8
FNS 254 PO	−90.6	−92.7	−97.3	−95.5

September 1, 1999–	IOs			
March 14, 2000	FNS 249	FNS 240	FNS 254	FNS 251
10-Year Treasury	−86.4	−92.4	−92.6	−94.1
10-Year swap	−85.7	−91.5	−92.8	−92.4
10-Year agency	−85.6	−91.5	−93.1	−92.5
6.5% Collateral	−84.0	−90.4	−91.9	−90.8
7.5% Collateral	−81.4	−88.2	−89.6	−87.8
FNS 249 PO	−90.3	−93.1	−94.3	−94.2
FNS 254 PO	−89.0	−93.8	−97.6	−95.2

November 1, 1995–	IOs			
March 14, 2000	FNS 249	FNS 240	FNS 254	FNS 251
10-Year Treasury	−84.2	−88.9	−91.7	−92.1
10-Year swap	−80.8	−85.9	−89.2	−90.1
10-Year agency	−82.4	−86.9	−90.1	−90.5
6.5% Collateral	−70.9	−77.2	−82.4	−85.6
7.5% Collateral	−54.8	−62.2	−69.7	−75.2
FNS 249 PO	−93.6	−94.3	−94.3	−92.8
FNS 254 PO	−85.4	−91.1	−96.7	−94.7

HEDGING EFFECTIVENESS

Correlations are, for many of us, unintuitive. An alternative approach is to look at the effectiveness of hedging IOs with various alternatives. This method is very similar to that used in Chapter 32:

1. Calculate the empirical hedge ratios for a given IO, using 20 days of empirical data. This allows us to set up a position in which we were long $100 of IOs and long ($100 times the empirical hedge ratio) of Treasuries, agencies, swaps, collateral, or POs. Note that the empirical hedge ratios will be different for each instrument.

2. Rebalance our hedge each successive 20-day period. We closed out the prior position and tabulated hedged performance (of the long IO-long hedging instrument position). We assumed all mortgages were rolled at actual roll levels. We calculated IO rolls, assuming financing at 1-month London interbank offered rate (LIBOR). Treasuries were assumed to be funded at the 10-year repurchase rate, which is generally on special. The 10-year agency debentures were assumed to be funded at general collateral levels. After the tabulation, we derived a new position by recalculating the then-current 20-day hedge ratios.

3. Look at measures of hedging effectiveness. Our favorite is cumulative absolute performance (annualized). Under that measure, absolute hedging errors are aggregated, then annualized. We also show the annualized variance of performance (which uses the square of the absolute errors). Hence, for this measure, a series with many small errors tracks better than one with several very large errors.

4. We also used shorter (10- and 5-day) holding periods, following the same method as in steps 1 to 3 above. Note that shorter holding periods allow for more frequent rebalancing. We continued to set the size of the hedge with 20-day empirical hedge ratios, since that length was needed to provide sufficient data to be meaningful.

The Results

Our analysis of hedging Trust 240 IOs backed by FNMA 7s is shown in Exhibit 34–6. Results for each of the other IOs are very similar and are not shown in this chapter.

Exhibit 34–6 is divided into three sections. The first section shows the results for 20-day holding periods, the middle section shows the results for 10-day holding periods, and the bottom part shows results from the shorter 5-day holding periods. Focus first on the 20-day holding periods shown at top. For the November 1, 1995–June 30, 1998 period, POs provided the best hedge for FNS 240 IOs, with cumulative absolute performances (annualized) of $4.64 for the 6.5% PO and $3.28 for the 7.5% PO. The next best hedge was the Treasury at $5.41, followed closely by swaps, agencies, and 6.5% collateral. FNMA 7.5 collateral was the worst hedge. During the period July 1, 1998–March 14, 2000, most hedging errors

Hedging Analysis of 7.0% IO (FNS 240)

					6.5%	7.5%	6.5%	7.5%
						Hedge Instrument		
Begin	**End**	**Treasury**	**Swap**	**Agency**	**Collateral**	**Collateral**	**PO***	**PO***
Hedging over 20-Day Holding Periods								
Cumulative Absolute Performance, Annualized								
11/1/95	6/30/98	$ 5.41	$ 5.70	$ 5.81	$ 5.75	$ 7.66	$ 4.64	$ 3.28
7/1/98	3/14/00	7.79	9.10	7.69	10.28	18.81	4.31	6.71
11/1/95	3/14/00	6.33	7.02	6.54	7.51	12.00	4.51	4.62
Annualized Variance of Performance								
11/1/95	6/30/98	4.23	5.17	6.15	5.03	9.11	4.05	1.49
7/1/98	3/14/00	9.57	11.11	6.96	15.09	61.96	2.25	6.27
11/1/95	3/14/00	6.33	7.39	6.36	8.85	29.57	3.28	3.33
Hedging over 10-Day Holding Periods								
Cumulative Absolute Performance, Annualized								
11/1/95	6/30/98	$ 7.04	$ 8.13	$ 8.54	$ 9.69	$12.67	$ 6.75	$ 5.81
7/1/98	3/14/00	10.88	11.74	11.70	13.09	24.28	6.76	7.91
9/1/99	3/14/00	7.30	9.09	9.42	9.74	10.00	7.16	6.56
11/1/95	3/14/00	8.53	9.54	9.77	11.01	17.18	6.75	6.63
Annualized Variance of Performance								
11/1/95	6/30/98	4.30	5.62	6.60	7.28	12.48	4.21	2.49
7/1/98	3/14/00	8.75	9.86	9.60	11.23	47.44	2.90	4.28
9/1/99	3/14/00	3.50	3.95	4.30	4.27	4.27	2.18	1.97
11/1/95	3/14/00	6.07	7.24	7.73	8.77	26.16	3.65	3.18
Hedging over 5-Day Holding Periods								
Cumulative Absolute Performance, Annualized								
11/1/95	6/30/98	$ 9.45	$10.43	$11.05	$12.24	$15.59	$ 9.11	$ 7.50
7/1/98	3/14/00	14.04	18.43	16.53	19.62	31.21	9.67	10.90
9/1/99	3/14/00	9.62	10.32	10.83	11.05	11.75	8.98	7.69
11/1/95	3/14/00	11.23	13.54	13.18	15.11	21.67	9.32	8.82
Annualized Variance of Performance								
11/1/95	6/30/98	3.78	4.34	5.11	6.26	10.86	3.45	2.28
7/1/98	3/14/00	10.32	13.24	9.76	13.75	44.18	3.17	4.81
9/1/99	3/14/00	2.99	3.18	3.52	3.41	4.02	2.07	1.74
11/1/95	3/14/00	6.37	7.79	6.92	9.16	23.81	3.33	3.26

*6.5% PO used is from FNS 249; 7.5% PO used is from FNS 254.
Note: Treasury, swap, and agency hedge instruments have 10-year maturities.

were larger, but the ordinal ranking was very similar. The POs were the best hedge, with errors of $4.31 and $6.71. Agency debentures and Treasuries were next, with errors of $7.69 and $7.79, respectively. Swaps weighed in at $9.10, and collateral again provided the poorest hedge, with cumulative absolute error of $10.28 and $18.81 for the 6.5% and 7.5% collateral, respectively. Variance measures were consistent with the cumulative absolute performance rankings.

The 10-day results (middle section) and 5-day results (bottom section) were again consistent. POs provided the best hedge. Treasuries provided the second-best hedge, followed closely by swaps and agencies. Collateral provided the worst hedge.

Reasons for Poor Mortgage Performance

It is not surprising that POs have delivered the best hedge, since they are the only hedge providing substantial positive convexity. It is also not shocking that hedging errors on most instruments were higher in the later period than in the earlier period. At first it surprised us that Treasuries were consistently a better hedge than swaps or agencies, whereas pass-throughs were a worse hedge, regardless of the period chosen. Let's look into those relationships more closely.

The poor performance of pass-throughs reflects the fact that they are actually negatively convex, and so the negative convexity of the IOs is magnified in a rally. This doubling up of negative convexity must be offset by the purchase of options product, which we did not allow in our simple analysis. If this is a contributing factor, Exhibit 34–6 should demonstrate that 6.5% collateral is a consistently better hedge than 7.5% collateral. This is virtually always the case. Exhibit 34–6 also demonstrates that 6.5% FNMA collateral performed much closer to swaps and agencies in the earlier period than during the later period, since the FNMA 6.5 collateral was under par for most of the earlier period. We should also see this result for the last 6 months (September 1, 1999–March 14, 2000). In fact, that is also clearly the case. Another factor contributing to the poor mortgage performance is that any flattening of the yield curve is detrimental to both IOs and pass-throughs, and the yield curve has flattened dramatically over our evaluation period.

Why Treasury Hedges Did So Well

At first it seemed very unintuitive to us that Treasury hedges outperformed swap, agency, and mortgage hedges. Then we realized that IOs had cheapened over the estimation period. Treasuries have richened, which cushioned the effect. Moreover, much of the poor performance of IOs versus mortgages, swaps, and agency debentures reflects the fact that these hedging instruments had cheapened as well.

It is useful to explore this further. The cheapening in IOs can be best seen by looking at the current-coupon IO multiplier though time. The current-coupon IO multiplier (shown in Exhibit 34–7) is the value of 100 bps of IO. It is calculated by taking the price on the current-coupon IO (calculated by interpolation) and dividing by the current-coupon itself. As can be seen from the results, IOs are cheaper than they were in 1995 (although not as cheap as in October of 1998).

E X H I B I T   34–7

Current-Coupon IO Multiplier

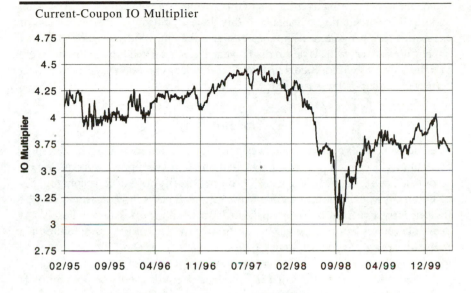

E X H I B I T   34–8

Mortgage, Swap, and Agency Spread to the 10-Year Treasury

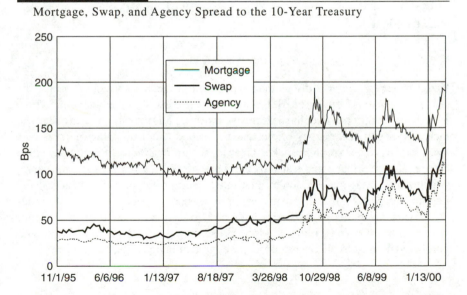

Exhibit 34–8 shows how much mortgages, agencies, and swaps have all cheapened versus Treasuries. We are very wide by any historical measure. Thus, when we look at historical hedging effectiveness, we capture the fact that IOs have cheapened while Treasuries have richened, making Treasuries a better hedge than spread product.

We believe that hedge profitability should be as important a consideration in a hedge as hedge effectiveness. As of this writing, spread product is very cheap, and servicers should take advantage of this. Indeed, much of the effectiveness of Treasuries as a hedge has been their secular richening. With the perfect current coupon now at very wide levels to the 10-year Treasury, spreads are far more likely to tighten than to widen. Stated differently, it is clear that one would not bet on a further richening of Treasury securities from these levels.

Caveats

There are a number of important caveats to keep in mind reviewing these results. First, in this discussion, we are totally excluding the accounting treatment. We realize that Treasuries, agencies, and POs do not qualify for hedge accounting because they are physical instruments. However, in all cases, it is possible to do the trade in derivative form and hence make hedge accounting a possibility. That is, 10-year note futures can be used instead of the 10-year Treasury, agency futures can replace the 10-year agency (although this contract is new, and the open interest is low), and total rate-of-return PO swaps can be used in place of the POs themselves.

Second, we are not considering purchased options, nor the possibility of multiple hedges (such as a combination of mortgages and purchased options). This would certainly improve the correlations and hedge effectiveness of all products. Mortgages will benefit more than would other products from the ability to add purchased options.

CONCLUSION

Hedge servicing is more difficult than ever before. We can draw a number of interesting conclusions from the analysis in this chapter. First, POs are likely to increase in hedging importance over the next few years, since it is the only way to hedge the increased negative convexity of mortgages. Second, the decoupling of Treasuries from spread product certainly makes Treasury securities a more difficult hedge than before. This is further complicated by the shape of the Treasury forward rate curve, which makes hedge calibration all that much more difficult. Third, from a profitability perspective, it certainly makes sense to hedge servicing with spread product. Finally, using mortgage pass-throughs as a hedge exacerbates the negative convexity on the IO. Thus, it is necessary to use pass-throughs in conjunction with purchased options to obtain a satisfactory degree of hedge effectiveness.

COMMERCIAL MORTGAGE-BACKED SECURITIES

CHAPTER **35**

COMMERCIAL MORTGAGE-BACKED SECURITIES

Anthony B. Sanders, Ph.D.
Professor of Finance and Galbreath Distinguished Scholar
The Ohio State University

Commercial mortgage-backed securities (CMBS) represent an interesting depar-
ture from residential MBS. With residential MBS, the underlying collateral is
loans on residential properties (1 to 4 units). With CMBS, the underlying collateral is loans on retail properties, office properties, industrial properties, multifamily housing, and hotels. Unlike residential mortgage loans, commercial loans tend
to be "locked out" from prepayment for 10 years. Counterbalancing the reduction
of prepayment risk for CMBS is the increase in default risk.

Both CMBS and real estate investment trusts (REITs) have grown tremen-
dously since 1995 as investors' tastes for new real estate–related products have increased. Investment banks were able to apply what they have learned from residential MBS and apply it (with some interesting twists) to the commercial real estate loan
market. Not only is the U.S. market continuing to expand, but also CMBS is growing at an ever-increasing rate in Europe (albeit at a much smaller scale). This chapter
focuses on the interesting twists that make CMBS such a fascinating product.

THE CMBS DEAL

A CMBS is formed when an issuer deposits commercial loans into a trust. The issuer then creates securities in the form of classes of bonds backed by the commercial loans. As payments on the commercial loans (and any lump-sum repayment of principal) are received, they are distributed (passed through) to the
bondholders according to the rules governing the distribution of proceeds.

Bond Pass-through Rates

An example of a recent CMBS deal can be used to highlight the distribution of
cash flows to the bondholders and the rules governing the distribution. The
GMAC 1999-C3 deal, underwritten jointly by Deutsche Bank and Goldman

---

This chapter is reprinted with permission from Frank J. Fabozzi (ed.), *Investing in Asset-Backed Securities* (New Hope, PA: Frank J. Fabozzi Associates, 2000).

Sachs, is summarized in Exhibit 35–1. The balance of the bonds as of the cutoff date (September 10, 1999) is $1,152,022,048. The gross weighted average coupon (WACg) is 7.90% and the net weighted average coupon (WACn) is 7.79%. The weighted average maturity (WAM) is 117 months.

The bonds are sequential-pay. The pass-through rate for class A-1-a is 6.97% and fixed. The pass-through rates for classes A-1-b, A-2, B, C, G, H, J, K, L, M, and N are equal to the lesser of the fixed pass-through rate and net WAC of the mortgage pool. For example, the A-1-b bondholders will receive the lesser of the fixed pass-through rate (7.27%) and the net WAC (7.79%). Pass-through rates for classes D, E, and F are equal to the WAC of the mortgage pool.

Class X is an interest-only (IO) class. Class X receives the excess of the net WAC received from the pool over the weighted average pass-through rate paid to the sequential-pay bonds. Class X's notional balance equals the outstanding balance of the sequential-pay bonds.

CMBS Ratings and Subordination Levels

The rating agencies play a critical role in the CMBS market. The role of the rating agency is to provide a third-party opinion on the quality of each bond in the structure (as well as the necessary level of credit enhancement to achieve a desired rating level). The rating agency examines critical characteristics of the underlying pool of loans such as the *debt service coverage ratio (DSCR)* and the *loan-to-value (LTV) ratio*. If the target ratios at the asset level are below a certain level, the credit rating of the bond is reduced. Subordination can be used at the structure level to improve the rating of the bond. For example, suppose that a certain class of property requires a DSCR of 1.50× to qualify for an A rating; if the actual DSCR is only 1.25×, additional subordination can be added at the deal level to bring the rating to an A rating.

The credit ratings for the bonds in the GMAC 1999-C3 deal are presented in Exhibit 35–1. Fitch rated the first three bonds (A-1-a, A-1-b, and A-2) AAA Moody's rated the same bond classes as Aaa. The B through F bonds have progressively lower ratings. The subordination levels decline with the bond ratings: 27% subordination for the AAA bond down to 10.5% for the BBB− bond. The subordination levels continue to drop for the C bond (17.5%) through the N bond (0%).

Prioritization of Payments

The highest-rated bonds are paid off first in the CMBS structure. Any return of principal caused by amortization, prepayment, or default is used to repay the highest-rated tranche first and then the lower-rated bonds. Any interest received on outstanding principal is paid to all tranches. However, it is important to note that many deals vary from this simplistic prioritization assumption.

For example, consider the GMAC 1999-C3 deal. The bonds that are rated AAA by Fitch (Classes A-1-a, A-1-b, and A-2) are the senior certificates. Classes B through M are organized in a simple sequential structure. Principal and interest

EXHIBIT 35–1

Bonds for GMAC 1999-C3 Deal

Bond	Moody Rating	Fitch Rating	Original Amount	Subordination Original	Coupon	Coupon Type
A-1-a	Aaa	AAA	$ 50,000,000	0.2700	0.0697	Fixed
A-1-b	Aaa	AAA	190,976,000	0.2700	0.0727	Fixed
A-2	Aaa	AAA	600,000,000	0.2700	0.0718	Fixed
B	Aa2	AA	51,840,000	0.2250	0.0754	Fixed
C	A2	A	57,601,000	0.1750	0.0779	Fixed
D	A3	A−	20,160,000	0.1575	0.0779	WAC-0b
E	Baa2	BBB	37,440,000	0.1250	0.0779	WAC-0b
F	Baa3	BBB−	23,040,000	0.1050	0.0779	WAC-0b
G	NA	NA	57,601,000	0.0550	0.0697	Fixed
H	NA	NA	8,640,000	0.0475	0.0697	Fixed
J	NA	NA	11,520,000	0.0375	0.0697	Fixed
K	NA	NA	14,400,000	0.0250	0.0697	Fixed
L	NA	NA	11,520,000	0.0150	0.0697	Fixed
M	NA	NA	5,760,000	0.0100	0.0697	Fixed
N	NA	NA	11,524,048	0.0000	0.0697	Fixed
X	NA	NA	1,152,022,048n	NA	0.0053	WAC/IO
R	NA	NA	0r	NA	0	

Source: Charter Research.

are distributed first to the Class B and last to the Class N. Unfortunately, the senior certificates are not as simple in their prioritization.

The loans underlying the GMAC 1999-C3 are divided into two groups. Group 2 consists of the multifamily loans and Group 1 consists of the remaining loans (retail, office, warehouse, and so on). In terms of making distributions to the senior certificates, 61% of Group 1's distribution amount is transferred to Group 2's distribution amount. Group 1's distribution amount is used to pay

1. Interest on bond Classes A-1-a, A-1-b, and the portion of interest on the Class X on components A-1-a and A-1-b pro rata

2. Principal to the Class A-1-a and A-1-b in that order

   Loan Group 2's distribution amount is used to pay

1. Interest on Class A-2 and the portion of interest on the Class X components from A-2 to N pro rata

2. Principal to the Class A-2

In the event that the balances of all the subordinated classes (Class B through Class M) have been reduced to zero because of the allocation of losses, the principal and interest will be distributed on a pro rata basis to Classes A-1-a, A-1-b, and A-2.

Loan default adds an additional twist to the structuring. Any losses that arise from loan defaults will be charged against the principal balance of the lowest-rated CMBS bond tranche that is outstanding (also known as the *first loss piece*). For the GMAC 1999-C3 deal, losses are allocated in reverse sequential order from Class N through Class B. After Class B is retired, Classes A-1-a, A-1-b, and A-2 bear losses on a pro rata basis. As a consequence, a localized market decline (such as a rapid decline in the Boston real estate market) can lead to the sudden termination of a bond tranche. Hence, issuers seek strategies that will minimize the likelihood of a "microburst" of defaults.

As long as there is no delinquency, the CMBS tranches are well-behaved. Unfortunately, delinquency triggers intervention by the servicer (whose role is discussed later in the chapter). In the event of a delinquency, there may be insufficient cash to make all scheduled payments. In this case, the servicer is supposed to advance both principal and interest. The principal and interest continue to be advanced by the servicer as long as these amounts are recoverable.

Call Protection

In the residential MBS market, the vast majority of mortgages have no prepayment penalties. In the CMBS market, the vast majority of mortgages have some form of prepayment penalty that can impact the longevity and yield of a bond. Call protection can be made at both the loan level and in the CMBS structure. The loan level offers several forms of call protection: prepayment lockout, yield maintenance, defeasance, and prepayment penalties.

Prepayment lockout occurs when the borrower is contractually prohibited from prepaying the loan during the lockout period. The lockout is the most stringent form of call protection since it removes the option for the borrower to prepay before the end of the lockout period. The prepayment lockout is commonly used in newer CMBS deals.

Under *yield maintenance,* the borrower is required to pay a "make whole" penalty to the lender if the loan is prepaid. The penalty is calculated as the difference between the present value of the loan's remaining cash flows at the time of prepayment and principal prepayment. Yield maintenance was a common form of call protection in older CMBS deals, but it is less common in newer deals.

Defeasance is calculated in the same manner as yield maintenance. However, instead of passing the loan repayment and any penalty through to the investor, the borrower invests that cash in U.S. Treasury securities (strips or bills) to fulfill the remaining cash flow structure of the loan. The Treasuries replace the building as collateral for the loan. The expected cash flows for that loan remain intact through to the final maturity date. Like yield maintenance, it was more popular with older CMBS deals and is less common in newer deals.

EXHIBIT   35–2

The 20 Largest Loans Underlying the GMAC 1999-C3 Deal

	Name	Location, MSA	Category	Loan Amount
1	Biltmore Fashion	Phoenix, Arizona	Retail	$80,000,000
2	Prime Outlets	Niagara Falls, New York	Retail	62,835,426
3	Equity Inns	Various	Hotel	46,511,317
4	One Colorado	Pasadena, California	Retail	42,628,093
5	Comerica Bank	San Jose, California	Office	33,640,510
6	120 Monument	Indianapolis, Indiana	Office	28,955,362
7	125 Maiden	New York, New York	Office	28,500,000
8	Texas Development	Houston, Texas	Apartment	26,926,701
9	Sherman Plaza	Van Nuys, California	Office	25,984,904
10	Alliance TP	Various	Apartment	24,888,157
11	Bush Tower	New York, New York	Office	23,000,000
12	County Line	Jackson, Mississippi	Retail	20,990,264
13	Sherwood Lakes	Schereville, Indiana	Apartment	20,162,442
14	Laurel Portfolio	Various	Apartment	17,950,331
15	Sweet Paper	Various	Warehouse	17,420,000
16	Sheraton Portsmouth	Portsmouth, New Hampshire	Hotel	15,949,087
17	Trinity Commons	Fort Worth, Texas	Retail	15,242,981
18	Village Square	Indianapolis, Indiana	Apartment	14,993,950
19	Golden Books	Fayetteville, North Carolina	Warehouse	14,493,350
20	Air Touch	Dublin, Ohio	Office	13,992,523

Source: Charter Research.

With *prepayment penalties,* the borrower must pay a fixed percentage of the unpaid balance of the loan as a prepayment penalty if the borrower wishes to refinance. The penalty usually declines as the loan ages (e.g., starting with 5% of the outstanding principal in the first year, 4% in the second year, and so on, until the penalty evaporates).

Exhibits 35–2 and 35–3 examine the largest 20 loans underlying the GMAC 1999-C3 deal. In terms of call protection, each of the loans is locked out. The average lockout has about 114 months remaining. Hence, the loans underlying this CMBS deal have just less than 10 years of prepayment protection.

In addition to call protection at the loan level, call protection is available in structural form as well. Since CMBS bond structures are sequential-pay, lower-rated tranches cannot pay down until the higher-rated tranches are retired. This is the exact opposite of default where principal losses hit the lowest-rated tranches first.

EXHIBIT 35-3

Loan Characteristics for the 20 Largest Loans Underlying the GMAC 1999-C3 Deal

	Name	Coupon	Maturity	Current Occupancy	DSCR	LTV	Prepay Lockout
1	Biltmore Fashion	7.68%	07/01/09	96.00%	1.43	60.40%	114
2	Prime Outlets	7.60	05/01/09	96.00	1.36	72.70	109
3	Equity Inns	8.37	07/01/09	NA	1.90	49.50	114
4	One Colorado	8.29	07/01/09	91.00	1.25	72.30	114
5	Comerica Bank	7.55	05/01/08	99.00	1.43	65.20	32
6	120 Monument	8.09	06/01/09	100.00	1.23	74.40	113
7	125 Maiden	8.12	09/01/09	97.00	1.31	73.80	116
8	Texas Development	7.44	05/01/09	NA	1.34	72.00	114
9	Sherman Plaza	7.68	08/01/09	95.00	1.24	68.40	115
10	Alliance TP	7.32	08/01/09	NA	1.19	86.40	112
11	Bush Tower	7.99	08/01/09	97.00	1.27	46.00	115
12	County Line	7.91	08/01/09	98.00	1.39	84.00	115
13	Sherwood Lakes	6.99	02/01/08	94.00	1.32	76.70	94
14	Laurel Portfolio	7.37	05/01/09	NA	1.22	73.60	112
15	Sweet Paper	8.26	06/01/09	NA	1.25	71.40	113
16	Sheraton Portsmouth	8.53	05/01/09	71.00	1.28	72.50	116
17	Trinity Commons	7.93	08/01/09	97.00	1.44	68.80	115
18	Village Square	7.80	10/01/07	97.00	1.28	79.30	93
19	Golden Books	8.50	08/01/09	100.00	1.69	67.40	119
20	Air Touch	7.98	08/01/09	100.00	1.20	77.70	117

Source: Charter Research.

Timing of Principal Repayment

Unlike residential mortgages that are fully amortized over a long time period (say, 30 years), commercial loans underlying CMBS deals are often balloon loans. *Balloon loans* require substantial principal payment on the final maturity date although the loan is fully amortized over a longer period of time. For example, a loan can be fully amortized over 30 years but may require a full repayment of outstanding principal after the tenth year. The purpose of a balloon loan is to keep the periodic loan payment of interest and principal as low as possible.

Balloon loans pose potential problems for investors due to the large, lump-sum payment that must be refinanced. If there is a change in the quality of the underlying asset (such as a decline in the real estate market or increased competition leading to a decline in lease rates), there is a danger that the loan will not be refinanced; this can result in default. In order to prevent this type of loan failure at the balloon date from occurring, there are two types of loan provisions: the internal tail and the external tail.

The *internal tail* requires the borrower to provide evidence that an effort is under way to refinance the loan prior to the balloon date (say, 1 year prior to the balloon date). The lender would require that the borrower obtain a refinancing commitment before the balloon date (say, 6 months prior to the balloon date). With an *external tail*, the maturity date of the CMBS deal is set to be longer than that of the underlying loans. This allows the borrower more time to arrange refinancing while avoiding default on the bond obligations. The servicer advances any missing interest and scheduled principal in this buffer period.

THE UNDERLYING LOAN PORTFOLIO

There are two sources of risk relating to the underlying loan portfolio. The first risk is prepayment risk and the second risk is default or delinquency risk.

Diversification

A factor that is often considered when analyzing the risk of a CMBS deal is the diversification of the underlying loans across space. The reasoning for what is termed "spatial diversification" is that the default risk of the underlying pool of loans is lessened if the loans are made on properties in different regions of the country. Rather than have the entire portfolio of loans subject to an idiosyncratic risk factor (e.g., the decline in oil prices and the collapse of the Houston real estate market), the portfolio can spread its risks across numerous economies. Thus, a collapse of the Houston real estate market (which may lead to higher defaults on commercial loans) will be less of a concern if the commercial property markets in Chicago, Kansas City, New York, and Seattle remain strong.

The strategy of spatial diversification can be seen in Exhibit 35–4. Approximately 22% of the loans underlying the GMAC 1999-C3 are on properties in California, 14% on properties in Texas, and 11% on properties in New York. The remaining loans are spread out among other states such as New Hampshire, Missouri, Illinois, and Mississippi. Thus, the GMAC 1999-C3 deal has achieved a significant degree of

EXHIBIT 35–4

Aggregate Loan Amounts by State for GMAC 1999-C3 Deal

State	Loan Amount	No. of Loans	Percent of Pool
California	$ 257,522,410	33	22.35%
Texas	162,355,125	26	14.09
New York	130,070,471	7	11.29
Arizona	99,942,794	5	8.68
Indiana	68,623,516	5	5.96
Ohio	44,982,528	5	3.90
Mississippi	23,067,864	2	2.00
New Jersey	22,983,973	5	2.00
Other	342,473,371	50	29.73
Total	$1,152,022,052	138	100.00%

Source: Charter Research.

EXHIBIT 35–5

Aggregate Loan Amounts by Property Type for GMAC 1993-C3 Deal

Property Type	Loan Amount	No. of Loans	Percent of Pool
Apartment	$ 259,779,802	39	22.55%
Office	322,053,844	36	27.96
Retail	350,683,062	34	30.44
Warehouse	99,126,075	15	8.60
Hotel	105,832,139	8	9.19
Other	14,547,130	6	1.26
Total	$1,152,022,052	138	100.00%

Source: Charter Research.

spatial diversification. Although a 22% concentration factor for California is still quite large, it is considerably lower than a 100% concentration factor (which is often referred to as a "pure play" strategy). Furthermore, California, Texas, and New York represent the states where most of the commercial loans are being originated.

In addition to spatial diversification, CMBS pools can be diversified across property types. Rating agencies tend to give lower levels of credit enhancement to deals that contain diversification across property types since a pool that is diversified across residential, office, industrial, and retail will likely avoid the potential of a national glut in one of the sectors (such as the retail market).

The degree of property type diversification can be seen in Exhibit 35–5. Approximately 90% of the loans are on retail, apartments, and office properties, with

EXHIBIT 35-6

Characteristics for Loans Underlying the GMAC 1999-C3 Deal by Property Type

Property Type	Coupon	Due	Current Occupancy	DSCR	LTV	Prepay Lockout
Apartment	7.62%	06/29/09	92.92%	1.29	76.51%	113
Office	7.79	04/03/09	96.17	1.33	67.84	107
Retail	7.95	09/19/09	95.21	1.36	69.77	116
Warehouse	8.13	06/27/09	99.56	1.42	68.28	115
Hotel	8.50	12/31/08	75.18	1.65	58.93	109
Other	7.83	05/13/09	95.11	1.54	67.00	113

Source: Charter Research.

retail having the largest percentage (30.44%). As a consequence, the GMAC 1999-C3 deals have reduced the risk of default by not being heavily concentrated in only one of the property groups.

The loan characteristics of the pool underlying the GMAC 1999-C3 pools are presented in Exhibit 35–6. The hotel properties are viewed as being the riskiest given that they have the highest coupon (8.50%), the highest DSCR (1.65×), and the lowest LTV (58.93%). The apartment properties are viewed as the safest risk with the lowest coupon (7.62%), the lowest DSCR (1.29×), and the highest LTV (76.51%). As can be seen in Exhibits 35–5 and 35–6, 90% of the underlying loans are in the three least-risky property types: apartment, office, and retail.

Cross-Collateralization

Diversification of the underlying collateral is one way of reducing default risk. Another way to reduce default risk is to use cross-collateralization. *Cross-collateralization* means that the properties that serve as collateral for the individual loans are pledged against each loan. Thus, the cash flows on several properties can be used to make loan payments on a property which has insufficient funds to make a loan payment. This "pooling" mechanism reduces the risk of default. To add some additional enforcement penalties to the cross-collateralization mechanism, the lender can use cross-default which allows the lender to call each loan within the pool, when any one defaults.

Loan Analysis

Several products are available that provide analysis of the underlying collateral for CMBS deals. An example of a package that allows for the analysis of the CMBS deal and the underlying collateral is Conquest, an on-line service provided by Charter Research in Boston. Conquest provides for a detailed examination of each loan in the underlying portfolio. In addition to simply describing the loan data (DSCR, LTV, loan maturity, prepayment lock type, etc.), Conquest provides default risk (delinquency) analysis as well. Using vendors such as Torto Wheaton, Conquest forecasts the growth in net operating income and value for each property in the underlying portfolio.

Torto Wheaton, for example, provides 10-year forecasts of net operating income and value by geographic area (MSA) and property type (office, industrial, retail, and apartments). These forecasts are updated quarterly. Torto Wheaton provides five scenarios ranging from best to worst cases. Given these five scenarios, the user is able to examine the future path of debt service coverage and LTV for each loan in the pool. Thus, the user is able to examine default and extension risk tendencies on a loan-by-loan basis. This information is aggregated to the deal level so that changes in the riskiness for each of the underlying loans are reflected in the cash flows for each tranche at the deal level.

Stress Testing at the Loan Level

Stress testing the collateral in a CMBS deal is important from both the underwriter and investor perspective. By allowing the forecasts on net operating income and value to be varied over time, underwriters and investors can better understand the default risk and extension risk likelihoods and how these in turn impact CMBS cash flows.

For CMBS markets, stress tests must be performed in a manner that is consistent with modern portfolio theory. Although diversification across property type and economic region reduces the default risk of the underlying loan pool, the effects of diversification are negated if the stress test ignores the covariance between the properties. For example, there should be some degree of common variance across all properties (reflecting general economic conditions). Furthermore, there should be some degree of common variance across property type and economic regions.

The Torto Wheaton approach of generating five forecast paths by property type and geographic location permits the construction of a distribution of future outcomes for property value and net operating income growth for the loan pool. Based on Torto Wheaton forecasts, the user can determine the degree to which the portfolio is diversified (by reducing the variance of the distribution of future outcomes). An index of diversification can be created that allows users to compare the degree of diversification across different CMBS deals. Thus, stress testing the underlying properties can be measured in the aggregate by how much the diversification index is changed.

In addition to being able to create a diversification index, the user can construct a default risk–extension risk index as well. As the underlying loans are stressed, a distribution of outcomes in terms of default and extension risk can be obtained. This would allow users to compare CMBS deals not only for the diversification of the underlying loan portfolio but also to compare CMBS deals for sensitivity to the stress test.

Historical Aspect on Loan Performance

Although a detailed analysis of loan performance models is beyond the scope of this chapter, it is important to recognize that CMBS deals are not free of prepayment, default, and delinquencies. In Exhibit 35–7, the historical default and prepayment information for deals with a cutoff date in 1994 (from the Conquest database) are presented. As one can see, there is a wide range in terms of the ratio of performing loans to original loans in the pool. The KPAC 1994-M1 deal has the lowest-performing loan ratio of 11.48%. On the other hand, the DLJ 1994-MF 11 has a performing loan ratio of 98.72%. The average performing loan ratio is 46.34% for the 13 deals from 1994.

It should be noted that the average performing loan ratio of 46.34% could be explained, in part, by underlying loan maturity. On average, 20.58% on the loans underlying deals from 1994 matured. Mortgage prepayments account for approximately 30.33% of the original loans terminating. Foreclosures, defaults, and real estate owned (REO) comprise only 2.50% of the 13 deals from 1994. Interestingly, the DLJ CMBS deals have a very high performance loan ratio (90% and 98%) with few loan maturities and prepayments (and no defaults or foreclosures).

Despite the historical performance of these deals, analysts must be careful about projecting these results for current deals. Prepayment lockouts, which are more popular now than they were in 1994, will be more effective in determining prepayments than simple yield maintenance provisions. Also, longer-term mortgage loans will extend the duration of the underlying loan pool (keeping the performance loan ratio higher for a longer period of time). Finally, improvements in underwriting and the investor's ability to understand the underlying collateral should improve default and foreclosure risk over time.

CREATING A CMBS MODEL

As mentioned before, a number of CMBS models are available in the marketplace. Whether someone chooses one of the "one size fits all" models or designs a customized model tailored to specific needs, several key features should be included in a CMBS model.

1. An econometric model of historical loan performance using logit or proportional hazards model. This permits a better understanding of property and loan attributes that predict default and prepayment.

2. If default does occur, empirical estimates of loss severity by property type and state are needed.

3. Database of actual net operating income (NOI) and Value volatility by property type and geographic location (see the discussion of Torto Wheaton earlier in this chapter). This step permits the construction of default risk indicators.

4. Monte Carlo simulation of interest rates and NOI paths should be included to estimate foreclosure frequency and prepayment risk.

EXHIBIT 35–7

Historical Default and Prepayment for CMBS Deals with Cutoff Dates in 1994

Deal	Loans	Performing	Matured	Prepaid	Bankrupt	Foreclosures	REO*
ASC 1994-C3	40	21	3	13	0	3	0
ASC 1994-MD1	9	7	1	1	0	0	0
ASFS 1993-2	30	19	4	5	1	1	0
ASFS 1994-C2	39	6	26	7	0	0	0
CLAC 1994-1	89	37	33	19	0	0	0
CSFB 1994-CFB1	63	21	8	34	0	0	0
DLJ 1993-MF 17	42	38	0	3	0	0	0
DLJ 1994-MF 11	78	77	0	1	0	0	0
KPAC 1994-M1	61	7	13	41	0	0	0
MCFI 1994-MC1	44	9	9	26	0	0	0
MLMI 1994-M1	80	32	28	20	0	0	0
SASC 1994-C1	185	67	51	53	0	0	14
SASC 1995-C1	142	30	21	71	0	5	15

*REO = real estate owned.
Source: Charter Research.

EXHIBIT 35–8

Percentage Disposition of Loans Underlying 1994 CMBS Deals

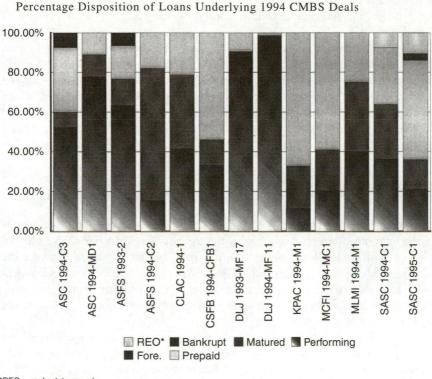

REO* ■ Bankrupt ■ Matured ■ Performing
■ Fore. ▨ Prepaid

*REO = real estate owned.
Source: Charter Research.

5. Finally, the deal structure (and waterfalls) should interface cleanly with loan-by-loan simulations.

A CMBS model with these features should be able to capture the critical elements of pricing, risk, and return.

THE ROLE OF THE SERVICER

The servicer on a CMBS deal plays an important role. The servicer collects monthly loan payments, keeps records relating to payments, maintains escrow accounts, monitors the condition of underlying properties, prepares reports for trustee, and transfers collected funds to trustee for payment.

There are three types of servicers: the subservicer, the master servicer, and the special servicer. The *subservicer* is typically the loan originator in a conduit deal who has decided to sell the loan but retain the servicing. The subservicer will then send all payments and property information to the master servicer. The *master servicer* oversees the deal and makes sure the servicing agreements are maintained. In addition, the master servicer must facilitate the timely payment of interest and principal. When a loan goes into default, the master servicer has the responsibility to provide for servicing advances.

Unlike the subservicer and the master servicer, the *special servicer* enters the picture when a loan becomes more than 60 days past due. Often, the special servicer is empowered to extend the loan, restructure the loan, and foreclose on the loan (and sell the property). This critical role is of great importance to the subordinated tranche owners because the timing of the loss can significantly impact the loss severity, which in turn can greatly impact subordinated returns. Thus, first-loss investors usually want to either control the appointment of the special servicer or perform the role themselves. This creates a potential moral hazard problem since the special servicer may put self-interest first, potentially at the expense of the other tranche holders.

INNOVATIONS IN THE CMBS MARKET: "BUY-UP" LOANS

A recent innovation in the CMBS market is the "buy-*up*" loan. Most participants in the mortgage market are familiar with the "buy-*down*" loan in the residential market. With a buy-down loan, a borrower pays "points" up front to reduce the mortgage interest rate. The resulting loan, having a lower interest rate, is less sensitive to prepayment and has a greater duration than a higher interest rate loan. The buy-up loan in the commercial mortgage market is the exact opposite, but with a twist.

Consider a borrower who approaches a commercial mortgage lender for a $1 million loan. They agree on an 8.00% interest rate with the loan being fully amortized over 30 years (using monthly amortization). The resulting monthly mortgage payment would be $7,337.65. The DSCR for the loan (based on annual NOI of $100,000) is 1.14×, while the LTV is 71.40%. (See Exhibit 35–9.)

E X H I B I T   35–9

Comparison of a Standard Loan and a Buy-up Loan

	Standard	Buy-up
NOI (annual)	$100,000.00	$100,000.00
Loan size	$1,000,000.00	$911,936.30
Amount to borrower	$1,000,000.00	$1,000,000.00
Loan term	360	360
Mortgage rate	8.00%	9.00%
Monthly payment	$7,337.65	$7,337.65
DSCR	1.14	1.14
LTV—PV of loan	71.4	64.9
LTV—amount to borrower	71.4	71.4

Suppose that the rating agency requires additional loan subordination (or gives a lower rating) if the loan in question has an LTV in excess of 65%. In this case, the subordination level would be reduced (and/or the rating increased) if the loan has an LTV of 65% or less. With a buy-up loan, the monthly payments of $7,337.65 are discounted at an interest rate of 9.00% (instead of 8.00%), resulting in a present value of the loan being $911,936.30. Although the DSCR remains the same, the LTV declines to 64.9%, thus qualifying the loan for lower subordination levels (and/or a higher rating).

The problem facing the rating agency is selecting the correct LTV. Clearly, for the purpose of correctly identifying default risk, an LTV should be used that is based on the actual amount disbursed to the borrower, not the present value of the mortgage payments. The definition of LTV caused some problems when buy-up loans were first used since it was unclear which definition of LTV the lender was using. Once the rating agencies recognized that there were multiple definitions of LTV, the lenders began to report both LTVs.

Technically, the difference between the amount disbursed to the borrower ($1,000,000) and the present value of the buy-up loan ($911,936.30) is the buy-up premium. The documents on a CMBS deal containing buy-up loans will most likely say that the buy-up loan is locked out; furthermore, in case of prepayment, the borrower would owe both the buy-up loan amount and the buy-up premium. The higher interest rate on the buy-up loan (with its lockout provision) means that there is more interest for an IO class.

SUMMARY

This chapter provided a broad overview of the CMBS market from the point of view of a sample CMBS deal. Although CMBS deals tend to be prepayment-insensitive, bonds (or tranches) will still be somewhat sensitive to interest rate changes since lockouts usually dissolve after 10 years. Default risk is a concern with CMBS and the underlying collateral needs to be examined on a loan-by-loan basis. Products currently available make this task much more tractable.

CHAPTER 36

MULTIFAMILY PROJECT SECURITIES

Ed Daingerfield
Managing Director
Nomura Securities International, Inc.

Projects are mortgages on multifamily homes that are insured by the Federal Housing Administration (FHA) under various federal programs of the National Housing Act of 1934, as amended. For more than 65 years, one of the primary goals the government has set for the FHA is to enhance the nation's supply of multifamily housing. Several FHA programs have evolved to provide federal insurance for the construction financing and permanent mortgage financing on many types of multifamily residences (including rental apartments, condominiums, and cooperatives), on nursing homes, residential facilities for the elderly, hospitals, and on other health care units. In addition, the FHA has long-established insurance programs used for refinancing mortgages on these types of properties and/or rehabilitating them.

FHA AND GNMA PROJECTS: TWO PRIMARY STRUCTURES OF PROJECT SECURITIES

Projects most commonly trade in two forms: either as FHA-insured pass-through participations or as Ginnie Mae (GNMA) securities. Regardless of form, all projects are guaranteed by the U.S. government through the Department of Housing and Urban Development (HUD) and the FHA insurance funds. Projects may only be originated by mortgage lenders in good standing with the FHA and HUD, and all projects are first created as *FHA-insured multifamily loans*. However, FHA-insured whole loans may only be purchased by FHA-approved lenders, and so the secondary market for projects in whole-loan form is relatively small. More common are *FHA Participation Certificates (PCs)* or *FHA pools*. FHA PCs are created whenever an FHA-insured project loan is used to collateralize a pass-through security issued by an approved mortgage banker. FHA pools are simply a collection of FHA-insured projects aggregated together.

This chapter is reprinted with permission from Frank J. Fabozzi (ed.), *Investing in Commercial Mortgage-Backed Securities* (New Hope, PA: Frank J. Fabozzi Associates, 2001).

GNMA project pass-through securities are created when a mortgage banker originates an FHA-insured multifamily loan but then selects the additional guarantee and standardization provided by GNMA securities. This is analogous to the single-family market, where the FHA or VA insures mortgages that are then issued as GNMA pass-throughs. The credit backing of all FHA and GNMA projects derives from the FHA insurance fund, and so projects issued in both GNMA and FHA form enjoy the full faith and credit backing of the U.S. Government.

DIFFERENCES BETWEEN FHA AND GNMA PROJECTS

There are several important differences between projects issued in FHA-insured form and projects issued as GNMA securities, and as a result GNMA project securities command a price premium over FHA projects. (These differences are summarized in Exhibit 36–1.) Like single-family GNMA securities, GNMA projects pay principal and interest with a 44-day delay, while FHA projects pay with a 54-day delay. In the event of default, GNMA project pass-through securities incorporate the same standardized procedures as single-family GNMA pass-throughs: full and timely reimbursement of principal and interest is guaranteed in the event of default, and claims for GNMA insurance are paid out in cash, in a timely manner.

In contrast, in the event of default, procedures are not standardized with FHA project securities: Investors may have to rely on specific information written into the servicing agreement to determine the exact default proceedings. Also, although FHA projects do insure full payment of principal and interest, the FHA takes a 1% administrative fee when a project defaults and is assigned to HUD, and so the investor receives only 99% of principal in default. In addition, the FHA does

E X H I B I T   36–1

Primary Differences Between GNMA and FHA Projects

GNMA	FHA
If Default:	If Default:
100% of principal paid upon default	99% of principal upon default
Full and timely payment of principal and interest	Ultimate payment of principal and interest less 1 month interest
Forty-four-day payment delay	Fifty-four-day payment delay
Securities wired through depository; denominations of $\geq 25{,}000$	Physical delivery of certificates; standard piece limit: 3 – 4 per pool
Delivery of GNMA prospectus; supplement available	Delivery of participation and servicing agreement is recommended
Pool data on Bloomberg	Pool data not on any central database
Supplemental data available on GNMA's web site	Supplemental data available on the FHA's web site

not guarantee timely payment of principal and interest. Investors may have to wait several months in the event that an FHA-insured project defaults, although interest does continue to accrue during this time (with the exception of a 1-month grace period for which no interest is paid, although no interest is lost on a GNMA project). Finally, although all projects issued in GNMA form pay cash in the event of default, claims on some FHA project defaults are paid in cash, whereas others are paid in FHA debentures, which are federal agency debt issues of the FHA. Many FHA projects are designated either "cash pay" or "debenture pay" at origination, and others are designated cash or debenture pay at the time of default, at the option of either the mortgagee or of HUD. FHA projects designated "cash pay" pay default claims in cash, whereas those designated "debenture pay" may pay default claims either in FHA debentures with a 20-year maturity or in cash, at the option of HUD. Given all these differences it is no surprise that FHA projects trade cheaper than GNMA projects, nor that the spread differential between GNMA and FHA projects widens or tightens in response to market factors.

GNMA AND FHA TRENDS IN ORIGINATIONS

Whether projects are issued in FHA or GNMA form is a function of the rates at which either can be sold in the secondary market, as well as the costs to issue and insure either form of project. GNMA projects are more expensive to issue than FHAs, given the increased costs of GNMA's wrap. However, this cost difference has varied widely in recent years, as GNMA has adjusted its costs. Consequently, at various points in time new issuance in projects shifts back and forth between predominantly FHA to predominantly GNMA originations. Prior to 1981, the majority of all projects were issued as FHA pass-through certificates or in FHA pools. With the advent of the coinsurance program (see below) in 1983, issuance shifted and most projects were issued as GNMA securities until 1990, when the coinsurance program was terminated. After coinsurance, issuance shifted back to favor FHA projects, which dominated new originations from 1990 through early 1993. In March of 1993, GNMA lowered its guarantee fee, which reduced the cost of issuing GNMA project securities, and from that time to the present, most new projects have been issued as GNMAs.

PREPAYMENTS

Most project pools consist of one large mortgage loan, unlike single-family pools which are backed by numerous smaller mortgages. Consequently, projects do not trade to estimates of prepayment speeds like single-family mortgage-backed securities. Rather, prepayments on projects are driven by the definite incentives most mortgagors have to prepay their mortgages. The likelihood that a project will prepay is based largely on the economics of the underlying building and the characteristics of the mortgagor, as well as on the specific prepayment restrictions and penalties of each project. A key determinant of prepayment likelihood in projects is whether the borrower is a profit-motivated private enterprise or a not-for-profit group. As a general rule, profit-motivated developers prepay project mortgages as early as is economically feasible, while nonprofit developers are less likely to prepay.

Prepayments Less Likely on Projects Owned by Nonprofit Groups

Most nonprofit groups that operate projects are either state or local housing authorities, church groups, or community organizations. As nonprofit entities, these groups are not concerned with prepaying a mortgage to access built-up equity or with refinancing to generate increased tax benefits. Also, nonprofit organizations are not likely to convert a rental property to a cooperative or sell out to another developer for a profit, and nonprofits often receive government and/or private subsidies that effectively limit default risk. As a result, prepayments on not-for-profit projects are rare. These projects provide reliable call protection, and since their cash flows are consistent, most nonprofit projects trade to their final maturity rather than to any assumed prepayment date.

Prepayments Less Likely on Projects with Section 8

One feature of projects that provides call protection to investors exists when a project has a Section 8 rental subsidy contract between the project owner and the FHA (called a "Project-Based Section 8" contract). Under these Section 8 Housing Assistance Payment (HAP) contracts, the FHA agrees to pay the difference between what a tenant can afford to pay for rent (based on tenant income) and the prevailing market rate for a similar apartment in the same area. Typically, tenants pay 30% of their monthly income for rent, and Section 8 subsidies cover the balance. To be eligible for Section 8 payments, tenants must be low-income families whose incomes do not exceed 50% of the median income for the area; close to 4 million families are currently served by some form of Section 8 subsidy.

Project-based Section 8 payments are made directly to the owner of the project, which assures a reliable cash flow from the project and makes prepayments from default less likely. Section 8 subsidy payments also provide additional call protection since the project owner may not prepay the mortgage while the HAP contract is in force (most project-based HAP contracts are for 20 years and are renewable). Section 8 contracts cannot be transferred or terminated, and remain with the project under a change of ownership. Section 8 HAP contracts may cover fewer than 100% of the rental apartments in a given project; obviously, projects with higher percentages of Section 8 provide greater call protection.

The Section 8 program has been modified several times in the past decade, as HUD worked to preserve and expand the number of affordable multifamily apartments, and these program changes do affect the prepayment characteristics of bonds backed by Section 8 projects. In the early nineties, the Low-Income Project Preservation Act (LIPPRA) and successor laws were established to preserve low-income apartments. Section 8 projects covered by LIPPRA are expressly prohibited from prepaying. If the developers of such projects wish to refinance for any reason, they must take a HUD-insured Section 241 second mortgage (see below) rather than prepay the first Section 8 mortgage. Bonds backed by the initial Section 8 project mortgage covered by LIPPRA provide significant call protection.

By 1994, HUD realized that the agency had significant problems brewing, since a substantial majority of their original project-based 20-year Section 8 HAP contracts were up for renewal between 1999 and 2003. Although the social policy goals of HUD suggested that the agency renew these Section 8 contracts, the subsidized rents at many of these properties exceeded market rents. As a result, concern grew at HUD that the fiscal realities of renewing Section 8 HAP payments could be at odds with the government's goal for a balanced federal budget. Another issue complicated HUD's ability to insure Section 8 housing, since in many cities across the nation, select urban neighborhoods have improved in recent years. Borrowers at Section 8 properties located in these so-called gentrified neighborhoods often did not want to renew their Section 8 contracts, since by refinancing and exiting the Section 8 program, they might generate higher, nonregulated rents from their properties. Political issues and staff reductions slowed HUD's response to these problems, and throughout the late 1990s HUD instituted several different, short-lived programs to address fiscal problems caused by the large number of expiring Section 8 contracts.

As a result of these regular changes in the Section 8 program, estimating the prepayment likelihood of project bonds with Section 8 became difficult. After various studies and pilot programs over several years, the FHA has finally decided to renew some expiring project-based Section 8 HAP contracts, while providing Section 8 rental vouchers directly to tenants at other projects. Under HUD's voucher program, low-income tenants receive direct credits which can be used to subsidize their rent at any apartment of their choosing. While Section 8 payments remain linked to specific properties under the project-based HAP contracts the FHA renews, the new voucher-based Section 8 subsidies are portable. Although this new Section 8 voucher program is untested as of this writing, low-income tenants will likely have more choice in selecting where they'll live under Section 8 vouchers than they would have under the more established project-based subsidies. This suggests that to the degree the FHA expands voucher-based Section 8 subsidies, investors may anticipate some increase in prepayments on bonds backed by these properties. In the future, the prepayment likelihood of Section 8 projects will depend as much on the location and underlying economics of the property as on the specific type of Section 8 subsidy program at that project.

Prepayments Likely on For-Profit Projects

Private sector, profit-motivated borrowers may refinance projects if interest rates decline, but they also have incentives to refinance loans at current or even somewhat higher rates. Higher interest rates increase the expenses for project owners, but higher debt service costs can often be offset or exceeded by increasing rents. For existing properties that have increased in value, selling the property or refinancing at a higher loan-to-value (LTV) ratio enables developers to access equity that has built up in a project. The economics of a profit-motivated developer's business often dictate that private sector project borrowers refinance to capitalize available equity. Refinancing a for-profit project may also be driven by a need for the mortgagor to raise money to refurbish or rehabilitate a property without putting up scarce equity. This is very common since most developers maximize profits by gradually increasing rents over time as leases expire and tenants move. The ability to increase rents is obviously dependent on the physical condition of the property. As projects age, developers frequently refinance the mortgage to generate money for refurbishing the building, which in turn protects their long-term investment and encourages higher rents.

As for-profit projects age and the mortgage is paid down, the probabilities increase that private developers will prepay the mortgage to rehabilitate the project or to take out equity. The likelihood and timing of prepayments on profit-motivated projects depends on several factors, including the LTV ratio of the project, the type and location of the project, the physical condition of the property, and the type of borrower. Borrowers are more likely to prepay projects with lower LTV ratios, since this permits them to access a substantial amount of equity quickly. Also, projects built for upper- and middle-income rather than low-income tenants are more likely to refinance, since they typically have more amenities (pools, dishwashers, microwave ovens, etc.), generally are located in better neighborhoods, and so are more likely to increase in value or to be converted to condominiums. Under FHA regulations, if a project does not continue to serve the same use, its mortgage must be prepaid. Thus before an owner of a rental project can convert the property to a cooperative or condominium, the HUD mortgage must be prepaid. Moderate- and higher-income projects also tend to prepay faster since, as the building ages and amenities deteriorate, developers often need to refinance to access equity to refurbish and maintain the project in order to protect their investment. Also, projects in high-growth areas and other favorable locations more frequently increase in value and so tend to prepay faster. Exhibit 36–2 illustrates that even assuming a conservative 1% annual increase in property values, equity in a project increases by as much as one third after 10 to 12 years.

Tax considerations also provide motivation for many private investors and limited partnerships to refinance projects. The Tax Reform Act of 1986 curtailed accelerated depreciation, which had provided significant incentives to refinance older projects. Projects originated after 1986 must be depreciated over 27½ years, using a straight-line method. However, tax factors remain a consideration in refinancing decisions. The tax shelter provided by deducting mortgage interest payments, coupled with the tax advantages that remain under the current depreciation rules, begin to abate during years 10 to 12 as the project mortgage amortizes. Exhibit 36–3 shows that, typically, passive tax losses in a project partnership dissipate and begin to generate taxable income by years 10 to 12. This makes it advantageous for partnerships and individual owners to refinance project mortgages to reset the passive tax losses that are vital to many real estate owners.

Taken together, Exhibits 36–2 and 36–3 illustrate how profit-motivated projects often refinance in 10 to 12 years for two complementary reasons: (1) owners access equity in order to refurbish their property and maintain competitive rents in their local apartment market, to consolidate ownership by paying off limited partners, and to purchase other projects; and (2) refinancing or sale of the property is a common exit strategy for owners focused on the tax-shelter advantages of projects.

Project Equity Accrues over Time

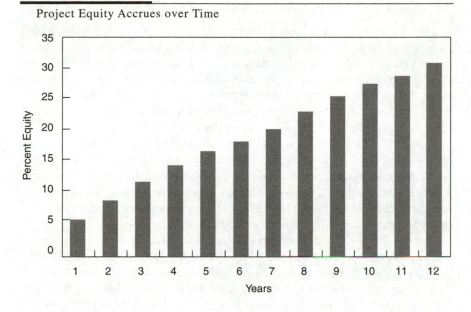

Tax Advantages Erode over Time

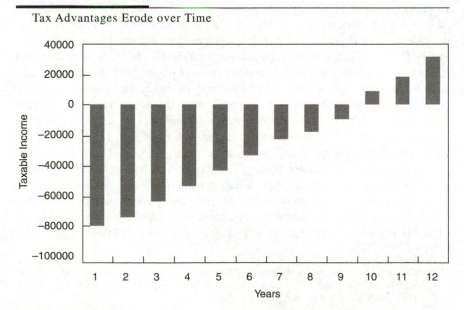

PREPAYMENTS, CALL PROTECTION, LOCKOUTS, AND PENALTIES

The FHA-HUD administration does not prohibit profit-motivated developers from prepaying or refinancing project mortgages, although prepayments on nonprofit projects are generally restricted by the agency. Nonprofit projects built under several FHA programs may not be prepaid, whereas under other programs prepayments on nonprofit projects are permitted only if the mortgagor is able to secure HUD's approval. In addition, prepayments on projects with Section 8 are restricted, some by formal HUD regulations and others by economic forces (see above).

Most project pass-throughs are whole pools backed by one building, and so a full prepayment effectively generates a call at par on the security. As a result, prepayment restrictions and penalties are written into the documentation that governs project trades. HUD has approved three basic types of prepayment restrictions and penalties (see HUD mortgagee letter 87-9): (1) prepayment lockout restrictions that extend to a maximum of 10 years plus the stated construction period, (2) prepayment penalties of 1% or less, 10 years after the stated construction period, and (3) some combination of prepayment lockout and penalties with a lockout of less than 10 years and a premium of no more than 1% 10 years after the stated construction period.

At present the most common form of call protection is a 5-year lockout with prepayments then permitted in year 6 at a 105% of par, declining to 101% in year 10. HUD also provides 10-year lockouts. A review of actual prepayment history on GNMA multifamily securities shows that projects do begin to prepay as soon as any lockouts expire.[1]

PREPAYMENTS AND DEFAULT: BACKGROUND

Default generates an unanticipated prepayment, received in cash at par for GNMA projects and at 99% in cash or debentures (depending on program) for FHA projects. Defaults on HUD-insured projects have primarily occurred in two older programs: (1) The 221(d)3 below market interest rate (BMIR) program, which insured urban low-income projects in an effort to ameliorate poverty and provide inner-city housing (however, construction design, planning, location, and underwriting later proved to be flawed). (2) The coinsured program of the 1980s. The structural failures of HUD's GNMA coinsurance program are now widely acknowledged (see coinsurance, below). Accurate numbers are difficult to obtain from HUD, but default rates on BMIRs and coinsurance projects are generally assumed to exceed 35% (that's over 35% in each program). For investors, the economic consequences or return characteristics of defaulting bonds depend purely on interest rates.

Actual prepayment history on GNMA multifamily bonds shows a modest but consistent default pattern over the first 5 years of the securities' history. This pattern should be considered when evaluating prepayment likelihood of GNMA projects.[2]

---

[1]Steve Banerjee, Lisa Pendergast, and Weisi Tan, "Project-Loan Prepayments and Defaults," Chapter 11 in Frank J. Fabozzi (ed.), *Investing in Commercial Mortgage-Backed Securities* (New Hope, PA: Frank J. Fabozzi Associates, 2001).

[2]Ibid.

When a project goes into default, the servicer assigns it to the FHA, and over the years the agency has accumulated a significant inventory of defaulted projects. Cumbersome regulations have prevented HUD from foreclosing on many troubled properties, and budget constraints have left HUD ill-equipped to manage problem properties. As a result, HUD has begun to sell the projects that have been assigned to the agency. Some of the properties in HUD's inventory are seriously troubled, others are performing, and still other loans have been helped by recovering real estate values and lower interest rates. As HUD continues to liquidate this portfolio, investors can expect to see HUD-insured mortgage pools, senior-subordinate pools, and structured securities transactions backed by these loans.

COINSURANCE

For most of its existence, HUD has been a thinly staffed and lightly funded federal agency. Also, as the nation's largest insurer-provider of multifamily rental housing, HUD has frequently been subject to political pressures at the city, state, and particularly the national levels. Significant political pressures were brought to bear on HUD with the advent of the Reagan administration in the early 1980s, when the department suffered substantial reductions in staffing. FHA loan underwriters and auditors bore the brunt of these cutbacks, and this vitiated HUD's ability to implement strict underwriting standards. In response, in 1983, HUD introduced the coinsurance program.

Under this coinsurance program, private GNMA mortgage bankers took on the role of HUD staffers and were responsible not just for originating loans, but also for all due diligence and underwriting for project loans. In an attempt to preserve credit standards, HUD required mortgage originators to reimburse the agency for 20% of any insurance claims the agency paid out on any projects that defaulted. This 20% liability was intended to keep mortgage bankers in the coinsurance program honest. At that time, the feeling was that the government could minimize risk to the FHA insurance fund by enabling private sector lenders to risk their own capital on a project in return for greater origination fees. Predictably, the program ran into problems. By the late 1980s, it became clear that underwriting standards had generally received a lower priority than the mortgage bankers' desire for the lucrative fees generated by new loan originations. HUD also lacked the systems needed to monitor the thinly capitalized coinsured mortgage bankers. In addition, cases of outright fraud in loan originations were well-publicized, and senior management at HUD became embroiled in several well-publicized scandals. HUD eventually canceled the coinsurance program in 1990.

A significant number of coinsured GNMA project securities remain in circulation and trade regularly in the secondary market. Since these outstanding projects are in GNMA form, investors are shielded from credit risk by the U.S. Government guarantee of Ginnie Mae. However, since most coinsured GNMAs were originated with high coupons, they generally trade at significant price premiums. Investors should exercise caution in evaluating premium projects underwritten with coinsurance; to the degree that questionable underwriting increases the likelihood of default (i.e., par call), the return characteristics of premium-coinsured GNMAs can shift dramatically.

CLCs and PLCs

Under HUD's multifamily insurance programs, the government insures the construction financing of projects as well as the permanent mortgage on the completed structures, unlike single-family mortgage pass-throughs in which the government only insures mortgages on completed homes. Investors purchase construction projects by investing in bonds that fund construction costs on a monthly basis until the project is built. When construction is completed, the investor's cumulative monthly construction securities are rolled into a permanent mortgage security on the building. The construction financing portion of a project trades in the secondary market as insured *Construction Loan Certificates* (*CLCs*), in either FHA-insured or GNMA form. CLCs operate as follows: each month during a predetermined construction period (typically 14 to 18 months), the contractor completes a specified portion of the construction and then submits a bill for the work to the local FHA office. The FHA then sends an inspector to the job site, and after the work meets specifications, GNMA issues an insured CLC for that month's work (FHA issues the insured CLC if the security is in non-GNMA form). The investor funds the work by fulfilling a commitment to purchase each monthly CLC. When the project is completed, the bond servicer exchanges all the monthly CLCs for an insured *Permanent Loan Certificate* (*PLC*). The PLC is an insured GNMA (or FHA) pass-through security backed by the final mortgage on the completed property. There are vastly more PLCs than CLCs in the market, owing to the long economic lives of project structures, and although CLCs are generally held by one investor over a relatively short construction period, PLCs trade frequently in the secondary market.

Determining the relative value of insured construction-permanent securities is a function of the coupon, seasoning, and call protection of the CLC or PLC, as well as the length of the construction period. During construction, each month the investor funds another insured CLC, which represents the construction work completed in the prior month, and bond interest is paid monthly on all the CLCs already funded. The present value of CLC interest payments is primarily a function of the opportunity cost of earning coupon payments as the investment is phased in gradually over the construction time. As a result, CLCs trade at a discount to fully funded project securities, and CLCs with shorter construction periods offer more value than do CLCs with lengthy construction periods.

STRUCTURED PROJECT SECURITIES

In 1996, projects began to be used as collateral for structured securitizations, and at present $7.4 billion of project loans have been used as collateral for 23 separate structured transactions. A large majority of these securitizations (close to $6 billion) have structured GNMA projects into sequential-pay securities, and have been completed under Fannie Mae's shelf. In early 2001, Ginnie Mae expanded its shelf to include multifamily REMICs backed by GNMA projects. As of February 2001, over $1 billion additional project REMICs were being planned for Ginnie Mae's new multifamily shelf.

Structuring projects directs the cash flows and prepayment protection of project collateral to minimize extension risk, target appropriate prepayment scenarios, and so produce more efficiency from the underlying project bond collateral. Also, just as structured financings have increased the market value of many other asset classes, structuring projects has augmented the secondary trading value of project securities.

SPECIFIC PROJECT PROGRAMS

Since its creation under the National Housing Act of 1934, the FHA has established numerous multifamily insurance programs. Each program serves a specific purpose, and is referred to by the section of the housing act under which it was created. Specific characteristics vary from program to program, since the types of projects, their purposes, allowable mortgage limits, prepayment features, and other criteria often differ. As discussed above, regardless of which program insures a project, securities backed by insured mortgages may exist in either GNMA form or as FHA passthroughs. Exhibit 36–4 provides a quick reference chart outlining these programs.

E X H I B I T   36–4

Quick Reference Chart: FHA-GNMA Projects

Section 202	
Type of program	Direct loans for housing the elderly or handicapped
Type of borrower	Private, nonprofit sponsors (including nonprofit cooperatives)
Maximum loan amount	The lesser of 95% of anticipated net project income or 100% of the project's development costs
Maximum term	50 years by statute, but HUD has limited loans to 40 years
Date program enacted	1959 (amended 1974)
Additional features	Older loans fixed rate; newer loans adjust annually at a HUD-determined margin over Treasuries; all projects under Section 202 have 100% Section 8 HAP contracts (see Section 8)
Program status	Active
Insurance in force	$7.7 billion
Section 207	
Type of program	Construction or rehabilitation of rental housing
Type of borrower	Primarily profit-motivated sponsors
Date program enacted	1934
Prepayment restrictions	Negotiable
Program status	Authorized but not used; multifamily rental projects now issued under Sections 221(d)3 and (4)
Insurance in force	$2.9 billion
Section 213	
Type of program	New construction, rehabilitation, acquisition, conversion , or repair of cooperative housing projects

Continued

EXHIBIT 36–4

Continued

Type of borrower	Profit-motivated co-op sponsors as well as nonprofit corporations or trusts
Date program enacted	1950
Prepayment restrictions	Negotiable
Program status	Authorized but not used; cooperative projects now issued under Sections 221(d)4, 221(d) 3 and 223(f)
Insurance in force	$678 million

Section 220

Type of program	New construction or rehabilitation of projects in designated urban renewal areas
Type of borrower	Profit-motivated and nonprofit sponsors
Date program enacted	1949 (expanded 1980)
Prepayment restrictions	Negotiable
Program status	Active but infrequently used; urban renewal projects are being eliminated
Insurance in force	$1.1 billion

Sections 221(d)3 and 221(d)4

Type of programs	Construction or rehabilitation of multifamily rental or cooperative housing
Type of borrower	For-profit corporations or partnerships (developers, builders, investors); also nonprofit public or community groups
Maximum loan amount	221(d)4: 90% of FHA-estimated replacement cost (maximum can be higher only with explicit FHA approval) 221(d)3: 100% of FHA-estimated replacement cost
Maximum term	40 years from origination
Date programs enacted	221(d)3: 1954; 221(d)4: 1959
Additional features	FHA pass-throughs auctioned before January 1, 1984, have an option that permits investor to put the mortgage to HUD in its 20th year
Prepayment restrictions	Negotiable between mortgagor and mortgagee unless project has a low-income use restriction within a Section 8 HAP contract
Program status	Active
Insurance in force	221(d)4: $28.9 billion; 221(d)3 market rate only: $2.2 billion

Section 223(f)

Type of program	Purchase or refinancing of existing multifamily projects
Type of borrower	Primarily profit-motivated sponsors
Maximum loan amount	85% of HUD estimated value (may be raised to 90% with HUD approval)
Maximum term	35 years from origination
Date program enacted	1974
Prepayment restrictions	Negotiable
Program status	Active
Insurance in force	$16.4 billion

E X H I B I T   36–4

Continued

Section 231
   Type of program   Rental housing for the elderly or handicapped
   Type of borrower   Profit-motivated and nonprofit sponsors
   Maximum loan amount   90% (for-profit project) 100% (nonprofit project) of the
                                            FHA-estimated replacement cost
   Maximum term   40 years, or 75% of the project's estimated economic life
   Date program enacted   1959
   Prepayment restrictions   Negotiable
   Program status   Active
   Insurance in force $640 million

Section 232
   Type of program   Construction or rehabilitation of nursing homes,
                                            intermediate-care facilities, and board and care homes
   Type of borrower   Profit-motivated and nonprofit sponsors
   Maximum loan amount   90% of FHA-estimated value of property (includes the
                                            value of equipment used to operate the facility)
   Maximum term   40 years from origination
   Date program enacted   1959
   Prepayment restrictions   Negotiable
   Program status   Active
   Insurance in force $7.4 billion

Section 236
   Type of program   Interest rate subsidies for low- to moderate-income
                                            families and elderly individuals
   Type of borrower   Profit-motivated and nonprofit sponsors
   Maximum loan amount   90% of FHA-estimated replacement cost (100% or
                                            higher permissible for nonprofit sponsors)
   Date program enacted   1968
   Prepayment restrictions   Negotiable
   Program status   Inactive
   Insurance in force $4.9 billion

Section 241
   Type of program   FHA-insured second mortgage for preservation-desig-
nated
                                            Section 8 projects
   Type of borrower   Profit-motivated and nonprofit sponsors
   Maximum loan amount   90% of FHA-estimated replacement cost of first and
                                            241 second mortgage combined
   Date program reactivated   1993
   Prepayment restrictions   Negotiable
   Program status   Active
   Insurance in force $1.5 billion

Section 242
   Type of program   Construction or rehabilitation of public or private
                                            hospitals (includes major movable equipment)

Continued

EXHIBIT 36–4

Continued

Type of borrower	Profit-motivated or nonprofit sponsors
Maximum loan amount	90% of FHA-estimated replacement cost
Maximum term	25 years from origination
Date program enacted	1968
Prepayment restrictions	Negotiable; nonprofit sponsors may make prepayments only with HUD's written consent
Program status	Active
Insurance in force	$5.4 billion

EXHIBIT 36–5

Relative Size of the Various Programs That Constitute the $74 Billion
Project Securities Outstanding as of October 31, 1999 (HUD Data)

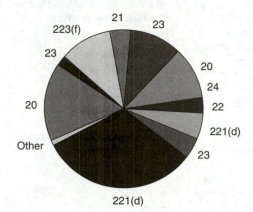

Exhibit 36–5 shows a graph that illustrates the relative size of each program within
the project market. The chapter closes with brief descriptions of several of the most
common multifamily insurance programs.

Multifamily Housing

Section 221(d)4: Rental Housing for Low- to Moderate-Income Families
The 221(d)4 program is the largest project program, with $35.1 billion in cumula-
tive insurance issued on 9,960 projects and $28.9 billion insurance remaining in
force since the program began in 1959.[1] This program insures mortgages made by
private lenders to finance construction or substantial rehabilitation of multifamily

---

1. All data reported in this chapter are from the U.S. Department of Housing and Urban Development,
    as of October 31, 1999.

rental or cooperative housing for low- to moderate-income or displaced families. Projects insured under Section 221(d)4 must have five or more units, and may consist of detached, semidetached, row, walk-up, or elevator structures.

Section 221(d)4 projects may be owned by either nonprofit or profit-motivated developers, and these projects may be insured for up to 90% of their FHA-determined replacement cost. Although 100% of the funds invested in project securities is insured, the mortgagor borrows only 90% or less of replacement cost; the balance represents owner equity. The majority of loans insured under Section 221(d)4 and most new loan originations are unsubsidized, market rate projects. That is, project developers set the rental rates at whatever levels their local real estate market can command (subject to HUD approval), and there are no income restrictions on tenants. Since the early 1990s, a significant majority of 221(d)4 issuance has been on these market rate projects. Developers have selected HUD financing as the most cost-efficient way to finance new apartment construction, and most projects insured under Section 221(d)4 are suburban garden apartments and other higher-end apartment complexes. Non-market-rate projects may also be insured under Section 221(d)4, and most Section 8 subsidized projects have been financed through the 221(d)4 program. Unlike market rent projects, Section 8 projects have restrictions on monthly rents and tenant income (see Section 8, above).

The maximum term of mortgages insured under Section 221(d)4 is either 40 years or 75% of the FHA-estimated remaining economic life of the project, whichever is less. The majority of these projects carry 40-year terms. FHA-HUD does not restrict prepayments on Section 221(d)4 mortgages, although prepayment lockouts and penalties are usually negotiated between the mortgagee and mortgagor (see prepayment section, above). HUD may allow mortgagors to prepay up to 15% of a mortgage per year, unless documents that record the transaction specify in the lockout that the bonds are noncallable in whole or in part for a specified period of time. However, even if documents do not prohibit prepayments, the 15% prepayment option is not exercised often, since U.S. government backing makes project financing much less expensive for developers than private financing alternatives.

Section 221(d)3: Rental and Cooperative Housing for Low- to Moderate-Income Families

The 221(d)3 program has two components. The first was an older, below-market interest rate (BMIR) program that provided financing to sponsors of lower-income housing projects. The default rate on BMIRs has been high, over 35% as discussed above, and so the BMIR program was closed in 1972 (of the $2.87 billion BMIRs originally insured, only $1.2 billion remain outstanding).

The second component of Section 221(d)3, the market rate program, has been replaced by the 221(d)4 program (see above). The market rate 221(d)3 program remains in force, with $3.2 billion in cumulative insurance issued on 2,058 projects and $2.2 billion insurance in force since the program began in 1954 (2). The primary difference between the 221(d)3 and the 221(d)4 program is that Section 221(d)3 provided developers with more leverage, since HUD could insure up to 100% of a project's FHA-determined replacement cost under this program, as opposed to only 90% under Section 221(d)4. The majority of market rate projects insured under Section 221(d)3 have Section 8 rental subsidies, and unlike projects insured under Section 221(d)4, 221(d)3 projects can include cooperatives. Finally, during the first 20 years of a mortgage insured under Section 221(d)3, borrowers must obtain HUD's permission before making any prepayments on the mortgage. Aside from these differences, the 221(d)3 market rate program closely resembles the 221(d)4 program. The program may be used for new construction or substantial rehabilitation of various types of buildings.

7.43 Putable Projects: Older FHA Projects Insured Under Sections 221(d)3 and 221(d)4

FHA projects insured under Sections 221(d)3 and 221(d)4 before 1984 included a 20-year put feature. This put option gives the FHA pass-through holder the right to assign, or put, the mortgage to HUD for a 1-year period 20 years after the original mortgage was endorsed by HUD-FHA. When investors put the securities under the FHA's initial program, they received FHA series MM debentures; to the FHA MM debentures are bonds with a 10-year maturity, callable after 6 months. These MM debentures are obligations of the FHA, and as such are unconditionally guaranteed by the U.S. Government as to payment of interest and principal. The debentures' face value equals the unpaid principal balance of the mortgage that is put to HUD, plus accrued interest.

Before December 1983, many FHA projects were auctioned by GNMA. The majority of these projects were purchased by servicers as 7.50% loans, and issued as FHA pass-through securities with 7.43 coupons. They are commonly referred to as 7.43s, since the issuers often retained 7 bps of servicing. The vast majority of 7.43s were auctioned between 1979 and 1983; consequently, most 7.43s are putable between 1999 and 2003, and trade at a spread over comparable Treasury bonds. Most of the projects underlying 7.43s carry Section 8 contracts (see above), which provide the investor with a defined cash flow and also limit prepayments. This cash flow certainty coupled with their put feature make putable 7.43s very convex securities.

The exact value of the FHA debentures definitely affects the value of the put option. To compensate for the additional market risk and record keeping associated with debentures, investors have typically valued FHA debentures at between 96 and 98 cents on the dollar. However, the FHA changed the put process on 7.43s in 1992. For several years thereafter, investors in 7.43 putable bonds received cash, or par, in lieu of debentures when the bonds were put. As a result, the put option became worth more than the 96% to 98% most investors assumed upon purchase. HUD funded the cash put by auctioning the bonds that were put to the FHA; several successful auctions were held in the mid-1990s, but the auctions stopped by 1996. Since interest rates trended lower during that time, few bonds were put to HUD and the agency had an insufficient number of bonds to hold further auctions. Consequently, by 1999, the FHA again began paying puts with FHA debentures, and as of this writing, 7.43s are being paid in Series MM debentures, although the cash put auctions are still authorized by HUD.

An accurate valuation of 7.43 puts is linked to the assumed strike price of the put which, in turn, depends primarily on whether HUD funds the put in cash or in debentures. The shift from paying puts in Series MM debentures to paying puts with the cash generated by auctions creates budgetary savings for HUD, and so shaves the federal budget deficit. As a result, many observers think it likely that HUD will resume their put auctions and reinstitute the change from debenture pay to cash pay. Investors should realize that an overwhelming majority of all 7.43s (just over $7 billion) are eligible to be put in between 2000 and 2003, whereas only 2½ billion were eligible to be put during the entire period 1992–1999. Should HUD elect to continue using Series MM debentures to fund the 7.43 puts, the increased supply of debentures could weaken their secondary market value and further erode the value of the put option. Until HUD clarifies the cash versus debenture funding mechanism, the value of 7.43 putable bonds will remain in question.

Finally, investors should note that not all 7.43s are putable; 7.43s issued under some project programs are not putable. Most of these nonputable 7.43s also carry Section 8 contracts, and so provide defined cash flows. Nonputable 7.43s trade in the secondary market at a spread over the U.S. Treasury curve.

Section 223(f): Purchase or Refinancing of Existing Multifamily Projects

The 223(f) program was created to insure the purchase or refinancing of existing rental apartment projects, to refinance existing cooperatives, or to purchase and convert existing rental projects to cooperative housing. Section 223(f) was added to the National Housing Act by the Housing and Community Development Act in 1974, in response to private sector demands for an FHA-insured refinancing vehicle and to help preserve an adequate supply of affordable housing. Conventionally financed apartment projects, as well as FHA-insured housing projects issued under any section of the National Housing Act, can be refinanced by using Section 223(f). Since 1974, 3,823 projects have been originated under Section 223(f), representing $19.4 billion of insurance written with $16.4 billion remaining in force.

Section 223(f) is a market-rate, unsubsidized program created primarily to improve the financing flexibility for profit-motivated project developers by making it easier for owners to refinance, convert a project to a co-op, and buy or sell an existing building. To qualify for insurance under Section 223(f), a project must be at least 3 years old, must contain five or more units, and must have sufficient occupancy to pay operating expenses, annual debt service, and maintain a reserve fund for replacement requirements. A mortgage insured under Section 223(f) cannot exceed 85% of the HUD-FHA estimated value of the project, although this requirement can be raised to 90% for cooperatives and those projects located in target preservation areas as designated by HUD.

The maximum term for mortgages insured under Section 223(f) is either 35 years or 75% of the FHA-estimated remaining economic life of the project, whichever is less. Most 223(f) projects carry 35-year terms. As with other programs, HUD-FHA permits prepayments on mortgages insured under Section 223(f), although prepayment lockouts and penalties are usually negotiated between the mortgagee and mortgagor.

Section 207

Section 207 was enacted in 1934 as the first program used by the FHA to finance construction or rehabilitation of multifamily housing projects. Section 207 projects are primarily moderate-income projects sponsored by for-profit developers. The 207 program is rarely used today, as multifamily projects are now originated under Sections 221(d)3 and 221(d)4. However, seasoned Section 207 projects continue to trade in the secondary market. Total cumulative insurance issued under Section 207 was $4.2 billion, with $2.9 billion insurance remaining in force.

Section 213

The Section 213 program was enacted in 1950 to provide mortgage insurance on cooperative projects. Section 213 insurance was used for new construction, rehabilitation, acquisition, and conversion or repair of existing housing in several types of cooperative projects that consist of five or more units. The program was available for both nonprofit cooperative corporations as well as for profit-motivated developers who build or rehabilitate a project and sell it to a cooperative corporation. The 213 program is no longer used, as cooperative apartments are now insured under Sections 221(d)4 and 223(f). Total cumulative insurance written under Section 213 is $1.6 billion on 2,043 projects, with $640 million insurance remaining in force.

Section 220

The Section 220 program was created to insure mortgages and home improvement loans on multifamily projects in urban renewal areas. Before 1980, Section 220 insurance was available in urban renewal areas in which federally assisted slum clearance and urban redevelopment projects were being undertaken. In 1980, the Housing and Community Development Act expanded the scope of the Section 220 program to include those areas in which housing, development, and public service activities will be carried out by local neighborhood improvement, conservation, or preservation groups. The main focus of Section 220 is to insure mortgages on new or rehabilitated multifamily structures located within designated urban renewal areas. Over 540 projects have been insured under Section 220, which represents $3.1 billion in total cumulative insurance, with $1.1 billion remaining in force.

Section 236: Interest Rate Subsidies for Low- to Moderate-Income Families and Elderly People

Section 236 was added to the National Housing Act in 1968, but was suspended during the subsidized housing moratorium of 1973 and has never been revived. The 236 program combined governmental mortgage insurance on projects with subsidized payments to reduce the project owners' monthly debt service payments. These reduced interest payments, in turn, are passed on to tenants of the project in the form of lower rents. To qualify for rental assistance under Section 236, tenants' annual income must be lower than 80% of the median income of the area. The program served both elderly people and low-income families.

The maximum mortgage amount for limited-dividend sponsors is 90% of replacement cost; for nonprofit sponsors, the maximum mortgage amount can be 100 percent. In certain defined high-cost areas, maximums may be increased up to an additional 75%. The maximum term under this program is 40 years, and prepayments are prohibited for at least 20 years without prior approval from HUD. Total cumulative insurance issued under Section 236 was $7.5 billion on over 4,000 projects; $4.9 billion insurance remains in force.

Section 241(f): Section 8 Refinancings

Section 241(f) was reactivated early in 1993 to address the refinancing of low-income housing that receives Section 8 rent subsidies (see above). Section 8 projects that fall under the Low Income Housing Preservation Acts of 1987 (Title I) and 1990 (Title II) are designated preservation projects and cannot be refinanced. However, owners whose preservation properties have increased in value can access that equity with a second mortgage loan insured under this Section 241, without refinancing the project's underlying Section 8 first mortgage. Under Section 241, HUD reunderwrites the entire project to a maximum 90% LTV, subtracts the remaining balance on the first mortgage, and then insures a 241 loan for the balance. The 241 loan is fully insured by HUD; there is no credit difference between the original HUD mortgage and the new 241 loan. Obviously, given the use of the 241 program, securities backed by first mortgages with Section 8 subsidies provide significant call protection to investors. In addition, the 241 loans are usually originated with 10 years of call protection. Total cumulative insurance written under Section 241(f) is $1.6 billion, with $1.5 billion insurance remaining in force.

Health Care and Housing for Elderly and Handicapped People

Section 231: Rental Housing for Elderly or Handicapped People

In 1959, Congress enacted Section 231 of the National Housing Act to provide insurance for the construction or rehabilitation of rental housing for elderly people. Section 231 was expanded to include housing for handicapped people in 1964. Residents of projects for the elderly people must be at least 62 years old, and residents in projects for handicapped people must have a long-term physical impairment that substantially impedes an independent living arrangement, but who could live independently in suitable housing.

Projects must have eight or more units to qualify for insurance under Section 231, and the maximum term for mortgages insured under Section 231 is 40 years or 75% of the project's estimated economic life. In addition, HUD may insure up to 100% of the estimated replacement cost for projects originated by nonprofit and public borrowers, but only up to 90% of replacement cost for profit-motivated mortgagors. Section 231 is no longer used for new loans; housing for elderly people is now financed under the 221(d)4 and the 232 programs. Total cumulative insurance issued under Section 231 was $1.1 billion, with $640 million insurance remaining in force.

Section 232: Nursing Homes, Intermediate-Care Facilities, and Board and Care Homes

Under Section 232, HUD insures mortgages to finance new construction or rehabilitation of nursing homes for patients who require skilled nursing care and related medical services, as well as intermediate-care facilities and board and care homes for patients who need minimum but continuous care provided by licensed or trained people. Section 232 insures mortgages on any of these facilities; also, nursing, intermediate-care, and board and care homes may be combined within the same facility and insured under Section 232. Board and care homes must have a minimum of five one-bedroom or efficiency units, whereas nursing homes and intermediate-care facilities must have 20 or more patients who are unable to live independently but are not in need of acute care. Mortgage insurance under Section 232 may also cover the purchase of major equipment needed to operate the facility. Also, Section 232 may be used to purchase, rehabilitate, and/or refinance existing health care projects already insured by HUD.

Legislation establishing Section 232 was enacted in 1959. Borrowers may include private nonprofit associations or corporations as well as for-profit investors or developers. To qualify for insurance under Section 232, sponsors must first qualify for licensing in the state of the facility, and must comply with all relevant state regulations. Total cumulative insurance issued under Section 232 is $8.6 billion on 3,320 projects; total insurance remaining in force is $7.4 billion.

Section 242: Mortgage Insurance for Hospitals

In 1968, Congress enacted Section 242 of the National Housing Act to provide insurance for the construction or rehabilitation of hospitals. Major equipment used in the hospital may also be included in an insured mortgage under Section 242. Hospitals built or rehabilitated under Section 242 must have appropriate licenses, must meet the regulatory requirements of the state in which they are located, and must be approved by the U.S. Department of Health and Human Services. A Section 242 mortgage may not exceed 90% of the FHA-estimated replacement cost, and the maximum term for these mortgages is 25 years.

Borrowers under Section 242 may be either profit-motivated or not-for-profit hospitals. HUD permits full or partial prepayments on profit-motivated Section 242 projects, subject to prepayment restrictions and penalties negotiated between the mortgagor and mortgagee, but prepayments by nonprofit mortgagors are permitted only with the written consent of HUD. Total cumulative insurance issued under Section 242 is $7.7 billion on 305 projects, with $5.4 billion insurance remaining in force.

CHAPTER 37

VALUE AND SENSITIVITY ANALYSIS OF CMBS IOs

Philip O. Obazee
Vice President
Quantitative Research
First Union Securities, Inc.

Commercial mortgage-backed securities (CMBS) interest-only (IOs) issues are coupons stripped from an underlying pool of commercial mortgages. Stripping the coupon allows issuers to sell a bond with premium collateral at a price close to par. For example, a 9% coupon commercial mortgage collateral could be stripped to create a 2% IO, so that the bond created out of the collateral would be priced at par with a 7% coupon. In Exhibit 37–1, we show an example of a weighted average coupon (WAC) IO created from AAA and AA bonds, with 7% and 7.5% coupons, respectively. The collateral WAC is 9.5%, so 2.5% and 2% coupons are stripped from the AAA and AA bonds, respectively.

To understand the value drivers for an IO, we need to break down CMBS. An investor who purchases CMBS holds a long position in a noncallable bond, a short call, and default put options. When selling the options, the investor is compensated in the form of enhanced coupon payments. Part of this enhanced coupon is stripped off to create the IO, hence the basic value drivers for IOs come largely from prepayments and default put options. Unlike residential mortgage-backed securities (RMBS) for which the prepayment option predominates, the default option has greater impact in a CMBS transaction. The option embedded in a CMBS transaction derives its value from the

- Time to maturity of the underlying collateral
- Collateral coupon and scheduled and unscheduled principal payments
- Interest rate
- Volatility of the interest rate
- Prepayment restriction (e.g., lockout)
- Net operating income (NOI) from the collateral and the volatility of the NOI
- Correlation between the interest rate and the NOI
- Collateral default clause

Although this option-theoretic approach is useful in identifying the factors that determine the value of CMBS, the analytic complexity it presents makes investors

E X H I B I T   37–1

A Typical WACO IO* Structure

Bond Class	Principal Balance	Investment Class Coupon	Pool WAC	Class WAC IO
AAA	375	7.00%		2.500%
AA	125	7.50	9.50%	2.000
WAC IO	0			
Total	500	7.125%		2.375%

*WAC IO: weighted average coupon interest-only.
Source: First Union Securities, Inc.

more likely to value IOs by looking at the contribution to return from prepayment and default as well as the sensitivity of their IO position to changing prepayment and default assumptions.

In this chapter, we examine the various types of IOs and show how the value of an IO is affected by a number of scenarios related to the magnitude and timing of prepayments, defaults, and interest rates.

TYPES OF CMBS IOs

Fixed-Strip IOs
The holder of a fixed-strip IO receives a fixed-stripped coupon off a collateral WAC. For example, a 1% IO stripped off a 9% collateral WAC will pay an 8% coupon to the bond classes. Any change in the collateral WAC is absorbed by the bond classes. Thus, if the collateral WAC changes to 8.5%, the IO will remain at 1%, with the WAC bond changing to 7.5%.

WAC IOs
With WAC IOs, bondholders receive a fixed coupon and the change in the WAC is passed on to the IO holders. For example, if a 1% IO is stripped off a 9% collateral WAC, the coupon to the bond classes is 8%, and the change in the collateral WAC to, say, 8.5% will result in a new IO coupon of 0.5%. As the loan with the high coupon prepays, the WAC IO coupon is lower and, conversely, as the loan with the low coupon prepays, the coupon on the WAC IO is higher.

Notional IOs
The holder of a notional IO receives varying strips of coupons from different tranches. For example, the notional IO structure could consist of 1.5% stripped from the A1 tranche and 1% from the A2 tranche. Both bonds are off collateral WAC, so that as the collateral WAC changes, the coupon on the bond changes and the IO remains the same. Moreover, the cash flow of a notional IO is affected by

the paydown in the bond class; the cash flow decreases the most as the bond with the higher stripped coupon pays down.

Component IOs

A component IO is a combination of a WAC and a notional IO. The WAC IO is stripped from the collateral and the notional IO is stripped from the bond classes. Changes in the collateral WAC are passed on to the WAC IO, and the notional IO remains unchanged.

IMPACT OF PREPAYMENT ON CMBS IOs

A CMBS IO has low convexity cost because, unlike residential mortgages that can prepay in response to refinancing incentives, commercial mortgages usually have prepayment restrictions. The restrictions in CMBS structures are lockouts, defeasance, point penalties, and yield maintenance.

Lockouts

The lockout period, generally 2 to 5 years, prohibits a borrower from prepaying a loan prior to the scheduled maturity.

Defeasance

From an investor's perspective, a loan that is defeased is locked out from prepayment. In a defeased structure, prepayments from borrowers do not change the cash flows to investors. The borrower replaces a mortgage with a series of U.S. Treasury strips that match the payment stream of the mortgage loan. The defeasance option improves the credit quality of the collateral with a corresponding decline in yield. For example, NASC 98-D6 is backed by collateral with defeasance.

Penalty Period

The penalty period, which follows a lockout period, allows a borrower to repay a loan by compensating the lender for the right to terminate early. There are two types of penalties: yield maintenance and fixed percentage penalty points.

Yield Maintenance   Yield maintenance is designed to compensate the lender for interest lost as a result of prepayments by making borrowers indifferent to prepayments. If the prevailing market rate is higher at the time of prepayment than at origination, the borrower would not be required to make a penalty payment. The key variable determining yield maintenance is the reference rate, which is the comparable maturity Treasury rate or the comparable maturity Treasury plus spread. Investors prefer Treasury flat because it results in higher present value in terms of prepayment penalty. As the term to maturity of the mortgage shortens, the yield maintenance as a percentage of the remaining balance decreases and the remaining loan payment represents a lower percentage of total investor return.

Fixed Percentage Penalty Points   These points are the fixed percentage assessed on the remaining loan balance, and this percentage declines over the life of the loan. Typically, the points penalty is distributed as follows.

Lockout: 5 Years

Year	Penalty (%)
6	5
7	4
8	3
9	2
10	1

Significant movement in interest rates and increases in property values would affect these fixed economic disincentives to prepay a penalty loan because the penalties do not change with interest rates.

ALLOCATION OF PREPAYMENT PENALTIES

The allocation of prepayment penalties differs by deal. In general, for a deal issued prior to and including 1996, the prepayment penalties were 75% to 100% allocated to IOs and the penalties paid to the coupon bondholders were capped between 0% and 25%. Recent deals allocate the prepayment penalties such that the currently paying bonds are "whole" and the remaining penalties are distributed to the IOs. In this newer allocation method, the investor holding the currently paying bond receives compensation for the early return of principal in a lower-rate environment. The IO holder generally receives 65% to 75% of the penalty, and the current principal paying bond receives the remainder—making it "whole" to the bond's coupon and not flat to Treasuries. The penalty point allocated to a bond is computed as the product of the prepayment distribution and yield maintenance.

PREPAYMENT RESTRICTIONS
AND RELATIVE VALUE ISSUES

The cash flow variability in lockout and defeased bonds comes from credit events. Movements in interest rates, spread levels, and the credit performance of the underlying loan determine total return. Lockout and defeased structures are not exposed to prepayment risk. Exhibit 37–2 shows the yield to maturity of NASC 98-D6 PS1

E X H I B I T   37–2

Yield to Maturity of NASC 98-D6 PS1 by Prepayment Restriction

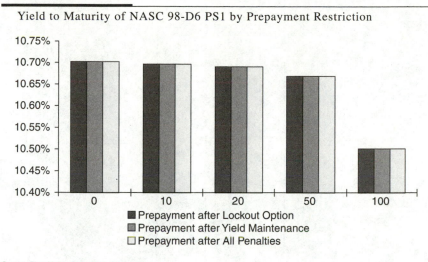

■ Prepayment after Lockout Option
■ Prepayment after Yield Maintenance
☐ Prepayment after All Penalties

Source: First Union Securities, Inc.

under different prepayment restrictions. The yield is not affected by prepayment protection because of its defeasance feature. NASC 98-D6 PS1 exhibits greater average life stability than FULBA 98-C2 (Exhibit 37–3). As a rule of thumb, a change in average life of less than half a year as prepayment speed increases from a constant prepayment rate (CPR) of 0% to 100% CPR is a good indicator of how well the structure is call-protected. For example, NASC 98-D6 PS1 has approximately two months weighted average life (WAL) drift for an increase in prepayment speed from 0% CPR to 100% CPR.

Although yield maintenance leaves investors indifferent to prepayments, the variety of securities within a deal and differences across deals cause diverse bond performance, depending on the prepayment and rate scenarios. The credit performance of the loan, interest rates, prepayment speed, and the allocation of penalties will determine the yield of a bond with a yield maintenance provision. Market convention assumes that the loans do not prepay during the yield maintenance period and a pricing speed of 100% CPR for an IO. If the actual prepayment is less than 100% CPR, the investor benefits. For example,

E X H I B I T 37–3

YTM and WAL of NASC 98-D6 PS1 by Prepayment Scenario*

CRP	Prepay after Lockout Option					Prepay after Yield Maintenance					Prepay after All Penalties				
	0	10	20	50	100	0	10	20	50	100	0	10	20	50	100
Yield	10.70	10.70	10.69	10.67	10.50	10.70	10.70	10.69	10.67	10.50	10.70	10.70	10.69	10.67	10.50
WAL	9.83	9.82	9.82	9.80	9.67	9.83	9.82	9.82	9.80	9.67	9.83	9.82	9.82	9.80	9.67

CPR: constant repayment rate; IO: interest-only; WAL: weighted average life; YTM: yield to maturity.
*Pricing assumption: 470 bps at 100 CPR.
Source: First Union Securities, Inc.

EXHIBIT   37–4

Yield to Maturity of FULBA 98-C2 IO by Prepayment Restriction

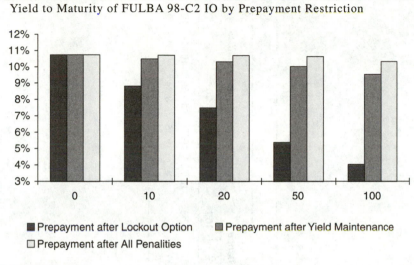

■ Prepayment after Lockout Option   ■ Prepayment after Yield Maintenance
□ Prepayment after All Penalities

IO = Interest-only.
Source: First Union Securities, Inc.

Exhibit 37–4 shows the yield to maturity of FULBA 98-C2 with prepayments that occur under different prepayment scenarios. Exhibit 37–5 shows a yield pickup of 77 basis points (bps) if the realized prepayment for FULBA 98-C2 is 20% CPR. Exhibit 37–7 shows the yield to maturity of FULBA 98-C2 with prepayments that occur under different prepayment scenarios.

Exhibit 37–6 shows the pickup in yield that results in a drop or slope in spread, that is, the difference between the actual prepayment and the pricing speed.

In general, IOs benefit as prepayment speed increases during the yield maintenance period. The present value of the yield maintenance penalty paid to the IO is usually greater than the present value of the forgone interest that would have been received from the loan that prepaid. If interest rates rise to the level where there is no prepayment penalty, the IO holder does not benefit from faster prepayments and the IO loses the income from the prepaid loan and does not receive a compensating penalty payment.

EXHIBIT 37–5

YTM and WAL of FULBA 98-C2 IO by Prepayment Scenario*

	Prepay after Lockout Option					Prepay after Yield Maintenance					Prepay after All Penalties				
CRP	0	10	20	50	100	0	10	20	50	100	0	10	20	50	100
Yield	10.73	8.81	7.49	5.37	4.03	10.73	10.47	10.301	0.01	9.53	10.73	10.71	10.69	10.63	10.31
WAL	9.37	8.56	8.14	7.61	7.36	9.37	9.12	8.99	8.82	8.61	9.37	9.35	9.34	9.31	9.15

CPR: constant repayment rate; IO: interest-only; WAL: weighted average life; YTM: yield to maturity.
*Pricing assumption: 375 bps at 100 CPR.
Source: First Union Securities, Inc.

E X H I B I T   37–6

Yield Pick from the Slope in Spread for FULBA 98-C2 IO

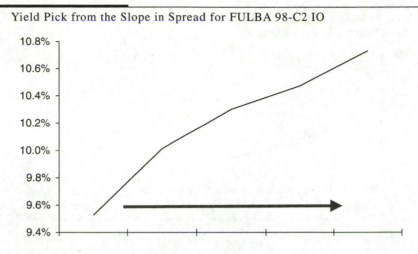

CPR = constant prepayment rate; IO = interest-only.
Source: First Union Securities, Inc.

E X H I B I T   37–7

YTM and WAL of FULBA 98-C2 IO by Prepayment Scenario—Shock Versus No Shock

	Prepay during Yield Maintenance (no shock)					Prepay during Yield Maintenance (shock + 300 bps)				
CRP	0	10	20	50	100	0	10	20	50	100
Yield	10.71	11.26	11.75	12.63	13.56	10.71	9.46	8.59	7.06	6.53
WAL	9.37	8.56	8.14	7.60	7.16	9.37	8.56	8.14	7.60	7.16

CPR: constant prepayment rate; IO: interest-only; WAL: weighted average life; YTM: yield to maturity.
Source: First Union Securities, Inc.

Unlike a defeased IO, an IO from a deal backed by yield maintenance offers investors the potential for a higher return with faster prepayment under stable interest rate scenarios. Exhibits 37–7 and 37–8 show the yield to maturity of FULBA 98-C2 IO for an unchanged rate and a 300 bps rate increase.

IMPACT OF DEFAULT ON CMBS IOs YIELD

The impact of defaults on a CMBS bond depends on various factors. Some of these factors are the bond's position in the distribution priority, loan characteristics in the pool, timing of default, amount of recovery, and servicer advance feature. For an IO, the lower the default rate and the later the default occurs, the better the IO's

E X H I B I T   37–8

Yield to Maturity of FULBA 98-C2 IO by Prepayment Scenario During
Yield Maintenance

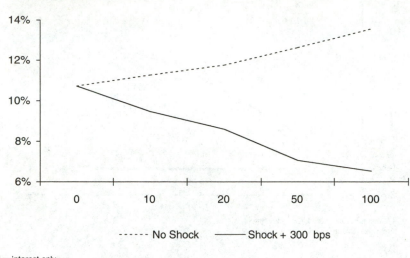

IO = interest-only.
Source: First Union Securities, Inc.

performance profile. To assess the default probability and the timing of the default, the investor has to understand the characteristics of each of the loans in the pool. In a WAC IO, one approach is to take the difference between each of the loan rates and the current weighted average coupon and determine which loans contribute the most to the IO. After that, one must examine the loans by using the historical default rate for each type of loan.

Investors generally make assumptions about the default rate. A recent industry study of default rates on commercial mortgages held by insurance companies showed that the 10-year cumulative default rate ranged from 9% for 1977 origination to about 28% for 1986.[1] These cumulative default rates translate to about 1% and 4% conditional default rates (CDRs), respectively, for 10-year collateral. Although this study provides useful insights into default rates, there are differences between insurance companies and mortgage conduit originations. Another industry study that examined default rates on conduit loans originated and securitized between 1995 and 1999 showed that the cumulative default rate was 0.78% on a loan basis and 0.48% on a balance basis. We believe this impressive performance is partly explained by the absence of term defaults for these loans (that is, a default that occurs prior to the balloon date), the strong real estate market, and the oversight and discipline provided by the capital markets and the rating agencies.

1. Howard Esaki, Steven L'Heureux, and Mark P. Snyderman, "Commercial Mortgage Defaults," *Real Estate Finance,* (Spring 1999).

Although there is no standard CDR to use, there is an emerging consensus favoring a 2% to 3% CDR, with 30% to 35% loss severity and 12 months to recover as reasonable numbers to evaluate conduit IOs. In Exhibits 37–9 and 37–10, we show the results for FULBA 98-C2 and NASC 98-D6 using various CDRs. At 3% CDR, FULBA 98-C2 suffers a yield loss of 381 bps and NASC 98-D6 incurs a yield loss of 335 bps. We decided to look at the degree of structural leverage in the FULBA 98-C2 and NASC 98-D6 IOs. What we found is that, on average for a 1% change in CDR, there is a 10.31% yield compression for FULBA 98-C2 and a 10.24% for NASC 98-D6. However, when we examine the volatility of the yield compression, FULBA 98-C2 has a standard deviation of 3% compared with 1.4% for NASC 98-D6. FULBA 98-C2 suffers a 15.7% yield compression for the first 1% of CDR shock compared with 10.5% for NASC 98-D6. Ignoring that series for a moment, the average and standard deviations of the yield compression for FULBA 98-C2 become 8.97% and 0.2%, respectively, compared with 10.17% and 1.6% for NASC 98-D6. A telling detail is that there is larger swing in yield for the FULBA 98-C2 IO for the first 1% default rate, but the yield stabilizes as the default rate increases. Exhibits 37–11 and 37–12 contain the results for percentage yield compression for the FULBA 98-C2 and NASC 98-D6 IOs.

PUTTING IT ALL TOGETHER:
CMBS IOs SENSITIVITY ANALYSIS

To properly evaluate the prepayment and default risk in CMBS IOs in one shot, we designed a sensitivity report that contains carefully chosen scenarios which we believe will help investors identify relative value in this sector. Typically, investors need to see the effect of a large number of scenarios relating to the magnitude and timing of prepayments, defaults, and interest rates.

In Exhibits 37–14 and 37–15, we present a CMBS Sensitivity Report that includes 27 carefully chosen scenarios and a summary table. In this way, an investor can get one comprehensive report for each bond and use the summary table to compare value among bonds. Scenarios in the report are defined in terms of prepayment and default risk measures.

• Scenario 1: Base scenario at 0% CPR and 0% CDR, no yield shock

• Scenarios 2–4: Prepay at 10%, 50%, and 100% CPR after all penalties (measures the effect of prepayments at the tail of a deal)

• Scenarios 5–7: Prepay at 10%, 50%, and 100% CPR after yield maintenance (measures the effect of prepayments during and after fixed-point penalty periods)

• Scenarios 8–10: Prepay at 10%, 50%, and 100% CPR after lockout periods (measures the effect of prepayments during and after yield maintenance and fixed-point penalty periods)

• Scenarios 11–13: Prepay at 10%, 50%, and 100% CPR after lockout periods with negative 1% yield shock (lower rates mean higher yield maintenance penalties)

EXHIBIT 37–9

YTM of FULBA 98-C2 IO by CDR Variance

CPR	0						100					
CDR	1.0%	2.0%	3.0%	4.0%	5.0%	6.0%	1.0%	2.0%	3.0%	4.0%	5.0%	6.0%
Yield	9.33	7.84	6.95	6.11	5.26	4.42	8.14	6.63	5.72	4.93	4.10	3.28
WAL	8.94	8.55	8.19	7.85	7.54	7.24	8.26	7.94	7.64	7.36	7.09	6.83

CDR: conditional default rate; CPR: constant prepayment rate; IO: interest-only; WAL: weighted average life; YTM: yield to maturity
Source: First Union Securities, Inc.

EXHIBIT 37–10

YTM of NASC 1998-D6 PS1 by CDR Variance

CPR	0						100					
CDR	1.0%	2.0%	3.0%	4.0%	5.0%	6.0%	1.0%	2.0%	3.0%	4.0%	5.0%	6.0%
Yield	9.63	8.52	7.36	6.10	5.12	4.25	9.42	8.31	7.15	5.88	4.89	4.01
WAL	9.40	9.00	8.62	8.26	7.93	7.61	9.26	8.87	8.50	8.16	7.83	7.53

CDR: conditional default rate; CPR: constant prepayment rate; WAL: weighted average life; YTM: yield to maturity.
Source: First Union Securities, Inc.

EXHIBIT 37–11

Yield and Percentage Yield Compression for FULBA 98-C2 and NASC 98-D6 by CDR Variance

CDR	FULBA 98-C2 Yield	NASC 98-D6 Yield	FULBA 98-C2 Yield Compression	NASC 98-D6 Yield Compression
0.01	9.33	9.63		
0.02	7.84	8.52	15.7%	10.5%
0.03	6.95	7.36	9.3	11.0
0.04	6.11	6.10	8.8	12.0
0.05	5.26	5.12	9.0	9.3
0.06	4.42	4.25	8.8	8.3
		Average	10.3%	10.2%
		Standard deviation	3.0%	1.4%

CDR: conditional default rate.
Source: First Union Securities, Inc.

EXHIBIT 37–12

Percentage Yield Compression for FULBA 98-C2 and NASC 98-D6

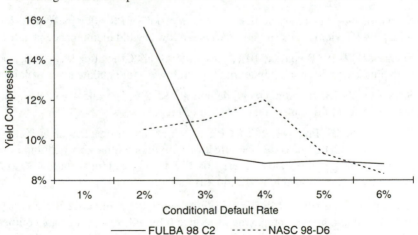

Source: First Union Securities, Inc.

E X H I B I T   37–13

CMBS IO and BBB1 Corporate Industrial Spreads

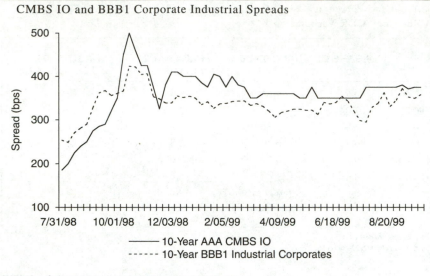

CMBS IO = Commercial mortgage-backed securities interest-only.
Source: First Union Securities, Inc.

- Scenarios 14–16: Prepay at 10%, 50%, and 100% CPR after lockout periods with plus 1% yield shock (higher rates mean lower yield maintenance penalties)

- Scenarios 17–19: Prepay at 10%, 50%, and 100% CPR after lockout periods with plus 2% yield shock (higher rates mean lower yield maintenance penalties)

- Scenarios 20–23: No prepayment, default at 1%, 2%, 3%, and 4% CDR (measures the effect of defaults in the absence of prepayments)

- Scenarios 24–27: Prepay at 100% CPR after lockout periods, default at 1%, 2%, 3%, and 4% CDR (measures the effect of defaults in situations with high prepayments and penalties); loss severity of 25% is assumed for scenarios 20 to 27 and recovery is assumed to be 12 months

In the top portion of the CMBS Sensitivity Report, we summarize these various effects. In a nutshell, high prepayments reduce IO yields unless they are compensated for with large penalties. The report and summary table allow an investor to effectively evaluate the interaction among prepayments, defaults, interest rates, loan penalty terms, and deal structures. Exhibits 37–14 and 37–15 show the sensitivity analysis results for the FULBA 98-C2 and NASC 98-D6 IOs.

CONCLUSION

Determining value in CMBS IOs may look daunting, but the challenges can be easily overcome if the investor understands the contribution of each value driver—prepayments and defaults. From the prepayment angle, the market convention of pricing an IO at 100% CPR provides a "drop" advantage that is the difference in spread using 0% and 100% CPRs. Although there is a dearth of historical data on commercial mortgage prepayments, from the little we know about the pools issued by Resolution Trust Corporation, the lifetime prepayment speeds for those pools were 20% to 30%. More important, these deals did not enjoy the type of prepayment protections found in recent deals. In this respect, we believe the market convention of pricing IOs with a 100% CPR assumption provides the potential for higher yield if the actual prepayment is below the pricing speed.

On the default front, a recent report by the American Council of Life Insurance (ACLI) shows that the delinquency rate on loans held by insurance companies fell to 0.30% in the second quarter of 1999—the lowest level in the past 34 years. Moreover, an industry study of defaults on commercial mortgages originated in the conduit loan market shows a cumulative default of 0.48% for the past 5 years. A spate of negative reports about the viability of some retail-type properties notwithstanding, we believe the short-term fundamentals on the credit front are sound.

Adjusting for the value drivers (prepayments and defaults), we believe CMBS IOs provide yield-enhancing opportunities for investors. The 10-year AAA IO spread has retraced about 2.5 standard deviations from its high in October 1998, whereas the BBB1 corporate industrial has retracted 2.6 standard deviations from its high. Exhibit 37–13 shows the CMBS IO and BBB1 corporate industrial spreads from July 31, 1998 to September 24, 1999.

E X H I B I T   37–14

CMBS Sensitivity Report for FULBA 98-C2 IO

Issue	fulb98c2
Tranche	IO
Cusip	337367ag1
Price	3 50/64
Settle Date	10/1/99
Price Date	9/28/99

Yield Curve 9/28/99

3MO	6MO	1YR	2YR	5YR	10YR	30YR
4.851	4.988	5.165	5.575	5.700	5.808	5.994

	10% CPR	50% CPR	100% CPR
Yield Change (bp) for *Prepayments* After LO,YM, and Penalties	-2	-10	-42
Yield Change (bp) for *Prepayments* During Penalty Period	-26	-72	-120
Yield Change (bp) for *Prepayments* During YM (Yield Curve Unch)	53	186	170
Yield Change (bp) for *Prepayments* During YM (Yield Curve -100bp)	57	200	193
Yield Change (bp) for *Prepayments* During YM (Yield Curve +100bp)	-15	-21	-114
Yield Change (bp) for *Prepayments* During YM (Yield Curve +200bp)	-120	-349	-499

	1% CDR	2% CDR	3% CDR	4% CDR
Yield Change (bp) for Defaults Assuming No Prepayments	-126	-261	-392	-486
Yield Change (bp) for Defaults Assuming 100 CPR During YM (Yield Curve -100 bp)	-118	-242	-377	-502

Scenario #	PrePay Assumptn Unit	Rate	Yield Shock(bps)	Default Assumptn Unit	Rate	Prepay when....	Yield	Wal	ModDur	Sprd(bp)	TSY Mat	Win Beg	Win End
1	CPR	0.00%	0	CDR	0.00%	After All Penalties	10.732	9.369	3.954	494	9.37	Nov-99	May-28
2	CPR	10.00%	0	CDR	0.00%	After All Penalties	10.708	9.354	3.950	491	9.35	Nov-99	May-28
3	CPR	50.00%	0	CDR	0.00%	After All Penalties	10.628	9.307	3.942	484	9.31	Nov-99	May-28
4	CPR	100.00%	0	CDR	0.00%	After All Penalties	10.314	9.145	3.933	452	9.15	Nov-99	Apr-28
5	CPR	10.00%	0	CDR	0.00%	After Yield Maintenance	10.473	9.123	3.895	468	9.12	Nov-99	May-28
6	CPR	50.00%	0	CDR	0.00%	After Yield Maintenance	10.012	8.821	3.835	423	8.82	Nov-99	Apr-28
7	CPR	100.00%	0	CDR	0.00%	After Yield Maintenance	9.528	8.610	3.816	**375**	8.61	Nov-99	Apr-28
8	CPR	10.00%	0	CDR	0.00%	After Lock Out Periods	11.267	8.561	3.671	549	8.56	Nov-99	May-28
9	CPR	50.00%	0	CDR	0.00%	After Lock Out Periods	12.596	7.611	3.186	684	7.61	Nov-99	Apr-28
10	CPR	100.00%	0	CDR	0.00%	After Lock Out Periods	12.435	7.358	3.050	668	7.36	Nov-99	Apr-28
11	CPR	10.00%	-100	CDR	0.00%	After Lock Out Periods	11.306	8.561	3.672	553	8.56	Nov-99	May-28
12	CPR	50.00%	-100	CDR	0.00%	After Lock Out Periods	12.731	7.611	3.175	697	7.61	Nov-99	Apr-28
13	CPR	100.00%	-100	CDR	0.00%	After Lock Out Periods	12.664	7.358	3.028	691	7.36	Nov-99	Apr-28

14	CPR	10.00%	100	CDR	0.00%	After Lock Out Periods	10.586	8.561	3.748	481	8.56	Nov-99	May-28
15	CPR	50.00%	100	CDR	0.00%	After Lock Out Periods	10.519	7.611	3.419	476	7.61	Nov-99	Apr-28
16	CPR	100.00%	100	CDR	0.00%	After Lock Out Periods	9.596	7.358	3.400	385	7.36	Nov-99	Apr-28
17	CPR	10.00%	200	CDR	0.00%	After Lock Out Periods	9.534	8.561	3.852	376	8.56	Nov-99	May-28
18	CPR	50.00%	200	CDR	0.00%	After Lock Out Periods	7.238	7.611	3.812	148	7.61	Nov-99	Apr-28
19	CPR	100.00%	200	CDR	0.00%	After Lock Out Periods	5.746	7.358	3.979	-1	7.36	Nov-99	Apr-28
20	CPR	0.00%	0	CDR	1.00%	After All Penalties	9.472	8.948	3.926	369	8.95	Nov-99	May-29
21	CPR	0.00%	0	CDR	2.00%	After All Penalties	8.120	8.557	3.865	234	8.56	Nov-99	May-29
22	CPR	0.00%	0	CDR	3.00%	After All Penalties	6.814	8.193	3.800	104	8.19	Nov-99	May-29
23	CPR	0.00%	0	CDR	4.00%	After All Penalties	5.873	7.855	3.834	11	7.85	Nov-99	May-29
24	CPR	100.00%	-100	CDR	1.00%	After Lock Out Periods	11.486	7.084	3.022	574	7.08	Nov-99	Apr-29
25	CPR	100.00%	-100	CDR	2.00%	After Lock Out Periods	10.240	6.826	3.001	450	6.83	Nov-99	Apr-29
26	CPR	100.00%	-100	CDR	3.00%	After Lock Out Periods	8.894	6.584	2.960	316	6.58	Nov-99	Apr-29
27	CPR	100.00%	-100	CDR	4.00%	After Lock Out Periods	7.647	6.355	2.942	192	6.35	Nov-99	Apr-29

CMBS = Commercial mortgage-backed securities; IO: interest-only.
Source: First Union Securities, Inc.

EXHIBIT 37-15

CMBS Sensitivity Report for NASC 1998-D6 IO

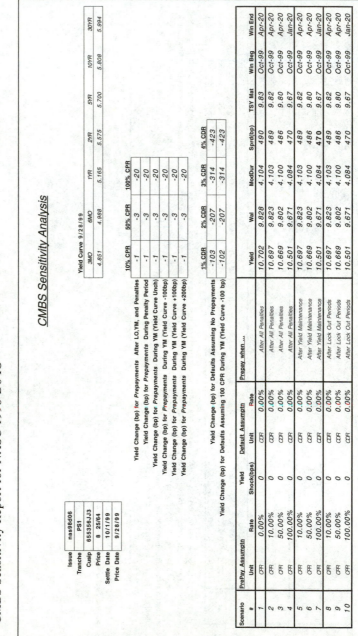

CMBS Sensitivity Analysis

Issue	nas98d06
Tranche	PS1
Cusip	655356JJ3
Price	8 25/64
Settle Date	10/1/99
Price Date	9/28/99

Yield Curve 9/28/99

3MO	6MO	1YR	2YR	5YR	10YR	30YR
4.851	4.988	5.165	5.575	5.700	5.808	5.994

	10% CPR	50% CPR	100% CPR
Yield Change (bp) for *Prepayments* After LO,YM, and Penalties			
Yield Change (bp) for *Prepayments* During Penalty Period			
Yield Change (bp) for *Prepayments* During YM (Yield Curve Unch)	-1	-3	-20
Yield Change (bp) for *Prepayments* During YM (Yield Curve -100bp)	-1	-3	-20
Yield Change (bp) for *Prepayments* During YM (Yield Curve +100bp)	-1	-3	-20
Yield Change (bp) for *Prepayments* During YM (Yield Curve +200bp)	-1	-3	-20
	-1	-3	-20
	-1	-3	-20

	1% CDR	2% CDR	3% CDR	4% CDR
Yield Change (bp) for Defaults Assuming No Prepayments	-103	-207	-314	-423
Yield Change (bp) for Defaults Assuming 100 CPR During YM (Yield Curve -100 bp)	-102	-207	-314	-423

Scenario #	PrePay Assumptn Unit	Rate	Yield Shock(bps)	Default Assumptn Unit	Rate	Prepay when	Yield	Wal	ModDur	Sprd(bp)	TSY Mat	Win Beg	Win End
1	CPR	0.00%	0	CDR	0.00%	After All Penalties	10.702	9.828	4.104	490	9.83	Oct-99	Apr-20
2	CPR	10.00%	0	CDR	0.00%	After All Penalties	10.697	9.823	4.103	489	9.82	Oct-99	Apr-20
3	CPR	50.00%	0	CDR	0.00%	After All Penalties	10.669	9.802	4.100	486	9.80	Oct-99	Apr-20
4	CPR	100.00%	0	CDR	0.00%	After All Penalties	10.501	9.671	4.084	470	9.67	Oct-99	Jan-20
5	CPR	10.00%	0	CDR	0.00%	After Yield Maintenance	10.697	9.823	4.103	489	9.82	Oct-99	Apr-20
6	CPR	50.00%	0	CDR	0.00%	After Yield Maintenance	10.669	9.802	4.100	486	9.80	Oct-99	Apr-20
7	CPR	100.00%	0	CDR	0.00%	After Yield Maintenance	10.501	9.671	4.084	470	9.67	Oct-99	Jan-20
8	CPR	10.00%	0	CDR	0.00%	After Lock Out Periods	10.697	9.823	4.103	489	9.82	Oct-99	Apr-20
9	CPR	50.00%	0	CDR	0.00%	After Lock Out Periods	10.669	9.802	4.100	486	9.80	Oct-99	Apr-20
10	CPR	100.00%	0	CDR	0.00%	After Lock Out Periods	10.501	9.671	4.084	470	9.67	Oct-99	Jan-20

11	CPR	10.00%	-100	CDR	0.00%	After Lock Out Periods	10.697	9.823	4.103	489	9.82	Oct-99	Apr-20
12	CPR	50.00%	-100	CDR	0.00%	After Lock Out Periods	10.669	9.802	4.100	486	9.80	Oct-99	Apr-20
13	CPR	100.00%	-100	CDR	0.00%	After Lock Out Periods	10.501	9.671	4.084	470	9.67	Oct-99	Jan-20
14	CPR	10.00%	100	CDR	0.00%	After Lock Out Periods	10.697	9.823	4.103	489	9.82	Oct-99	Apr-20
15	CPR	50.00%	100	CDR	0.00%	After Lock Out Periods	10.669	9.802	4.100	486	9.80	Oct-99	Apr-20
16	CPR	100.00%	100	CDR	0.00%	After Lock Out Periods	10.501	9.671	4.084	470	9.67	Oct-99	Jan-20
17	CPR	10.00%	200	CDR	0.00%	After Lock Out Periods	10.697	9.823	4.103	489	9.82	Oct-99	Apr-20
18	CPR	50.00%	200	CDR	0.00%	After Lock Out Periods	10.669	9.802	4.100	486	9.80	Oct-99	Apr-20
19	CPR	100.00%	200	CDR	0.00%	After Lock Out Periods	10.501	9.671	4.084	470	9.67	Oct-99	Jan-20
20	CPR	0.00%	0	CDR	1.00%	After All Penalties	9.676	9.399	4.089	388	9.40	Oct-99	Apr-20
21	CPR	0.00%	0	CDR	2.00%	After All Penalties	8.629	8.997	4.076	284	9.00	Oct-99	Apr-20
22	CPR	0.00%	0	CDR	3.00%	After All Penalties	7.561	8.618	4.061	178	8.62	Oct-99	Apr-20
23	CPR	0.00%	0	CDR	4.00%	After All Penalties	6.468	8.262	4.043	70	8.26	Oct-99	Apr-20
24	CPR	100.00%	-100	CDR	1.00%	After Lock Out Periods	9.477	9.257	4.070	368	9.26	Oct-99	Apr-20
25	CPR	100.00%	-100	CDR	2.00%	After Lock Out Periods	8.430	8.867	4.057	265	8.87	Oct-99	Apr-20
26	CPR	100.00%	-100	CDR	3.00%	After Lock Out Periods	7.360	8.501	4.041	158	8.50	Oct-99	Apr-20
27	CPR	100.00%	-100	CDR	4.00%	After Lock Out Periods	6.266	8.155	4.022	50	8.15	Oct-99	Apr-20

This is for your information only and is not an offer to sell, or a solicitation of an offer to buy, the securities or instruments mentioned. The information has been obtained or derived from sources believed by us to be reliable, but we do not represent that it is accurate or complete. Any opinions or estimates contained in this information constitute our judgment as of this date and are subject to change without notice. First Union Securities, Inc. or its affiliates may provide advice or may from time to time acquire, hold, or sell a position in the securities mentioned herein. First Union Securities, Inc. is a subsidiary of First Union Corporation and is a member of the NASD and SIPC. First Union Securities, Inc. is a separate and distinct entity from its affiliated banks and thrifts.

CMBS = Commercial mortgage-backed securities; IO: interest-only.
Source: First Union Securities, Inc.

CHAPTER **38**

CMBS COLLATERAL PERFORMANCE

Philip O. Obazee
Vice President
Quantitative Research
First Union Securities, Inc.

There have been several industry reports on commercial mortgage-backed securities (CMBS) default studies and collateral performance analysis. One such report updates Mark P. Snyderman's default analysis of commercial mortgages originated by insurance companies.[1] This report found that commercial mortgages held by insurance companies showed a 10-year cumulative default rate ranging from 9% for 1997 originations to 28% for those originating in 1986. These cumulative default rates translate into 1% and 4% conditional default rates (CDRs), respectively, for 10-year collateral. A quarterly report issued by the American Council of Life Insurance shows the delinquency rate on loans held by insurance companies fell to 0.30% in the second quarter of 1999—the lowest level in 34 years (Exhibit 38–1).

In this chapter, we review defaults in conduit loans, attempt to shed some light on how to monitor the frequency of default, and examine how the value of CMBS tranches are affected by scenarios related to the frequency of defaults and loss severity.

DEFAULTS IN CONDUIT LOANS

Other industry reports have focused on deals that originated in the conduit loan market. One of these reports, which is based on analysis that tests for the statistical significance of its findings, showed a cumulative default rate of 0.78% on a loan basis and 0.48% on a balance basis for commercial mortgages originated and securitized from 1995 to 1999. Furthermore, this report follows the lead of a 1998

Parts of this chapter are adapted from Philip O. Obazee, "Valuation and Analysis of Credit-Sensitive CMBS Tranches," in Frank J. Fabozzi (ed.), *Investing in Commercial Mortgage-Backed Securities* (New Hope, PA: Frank J. Fabozzi Associates, 2001).

1. Howard Esaki, Steven L'Heureux, and Mark P. Snyderman, "Commercial Mortgage Defaults," *Real Estate Finance* (Spring 1999).

E X H I B I T   38–1

Life Insurance Companies' Commercial Mortgage Delinquencies

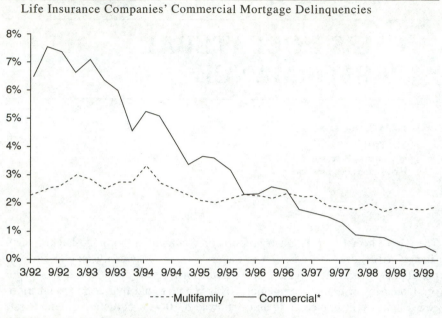

*Apartments, retail, office, industrial, hotel and motel, mixed use, and others.
Source: American Council of Life Insurance.

Fitch IBCA study that cited the factors discussed below as statistically significant in explaining defaults.[2]

Loan to Value and Debt Service Coverage Ratio

The incidence of default rises with the loan-to-value ratio (LTV); that is, if all other factors are held constant, the probability of default for a loan increases as the LTV increases, but the increases are not equal. For example, an increase in the original LTV from 60% to 70% resulted in about a 50% rise in the probability of default from 0.54% to 0.80% CDR. An increase in the LTV from 50% to 60% raised the probability of default by 0.18%, whereas increasing the LTV from 80% to 90% boosted the probability of default by 0.58%.

---

2. Rodney Pelleiter and Andrew Rudenstein, "Trends in Commercial Mortgage Default Rate and Loss Severity—1997 Update."

Unlike the LTV, where the probability of default increases as the LTV rises, the incidence of default is a decreasing function of the debt-to-service coverage ratio (DSCR). However, the relationship between the DSCR and the probability of default is weaker than the relationship between the LTV and default. One explanation is that borrowers have an incentive to negotiate with lenders about payment rescheduling and debt restructuring, but that incentive wanes quickly when the LTV is significantly greater than 1.0.

Age

The incidence of default increases with age. On a loan count basis, the aging curve is steeper in the 12- to 24-month range with the CDR rising from 0.2% to 1.0% and remaining at 1.0% thereafter.

Property Type

A 1999 Fitch IBCA study examined 9,760 commercial mortgage loans in 69 conduit deals issued since 1993 and found that loans secured by hotel properties have the highest cumulative default rate, at 1.07%, followed by multifamily loans at 0.81%.[3] Exhibit 38–2 show the defaults by property type.

---

3. Mary Stuart C. Freydberg and Keith Lee, "CMBS Conduit Loan Defaults by Property Type," *Fitch IBCA,* April 6, 1999.

E X H I B I T   38–2

Commercial Mortgage Default by Property Type

Property Type	No. of Loans	% of Total Loans	No. of Defaults	% of Total Defaults
Multifamily	3,078	33.2	25	50.0
Retail	2,373	25.6	7	14.0
Other/Mixed	1,534	16.6	4	8.0
Office	905	9.8	3	6.0
Hotel	839	9.1	9	18.0
Industrial	535	5.8	2	4.0
Total	**9,264**	**100.0**	**50**	**100.0**

Source: Fitch IBCA.

Coupon Spread

The difference between the loan rate and the average interest rate of a loan cohort is a determinant of default. A loan cohort is defined in terms of origination month, property type, and loan size. In the home equity loan market, for example, the initial coupon spread is used as an indicator of involuntary prepayment. In theory, borrowers willing to pay a high initial credit spread have weak credit histories, which implies an extended period of credit curing. Therefore, they are assigned a higher probability of default—a higher percentage of the standard default assumption (SDA) curve. In contrast, commercial mortgage loans with a higher-than-average coupon in a cohort reflect the increased likelihood of default.

Loan Size

Large loans have lower default probabilities than small loans. For example, an industry study showed that the probability of default for a $2 million loan was 2.5 times greater than for a $20 million loan with the same characteristics. One explanation is that the management quality and control for borrowers seeking larger loans are far superior to those for borrowers of small loans.

Amortization Schedule

The conventional wisdom that the quicker a loan amortizes, the lower the default risk was not supported by this report. A loan with a 240-month amortization schedule has about 35% greater probability of default than a similar loan with a 360-month schedule.

Loan Underwriting

Bank-originated collateral exhibited a better credit performance than non-bank-originated collateral. An industry study showed that, on average, bank-originated collateral has a 0.27% default rate on a balance basis compared with a rate of 0.56% for nonbank conduits. The report attributes the difference in performance to the banks' superior underwriting standards. This finding that bank-originated loans have better collateral performance than non-bank-originated loans has sparked so much debate among the investment banking community that some Wall Street analysts have been mining databases and surveillance reports trying to refute this evidence.

One such recent report from a Wall Street firm concluded some bank-contributed loans have a higher delinquency rate than some non-bank-contributed collateral. This report found that, for example, the loans contributed by First Union National Bank had a delinquency rate of 1.47% compared with 0.12% for loans contributed by Nomura Securities, Inc. First Union's high delinquency rate is attributable to retail properties, particularly Service Merchandise Co., Inc., which filed for bankruptcy protection in March 1999. Retail property in general continues to exhibit greater uncertainty because of concern about the impact of an economic downturn on supply and demand, the realignment of the retail industry as a result of the internet revolution, and changes in personal income growth and spending. Although we are not suggesting a direct correlation between industry categories and property-type performance, Standard and Poor's reports a default rate of 12.7% in the consumer-service sector for the period 1981–1998. A large percentage of the borrowers in the consumer-service sector are tenants of retail properties. Moreover, recent bankruptcies in the retail industry, for example, Hechinger Co., Caldor Corp., and JumboSports, Inc., have increased the overall default frequency in CMBS transactions.

Although we share this Wall Street firm's enthusiasm for sensitizing investors to the relationship between the quality of loan underwriting and the frequency of default, we believe the report's results are statistically biased to the time period the data covers. In our view, given that conduit origination came of age in 1995 and that real estate markets have been strong, richer statistical data is too sparse to conclusively support the quality of loan underwriting claims. That said, we strongly believe that the quality of loan underwriting should improve as surveillance efforts and market discipline increase. Moreover, we believe the market's perception that bank-originated collateral would, on average, exhibit a better credit performance than non-bank-originated loans is a valid extrapolative assessment, based on the history of commercial banks and their expertise in credit management.

More important, we believe that although the frequency of default is a part of the value equation, we should not lose sight of the most significant part—loss severity. Indeed, an investor who purchases CMBS holds a long position in noncallable bonds and short positions in both call and default put options. For selling the options, the investor is compensated in the form of enhanced coupon payments. A larger share of this enhanced coupon is attributable to the default option, which gives the borrower the right to put the property to the trust. If the borrower exercises this option, the investor looks at how much could be recovered by liquidating the property, in other words, the recovery rate risk. This risk is inversely related to loss severity and apparently explains why property value and the LTV are given primary roles by rating agencies and B-piece investors.

The LTV is used to measure the likelihood of default as well as the potential loss severity after foreclosure and liquidation. The LTV is the ratio between the loan amount and the property value. The property value is estimated as the stabilized net operating income divided by the appropriate capitalization rate, which is the minimum acceptable rate of return for the level of cash flow variability inherent in the property type. Which capitalization rate to use is a thorny question. However, whatever rate is chosen, it must reflect the operating and financial risks of the property type. Operating risk depends to a large extent on the nature of the property type and to a lesser degree on the operating leverage—the mix of fixed and variable costs. In contrast, financial risk depends principally on financial leverage—the mix of debt to equity. By approaching the analysis this way, we see that LTV estimation is built on two fundamental principles: incremental benefits (identification and estimation of the cash flow) and risk-return trade-off (consideration of the risk when determining a

E X H I B I T   38–3

Change in Market Value by Property Type*

Property Type	Change in Market Value
Office	−50.2%
Industrial	−33.6%
Retail	−26.4%
Apartment	−16.6%

*Change from the first quarter of 1986 to the third quarter of 1995.
Source: National Council of Real Estate Investment Fiduciaries (NCREIF) and Standard & Poor's Corp.

required rate of return). We make this point to emphasize the importance of property value and the LTV in assessing credit risk as well as to foreshadow our argument that the recovery rate matters more than the frequency of default. In Exhibit 38–3, we show the changes in market value for different property types as reported by the National Council of Real Estate Investment Fiduciaries (NCREIF).

The NCREIF data indicate that the value of office property declined 50.2% from the first quarter of 1986 to the third quarter of 1995. These figures reflect changes in market value at the national level and the results would vary from one local economy to another. This past performance further reinforces our argument that property value and recovery rate are more important to the credit quality of CMBS bonds, at least for most investors, than a temporal phenomenon such as the frequency of defaults.

MONITORING THE FREQUENCY OF DEFAULTS

A common technique used by investors and rating agencies to model the frequency of defaults is called *survival analysis*. This survival analysis model relates a credit rating probability of default to factors such as the original credit rating, the current rating, and the historical volatility of the credit quality based on rating actions (upgrades and downgrades). However, investors who do not have access to this analytic framework look to the credit rating and rating agencies when assessing the probability of default risk. Rating agencies continually monitor a deal to determine if the current rating correctly reflects the credit risk. The rating agencies and investors use the sources of information discussed below.

Trustee
The reports provided by the trustee contain transaction-level information including certificate balances, collateral balances, cumulative realized losses, delinquencies, and cumulative advances. The trustee depends on the master and primary servicers for this information.

Master and Primary Servicers

By mandate, there is only one master servicer in a deal who is responsible for supervising the primary servicer while the loan is performing. The primary servicer collects loan payments, operating financial statements, and other information specified in the pool and servicing agreement.

Special Servicer

Troubled loans and loans 60 to 90 days delinquent are transferred to a special servicer. The effectiveness of the special servicer is reflected in the ability to maximize the proceeds from troubled loans.

Borrowers and Property Management Companies

On single-transaction deals, borrowers and property management companies are good sources of information. Rating agencies review information from these sources as well as other pertinent information to determine whether a rating alert or action is required. A rating action would result in either an affirmation, an upgrade, or a downgrade. As a rule of thumb, because of the sequential nature of the CMBS transactions, senior tranches are more likely to be upgraded than lower-rated classes. Moreover, we note a correlation between credit quality and default remoteness; that is, the higher the credit rating of a bond, the lower the probability of default. Conversely, the lower the original rating on the bond, the shorter the time to default.

Affirmation

Most rating actions are affirmations of the existing rating, which indicate that no material change has occurred in the rating agency's assessment of the probability of a tranche's default.

Upgrade

The key determinant of upgrade is the current level of credit enhancement. In addition, rating agencies also consider the diversification and concentration of the remaining loans in a deal in determining whether to issue an upgrade. As the loan pays down and realized losses are low or nonexistent, the credit enhancement in the senior tranches will increase. Transactions upgraded by a rating agency include those without prepayment lockouts, those with no or low prepayment penalties, and those with some seasoned loans. From the first quarter of 1993 to the third quarter of 1999, Fitch IBCA upgraded 363 tranches with a total of $9.7 billion.

Downgrade

Unlike upgrades driven by increases in the level of credit enhancement, downgrades are caused by decreases in the credit enhancement that result from losses. High delinquency rates that lead to decreases in projected credit enhancement could, in somewhat rare cases, result in a tranche being downgraded. Fitch IBCA downgraded 47 tranches totaling $1.3 billion from the first quarter of 1993 to the third quarter of 1999. The ratio of downgrades to upgrades was 0.12.

DEFAULT RATE, LOSS SEVERITY, AND VALUATION ISSUES

The price of credit-related transactions generally incorporates the credit rating. The credit rating reflects the rating agency's assessments of the likelihood of default. For each rated class, an applicable credit spread provides information about the following:

• Likelihood of default

• Expected recovery rate in the event of default

• Market credit risk premium

Dividing credit spread into its various components allows us to write the following equation for the price of a credit-sensitive bond.

Price of a zero-coupon credit-sensitive bond = Price of a risk-free bond with the same maturity (or average life)

    − Loss severity × Adjusted probability of default

    × Price of risk-free bond with the same maturity (or average life)

   The loss severity is equal to 1.0 minus the recovery rate. Pricing a security in the absence of arbitrage opportunity requires that a credit-sensitive bond trade at a value less than its risk-free counterparts. This means that the credit-sensitive bond's yield will be higher than that of a corresponding risk-free yield (e.g., Treasury). The difference in yields is the credit spread. In the equation, the value of the credit-sensitive bond equals the value of a risk-free bond of the same average life minus the adjustment for the default risk. This adjustment is the product of the adjusted probability of default, loss severity, and the value of a risk-free bond of the same average life. So, the equation expresses a credit event as the product of the frequency of default and loss severity. Another way of interpreting the equation is that the value of a credit-sensitive bond is the expected value of all its possible cash flows (for both default and no default scenarios) discounted at the risk-free rate.

   Under the pricing rule that makes the equation consistent, one cannot value securities using the objective probability but must price them using a normalized probability, that is, the equivalent probability measure. This measure is the product of a risk-adjustment factor for the default risk premium and the objective probability. For a given frequency of default associated with a bond, the market consensus—the risk adjustment factor for the default risk premium—must be taken into consideration. We observed that when valuing a bond, the correct probability measure is the equivalent (risk-neutral) measure, whereas in scenario analysis the objective probability is more appropriate.

   In short, the frequency of default must be adjusted based on the market's prevailing default premium. For example, in October 1998 when CMBS spreads widened, the frequency of default was not necessarily increasing but the adjustment for the default premium was. The market determines the adjustment factor for the default risk premium.

Could this explain why bank-originated CMBS are fairly priced in the market? The market may be looking at bank-originated deals, recognizing banks' conservative credit culture and their expertise in credit management and then correctly adjusting risk for the default risk premium. On the contrary, some researchers are working on theories using objective default probabilities with no adjustment, and then questioning why bank-originated deals are spread tightly and challenging the authenticity of market levels.

The most important points in valuing credit-related instruments such as CMBS are as follows:

- The frequency of default does not directly enter the equation because it must be adjusted as a function of the default risk premium.

- The loss severity, which is 1.0 minus the recovery rate, enters the equation directly.

Invoking Nobel-laureate Paul Samuelson's famous dictum, "a dollar is a dollar," a CMBS is a bond, and we argue that a CMBS's value is the expected discounted cash flow adjusted for the risks priced in the market. For CMBS, aside from the interest rate and prepayment risks, the other inherent risks are the default rate and the recovery rate. For these risks, there are two market variables—credit rating and credit spread—that contain the information necessary to price CMBS. Moreover, the frequency of default enters into the equation indirectly, whereas loss severity enters the equation directly. This leads us to conclude that the frequency of default matters, but how much is recovered in the event of a default matters more for most investors.

As an example, we considered the mezzanine tranche of FULBA 1998-C2, in particular, class C, rated A or A2, and the result of our analysis is as follows:

Case 1   At a loss severity of 0%, the yield to maturity increases as the CDR rises and the weighted average life (WAL) decreases (see Exhibit 38–4).

Case 2   Holding the CDR at the same level, for example at 2%, the yield to maturity decreases as the loss severity increases and the WAL also increases (see Exhibit 38–5). Note the "hockey stick" shapes, a common feature of structures with embedded optionality.

Case 3   Holding loss severity at the same level, for example, 35%, the yield to maturity decreases as the CDR increases and the WAL also increases (see Exhibit 38–6).

Exhibits 38–7 and 38–8 show the sensitivity of yield and the WAL to changes in the CDR and loss severity. Exhibit 38–9 shows the yield compression resulting from these changes.

EXHIBIT 38–4

Change in Yield and Weighted Average Life Varying the Conditional Default Rate*

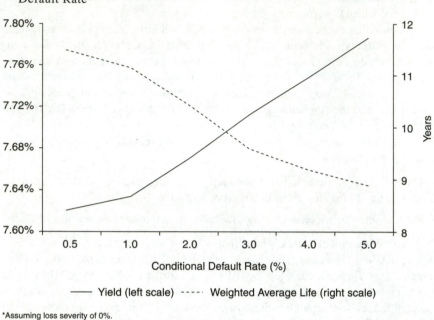

*Assuming loss severity of 0%.
Source: First Union Securities, Inc.

EXHIBIT 38–5

Change in Yield and Weighted Average Life Varying Loss Severity*

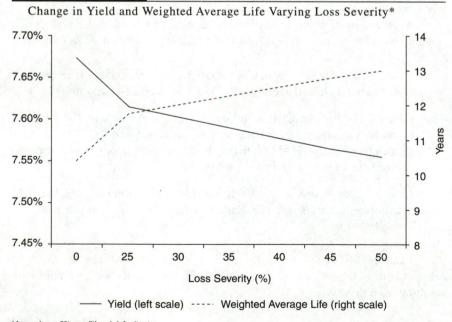

*Assuming a 2% conditional default rate.
Source: First Union Securities, Inc.

Change in the Yield and Weighted Average Life Varying the Conditional
Default Rate*

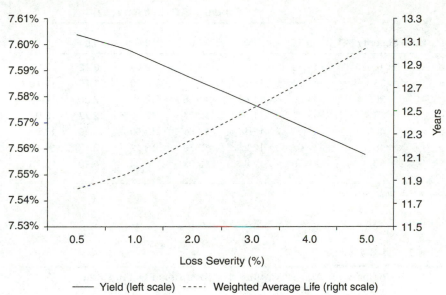

*Assuming 35% loss severity.
Source: First Union Securities, Inc.

E X H I B I T 38–7

Sensitivity of Yield to Change in CDR and Loss Severity

	Conditional Default Rate (%)					
Loss Severity (%)	0.5	1.0	2.0	3.0	4.0	5.0
0	7.62	7.64	7.67	7.72	7.75	7.77
25	7.61	7.61	7.61	7.61	7.61	7.61
30	7.61	7.60	7.60	7.59	7.59	7.58
35	7.60	7.60	7.59	7.58	7.57	7.56
40	7.60	7.59	7.58	7.56	7.55	7.54
45	7.60	7.59	7.57	7.55	7.54	7.51
50	7.59	7.58	7.56	7.55	7.52	7.46

Source: First Union Securities, Inc.

EXHIBIT 38-8

Sensitivity of Weighted Average Life to Change in CDR and Loss Severity

Loss Severity (%)	Conditional Default Rate (%)					
	0.5	1.0	2.0	3.0	4.0	5.0
0	11.45	11.14	10.48	9.69	9.22	8.89
25	11.74	11.73	11.71	11.70	11.70	11.70
30	11.80	11.86	11.98	12.11	12.25	12.40
35	11.87	11.99	12.24	12.50	12.77	13.03
40	11.93	12.12	12.51	12.90	13.20	13.51
45	12.00	12.26	12.79	13.19	13.47	14.69
50	12.06	12.40	13.03	13.34	14.20	16.76

Source: First Union Securities, Inc.

EXHIBIT 38-9

Yield Compression Matrix Varying the Conditional Default Rate
and Loss Severity

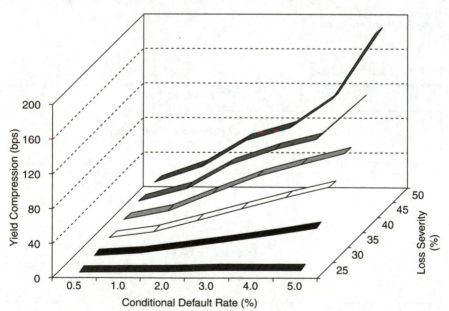

Source: First Union Securities, Inc.

SERVICER'S FLEXIBILITY AND LOSS SEVERITY

When a loan is defaulted, it can either be restructured or foreclosed. If a loan is foreclosed, the property value and the foreclosure and liquidation costs are important determinants of the recovery rate. Whether a loan is restructured or foreclosed, the servicer's effectiveness and flexibility are important in working out successful outcomes for the defaulted loans. Some of the factors that contribute to loss severity are as follows:

- Foreclosure process (state laws and ownership structure)
- Ease of sale (property type, condition of the property, and location)
- Foreclosure and liquidation costs (legal fees, carrying costs, improvement costs, and commissions)

The amount recovered in the event of default is the cash flow of the property estimated over the foreclosure period minus the foreclosure and liquidation costs. An important role for the servicer is to maximize the cash flow from a defaulted loan. In performing this role, the servicer has the flexibility to decide whether modifying or foreclosing the loan would maximize returns for the stakeholders. The servicer's flexibility in modifying a defaulted loan is crucial to loss mitigation. For example, the 1998 Fitch IBCA study showed a slight trend toward lower losses when servicers had more flexibility. Servicers can modify a defaulted loan in the following ways:

- Adjust the interest rate and amortization schedule
- Extend the loan maturity
- Forgive interest or principal
- Change other terms of the loan

CONCLUSION

It is probably too early to tell how conduit-originated collateral will perform over real estate cycles. A careful review of surveillance reports is one way of keeping a scorecard on collateral performance. However, the transitory nature of the frequency of default should be acknowledged. Moreover, we should not lose sight of the fact that credit-event risk is the product of frequency of defaults and loss severity. In market valuations, the frequency of default enters the equation adjusted for the default premium, whereas loss severity (1.0 minus the recovery rate) enters the equation without adjustment. The adjustment to the frequency of default reflects market consensus about the default risk premium. The product of the adjusted frequency of default and loss severity is responsible for the magnitude and variability of credit spread.

NON-U.S. MORTGAGE-BACKED PRODUCTS

CHAPTER 39

MORTGAGE-BACKED SECURITIES IN GERMANY

Alexander Batchvarov
Managing Director
Merrill Lynch & Co.

Ganesh Rajendra
Vice President
Merrill Lynch & Co.

Xavier De Pauw
Assistant Vice President
Merrill Lynch & Co.

With 37 million dwellings in 1997, or approximately one-fifth of the total dwellings in the European Union (e.g., 21.4% in 1995), Germany has the greatest number of dwellings.[1] The level of owner occupation in Germany was 40% in 1993, according to the most recent information available from the European Mortgage Federation (EMF). This is by far the lowest level in Europe where the average level of owner occupation is 64%[2] and the highest is 80% (Ireland). Germany has the most extensive private rented sector in Europe (40% of dwellings) and a well-developed social rented sector. Similar to the Netherlands, Sweden, and the United Kingdom, mortgages in Germany are used not only to finance owner-occupied and private rented dwellings but also to finance social rented dwellings.

The high number of dwellings and the use of mortgages in every part of the housing sector (including the social rented one) contribute to the fact that Germany's outstanding mortgage loans account for more than 50% of its GDP (50.9% in 1997, EMF). This level is less than in Denmark (65%), the Netherlands (60%), the United Kingdom (57%), and Sweden (57%) but much higher than in other European countries, which have an average residential mortgage to GDP ratio of 21%.

In this chapter we discuss the MBS market in Germany. Specifically, we cover the mortgage lenders, mortgage products, indicators of mortgage loan performance, housing market trends, the regulatory framework for some MBS transactions.

---

1. All data in this paragraph was sourced from *Hypostat 1987–1997*, a 1998 publication of the European Mortgage Federation (EMF).
2. Estimates based on EMF data, 1998 (see, footnote 1).

MORTGAGE LENDERS AND MORTGAGE PRODUCTS

Germany boasts a well-developed housing market with a large number of mortgage-lending institutions that offer a variety of mortgage products to meet the needs of their respective client bases. Several types of financial institutions account for the large chunk of the mortgage business: mortgage banks, *Bausparkassen,* universal banks, savings banks, and cooperatives.

Mortgage Lenders

The four main groups of mortgage lenders are described below.

Private and Public *Pfandbriefe-Institutes* (Private mortgage banks and public sector banks)

Private mortgage banks are subject to the restrictions of Germany's Mortgage Banking Law, and like the public mortgage banks they are entitled to issue *Pfandbriefe*—mortgage bonds. Mortgage banks are sometimes referred to as capital market institutions because they mainly finance themselves by selling *Pfandbriefe* on the financial markets.[3]

Mortgage banks are also called *Realkreditinstitute* because they focus exclusively on granting real estate loans *Objektkredite* contrary to other banks, which issue loans with more diverse purposes *Personalkredite.* The *Objektkredite* are granted mainly based on the characteristics of the property and benefits from a mortgage—a lien on the property in case the borrower defaults. *Personalkredite* are personal loans, which are granted while taking into consideration the characteristics of the borrower (income, employment, etc.) and can be used for different purposes; usually, they are not linked to a mortgage.

Mortgage banks have almost no branches of their own, but sell their products through intermediaries. Similarly to mortgage banks, public banks and central Giro institutions can finance first ranking mortgages through mortgage bonds. However, their main financing instruments are regular bonds and deposits of customers, more specifically institutional investors and credit institutions.

Private and Public *Bausparkassen*

Bausparkassen are a closed system mainly financed by the deposits of their customers and by savings certificates. Potential house buyers agree to save at an interest rate below the market rate in order to take out a below-market-rate loan in the future. *Bausparkassen* function in a way similar to United Kingdom mutuals.

---

3. *Pfandbriefe* can finance mortgages with a loan-to-value (LTV) ratio up to 60%. In practice, the total financing of a property can be well in excess of 60%, but then this excess above 60% is financed with instruments other than *Pfandbriefe.*

Universal Credit Institutions (savings banks, *Landesbanken*, commercial banks, and cooperative banks)

The savings banks and the *Landesbanken* are public law institutions. The former banks have a mandate to promote savings. The latter play a threefold role: that of a central clearing bank to their savings banks (*Sparkassen*), a house bank to their respective federal state (*Bundesland*), and a wholesale commercial bank.

The *Landesbanken* and the savings banks benefit from public sector support mechanisms of *Anstaltslast* (a maintenance obligation) and *Gewährträgerhaftung* (a statutory guarantee on the bank's liabilities to its clients).

- *Anstaltlast* is a guarantee of the owner of the *Landesbank* (the federal government or one of the federal states' government) to support the bank at all times.

- *Gewärträgerhaftung* is a more traditional guarantee on the claims against the bank. The government owning the bank assumes the claims against the banks in case of bank's default. In case of a privatization of such a bank, the government will grandfather the liabilities created during its ownership.

Compared to the savings banks, German credit cooperatives are more numerous but much smaller on average. They are usually located in rural areas.

The three *Grossbanken* (Commerzbank AG, Dresdner Bank AG, and Deutsche Bank AG) constitute the group of private sector commercial banks and hold approximately 10% of the mortgage market. Another major player was introduced in the market on September 1, 1998, when the Bayerische Hypo- und Vereisbank (HVB) was created. This entity resulted from the merger of Bayerische Hypotheken und Wechsel Bank with Bayerische Vereinsbank and is now the largest mortgage lender in Europe.

Insurance Companies

Insurance companies issue mortgage loans that are linked to life assurance contracts. Their main source of funding comes from insurance premiums.

Market Shares According to the Type of Lender

Because there is such a wide variety of lenders in Germany, no one type of institution dominates the mortgage market. The mortgage banks and the savings banks are the only two groups that have a market share larger than 20%.

As we can see by comparing Exhibits 39–1 and 39–2, the EMF and the Bundesbank classify the financial institutions in a slightly different manner. Data from the Bundesbank gives a more detailed view on the market shares of different lenders. Its category real estate credit institutions (*Realkreditinstitute*) groups only the "pure" mortgage banks. Mortgage banks with diversified financial and business activities are included in other categories.

The savings banks specialized in the construction (*Bausparkassen*) and cooperative sectors are included in both exhibits. Their market shares seem to remain more or less stable over the period from 1997 to the end of 1998.

EXHIBIT 39–1

1997 Market Shares by Mortgage Originator, EMF Classification

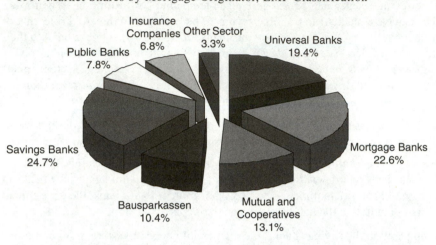

Source: European Mortgage Federation.

EXHIBIT 39–2

Market Shares, Bundesbank Classification

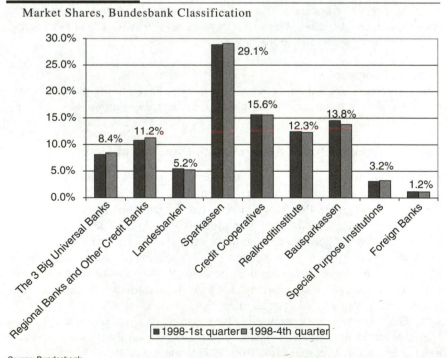

Source: Bundesbank.

MORTGAGE PRODUCTS AND CHARACTERISTICS

In the following section, we discuss the various mortgage products and their characteristics.

Mortgage Products

The type of products available to mortgage borrowers in Germany depends very much on the type of lending institution the borrower approaches.

Mortgage Banks
Products created by mortgage banks include:

- Loans for a term of 25 or 30 years   Initially the interest rate is fixed for 5 to 15 years. At the expiration of the initial term, the interest rate is renegotiated. If the loan-to-value (LTV) ratio is less than 60%, the mortgage can be financed through the issuance of *Pfandbriefe.*

- Variable-rate mortgages   Since borrowers carry all the interest rate risk, they are allowed to prepay the loan 3 months after giving the bank notice of their intention to do so.

Savings Banks
Products created by savings banks include:

- Loans extended by *Bausparkassen,* typically with a term of 7 to 16 years. As mentioned earlier, though, they require a future borrower to save during an average period of 6 to 7 years before drawing a loan.

- Variable-rate loans as well as fixed-rate loans with a term of up to 5 years.

Credit Cooperatives
Credit cooperatives and commercial banks issue loans with the same characteristics as the loans granted by the savings banks but not necessarily with such a short term.

Insurance Companies
Insurance companies issue mortgage loans in conjunction with a life assurance policy.

Mortgage Loan Characteristics

In addition to the maturity and the interest rate of the mortgage loans, we stress three additional loan characteristics, which to a large degree determine the servicing of those loans. Lenders resort to a number of debt ratios in order to determine the likelihood of default of a (potential) borrower.

First, the *LTV* ratio determines borrowers' motivation (willingness) to pay back their loans even when facing financial difficulties. The normal LTV ratio in Germany is between 60% and 80%. This is a result of the maximum LTV for loans extended by some institutions, specifically the ones funded with *Pfandbriefe*. The absolute maximum LTV acceptable to German lenders is 100%.[4]

Note that the default rates per LTV band have been lower in Germany than the other European countries, as concluded by some rating agencies in their rating analysis for German MBS.

Second, the *price-to-income (PTI)* ratio and the *debt-to-income (DTI)* ratio reflect the borrowers' ability to pay back their loans. Based on data from the mortgage banks, the average PTI ratio in Germany was estimated around 7.2 in 1994, by far the largest in Europe (in our estimates, using data from Empirica. November 1997, the average PTI in Europe is approximately 3.9). The average DTI ratio is approximately 5, almost two times higher than the European average of 2.73.[5]

SOME INDICATORS OF MORTGAGE LOAN PERFORMANCE

Notwithstanding the limited information about the performance of the mortgage industry as a whole, we make an attempt to derive some key performance indicators for German mortgage pools. In particular, we focus on prepayments, foreclosure, and seasonality in origination. From the very low foreclosure statistics, we can conclude that the delinquency and loss statistics should be very low indeed. Limited performance data about German mortgage-backed securities (MBS) deals support that conclusion.

To our knowledge, the Association of German Mortgage Banks is the only organization in Germany that distributes information on loan performance. We are aware that mortgage banks represent only 20% of the mortgage market but we believe that this review will at least provide investors with a general idea about the trends in German mortgage loan performance.

Prepayment and Prepayment Penalties

Prepayments on mortgage loans in Germany encounter distinctly different treatment, depending on the type of mortgage in question:

• Fixed-rate mortgages are protected against prepayments through prepayment penalties. This is because they are largely financed through *Pfandbriefe*. Lenders could ban prepayments for a period of up to 10 years. Once the initial restricted period has expired, the borrower could make a prepayment with a 6-month prior notice.

There are, however, exceptions to the prepayment restrictions. For example, if the borrower wants to sell the property or needs it to back a new and larger loan (refinancing) which a current lender refuses to grant, then the borrower is allowed to prepay the mortgage. The condition for prepayment is that the borrower compensates the initial lender for losses due to the prepayment of the mortgage. This

---

4. EMF, Hypostat 1987–1997, November 1998.
5. *Empirica,* November 1997.

E X H I B I T   39-3

Repayments

	1997	1998	Percent Change Between 1998 and 1997
Outstanding loans	563.0	616.6	9.5%
Repaid loans	52.8	65.2	23.5%
Repaid loans/Outstanding loans (%)	9.4%	10.6%	

Source: Association of German Mortgage Banks.

amounts to paying penalties (*Vorfälligkeitsentschadigung*), which depend on the remaining term to maturity and the prevailing level of interest.

• Variable-rate mortgages face no prepayment restrictions provided a 3-month advance notice is given. Lenders are not entitled to compensation.

As a consequence of the prepayment regulations, we expect prepayments to be relatively low in Germany. The fall of interest rates over the past few years, however, has had its effects and can explain the recent surge in repayments of mortgage loans (partially explained by increases in prepayments). The repayments of mortgages grew by 23.5% from 1997 to 1998 and reached 65.2 billion Deutsches Marks, or 10.57% of outstanding mortgages in 1998 as compared to 9.4% in 1997 (see Exhibit 39–3).

Foreclosures

From Exhibit 39–4 we can conclude that the number of foreclosure suits is very low in Germany. The number of executed foreclosures is even lower. The Association of German Mortgage Banks remarks that many pending foreclosures are not solved by a forced sale but by an arrangement between the debtor and creditor.

The procedure in case the lender insists on repossession and foreclosure is becoming increasingly lengthy. In a 1993 study[6] on foreclosure practices, the EMF has estimated that the average time needed to obtain funds through a forced sale is between 12 and 18 months. Since the Association of German Mortgage Banks reports that the length of foreclosure procedures is increasing, we believe it is safe to assume that the length of time for average foreclosure to take place is roughly 18 months. The same EMF study concluded that the costs of this procedure amounted to approximately 6% of the sales price.

---

6. Comparative Study on Real Estate Enforcement Procedures in EEC Countries, March 1993.

E X H I B I T   39–4

Foreclosure Suits and Foreclosures (for Residential and Commercial Properties) for Mortgages Issued by Mortgage Banks Only

		1997	1998	Percent of Increase or Decrease 1998–1997
1	Total number of mortgage-financed properties	1,600,000	1,890,000	18.1%
2	Foreclosure suits pending	8.900	7.600	−14.6
	2 / 1 (%)	0.6%	0.4%	
3	Forced sales executed	1,887	2,700	43.1
	3 / 1 (%)	0.12%	0.14%	
4	Of which owner-occupied	1,131	1,300	14.9
	4 / 1 (%)	0.07%	0.07%	

Source: Association of German Mortgage Banks.

Seasonality in Mortgage Origination

Exhibit 39–5 demonstrates that the mortgage loans origination follows a distinct cyclical pattern. Each year the number of new issues is modest in the first quarter but peaks in the last quarter. The peaks in loan issuance at the end of the year are due to tax regulations. A mortgage loan entitles German households to reductions in tax payments for the entire year, independent of the time during that year when the loan was issued. This means that a great number of households request a loan at the end of the year prior to the purchase of their property in order to enjoy the tax benefit over the past year.

We would expect the seasonal fluctuations in loan extension and its concentration in the last quarter to have a similar seasonal effect on prepayments due to refinancing of mortgage loans.

RECENT HOUSING MARKET TRENDS

Despite the vagaries of the German economy since reunification, the housing market has remained relatively healthy, supported by a lasting shortage of single-family properties and declining interest rates.

After the reunification boom of the early 1990s the economic growth fell sharply as a consequence of the Bundesbank's monetary tightening. Unemployment surged from 7.8% in 1992 to more than 11% and was still at 10.5% in June 1999. This depressed economic situation increased the number of insolvencies (both commercial and private) and credit costs to banks.

E X H I B I T   39–5

Issuance of House Loans to Private Persons*

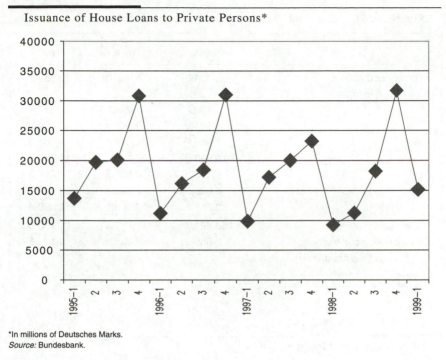

*In millions of Deutsches Marks.
Source: Bundesbank.

The housing sector, though, remained relatively healthy. Generally speaking, the housing market is supported by a persistent shortage of single-family properties, currently estimated at 2 million units. The situation, though, is different in different regions of the country, some of which were characterized by falling rents and property prices.

Increasing Number of Dwellings

In 1997 the number of dwellings amounted to approximately 37 million, which accounted for 161 million rooms (see Exhibit 39–6). The number of houses per 1,000 inhabitants totaled 452.

Falling Interest Rates

Interest rates on mortgage loans have been falling for the past few years (see Exhibit 39–7). Both the *average renegotiable rate* (i.e., effective rate on mortgage loans with a 10-year period of fixed interest rate and maximum term of 30 years) and the *variable rate* are at a much lower level than at the beginning of the nineties.

EXHIBIT 39-6

Number of Dwellings and Total Dwelling Surface (in thousands)

	1995	1996	1997
Number of dwellings	35,954.3	36,492.3	37,050.3
with . . . Rooms			
1	782.2	798.5	813.4
2	2,221.2	2,265.1	2,309.5
3	7,949.7	8,078.4	8,208.0
4	10,966.0	11,108.7	11,247.6
5	6,888.2	6.985.5	7,089.2
6	3,629.5	3,686.7	3,752.8
7 or More	3,517.6	3,569.5	3,629.8
Total number of rooms	156,520.7	158,818.4	161,256.0
Total dwelling surface	3,005.5	3,054.3	3,106.3
(minimum square meters)			

Source: Statistisches Bundesamt Deutschland.

EXHIBIT 39-7

Interest Rates on Mortgage Loans

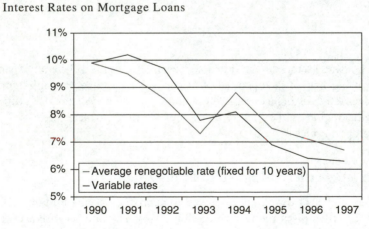

Source: European Mortgage Federation.

The renegotiable rate has been higher than the variable once since 1994.[7] The
falling interest rates, that is, the availability of cheap housing financing, is another
factor (along with the housing shortages) that explains the relative health of the
housing sector as indicated by house construction and number of building permits.

---

7. Hypostat 1987–1997, 1998.

House Construction in Germany

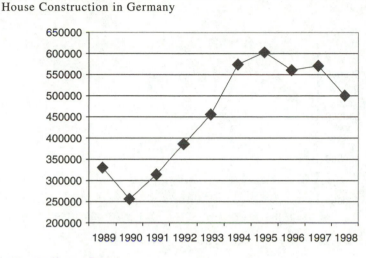

Source: European Mortgage Federation.

Housing Construction Boom

The number of new house constructions did not evolve evenly over Germany with a clear distinction between the former West Germany and the *Neue Länder* (the former East Germany):

• In the former West Germany the number of house constructions grew continuously from 238,617 in 1989 to 372,265 in 1998.

• The number of constructions in the Neue Länder fell from 92,347 in 1989 to 23,598 in 1993. This downward trend was reversed in 1997 with a record amount of new houses constructed 177,829. In 1998 another 128,453 new dwellings were erected.

The number of new house constructions in Germany as a whole is stagnating (see Exhibit 39–8), but can nevertheless be expected to remain at a historically higher level in the near future given the information on building permits.

Building Permits Peaked

As for the number of building permits, continuous growth between 1987 and 1994 was followed by a decline during the last few years (see Exhibit 39–9). Despite the recent fall, the number of building permits remains at a relatively high level—just a little less than 500,000 building permits were granted in Germany as a whole in 1998:

E X H I B I T   39–9

Building Permits

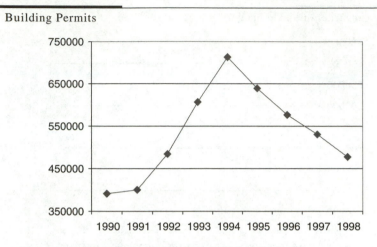

Source: European Mortgage Federation and Statistiches Bundesamt Deutschland.

- In the Neue Länder 114,014 building permits granted in 1998 after the record issuance of building permits in 1996 (185,155).

- In the former West Germany 363,692 building permits were granted in 1998.

Dropping Housing Construction Prices

The price of newly constructed houses has been decreasing since the fourth quarter of 1995 and is currently at a level below that of the beginning of 1995 (see Exhibit 39–10). The fall in prices makes the purchase of a property more affordable and could entice more households to buy rather than rent their home. If this is true, then the level of owner occupation could increase and so could the number of mortgage loans. On the other hand, the fall in house prices means that the LTV ratio would increase, thereby raising the probability of borrower's default on their mortgage. However, the practice of setting value at 10% to 20% below market for the purposes of calculating LTV acts as a damper on the falling price effect. It is also worth noting that severe negative equity situations have never occurred in Germany, as reported by some rating agencies working on German MBS.

REGULATORY FRAMEWORK

Germany has long-established traditions and practices in mortgage lending. The regulatory framework for mortgage lending and finance is well-developed. The legal framework for securitization is generally favorable, despite some recent ambiguities introduced by the new Insolvency Law.

E X H I B I T   39–10

Price Indices (Construction Plus Tax) for New House Construction (1995 = 100)

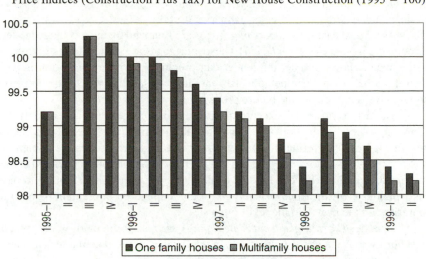

Source: Statistisches Bundesamt Deutschland.

Germany has a long-established legal framework regarding mortgage lending. Already in 1770 the basis was laid for the creation of *Landschaften*. These institutions were the precursors of mortgage banks, principally established in Prussia and focusing on providing funds for agriculture. Private credit institutions were established in the mid-nineteenth century and had as their main activity mortgage lending for the purpose of financing house construction (EMF).

More recently, the Credit Act of April 13, 1993, which governs all the German credit institutions, was implemented. This act lays down several operational rules (on funding, exposures, etc.) for credit institutions to follow and regulates the supervision of the credit institutions by the federal office for the supervision of the credit sector (*Bundesaufsichtsamt für das Kreditwesen*).

We mentioned in the beginning of this chapter that the German mortgage market is characterized by a wide variety of lenders. Specific laws along with the general Credit Act regulate some of these institutions and define their mortgage lending practices. For example the German Mortgage Bank Act, which entered into force on January 1, 1900, and was amended several times afterwards, imposes stricter rules on the private mortgage banks than the ones included in the Credit Act. Other examples are: the Act of December 21, 1927, Regarding Mortgage Bonds and Similar Instruments Issued By Public Law Institutions and the Insurance Companies Supervision Act.

Prepayment and Prepayment Penalties

The rules on mortgage loan prepayment for Germany can be found in the Civil Code, which entered into force on January 1, 1900.

As in most cases, *fixed-rate mortgages* are financed by the mortgage lenders through the issuance of *Pfandbriefe*. These mortgages are subject to restrictions to prepayments. For example, the lender can preclude the mortgage from prepayment for a period that can be up to 10 years long. After this period, the borrower should give 6 months notice before prepayment.

There are, however, exceptions to the ban on prepayments, namely for "hardship cases." If the borrower wants to sell the property or needs it to back a new and larger loan (refinancing) which a current lender refuses to grant, then the borrower is allowed to prepay the mortgage. The condition for prepayment is that the financial damage incurred by the bank is compensated. This amounts to paying penalties (*Vorfälligkeitsentschadigung*) that depend on the remaining term to maturity and the prevailing level of interest.

Penalties (*Vorfälligkeitsentschaedigung*) are also to be paid by the (potential) borrower when she is granted a loan but decides not to take it after all. These penalties are meant to compensate the lender for the costs incurred in raising funds on the capital market.

Prepayment of *variable-rate mortgages* is always allowed with 3 months notice. In this case, the lender is not entitled to compensation.

Valuation of the Property

Article 12 of the Mortgage Bank Act stipulates that the value of the property for lending purposes may not exceed the market value as established by prudent appraisal. For owner-occupied housing the appraisal of the property is based on its real value. For new buildings where the appraisal is based on the likely construction costs the Federal Office for the Supervision of the Credit Sector requires a safety margin to be built into the calculation (EMF).

The supervisory authority verifies the expertise and the reports of the appraiser. It also conducts regular checks to verify the current market value of the property.

For the purposes of calculating LTV ratios the value of the property is established at 10% to 20% below the current market value. It is important to emphasize that no official national statistics about real estate price developments exist.

Foreclosure

The Association of German Mortgage Banks remarks in its *1998 Annual Report* that a large number of pending foreclosure cases are not solved by a forced sale but by an arrangement between the debtor and creditor.

The procedure in case the lender insists on repossession and foreclosure is becoming increasingly lengthy.[8] Combining this information with data from a 1993 EMF study we believe it is safe to assume that 18 months are needed today for financial institutions to recuperate their loans. The same EMF study concluded that the costs of the procedure amounts to approximately 6% of the sales price.

Risk Weightings for Investors

Following the rules from the German Federal Office for the Supervision of the Credit Sector, banks are allowed to give zero weighting to mortgage bonds (*Pfandbriefe*) they acquire. Implementation of the European Community Solvency Directive would mean that these bearer bonds would be weighted at 10%, compared with 20% for other bank bonds and 100% for industrial bonds (EMF). MBS, on the other hand, are subject to 50% risk weighting. Risk weightings for bonds are expected to change under the new BIS proposal based on the type of the bond and its credit rating.

Regulatory Framework for Securitization

Germany is one of the few countries in Europe without a dedicated, detailed framework for securitization. This does not make securitization impossible, but simply requires more detailed legal work underpinning each new deal and asset type, as well as efforts at interpretation of changes in the laws with regard to attempted and existing securitizations.

A key document regarding securitization by German banks is the circular and covering note released after a long consultation process on May 20, 1997, by BaK—*Bundesaufsichtsamt für das Kreditwesen,* that is, the German Banking Supervisory Authority. This circular establishes the framework, and the covering note clarifies the purpose and the implementation of the circular. The circular deals with the issues of transfer of credit risk from the originating bank, the potential for deterioration of the credit quality of the retained assets, and the bank secrecy and customer data protection. Furthermore, the BaK establishes a requirement for notification about each proposed securitization by a German bank and for approval of each transaction should it fall beyond the established guidelines. Recent introduction of a new German Insolvency Act as of January 1, 1999, raised a number of issues regarding asset securitization.

A key element in every securitization is the "delinkage" between the assets subject to securitization (usually transferred to a bankruptcy-remote special purpose company—SPC) and the originator of those assets. Securitization requires that SPV have full right over the transferred assets and the proceeds from their liquidation, as well as a control over those assets and the decision to liquidate them. Such status of the SPC can be achieved through different legal mechanisms, namely a "true sale" and "secured loan" structures.

---

8. German Mortgage Banks Association, 1997.

The new German Insolvency Law drives a bigger wedge between a true sale and secured loan structures for the purposes of securitization. As it is aimed to promote more restructuring and support the unsecured creditors of an insolvent entity, the law limits the rights of the secured creditors. The short of it is that the new law strips the security assignee (*Sicherungsabtretungsempfanger*) from the right to separate the assets from the insolvency estate and to liquidate them. This right is now transferred to the insolvency representative (*Insolvenzverwalter*) who is also entitled to a "fee" of about 9% of the liquidation proceeds and has a control over the timing of the liquidation process itself. The consequences for the SPV in case of a secured loan as opposed to a true sale structure are obvious.[9] Hence, a need for clear understanding of:

• Whether a given deal structure is a true sale or not

• What is the risk of a recharacterisation of a true sale structure into a secured loan structure

• What are the possible consequences of the recharacterization for the deal's liquidity and expenses

• How such consequences can be mitigated by factoring delays in liquidation and insolvency representative fees in cash flow stress scenarios and deal enhancements (liquidity facilities, "springing" protections, etc.)

Transfer for the Purposes of Securitization

The mechanism of transfer of the mortgage loans included in the securitization mortgage loan pool depends on the type of mortgage loan:

• Certificated mortgages (*Briefgrundschulden*) are transferable and the transfer requires detailed description of each mortgage

• Uncertificated mortgages' (*Buchgrundschulden*) transfer requires an entry into the respective land register

In other words, a true sale can be achieved for certificated liens (*Briefgrundschulden*) easier, while uncertificated mortgages (*Buchgrundschulden*) cannot be perfected without land registration.

German mortgage deals to date have been executed without a true sale from the outset. The underlying mortgages, even those with certificated security, are not transferred given the administrative inconvenience in achieving perfection. Instead, all beneficial interests in the underlying assets are sold to the SPV, whereas the actual assets remain on trust with the seller-originator. Perfection of sale of the actual mortgages securing the loan portfolio will be effected only under certain credit events (e.g., insolvency of the seller-originator).

---

9. For a detailed discussion of the impact of the new German Insolvency Law on German securitization, *see* German *Securitsation and Delinkage by Mark Odenbach and Tom Schorling, International Securitisation and Structured Finance Report,* August 16, 1999.

INVESTMENT ANALYSIS FOR GERMAN MBS

The purpose of the investor's analysis of a MBS is to define its credit and non-credit-related characteristics and, ultimately, the security's fit with the investment objectives—current and expected status of investor's portfolio. MBS require a detailed analysis of the underlying mortgage pool, its servicing and expected performance, the financial and legal structure of the deal, the relationship between the underlying mortgage pool performance and its changes, and the performance of the MBS and each of its tranches. A case in point is the analysis of interest-only (IO) tranches of MBS.

The purpose of investment analysis is to determine the likelihood of full repayment of the bonds as well as the likely timing of the repayment cash flows. Investors should also be concerned with the occurrence of changes to any aspects of the deal that could have an effect on the bonds' pricing initially or on the secondary market, such as bond's rating and potential for rating changes during its life, the performance of the underlying collateral, or the performance of the servicer.

In their investment analysis, investors are aided by the rating agencies and the rating for the bonds, which they are buying. The purpose of the rating agencies' analysis is to determine the likelihood of timely payment of interest and principal (reflected in the rating) on the rated tranches of the MBS. This requires assessment of the credit quality of the underlying pool of mortgages and, on that basis, assessment of the necessary level of credit enhancement relevant to the assigned rating level. The rating agencies evaluate the credit characteristics of the collateral pool, the servicing capabilities of the servicer, the underwriting criteria of the originating entity, the matching of the cash flows generated by the collateral pool with the cash flows promised to investors under the mortgage-backed securities, and the soundness of the legal and financial structure of the deal. They subject the cash flows of the pool to stress scenarios whose severity is directly related to the assigned final rating on the bonds.

The credit rating of the bonds provides a proper indication of the creditworthiness of those bonds. However, investors should also look at a number of other features to understand the current and future performance of their investments. Such analysis includes the following:

1. Potential for rating changes affecting the bonds associated with

   - Status and ratings of the parties involved in the MBS: originator, servicer, swap counterparty, etc.

   - Collateral backing the MBS—assumptions related to expected pool performance and change in those assumptions over time

2. Liquidity characteristics of the MBS associated with

   - Size of the initial issuance

   - Syndicate members and their commitment as market makers

3. Prepayment characteristics of the MBS

- Prepayment speed assumed for pricing purposes
- Effects on prepayment speed changes on bond's duration, weighted average life, convexity

In the following sections we briefly discuss key aspects of MBS analysis, such as collateral pool, legal and the structural features, and prepayment characteristics.

Characteristics of the Collateral Pool

The key characteristics of the collateral pool are summarized below.

- Number and average size of the mortgages, distribution by mortgage balance.

- LTV ratio—average and distribution by LTV; key determinant of the LTV is the determination of the property value. LTV is considered the key determinant of the borrower's willingness to pay—especially related to the borrower's equity in the property.

- Price-to-income or net income-to-mortgage payment—determines the ability of borrower to pay.

- Weighted average interest rate on the mortgage pool at closing and its expected change as determined by the type of mortgages in the pool—fixed or variable interest rate mortgages, fixed-rate mortgages with periodic resets, etc.

- Type of underlying property—detached single-family or two-family property, semidetached property, block of flats, single flat, investment property, residential property, multipurpose property (e.g., part commercial, part residential)— each type of property has different characteristics from the point of view of the borrower's motivation to service the mortgage debt and from the perspective of the property liquidation and recovery value in case of borrower default.

- Type of mortgage products—such as annuity mortgages and life insurance mortgages—and the effects of the mortgage type on the debt servicing and debt recoveries.

- Seasoning of the mortgage pool—the seasoning (aging) of the mortgage is associated with the building up of equity of the borrower in the acquired property, which has a strong influence on borrower's motivation to continue servicing or to abandon the mortgage. The mortgages' seasoning (pool's aging) is associated with a loss curve—mortgage loss curves tend to be front-loaded, that is, losses occur early in the life of the mortgage pool and decrease and stabilize later in its life.

- Pool performance characteristics—levels and dynamics of delinquencies (late payments), charge-offs, gross and net losses; pool performance on a dynamic (pool "as is") and static basis (tracking performance of a fixed pool of mortgages since their origination).

- Pool prepayment dynamics and main determinants of prepayment behavior of mortgage borrowers in general and specifically for the mortgage borrowers in the pool.

- Characteristics of the obligors in the pool—salaried employed (employment history), self-employed (riskier); possible effects of social welfare.

- Security—first, second, third lien mortgages; in Germany some loans are "upper LTV" loans exceeding 60% LTV but secured by first-ranking mortgages.

- Geographic concentration of the mortgage loans related to the demographic and economic characteristics of the respective regions.

- House price movements by region, by valuation bracket, and so on.

- Recovery value—property value reduced by market value decline, foreclosure costs, and carrying costs from delinquency to foreclosure.

- Set-off risk—risk associated with the ability of borrower to offset mortgage debt against a deposit held with the bank originator of the mortgage.

- Possibility for addition of mortgages to the original pool and the effects on the evolution of the pool's credit quality.

- Insurance policies assuring balloon payments on IO mortgages.

Financial Structure of the Pool

The key features of the financial structure of the pool are summarized below.

- Credit enhancement and method of its provision—such as subordination and insurance—credit enhancement is established through subordination of several tranches with significantly different maturities, the paydown of the senior tranches and pool performance within or better than initial expectations are prerequisites for subordinated tranches upgrade or spread tightening.

- Cash flow mechanics of the structure—priority of cash flow distribution—interest and principal payments on the different tranches, trustee, servicer and issuer expenses, swap payments, missed payments of interest, and principal.

- Liquidity support—liquidity line or servicer advances for liquidity support for payments of interest and/or principal for borrowers in arrears.

- Swaps addressing potential cash flow mismatches between underlying pool WAC and WAC on the MBS; key elements include actions to be taken in case of swap counterpart default or downgrade and/or swap termination.

- Application of excess spread, if any; the excess spread is the difference between WAC of underlying mortgage pool and the sum of WAC of MBS, servicing fee and other trust expenses, and serves as a first level of protection against current and potential future losses on the mortgage pool.

Legal Structure

Legal structure considerations are summarized below.

- Bankruptcy remoteness of the issuing entity.

- Data protection trustee—custody over certain data lists in order to identify borrowers and enforce the loans and the collateral.

- Transfer of rights to the issuers.

- Transfer of mortgages securing the loans—transferred only upon the occurrence of certain events—downgrade of originator below certain level (A or A−).

- Transfer of the pool of loan claims and all corresponding economic rights— collateral remains with seller until occurrence of a specified event; borrowers may or may not have been notified.

- Legal transfer and perfection of security interest over the mortgages and the cash flows they generate.

- Representations and warranties by the seller-servicer.

Origination and Servicing

Origination and servicing considerations are summarized below.

- Underwriting criteria and guidelines—the conservativeness and the consistency of the underwriting criteria inevitably affect the performance of the mortgage pool. Mortgages originated through a bank branch network, and based on long-term relationship with a borrower, including the provision of other financial services to that same client tend to perform better than mortgages originated by a broker and sold to a mortgage consolidator for the purposes of an MBS deal.

- Payment methods—direct debit, that is, borrowers have a current account with the originator.

- Availability of credit scoring system for the purposes of faster and standardized assessment of borrowers' credit quality.

- Availability of information regarding borrowers debt burden and credit performance through a centralized, nationwide data-sharing system among the credit institutions.

- Property value assessment—availability of established practices and mechanisms for current determination and subsequent updates of property value information. In Germany it is a well-established practice to set the value of the property 10% to 20% below its market value.

- Servicing guidelines—generally speaking, the originator of the mortgages is at least initially their servicer for the purposes of the MBS transaction.

MBS Bond Features

MBS bond features are summarized below.

- Prepayments and their effect on floating-rate MBS (mainly WAL) and fixed-rate MBS (duration and convexity).

- Prepayment assumptions used in credit enhancement modeling and MBS pricing.

- Clear understanding of the differences between expected maturity and legal maturity for pass-through structures; for example, pass-through structures are rated by legal final, not by expected final.

- Investment characteristics of each specific MBS tranche—senior, subordinated, IO, or PO—effects of prepayments, resets on the fixed-rate loans, excess spread, WAC.
- Syndicate composition and commitment to secondary market-making associated with the expected securities liquidity.

Monitoring

Monitoring aspects of MBS are summarized below.

- Mechanisms for receiving timely information regarding pool performance (trustee reports, rating agencies reports, reporting on Bloomberg or a web site).
- Sufficiency of the information received for evaluation of pool performance—reporting criteria, clarity about calculation of different performance indicators, comparability of reported information among similar deals in the respected country and across countries.

Analyzing IO MBS

The economic incentive for issuers to launch IOs is the possibility to receive the excess spread on the mortgage pool up front; that is, instead of receiving the excess spread (difference between the revenue from the mortgage pool WAC on the mortgages and the expenses under the MBS—servicing, WAC on MBS and losses) on a monthly or quarterly basis, the issuer could receive it in the beginning of the deal by packaging the stream of excess spread payments into interest-only security. IOs can also be created by stripping the interest component of an MBS and creating two complimentary securities, one entitled to the principal payments only (PO) and another entitled to the interest payments only (IO).

Here we discuss only the IOs created on the basis of excess spread. By doing this the issuer in effect passes on to investors:

- Risk associated with the generation of excess spread—changes to WAC of the underlying mortgage pool due to voluntary prepayments and involuntary payments (borrower default and subsequent repossession and liquidation of the underlying property), as well as losses
- Market interest rate risks (as repayments on mortgages are heavily influenced by changing interest rate environment; differences in indexes used for pricing the underlying mortgages and the MBS)

IOs are structured (mainly) as notional amount securities, which promise to pay investors a specified interest on outstanding notional amount securities. The outstanding notional amount is determined based on a specified formula.

IOs are usually rated securities. However, investors should take little comfort in the assigned rating since these ratings address the likelihood of investors receiving a promised coupon rate on the outstanding notional balance, but not the return of the principal invested or the timing of the cash flow receipts.

Investors should focus on:

- Expected interest rate environment (yield curve shape) during the expected life of the IO.

- Changes in WAC of the mortgage pool during the IO life due to voluntary prepayments (mortgage prepayments are sensitive to declining interest rates) or losses (mortgagee defaults tend to increase in adverse economic conditions and rising interest rates); defaults tend to affect the IOs in two ways: by reducing the WAC yield available (mortgages paying interest rate) and by reducing the excess spread available (losses reduce the pool's gross yield).

- Original pool composition by interest rate, that is, the pool's coupon distribution— high concentration of high coupons on the underlying mortgages may negatively affect the pool in both declining (they tend to prepay faster) and rising (they tend to default more often) interest rate environments.

- Cash flow priority of the IO (what payments precede the interest payment on the IO in the overall deal "cash flow waterfall") and cash flow distribution to the respective IO (whether only interest collections or both interest and principal collections can be used for payments under the IO).

- Prepayment speed and loss assumptions for IO pricing purposes, as well as assumptions regarding the WAC deterioration of the mortgage pool.

GERMAN MBS DEALS OVERVIEW

As of 1999, Germany's experience with MBS was rather modest in terms of number of deals, yet quite innovative in terms of structures. There had been, to our knowledge, five deals—two public issuances and three private placements. The reasons for the current status of the German MBS market should be traced to the development of its capital markets and existing traditions and business practices. As those evolve, the potential for MBS market development will gradually be realized.

As indicated earlier, Germany has one of the largest housing markets in Europe with a long-established legal framework and tradition in mortgage lending and mortgage finance. Yet, it has one of the smallest functioning MBS markets. The following reasons provide an explanation for this apparent contradiction.

- Strong financial sector and a highly developed domestic mortgage finance system have undoubtedly affected the development of an MBS market.

- Regulatory and legal ambiguities remain as discussed in the previous section. Strict rules regarding banking confidentiality and customer data protection create additional barriers to overcome in structuring securitization deals.

Two public MBS transactions and two private transactions (the latter totaling $4.8 billion[10]) have been executed to date. The transaction details are summarized in Exhibits 39–11 and 39–12 and are discussed next.

---

10. Figures from: Moody's Investors Service.

EXHIBIT 39–11

Transaction Details

Date	Issuer	Originator	Class	Amount (DM, mln)	Redemption	Launch Spread	Rating	WAL[b]
4/4/95	GEMS BV	Rheinische Hypothekenbank AG	A-1	380.0	Bullet	+43 bps / November 1999 BOBL	AAA	5.0
			A-2	142.6	Controlled Amortization	N/A	NR	na
5/11/98	HAUS 1998-1	Deutsche Bank AG	A1	1,278.17	Pass-through	+17 bps / 1-month LIBOR	AAA	4.0
			A-IO	1,278.17[a]	Interest-only		AAA	–
			B1	56.18	Pass-through	+48 bps / 1-month LIBOR	A	8.4
			B2	42.14	Pass-through	+93 bps / 1-month LIBOR	BBB	8.4
			B-IO	98.32[a]	Interest-only		BBB	–
			B3	28.09	Pass-through	N/A	NR	8.3

[a]Notional amounts.
[b]WAL = weighted average life.
Source: Bloomberg.

E X H I B I T 39–12

Collateral Details

Date	Issuer	Pool Composition	Weighted Average LTV*	Credit Support for Senior Notes	Structure Notes
4/4/95	GEMS BV	Single-family (35%) and multifamily (20%) residential mortgages, commercial mortgages (45%)	74%	31%	Triple-A swap counterparty guarantees all interest and bullet payment on senior notes
5/11/98	HAUS 1998-1	Single-family (55%), multifamily (19%) residential mortgages, apartments (20%), mixed use mortgages (6%)	74%	9%	IOs; servicer advances

*LTV = loan to value.
Source: Rating Agency Reports.

GEMS BV

GEMS BV was the first public German MBS transaction, originated by Rheinische Hypothekenbank, the mortgage subsidiary of Commerzbank. The motivation behind the securitization appeared to be credit exposure management since the bank had allegedly been close to breaching a regulatory limit on the portion of second lien mortgages on its loan book at this time.

Assets securitized are fixed-rate mortgages (with reset) ineligible for *Pfandbriefe* funding. The transaction is structured such that the first 60% principal portion remains on the balance sheet for funding *Pfandbriefe*. The issuing vehicle has claim on any cash flow or recoveries accruing to the remaining portion of the underlying mortgages. Such claims are subordinate to the *Pfandbriefe*.

Senior notes structured as bullets. A triple A–rated swap counterparty absorbs *all* risks of cash flow timing mismatches in the structure, guaranteeing all interest and expenses due as well as the bullet principal payment to senior note holders. The swap agreement extends also to insuring any interest rate coverage risks since some of the underlying mortgage rates are reset periodically. Clearly, the credit quality of the bonds is strongly linked to that of the swap counterparty. The transaction is structured with a 10% liquidity line.

HAUS 1998-1 LTD

HAUS 1998-1 launches for the first time a repeat mortgage issuance program by a leading German universal bank. Unlike the GEMS transaction, we understand that balance sheet economics was the primary motivation behind this securitization.

Assets securitized are fixed-rate mortgages (with reset). The majority of underlying loans comprise junior portions (greater than 60% LTV) to first lien mortgages, covering the portion of loans ineligible for *Pfandbriefe* funding. There are also a number of second- and lower-ranking mortgages in the pool. No substitutions are allowed in the pool with the bonds paying down on a pass-through basis. The transaction is structured without a liquidity line, replaced by certain obligations of the servicer to provide advances.

The transaction breaks new ground in so far as being the first to introduce IOs to the Euroland securitization market. The A-IO note is based on notional amounts equal to the outstanding balance on the A1 notes, with interest-only holders receiving payments that equal the excess spread accruing to the A1 notes (i.e., the gross pool interest rate weighted against the amount of A1 notes outstanding, less all weighted transaction expenses). B-IO note holders are eligible for interest payments that are made up of two components. The first is based on excess spread accruing to the amount outstanding on the B1 notes, and the second on excess spread accruing to the amount outstanding on the B2 notes (the notional amount for the B-IO notes equals the sum of outstanding B1 and B2 notes). The first component of interest-only payments to the B-IO note holders ranks *pari passu* to the B1 notes interest, and the second component to the B2 notes interest. Similarly, interest payments to A1 and A-IO note holders rank *pari passu*.

In the absence of any excess spread or spread account to support the bonds, the B3 notes are in a first-loss position. There is no reserve fund in the deal.

E X H I B I T   39–13

HAUS 1998-1 A1 Spread History

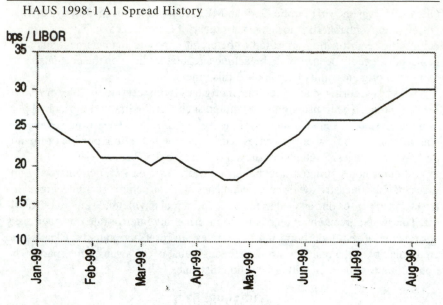

Source: Merrill Lynch.

Liquidity may be provided from advances by Deutsche Bank, to the extent that the bank deems such advances recoverable (i.e., any liquidity provision by the servicer will be used to cover noncredit-related delays in payments, as opposed to any delinquencies or losses). The Aa1/AA+ rating of Deutsche Bank, as the potential liquidity provider, is sufficiently high to support the rating on the bonds. From this perspective, downgrade triggers are built in to protect against a rating downgrade of Deutsche Bank. The transaction is structured so that the swap counterparty covers any risk arising from the reset of interest rates on the underlying mortgages.

The secondary market performance of Haus 1998–1 A1 is shown in Exhibit 39–13.

EUROPEAN MBS MARKET OVERVIEW

The development of the MBS market in Europe was initially confined to the United Kingdom. Favorable legal changes and the need for financing prompted MBS developments in France and Spain, which together with the United Kingdom form the stronghold of European MBS. In recent years, the Netherlands and Belgium issuers made their presence on the market permanent. Other European countries have also experimented with MBS. With the introduction of the Euro and recent increase in MBS issuance in the Euro zone, a relatively large Euro MBS market sector is beginning to emerge.

A quantitative review of the development of the European MBS market is provided in Exhibits 39–14, 39–15, and 39–16.

EXHIBIT 39–14

Growth of MBS Issuance Volumes (1987–Sept. 1999)

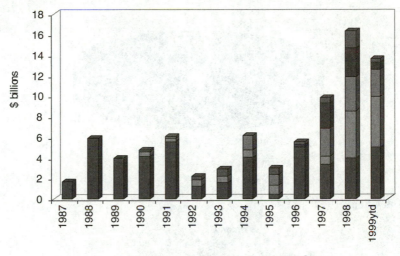

Source: Merrill Lynch.

EXHIBIT 39–15

Growth in the Number of MBS Transactions (1987–Sept. 1999)

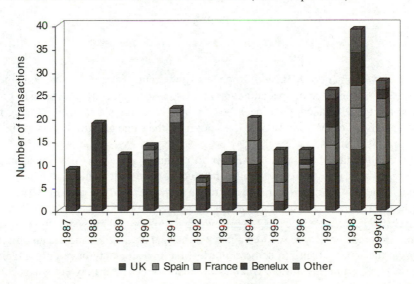

Source: Merrill Lynch.

EXHIBIT 39–16

European MBS Issuance by Country for the Years 1992–1994

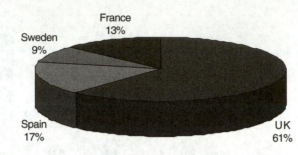

1997–Sept. 1999

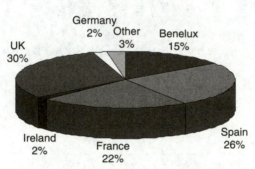

Development of MBS in Europe has significantly lagged that of the United States. In the absence of special government-sponsored agency programs to promote mortgage financing and because of a lack of active specialized housing finance companies, MBS in Europe does not have the same growth drivers as those in the United States.

Furthermore, a number of European countries have well-developed large mortgage bond (secured on residential mortgages) domestic markets that have existed for decades and have come to be known as the *Pfandbriefe* market. Mortgage bond markets exist in Austria, Finland, Germany, Holland, Scandinavia, Spain, and Switzerland, and are expected to develop in France and Ireland in the near future. Mortgage bonds are secured against a mortgage portfolio and are an obligation of the issuing bank. In some countries, the investor may have only a claim against the issuing institution, whereas in others the investor may enjoy a special conditional claim over a specific portfolio of underlying mortgages.

A Brief History of European MBS

The development of MBS in Europe began in the United Kingdom. The lack of any functional mortgage financing market (in contrast to much of the continent), a favorable regulatory framework, as well as a greater role of capital markets fed the growth in U.K. MBS issuance. In the late 1980s, the United Kingdom was the only country in Europe to boast a mortgage-backed sector, the bulk of which represented issuance from specialized mortgage lenders (SMLs), as opposed to the traditional mortgage financiers such as building societies and retail banks. Led by strong MBS issuance from SMLs, the U.K. MBS market reached a peak in 1988 (one that it has yet to surpass). The abrupt slowdown in MBS issuance that followed in the early 1990s was precipitated by the housing market collapse which, coupled with wider consumer credit deterioration, pushed many SMLs into financial difficulties and were eventually acquired by building societies and banks—none of them really keen on securitization.

In the early 1990s the European MBS market then began to find some support from Spanish and French issuers. France endorsed securitization in the late 1980s, but issuers came to market only when the authorities developed distinct regulatory methods for securitization, using special-purpose vehicles that resembled collective investment vehicles (FCCs). Spain enacted a law in 1991 allowing for the issuance of MBS, and, as in France, the new law also allowed for the creation of unique securitization vehicles that were compatible with Spanish domestic legal structures. Despite moderate MBS supply out of these countries and sporadic issues from originators in certain other countries (notably Sweden), there was generally not a strong consensus for mortgage securitization in Europe for much of the early 1990s. And it was only toward the mid-1990s that new players from Belgium and Holland entered the MBS market.

The resurgence of the MBS market in 1997 had a broader, more durable base than that seen in the late 1980s. U.K. MBS were complimented by stronger issuance out of France, Spain, and the Benelux. Issuers this time represented the more mainstream lenders, although in the United Kingdom, subprime and near-prime originators feature prominently (see Exhibit 39–17). More recently, Irish, German, Swiss, and Italian issuers have used securitization to finance mortgage portfolios.

Diversity of Asset Types Backing European MBS

First-ranking mortgages from status (or prime) borrowers continue to dominate collateral underlying MBS in Europe. In the United Kingdom, securitization of subprime mortgages has developed relatively rapidly, led by U.S. issuers setting up origination activities in the United Kingdom. Peculiar also to the United Kingdom is the securitization of shared appreciation mortgages, where borrowers sacrifice certain equity appreciation in their underlying properties in return for lower-than-market interest rates. Italian mortgage securitization as of 1999 has been limited to nonperforming assets. Social housing mortgage securitization is found in the Benelux, Finland, and the United Kingdom (see Exhibit 39–18).

Top 10 European MBS Originators Between 1993 and 1999

Originator	Country	Share of Total New MBS Issuance	No. of Deals
Union de Credit pour le Batiment	France	8.5%	8
Credit Lyonnais	France	7.0	4
Caja de Ahorros (Spanish savings banks)	Spain	5.8	11
Paragon Mortgages Ltd.[a]	United Kingdom	5.8	11
Ocwen UK plc[b]	United Kingdom	5.1	17
Comptoir des Entrepreneurs	France	4.0	7
Abbey National	United Kingdom	3.6	2
Banco Santander	Spain	3.1	5
ABN AMRO	The Netherlands	3.0	2
Bank of Ireland	United Kingdom	2.8	3

[a] Includes National Home Loans.
[b] Includes City Mortgage and Kensington Mortgage (33% ownership).
Source: Merrill Lynch.

Underlying Mortgage Types Since 1995

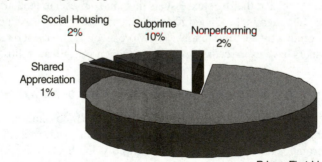

Social Housing 2%
Subprime 10%
Nonperforming 2%
Shared Appreciation 1%
Prime, First Lien 85%

Source: Merrill Lynch.

E X H I B I T   39–19

MBS Rating Distribution

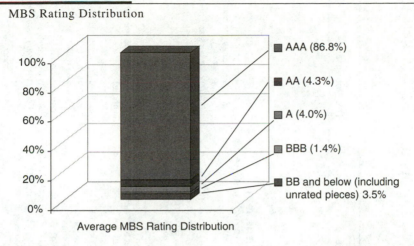

Average MBS Rating Distribution

Source: Merrill Lynch.

European MBS—Predominantly AAA Floaters

The European MBS market remains predominantly a floating-rate market (over 83% of issuance in the past 5 years). As such, prepayments are of little concern, very much unlike the United States. Notably, in late 1997 a Dutch bank became the first to issue fixed-rate pass-through MBS. Fixed-rate MBS in Europe, namely from the Netherlands and France, are normally structured as bullets (reflecting the as-yet-undeveloped appetite for prepayment-driven investments).

European MBS are predominantly AAA-rated, as evidenced by Exhibit 39–19. As with prepayments, most investors are not highly receptive to subordinate bonds, though there is every indication that this is changing. In certain jurisdictions regulators do not encourage issuers to retain the lowest subordinated (equity) tranches, thus forcing their sale to investors.

Despite strong growth in MBS in the second half of the 1990s, MBS has yet to play a significant role in housing finance as it does in the United States. In the United Kingdom, for example, (the largest MBS market in Europe) MBS finances about 5% of residential mortgages outstanding.

With the introduction of the Euro, the MBS market in the Euro zone stands to benefit from broader investor base, more transparency, and better understanding of the structures and underlying collateral pools. We expect the MBS market sector to gradually emerge as one of the more liquid and active sectors of the overall asset-backed market in Europe. In order to facilitate comparisons and better understanding of some of the main euro MBS markets, we summarize the market's characteristics in Appendix A.

European MBS Review: Comparisons Among Selected European MBS Markets and Transactions

	Germany	Belgium	France	The Netherlands
Size of the mortgage market[a] (outstanding loans / GDP)	51%	22%	20%	60%
House owner-occupation[b]	39%	65%	54%	50%
Types of issuers (market shares)	**Types (EMF, 1998)** Savings banks (24.7%) Mortgage banks (22.6%) Universal banks (19.4%) Mutual and cooperative banks (13.1%) Bausparkassen (10.4%) Public banks (7.8%) Insurance companies (6.8%) Other companies (3.3%)	**Types (UPC-BVK, 1998)** 7 large "universal" banks (68.6%) Other banks (18.2%) Other financial institutions (6.8%) Insurance companies (3.6%) Specialized mortgage companies (2.9%)	**Types (EMF, 1998)** Mutual and cooperative sectors (34%) Banks (33%) Savings banks (13%) Credit Foncier and Comptoir des Entrepreneurs (12%) Specialized institutions (8%)	**Types (EMF, 1998)** Commercial banks (74.1%) Mortgage banks and building funds (17.2%) Insurance groups and pension funds (8.6%)
Products Interest payment Loan categories	**Interest payment** Fixed-rate mortgage (fixed for the first 5 to 15 years followed by a reset) Variable-rate mortgages **Loan categories** Standard annuity mortgage Loan over 7–16 Years after an Initial Savings period of 6–7 years with a *Bausparkas* Loans with a life assurance	**Interest payment** Fixed-rate mortgages (fixed rate over the full life of the Loan) (70% market share in October 1998) Referenced-rate loans (limited variability of interest rates)	**Interest payment (1995 market share)** Variable rate (20%) Fixed rate (80%) **Loan categories** Government subsidised loans (PAP, PTZ) Regulated loans (PC, PAS, PEL, "1% patronal") Free market loans	**Interest rate (1995 market share)** Intermediate term (5–10 years) fixed-rate loans (65%) Variable rate (10%) Fixed rate (25%) **Loan categories** Annuity mortgage Endowment mortgage (interest only) Savings mortgage Traditional life assurance mortgage

Product characteristics				
Loan-to-Value[a]	LTV = Normal: 60–80% = Maximum: 100%	LTV = Normal: 80–85% = Maximum: 125%	LTV = Average: 80% 	LTV = Normal: 75% = Maximum: 125%
Price-to-Income[b]	PTI = 7.2	PTI = 2.5	PTI = 2.5	PTI = 3.5
Debt-to-Income[c]	DTI = 5	DTI = 1.5	DTI = 1.5	DTI = 2.5
Legal framework				
Prepayment	**Prepayment** No prepayment allowed during the first 10 years of fixed interest. Then 6-month notice required 3 month notice on variable rate loans	**Prepayment** Limitation of penalties to 3 months interest	**Prepayment** Prepayments on less than 10% of original loan can be forbidden Compensation limited to the lower of: 6 months interest 3% of the outstanding loan	**Prepayment** Maximum 10% of the initial amount without charges
Foreclosure[d]	**Foreclosure** Procedure: 12–18 months Costs: 6% of the sales price	**Foreclosure** Procedure: approximately 1 year Costs: 16–23% of sales price	**Foreclosure** Lengthy process (More than 2 years in 50% of the cases) Costs: 10–12% of allocation price	**Foreclosure** Procedure: on average 3 months Costs: 1.5% of the property sale
Guarantee			**Guarantee on loans** PCs are backed by a state guarantee Some loans are not backed by a mortgage but by a house loan guarantor ("Société de Caution")	**Guarantee on loans** National mortgage guarantee which covers all losses and costs.
Credit bureau	**Credit Bureau** SCHUFA	**Credit bureau** Union Professionnelle du Credit		**Credit bureau** Organization for credit registration (*Stichting Bureau Krediet registratie*), registers arrears greater than 120 days
Law on overindebtedness		**Law on overindebtedness** Encourages negotiations in case of delinquencies Possibility to seize part of the borrower's income	**Law on overindebtedness** Emphasis on renegotiations, otherwise renegotiation commission's recommendation is enforced by a judge	**Law on overindebtedness** Emphasis on negotiations and possible reduction in the borrower's dues Possibility to seize part of the borrower's income

Continued

APPENDIX A

Continued

	Germany	Belgium	France	The Netherlands
Performance Delinquencies Prepayments Losses (N/A)	**Delinquencies**[e] 0.4% of the financed properties are undergoing a foreclosure suit and 0.14% are loans effectively solved by a foreclosure **Prepayments** Limited data points to low prepayments	**Delinquencies**[f] <1% of the outstanding amount of mortgage **Refinancing**[g] On average 24% of the newly issued loans in 1998[(6)]	**Delinquencies** Data not available in France **Prepayments**[i] On average 9% of the newly issued loans	**Delinquencies**[h] <0.63% of the number of loans **Prepayments** 38.5% average for 1998; average 30% for 1993–1998
Mortgage bonds	*Pfandbriefe*		*Obligation Foncières*	
MBS issues (1993–Sept. 1999) Number of issues	2	9	22	7
New issuance volumes	$1.17 billion	$3.13 billion	$11.15 billion	$3.11 billion
Major originators	Deutsche Bank, Rheinische, Hypothekenbank	Bacob Bank, Kredietbank, Generale Bank	Credit Lyonnais, Comptoir des Entrepreneurs, Union de Credit pour le Batiment	ABN AMRO, Stad Rotterdam Bank NV (and other sellers associated with DNIB)
Main collateral types	First-ranking or second-ranking mortgages	First-ranking private mortgages, social housing loans	First- or second-ranking private mortgages, home loans to civil servants or company employees	First-ranking private mortgages only

MBS structures	Senior-subordinate, floaters, fixed rate, pass-throughs, controlled amortization; IO structures	Senior-subordinate; floaters; pass-throughs	Senior-subordinates, floaters, fixed rate, pass-throughs, soft bullets	Senior-subordinate; fixed rate, pass-throughs, soft bullets
Prepayment assumptions	15% CPR	6–8% CPR	4–16% CPR	5–8% CPR
Typical AAA credit support	9%	4–8%	4–10%	6–10%

Sources:

[a]Hypostat 1987–1997, European Mortgage Federation 1998.

[b]Study on the mortgage credit in the European Economic Area, Empirica, November 1997.

[c]Estimation based on data from Empirica, November 1997.

[d]Comparative study on real estate enforcement procedures in the EEC, European Mortgage Federation, March 1993.

[e]Estimation based on data from the Association of German Mortgage Banks, Annual Report 1998.

[f]Estimation based on data from the Belgian Central Bank (Nationale Bank van Belgie) 1997.

[g]Estimation based on data from UPC-BVK over the period July 1996 to October 1998.

[h]Estimation based on data from the SBKR ("Stichting Bureau Krediet Registratie") and CBS ("Centraal Bureau voor de Statistiek"), 1998.

[i]AFB (Association Francaise des Banques).

CHAPTER 40

MORTGAGE-BACKED SECURITIES IN THE NETHERLANDS

Alexander Batchvarov
Managing Director
Merrill Lynch & Co.

Wembo Zhu
Vice President
Merrill Lynch & Co.

Ganesh Rajendra
Vice President
Merrill Lynch & Co.

Xavier De Pauw
Assistant Vice President
Merrill Lynch & Co.

The Netherlands is characterized by a relatively low level of owner occupation. From 42% in 1981, the level of owner occupation in the Netherlands gradually reached 50% in 1997. This is low compared to the European level of 64%. The above estimates are based on EMF (European Mortgage Federation) data from 1998. The gradual increase in the number of owner-occupied dwellings is mainly due to Dutch government incentives such as a mortgage guarantee scheme introduced in 1956 and tax deductibility of mortgage interest rate payments.

The mortgage debt-to-GDP ratio for the Netherlands was 60% in 1997. This was the second-largest level in Europe after Denmark—(65% according to the EMF). Several factors explain the size of the Dutch mortgage market and the apparent contradiction between low owner occupation and high mortgage lending. First comes the popularity of IO mortgages in the Netherlands—the entire principal amount remains outstanding during the full term of the mortgage. Also, the recent increase in house prices (approximately 10% in 1997) has led to a rise in the size of mortgage loans by approximately 12% in 1997 and 14% in 1998. Price increases are a consequence of a mortgage rate–induced shift of preferences toward home ownership and lagging supply of dwellings.

In this chapter we discuss the MBS market in the Netherlands. Specifically, we cover the mortgage lenders, mortgage products, indicators of mortgage loan performance, housing market trends, the regulatory framework, investment analysis, and MBS deals. Our presentation is the same as in the previous chapter where we discussed the MBS market in Germany.

MORTGAGE LENDERS AND MORTGAGE PRODUCTS

A wide variety of lenders operate on the Dutch mortgage market—banks, insurance companies, pension funds—which are, however, increasingly represented by commissioned intermediaries. An array of equally diverse and constantly evolving mortgage products is available, ranging from more or less traditional amortizing (repayment) mortgages, through savings to repay mortgages to interest-only (IO) mortgages.

Mortgage Lenders

Mortgage lending in the Netherlands comes essentially from the sources described below.

Banks
Commercial, cooperative, and savings banks have the largest market share in the mortgage market (Exhibit 40–1). Mortgage credit is a part of their general lending business. The largest mortgage lender in Holland is Rabobank, which is, in fact, an umbrella association of 550 small cooperative banks.

Insurance Companies and Pension Funds
Insurance companies and pension funds also issue a substantial amount of residential loans. For them, mortgage lending is a form of investment and a cross-selling opportunity especially when selling life insurance and endowment policies as well as other products such as home contents or building insurance.

Mortgage Banks and Building Funds
Mortgage banks are specialized institutions for residential lending. They tend to concentrate on the top end of the mortgage market. Building funds grant mortgages for

E X H I B I T   40–1

Market Shares by Mortgage Originator During 1997

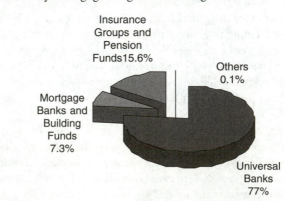

Insurance Groups and Pension Funds 15.6%

Others 0.1%

Mortgage Banks and Building Funds 7.3%

Universal Banks 77%

Source: European Mortgage Federation.

the sale of properties built by them in their role of developers of social housing. However, only about 10% of their mortgage lending is associated with such properties.

Private Persons and Mortgage Intermediaries

The role of private persons in mortgage lending is negligible, whereas that of mortgage intermediaries is rapidly increasing. It is interesting to note that in the Netherlands everyone is allowed to grant a mortgage credit. In the past, notaries often played the role of an intermediary for the extension of mortgage credit by one private person to another. More recently, this source of credit has become negligible.

Intermediaries (such as estate agents, insurance brokers, and mortgage brokers) are rapidly becoming major players in the mortgage origination process. Different sources, including the European Mortgage Federation, have indicated that the share of mortgages originated through intermediaries is as high as 50% of all new mortgage loans.

Mortgage Products and Characteristics

The typical term of a mortgage loan in Holland is 30 years, which is longer than in other European countries (Belgium 20 years, France 15 years, and Germany 25 to 30 years—EMF, 1998). The mortgage term, though, can be as long as 75 years.

According to mortgage rates, we can distinguish between three types of loans:

- Fixed loans with reset (65% of the market share in 1996, according to *Empirica,* November 1997). Fixed-rate loans with a reset have interest rates fixed for a term of usually between 2 and 5 years. Most frequently the rates on these loans were fixed for 5 years but this term is becoming longer (10 years and beyond is very popular now) due to the current low interest rates. At the reset date, the borrower may choose to alter the interest rate, the reset period, and even the type of mortgage.

- Variable-rate mortgages (10% market share in 1996).

- Fixed-rate mortgages without reset (25% market share in 1996).

According to repayment methods, housing loans in the Netherlands can be divided into three main categories—repayment mortgages, saving-to-repay mortgages, and IO mortgages.

Repayment Mortgages

Payments on this type of mortgage include both an interest and a principal component. At the end of the term the mortgage loan should be fully amortized. There are three types of repayment mortgages:

Annuity Mortgage (Annuiteitenhypotheek)   The borrower using an annuity loan pays fixed monthly amounts during the full term to maturity. The payments cover both principal and interest rate, where the interest rate component diminishes over time, while the principal payments increase.

Linear Redemption Mortgage (Lineaire Hypotheek)   Like the annuity mortgage, the linear redemption mortgage is a fully amortizing type of loan. However, the monthly payments vary in size—each period the same amount of principal is repaid together with a diminishing interest rate component.

Wage-Fixed Mortgage (Loonvast Hypotheek)   The wage-fixed mortgage must be fully repaid through amortization by the time the borrower is 65 years old. The principal repayments are subject to fluctuations, depending on the evolution of a wage index calculated on a yearly basis by the CBS (*Centraal Bureau voor de Statistiek*).

Saving-to-Repay and Investment Mortgages

The borrower under a saving-to-repay mortgage does not repay the principal directly to the lender, but instead periodically pays fixed amounts into a savings account or pays an insurance premium. The accumulated funds are used to make a lump-sum principal repayment at the end.

The popularity of the saving-to-repay mortgage is due to its double tax advantage for the borrower. First, interest rate payments are tax-deductible in the Netherlands, and since the outstanding principal does not diminish, this advantage remains high during the entire life of the mortgage. Next, return on the savings is not taxed as long as certain conditions are fulfilled.

Savings Mortgage (Spaarhypotheek)   The savings mortgage is linked to a life assurance, which can be used to pay back the loan in case of borrower's death. Under the terms of this mortgage, the borrower makes payments into a savings account instead of repaying the loan directly. The return on the deposit is such that at the end of the loan term, enough capital is accumulated to pay back the full principal amount. The deposit yields at a rate equal to the mortgage rate of the loan.

A savings mortgage enables the borrower to take advantage of favorable tax rules on long-term saving—the income on the savings account is not taxed. In addition, at given intervals during the term of the mortgage, the borrower can draw a specified amount from the savings account tax-free.

Traditional Life Insurance Mortgages (Traditionele Levenshypotheek)   This product is very similar to the savings mortgage. The borrower pays regular amounts into a savings account and pays an insurance premium. Contrary to the savings mortgage, the reinvestment rate on the deposits is not fixed (the borrower has some flexibility as to how the money is invested) and, therefore, it is possible that the capital accumulated at the end of the term does not cover the principal payment in full. However, the expectation of the borrower is that the accumulated amount will exceed the principal repayment and that he will benefit from that upside.

Investment Mortgage (Beleggingskeuzehypotheek)   The introduction of this mortgage was encouraged by the high returns on the Dutch stock market. Again the borrower pays regular amounts into an account. The return on the deposit, however, depends solely on the investment decisions made by the borrower who chooses how her money is invested. According to *Euromoney,* roughly 50% of the new mortgage loans issued in 1998 were investment mortgages.

Switch Mortgages   A switch mortgage allows borrowers to switch (with lender's consent) between an investment mortgage and a savings mortgage. Borrowers' decisions depend on their views on the comparative dynamics of the stock market, which determine the return on the investment fund, and the deposit rate, which determines the return of the savings mortgage deposit. Those returns will determine the amount of premium to be paid by the mortgage borrowers and the incentive to minimize it will affect the decision as to which mortgage to choose. In either case, the outcome is the amount of premium payable by the mortgagee and the borrowers' incentive to minimize it. This product was launched in the last 1 to 2 years. All the switch mortgages so far have been taken out in the form of investment mortgages and no switch has occurred yet.

Interest-Only Mortgages (*Aflossingsvrijehypotheek***)**
Interest-only (IO) mortgages require no regular principal amortization payments during the term of the loan. The monthly payments consist of interest only, and the principal is repaid in full at the end of the term, which can be up to 75 years long. Principal repayment can be achieved through the sale of the property or by taking a new mortgage loan. IO mortgages are subject to a 75% loan-to-foreclosure-value (LTFV) and are combined with another, usually savings, mortgage.

Mortgage Loan Characteristics
The loan-to-value (LTV) ratio determines the *willingness* of the borrower to pay back his loan. The CBS (the Dutch Central Bureau for Statistics) states that the standard LTV in the Netherlands is 75%. The absolute maximum LTV is 125%. The average house price in the first half of 1999 was NLG[1]272,000 whereas the average outstanding mortgage loan amounted to NLG242,000. Even though these figures are averages, we can calculate the LTV ratio for loans granted in the first 6 months of 1999 at approximately 89%.

However, in the definition of LTV in Holland, value is defined as the foreclosure value, that is, the estimated value of the property in case of a forced sale (*executiewaarde*). The Dutch Association of Estate Agents (the *Nederlandse Vereniging voor Makelaars*) and the lenders determine the foreclosure value. Foreclosure value can vary between 80% and 90% of market value due to the state of the dwelling, its age, its location, and its purpose. In short, the LTV ratio in the Netherlands is, in fact, an LTFV ratio.

Borrowers covered by the National Mortgage Guarantee can obtain a mortgage loan of a sufficient amount to finance the entire purchasing cost of their property including extra expenses (usually about 12%). This means that the LTV can be in excess of 100%, but the risk to lenders is not increased by the high LTV as they are protected by the national guarantee in case the borrower defaults.

---

1. NLG = Dutch gulden or guilders.

The price-to-income (PTI) ratio, together with the debt-to-income (DTI) ratio, assesses the borrower's *ability* to pay back the loan and to cope with unexpected changes in financial situation. These indicators are especially important in the Netherlands since the main reasons for defaults are divorce and unemployment. The typical PTI ratio in 1994 was 3.5, whereas the DTI was 2.5. These values are just below the European averages, which are 3.9 and 2.73, respectively.[2]

SOME INDICATORS OF MORTGAGE LOAN PERFORMANCE

Dutch mortgages are characterized by a low level of delinquencies and a minuscule level of losses. This can be explained by several factors, among them the way lending business is conducted and the legal framework for credit extension. Prepayments, traditionally low, have been on the rise. We believe that this change was caused by a sharp drop in interest rates, an active role of intermediaries in mortgage origination, diversification of available mortgage products, and upbeat borrowers' expectations about future developments in the market.

Delinquency Levels

Using data from the Credit Registration Office (*Stichting Bureau Krediet Registratie*, SBKR) and the Dutch Central Office of Statistics (*Centraal Bureau voor de Statistiek*, CBS) we estimated mortgage delinquencies in Holland during 1998. The Credit Registration Office registers every mortgage borrower who has payments in arrears in excess of 120 days.

Exhibit 40–2 provides a rough estimate of the level of delinquencies in Holland: we multiplied the number of delinquencies by the average mortgage loan size for 1998 and divided the result by the value of the total outstanding mortgages. We note, however, the approximation of this estimate given that mortgage values have increased steadily and the average size of loans issued in 1998 is larger than the average loan size among outstanding loans.

---

2. *Empirica,* November 1997.

E X H I B I T   40–2

Estimation of the Delinquent Loans as of End 1998

Delinquencies registered (number) (A)	17,310
Average mortgage value (B)	(NLG)* 175,000
Total outstanding mortgage loan value (C)	(NLG)* 486,000,000,000
Estimated percentage of delinquent loans (A+B)/C	0.62%

*NLG = Dutch gulden or guilders.
Source: 1: SBKR, 2-3: CBS.

Factors Explaining the Low Level of Delinquencies
The evidence points clearly to much lower delinquencies in Holland as compared to the United States and the United Kingdom. Three social and cultural factors explain the Dutch borrowers' reluctance to miss or default on loan payments. The first two arguments are personal and cultural, the third one, legal:

Branch-Based Banking Is Still the Norm in the Netherlands   Mortgage lending is generally carried out through the borrower's local bank branch. The borrower relies on other services from that branch in addition to her mortgage. The relationship with the lender is viewed as a personal relationship with the bank's manager and borrowers have greater incentives to pay.

The Second Argument Is a Geographic One   The small size of the country and low housing stock turnover is conducive to more stable housing market. Stable housing markets make a negative equity situation for borrowers less likely; hence borrower's incentives to abandon the property leading to lender's losses are small.

"Attachment of Earnings" Influences Borrowers' Behavior   Under the Debt Restructuring Law (*Wet Schuldsanering Natuurlijke Personen*), a lender in Holland can apply for an attachment on the borrower's income at any stage during the foreclosure process. The lender's ability to seize a portion of the borrower's earnings directly from his employer acts as a strong disincentive to default and limits losses if the borrower defaults for reasons other than unemployment.[3]

Defaults on Guaranteed Loans

The National Mortgage Guarantee (NMG) is an organization that covers all the losses incurred by the lenders in case the borrower defaults on guaranteed loans. Approximately one in three eligible borrowers (about 10% of all new borrowers are eligible) or 57,000 households joined this guarantee scheme in 1998. Notwithstanding the large number of borrowers who benefit from the guarantee, only 54 interventions of the NMG were necessary in 1998 (53 in 1997), which lead NMG to spend NLG2 million (less than $1 million) to cover associated losses.

Prepayments

Prepayments in Holland have traditionally been low mainly due to high prepayment penalties and tax disincentives. New information, though, points to rising prepayments in absolute terms during the last several years, yet their level remains

---

3. Ministry of Justice, The Netherlands, 1998.

low in comparison to other countries like the United States. A combination of factors could explain this ambivalent trend:

Prepayment Penalties and Tax Disincentives

Dutch mortgage lenders must pay prepayment penalties when they refinance their mortgage early, and may lose accumulated tax advantages. The prepayment penalty is meant to compensate the lender for lost income. It is calculated as the present value of the difference between a given mortgage loan rate and the market mortgage rate. In addition to the gap between the two different rates (which we later call the refinancing incentive), the prepayment penalty will also depend on the remaining time to reset of the mortgage. The longer the time remaining to reset, the bigger the refinancing incentive should be.

In the Netherlands, mortgage interest payments are tax-deductible. For saving-to-pay mortgages, interest earned on mortgage deposits is tax-free. On the other hand, mortgage deposit premiums are paid from after tax income and depend on the returns on the deposit, which is usually equal to the mortgage rate. Ironically, prepayment on a savings mortgage may put a borrower in a worse situation, in which the interest payment is lower due to the lower mortgage rate, but the return on the mortgage deposit is also lower and the borrower must compensate for that by paying a higher premium. With a lower income on the mortgage deposit, the borrower forgoes some of the tax benefits, and with higher premium on the mortgage deposit, the borrower must pay more from its after-tax income. This may explain, on one hand, a reluctance to prepay a savings mortgage and, on the other hand, the switch from savings into investment mortgages.

Falling Mortgage Rates and Increasing Mortgage Reset Terms   Interest rates have fallen significantly over the last several years. As the level of interest rates remains an important factor in determining the mortgage-servicing burden for a borrower, it is natural for a borrower to seek to reduce that burden through refinancing when interest rates fall. Interest rates, though, have to be considered together with all other factors, which could affect refinancing decisions—like prepayment penalties and tax treatment. As interest rates fell during the 1990s, as evidenced by Exhibit 40–3, it became more favorable to refinance mortgages with longer remaining period to reset. So, depending on the relative drop in interest rates, borrowers with mortgages having different reset dates can find it beneficial to refinance.

The prepayment penalties seem no longer sufficient to keep the borrowers from refinancing and their desire to lock in the low interest rates for a longer period of time. The prepayment penalty burden paid at refinancing can be financed through a new mortgage at a lower interest rate and longer term. By doing so, the borrower's payments under the new mortgage can still be lower despite the amount of prepayment penalty. The payments can further be reduced if the borrower takes an investment mortgage and the stock market performs in his favor. Anecdotal evidence points to the fact that the newly originated mortgages and reset mortgages tend to have a longer reset term. In the past mortgages were originated with first reset in 5 to 10 years, but more recently mortgages have tended to reset in 10 to 20 years.

EXHIBIT 40–3

Interest Rate (%)

Source: Datastream.

Investment Mortgages Outnumber Savings Mortgages   In a falling and low interest rate environment, reset or refinancing with a savings mortgage at a lower interest may not always be favorable for the borrower. Given that the interest rate on the mortgage loan is the same as the interest rate on the mortgage savings deposit, the benefit of a lower interest rate payment could be eliminated by the shortfall in income from the savings account, which leads to a higher premium payment. In other words, reduced interest payments can be outstripped by increased premium payments. One way to address this issue is to refinance with an investment mortgage whose premium depends on the stock market performance. Currently, many borrowers have expectations for a strong stock market performance in the future.

The previous section gives a partial explanation for the reasons why more investment mortgages (in comparison to savings mortgages) have been extended recently. About 50% of all new mortgages extended in 1998 were investment mortgages. Another reason for that is the continuing bullish outlook on the stock market, which many borrowers allegedly harbor.

Refinance to Upgrade—Turnover   We mentioned earlier that a Dutch borrower could fully prepay his mortgage without penalties if he moves to a new house. Due to the small size of the Netherlands, borrowers are less likely to move in case of job change. That leaves them with the opportunity to move in order to acquire a bigger dwelling, that is, to upgrade their housing or change dwelling type (from an apartment to a single-family house).

Seasonality in Refinancing   The housing turnover in the Netherlands usually peaks in the late summer and the early autumn and at year-end, and bottoms out in the winter. This pattern corresponds to holiday schedules, climate cycle, and bonus payments (say, an extra paycheck, or annual bonus).

Increasing Role of Mortgage Middlemen   Recently, as much as 60% of new mortgages originated through middlemen (a mortgage broker or real estate agent). There is reason to believe that these middlemen play an active role in prepayment dynamics of Dutch mortgages. Since these brokers work on commission, they benefit from a high turnover in mortgage loans. Hence, they have every reason to contact their clients and inform them about the benefits of falling interest rates and offer them new, suitable mortgage products as a marketing tool to convince them to refinance. However, in case a borrower prepays the mortgage soon after origination, the mortgage broker has to partially pay back the commission received at origination.

"Burnout" Yet to Be Seen   Borrowers most likely to respond to a given interest rate incentive tend do so relatively quickly and refinance their mortgages, leaving behind borrowers who are unwilling or unable to respond at the current interest rate. Burnout causes the refinancing response to fall with the age of the pool. If borrowers believe that interest rates will remain low, they may decide to delay refinancing until their mortgage reset date to avoid paying prepayment penalties. Such a decision would delay the response to an interest rate incentive and diminish the burnout effect.

RECENT HOUSING MARKET TRENDS

In recent years the Dutch housing market has been unusually active. The relatively low level of house ownership in an environment of falling to historically low interest rates is an ideal condition for mortgage lending further spurred by commissioned mortgage brokers (intermediaries) and new mortgage products. Voluntary repayments have reached a high, driven by low interest rates, proactive mortgage brokers, and switching between different mortgage products.

In the first 6 months of 1999, 313,000 mortgage loans were issued, which is 25% more than in the first semester of 1998. They amounted to NLG76 billion, which is a 37% volume increase over the first 6 months of 1998. As we can see from Exhibit 40–4, the number of mortgages issued and their volume have been increasing almost continuously since 1995.

The total number of outstanding mortgages increased less than one would expect, given the evolution of the yearly mortgage issues. This is due to a large degree to refinancing. Of the 313,000 mortgages issued in the first semester of 1999, 181,000 (or approximately 60%) were refinancings of existing mortgages. Refinancing of mortgages is more and more popular due to several factors:

Falling Interest Rates   The interest rate on mortgages has been falling during the past several years and has reached historical lows. The average interest rate of 5.56% in 1998 was the lowest since 1965. From Exhibits 40–5 and 40–6 we can see that the downward trend in interest rates persisted until June 1999.

EXHIBIT 40-4

Mortgage Loans

	Mortgage Loan Issues	Change in the Number Issued (YoY[a], %)	Mortgage Loan Issues (NLG[b] millions)	Change in the Amount Issued (YoY[a], %)	Average Mortgage Value (NLG)[b]	Total Mortgages Outstanding (NLG[b] millions)
1993	301,332		46,203		153,329	263,000
1994	384,233	+27.5	60,055	+30.0	156,298	292,000
1995	349,994	–8.9	57,049	–5.0	163,000	322,000
1996	470,178	+34.3	82,877	+45.3	176,267	368,000
1997	537,065	+14.2	106,456	+28.5	198,218	426,000
1998	577,241	+7.5	132,289	+24.3	229,175	486,000
1999[c]	313,000		76,000		242,812	520,000

[a] YoY = Year on Year.
[b] NLG = Dutch gulden, or guilders.
[c] First half.
Source: CBS.

EXHIBIT 40-5

Average Interest Rates on Mortgage Loans (%)

Year	1989	1990	1991	1992	1993	1994	1995	1996	1997	1998	1999*
Interest rate	7.61	8.78	9.25	8.84	7.5	7.26	7.12	6.25	5.82	5.56	5.0

*The interest rate for 1999 is the average over the first 6 months only.
Source: CBS.

779

E X H I B I T   40–6

Refinancing of Mortgages (Left Axis, in thousands) and Mortgage Rates
(right axis, %)

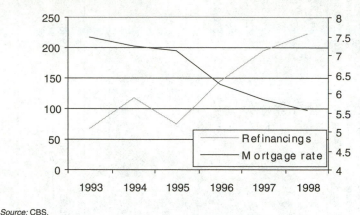

Source: CBS.

Increasing Role of Intermediaries   We mentioned earlier that intermediaries
grant a large number of mortgages in the Netherlands. Since these middlemen receive an up-front commission per mortgage, they benefit from borrowers who refinance their mortgage. The low level of mortgage rates is a strong marketing argument for these intermediaries to promote refinancing aggressively.

Rising Housing Prices   The increase in house prices has led to refinancing
where the house owner takes advantage of the upward revaluation of his property
to take cash out or to obtain a larger new loan at an attractive interest rate.

Introducing New Mortgage Products   The introduction of new products in the
mortgage market has also induced mortgage refinancing. The borrower repays her
old mortgage and borrows again using a new type of mortgage. The typical example is the investment mortgage, which was introduced in mid-1990s to allow
borrowers to benefit from high returns on the Dutch stock market. The market
share of this type of mortgage already exceeded 50% in 1998.[4]

Repaying Nonamortizing Mortgages   Most of the repaid loans are saving-to-repay
mortgages, which do not amortize any principal over the term of the mortgage. When
these loans are repaid, the total amount of prepayments increases more than when
amortizing loans are prepaid, due to their higher principal amount outstanding.

---

4. *Euromoney,* June 1999.

REGULATORY FRAMEWORK

The Netherlands has a long-established and developed (read "complicated") framework for mortgage lending. The system is, generally speaking, lender-friendly and imposes somewhat stiff conditions on the borrowers in terms of, say, their ability to prepay (limited), the speed of foreclosure (faster than anywhere else in Europe), ability to renegotiate (not that easy). Largely available credit information from a credit bureau allows lenders to make informed credit decisions. Framework for securitization is incomplete, yet favorable, which explains the recent development of the active mortgage-backed securities (MBS) market.

The origins of mortgage banks in Europe can be traced back to 1770 when a new form of land credit was created in favor of landowners in Silesia. Landowners could obtain mortgage bonds with a value up to 50% of the value of their estates from their *Landschaft* but were to sell these bonds themselves to the public.[5] In 1823 under the initiative of King William I of the Netherlands, the Society of Landowners and Mayors of the Province of Groningen (*Maatschapij van Landeigenaren en Vastbeklemde Meiers der Provincie Groningen*) was established based on the Silesian model. The mortgage market really developed, however, at the end of the nineteenth century with the development of urban areas and related need for house financing.

The regulatory framework developed over time. Most recently, a new Credit Act (*Wet Toezicht Kredietwezen*—WTK) was implemented in 1993 to introduce the second EC Banking Co-ordination Directive. The act put the Dutch Central Bank in charge of the supervision of all credit institutions.

The Dutch mortgage market is ruled by a self-regulatory system, to which virtually all lenders subscribe. This system is an agreement between umbrella organizations of mortgage lenders and some individual lenders. It consists of three agreements—an accord signed by all professional mortgage lenders in May 1990, the Code of Conduct of October 1, 1990, and regulations on the application of the Code of Conduct.

Early Repayments

Code of Conduct Article 8 states that the borrower should be allowed to repay his mortgage loan earlier than agreed in the initial contract. The borrower is allowed to repay up to 10% of the initial amount of the original loan every year without facing any penalties. The 10% (which some lenders extend to 15% or even 20%) is not cumulative in the sense that they cannot be saved and transferred to the next year. Beyond this limit, contractual prepayment penalties are usually levied.

Full early repayment is allowed without penalty in case

- A borrower dies and the loan is paid by means of a death benefit

- A borrower moves the house and transposes the mortgage on the new property. If the mortgage loan is not transposed and is fully repaid, penalties may be due.

---

5. European Mortgage Federation, 1993.

- Of a reset
- Of house damage and mortgage repayment from insurance proceeds

Article 10 of the Code of Conduct further specifies that the lender must not impose prepayment penalties on borrowers when two conditions are met simultaneously: (1) contractual terms of the loan specify a compensation equal to the present value of the difference between the market rate and the contractual rate, and (2) market rate of interest at the time of repayment is higher than the contractual one.

Default of a Borrower

A new Law on Debt Restructuring (*Wet Schuldsanering Natuurlijke Personen*) introduced in December 1998 defines the procedure to follow in case of a borrower default. Several remedies are available to the lender:

Seizure of Wages   First, it is possible for the lender to seize a part of the borrower's wage above a certain minimum. Repaying the loan in this manner can be a tedious and lengthy process since the cash flows available to the lender will typically be limited. However, the mere possibility for the lender to contact the borrower's employer in order to seize part of his wage puts a strong incentive on the borrower to make timely payments.

Deferment of Payments   A second possibility is a period of deferment (*surséance*) accorded to the borrower by a judge. This is a limited period of time when the borrower is authorized to stop making payments while he reorganizes his financial resources. With the introduction of the new law mentioned above borrowers can no longer ask for deferment.

Bankruptcy   The lender as well as the borrower can also ask for a judge to declare the borrower bankrupt. In this case an administrator is appointed to take control over the income, expenses, and possessions of the borrower. The aim of the administrator is to create cash flows to repay the debts. If any cash flows are created, they will first be used to pay the administrator's wage and then to pay the preferential lenders such as the government (taxes due). Foreclosure procedures normally take only 3 months, which is a lot less than in other European countries.

Renegotiations   Finally, when a private person is not capable of making the payments due on her loan she can contact her creditor to renegotiate the terms of the loan. The lender is obliged to meet the borrower for negotiations and can grant a period between 3 and 5 years to pay back as much of the debt as possible, after which the borrower is usually released from any remaining payment obligations. For lenders, this means that they will almost certainly recuperate only part of the loan. But, on the other hand, they incur only minor costs and know approximately what they recover.

Some lenders refuse to renegotiate the payments because of the concessions they would have to make. In that case the borrower can go to court and demand renegotiations. If the judge agrees, the borrower is assigned an administrator (*be-windvoerder*) who supervises his expenses and earnings and ensures that he pays his dues to the extent possible. This procedure can also last for 3 to 5 years, after which the borrower is no longer obliged to pay the remaining debt.

State Guarantee on Loans

On June 1, 1956, a Government Guarantee made it possible to finance housing up to 90% of the building costs. This was the start of a campaign to promote home ownership and house building. The effect of this guarantee was the relaunching of mortgage lending in Holland. Mortgage banks soon experienced the competition of universal banks, cooperative banks, savings banks, and other institutions. In the field of the housing market, the government's policy had increased home ownership from 29% in 1956 to 39% in 1975, which meant an increase of 950,000 dwellings.[6]

In 1995 the National Mortgage Guarantee (NMG) or *Nationale Hypotheek Garantie,* was created from the former Communal Guarantee scheme (*Gemeente Garantie*). The National Mortgage Guarantee is available almost everywhere in the Netherlands except in Arnhem and Rotterdam. These towns have their own guarantee systems with different conditions.

The National Mortgage Guarantee insures all losses incurred by the lenders in case of borrower default, covering remaining outstanding principal amount, overdue interest, and enforcement costs. As the risk of losses for the lenders is reduced, they can offer lower rates on the guaranteed loans, up to 50 basis points (bps).

Mortgage borrowers in Holland can benefit from the NMG if they meet certain conditions:

• The total purchase price including extra expenses, such as notary costs and initial outlays (*kosten van noodzakelijk onderhoud*), should not exceed NLG379,000 in 1999. This amount is adjusted each year according to the changes in the house price index.

• The owner must use the property as a primary residence (*hoofdverblijf*).

• The borrower's income must be high enough to carry the mortgage costs. For this reason, the level of income will determine the amount that can be borrowed. The cover by the NMG is not restricted to low-income households. No maximum limit is put on the income.

• Borrowers have to pay a one-time fee equal to 0.36% of the loan.

Borrowers who are covered by the National Mortgage Guarantee can fully finance the purchase of their property including extra costs. In summary, the guarantee may allow an LTV ratio in excess of 100%. Since 1999 NMG can also guarantee mortgage loans on home improvement along with mortgages for purchase or building of a house. The National Mortgage Guarantee reported that its funds were

6. European Mortgage Federation, 1993.

approximately equal to NLG270 million in 1998, which is 29% higher than the year before. With these funds the NMG covers around NLG70 billion of mortgages outstanding.

Credit Bureau (*Stichting Bureau Krediet Registratie*)

The lending sector developed strongly in the sixties. In several cases this led to financial problems. The *Stichting Bureau Krediet Registratie* (BKR) was founded in 1965 by request of the financial sector in order to avoid such problems. Meanwhile the credit registration has been adopted in the Law on Consumer Credit (*Wet op het consumentenkrediet.*)

The BKR is an organization that registers every person taking up some kind of credit, irrespective of the form (such as credit cards or mortgage loans). This allows lenders to check the credit history of potential borrowers. In the case of mortgage loans the BKR registers only the persons who have payments in arrears in excess of 120 days. One infraction is enough to be picked up in the statistics.

Legal Framework for Securitization

The regulatory status of securitization was not entirely clear until September 1997 and remains incomplete to date. In 1997 the Dutch Central Bank issued guidelines concerning securitization. These guidelines have not been confirmed yet, which leaves a requirement for explicit authorization of each MBS transaction by the authorities.

According to the New Civil Code (*Nieuw Burgerlijk Wetboek*) introduced in 1992, a full legal transfer of mortgage loans from an originator to a special purpose vehicle (SPV) (true sale) requires the notification of the borrowers. Dutch lenders are not keen on notifying the borrowers of a true sale because this could damage the relationship with their customers. Therefore, in order to circumvent the obligation of notification, a true sale does not take place but "a silent right of pledge" is created. Only when a "notification event" (e.g., insolvency or default of originator-seller) occurs is the borrower notified and true sale is legally fully achieved.

A potential problem in securitizing a residential mortgage loan portfolio is that Dutch law gives a borrower the right of setoff in case the financial institution defaults. In other words, the mortgage debt due to the financial institution can be set off against deposits the borrower holds with that institution. For securitization purposes it is important to know that the borrower retains his right of setoff even after the borrower is notified of the formal assignment of his mortgage to another party—the MBS issuer.

Another legal problem is related to the fact that so-called bank mortgages in Holland secure borrowers' liabilities to the lender other than and in addition to the liability under a loan to acquire a property. This creates the need for partial termination of the bank mortgage in order to release the property from securing liabilities other than the loan for property acquisition. Partial or full termination can be achieved only through notification of the borrower, which as explained above, many lenders are reluctant to give.

Yet another legal and regulatory problem is associated with the right to pledge insurance proceeds or NHG claims from the originator-seller to the issuer of the MBS and security trustee. The enforceability of this right is under dispute, since this is regarded as a future right, and future rights may not be enforceable in case of pledgor's bankruptcy or insolvency.

INVESTMENT ANALYSIS FOR DUTCH MBS

The purpose of the investor's analysis of an MBS is to define its credit and non-credit-related characteristics and, ultimately, the security's fit with the investment objectives and with the current and expected status of investor's portfolio. MBS require a detailed analysis of the underlying mortgage pool, its servicing and expected performance, the financial and legal structure of the deal, the relationship between the underlying mortgage pool performance and its changes, and the performance of the MBS and each of its tranches. A case in point is the analysis of prepayments for mortgage pools and how they affect fixed- and floating-rate MBS.

Analytical Framework

The purpose of investment analysis is to determine the likelihood of full repayment of the bonds as well as the likely timing of the repayment cash flows. Investors should also be concerned with the occurrence of changes to any aspects of the deal that could have an effect on the bonds' pricing initially or on the secondary market, such as the bond's rating and potential for rating changes during its life, the performance of the underlying collateral, or the performance of the servicer.

In their investment analysis investors are aided by the rating agencies and the rating for the bonds that they are buying. The purpose of the rating agencies' analysis is to determine the likelihood of timely payment of interest and principal (reflected in the rating) on the rated tranches of the MBS. This requires assessment of the credit quality of the underlying pool of mortgages and, on that basis, assessment of the necessary level of credit enhancement relevant to the assigned rating level. The rating agencies evaluate the credit characteristics of the collateral pool, the servicing capabilities of the servicer, the underwriting criteria of the originating entity, the matching of the cash flows generated by the collateral pool with the cash flows promised to investors under the mortgage-backed securities, and the soundness of the legal and financial structure of the deal. They subject the cash flows of the pool to stress scenarios whose severity is directly related to the assigned final rating on the bonds.

The credit rating of the bonds provides a proper indication of the creditworthiness of those bonds. However, investors should also look at a number of other features to understand better the current and future performance of their investments. Such analysis includes the following:

- Potential for rating changes affecting the bonds associated with:
  - Status and ratings of the parties involved in the MBS: such as originator, servicer, swap counterparty

- Collateral backing the MBS—assumptions related to expected pool performance and change in those assumptions over time
- Liquidity characteristics of the MBS associated with:
  - Size of the initial issuance
  - Syndicate—its breadth and commitment as a market maker
  - Prepayment characteristics of the MBS
  - Prepayment speed assumed for pricing purposes
  - Effects of prepayment speed changes on bond's duration, weighted average maturity (WAM), convexity

Hereon, we briefly discuss key aspects of MBS analysis of collateral pool such as legal and structural features, and prepayment characteristics.

Characteristics of the Collateral Pool

The key characteristics of the collateral pool include:

- Number and average size of the mortgages, distribution by mortgage balance
- Loan-to-value (LTV) ratio—average and distribution by LTV
- Price-to-income or net income-to-mortgage payment—determines the ability of borrower to pay
- Weighted average interest rate on the mortgage pool at closing and its expected change as determined by the type of mortgages in the pool—fixed- or variable-rate mortgages, fixed-rate mortgages with periodic resets, and so on.
- Type of underlying property—detached single-family or two-family property, semidetached property, block of flats, single flat, investment property, residential property, multipurpose property (e.g., part commercial, part residential)—each type of property has different characteristics from the point of view of the borrower's motivation to service the mortgage debt and from the perspective of the property liquidation and recovery value in case of borrower default.
- Type of mortgage products—for example, annuity mortgages and life insurance mortgages—and the effects of the mortgage type on the debt servicing and debt recoveries
- Seasoning of the mortgage pool—the seasoning (aging) of the mortgage is associated with the building up of equity of the borrower in the acquired property, which has a strong influence on borrower's motivation to continue servicing or to abandon the mortgage. A mortgage's seasoning (the pool's) aging is associated with a loss curve: Mortgage loss curves tend to be front-loaded, that is, losses occur early in the life of the mortgage pool and decrease and stabilize later in its life.
- Characteristics of the obligors in the pool—salaried employed (employment history), self-employed (riskier); possible effects of social welfare

- Security—first, second, third lien mortgages
- Geographic concentration of the mortgage loans related to the demographic and economic characteristics of the respective regions
- House price movements by region
- Recovery value—property value reduced by market value decline, foreclosure costs, and carrying costs from delinquency to foreclosure
- Setoff risk—risk associated with the ability of borrower to offset mortgage debt against a deposit held with the bank originator of the mortgage
- Possibility for addition of mortgages to the original pool and the effects on the evolution of the pool's credit quality
- Insurance policies assuring balloon payments on interest-only mortgages

Financial Structure of the Pool

Key features of the financial structure of the pool include:

- Credit enhancement and method of its provision, such as subordination and insurance; when credit enhancement is established through subordination of several tranches with significantly different maturities; the paydown of the senior tranches; and pool performance within or better than initial expectations are all prerequisites for subordinated tranches upgrade or spread tightening
- Cash flow mechanics of the structure—priority of cash flow distribution—interest and principal payments on the different tranches, trustee, servicer and issuer expenses, swap payments, missed payments of interest and principal
- Liquidity support—liquidity line or servicer advances for liquidity support for payments of interest and/or principal for borrowers in arrears
- Swaps addressing potential cash flow mismatches between underlying pool weighted average coupon (WAC) and WAC on the MBS; key elements include actions to be taken in case of swap counterpart default or downgrade and/or swap termination
- Application of excess spread, if any; the excess spread is the difference between the WAC of underlying mortgage pool and the sum of WAC of MBS, servicing fee, and other trust expenses, and serves as a first level of protection against current and potential future losses on the mortgage pool

Legal Structure

Legal structure considerations include:

- Bankruptcy remoteness of the issuing entity
- Data protection trustee—custody over certain data lists in order to identify borrowers and enforce the loans and the collateral

- Transfer of rights to the issuers
- Transfer of mortgages securing the loans—transferred only upon the occurrence of certain events, downgrade of originator below certain level (A or A−)
- Transfer of the pool of loan claims and all corresponding economic rights; collateral remains with seller until occurrence of a specified event; borrowers may or may not have been notified
- Legal transfer and perfection of security interest
- Representations and warranties by the seller-servicer

Origination and Servicing

Considerations including origination and servicing are:

- Underwriting criteria and guidelines—the conservativeness and the consistency of the underwriting criteria inevitably affect the performance of the mortgage pool; mortgages originated through a bank branch network, and based on long-term relationship with a borrower, including the provision of other financial services to that same client tend to perform better than mortgages originated by a broker and sold to a mortgage consolidator for the purposes of an MBS deal
- Payment methods—direct debit, that is, borrowers have a current account with the originator
- Availability of credit scoring system for the purposes of faster and standardized assessment of borrowers' credit quality
- Availability of information regarding borrowers' debt burden and credit performance through a centralized, nationwide data-sharing system among the credit institutions
- Property value assessment—availability of established practices and mechanisms for current determination and subsequent updates of property value information
- Servicing guidelines—generally speaking, the originator of the mortgages is at least initially their servicer for the purposes of the MBS transaction

MBS Bond Features

MBS bond features include:

- Prepayments and their effect on floating-rate MBS [mainly weighted average life (WAL)] and fixed-rate MBS (duration and convexity)
- Prepayment assumptions used in credit enhancement modeling and MBS pricing
- Clear understanding of the differences between expected maturity and legal maturity for pass-through structures; for example, pass-through structures are rated by legal final, not by expected final

- Investment characteristics of each specific MBS tranche—senior, subordinated, IO or PO; IO—effects of prepayments, resets on the fixed-rate loans, excess spread, weighted average net mortgage rate

- Syndicate composition and commitment to secondary market making associated with the expected securities liquidity

Monitoring

Monitoring considerations include:

- Mechanisms for receiving timely information regarding pool performance (trustee reports, rating agencies reports, reporting on Bloomberg or a specified web site)

- Sufficiency of the information received for evaluation of pool performance—reporting criteria, clarity about calculation of different performance indicators, comparability of reported information among similar deals in the respected country and across countries

Analyzing MBS Prepayments

An important aspect of MBS deals and underlying pools for investors to understand is that of prepayments. Mortgage borrowers have the right and are often induced by a number of circumstances (e.g., market interest rates have fallen well below borrower's initial mortgage rate, increased income and desire to move to a bigger house, or change of job location and need to move house) to prepay their mortgage loans voluntarily. Alternatively, mortgage borrowers may face another set of conditions (increasing mortgage payments due to interest rate hikes or loss of income due to unemployment or disability) that may force them to default on their mortgages and lead to involuntary mortgage paydown as a result of a foreclosure on the mortgaged property.

Both voluntary and involuntary paydowns of the outstanding mortgages have the effect of changing the composition of a given mortgage pool backing an MBS, thus changing the cash flows generated by the pool and ultimately affecting the MBS amortization schedule. This is why investors must understand the effects prepayments have on MBS and must form adequate expectations as to when they will be repaid.

Effects of Prepayments on MBS

The effects depend on the type of MBS: whether it is an interest-only (IO) or principal-only (PO) security, or whether it is a fixed-rate or floating-rate security. We discussed the analysis of IOs in the previous chapter, since IO securities were issued as part of a German MBS deal to help monetize the excess spread in the transaction.

Now we will focus on the analysis of the effects of prepayments on fixed- and floating-rate MBS. Those effects can be summarized as follows:

- Prepayments may affect the weighted average yield generated by the mortgage pool as compared to the weighted average coupon as paid under the MBS. The difference between the two is the excess spread (after deduction of losses and servicing fees), which serves to investors as the first protection against losses: Reduction in excess spread diminishes the cushion protecting investors against losses. Reduction in excess spread due to prepayments occurs as mortgage borrowers prepay or default first on higher interest rate loans, thus reducing the weighted average yield generated by the mortgage pool in a respectively falling or rising interest rate environment.

• Prepayments shorten the WAL of MBS since investors receive principal repayments earlier than expected.

• Receiving principal repayments earlier than anticipated may have little effect for floating-rate MBS investors since the reinvestment risk of the repaid principal is relatively small: The floating-rate coupon on an MBS should trace closely the reinvestment rate, save for a spread over a common index.

• The effect on fixed-rate MBS could, however, be significant and can be expressed in:
  • Reinvestment risk—MBS prepay mainly when interest rates are declining and low, hence an MBS investor may have to reinvest prepaid principal at a rate below that of the MBS coupon
  • Convexity risk—prepayments lead to decreasing convexity for MBS; in a declining interest rate environment, the value of a portfolio with decreased convexity increases by a smaller percentage than that of a portfolio with larger convexity

Hence, the need for investors in fixed-rate MBS to understand the prepayment dynamics of a pool backing the respective MBS, the prepayments of which give rise to the prepayments under the MBS itself.

Voluntary and Involuntary Prepayment Drivers and Deterrents
As mentioned above, prepayments may be:

• Involuntary, that is, default and subsequent repossession, which depend on what has become known as the four D's: default, disease, divorce, and death. The first of the four is mainly associated with loss of employment. Hence, the need for investors to understand the employment conditions in the respective country, the employment characteristics of the mortgage borrowers in the specific pool (mainly employed versus self-employed for example), the availability and scope of social safety net and unemployment support, the availability and coverage of unemployment insurance and other social guarantees. Further, it is important to understand the foreclosure practices in a given country such as length of procedure, mechanisms of sales, and related expenses.

• Voluntary, which depend on the decision of the mortgage borrower to prepay a given mortgage loan because of
  • Refinancing (obtaining a new mortgage loan at a lower interest rate in a falling interest rate environment or to buy a bigger house)

- Relocation (usually associated with change of jobs and change of residence)

- Monetization of equity in an existing home (replacing an existing mortgage loan with a higher LTV loan or same LTV loan in case of a rising property values environment, i.e., borrowing against an upward revalued property)

- Using a tax benefit (ability to realize a capital gain on a property when the property values have increased without paying capital gains tax)

The mortgage borrower's decision to prepay in case of voluntary prepayments, though, depends on a number of additional factors:

- Existence of prepayment penalties or other restrictions on prepayments

- Transaction costs associated with the property transfer, legal and surveyor expenses, stamp duties

- Potential loss of tax benefits attached to an initial mortgage but not transferable to a subsequent mortgage

The above factors are translated into refinancing expenses and lead to a trade-off decision as to whether the expenses under the new mortgage are sufficiently lower than the expenses under the current mortgage to allow for absorption of all refinancing expenses and leave room for some savings. In some cases, that may be impossible, especially if mortgage prepayment is subject to a requirement that the prepaying borrower must compensate the lender for any lost income stemming from the difference between the original mortgage rate and the current mortgage rate.

Pool-Specific Prepayment Drivers and Deterrents
When analyzing fixed-rate MBS, investors must understand the prepayment history of a given mortgage pool within the context of the respective housing and mortgage market environment. A number of specific pool characteristics also have effects on prepayments:

- LTV distribution of the pool—High LTV loans have a higher incentive to prepay in a falling interest rate environment as they realize bigger savings.

- Seasoning of the pool—As the pool ages, prepayments follow a distinct pattern usually rising initially and then stabilizing at some plateau level.

- Way of mortgage origination—Mortgages originated through brokers compensated through commission on mortgage origination tend to prepay faster than mortgages originated through banks, since the commission that brokers receive for each new mortgage provides an incentive for them to encourage their clients to prepay at the first available opportunity.

- Prepayment burnout—As fewer borrowers seize the opportunity to prepay and refinance their mortgage loan, the prepayment rate decreases.

The term *burnout* means that prepayment rates depend not only upon the interest rate differential between a given mortgage rate and the prevailing primary market mortgage rates, but also on the path taken by mortgage rates to arrive at this level.

This is referred to as the *path dependency* of prepayments. This alert occurs because when faced with a refinancing opportunity, the most aware borrowers will react and prepay their mortgages, but after a while, given the same refinancing incentive, a decreasing share of the remaining borrowers will respond. Those remaining in the pool are either unaware of the refinancing opportunity, unwilling to take advantage of it, or cannot qualify for a new mortgage.

• Pool composition in terms of type of mortgages, type of properties that back the mortgage loans, etc.

Prepayment Modeling and MBS Pricing Speed

When determining the conditional prepayment rate (CPR) speed for a given MBS, that is, the underlying mortgage pool, all the factors mentioned are taken into consideration through relevant prepayment modeling. A prepayment model for a specific issuer is developed based on a detailed quantitative and qualitative analysis of that issuer's mortgage pool. The analysis is meant to determine the factors that affect its prepayment behavior and prescribe to each of these factors a given weight to be used to determine potential future prepayment behavior of a given MBS pool based on its particular characteristics. When buying fixed-rate MBS, investors should understand the prepayment assumption used when it is being priced. The prepayment assumptions are expressed using the following prepayment conventions:

Conditional Prepayment Rate   The conditional prepayment rate (CPR) measures prepayments as a fraction or percentage of the remaining principal balance at the beginning of the measurement period (hence, "conditional" on the principal balance). It can be employed to express an average or compound rate over many periods, or a single-period rate. The resulting rate sometimes is expressed as annualized percentage. In recent years CPR has increasingly come to refer to an annualized prepayment rate, single monthly mortality (SMM) to the monthly rate. In calculating yields, investors may employ a single or "constant" CPR assumption across the term of the investment to project the cash flows. A varying CPR assumption has also been used to reflect historical experience or projections from a prepayment model.

Public Securities Association   The Public Securities Association (PSA) prepayment model combines the simplicity of the CPR method with the intuition of the empirical survivorship schedules from the Federal Housing Administration (FHA) method. The FHA method predicts the prepayment on a mortgage based on aggregate data on FHA mortgage pools. The PSA benchmark (denoted 100% PSA) assumes a series of CPRs beginning at 0.2% in the first month and increasing afterward by 0.2% every month until the CPR reaches 6% (30 months after mortgage origination) and remains constant at 6% CPR thereafter. Prepayment levels are then expressed as multiples of the benchmark PSA: For example, a prepayment rate of 200% PSA means that the prepayment will be twice as high as the benchmark every month.

Option-Adjusted Spread

The option-adjusted spread (OAS) model has been developed to reflect the risks to an MBS investor arising when mortgage borrowers in the MBS mortgage pool exercise their options to prepay (refinance) their mortgage loans. If interest rates fall sufficiently, the borrower will prepay his mortgage in order to refinance at the lower prevailing interest rate. The investor who holds mortgage-backed securities receives the prepaid principal and has to reinvest it at a lower market rate.

OAS determines the cost of the mortgage prepayment option as a basis-point value, which should be deducted from the yield spread on the MBS. If the yield curve is flat, the following relationship holds: Option cost = Yield spread − OAS.

As rates fall, the option cost on a current-coupon increases. Traders and investors will then ask for higher spreads in order to compensate for the increased likelihood that the option is exercised and investors have to reinvest prepaid principal at a lower rate.

The OAS provides a benchmark for the bond value after accounting for the embedded option cost assumed by the bondholder. This measure is used to evaluate the relative cheapness or richness of securities with embedded options such as MBS.

CASE STUDY: DNIB'S "DUTCH MBS" DEALS

DNIB is the most active issuer of fixed-rate pass-through MBS, not only in the Netherlands but also in Europe. We briefly examine its origination, structuring, and underwriting practices in the area of mortgage lending and financing through securitization.

Principal Actors in DNIB's MBS Deals

The principal actors in the deal are described below.

De Nationale Investeringsbank N.V. (DNIB)

DNIB is fully owned by the two largest Dutch pension funds ABP and PGDM. Both its strong financial performance and its sound risk profile (Cooke Ratio = 13.7% and Core Capital Ratio = 9.7%) point to strong creditworthiness reflected in ratings in the AA range. DNIB businesses span long-term lending, equity investments, capital market transactions, and various financial brokerage and consultancy services.

DNIB has been actively acquiring residential mortgages from diverse mortgage brokers (especially insurance companies) since the early 1990s. Servicing of the mortgage pools is outsourced, and a growing amount of loan portfolios is financed off-balance-sheet through securitization. About 60% to 70% of its mortgage book DNIB originates through subsidiaries; another 20% it purchases from several mortgage originators such as Stad Rotterdam, Deutsche Beambte Verzicherung, Royal Life, which is a 100% subsidiary of Royal Netherlands, and Swiss Life. The remaining 10% of its mortgage book are mortgages received as a security against loans extended to insurance companies.

Royal Residentie Hypotheken B.V. (Royal Residential Mortgages)
Royal Residentie Hypotheken B.V. is a fully owned subsidiary of DNIB and originates residential mortgages through the brokerage network of Royal Nederland Verzeker-ingsgroep N.V. following acceptance criteria established by DNIB. It also finances (warehouses) residential mortgages while outsourcing their servicing to STATER B.V.

STATER Portfolio Performance Management B.V. (STATER)
STATER, previously part of Bouwfonds and now its fully owned subsidiary, is the largest independent residential mortgage loan servicer in the Netherlands. It ser-vices portfolios of numerous institutions including DNIB along with the entire NLG25 billion loan portfolio of Bouwfonds. STATER plays a crucial role in the processes of mortgage origination and securitisation.

STATER currently services about 30% of all newly originated mortgages, and its share is expected to increase in the future. The remainder of the mortgages are serviced by banks and insurance company originators; another, say 2%, of the new mortgages are serviced by Hypotrust. In other words, qualified servicers do exist in Holland, and replacement servicers, should the need arise, are available.

N.V. Bouwfonds Nederlandse Gemeenten
Bouwfonds was created in 1946 with the mandate to promote home ownership, es-pecially low-income housing. It was fully owned by its founders—27 Dutch municipalities—and most recently was acquired by ANB Amro. Through its three subsidiaries Bouwfonds occupies a leading position in the real estate sector. It is the largest developer of owner-occupied houses (Bouwfonds Woningbouw B.V.), the second-largest (after the four largest Dutch commercial banks) originator of residential mortgages (Bouwfonds Hypotheken B.V.), and the largest property manager (Vastgoedbeheer ABC) in the Netherlands.

Mortgage Origination and Servicing

Mortgage origination through mortgage brokers and mortgage servicing are de-scribed below.

The Origination Process
A potential borrower does not deal with DNIB directly but turns to a mortgage broker, which is quite often an insurance company. STATER checks the client's credit history with the Dutch Credit Bureau, SBKR. If no irregularities are found, he uses the infor-mation supplied by the borrower regarding income and the underlying property to cal-culate the maximum loan size he can grant. Also, this information is run through the STATER credit-scoring model (based on DNIB criteria), after which the decision is made whether to offer the loan. If the mortgage broker makes an offer, the borrower has approximately 3 weeks to decide whether to accept it. In case the borrower accepts the offer, the information supplied earlier is thoroughly checked and only then will DNIB transfer the money to the notary for the purchase of the property.

DNIB Acceptance Criteria

Acceptance criteria specified by DNIB are applied through the STATER Credit-Scoring Model. These criteria include:

- Maximum-allowed LTFV is 125%. The older the borrower, the lower the maximum-allowed LTFV
- Loan size can not exceed five times borrower's income
- Property must be used by the owner for its primary residence and not for commercial purposes

Overruled Decisions

The decision taken by STATER is based on its credit-scoring model and on the above-specified acceptance criteria. It can, therefore, be only "accept" or "reject." To preserve flexibility in its origination process, DNIB has the right to reconsider and overrule the rejects. In reality, about 30% of the decisions not to grant a loan are overruled by DNIB as a result of a more detailed individual assessment. In 20% of those cases the initial reject was due to minor administrative problems (e.g., missing documents) and the remaining 10% to minor credit impediments.

Mortgage Servicing

STATER services all of DNIB's loan portfolios in return for a fee. In the case of payments in arrears, STATER contacts the delinquent borrower and DNIB intervenes to renegotiate the loan or foreclose the property only if the problem persists for more than 4 to 6 months.

Dutch MBS Deals Overview

The first MBS transaction in the Netherlands was structured as a soft bullet and took place in 1996. Since then, eight MBS transactions have been completed. The details are summarized in Exhibit 40–7.

DNIB is the most active issuer of MBS in the Netherlands, and one of the few fixed-rate pass-through MBS issuers in Europe. Under this form, all risks, including prepayment risks, are transferred to the investors, which, in turn, receive higher yields on their investment. Credit risk to investors is mitigated through credit enhancement, and DNIB retains the most junior tranche in the subordination (credit enhancement) structure.

Dutch MBS 97-1 B.V.

Dutch MBS 97-1 and Dutch MBS 97-II notes are the first publicly offered mortgage-backed securities in the Dutch market, which are structured as pass-throughs. Dutch MBS 97-1 was originated by Bouwfonds Hypotheken on behalf of Bouwinvest B.V. The mortgage pool consists of interest-only mortgages (38.6%), savings mortgages (34.8%), life mortgages (22.9%), and annuity mortgages (3.7%). The average LTV of nonguaranteed loans in the pool is 74.9%.

E X H I B I T 40–7

Dutch MBS Deals

Date	Issuer	Originator	Class	Currency	Total Amount (million)	Redemption	Coupon	Rating
1996	Fortis Investment Mortgage Securities BV	Dutch Municipalities	A	NLG[a]	500	Bullet	Fixed	AAA
							Fixed	
							Fixed	
1997	European Mortgage Securities 1 BV (EMS 1)	ABN AMRO	A1	NLG	200	Soft bullet	Fixed	AAA
			A2	NLG	250		Fixed	AAA
			A3	NLG	250		Fixed	AAA
			A4	NLG	1,200		Fixed	AAA
			M	NLG	100		Fixed	A
1997	Dutch MBS 97-I	Bouwfonds Hypotheken	A	NLG	368	Pass-through	Fixed	AAA
								NR[c]
1997	Dutch MBS 97-II	Stad Rotterdam Bank NV	A1	NLG	105	Pass-through	Fixed	AAA
			A2	NLG	453		Fixed	AAA
			B	NLG	30		Fixed	A
1998	European Mortgage Securities 2 BV (EMS 2)	ABN AMRO	A1	FFR[b]	1,000	Soft bullet	Fixed	AAA
			A2	NLG	1,000		Fixed	AAA
			M	FFR	260		Fixed	AA
			C	FFR	40		Fixed	BBB

Year	Issue	Issuer	Tranche	Currency	Amount	Structure	Coupon	Rating
1998	Dutch MBS 98-I	Stad Rotterdam Bank NV	A1	NLG	141	Pass-through	Fixed	AAA
			A2	NLG	420		Fixed	AAA
			B	NLG	27		Fixed	A
1999	Dutch MBS 99-I	Royal Residentie Hypotheken BV	A1	Euro	66.5	Pass-through	Fixed	AAA
			A2	Euro	195		Fixed	AAA
			B	Euro	13.5		Fixed	A
			C	Euro	7		Fixed	BBB
			D	Euro	4		Fixed	BB
1999	European Mortgage Securities III	ABN AMRO	A1	Euro	1,400	Soft bullet	Floating	AAA
			A2	Euro	1,000		Fixed	AA
			M	Euro	100		Fixed	A
			C	Euro	23		Fixed	BBB

[a]NLG = Dutch gulden, or guilders.
[b]FFR = French francs.
[c]NR = not rated.
Source: Merrill Lynch.

Two classes of notes are issued: a senior and a subordinated class. DNIB covers any shortfall in the cash flows aimed to pay interest on the senior notes. A special arrangement is made to address the fact that savings mortgages in the pool do not make any principal payments before the final maturity of the loan. A GIC and a put option mitigate the reinvestment and interest rate risks.

Credit enhancement of the mortgage pool is achieved through several layers of protection, namely, excess spread, a cash reserve (initially zero, increases with excess spread until the "target balance" is reached), subordination, and the National Mortgage Guarantee on 17% of the loans.

Dutch MBS 97-II

The four classes of notes issued are backed by 2,980 residential life mortgage loans on properties in Holland. The mortgage loans were originated by N.V. Bouwkas Rohyp and SR-Bank N.V. and then sold to S.R. Hypotheken N.V., which is the actual seller of the mortgages for the purposes of the deal.

The average LTFV of the pool is 71.1%.

Reinvestment and interest rate risks on DMBS 97-II are minimized by a GIC and a put option, respectively.

Credit enhancement is provided through the excess spread, subordination, and National Mortgage Guarantee on 24% of the loan pool.

Dutch MBS 98-I

Similar to the Dutch MBS 97-II, the Dutch MBS 98-I consists of four classes of notes backed by residential life and savings mortgage loans on properties in the Netherlands. The average LTFV of the pool is 78%. N.V. Bouwkas Rohyp and SR-Bank N.V. originated the loans initially, and the latter is the actual seller of the mortgage loans.

The structure of the deal is the same as for the Dutch MBS 97-I, but special provisions have been added in order to receive regular cash flows from the non-amortizing savings mortgages. Again, a put option and a GIC are used to control the reinvestment and the interest rate risk. Credit enhancement is achieved through excess spread, subordination, a reserve fund, and National Mortgage Guarantee on 29% of the loans.

Dutch MBS 99-I

The two senior and the four subordinated classes of notes are backed by 2,331 performing residential mortgage loans secured by first mortgages on properties in the Netherlands and by life insurance policies. The average LTV of the loans is approximately 76%.

Royal Nederland Levensverzekering (RNL) originated the mortgage loans through its insurance broker network under a joint-venture agreement with DNIB signed in 1997. The legal seller of the mortgages is Royal Residentie (RR). Credit enhancement on the transaction is obtained by protection through an arrears liquidity facility provided by DNIB, excess spread, and subordination. DNIB provides an interest rate swap in order to address interest rate risk, and a GIC mitigate reinvestment risk.

Performance: Delinquencies, Losses, Prepayments

As we saw earlier, the level of delinquencies and losses in the Netherlands are as a whole very low. DNIB's mortgage pools are no different and demonstrate exceptionally low levels of delinquencies and losses.

Delinquencies
Earlier in the chapter we estimated that the delinquencies on Dutch mortgage loans are below 0.63% of the outstanding mortgages. Delinquencies on DNIB deals are even lower. To illustrate that, we use delinquency information about the pool backing Dutch MBS 97-2 and 98-1 (see Exhibits 40–8 and 40–9).

Losses
As reported in Exhibit 40–10, the level of losses on DNIB's total mortgage loan portfolio is extremely low. This is similar to the Dutch mortgage market in general.

Prepayments
Data about prepayments point to their recent higher level. In previous sections we discussed the combination of the unique circumstances that explain such developments. In brief, we believe that the observed increase in prepayments is driven by:

- Substantial interest rate drop to historically lowest levels

- Increasingly aggressive role of intermediaries in mortgage origination

- Introduction of new mortgage products

- Increases in housing values and favorable stock market performance

EXHIBIT   40–8

Dutch MBS 97-II: Delinquencies

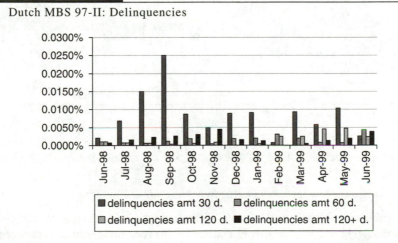

Source: FitchIBCA.

E X H I B I T   40–9

Dutch MBS 98-I: Delinquencies

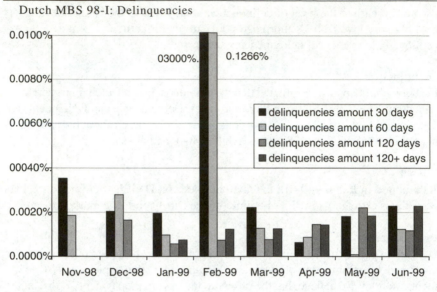

Source: FitchIBCA.

E X H I B I T   40–10

DNIB Mortgage Loan Loss Experience

Year	Portfolio (in Euros, minimum)	Net Loss (in Euros, minimum)	Loans Foreclosed	Net Loss Percent of Portfolio
1993	268	0	0	0.000%
1994	1,234	0	0	0.000
1995	1,535	0.05	1	0.003
1996	2,106	0.1	5	0.005
1997	2,097	0.04	5	0.002
1998	3,206	0.19	9	0.006

Source: Moody's Investor Service.

- Ability to replace a mortgage with a shorter period to reset with a mortgage with a longer period to reset

- Expectation for low interest rate that may have slowed burnout

The combination of these factors makes refinancing at a mortgage reset date and also refinancing of mortgages with relatively short remaining term to reset beneficial for the respective borrowers. The expectation that the interest rate will re-

E X H I B I T   40–11

DNIB MBS Mortgage Pool Composition by Reset Window

Deal	WAM* (Year)	Percentage Loans Reset
97–1	<3.1	14.7%
	3–7	0
	>7	85.3
97–2	<5	30
	5–7	40
	>7	30
98–1	<5	8
	5–7	45
	>7	47
99–1	<7	0
	>9	100

*WAM = weighted average maturity.
Source: DNIB.

main low may have delayed the burnout effect, as borrowers expect to refinance later with a shorter remaining term to reset and pay less penalty. However, recent mortgage rate increases indicate that such expectations may have been misguided. That will probably lead to prepayments for mortgages originated in the past to stabilize in the foreseeable future at or below their current levels.

We illustrate our reasoning with the following example. Exhibit 40–11 shows the composition of the mortgage pools (backing various DNIB deals) by various reset periods. We argue that the prepayment penalty depends on the remaining period to next reset (the reset window). For example, to refinance a loan of NLG100,000 from 7% to 6%, the prepayment penalty increases, depending on the reset window from 2.74% of the loan amount for the 36-month reset window to 9.88% for the 180-month reset window (see Exhibit 40–12).

This example alone illustrates one of the reasons for the increased prepayments in earlier DNIB deals. Generally, they included higher percentage of loans with small reset windows. Currently, an increasing amount of loans is being originated with longer reset windows (extended from 5 to 10 years in 1997 and 1998 to 10 to 20 years in 1999), as evidenced by later DNIB deals (see Exhibit 40–11). A higher prepayment penalty associated with longer reset window should discourage prepayments in the future.

DNIB's Prepayment Model

DNIB started developing its own model in the beginning of 1998 for the purposes of analyzing the prepayments of the mortgage pools backing the securities issued and for determining pricing speed for new MBS deals.

E X H I B I T   40–12

Prepayment Penalties*

Penalty (%)	Period to Next Reset (Months)
2.74%	36
3.55	48
4.31	60
7.51	120
9.88	180

*As a percent of mortgage amount (calculated on the basis of NLG100,000 mortgage, mortgage rate drop from 7% to 6%, and varying period to next reset).
Source: Merrill Lynch.

The proprietary model (a proportional hazard model) uses two functions:

- A turnover function, which determines the baseline as a function of variables such as age, property type (single-family or apartment), mortgage type (first or second lien), and seasonality. Coefficients are used to modify the baseline due to deviating characteristics of the analyzed pool.

- An interest rate function, which uses the following variables: interest rate, property type (single-family or apartment), mortgage type (first or second lien mortgage), type of mortgage amortization (annuity, savings mortgage, interest rate only mortgage).

Overall, according to the model, prepayments are most sensitive to mortgage age and interest rate change, that is, a refinancing incentive. The refinance incentive is expressed as a change between the interest rate at which the mortgage was initially issued and the current average mortgage rate of all mortgages issued during a given month. The refinancing incentive function is set in a way that reflects not only the relative change of interest rates, but also the starting point of that change. To illustrate, if the mortgage rate at origination (A) of a given mortgage is 10% and the current mortgage rate (B) is 8%, the refinancing incentive (C) is calculated to be 10%/8% − 1, or 0.25%. If $A = 7\%$ and $B = 5\%$, then $C = 0.4\%$. In other words, the refinancing objective is higher starting from a lower point for the same amount of interest rate drop. Refinancing objective is denoted as Relative Spread in Exhibit 40–13.

We caution that direct comparisons of the refinancing incentives with U.S. MBS and HEL may be misleading. In the United States, the relationship between prepayments and interest rate change are expressed in terms of absolute change in mortgage rate. For example, a clear change in prepayments can be observed as soon as mortgage rates drop or increase by 50 bps.

Prepayments as a function of aging of the mortgage follow a different path, depending on whether the mortgage loan is to finance the purchase of an apart-

E X H I B I T   40–13

Dutch MBS 99-II—Interest Rates and CPR

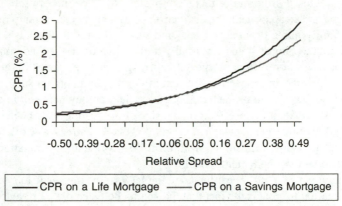

Source: DNIB—Based on proprietary prepayment model.

E X H I B I T   40–14

Dutch MBS 99 II—Seasoning

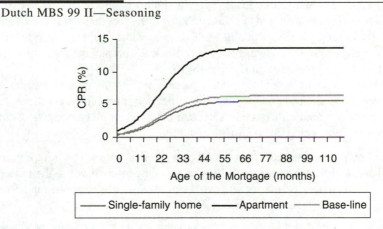

Source: DNIB—Based on proprietary prepayment model.

ment or a single-family house. Apartments are subject to higher prepayments as the loans in the pool progressively age. The rationale behind this is the practice that young people usually buy an apartment, which they replace with a single-family house when they are ready to start a family or gain higher income in their careers. The results of a simulation using DNIB's proprietary prepayment model regarding the expected prepayment dynamics as a function of mortgage aging based on the characteristics of mortgage pool backing Dutch MBS 99-2 are shown in Exhibit 40–14. The ratio between apartment and single-family house loans in the pool should help determine the average pool prepayment speed.

Comparisons with U.S. MBS may again be misleading. In the United States, for example, the ramp-up is usually 30 months, and for HEL, it is much shorter—about 15 months. Furthermore, there is no clear distinction between a single-family home and an apartment; the distinction is rather between primary residence (a single-family home or an apartment) and second home. In that case, the prepayments on the primary home are usually higher than on the second home.

Prepayments on different types of mortgages demonstrate different sensitivity to the refinancing incentive. For example, prepayments on savings mortgages are less sensitive to refinancing incentive than prepayments on investment mortgages. We relate it to the effects on the size of the premiums to be paid by the borrower in the mortgage deposit and the related tax incentives, as explained earlier. This relationship is illustrated in Exhibit 40–13 based on simulations using DNIB's proprietary prepayment model.

Prepayments do not appear linked to the LTV of the mortgage loans. A plausible explanation for that is the fact that the spread between the mortgage rates on high LTV and low LTV mortgages is relatively small.

This is not the case in the United States, where LTV and prepayments are closely linked—the higher the LTV, the lower the expected prepayment. For example, for an increase in LTV by 10%, prepayment likelihood decreases by 7% to 8% in the case of home equity loans (alias for subprime mortgages). The reasoning behind such relationship in the United States is the fact that a high LTV entails low equity in the property, which in itself decreases the chances for refinancing and increasing leverage. Comparison of specific deal's prepayment behavior in the US and in Holland is shown on Exhibit 40–15.

There are several variables, which the model cannot take into account, but which may have an effect on prepayments especially in recent years. Such variables are not captured either because of lack of information or because of difficulty in their forecasting. Such variables include:

- Role of mortgage intermediaries—mortgage intermediaries work on a commission basis and have interest in pushing refinancing alternatives to their clients. The aggressiveness of the intermediaries is a relatively new phenomenon in Holland and its effects are yet to be fully assessed.

- Borrowers' take advantage of reset dates to approach new mortgage products or extend the term of their mortgages.

- Borrowers' expectations of generally low interest rates and low inflation in concurrence with the understanding that demand will continue to outstrip supply in the foreseeable future underpin their expectations for rising housing values.

To summarize, the recent increase in prepayments in our view can be explained by the simultaneous influence of several factors discussed above in detail. Briefly, it is the unique mix of substantial interest drops to historically lowest levels, the aggressive role of intermediaries in mortgage origination, the pursuit of new mortgage products, and the increase in housing values. The combination of these factors makes refinancing at reset date and also refinancing of mortgages

E X H I B I T   40–15

Prepayments—Dutch MBS 97-1 Versus FNMA-30 (Left-hand Axis: CPR %, Right-hand Axis Mortgage Rate %)

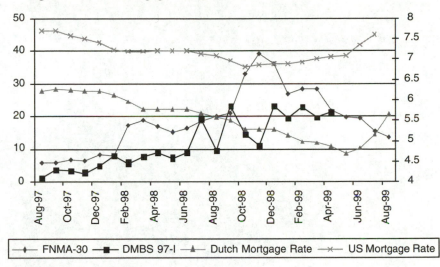

Note: (1) FNMA, 30 yr, 7%, No prepayment penalties; (2) DMBS 97-1: WAL 6.60 years and coupon, 5.50, Prepayment penalties; (3) monthly CPR, annualized.
Source: Merrill Lynch, Datastream.

with relatively short term to reset beneficial for the respective borrowers. Many of these factors will persist in the near term, whereas others show signs of change (e.g., mortgage interest rates have increased since June 1999). This will probably lead prepayments to stabilize and gradually slow down, especially for mortgages originated in the past.

The question, then, becomes whether the recently seen prepayment experience will persist in the longer term. As we explained, the higher-than-usual prepayment levels are due to a unique combination of factors. The influence of some of these factors, though, should wear off over time. Interest rates are unlikely to see as significant a drop as seen in the last several years—this would diminish the refinancing incentive going forward. In addition, many of the recently refinanced mortgages have a reset term longer than usual (beyond 10 years), which will make their refinancing more expensive or would require a very steep and unlikely drop in interest rates. This will probably act to dampen prepayments for such more recently originated mortgages.

CHAPTER 41

MORTGAGE-BACKED SECURITIES IN AUSTRALIA

Karen Weaver, CFA

Managing Director
Global Head of Securitization Research
Deutsche Banc Alex. Brown Inc.

Eugene Xu

Director
Deutsche Banc Alex. Brown Inc.

Nichol Bakalar

Vice President
Deutsche Banc Alex. Brown Inc.

Trudy Weibel

Assistant Vice President
Deutsche Banc Alex. Brown Inc.

Australian mortgage-backed securities (MBS) are playing a growing role in global fixed income markets. Since its inception in the mid-1980s, the Australian MBS market has been enjoying impressively healthy growth, and increasingly, large portions of the securitization programs are reaching the U.S. and European markets. The Australian MBS market is now the third largest MBS market in the world, after the United States and Germany (including *Pfandbriefe*). Australian MBS are gaining favorable recognition from an increasing number of U.S. and European investors because of the high credit quality and benign prepayment behavior exhibited by the underlying collateral. With more frequent issuance, liquidity is also improving. Lastly, securitization structures are likely to become more flexible over time, allowing issuers to reach a more extensive market.

The first Australian MBS were issued in the mid-1980s, but MBS remained a domestic market until 1997. Furthermore, before 1992, most issuance was done through state government–sponsored programs. Private sector programs have since rapidly replaced the government programs in issuance, and the latter have almost completely faded from the picture. Withholding tax treatment for mortgage-backed securities changed in 1997, which paved the way for European market access first,

The authors wish to thank Glenn McDowell of Deutsche Bank Australia for his important contributions to this chapter.

EXHIBIT 41–1

Australian Mortgage Issuance Has Quadrupled in 5 Years

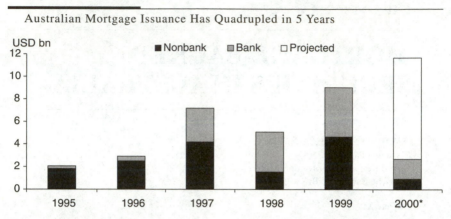

*Actual data for 2000 consists of only first-quarter issuance. Projection is for the rest of the year.
Source: Deutsche Bank Securities.

and U.S. market access later. With the expanded markets to tap, issuance of Australian MBS surged. Total MBS issuance increased 160% from 1996's Australian dollars (A$) 3.7 billion (USD 2.9 bn) to 1997's A$ 9.6 billion (USD 7.2 billion). In 1999, total MBS issuance reached A$ 14 billion (USD 9 bn).

As in the United States, Australian MBS issuers can be divided into banks and nonbanks. Nonbank entities, like mortgage finance companies in the United States, rely mostly on the capital markets for their funding. Saturation within the (relatively small) domestic MBS market has raised nonbank funding costs. Banks had, in the past, preferred to use other means such as on-balance-sheet bond issues or deposits to fund their mortgage lending. However, since the opening of the U.S. and European markets to Australian MBS, the international capital market has brought a more efficient, flexible, and diversified venue to obtain funding. Australian bank issuers have been increasingly attracted to the MBS market as a result.

Exhibit 41–1 shows Australian MBS issuance since 1995, in U.S. dollars.

Notwithstanding such rapid growth, the issuance volume of Australian MBS was likely hampered by a series of mishaps in global financial markets. The Australian dollar was adversely affected by Asian financial turmoil in late 1997; the Russian default crisis caused extensive spread widening in the global fixed income markets in 1998; and the Y2K liquidity squeeze in mid-1999 widened most credit-related spreads, especially on off-the-run asset classes. The market for Australian MBS might have been larger than it is today had these crises not occurred.

Currently, only about one-fifth to one-quarter of Australian mortgage loans are securitized each year. In particular, although banks originate the bulk of mortgage loans in Australia (see Exhibit 41–2), they made up only about half the volume in the securitization market. This means that about 80% of their portfolios currently are not securitized. We believe that great potential exists for the Australian MBS market to grow into a larger and even more efficient and more liquid asset sector over the next few years.

EXHIBIT 41–2

Banks Originate the Bulk of Australian Mortgage Loans

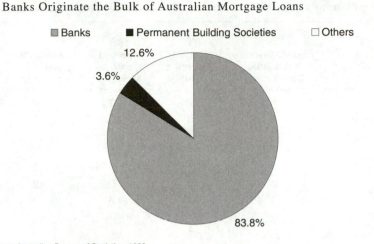

Source: Australian Bureau of Statistics, 1999.

COLLATERAL CREDIT CONSIDERATIONS

One of the hallmarks of Australian MBS is their outstanding historical credit performance. The collateral in these pools has exhibited low delinquencies, low defaults, and miniscule losses relative to U.S. mortgages. Such credit robustness is due to a favorable economy and a strong housing market, as well as government policies, lending and insurance practices, and Australian borrowers' financial conservatism.

Australia, like the United States, is characterized by high rates of home ownership. According to the Australian Bureau of Statistics (AusBS), in 1998, about 4.9 million Australian households owned their residence. This represents about 70% of all Australian households. According to the Current Population Survey (CPS), a joint project between the U.S. Bureau of Labor Statistics and the Bureau of the Census, U.S. home ownership was 67% for the same year.[1]

An unusually high percentage of Australian homes are owned by their occupants without a mortgage. The AusBS data shows that, out of the 4.9 million households that owned their homes in 1998, more than 56% of them owned the home outright. In contrast, the percentage of U.S. households that own their residence mortgage-free is below 39%. The low level of Australian home-owners' indebtedness provides added protection to the Australian housing market in an economic

---

1. Note that Australia and U.S. home-ownership rates are calculated differently. In Australia, the home-ownership rate is calculated as the number of households that own the residence they occupy divided by the number of all households. In the United States, home-ownership rates are calculated as the number of units that are occupied by their owners divided by the total number of housing units. Since a household can own and occupy more than one housing unit (i.e., a vacation home), the U.S. rate should have an upward bias.

E X H I B I T 41–3

Housing Costs as a Proportion of Income Are Moderate in the Australian Market

	Home-Owner Household Distribution	(1) Owned Without a Mortgage	(2) Owned with a Mortgage	(3)* Estimated Debt-to-Income Ratio
Sydney	31%	2%	20%	18%
Melbourne	30	3	17	14
Brisbane	12	3	16	13
Adelaide	10	3	17	14
Perth	12	2	17	15
Hobart	2	3	15	12
Darwin	1	N/A	N/A	N/A
Canberra	29	2	20	18
All Capital Cities	100%	3	18	15

*(2) − (1) = (3)
Source: Australian Bureau of Statistics, 1998.

downturn. All else being equal, relatively fewer Australians would need to sell their properties in an economic downturn, which should help stabilize home prices.

In addition, housing costs, including mortgage payments and other recurring costs such as property tax and other expenses to maintain a property, expressed as a proportion of income, are relatively low in Australia. Exhibit 41–3 shows the mean housing cost, as a proportion of income, in the eight Australian capital cities. To express this in debt-to-income terms, we estimated the debt-to-income ratio as the difference in total housing costs for mortgagees versus cash owners.

Another indicator of the generally low level of indebtedness among Australian home owners is loan-to-value (LTV).[2] Exhibit 41–4 shows that overall, the mean LTV ratio among Australian home owners is only 16%. Even among home owners under age 35, who can be considered "starters" and whose home often represents their only asset, the mean LTV ratio is only 42%. In contrast, the median LTV ratio for all U.S. home owners, according to U.S. Bureau of Census, is estimated at about 55%.[3]

---

2. In the Australian mortgage market, what we know in the United States as the LTV (loan-to-value) ratio is often called the "LVR."

3. U.S. Bureau of Census, *American Housing Survey for the United States; 1997.* It should be noted that both the Australian Bureau of Statistics and the U.S. Bureau of Census calculated the LTV ratio by dividing the current outstanding mortgage loan balance by the estimated home value at the time of survey. The samples in both countries include home owners who own the home mortgage-free. Because the home values were estimated and reported by the respondents, they tend to have upward biases. This in turn may result in downward biases of estimates of LTV in both countries.

E X H I B I T   41–4

Debt as a Percentage of Home Value Among Australian Home-owners

Age	Mean Loan-to-Value Ratio	Percentage of Total
Under 35	42%	16.4%
35–44	26	22.6
45–54	12	22.2%
55–64	4	15.7
65 and Over	1	23.1
Total	16%	100.0%

Source: Australian Bureau of Statistics, 1998.

E X H I B I T   41–5

Australian Home Prices Outpaced Consumer Price Index Since Late-1980s

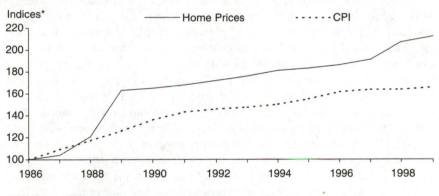

*1986 indices = 100.
Source: Reserve Bank of Australia, Australian Bureau of Statistics and Deutsche Bank Securities.

Australia's fast-expanding economy,[4] along with vibrant population growth[5] has been the foundation of a strong, healthy housing market. According to the Australian Bureau of Statistics, the weighted average housing price in the eight capital cities rose 30% from 1990 through 1999, cumulatively. In the same period, the country's Consumer Price Index (CPI) increased only 22% (see Exhibit 41–5).[6]

---

4. Australia's gross domestic product (GDP) growth rate in 1999 was 4.3%.
5. Population growth rate in 1997 was 1.3%.
6. A history of steadily rising home prices notwithstanding, rating agencies generally require a more onerous home price stress test for Australian MBS than for their U.S. counterparts. Standard & Poor's for example, usually requires that Australian MBS with a AAA rating should withstand a 45% home price decline, whereas for U.S. MBS, the standard stress test calls for only a 35% decline in home prices.

Steadily rising home prices are only one of the causes for the lower indebtedness level of home owners in Australia. There seems to be a stronger aversion among the Australian population toward debt and a higher tendency to save than in the United States. Australian government policies also encourage people to build home equity. Unlike in the United States, interest charged on mortgage loans for owner-occupied properties is not tax-deductible, whereas interest earnings on savings accounts and other investment income is fully taxed. Australian mortgages generally carry adjustable rates, with margins usually higher than their U.S. counterparts. This gives Australian mortgage borrowers further incentive to pay down debt and build home equity quickly vis-à-vis their U.S. counterparts.

Underwriting practices in Australia have arguably been much more rigorous than those in the United States. Borrowers with impaired credit history in Australia may find it impossible to find a lender, particularly if they have any default history. Socially, bankruptcy still carries a stronger stigma in Australia than in the United States. This results in higher levels of prudence both on the part of the borrowers and the lenders. Subprime mortgage lending, in the U.S. sense, is almost nonexistent in Australia.

Most Australian mortgages carry a redraw feature. Borrowers who have partially prepaid their mortgage can redraw their mortgage account up to the amount that has been prepaid (the excess equity above the scheduled amount). In practice, this feature enables the mortgage account to serve as a redrawable savings account, which carries an implicit nontaxable interest rate that equals the mortgage rate. Borrowers can freely stash their surplus funds into their mortgage account, knowing that they are able to redraw these funds later if a need arises. In contrast, in the United States, partial prepayments on a closed-end mortgage cannot be redrawn. Once a curtailment payment is made, the balance has been permanently decreased. If the cash is needed later, the borrower will have to apply for a cash-out refinancing or a second lien mortgage, paying a fee that is not always negligible and running the risk of a higher interest rate or being rejected for credit. This makes it less appealing for U.S. borrowers to curtail their mortgage.

Most Australian lenders also provide their existing borrowers with an "add-on" feature to existing loans. If the borrower shows a good payment history and the property value meets certain LTV requirements, he may choose to take out a loan from the original lender in addition to the original loan. This add-on loan is like a second mortgage, except it often carries the same loan rate as the first loan, and the lender isn't handicapped in the case of a recovery from a default, since it holds the first lien claim as well. The add-on amount usually is not included in the securitization if the first loan has already been securitized, and the add-on activity doesn't cause a cash-out prepayment event for the first loan. The add-on feature is useful to both borrowers and lenders when the property value has increased and the borrower needs additional cash. It helps the lender retain existing customers and minimize cash-out prepayments, and the borrower gets financing in an inexpensive fashion.

Not surprisingly, lower LTV ratios reduce both the probability of default and the loss severity if defaults occur. This shows up first in delinquency data. The levels of Australian mortgage delinquencies versus their U.S. counterparts illustrate the strong credit performance of Australian MBS. Exhibit 41–6 compares average

EXHIBIT 41–6

Delinquencies on Australian MBS Are a Fraction of Those on Even U.S. Prime Mortgage Pools

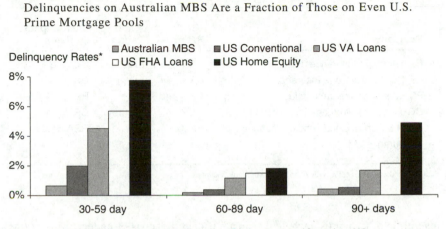

*Dollar amount of delinquent loans as a percentage of outstanding. Levels are as of September 1999.
Source: Inside Mortgage Finance Publications, Inc, Deutsche Bank Securities.

levels of delinquencies for Australian MBS to U.S. conventional mortgages, VA loans, FHA loans, and subprime mortgages. By all measures, Australian mortgage delinquency levels are far lower than those of U.S. loans. Even compared to U.S. *conventional* mortgages, which are of prime quality, Australian mortgage delinquencies are only a third to a half as high.

Low delinquencies help illustrate the high credit quality of Australian mortgages. More important, however, are historical losses. Net collateral losses have been extremely low, even by the standard of U.S. prime mortgages. Data from the Australian mortgage insurance industry shows that since 1965, the average annual default rate has been only 0.73% CDR, with the highest annual CDR being barely over 2%. The average annual net loss rate was only 0.17%, with the high being just a little more than 0.5%.[7] In comparison, it is estimated that the mortgage default rate for the United States (including subprime loans) has been 5%; for the United Kingdom, 6%; and for Canada, 4%.

Almost all Australian mortgage loans are insured by mortgage insurers, called Lenders Mortgage Insurance (LMI) providers. Until 1993, LMI only provided coverage for the amount in excess of 80% LTV. Rating agencies favored 100% LMI and today, as securitizations of loans have become more frequent, most policies cover 100% of the loan balance. Importantly, coverage exclusions for LMI policies are quite limited. Historically, it is much harder to deny a claim in Australia than in other jurisdictions. Under Australia's Insurance Contracts Act 1984, an insurer's ability to deny a claim is limited to circumstances where the lender has failed to disclose relevant information about the borrower or the property, which subsequently gives rise to a *material* disadvantage (or loss) to the

---

7. Standard & Poor's, *Australian Residential MBS Criteria.*

E X H I B I T   41-7

Five Dominant LMI Providers Are All Backed by International Parents

Company	S&P Rating	Fitch Rating	International Parent
GE Mortgage Insurance (HLIC Ltd.)	AAA	AAA	GE (U.S.)
GE Capital Mortgage Insurance Ltd.	AA	AA	GE (U.S.)
PMI Mortgage Insurance Ltd.	AA−	AA	PMI (U.S.)
CGU Lenders Mortgage Insurance Ltd.	AA−	AA	CGU (U.K.)
Royal & Sun Alliance Lenders Mortgage Insurance Ltd.	AA−	—	RSA (U.K.)

Source: Standard & Poor's, Fitch IBCA, and Deutsche Bank Securities.

insurer. In other words, technical or insignificant breaches of underwriting policy are not alone sufficient.

The five LMI providers that dominate the market are all rated AA− or above by Standard and Poor's, and, except for Royal & Sun Alliance (which is not rated), all are rated AA and above by Fitch IBCA. (See Exhibit 41–7.) These five companies are Australian subsidiaries of international parents. Each LMI provider is separately capitalized, with its rating maintained independently from its parent. Since it is crucial for an LMI provider to stay highly rated in order to continue to operate, an LMI provider with international backing would arguably benefit both from the parent company's diversification and their resources. In cases where loans are securitized, sometimes an additional mortgage protection policy is purchased for the benefit of the trust, to provide extra coverage in the event that the primary insurance policy fails. These policies are usually provided by insurance companies that are not in the LMI business and often are located overseas. Because the overwhelming majority of LMI insurance is provided by very highly rated companies, additional policies are very rare.

The loans are covered either at the individual loan level or pool level. The rating agencies view the LMI as a form of credit enhancement on the collateral. The level of required enhancement varies according to the LMI provider's credit rating. Exhibit 41–8 below shows Fitch and S&P's haircut percentages associated with each LMI rating. Assume, for rating purposes, a stress scenario where an A\$100,000 loan defaults, and the loss severity ratio assumed is 50%. The net loss amount to be covered by credit enhancement before insurance is A\$50,000 (100,000 × 50%). If the loan were covered by a policy issued by a AAA-rated LMI provider, according to Exhibit 41–7, 100% credit is given to the LMI protection for rating agency purposes. Thus the resulting effective net loss on the loan for rating purposes is zero. If, instead, the loan were covered by a policy issued by a AA-rated provider, the insurance credit is 75%. For rating purposes, the resulting net loss on the loan is then A\$12,500 (50,000 × 25%). This calculation, together with a set of prescribed loss

E X H I B I T   41–8

Fitch and S&P Adjust for the LMI's Credit Rating in Sizing Enhancement

	Credit Given to Mortgage Insurance	
LMI Provider's Rating	**Fitch**	**S&P**
AAA	100% weight	100% weight
AA	75% weight	75% weight
AA−	68% weight	75% weight
A	50% weight	50% weight
BBB	25% weight	25% weight
BB	0% weight	0% weight
None	0% weight	0% weight

Source: Fitch IBCA and Standard & Poor's.

probabilities, is used to determine the subordinate credit enhancement for an MBS bond, which provides investors with protection over and above LMI.

In most circumstances, LMI not only provides protection against principal losses (including losses arising out of the foreclosure costs), but also guarantees timely payment of interest and scheduled principal payments on each loan for a given time period, usually 24 months. Given that, historically it only takes approximately 9 to 12 months from the time of borrower default to property liquidation in Australia. The liquidity coverage on the payments provided by LMI is more than adequate. If a securitization contains loans where timely payments are not covered, an appropriately sized liquidity facility is included in the transaction to offset the risk of a possible shortfall.

Finally, the legal process in Australia for real estate foreclosures is relatively lender-friendly. Most Australian home mortgages are full recourse to the borrower. This means the lender is allowed to pursue further recoveries against the borrower's other assets should the property sale fail to cover the amount due to the lender. By contrast, in a significant portion of the U.S. market, (e.g., California) there is a "one-action" rule. The lender can take back the property or pursue the borrower's personal assets, but not both. The lender-friendly nature of the legal process in Australia benefits both mortgage lenders and LMI providers.

PREPAYMENTS

Historical prepayment data on existing Australian MBS is relatively stable. This is not surprising giving the mechanisms of the country's mortgage market.

Almost all Australian home loans are adjustable rate. More accurately, Australian home loans are either discretionary variable-rate loans or hybrids (in Australia also called *split* or *fixed-rate*). A discretionary variable-rate loan, unlike a U.S. adjustable-rate mortgage (ARM) loan, does not fluctuate according to an index. The rate of the loan is determined by the lender based on their full discretion with very few restrictions. There is no fixed frequency of adjustment. The lenders have full discretion to change the rate at any period.

A hybrid home loan is somewhat like a hybrid ARM in the United States. It has a fixed interest rate for an initial period, usually 3 to 5 years, and upon the end of the initial period, it converts to a discretionary variable-rate loan. Many lenders offer borrowers the option to fix the interest rate for another period, at a rate dictated by the lender. Full-term fixed-rate loans (in the U.S. sense) have attracted little following thus far and are not currently an option for most home loan borrowers, due to Australian lenders' funding pattern and lending practice. The hybrid loans are often subject to a prepayment penalty on partial or full prepayments during the fixed-rate period. This discourages the borrower from prepaying when market mortgage rates decline.

Since Australian mortgages carry discretionary rates, Australian lenders have the advantage of exerting some influence on the existing borrowers. This includes the timely lowering of rates to forestall prepayments and, like credit card issuers in the United States, the raising of rates to cover rising defaults. Although Australian lenders have a wide range of discretion in determining the rates, certain restrictions apply after the loan is securitized. At the time of securitization, a minimum threshold for the loan rate is set by the rating agencies, to ensure that the collateral will generate enough interest cash flow to cover bond coupons and other expenses. This mechanism prevents the trust from running a negative excess spread.

Because of the lack of availability of full-term fixed-rate loans (i.e., the rate is fixed for the entire life of the loan), certain refinancing activities that are commonplace in the United States rarely take place in Australia. In the United States, whenever the yield curve flattens or long-term interest rates decline, many ARM borrowers will either refinance or, in cases of convertible ARM loans, convert their loans into fixed-rate loans in order to lock in the new, low interest rate. Australian borrowers' options are more limited. They may choose to fix their loan rates for a period, that is, to convert into a hybrid loan. Once this is done, the loan is subject to a prepayment penalty for the fixed-rate period. As a result, the prepayment response of Australian MBS to interest rate changes is very much muted.

In the United States, converting an ARM loan into a fixed-rate loan will result in the loan's being taken out of a securitized pool as a prepayment. In Australia, a refix of the interest rate on a hybrid loan usually will not result in prepayment. In a rapidly changing interest rate environment, this Australian practice should forestall a prepayment surge due to loan conversion.

In contrast to some other market participants, we believe that the redrawable feature plays a role in stabilizing prepayments, instead of making the speeds more volatile. Since Australian borrowers tend to pay down their loan much faster than scheduled, most loans are likely to build up a sizable level of extra equity. Thus, the redraw can serve as a reservoir to absorb the cash-out refinancing wave that might otherwise occur when rates are low, as well as generate incentive for extra paydown when interest rates are high. It might be true that as an individual, each borrower's prepayment behavior might become more volatile regarding when to make an extra payment and when to redraw. But as a large number of mortgages

EXHIBIT 41–9

Large Swings in Mortgage Rates Had Little Effect on Prepayments

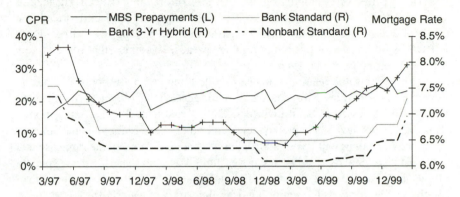

Source: Reserve Bank of Australia and Deutsche Bank Securities.

are pooled together, the random effect of individual decisions on paying and re-drawing extra equity due to personal reasons should average out. This activity is likely to be benign for investors and distinct from U.S.-style prepayments, which have strong interest rate correlation.

As we have discussed above, the add-on feature provided by most Australian lenders also helps to minimize cash-out prepayments when property values are rising.

Historical data on Australian MBS prepayments is limited. However, from the data available to us, we see very stable behavior. Exhibit 41–9 shows the aggregated PUMA prepayments in terms of CPR, with a history of various Australian mortgage interest rates also shown. The stability of prepayments is quite impressive. During the 3-year period from March 1997 to February 2000, mortgage rates in Australia went through a large-scale swing. According to the Reserve Bank of Australia, standard mortgage rates from banks declined 105 bps from April 1997 to December 1998 and then climbed 80 bps from June 1999 to February 2000. Non-bank standard rate changes were similar: a 125-bp drop followed by an 85-bp increase. The changes in the 3-year fixed-rate (hybrid) mortgage were even more dramatic. The decline was 190 bps and the increase was 155 bps. The prepayment response to such rate changes, however, has been very muted. In February 2000, PUMA's aggregate prepayment speed was even a few CPR points faster than that in February 1999, despite large interest rate increases. (See Exhibit 41–8.)

Such prepayment insensitivity toward interest rate changes is akin to that of home equity loans in the United States, and in sharp contrast to U.S. agency mortgages.

SECURITIZATION STRUCTURES

Securitization of Australian MBS is relatively straightforward in structure. There are, however, a few fine points on which Australian MBS differ from their U.S. counterparts. One most obvious difference is that most Australian MBS have been quarterly-pay[8], in contrast to U.S. MBS products, which are overwhelmingly monthly-pay. Because of this, the floating-rate bonds in an Australian MBS are usually priced off 3-month London interbank offered rate (LIBOR) instead of 1-month LIBOR. Given that the 1- to 3-month basis swap is usually priced in a range of 2 to 4 bps, one can convert Australian MBS pricing levels to 1-month LIBOR by adding 2 to 4 bps to the pricing spreads. It is likely that some issuers will begin monthly pay issues in the future.

The redrawable feature of loans in underlying collateral pools also has an impact on the securities. Most deals are structured such that only net principal payments will be passed to bond investors. This means that, if in the same month, some borrowers have made prepayments and others have redrawn some amount, the redrawn amount will be netted from prepayment amount. In the rare case that principal payments received do not cover the redrawn amount, the deal typically allows the trustee to issue a redraw funding facility (with the newest paper carrying the same priority as the senior bonds in the payment waterfall).

Another difference between MBS in Australia and the United States is that it is common for Australian MBS to have an initial revolving period (usually from 1 to 2 years), while U.S. MBS usually do not have a revolving period. The revolving period serves both to stabilize prepayments and to help issuers to manage the origination pipeline.

Many Australian MBS, like their counterparts in the United States, include a cleanup call provision, often 10%. However, higher levels for the cleanup calls are not uncommon. Many recent Australian MBS transactions have also used a "step-up and call" provision in their structures. This specifies a step-up and call date in the future, usually six or seven years after the issuance, after which the bonds step up their coupon margins and become callable. Because of the step-up and call feature, there is no cash-flow crossover or subordinate step-down mechanism in a typical Australian MBS transaction. Given the coupon step-up and lack of cash-flow crossover mechanism, the deal economy at the time of call date usually makes the exercise of the call very likely, unless a dramatic spread widening occurs. The high probability that the call is exercised, together with the initial revolving period, reduces average life variability and further enhances the convexity of the bond.

RELATIVE VALUE ANALYSIS

Many investors, particularly in the United States, have yet to become active players in Australian MBS. One concern has been the relatively small size of the sector and, in some cases, small transaction sizes. However, liquidity for the Australian MBS market is poised to improve. Already in the first quarter of 2000, nearly U.S.$3 billion of Australian MBS was issued. One of the most recent transactions done outside Australia, the Medallion 2000-1G, issued by CBA, contains a senior global class with a size of close to U.S. $1 billion.

---

8. This is particularly true for Australian MBS placed in Europe and the United States. For domestic issuance, many MBS are actually monthly-pay.

Some U.S. investors compare Australian MBS with U.S. home equity products. Indeed, currently, Australian MBS trade at levels close to U.S. home equity bonds (see Exhibit 41–10). The pricing level on the global class of Medallion 2000-1G, a 3.2-year senior tranche that was priced on March 21, 2000, was 23 bps above 3-month LIBOR. If we allow 2 bps for the 1- to 3-month LIBOR basis swap, this equates to 25 bps over 1-month LIBOR. This pricing level is comparable to a typical 3-year U.S. floating-rate home equity sequential bond at that time. However, Australian MBS offer superior credit quality with regard to both collateral and issuer, and comparable convexity.

One more advantage which Australian MBS enjoy versus U.S. home equity products is the low regulatory risk weighting assigned to Australian MBS for U.S. bank investors. Since most Australian mortgages are first lien (to date, no Australian MBS contain second lien loans), the risk weighting for Australian MBS is 50%. On the other hand, since U.S. home equity pools often contain second lien loans, their risk weighting is 100%.

When we compare Australian MBS with agency collateralized mortgage obligations (CMOs), we see a substantial pickup to compensate for the lesser liquidity and lack of government guarantee (implied in U.S. agency CMOs). At the time the CBA issue was priced, a U.S. agency floating-rate CMO with a 3-year average life, a 9.5% cap, and similar average life variability, would have traded at about 35 bps over 1-month LIBOR (see Exhibit 41–9). However, agency CMOs pay with 30/360 accrual. If converted into actual/360 accrual (as Australian MBS pay), the CMO pricing spread would have been about 10 bps lower. Furthermore, the 9.5% cap on the floating-rate CMO costs about 14 bps (for a nonbalance guaranteed cap). All things considered, the Australian MBS was about 14 bps cheaper than the U.S. agency CMO in March 2000.

To be sure, Australian MBS are not as liquid as CMOs. The current 14 bp pickup in spread, however, is attractive compensation for such a shortcoming. In the United States, pricing spreads for similar assets with differences in liquidity, such as publicly registered securities versus securities sold in the 144A market, usually have spread differences of only a couple of basis points.

CONCLUSION

Characterized by strong underlying collateral, LMI protection, large and well-funded servicers, and little refinancing risk, Australian MBS offer attractive investment value in today's fixed income market. With the market size poised to increase and liquidity likely to improve accordingly, the asset is a prime choice for investors looking for diversification and quality.

EXHIBIT 41–10

Australian MBS Trade Flat with U.S. Home Equity and Offer Attractive Pickup to U.S. Agency CMOs

	Medallion 2000-1 A1	Three-Year U.S. HEQ Floater	Three-Year U.S. CMO Floater
Cap	None	Available funds	9.5%
Pricing	3-month LIBOR (actual/360)	1-month LIBOR +25 (actual/360)	1-month LIBOR +35 (30/360)
1- to 3-month basis swap	2 bps	NA*	NA*
Convert to actual/360	NA*	NA*	–10 bps
DM over 1-month LIBOR with actual/360	25 bps	25 bps	25 bps
Deduction: cap value	NA*	NA*	–14 bps
Net DM	25 bps	25 bps	11 bps
Medallion Pickup		0 bps	14 bps

*NA = not applicable.

Source: Deutsche Bank Securities.

CHAPTER 42

COMMERCIAL MORTGAGE-BACKED SECURITIES IN JAPAN

Patrick Corcoran, Ph.D.
Vice President
J.P. Morgan Securities Inc.

Joshua R. Phillips
Vice President
Nomura Securities International, Inc.

The emergence of a burgeoning commercial mortgage-backed securities (CMBS) market at the bottom of the commercial property cycle in Japan in some ways parallels the U.S. experience in the early 1990s. This chapter compares the growth of CMBS and recovery of commercial property markets in Japan with that in the United States. During 1999 and 2000, the differences between Japan and the United States in both CMBS and property markets are what is most striking. However, the comparison of the two country's markets, in our view, continues to provide an illuminating perspective on the future of CMBS in Japan.

THE EXPANDING CMBS MARKET

There are both parallels and differences between Japan's emerging CMBS market and conditions in the United States in the early 1990s. One important difference is that the United States had a much more extensive experience with public markets and securitization. In the U.S. early 1990s episode, the Resolution Trust Corporation (RTC) built on the foundation of earlier securitization in residential mortgages and other assets. The RTC pioneered securitization of commercial mortgage collateral by selling off the seasoned performing and nonperforming loans of failed banks and thrifts in the form of CMBS. This early effort paved the way for the securitization of newly originated performing loans, which only came several years later.

Mr. Phillips was employed at J.P. Morgan Securities when this chapter was written.
This chapter is reprinted with permission from Frank J. Fabozzi (ed.), *Investing in Commercial Mortgage-Backed Securities* (New Hope, PA: Frank J. Fabozzi Associates, 2001).

E X H I B I T   42–1

CMBS Issuance in Japan and the United States

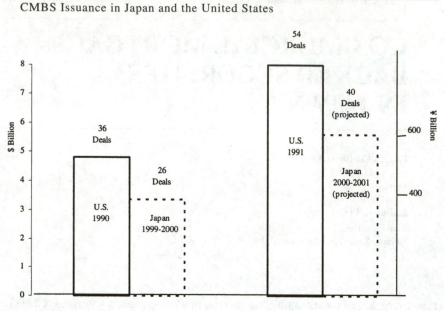

Source: J.P. Morgan Securities Inc.

By contrast, Japan's market in nonperforming loans (NPLs) has been relatively unimportant for the development of the CMBS market. In part, this reflects government policy to support ailing banks with infusions of public money rather than sell off the bad assets RTC-style. It also reflects an absence of property cash flow in the real estate collateral underlying many NPLs. Taking note of such differences, we believe that the new loan CMBS market may play an even more important role in Japan than it has in the United States.

Beginning in February 1999, up to the end of March 2000, we counted 26 CMBS transactions with total value of ¥370.8 billion. This compares with just under $5 billion of RTC CMBS deals (about ¥550 billion) done in the United States in 1990 (Exhibit 42–1). Moreover, we expect that Japan's expanding CMBS market will continue to keep pace with the United States' early 1990s track record. This implies issuance of about ¥600 billion between April 2000 and the end of March 2001.

WHAT IS DRIVING THE EXPANSION IN CMBS DEALS?

Weakness of the Portfolio Lender Model

To see CMBS issuance about 70% that of the United States in the early 1990s is quite striking and suggests that Japan is following a similar path. Measured by its gross domestic product (GDP), Japan is about half the size of the United States.

On the other hand, debt held by banks in Japan is substantially larger than that in the United States. This is also true for total real estate–related debt outstanding.

Similar to the U.S. experience in the early 1990s, a major part of Japanese borrower demand for nonrecourse commercial mortgage loans arises from the inherent weakness of the "portfolio lender model." United States bank and life company lenders traditionally made mortgage loans on their own balance sheets as "portfolio lenders," thereby earning a spread over their liability cost of funds. However, the late 1980s–early 1990s sharp downturn in real estate underscored overly aggressive lending and an inadequate return on capital earned by these lenders. As a result, traditional U.S. lenders at that time scaled back lending activity and the CMBS market accounted for a major new share of loans to borrowers.

The beginning of the U.S. CMBS in the 1990s market might also be contrasted with its "false start" in the late 1980s. In the earlier period, a few CMBS deals took place in the United States. However, because of overly aggressive lending by life companies and banks, securitizers won very little of the lending business. Moreover, to win business, portfolio lenders made new loans at very tight spreads. Since capital market skepticism about real estate in the late 1980s resulted in relatively wide CMBS spreads, very little securitization profit was left on the deals that took place.

In contrast with the approach of traditional portfolio lenders, the CMBS market allows the capital markets to judge the adequacy of the risk-return profile in commercial mortgage loans. In the United States during the early 1990s, the growth of the CMBS market was aided by a credit crunch, as traditional portfolio lenders ceased lending altogether. However, as these lenders gradually returned to the lending markets, CMBS pricing provided explicit signals about how the underlying loans should be priced. This pricing provided a capital market "discipline" to lenders that had been absent previously in the private U.S. markets.

Parallel to the U.S. experience, Japan also experienced an initial credit crunch, which is less severe in 2000–2001 than several years ago. However, the policy of providing capital infusions to ailing banks rather than RTC-type asset sales seems likely to extend the weak position of financial intermediaries. Banks still have large NPL positions, which should limit their competitiveness as portfolio lenders for some time to come. In addition, Japanese banks must repay government loans of ¥8.8 trillion. Thus, both the large initial scale of financial system problems as well as their likely protraction suggest that demand by borrowers for nonrecourse commercial mortgages will have to be met by loans that are securitized in the capital markets.

Exhibit 42–2 shows our count of 1999–2000 CMBS deals. This information may not cover every deal, but represents our best efforts to monitor activity in the market. As shown in Exhibit 42–3, almost half the deals (41% of issuance by volume or 7 out of 26 deals) were sale-leaseback transactions. Many corporations have experienced reduced ability to obtain debt or equity funding. For these entities, the ability to sell and lease back real estate assets is an attractive alternative funding source. Most Japanese financial institutions and corporations are under pressure to focus on core business operations and improve earnings. Sale leasebacks of owner-

EXHIBIT 42-2

March 1999–March 2000 CMBS Deals

Deal No.	Issuer	Property Type	Transaction Type	Arranger	Arranger Type	Rating	Amount (in billions of yen)	Closing
1	Kilimanjaro Limited	Office	Leveraged finance	NSSB	Foreign	Moody's/S&P	6.60	3/2000
2	Red Lions Capital	Office	Leveraged finance	JP Morgan	Foreign	Moody's	10.80	3/2000
3	Millenium Capital	Office	Leveraged finance	IBJ Securities	Group	Moody's	11.50	3/2000
4	Forester SPC	Retail	Sale leaseback	N/A	Unknown	R&I	28.50	3/2000
5	Prime Quest	Office	Leveraged finance	Daiwa SBCM	Group	Moody's/JCR	5.15	3/2000
6	M's Fort Co., Ltd.	Apartment	Leveraged finance	IBJ Sec.	Nongroup	S&P	24.00	3/2000
7	NEST Funding Corp.	Office	Sale leaseback	Daiwa SBCM	Group	Moody's	51.40	3/2000
8	Urbanity Capital TMK	Office	Leveraged finance	Daiwa SBCM	Nongroup	Moody's	9.30	3/2000
9	Millenium Residential SPC Co., Ltd.	Apartment	Development	Sakura Securities	Group	Moody's	11.70	3/2000
10	Kyodo Jutaku Securitization SPC	Apartment	Leveraged finance	Starts Co.	Group	N/A	0.25	3/2000
11	Amco Ventures Corp.	Office	Acquisition finance	JP Morgan	Foreign	Moody's	30.70	2/2000
12	MM Property Funding	Office	Sale leaseback	DKB Securities	Nongroup	R&I	13.50	2/2000
13	Ohmori Kaigan SPC	Factory	Development	Daiwa SBCM	Group	JCR	12.00	2/2000
14	Feris K.K.	Office	Sale leaseback	N/A	Unknown	N/A	N/A	2/2000
15	NeopasTMK	Office	Development	DKB Securities	Group	N/A	2.60	1/2000

No.	Name	Property	Finance Type	Arranger	Category	Rating	Amount	Date
16	International Credit Recovery Japan One Ltd.	NPL	Acquisition finance	MSDW	Foreign	Moody's/S&P/Fitch	21.00	11/1999
17	Pacific Century Residential One	Apartment	Leveraged finance	Jardine Fleming Securities	Foreign	N/A	6.63	10/1999
18	Start Capital	Office	Leveraged finance	Nomura Securities	Nongroup	Moody's	9.60	9/1999
19	New Shopping Center Funding Corp	Retail	Sale leaseback	Paribas	Foreign	Moody's	41.00	9/1999
20	N/A	Warehouse	Sale leaseback	Sakura Bank	Group	JCR	3.60	8/1999
21	Azuchi Estate Funding Limited	Office	Acquisition finance	N/A	Group	Moody's	18.35	8/1999
22	Takanawa Apartment SPC	Apartment	Leveraged finance	Fuji Bank	Group	S&P	3.00	6/1999
23	Sumquest Co. Limited	Office	Leveraged finance	Daiwa SBCM/IBJ Securities	Group	Moody's	24.50	6/1999
24	Network Capital	Office	Sale leaseback	Daiwa SBCM	Group	JCR	13.50	4/1999
25	Someino S.C.	Retail	Leveraged finance	Wako Securities	Nongroup	R&I	5.10	3/1999
26	LM Capital	Apartment	Acquisition finance	JP Morgan	Foreign	Moody's	6.50	3/1999
						Total	370.8	

Source: J.P. Morgan Securities Inc.

E X H I B I T   42–3

Japanese CMBS by Transaction Type

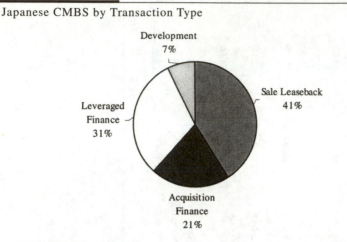

occupied real estate can help accomplish this goal. Looking at the sale-leaseback transactions in Exhibit 42–2, we see that a wide variety of companies have used the technique, including banks and financial companies, industrial concerns, and retailers.

Among the nonsale-leaseback transactions in Exhibit 42–2, four deals (21% by volume) represented mortgages to finance property acquisitions while eleven deals (31% by volume) helped meet the "leveraged finance" needs of existing property owners.

Looking at underlying property collateral (Exhibit 42–4), we see that fourteen transactions (56% by volume) involve the financing of office properties. Of these, four transactions involve real estate companies and six life insurance companies. In a macro environment where many companies have weakened balance sheets, companies with valuable real estate assets can use them to obtain scarce new financing.

Some of the 1999–2000 transactions benefited from off–balance sheet treatment to originators for loans, as long as senior CMBS tranches were sold. This is likely to change soon. The Japanese Institute of Certified Public Accountants is likely to recommend on–balance sheet treatment for loans in which B pieces are retained. This obviously increases the importance of the B-piece market. As discussed in the Rating Agency section, the supply of B-piece investments has been quite limited. We expect modest growth in the supply of B-piece investments to be matched by increased investor demand for B pieces to take up some of the slack (see Demand for CMBS section below).

A striking feature of Japan's emerging CMBS market is that several deals focused on new development (Exhibit 42–2). In the early 1990s U.S. market, this did not occur at all. Partly, the U.S. experience reflected low demand for development financing at the bottom of the real estate cycle and partly significant supply of de-

E X H I B I T   42–4

Japanese CMBS by Collateral Type

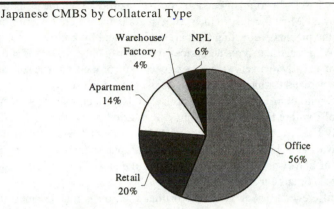

Source: J.P. Morgan Securities Inc.

velopment financing by banks. By contrast, replacement demand for real estate is far higher in Japan, even at the bottom of the property cycle. In turn, this reflects fundamental differences in the property markets (see Property Markets section below). A recent-development CMBS deal is also discussed in more detail below.

Demand for CMBS

The emergence of a new market in structured product, including CMBS, in Japan clearly required that investors become more familiar with these new structures. During 1999 and 2000, the strong initial reception by investors for CMBS has been striking. From a U.S. perspective, Japan's financial system is at an earlier point with relatively few capital market instruments available to investors. In the bond market, there is relatively little competition from other capital market instruments for Japanese investors' ¥1,430 trillion ($13 trillion) in savings. Reflecting a scarcity of spread product, many institutional investors have recently begun to allocate part of their funds to "alternative" investments, a category that includes mezzanine or subordinate CMBS.

Investors' appetite for CMBS has also been bolstered by increasing recognition of Japan's solid "bottom of the market" real estate fundamentals (see Property Markets section) and by progress in legal reform that is necessary to accommodate structured bonds [see section on Special Purpose Corporations (SPCs)].

DEAL OVERVIEW

Growth in Japan's CMBS market during 1999 and 2000 has paralleled that in the early 1990s U.S. experience in a number of ways. First, like the U.S. market, Japanese CMBS deals have been primarily fixed-rate borrowings with prohibition against prepayment prior to the balloon date. There have been a few Japanese floating-rate deals. One was the LM Capital Ltd. Deal in March 1999, an interim financing deal permitting the purchaser of a group of condominium properties to sell the properties as the market allowed. More recently in the spring of 2000, there were several floating-rate deals in the pipeline, reflecting an increased demand by borrowers for interim financing. With real estate rents and prices in higher-quality properties showing the firmness of an early recovery stage, we expect more properties to be sold and repositioned. The demand for interim financing is likely to increase.

The CMBS market in Japan has been entirely a large loan market with single borrower deals, with either single property or multiproperty, the norm. This parallels the early U.S. experience in new loans, beginning in 1994, with its emphasis on large loan deals. However, the difference in Japan so far is that there has been no pooling of borrowers' large loans into what the early U.S. market called megadeals, or pools of large loan borrowers.

Why the difference? In our view, the primary reason is that Japanese investors have a larger learning curve to climb than U.S. investors in the early 1990s. In part, this is so because the United States had a richer capital markets history that witnessed residential loans and other assets securitized beginning in the 1970s. Secondly, and even more importantly, U.S. nonrecourse real estate finance was already well-established by life insurance companies, banks, and thrifts in the private commercial mortgage market in the 1950s and 1960s.

In Japan, by contrast, real estate loans were made corporate-style with little meaningful reference to real estate underwriting criteria. In the early 1990s U.S. experience, investors had to learn the differences in rating agency approaches to underwriting real estate loans compared to previous insurance company underwriting. The rating agencies' heavy emphasis on current property cash flow was a new development at that time.

In Japan, by contrast, it is fair to say that there was no real estate–based lending market in commercial properties prior to the period 1998–1999. In the past, Japanese banks made loans corporate-style to industrial and real estate companies secured by real estate but with recourse. CMBS investors in Japan have to learn structural and other issues related to securitization. In addition, they also have to learn genuine real estate–based underwriting itself, which is a new development.

The hallmark of real estate–based lending is that the loans made are nonrecourse to the borrower. In the event that such a nonrecourse loan (NRL) defaults, the lender or investors have recourse to the property but not to the borrower's other assets. During 1999 and 2000, most of the nonrecourse loans made were done with securitization as the intended exit strategy. In some cases, however, such loans were made and not intended for securitization. A number of these transactions, parallel to nonrecourse whole loans in the U.S. market, are shown in Exhibit 42–5.

These nonsecuritized loans add materially to the volume of nonrecourse loans. If we add the Exhibit 42–5 transactions (¥82.8 billion) to the Exhibit 42–2 securitized transactions (¥370.8 billion), we get a total nonrecourse loan figure of about ¥453.6 billion. The point to emphasize along with this impressive total is that this is a market that did not previously exist. In two of the Exhibit 42–5 transactions, the loans are not strictly nonrecourse because the lender looked either to

E X H I B I T   42–5

Nonsecuritized Real Estate Loans

Deal No.	Original Real Estate Owner	Underlying Assets	Transaction Type	Arranger	Arranger Type	Rating	Amount (in billions of yen)	Closing or Announcement
1	Daiichi Life	Four office buildings	Office	IBJ	Group	Moody's	10	2/1999
2	Tokyu Land	Akasaka Tokyu Building	Office	IBJ	Nongroup	NA*	18.1	9/1999
3	Mazda	Research facilities, etc.	Sale leaseback	Citibank	Foreign	NA*	38.2	9/1999
4	Sumitomo Light Metal Inds.	Factory	Sale leaseback	NA	Group	NA*	16	9/1999
5	Nippon Tochi Tatemono	Kawasaki branch office of DKB	Development	DKB Securities	Group	NA*	0.5	1/2000
6	Izumiya	Two existing properties in Osaka-fu	Sale leaseback	Sumitomo Trust	Nongroup	NA*	NA*	NA*
						Total	82.8	

*NA = not available.
Source: J.P. Morgan Securities Inc.

the borrower's broader credit (the Mazda deal) or to other additional collateral (the Daiichi Life deal). In addition, some of the sale-leaseback transactions (Exhibit 42–5) provided off–balance sheet treatment to originators. As discussed above, this benefit is likely to change.

The historical absence of a real estate finance market in Japan might also be expected to slow the evolution of CMBS in other areas. For example, in the U.S. early 1990s experience, large loans were the "trailblazers" in the early CMBS market. However, they were soon eclipsed by the growing market in conduit, or small loan securitization. In the latter development, mortgage bankers and mortgage brokers helped bring together borrowers and lenders just as they had previously in the old private loan market. In Japan, this type of infrastructure has naturally been absent and there has essentially been no conduit-style lending so far.

WHO IS DOING THE DEALS?

A variety of domestic and foreign firms have completed CMBS deals. As indicated in Exhibit 42–2, many CMBS transactions were completed in Keiretsu (related group company) transactions, where the borrower and the securities firm are closely related. These transactions are labeled "Group" under the column "Arranger Type." About half the transactions involve nonrelated borrower and security firm entities (Exhibit 42–6). Of these latter transactions, the largest share (33%) have been arranged by foreign securities firms with a smaller portion arranged by domestic securities firms (17%).

For example, as shown in Exhibit 42–7, Daiwa SBCM has done the largest amount of CMBS in Japan. These deals primarily involve Sumitomo group companies. In these transactions, CMBS was utilized as a new restructuring method under

E X H I B I T   42–6

Types of CMBS Arrangers

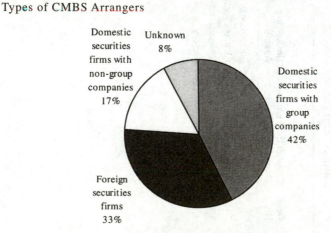

Source: J. P. Morgan Securities Inc.

E X H I B I T   42–7

Top 10 Underwriters of Japanese CMBS Including Keiretsu Transactions

Rank	Bank	Amount (in billions of yen)	No. of deals
1	Daiwa SBCM	115.9	6
2	J.P. Morgan	48.0	3
3	Paribas	41.0	1
4	IBJ Securities	35.5	2
5	MSDW	21.0	1
6	DKB Securities	16.1	2
7	Sakura Securities	15.3	1
8	Nomura Securities	9.6	1
9	Jardine Fleming Securities	6.6	1
10	NNB	6.6	1
	Total	315.5	

Source: J.P. Morgan Securities Inc.

E X H I B I T   42–8

Underwriters of Japanese CMBS Excluding Keiretsu Transactions

Rank	Bank	Amount (in billions of yen)	No. of deals
1	J.P. Morgan	48.0	3
2	Paribas	41.0	1
3	IBJ	24.0	1
4	MSDW	21.0	1
5	DKB	13.5	1
6	Nomura Securities	9.6	1
7	Daiwa SBCM	9.3	1
8	Jardine Fleming Securities	6.6	1
9	Nikko Salomon Smith Barney	6.6	1
10	Wako	5.1	1
	Total	184.7	12

Source: J.P. Morgan Securities Inc.

the leadership of Sumitomo Bank and Daiwa Securities. If the Keiretsu transactions are removed from the totals, the revised league table result, with much stronger show-ing by the foreign securities firms, as shown in Exhibit 42–8. In addition to the foreign securities firms shown in Exhibit 42–8, other firms are gearing up to do business.

RATING AGENCY APPROACH TO CMBS

Of the 26 deals counted in Exhibit 42–2, Moody's has taken a preeminent role (Exhibit 42–9), rating 11 deals by itself and 3 deals jointly with other agencies. The domestic Japanese rating agencies, R&I and JCR, have rated 3 and 4 deals, respectively. Moody's has largely adopted the approach honed in the earlier U.S. experience with a tight focus on sustainable property cash flows, debt service coverage ratios (DSCR), and loan-to-value (LTV) ratio measures to monitor balloon risk. Their approach also takes account of some differences in Japanese property markets, particularly the uncertainty surrounding valuation in a market with relatively few transactions (as of early 1999).

Exhibit 42–10 shows Moody's calculated DSCR and LTV ratios in the LM Capital Ltd. deal. The DSCR calculation employs an assumed debt service or loan

E X H I B I T   42–9

Rating Agency Activity in Japanese CMBS

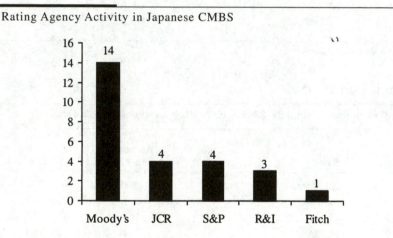

Source: J.P. Morgan Securities Inc.

E X H I B I T   42–10

Moody's Calculated LTV and DSCR Levels in the LM Capital Deal

Series	LTV (%)	DSCR*
A	39.8%	2.24
B	54.7	1.63
C	69.6	1.28
D	80.7	1.11

*DSCR based on an assumed loan constant of 6.5%.
Source: J.P. Morgan Securities Inc.

constant of 6.5%. Although the LM Capital deal is a floating-rate interim financing, Moody's gave no credit for cash flow generated through planned property sales. Thus, the deal was effectively rated as a permanent financing. Recently, in May 2000, as the borrower successfully sold condominiums as planned, the deal's pool balance was reduced by 48%, and Moody's upgraded Classes B (to Aaa from A2), C (to A2 from Baa3), and D (to Baa3 from B2). As a result of the property sales, the rating agency DSCR measure improved from 1.13× to 1.30× and Moody's stressed LTV measure improved from about 79% to 65%. The borrower's ability to sell the properties also testifies to the stability of the condominium market more generally. The LM Capital Ltd. deal is the first Japanese CMBS transaction to be upgraded by Moody's.

In general, it appears thus far that loan leverage has been conservative by the standards of the better-developed U.S. market. The 39.8% LTV (February 1999) calculated at the AAA bond level was achieved with a Moody's LTV of 80.7% and AAA subordination of about 50%. As shown in Exhibit 42–11 for a sample of deals, the AAA-equivalent LTV exhibited in LM Capital is generally representative of deals during 1999 and 2000. Both LTV and rating agency DSCR look conservative at the level of the bond classes, compared to U.S. standards, as well.

One result of the cautious leverage evident in Japan's CMBS market has been that the supply of below-investment-grade CMBS has been very limited. This has been the case because the rating agencies assign relatively few lower-rated bonds in deals where leverage in the underlying loan pool is prudent. In general, we expect the rating agencies to continue to require borrowers to supply substantial equity in their properties in order to qualify for lower-leverage securitizable commercial mortgage loans. This will mean that, at least by U.S. standards, the supply of lower-rated bonds is likely to remain small. At the same time, there has been increased activity in the market for B pieces in early 2000, reflecting marginal increases in both demand and supply (see discussion above).

EVOLUTION OF SPECIAL PURPOSE CORPORATIONS

The early CMBS transactions completed in Japan employed an offshore special purpose corporation (SPC) structure. This structure is shown in Exhibit 42–12.[1] Following the passage of the September 1998 SPC law, there has been increasing use of domestic SPCs in CMBS deals. The major problems cited with the 1998 law include (1) taxes on transfer profits that are imposed on sellers when assets are transferred to the SPC, (2) limitations on the use of loans as a funding source, (3) an absence of bankruptcy remoteness, and (4) a lack of flexibility in managing and disposing of the underlying assets. A number of amendments to the 1998 law addressing these issues passed the Diet in Spring 2000.

---

1. Japanese legal issues are discussed in International Structured Finance Special Report, "Japanese CMBS: 2000 Outlook," *Moody's Investor Service* (June 29, 2000).

EXHIBIT 42–11

Rating Agency Approach to CMBS

Settlement Date	Issuer	Underlying Assets	Rating Agency
03/26/1999	LM Capital	Lions Mansion condominiums: 1,090 primarily residential units	Moody's
03/30/1999	Someino S.C.	Itoyokado in Chiba	R&I
04/27/1999	Network Capital	Sumitomo Bank's 20 branch office buildings	JCR
06/30/1999	Sumquest Co. Limited	Five office buildings located in central Tokyo and Kawasaki	Moody's
08/01/1999	Azuchi Estate Funding Limited	Single Property	Moody's
09/26/1999	Star Capital	Five office buildings	Moody's
09/30/1999	New Shopping Center Funding Corp.	Ten general merchandising stores	Moody's
02/25/2000	Amco Ventures Corp.	Japan Energy HQ building	Moody's
03/24/2000	Millenium Capital	Five properties (office buildings in Tokyo, Nagoya, Osaka)	Moody's
03/28/2000	Red Lions Capital	Twelve properties	Moody's
03/29/2000	Kilimanjaro Limited	Five office buildings in Tokyo	Moody's, S & P
03/2000	NEST Funding Corp.	NEC headquarters building	Moody's

Source: J.P. Morgan Securities Inc.

AAA		AA		A		BBB		
Rating Agency	Other	Rating Agency	Other	Rating Agency	Other	Rating Agency	Other	Appraisal Corporation
38.9%	37.0%	53.6%	50.9%	68.3%	64.9%	79.2%	75.3%	Mitsui Fudosan Investment Advisors, Inc.
13.0%		29.6%						
		25.8%		49.8%				
		43.2%	35.4%	52.2%	42.8%	65.0%	53.3%	REAC
				54.0%		61.0%		
		48.1%		56.3%				
		40.6%						
35.8%	29.8%	42.9%	35.7%	49.9%	41.5%			Blake & Sanyu
		44.5%	43.5%	56.8%	56.0%	66.0%	65.0%	JREI (Fudoken)
		47.2%	46.2%	56.9%	55.8%	58.5%	57.4%	JREI (Fudoken)
36.6%		44.3%		53.9%		63.5%		
38.0%		46.0%		56.0%		67.0%		

EXHIBIT 42–12

Offshore SPC Structure (LM Capital Deal)

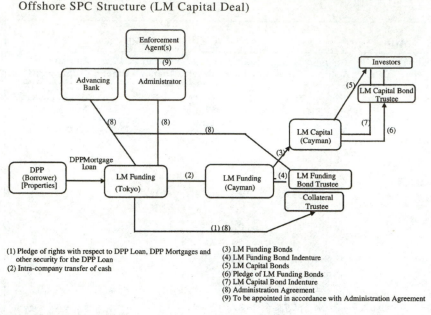

(1) Pledge of rights with respect to DPP Loan, DPP Mortgages and
 other security for the DPP Loan
(2) Intra-company transfer of cash

(3) LM Funding Bonds
(4) LM Funding Bond Indenture
(5) LM Capital Bonds
(6) Pledge of LM Funding Bonds
(7) LM Capital Bond Indenture
(8) Administration Agreement
(9) To be appointed in accordance with Administration Agreement

Source: J.P. Morgan Securities Inc.

Of our 26 CMBS deals, we had SPC information on 25 deals (see Appendix A). Of these, 13 deals employed the domestic Japanese SPC (TMK) structure and 11 deals employed the offshore SPC structure. One deal employed a domestic stock corporation (Kabushiki Kaisha) and did not use an SPC. In addition, many deals utilizing the domestic SPC structure also employed an offshore SPC to further improve the bankruptcy remoteness. An example of this latter type of structure is shown in Exhibit 42–13 for the Red Lions Capital deal.

The point of bankruptcy remoteness is to ensure separation between the assets being securitized and the bankruptcy risk of the issuer or borrower. To ensure a perfected security interest, it is important to preclude the borrower or issuer SPC from filing voluntarily for "corporate reorganization." In this case, the enforceability of the perfected security interest will be controlled by the bankruptcy trustee. However, as noted in a Moody's report,[2] only a Kabushiki Kaisha (KK), a stock corporation, can file for a corporate reorganization. This risk is not so great for a Yugen Kaisha (YK) or the new domestic SPC (TMK).

In the Red Lions structure (Exhibit 42–13), the offshore bankruptcy-remote SPC is the sole shareholder of the common equity in the domestic SPC (Red Lions Capital TMK). Since it is difficult to limit the shareholders' right to change di-

---

2. "Japanese CMBS: 2000 Outlook."

Domestic SPC Structure (TMK) with Offshore SPC (Red Lions Capital)

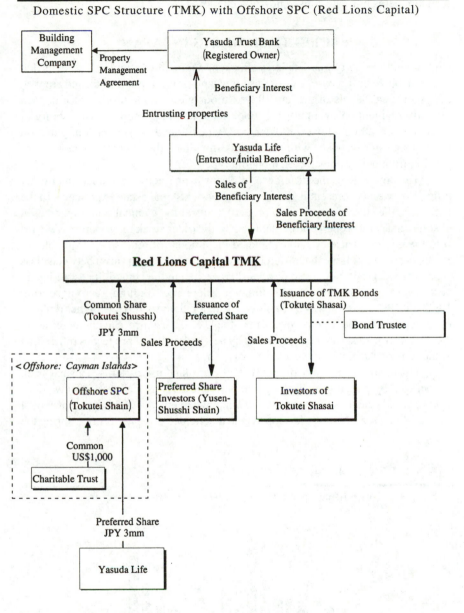

rectors in Japan and any director may petition a corporation into bankruptcy, the structure helps mitigate bankruptcy-related risk.

PROPERTY MARKETS IN JAPAN

High-quality property markets in every major segment continue to see rents and prices stabilize or increase. By contrast, raw land prices remain weak and are well below the peak levels of the late 1980s. In our view, modern properties in each property segment enjoy a bullish outlook for rent and property price stability or modest appreciation. However, older, poorly positioned properties configured on inadequate floor plates or with outdated designs face the prospect of more competition from newly constructed modern properties.

To some extent, the difference in performance between modern and older properties was also present in the early recovery U.S. real estate experience. In the U.S. case, the sharp depression in property rents at the cyclical bottom increased obsolescence and property retirements out of the older stock of properties. As a result, the nominal vacancy rate overstated the amount of total space available. In Japan's case, we believe that differentials (in quality and cash flow) between class A and class C properties are somewhat sharper than in the United States. In Japan, new construction has resurfaced, following depressed building activity during 1993 and 1997 (Exhibit 42–14). This construction activity reflects higher replacement demand for older properties than in the U.S. experience. Steady increases in the demand for space are being matched by newly developed properties rather than reductions in vacancies on the oldest real estate.

Japan has had a legacy of highly inefficient land use patterns. This has been encouraged by policies favoring agricultural land uses as well as a variety of restrictions and penalties on the transfer of land ownership. All of this has contributed to an artificial scarcity of undeveloped land that helped drive up its price during the

E X H I B I T   42–14

Supply of New Office Space in Tokyo CBD (in millions of sq. ft.)

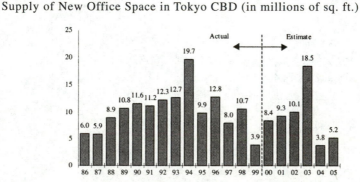

Note: New buildings with more than 107,642 sq. ft. for office usage in Tokyo CBD.
Source: Mori Building, Mitsui Fudosan.

"bubble" years. Low land prices in mid-2000 combined with the prospect of more "laissez faire" land use policies point to many opportunities to develop lower-cost property locations. These include faster growth in property markets at the edge of Tokyo and movement from higher-cost to lower-cost urban centers. Although such directions for new development will be familiar to U.S. investors, they are very new for Japan. Nonetheless, they are directions that are greatly encouraged by the dramatic decline and continuing softness in undeveloped land values.

In our view, this suggests that properties in each of the major segments with modern amenities are comparable in risk to class A properties in the United States (or perhaps even lower in risk), whereas older inefficient class C properties are more risky. In each of the major property segments, we favor more modern properties as well as locations that may benefit from possible shifts in land use patterns driven by the low price of undeveloped land. Put somewhat differently, we think commercial mortgage underwriting guidelines should be more stringent for what we are calling class B and C properties. With genuine real estate underwriting at such an early point in Japan, we are in effect highlighting some of the risk criteria that underwriters and investors need to consider. The new J-REIT legislation before the Diet offers the prospect that newly organized public real estate companies will be leaders (and mortgage borrowers) in what is potentially a new phase for Japanese real estate.

PROPERTY MARKETS AND CMBS DEVELOPMENT FINANCING

In the U.S. real estate market bottom of the early 1990s, demand for development financing was minimal and bank willingness to supply development lending easily supplied the limited demand. In Japan, the situation is the opposite. With the balance sheets of large financial intermediaries generally weak and with the demand for development financing strong, development financing has spilled over into the CMBS market. Three of the deals listed in Exhibit 42–2 involve development.

In one recent deal, Mitsui Fudosan Co., the largest real estate company in Japan, is securitizing eight condominium properties through Millennium Residential TMK, an SPC registered under the domestic SPC law. Like the Red Lions deal discussed above, the ordinary shares of the domestic SPC are solely owned by a bankruptcy-remote Cayman Island SPC.

In one sense, the Mitsui deal is similar to the LM Capital Ltd. deal in that it provides interim financing to a condominium developer while the individual units are being sold to households. However, the uniqueness of the deal is that it securitizes development projects both before and after construction authorization. In order to avoid project completion risk, Mitsui Fudosan is teaming up with Tokio Marine and Fire Insurance Corporation (Aa1/AAA), which will provide a performance bond. Tokio Marine's guarantee relates solely to project completion risk. The guarantee does not wrap the principal and interest cash flows of the CMBS. If completed properties are sold at prices representing a revenue shortfall, CMBS investors bear this risk.

Moody's analysis of the deal utilizes a stress scenario under which 40% of the properties are assumed to be sold at an early point prior to completion of construction but at a discount of 15%. Of the remaining property sales, 30% are assumed to take place at the end of construction at a 30% discount. The final 30% of the properties are assumed to be sold at the CMBS legal maturity date at a 50% discount. Additional protection for investors comes in the form of required property sales at severe discounts if Mitsui's property sales revenues fall below critical targets in mid-2001.

We expect continued evolution in development financing within CMBS. The presence of such financing within CMBS reflects some important differences in Japan's bottoming property markets and financing markets, relative to the U.S. early 1990s experience.

RELATIVE VALUE AND OUTLOOK

The cyclical parallels in property markets and financial systems between the United States in the 1990s and Japan in 2000 are striking. Rebounding property markets combined with important changes to the legal system and financial markets have all been stimulants to the rapidly expanding market in CMBS.

The growth of a CMBS market is all the more impressive, given the historical absence of real estate–based finance and less developed capital markets. But things are changing fast, and we look for the rapid expansion of CMBS to continue.

Property market fundamentals on more modern properties look very solid at the bottom of Japan's real estate cycle, just as they did several years earlier in the United States. Compared to the huge savings pool of Japanese investors, CMBS face only limited competition from other capital markets instruments. CMBS deals in mid-2000 have seen AAA bonds priced at about 30 basis points (bps) over the yen swap curve. This represents a significant tightening from pricing in the LM Capital Ltd. deal in February 1999. The AAA bonds in the latter floating-rate deal priced at a spread 60 bps over yen-LIBOR. CMBS spreads as of mid-2000 offer significant premiums to both ABS and corporate bond spreads, which are shown on a swap-adjusted basis in Exhibit 42–15. The combination of wide spreads and solid fundamentals is compelling.

Sharp declines in land values point to incentives for redirecting future development in lower cost directions and possibly repositioning much of Japan's older property markets. If land is not nearly as scarce as it appeared in the "bubble" real estate years, but is in fact much cheaper, it points to possible development of modern office properties in the suburban areas at the fringe of urban centers. If prohibitive transfer taxes no longer force tiny urban land parcels to remain uneconomically subdivided, such land parcels can possibly be assembled for the construction of larger modern office and other properties. Assuming that land use policy continues to move in the laissez-faire direction, there is a case for rebuilding a much more modern Japan. It's an exciting thought and one in which CMBS are poised to play a major role.

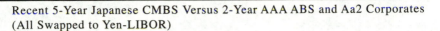

Recent 5-Year Japanese CMBS Versus 2-Year AAA ABS and Aa2 Corporates
(All Swapped to Yen-LIBOR)

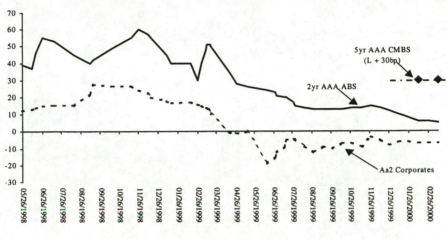

Source: J.P. Morgan Securities Inc.

APPENDIX

Lakhbir S. Hayre, DPhil.
Director of Mortgage Research
Salomon Smith Barney

Cyrus Mohebbi, Ph.D.
Managing Director
Prudential Securities Inc.
and
Adjunct Professor
New York University

MORTGAGE MATHEMATICS

Mortgage Cash Flow Without Prepayments

Monthly Payment   For a level-payment mortgage, the constant monthly payment is

$$M_n = \frac{B_0 \left(\dfrac{G}{1200} \right) \left(1 + \dfrac{G}{1200} \right)^N}{\left[\left(1 + \dfrac{G}{1200} \right)^N - 1 \right]}$$

where M_n = Monthly payment for month n
B_o = Original balance
G = Gross coupon rate (%)
N = Original term in months (e.g., 360)

Remaining Balance   The remaining balance after n months is

$$B_n = \frac{B_0 \left[\left(1 + \dfrac{G}{1200} \right)^N - \left(1 + \dfrac{G}{1200} \right)^n \right]}{\left[\left(1 + \dfrac{G}{1200} \right)^N - 1 \right]}$$

where B_n = Remaining balance at the end of month n.

Principal Payment   The amount of principal paid in month n is given by

$$P_n = \frac{B_0 \left(\dfrac{G}{1200} \right) \left(1 + \dfrac{G}{1200} \right)^{n-1}}{\left[\left(1 + \dfrac{G}{1200} \right)^N - 1 \right]}$$

where P_n = Principal paid in month n.

Interest Payment   The amount of interest paid in month n can be written as

$$I_n = \frac{B_o\left(\dfrac{G}{1200}\right)\left[\left(1 + \dfrac{G}{1200}\right)^N - \left(1 + \dfrac{G}{1200}\right)^{n-1}\right]}{\left[\left(1 + \dfrac{G}{1200}\right)^N - 1\right]} = B_{n-1}\left(\frac{G}{1200}\right)$$

where I_n = Interest paid in month n.

It should be noted that

$$G = S + C$$

where S = Service fee (%)

C = Security coupon rate (%)

and so the

$$Servicing\ amount = \left(\frac{S}{C + S}\right)I_n$$

Therefore, the cash flow to the security holder in month n is given by

$$CF_n = P_n + I_n - Servicing\ amount = P_n + \left(\frac{C}{C + S}\right)I_n$$

Prepayment Measuring Conventions

For a given pool of mortgages, let

B_n = Remaining principal balance per dollar of mortgage at the end of month n if there are no prepayments

C_n = Pool factor (*i.e.*, actual remaining principal balance per dollar of mortgage) at the end of month n

Let $Q_n = C_n/B_n$. If one thinks of the pool as consisting of a very large number of $1 mortgages, each of which can terminate separately, then Q_n represents the percentages of mortgages still remaining at the end of month n. Then,

$$Percentage\ of\ initial\ balance\ that\ has\ been\ prepaid = 1 - Q_n$$

For month n, the single monthly mortality, or SMM, stated as a decimal, is given by

SMM = Proportion of $1 mortgages outstanding at the beginning of the month that are prepaid during the month, or

$$\frac{Q_{n-1} - Q_n}{Q_{n-1}} = 1 - \frac{Q_n}{Q_{n-1}}$$

For the period from month m to month n, the constant SMM rate that is equivalent to the actual prepayments experienced is given by

$$(1 - \text{SMM})^{n-m} = \frac{Q_n}{Q_m}$$

That is,

$$\text{SMM} = 1 - \left(\frac{Q_n}{Q_m}\right)^{\frac{1}{n-m}}$$

The conditional prepayment rate, or CPR (also expressed as a decimal), is the SMM expressed as an annual rate, and is given by

$$1 - \text{CPR} = (1 - \text{SMM})^{12}$$

That is,

$$\text{CPR} = 1 - (1 - \text{SMM})^{12}$$

Inverting,

$$\text{SMM} = 1 - (1 - \text{CPR})^{\frac{1}{12}}$$

Percentage of PSA   If a mortgage prepays at a rate of 100% PSA, then the CPR for the month when the mortgage is n months old is

$$\text{CPR} = 6\% \times \frac{n}{30} \qquad \text{if } n \leq 30$$

$$= 6\% \qquad \text{if } n > 30$$

$$= 6\% \times \text{Min}\left(1, \frac{n}{30}\right) \qquad \text{for any } n$$

For a general prepayment rate of $x\%$ PSA, for age n,

$$\text{CPR} = 6\% \times \frac{x}{100} \times \frac{n}{30} \qquad \text{if } n \leq 30$$

$$= 6\% \times \frac{x}{100} \qquad \text{if } n > 30$$

$$= 6\% \times \frac{x}{100} \times \text{Min}\left(1, \frac{n}{30}\right) \qquad \text{for any } n$$

Conversely, if a mortgage of age n months prepays at a given CPR, the PSA rate for that month is given by

$$\text{Percent of PSA} = \text{CPR} \times \frac{100}{6} \times \frac{30}{n} \qquad \text{if } n \leq 30$$

$$= \text{CPR} \times \frac{100}{6} \qquad \text{if } n > 30$$

$$= \text{CPR} \times \frac{100}{6} \times \text{Max}\left(1, \frac{30}{n}\right) \qquad \text{for any } n$$

Mortgage Cash Flow with Prepayments

Let $\hat{M}_n, \hat{P}_n, \hat{I}_n$, and $\hat{B}_n$ denote the actual monthly scheduled payment, scheduled principal, interest, and remaining (end-of-month) balance for month n, respectively. Let SMM_n be the prepayment rate in month n, stated as a decimal, and let

$$Q_n = (1 - \text{SMM}_n)(1 - \text{SMM}_{n-1}) \ldots (1 - \text{SMM}_1)$$

The *total monthly payment* in month n is given by

$$\hat{M}_n = \frac{\hat{B}_{n-1}\left(\dfrac{G}{1200}\right)\left(1 + \dfrac{G}{1200}\right)^{N-n+1}}{\left[\left(1 + \dfrac{G}{1200}\right)^{N-n+1} - 1\right]} = M_n Q_{n-1}$$

The *scheduled principal* portion of this payment is given by

$$\hat{P}_n = \frac{\hat{B}_{n-1}\left(\dfrac{G}{1200}\right)}{\left[\left(1 + \dfrac{G}{1200}\right)^{N-n+1} - 1\right]} = P_n Q_{n-1}$$

The *interest* portion is given by

$$\hat{I}_n = \hat{B}_{n-1}\left(\frac{G}{1200}\right) = I_n Q_{n-1}$$

The *unscheduled principal payment* in month n is written as

$$PR_n = (\hat{B}_{n-1} - \hat{P}_n)\, \text{SMM}_n$$

The *remaining balance* is given by

$$\hat{B}_n = B_{n-1} - \hat{P}_n - PR_n = B_n Q_n$$

The total cash flow to the investor is

$$\hat{CF}_n = \hat{P} + PR_n + \left(\frac{C}{C+S}\right)\hat{I}_n$$

Average Life

Average life assigns weights to principal paydowns according to their arrival dates.

$$\text{Average Life (in years)} = \frac{1}{12} \sum_{t=1}^{N} \frac{(t + \alpha - 1)(\text{Principal}_t)}{\sum_{t=1}^{N} \text{Principal}_t}$$

where t = Time subscript, $t = 1, \ldots N$

Principal$_t$ = Principal arriving at time t

N = Number of months until last principal cash flow comes in

α = Days between settlement date and first cash flow date, divided by 30 (*i.e.*, the fraction of a month between settlement date and first cash flow date)

Macaulay Duration

Duration assigns time weights to the present values of all cash flows.

$$\text{Macaulay duration (in years)} = \frac{1}{12} \sum_{t=1}^{N} \frac{\dfrac{(t + \alpha - 1)\, C(t)}{(1 + r/1200)^{t + \alpha - 1}}}{\sum_{t=1}^{N} \dfrac{C(t)}{(1 + r/1200)^{t + \alpha - 1}}}$$

where $C(t)$ = Cash flow at time t

r = Cash flow yield of mortgage (%)

Cash Flow Yield

To obtain the cash flow yield, the present value of the security's cash flows on the settlement date is equated to its initial price P plus its accrued interest I.

$$P + I = \sum_{t=1}^{N} \frac{C(t)}{(1 + r/1200)^{t + \alpha - 1}}$$

This equation is solved iteratively for r. The solution is called the *mortgage yield*.

Bond-Equivalent Yield

The interest on a mortgage security is compounded monthly, whereas the interest on bonds such as Treasuries and corporates is compounded semiannually. The compounding frequency is reflected in the yield of a security. Therefore, to make mortgage yields and bond yields comparable, the yield of a mortgage is normally converted to a bond-equivalent yield, that is, a yield based on semiannual compounding of the mortgage's interest payments.

A yield based on monthly compounding can be converted to a bond-equivalent yield and vice versa as follows:

r = Mortgage yield based on monthly compounding (%)
y = Bond-equivalent yield (%)

$$y = 200\left[\left(1 + \frac{r}{1200}\right)^6 - 1\right]$$

$$r = 1200\left[\left(1 + \frac{y}{200}\right)^{1/6} - 1\right]$$

Total Return

$$y_h = \begin{array}{c}\text{Total return} \\ \text{over a holding period } h = \\ \text{(percent)}\end{array} \frac{\begin{array}{c}\text{Sales} \quad \text{Total} \quad \text{Total net cash flow} \quad \text{Total reinvestment} \\ \text{proceeds} - \text{price} + \text{received during} + \text{income during} \\ \text{paid} \quad \text{the holding period} \quad \text{the holding period}\end{array}}{\text{Total price paid}} \times 100$$

The bond-equivalent total return rate y_{BE} is given by

$$\left(1 + \frac{y_h}{100}\right)^{12/h} = \left(1 + \frac{y_{BE}}{200}\right)^2$$

Modified Duration

Modified duration is given by

$$\text{Modified duration} = \frac{\text{Macaulay duration}}{1 + \dfrac{y}{200}}$$

where y = Bond-equivalent yield (%)

INDEX

ABOUT THE EDITOR

Frank J. Fabozzi, Ph.D., is adjunct professor of finance at Yale's School of Management and is editor of *The Journal of Portfolio Management*. Dr. Fabozzi—a Chartered Financial Analyst, a Certified Public Accountant, and the editor or author of dozens of acclaimed financial books—is widely regarded as one of the world's foremost authorities on fixed income securities. Prior to joining Yale's faculty, he was on the faculty of MIT's Sloan School of Management.